The Story of *Opera*

The Story of *Opera*

JAMES PARAKILAS
Bates College

W. W. NORTON & COMPANY
NEW YORK · LONDON

W. W. NORTON & COMPANY has been independent since its founding in 1923, when William
Warder Norton and Mary D. Herter Norton first began publishing lectures delivered at the People's
Institute, the adult education division of New York City's Cooper Union. The Nortons soon expanded
their program beyond the Institute, publishing books by celebrated academics from America and
abroad. By mid-century, the two major pillars of Norton's publishing program—trade books and
college texts—were firmly established. In the 1950s, the Norton family transferred control of the
company to its employees, and today—with a staff of four hundred and a comparable number of
trade, college, and professional titles published each year—W. W. Norton & Company stands as the
largest and oldest publishing house owned wholly by its employees.

First Edition

Editor: Maribeth Payne
Developmental editor: Susan Gaustad
Electronic media editor: Steve Hoge
Ancillaries editor: Justin Hoffman
Assistant editor: Ariella Foss
Director of production, College: Jane Searle
Design director: Rubina Yeh
Designer: Lissi Sigillo
Photo researcher: Michael Fodera
Permissions manager: Megan Jackson
Marketing manager: Amy Parkin
Indexer: Marilyn Bliss
Composition and layout: cM Preparé
Manufacturing: RR Donnelley, Crawfordsville, Indiana

Library of Congress Cataloging-in-Publication Data

Parakilas, James.
    The story of opera/James Parakilas.—1st ed.
        p. cm.
    Includes bibliographical references and index.
    ISBN 978-0-393-93555-4 (pbk.)
1. Opera. I. Title.
ML1700.P36 2013
782.1—dc23

                                    2012028596

W. W. Norton & Company, Inc., 500 Fifth Avenue, New York, NY 10110
www.wwnorton.com

W. W. Norton & Company, Ltd., Castle House, 75/76 Wells Street, London W1T 3QT

1 2 3 4 5 6 7 8 9 0

For Mary,
the music of my life

The opera poster, like everything about opera, has its story, as the three posters reproduced here and on succeeding pages indicate. This poster for Puccini's *Madama Butterfly*, created by Leopoldo Metlicovitz for the premiere at Milan's La Scala in 1904, takes us into the inner life of the heroine through an image, partly photographic and partly

BRIEF CONTENTS

The poster by Georges Rochegrosse for the second production of Massenet's *Don Quichotte* (*Don Quixote*), staged at Paris's Gaîté Lyrique in 1910, was created six years after the *Madama Butterfly* poster, but is older in its painterly style and advertising concept, resorting to an inset of Dulcinée to cover the third main character.

CONTENTS

III

Opera of the Eighteenth Century 175

CHAPTER 8

Opera on Classical Subjects 177

CHAPTER 9

Opera on Comic Subjects 217

IV

Opera of the Nineteenth Century 257

V

Opera of the Twentieth Century and Beyond 373

CHAPTER 14

Operas of Dreaming 423

TEATR WIELKI

ALBAN BERG WOZZECK

Half a century after *Don Quichotte*, Jan Lenica's 1964 poster for a production of Berg's *Wozzeck* (first staged in 1925) at Warsaw's Teatr Wielki captures the agony and madness at the heart of the work without revealing any particulars of character or setting.

PREFACE

Opera is the human voice pushed to its limits so that it may take us to the limits of human experience. It is drama with all the stops pulled out—drama told in word, song, orchestral sound, dance, and visual spectacle. An art form as old as Shakespeare, opera is a stage on which the latest ideas of story and action, musical expression, visual display, and staging are being tested today. It is a medium that transports you to a unique world, giving you indelible memories of works you want to hear again and again and performances you can never get over, as well as the thrill of adding new works, new performers, and new concepts of favorite works to those memories.

The Story of Opera takes you into this all-encompassing world, from its beginnings to the present day, through the works that have spoken to audiences in each era of its four-hundred-year history. The book can be an enticing introduction to opera for those who have never experienced it, just as it can offer new, revelatory ways of thinking about opera to those who already love or perform it. If you have studied literature, theater, visual arts, languages, history, or music, opera is of vital interest to you, as it draws on all these subjects.

The Plan of the Book

PART I (Chapters 1–4) charts the experience of going to an opera: how people dress for it, where it is performed, who sits where, how an opera is staged, what the orchestra does, what the singers and dancers do, and how the story is told in actions, words, stage effects, and music. But since opera has developed for over four centuries and is still changing, each of these aspects has its own fascinating story, showing us how society has evolved over that time. Chapter 4, on operatic storytelling, focuses on a single classic

opera, Verdi's *La traviata*; you learn scene by scene how a compelling story that was originally told in a novel and then a play takes on its own, everlasting life in Verdi's masterpiece.

PARTS II–V, the remainder of the book, present the story of opera as a historical survey of works, both canonical (Mozart's *Marriage of Figaro*) and lesser known (Saariaho's *L'Amour de loin*). At every stage of that history certain kinds of story spoke most strongly to audiences, and so these parts of the book are organized according to story types and themes. We explore the reasons those stories were favored and the ways stagecraft, language, and music were adapted to make them powerful and beautiful.

Within the text there are three kinds of special sections. **On Stage and Off** highlights a particular aspect of the operatic experience: for example, what a conductor does, how a song became a hit in the late seventeenth century, how opera houses staged the supernatural in the nineteenth. **In Their Own Words** provides excerpts from the writings of people involved in making, performing, and analyzing opera. And for certain operas discussed in detail, a list of the **Principal Characters** is given.

Each chapter concludes with a list of works for further reading and questions for research and reflection. These questions encourage you to think about the issues covered in that chapter and set off on creative explorations of your own. As you delve into each chapter, **Playlists** on the StudySpace website will direct you to relevant audio and video performances, often thrilling classic ones; listening to a recording while studying the text or score is the best way to understand the relationship of words and music. Operatic terms are given in boldface where defined in the text; these along with other useful musical terms are also included in the Glossary at the back of the book.

Finally, the illustrations in the text are more than images of famous performers and remarkable productions. Many show how the story of an opera was visualized, and therefore how it was understood, when it was composed—either in original set and costume drawings or in contemporary paintings of the same subject. And because the visual is the element of opera that is used most freely to reinterpret a classic opera, comparisons of production images from different eras allow you to observe changing concepts of a given work, and of opera staging in general, over time.

Online: StudySpace

This website, available at www.wwnorton.com/studyspace, offers some exciting features to enrich your study of opera.

- **Chapter Outlines** will help you review each chapter's content.
- **Chapter Playlists** combine audio and video performances of fifty-eight operas from the book, with timings in some cases that allow you to locate a particular scene or moment.
- *Audio selections* are linked to purchases on iTunes and other available music-download sites.
- *Netflix video performances* are available with a personal Netflix subscription for offline DVD viewing.
- And the *Norton Opera Sampler* provides stunning excerpts from the Metropolitan Opera for sixteen operas discussed in the text; you can opt in to stream these performances for a modest fee. If you do opt in, you may also subscribe to a discounted student membership to the new *Met-on-Demand*.

For Instructors

There are several good ways to construct a course using this book. Some teachers prefer to teach a relatively small number of operas whole; others introduce students to excerpts from as many operas as possible; still others mix the two methods. *The Story of Opera* provides a conceptual frame of discussion within which any of these methods will work, and many good choices for inclusion and exclusion and substitution can be made. The opportunity for a class to see a live production of a given opera, for example, can be a reason to focus on that work one semester.

The text features a relatively small number of music examples and a larger number of text passages, with the original language and an English translation side by side. These may most profitably be read while listening to an audio recording of the passage. In that way students will incidentally learn the skill of following a foreign text and its translation simultaneously. Similarly, those with no experience reading musical notation will nonetheless find that by following the lyrics in a music example, they can actually see and therefore hear something in the music they might otherwise have missed.

An **Instructor's Manual**, by Karen Hiles, Muhlenberg College, includes sample syllabi and detailed teaching advice for new and experienced instructors alike. Each chapter offers an overview and outline; a list of learning objectives; lecture suggestions and class activities; suggested writing assignments; advice for responding to the challenges of teaching opera; an annotated bibliography; and an annotated videography. Finally, all of the book's exceptional art and photographs are available to adopters in both PowerPoint and raw JPG format.

Acknowledgments

The creation of this book has been aided by many illustrious scholars who have read partial or full drafts of the text and in some cases tried out parts with their students. It is a pleasure for me to thank those students (who are unknown to me) for their reports and to name those scholars and teachers in order to thank them for the benefit of their expertise, wisdom, and generosity: Katherine Axtell, Charles Dill, Rebecca Harris-Warrick, Wendy Heller, Steven Huebner, Shelagh Hunter, Ralph Locke, Ryan Minor, Michael Pisani, Hilary Poriss, John Platoff, Anthony Sheppard, Richard Sherr, and Jennifer Williams Brown.

For their help with access to materials, I am grateful to many librarians, especially Christopher Schiff of Bates College and Sarah Adams of Harvard University. I am indebted to Sophia Budianto for her impressive work on the music examples and glossary during a summer internship at Bates. For assistance of several sorts related to seventeenth-century opera, I thank Will Ash, Ellen T. Harris, Edward Harwood, and Thomas Lin, along with Michael Beckerman on Janáček. I am indebted to Bates College and especially to Jill Reich, Dean of the Faculty, for providing time and support for my scholarly work, and to Bates colleagues in many fields for their thoughts directly or indirectly related to opera.

I salute Maribeth Payne, who has profoundly influenced music scholarship and music-history teaching in America, for championing this project at Norton; Susan Gaustad, who couldn't have been more committed to my text if it were her own, yet persuaded me to read my sentences as if they were not my own; and many others at Norton, who brought their expertise, enthusiasm, and artistry to the project. The book is dedicated to my wife, Mary Hunter. She has earned a place in several of the earlier sentences of this section, as well as her place among the great opera scholars cited in the text; in my mind the whole book issues from our ongoing dialogue.

James Parakilas
September 2012

The Story of Opera

MILESTONES IN THE EXPERIENCE OF OPERA

SEVENTEENTH CENTURY

The Globe Theatre, built by the Lord Chamberlain's Men (including William Shakespeare), opens in London (1599).

First public opera house, the San Cassiano Theater, opens in Venice (1637).

Public commercial theaters are established across Western Europe.

Venetian opera houses pioneer seating in boxes, which line the theater walls.

Sets are designed with a central vanishing point.

Stage effects include set changes in plain view and performers lowered to the stage from above.

Candles provide dim lighting of stage and house.

Costumes are adapted from current aristocratic fashion.

Women singers and dancers are prominent in opera, but banned in Rome; castrati sing many male roles, except in France.

Dance sequences are often performed between acts.

Bass and chord instruments provide most of the accompaniment, with a string ensemble added for some numbers.

Librettos are regularly published in time for the first performance.

EIGHTEENTH CENTURY

Italian opera is a favorite public entertainment from London to St. Petersburg. New operas are created in Lima, Peru (1701) and Mexico City (1711).

Early in the century: scenery with off-centered and multiple perspective created by Ferdinando Galli-Bibiena and members of his family.

Late in the century: historically and geographically specific scenery and costumes designed.

Whole orchestra is used more in arias and other numbers; harpsichord with cello and double bass are generally used for basso continuo in recitatives.

NINETEENTH CENTURY

Chestnut Street Theater, Philadelphia, becomes the first theater illuminated by gaslight (1816).

Salle Le Peletier inaugurated, home of the Paris Opera and the tradition of grand opera and massive spectacle (1821).

Spotlighting, by means of limelight, introduced at the Royal Opera House, Covent Garden, London (1837).

Chorégies d'Orange in Orange, France, starts a trend of outdoor opera at summer festivals (1869).

Bayreuth Festival Theater, built by Richard Wagner for the production of *The Ring of the Nibelung*, opens in Bayreuth, Germany (1876).

Savoy Theatre, London, becomes the first theater to be illuminated with electric lighting (1881).

Orchestras are larger; basso continuo group is phased out.

Choruses are larger and more active participants in the action.

TWENTIETH CENTURY AND BEYOND

Tenor Enrico Caruso makes the first of his 260 recordings (1902).

History of opera on film opens with Georges Méliès's short silent-film version of Gounod's Faust (1904).

Selected acts of performances at the Metropolitan Opera, New York, are broadcast live on the radio in 1910. Regular broadcast of complete operas begin there in 1933.

Supertitles are introduced in opera productions by the Canadian Opera Company, Toronto (1983).

High-definition broadcast of opera performance from the Metropolitan Opera begin in movie theaters (2006).

PART I

Experiencing Opera

Opera is a kind of drama: one of many kinds of drama in the world that use singing and instrumental music and dancing, as well as sets and costumes, to enact a story. It is also a repertory: the accumulated body of operatic works created over the last four centuries. And it is also a theatrical experience: one that people enjoy today as they have for all those centuries.

When people go to the opera today, they see and hear works from throughout its long history, including some as new as the latest movies. One way to learn about opera is to study the development of that long and still-growing repertory, as you will do in the later parts of this book. But to learn what kind of drama opera is, you need to study the experience as well, to ask what the audience takes in as well as what the performers deliver. And so this first part offers an imagined trip to the opera, examining the elements of the show as we encounter them in the opera house. The experience of opera has its own history, just as the repertory does, a story with continuities and changes over the course of four centuries.

Gabriel de Saint-Aubin, *Lully's Opera "Armide" Performed at the Palais-Royal, 1761*. This painting of the experience of opera 250 years ago gives a sense of how the different kinds of participants impinged on each other's realms: the principals crowded in by choristers, the audience members in boxes that hang over the stage, the guards in the orchestra tucked in between the musicians and the audience — and the actors dressed very much like the people watching them.
Museum of Fine Arts, Boston/Wikimedia Commons

CHAPTER 1

Going to the Opera House

Dressing for the Opera

Today it is possible to experience opera at home, in a movie theater, a classroom, a car, or anywhere there is internet access. But opera continues, as in past centuries, to be performed live in opera houses: theaters with a large stage and elaborate staging facilities as well as a pit in front of the stage that can hold a large orchestra. And when people set out for an opera house, they have to decide what to wear. They are apt to take that question more seriously than they do for the movies or a concert—almost as seriously as for a wedding. When the music critic Anthony Tommasini reported from Germany recently on performances at the Bayreuth Festival, one of the most prestigious places in the world to experience opera, he devoted one of his columns in the *New York Times* to what people were wearing.[1] Why would readers of the *Times* care what operagoers in Germany wear? Isn't the spectacle onstage the one that counts? The fact that people worry about what to wear suggests that they think of opera as a social experience, not just an artistic one. Opera has always been defined by who goes to it and how they present themselves to each other.

The First Two Centuries

The very first operagoers dressed as if they *were* going to a wedding, because they were. The time was the beginning of the seventeenth

Pierre-Auguste Renoir, *The Box* (*La Loge*), 1874. A century after the performance that Saint-Aubin painted, women still dressed fashionably for the opera, but men wore what the sumptuary regulations dictated. At this date theater lights stayed up during the performance, and the man pictured here is taking advantage to look elsewhere than the stage. The Courtauld Gallery, London.

Jean Berain, costume design for the goddess Cérès in the original production of Lully's *Proserpine* at the French court and Paris Opera, 1680. The costume is in the high fashion of the day; what identifies the character as the goddess of the harvest are the ears of wheat on the front of her headdress. Nationalmuseum, Stockholm.

century, the marriages were princely alliances, the places were the palaces of the rulers of Northern Italian principalities, and the operas were part of the lavish entertainments put on for the wedding participants. But by the 1630s opera took on a life apart from court weddings. It became a commercial enterprise, staged regularly for paying audiences in theaters built for the purpose. Operagoing became a routine form of going out. People began to dress specifically for the opera. And what the performers wore began to influence what the operagoers wore, as it does today.

Costumes in the seventeenth century were extravagant and expensive, covered in jewels and shiny thread and ribbons, so that they would sparkle on a stage lit only by candles. The characters in those operas—at least the serious operas—were figures from Greek and Roman mythology, epic, or history, but no attempt was made to dress them the way artists of Greek and Roman antiquity depicted them. For that matter, singers did not wear separate costumes for each role they played. Their costumes might be more or less fantastic, especially for the roles of monsters or spirits. But for the divinities, heroes, and historical figures, the costumes were more apt to be splendid examples of the fashions of the day, associated with a particular character by the addition of identifying markers—seashells and pearls, for instance, for a sea goddess. In fact, the clothes themselves were sometimes cast-offs from the rich and noble, donated to the opera house.

These familiar-looking costumes helped people in the audience to recognize themselves in the characters, or perhaps to recognize their better selves, since contemporary dramatic theory told them that they were supposed to admire and emulate the classical nobility of dramatic characters. It is hard to know how much operagoers in the seventeenth and eighteenth centuries really emulated the nobility they saw modeled on the stage, but it is clear that the costumes sometimes created a fashion rage. One way or the other, costume created a bond between performers and patrons.

The Second Two Centuries

Two changes disturbed that bond. One was that, starting late in the eighteenth century, costuming became a device for placing the actors in a specific time and place, often distant from that of the audience. New costumes were created for each opera, based on evidence of how people dressed in ancient Greece or medieval Russia or the American West (settings were getting more varied, too).

Sometimes the charm of foreign and historic costuming was balanced with a grounding in the familiar: operagoers might still feel a bond with a singer dressed as an Aztec princess so long as her hairdo was in the current fashion.

The other change took place early in the nineteenth century: men in the audience no longer dressed to show off. Previously the men were as decked out as the women, but now the older and more respectable of them withdrew into a tuxedoed uniformity, condemning young men who persisted in dressing colorfully to be described as "dandies." Eventually many opera houses established rules that required men to wear "evening dress" (tuxedo, white tie). These "sumptuary regulations" were designed to control the expense of dressing for the event, but since they applied only to men and since men generally paid for their wives' or mistresses' gowns and jewels, there was still ample opportunity for men to display their wealth in the dress of their companions.

Alfredo Edel, costume design for the Venetian general Otello arriving on land after his naval victory, in the original production of Verdi's *Otello* at La Scala, Milan, 1887. The costume is modeled accurately on armor of the late fifteenth century, when the opera takes place. The armor serves the symbolic purpose of introducing the character as apparently invulnerable.
Archivio Storico Ricordi, Milan

The sumptuary system and its abuses were ridiculed in a letter that the great Irish dramatist and music critic George Bernard Shaw wrote to the *London Times* in 1905:

> On Saturday night I went to the Opera. I wore the costume imposed on me by the regulations of the house. I fully recognize the advantage of those regulations. Evening dress is cheap, simple, durable, prevents rivalry and extravagance on the part of male leaders of fashion, annihilates class distinctions, and gives men who are poor and doubtful of their social position (that is, the great majority of men) a sense of security and satisfaction that no clothes of their own choosing could confer, besides saving a whole sex the trouble of considering what they should wear on state occasions.

Shaw has no quarrel, then, with sumptuary rules for men; on the contrary, he says he wants them extended to women, on the grounds that "what is sauce for the gander is sauce for the goose":

> At 9 o'clock (the Opera began at 8) a lady came in and sat down very conspicuously in my line of sight. She remained there until the beginning of the last act. I do not complain of her coming late and going early; on the contrary, I wish she had come later and gone earlier. For this lady, who had very black hair, had stuck over her right ear the pitiable corpse of a large white bird, which looked exactly as if someone had killed it by stamping on its breast, and then nailed it to the lady's temple, which was presumably of sufficient solidity to bear the operation. I am not, I hope, a morbidly squeamish person, but the spectacle sickened me. . . . Had the lady been refused admission, as she should have been, she would have soundly rated the tradesman who imposed the disgusting headdress on her

Magdalena Kožená as Idamante at a dress rehearsal for Mozart's *Idomeneo* at the Salzburg (Austria) Festival, 2006. This costuming does not reflect the time either of the opera's setting (the time of the Trojan War) or of its creation (1781), and its symbolism overwhelms any connection to contemporary dress. Ms. Kožená's pants and necktie remind us that she is playing a male character; the bloodstains remind us that her character is marked for death.
Andreas Schaad/AP

under the false pretense that "the best people" wear such things, and withdrawn her custom from him; and thus the root of the evil would be struck at; for your fashionable woman generally allows herself to be dressed according to the taste of a person whom she would not let sit down in her presence.[2]

Sumptuary regulations merely reinforced a gender distinction that was deeply inculcated in Shaw's culture and is by no means gone from ours: that women were at the opera (or any public event) to be seen and men to see.

Lighting and Dress

It may seem odd that women would put so much effort and money into dressing for the opera, when the whole audience was going to spend most of the evening sitting in the dark. But in fact, up through the age

of candlelight and even after the introduction of gas lighting in the early nineteenth century, the house lights were generally left on throughout the performance. It was only in the 1880s, when opera houses converted to electric lighting, that house lights came to be turned completely off.

The darkening of the house is now such a universal practice that it is hard for us to imagine how different the social experience, let alone the artistic experience, of opera and other theater was when the lights were left up. The French painter Pierre Auguste Renoir, a lifelong operagoer in Paris, first encountered a darkened house when he went to the Bayreuth Festival in 1896, to see Richard Wagner's *Die Walküre* in the recently built opera house there. He found the experience disturbing: "They've no right to shut people up in the dark for three solid hours. It's taking a mean advantage of you. . . . You are forced to look at the only place where there's any light: the stage. It's absolute tyranny. I might want to look at a pretty woman sitting in a box."[3] From Renoir's point of view, the happy experience of seeing and being seen was being crammed into the corners of the operatic experience: the times of arrival and departure and the intermissions.

In the first two centuries of opera, then, the lighting was similar in the house and onstage, and the costuming was designed to make the spectators feel at home with the characters. In the nineteenth and twentieth centuries the continuity between stage and audience was severed by darkening the house and by dressing the performers in ways that the spectators would not try to emulate, or could not compete with if they tried. In the twenty-first century the costuming is less predictable than ever before. From one production to the next it might be historical or contemporary, true to the text in time and place or evocative of some different time and place, close to the dress of the audience or utterly fantastic. Likewise, both formal and implied dress codes for the audience are gone, and patrons enjoy greater freedom in how they choose to dress than they ever have. That unpredictability and that freedom constitute an invitation to think about the significance of dress, both onstage and off, at the opera.

Housing Opera

Although opera is seen on movie and television and computer screens, in outdoor amphitheaters, sports arenas, and concert halls, the traditional place to experience it is in an opera house. An opera house is in most respects

Interior of the Margravial Opera House in Bayreuth, Germany, seen from the stage. The house was built in the 1740s, its interior designed by Giuseppe Galli Bibiena with his son Carlo. The design focused performers' attention on the box occupied by the rulers who built the opera house: Friedrich, Margrave of Brandenburg-Bayreuth, and his wife, the Margravine Wilhelmine.

Svenja-Foto/Corbis

an ordinary theater, yet spoken plays are hardly ever presented there. And, though it has an orchestral pit, neither are Broadway musicals. On the other hand, ballet, which requires the same facilities as opera, is often performed in opera houses. Concerts are sometimes given there too, as well as balls and banquets. So why is this particular kind of theater used for so few kinds of theater and so many nontheatrical events?

Part of the answer is musical. The acoustics of an opera house tend to favor the resonance of music over the clarity of speech. An opera house can be considerably bigger than most Broadway theaters, and opera singers are expected to sing unamplified, over an orchestra larger than the typical Broadway band. And so they are trained to sing loudly and with great endurance, thrilling large audiences with what seems to be a superhuman sound. By contrast, Broadway singers are trained to sing in a talkier way; the sound they aim for is not superhuman. An intimate theater suits their art.

The uses of an opera house are also based on what it represents in the community, beginning with what it looks like and where it is to be found.

Civic Setting and Social Status

In New York City the Metropolitan Opera is sheathed in marble and set up and back from the street in Lincoln Center, the city's primary cultural center. Most other theaters in the city sit right on the street, concentrated on and off Broadway, near Times Square, in what is called the Theater District, twenty blocks from Lincoln Center. So, though the Met is a theater, it does not seem like part of the theatrical scene of its city, and though the other theaters certainly offer a cultural product, they are not proclaimed as culturally central by being placed in a cultural center. Opera presents itself as a more rarefied pleasure, while the Broadway show—named for a major street in New York—presents itself as more characteristic of New York. Likewise ballet, which is performed at Lincoln Center, is designated by this location as more rarefied than modern dance, which is performed in less prestigious venues all around the city and is more closely identified with New York.

The Palau de les Arts Reina Sofia, the opera house of Valencia, Spain, designed by Diego Calatrava and opened in 2008, is one of several striking buildings clustered together in a monumental civic cultural center.
© View Pictures LTD/Lebrecht Photo Library

In the seventeenth and eighteenth centuries opera houses were often undistinguished buildings located on crowded streets. Only in the nineteenth century were they conceived as civic or national monuments and built with imposing facades on important squares. Starting with the Sydney Opera House in 1973, a number of striking-looking structures have been built on dramatic harborside sites—away from the bustle of city life, yet photogenic symbols of their cities.

Of all the ways an opera house may be used, the opera ball says the most about opera's social status. For several centuries houses were built with flat floors that could be cleared of seats for dancing. A ball given there—the opera ball—was often the most elegant and elite ball in a city's annual social calendar, a sign that opera belonged to the privileged. Today balls are still held in a few European houses from the nineteenth century, such as the Vienna State Opera. Newer houses, including most in North America, are not suitable for balls because their floors are raked (slanted toward the stage). This change in design gives the opera house a new social identity as well as a new focus. Raking the floor not only makes the auditorium unusable for the balls of the upper classes, but also encourages those who sit there to concentrate on the performance rather than glance around to see who else is in attendance. In that sense the raked floor has helped to democratize opera: a broad public is apt to feel more comfortable when no one there expects to know the rest of the audience, but everyone expects to have a decent view of the stage.

Opera houses have always been used for fashionable balls, the floor cleared for dancers and others watching from the sides or the boxes. **Above:** an opera ball at the Regio Ducal Teatro in Milan in 1747, engraved by Marc'Antonio dal Re, from the Civica Raccolta delle Stampe Achille Bertarelli, Castello Sforzesco, Milan. Conservatore Raccolta Bertarelli

Below: the first waltz at a recent Opera Ball of the Vienna State Opera. Erich Lessing Culture and Fine Arts Archive

An Enclosed Space

From the start, opera was almost always performed indoors, whether it was a room in a prince's palace or a theater built for the purpose. That is surprising when we think of the model that the creators of the genre were emulating, or as they saw it, reviving: classical, especially Greek, drama. The Greeks and Romans watched their drama in open-air theaters. Why did the Italian creators of opera, living in the same sunny climate, require a closed, roofed building for their drama? Especially when the creators of Elizabethan drama in London and kabuki drama in Japan, developing their theatrical forms at practically the same date and in much soggier places, performed generally in open-air spaces or partly-roofed buildings, canceling their shows whenever it rained?

For one thing, opera requires by far the most elaborate and sustained musical accompaniment, and the instruments used, largely string instruments, are more effective and reliable indoors than out. But what most clearly gives opera its need for an indoor theater is its spectacle. Opera can no more exist without spectacle than it can without music—or maybe it should be said that the music is just one part of the spectacle that defines opera as a dramatic form.

In the princely Italian wedding festivities that are considered the birthplace of opera, all the entertainments combined elaborate staging with music, though in different balances. These differences are exemplified in two entertainments, both staged in Florence in 1600 to mark the wedding of Maria de' Medici, niece of the Grand Duke of Tuscany, to the King of France, Henri IV. The first of these, *L'Euridice* (*Eurydice*), was performed in a small hall with a platform at one end, and relied on just two sets (a meadow and the gates of hell). Nevertheless, its dramatic musical style marks this as a decisive work in the development of opera.

In the second work, *Il rapimento di Cefalo* (*The Abduction of Cephalus*), music was just one ingredient in a stupendous stage spectacle. Performed in the Great Hall of the Uffizi Palace, a room that may have held as many as 3,800 spectators, it boasted eight astounding scene changes performed by a multitude of stage machines: a thirty-eight-foot-high mountain, occupying the whole stage and bearing foliage and actors, that collapsed to the stage before the spectators' eyes; clouds, each carrying an actor, chasing each other high above the stage; a seascape with moving waves and an operational whale twenty-six feet long; a great cave that opened up from under the stage; and a pyramid (also bearing actors) that grew out of the stage floor until it reached the rafters. In this drama about the goddess of dawn, one of the most remarkable stage effects involved lighting: for a scene depicting

Designers and Directors

Operas have always required professional designers. In the seventeenth and eighteenth centuries the same person might design (or at least assemble) the scenery, machinery, special effects, costumes, and lighting, and that person might also have a large hand in the execution of the designs. The stage direction was entrusted to the librettist, just as the musical direction was customarily entrusted to the composer. When an opera was produced again elsewhere, a local librettist (author of the text) and a local composer might take over those roles.

In the nineteenth century, when operas began to be set in more specific times and places, designers were called on to recreate on the stage particular historic buildings, the costumes of a particular century, the flora and fauna of a particular part of the world. This, along with a move from painted backdrops to constructed sets, required the expansion of a single design position into a staff of scenic, costume, and lighting specialists, who in turn supervised teams of experts in the execution of their designs. At the same time, professional stage directors came on the scene, and the staging of the first production of a new work, down to the smallest details of blocking, was often recorded in a stage manual and published so that the work could be reproduced elsewhere.

In the twentieth century, as opera companies increasingly became museums presenting a repertory of classic works, they turned to stage directors and design teams to help keep those works alive with new interpretive ideas. Ironically, the same scenic means that in nineteenth-century productions had evoked the time and place specified in the text were now sometimes used to transfer the same work to a different time and place—even the audience's here and now. The staging might then be a way of testing the premises of a familiar opera in new contexts or simply of removing that work from the audience's comfort zone. Such a staging might seem to be at odds with the musicians' task of realizing more or less faithfully the words and notes of a responsibly edited score. But that task too could be subject to different interpretations: should musicians, for instance, continue performance practices that developed over the lifetime of a work, or restore practices they believed were associated with the birth of that work?

The illustrations in this book show what scenes from certain operas looked like, sometimes in their original production, sometimes in a more recent one. In a few cases there are images from more than one production of the same scene, exhibiting strikingly different concepts. Taken together, these illustrations give some idea of the evolution of the art of staging and the power of the visual elements to shape a spectator's experience of any opera.

the night, hundreds of oil lamps that lit both the house and the stage were dimmed all at once—"like lightning," a witness reported—and then were just as suddenly relit.[4]

Decades later, producers arrived at ways to bring the musical and scenic spectacles into a more even balance. The houses built in Venice in the 1630s

and 1640s provided the machinery for scenic extravaganzas, which were matched by extravagant displays of solo singing. Ever since then, opera has continued to offer far more visual spectacle than the spoken theater, along with its spectacular singing. Even in the seventeenth century it was commonly understood, as Mercedes Viale Ferrero tells us (noting exceptions), that "scene changes . . . were typical of opera, whereas plays were bound by the Aristotelian concept of unity and thus required no such thing."[5]

In *Il rapimento di Cefalo* sunlight would have hampered that sensational dimming of the lamps for the night scene. But there was a larger reason for excluding sunlight from opera. The flickering lights, whether oil lamps or candles, that lit opera houses for two centuries gave the actors a flickering, otherworldly presence. So too did the music, as it still does in our age of nonflickering electric lighting. In most opera all the words are sung, not spoken. The uninterrupted sounding of music, along with the magnificent scenic effects, take us into the opera's world and hold us there continuously. Both sonically and visually, then, opera cuts its spectators off from the world they left behind when they entered the theater and encloses them in its own imaginary world.

In that sense, opera has always been more like the movies, where the audience sits in the dark and is enveloped by the film's sounds and sights, than like the tragedy of the ancient Greeks, the theater of Shakespeare's London, or early kabuki theater—those sunlit, open-air forms of drama that relied on masked faces, stylized speech, and simple markers of setting to draw spectators into their imagined worlds. Open-air opera, heard in the summer at places like the Santa Fe Opera in New Mexico and the Baths of Caracalla in Rome, is almost always performed at night. Perhaps more remarkable is that seventeenth-century operas, occasionally performed in princely courtyards, also tended to be done at night. The people who put on opera have always sensed that its flickering, enveloping world dissolves at the touch of sunlight, just as it does at the sound of a speaking voice. Opera needs its opera house.

The Best Seat in the House

It matters where you sit. In a movie theater the seats are generally identical in comfort, all located on one floor in front of the screen, all costing the same. In a baseball stadium, by contrast, the seats are of different types and they wrap around the field, so that the spectators have radically different views of the game and different opportunities to catch a fly ball; a few fans get to sit isolated from the crowd, in more expensive boxes. Opera works more like baseball in its seating.

The box, in fact, is an invention of the opera house. In the earliest public opera houses—theaters in Venice that were converted to opera, starting in 1637—the walls were lined with three to six tiers of boxes, rather than with the traditional tiers of benches that we would call stadium seating. Patrons would buy a subscription to a box for the whole season, entitling them to that box every night the opera was open. The subscriptions gave a house its primary income, but also set the terms for social life there. For centuries opera boxes with their adjoining anterooms served as the evening retreats of the families who rented them. A box could be used for eating, playing cards or chess (some houses also had a gambling room set away from the auditorium), visiting friends in other boxes, pursuing love affairs or courtships or business deals, and of course taking in the opera, which sometimes meant loudly expressing pleasure or displeasure.

It is hard to appreciate how indispensable the box was as a scene for socializing in past centuries, when opera houses and other theaters were the only places other than church that rulers allowed their subjects to gather in large numbers. David Kimbell, writing of the opera box in seventeenth-century Venice, emphasizes its role as a meeting place for diplomats and the civic elite: "To have the noblest of diversions offered to you, at a modest price, in what felt like your own private apartment was to enjoy a matchless social amenity; and the curious condition of intimacy in a public place turned the theatre into an ideal centre for the exchange of commercial and political information."[6]

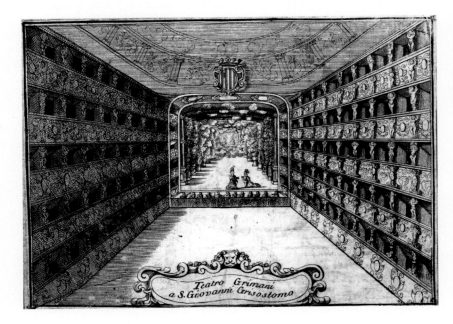

This rare drawing of one of the earliest opera houses, the seventeenth-century Teatro Grimani at San Giovanni Grisostomo in Venice, shows the sides of the theater filled with five ranks of boxes. Museo Correr (Civici Musei Veneziani d'Arte e di Storia), Venice.

Hulton Archive/Getty Images

In a different place and time—America around 1900—male patrons had other places they could meet. But women, especially unmarried young women of the upper classes, still lived shielded lives, and the opera box was one of the few places they could decently go to catch the eye of suitable young men. Ruth Solie finds evidence in American novels of the period that the box indeed offered "intimacy in a public place": "The opera box seems an ideal site: paradoxically both private and public—private in that access to it is strictly controlled, but nonetheless in public view—it functions as a glorious jewel-box to set off its prize. At the same time it is a sort of luxuriously upholstered trap; many a girl . . . must have experienced the opera box as cul-de-sac."[7]

Despite the fact that the stage was usually framed by a proscenium arch marking a boundary between the spectacle and the spectator, that boundary was often dissolved in the eighteenth century by seating spectators along the sides of the stage. We might wonder how anyone, including the performers, could concentrate on the show when part of the audience sat onstage. In fact, a great eighteenth-century satire on opera, Benedetto Marcello's *Il teatro alla moda* (*Operatic Fashion*, 1720), chides the singers of his day for giving their attention, at moments when they weren't singing, to friends for whom they had apparently procured onstage seats. "While the orchestra plays the introduction to his aria," Marcello mockingly advises, "[the singer] should take a stroll backstage, take some snuff, inform his friends that he is not in good voice tonight, and that he has a bad cold."[8]

All of this may suggest that the opera itself didn't matter to the performers, let alone the audience. But what seems like indifference may equally well be familiarity, or in David Kimbell's term, conviviality. Operagoers (and even singers) may have treated the performance casually because it was such a normal — and beloved — part of their lives. Baseball fans who sit in the stands at one game listening to the broadcast of another would understand.

In opera houses today the seats on the main floor of the auditorium are among the most desirable. But in the princely palaces where opera got its start, the floor was often used as part of the performing space, especially for dancers, just as the space in front of the stage was in Greek tragedy. For some time after that, in some royal opera houses the floor was kept clear to give an unimpeded view to a single spectator, the king, with his courtiers standing behind him. Wherever the king sat, others would compete for places as close as possible to him. In some houses the floor might be the rowdiest area, a place to stand or to deposit your rented bench and sit on it.

Social categories have usually determined who sits or stands where. Soldiers were often assigned to stand along the walls, keeping order but perhaps also enjoying the show. The servants of box holders used to stand in the auditorium or sit in the highest gallery (called "paradise" in French houses and "the gods" in British ones). Many opera houses still provide standing room behind the last rows of seats on various levels: students, retired people, and others snap up the tickets, the cheapest in the house, and

The royal party is seated in the center of the floor, with most of the floor kept clear to give them an unimpeded view, in this engraving of a performance of Giuseppe di Majo's *Sogno d'Olimpia* in the Theater of the Royal Palace in Naples, 1747. Engraving by G. Vasi after Vincenzo Re, from a publication marking the royal birth being celebrated at that performance.
Lebrecht Photo Library

race up flights of stairs when the doors are opened to claim choice spots. In the first few centuries of opera, only men were expected to stand, and even if the floor held seats, that was often considered an unsafe and improper location for women, filled as it was with unattached men. All in all, the opera house, despite its reputation as a preserve of the rich, has always been a place that brings together people of various classes and types, assigns them places that make them conscious of their social differences, but then unites them in a shared experience of the spectacle. Rather like a baseball stadium.

A Matter of Perspective

Differences in the price of seats reflect not just social distinctions but also differences in sight lines and sound quality. Consider the angle from which you view the set. Opera began in Italy at a time when Italian painters had developed the art of perspective for creating an illusion of three-dimensionality on a two-dimensional surface. Stage designers would paint a scene in perspective on a **backdrop** placed at the back of the stage. On each side of the stage they would put a half dozen **wing flats** (narrow vertical boards), each painted with a bit more of the backdrop scene, one placed in front of the other but slightly to the side, together extending the illusion of depth. The backdrop in two dimensions and the wings in three would create the illusion of a scene.

The Drottningholm Palace Theater at the royal palace in Drottningholm, Sweden, opened in 1776, was abandoned a couple of decades later. When it was reopened in the twentieth century, it was discovered to have original sets and stage machinery intact. This photo shows how an eighteenth-century backdrop and wing flats collaborate to produce the illusion of scenic depth.
Carmen Redondo/Corbis

An early Venetian scene design with a single, centered vanishing point. Giacomo Torelli's design for the courtyard of King Nasso in the opera *Venere gelosa* by Francesco Sacrati, produced at the Novissimo Theater in Venice, 1643.

Pinoteca Civica di Fano, Fano, Italy/Bridgeman Art Library

Actors standing in front of this scene would appear to be in it and of it, but because the wings were painted in perspective, using a diminution in size to represent distance, the actors couldn't move back into the wings without looming gigantic in relation to their surroundings. The early opera houses might have boasted a stage upward of sixty feet deep, but two-thirds of that depth was used to create the scenic illusion and only the front third for acting.

An eighteenth-century set-design drawing by Giuseppe Galli Bibiena, son of Ferdinando Galli Bibiena, with one vanishing point to the right and another to the left, both hidden from view. Engraving from the series *Architecture and Perspective*, 1740. Museu Nacional de Arte Antiga, Lisbon.

Divisão de Documentação Fotográfica/IMC

This perspective design was centered on a point at the rear of the stage toward which all the ostensibly horizontal lines in the design pointed—the **vanishing point**. Corresponding to that point was a central spot in the rear of the auditorium where the illusion of the scene was perfect. The royal box or seat could be placed at that point, and the order of the theater would reflect the order of the realm, with the ruler basking in the center and everyone else being reminded by their inferior viewing position that their social position was likewise inferior. Theater architects and set designers would consider it the duty of their art to reinforce symbolically the power of their ruler—who was also their employer. Even in Venice, which was an oligarchy rather than a monarchy, the artistic model that had so much political resonance elsewhere was hard to resist, and the single-perspective stage design prevailed for decades.

At the beginning of the eighteenth century, however, the designer Ferdinando Galli-Bibiena set off a revolution in stage design by creating sets that showed scenes from an angle. The vanishing point would no longer be at the center rear of the stage, but somewhere to the side, hidden from everyone's view no matter where they sat, by other elements of the scene. There might even be two vanishing points, or a profusion of them, some visible and others hidden. This may have had a kind of equalizing effect on the mass of spectators who sat everywhere but the royal box, though everything else about the experience would still have celebrated the established hierarchy of power.

The royalty were now free to move the royal box anywhere they liked. Already from the beginning of the eighteenth century, the royal box in English opera houses was placed along the side of the stage, where the royal family could display themselves to their subjects while enjoying the performance up close. The French royal boxes, one for the king and the other for the queen, were positioned on both sides of the stage as early as the seventeenth century. Most opera houses built in the eighteenth century, however, kept the royal box at the rear of the auditorium, far from the stage but with the straightest possible view.

A good seat for viewing has always meant a good seat for seeing the special stage effects, because those effects have been one of the glories of opera throughout its history. In the seventeenth century the special effects were illusionist tricks. Giacomo Torelli, the greatest engineer of stage marvels in the mid-seventeenth century, created machinery for changing an entire complex set in a few seconds, in full view of the audience (no curtain dropped, no lights going down, no waiting to get on with the show), causing what Edward Langhans calls "the visual effect of a dissolve in modern films."[9] Torelli and other stage engineers of the period also built machines that rolled on tracks high over the stage, lowering and raising characters, vehicles, and clouds from the rafters as if they were flying. These effects were essential in

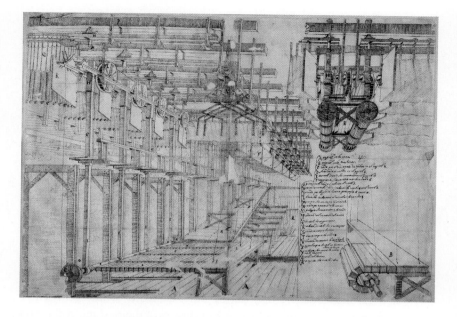

operas based on classical mythology, in which gods often descended from the heavens to rescue the human characters from their follies. Boxes close to the stage and especially those in the highest tier were the worst for viewing the flying effects, because the proscenium arch would have blocked the view.

In the nineteenth century opera houses were built with wider stages than before. Those stages were also shallower, but because the scenic design became less dependent on painted perspective effects and more on built structures, the whole depth of the stage could now be used for action, including the movements of large crowds. The stories catered to an audience that was increasingly middle class in outlook: less interested in the fates of classical gods and heroes than in the fates of nations and the lives of their people. Illusionistic effects depicting the supernatural were accordingly replaced by realistic scenes showing masses of people storming palaces, marching in civic processions, celebrating religious rituals in vast cathedrals or temples, swimming, ice-skating, and clinging to the decks of sailing ships as they rolled in operatic storms. For looking deep into the stage and catching the full effect of such scenes, the seats close to the sides of the stage were now more disadvantageous than ever, and by 1833 the French royal family returned to a box at the rear of the hall.[10]

Since the nineteenth century, increasingly sophisticated effects of lighting and image projection have only increased the pressure to design opera houses like movie theaters, where you can see everything almost equally well

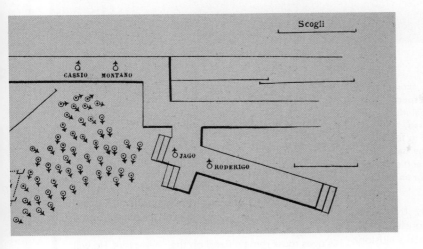

The movement of large crowds on large stages in nineteenth-century opera required elaborate blocking. Detailed books of blocking instructions, with moment-by-moment "snapshots" of the "disposition of the stage," were published in conjunction with the production of new works. **Above:** from the *Disposizione scenica* for the premiere of Verdi's *Otello* at La Scala, Milan (1887), the blocking drawing for a moment in Act 1 when a crowd gathers on the shore of Cyprus to watch the sea battle taking place at the back of the stage.

National Library of Scotland

Below: an engraving by A. Bonamore di C. Ferrario showing that moment as it looked to the audience on opening night. In "Verdi e Otello," the unique issue of *L'illustrazione italiana* (Milan: Fratelli Treves, 1887).

Harvard Theatre Collection, Houghton Library, Harvard University

Adolphe Appia

Adolphe Appia (1862–1928) was a Swiss scenery and lighting designer for whom opera, and especially the works of Richard Wagner, provided the ideal intellectual challenge. The following excerpts from his essay "Ideas on a Reform of Our Mise en Scène," published in 1904, give a sense of how his concepts challenged the naturalistic school of nineteenth-century stage design and set much twentieth-century practice on a new path. For an example of his work, see page 368.

Our present stage scenery is entirely the slave of painting—scene painting—which pretends to create for us the illusion of reality. But this illusion is in itself an illusion, for the presence of the actor contradicts it. In fact, the principle of illusion obtained by painting on flat canvas and that obtained by the plastic and living body of the actor are in contradiction. . . .

Lighting is an element in itself whose effects are limitless. . . . by means of light we can in a way materialize colors and forms, which are immobilized on painted canvas, and can bring them alive in space. No longer does the actor walk in front of painted shadows and highlights; he is plunged into an atmosphere that is uniquely his own. . . .

The second set of [Wagner's] **Siegfried** may serve as an example. . . . In order to create our setting we need not try to visualize a forest, but we have to imagine in detail the entire sequence of events that occur in this forest. Thorough knowledge of the score is therefore indispensable. It completely changes the nature of the vision that can inspire a stage director; his eyes must remain fixed on the characters. He will then think of the forest as an atmosphere around and above the performers—an atmosphere that can be realized only in relation to living and loving beings, on whom he must focus.

Essays, Scenarios, and Designs, ed. Richard C. Beacham, trans. Walther R. Volbach (Ann Arbor, Mich.: UMI Research Press, 1989), pp. 101–06.

from any seat. Still, houses of traditional design, despite their unequal sight lines, have proved to be unequaled at delivering the unamplified sound of singers and instruments clearly and warmly—and equally—to audiences.

FURTHER READING

On the history of stage costume, Anne Hollander, *Seeing Through Clothes* (New York: Viking Press, 1978); on early operatic costuming practices, ch. 10 of Beth L. Glixon and Jonathan E. Glixon, *Inventing the Business of Opera: The Impresario and His World in Seventeenth-Century Venice* (Oxford: Oxford University Press, 2006). On the cultural meanings of theater design and location, Marvin Carlson, *Places of Performance: The Semiotics of Theatre Architecture* (Ithaca: Cornell University Press, 1989). On the history of opera house design and staging, Mark A. Radice, ed., *Opera in Context: Essays on Historical Staging from the Late Renaissance to the Time of Puccini* (Portland: Amadeus Press, 1998). On the history of stage lighting, Gösta Bergman, *Lighting in the Theatre* (Stockholm: Almqvist & Wiksell International; and Totowa, N.J.: Rowman and Littlefield, 1977).

1. In our era, when you can buy a DVD of an opera for much less than the price of a ticket to a live performance, why do so many people still pay and go? Is it to be part of the social scene of the opera house? for the live aural and visual experience? for the thrill of being part of the event? How could you find out?

2. Visit any theatrical costume shop (such as the one at your institution), and learn how costumes are designed and made. Ask the designer how they contribute to the overall concept of a production, and what makes for a successful costume.

3. Examine costume drawings from opera productions of the last four centuries; you can find some in this book, in the article "Costume" in *The New Grove Dictionary of Opera*, and through internet image searches. How can you tell whether a costume design is recent or old? How do various designs relate to the time and place in which the opera is set?

4. When you watch an opera on video, are you conscious of changes in the lighting during and between scenes? When you go to the opera house, are those changes more striking? What purposes do they serve?

5. Compare the experience of open-air as opposed to indoor performances of a play, musical, ballet, concert, sports event, religious service, or an opera.

6. Examine some set designs and still photos of productions from every period of history, including the most recent. Look at illustrations in this book, in other books about opera, in magazines like *Opera News*, and through internet image searches. Compare different set designs for the same scene of a certain opera. What difference in concept of the work does each represent?

7. Look at some sets or set designs that represent a time and place very different from what the score of the opera specifies. What sense can you make of this alteration of the authors' concept?

8. When you watch a video recording of an opera, what happens to the idea of the best seat in the house? Does the camera seem to have that seat?

 Additional resources are available at wwnorton.com/studyspace.

CHAPTER 2

The Orchestra Plays

The **orchestra** provides a gate, in both space and time, into the opera. In space because the musicians are seated in the pit, a lowered, fenced-off area stretched in front of the stage. In time because the orchestra, by starting the proceedings with its **overture**, leads the spectators from the time frame of their own lives into the time frame of the opera's action. Other forms of drama may begin with an overture, but what is remarkable about the role of the orchestra in opera is the way it continues after that: except in some comic operas that are more like musicals, the orchestra plays from beginning to end. Opera is sometimes described as sung throughout, but it is truer to say that it is played throughout. The drama comes from the interaction of singers and dancers with an orchestra.

The ancient Greeks gave the name "orchestra," which means "a place for dancing," to the space in front of the stage of their outdoor theaters, the space in which the chorus danced as it declaimed its lines. When opera was first developed in Italy, the space in front of the stage was again called the orchestra, though now it referred to the whole floor of the hall, as it still does in opera houses (and concert halls). Instrumentalists sometimes hid behind the stage or crouched on the stage behind props; at other times they were onstage in full view, fitted into the action and costumed accordingly. Sometimes dancers descended stairs from the stage and danced in the vacant orchestra in front of the stage, as in the Greek theater. The early years were a time when people experimented with arrangement, sometimes allowing

The placement of the instrumentalists in a space between the stage and the audience was settled by the time commercial opera houses opened in Venice in the mid-seventeenth century. This painting by Pietro Domenico Olivero of a performance at the Teatro Regio in Turin, Italy, in 1740 shows the location that has persisted ever since, though the makeup and arrangement of the orchestra has changed considerably. Museo Civico, Turin.

the spaces of the spectators, the musicians, and the actors to flow into one another. But once theaters began to be designed specifically for opera, those three groups of people were boxed into distinct spaces, and "orchestra" eventually came to mean the body of instrumentalists in the pit.

This space gives the orchestra a visible role in the performance, if not the action. To the extent that we are absorbed in the dramatic action, we are ignoring the players. To the extent that we are conscious of the opera as a production, however, it is helpful if we are able to see the orchestra; seeing it may even help us hear the music better. The pit allows us to have it both ways, to keep the musicians present in our minds but separate from the action.

In the era when opera was emerging from diverse courtly entertainments, especially in Florence, it was common for the instrumentalists to be on the stage or hidden from view and for the space in front of the stage to be kept clear for dancers, who descended from the stage to perform. The first intermezzo in *The Liberation of Tirreno and Arnea*, designed by Giulio Parigi and performed at the Uffizi Palace, Florence, 1617. Etching by Jacques Callot.

National Trust Photo Library/
Art Resource, NY

Creating the Orchestra

In the earliest operas the instruments used the most to accompany the singers were plucked-string instruments: lutes, guitars, and citterns, as well as harps and harpsichords. They could be used one at a time rather than together, since any one of them could add full harmony, as well as counterpoint and rhythmic bite, to a singer's lines. In fact, for the first two centuries much of the singing was accompanied principally by a plucked-string instrument, sometimes joined by a melodic bass instrument, such as a cello. This accompaniment was called **basso continuo**—the composer wrote out just a "continuous bass" line, which would be played with the designated harmonies filled in above it.

Occasionally violins and other bowed-string instruments, reeds, brass, and drums were introduced, and instruments of the same family often played together to lend the appropriate color to a particular kind of scene: the reeds for a pastoral scene, the brass and drums for a military scene. But the earliest audiences seldom heard the whole ensemble play together, producing what we would call the sound of an orchestra.

The fact that opera wound up with around ninety instruments that did play together had more to do with dancing than singing. When opera was brought from Italy to France in the mid-seventeenth century, the French court already employed a large ensemble of violin-family instruments (called the King's Twenty-Four Violins) to accompany danced entertainments. In the operas a large string ensemble, joined by a group of wind instruments, was included in the pit to provide the music for the dance as well as choral numbers. Eventually the plucked-string instruments fell away, and this expanded dance band was used even to accompany solo singing. The French orchestra became the model for opera as well as symphony orchestras everywhere.

Controlling the Rhythm

Outside of Europe, in one tradition of musical drama after another, percussion instruments lead the music and guide the movement. In the Kathakali dance tradition of Kerala state in India, for instance, three different drums carry the whole action along, one of them featured specially in battle scenes and another in scenes with women. The tempos, meanwhile, are set by the singers

In the Kathakali dance-drama tradition of south India, movement and language respond to the drumming, and the drummers along with the singers share the same space as the dancer-actors.

Charles & Josette Lenars/Corbis

who narrate the action, using a gong and a pair of cymbals. In Peking Opera the instrumental ensembles are much larger and more varied, but a drummer still sets and changes the tempos, and signals the actors and players. In addition, the percussion group, according to Bell Yung, "not only [accompanies] every kind of stage movement, from long battle scenes to the roll of an eye, it also reflects the actors' thoughts and emotions, introduces sung passages, and occasionally imitates the sound of such nonexistent stage props as a boat rocking in water."[1]

In the opera orchestra, however, there are very few percussion instruments, and in most operas they are silent most of the time—even in the dance music. The principal percussion instruments are timpani—drums for marching more than dancing. That doesn't mean that opera lacks rhythm or a beat. It is often rhythmically electrifying. But how does it get that way with its percussion-poor orchestra?

Dance Rhythms and the Bass: Lully's *Armide*

To answer that question, we start by examining some music for a danced scene in the French opera *Armide*, first performed in 1686, by Jean-Baptiste Lully, who created French opera and built its orchestra around the royal dance band of violins, violas, and cellos. The title character, a Syrian sorceress, has called on a diabolical body of characters, the followers of Hate, to keep her from falling in love with the Crusader knight Renaud, whom she is sworn to destroy. In this number the followers of Hate are dancing with uncontrolled pleasure at the prospect of destroying the power of Love (see Example 2.1).

If the band for this dance had a percussion section, it would be able to lay down a pattern of beats, and the strings could give the music a suitably unbuttoned feeling by playing off against it. Something like that *is* done in this music, but without percussion. Here, as usual in opera, the **bass part** (the cellos with bassoons in this case, but in general the lowest part) provides the steady beat. This is the pulse against which the melody part (violins with oboes) marks out its more changeable rhythm. In fact, the interaction of these two parts gives the music its essential harmony as well as rhythm. The three inner parts, played by the violas, simply realize the harmonies that the outer parts imply.

2.1 Lully, *Armide*: Act 3, Air (Followers of Hate)

Further rhythmic interest in this dance comes from the flexible group-ing of the six quick quarter notes (♩) per measure. Sometimes, as in the first and third measures, the notes group into two beats of three quarter notes (or their equivalent); sometimes, as in the second and fourth mea-sures, into three beats of two quarter notes (or their equivalent). The beat pattern changes frequently and unpredictably, and following it is addition-ally intriguing because the bass and melody trade off controlling the pattern. Sometimes (as in mm. 11–12) the violins roll in endless eighth notes (♫), and the grouping of the bass notes dictates whether the music is heard in a pattern of two longer or three shorter beats. Sometimes (as in mm. 9–10) it is the bass part that flows along in eighth notes, leaving it to the violins to impose a pattern by the decisive grouping of their longer notes. If this violin

In 1874, two centuries after the premiere of Lully's *Armide*, Edgar Degas painted the orchestra accompanying a different ballet scene at the Paris Opera, the famous moonlit dance of the ghosts of dead nuns, from Meyerbeer's *Robert le Diable* (*Robert the Devil*, premiered in 1831). The conductor (far right) stands right up against the stage, with the players all around him. Victoria and Albert Museum, London.

Bridgeman Art Library

melody were heard against percussion instead of a bass line, the more powerful percussion would always determine the beat pattern. Here, there are instead two melody lines competing for our attention, and the game for the listener is to catch an ever-switching rhythmic message that emerges more strongly sometimes from one line and sometimes from the other.

If we do catch this complexity in the music, it is apt to make us giddy. But we are just listeners; there are dancers onstage who have to fit their steps to it.[2] Watching them may help us hear the music better, but it will make us no less giddy. And that effect is right for the drama: it allows us to feel what Armide feels. Having called on the powers of Hate, she watches Hate's minions move to this music, and we experience how the music and movement make her head spin, until she comes to her senses and banishes the whole hateful crew.

If this dance number derives its character from its rhythmic irregularity, there is also plenty of dance music in opera that is compellingly regular and repetitive, even obsessively so. Later in *Armide*, for instance, when the sorceress has cast her spell on Renaud, she leaves him in her enchanted palace to be entertained by a group of singers and dancers representing the Pleasures and happy lovers. They dance a *passacaille*, whose music casts its own spell by means of a lilting rhythm and a **ground bass**, a short bass phrase that endlessly repeats a progression, usually as here one that falls slowly from the tonic note (the resting note of the scale) to the dominant (the note that springs back to the tonic). Meanwhile everything else in the music is varied, and the bass line itself changes at times, but it never loses its step or its feeling of repeated progressions. After thirty-six repetitions in the bass line, solo singers and the chorus enter into the performance, keeping it going for another forty repetitions (Example 2.2 shows the first vocal entry, four phrases long). Through it all, the dancers vary their formations. All these variations have the effect of prolonging the spell of the music, holding us captive to the emotional cycle defined by the bass line, a cycle of yearning that forever leads to fulfillment that forever gives way to more yearning.

2.2 Lully, *Armide*: Act 5, Passacaille

The bass part of the orchestra, it seems, can both organize the rhythms of the other parts and control the movement of dancers—two of the functions generally taken by percussion instruments in dramatic traditions elsewhere in the world. Even in the sung dialogue of the characters, the bass instruments generally hold everyone else—the singers as well as the rest of the orchestra—together, when the rhythm is steady as well as when it changes. And they often perform that coordinating role by laying down a dance rhythm, even when no one onstage is going to dance to it.

Speaking Rhythms: Bizet's *Carmen* and Verdi's *La traviata*

In the centuries after Lully's time, dance types became more and more recognizable from the bass part alone, because it would repeat a simple but distinctive rhythmic figure over and over. Composers seized on this development, using bass figures not just to control the other performers rhythmically, but also to make complex dramatic effects. At the end of the first act of Georges Bizet's *Carmen* (1875), for instance, Carmen has been arrested. Her hands are tied together. She asks Don José, the officer who has been left in charge, to let her escape and meet her at a tavern, where she will dance the seguidilla for him. As she sings this, the lower string instruments play a figure over and over that suggests a guitar being strummed — in the rhythm, naturally, of a seguidilla: a quick triple rhythm with a short note into the second beat (one, a-two, three, one, a-two, three). The persistence throughout the song of this irrepressible dance figure, which the actress can sing to but can't dance to, makes us feel how irresistible her appeal is to Don José.

A very different case — where a character not only resists the dance, but even resists what the dance rhythm signifies — occurs in the first scene of Giuseppe Verdi's *La traviata* (*The Woman Gone Astray*, 1853). Violetta Valéry, a high-society Paris prostitute, is throwing a party and invites her guests into the next room to dance. There, offstage, a stage band of wind instruments is playing a waltz. But she is dying of tuberculosis and too sick to

Anna Caterina Antonacci as Carmen, singing her seguidilla, in which she promises to dance for Don José (Andrew Richards) when she is unbound. From Act 1 of Bizet's *Carmen*, directed by Adrian Noble at the Opéra Comique, Paris, in 2009.

Pierre Grosbois

join them, and Alfredo Germont, her secret admirer, takes this opportunity to press his love and concern on her. The overheard waltz music, with the relentless oom-pah-pah of its bass, forms a background to their conversation. On the one hand, it is a bitter reminder of Violetta's sickness, the sound of the pleasures she can no longer enjoy. On the other hand, the waltz is the musical embodiment of love in nineteenth-century opera, and the sound of a waltz as these two talk suggests that love, the one experience that a prostitute is supposed to deny herself, just may be possible for her.

In Carmen's seguidilla the orchestra introduces first the underlying rhythm, then the melody, which the singer picks up, fitting in with the orchestra as she continues. The orchestra's music counts as part of Carmen's utterance, and the rhythmic coordination between her and the orchestra assures the audience that the moment belongs exclusively to Carmen. The waltz number in *La traviata* works differently. Its stage band music counts as **diegetic**; that is, it belongs to the scene that the characters inhabit. They hear it from the next room and converse over it. The band sets a steady beat, and Violetta and Alfredo follow that beat in all their singing. But their phrases, which are irregular in length, cut across the four-bar phrases of the waltz melody. The regularity of the waltz allows us to hear the irregularity of the character's sentences as conversational.

Myrtò Papatanasiu as Violetta and Alfie Boe as Alfredo talk in one room while waltz music is heard from the next room, where the rest of the partygoers are dancing. From Act 1 of Verdi's *La traviata*, directed by David McVicar at the Welsh National Opera, 2009.
Bill Cooper

Recitative: Gershwin's *Porgy and Bess*

A good deal of the sung dialogue in opera, from the most ordinary to the most intensely dramatic, is not organized by a steady instrumental rhythm. Here the singers can pace their lines flexibly, suggesting the reluctance and the impulsiveness, the tirades and the pauses, of characters thinking on their feet. This kind of music is called **recitative** (reciting style), and in its classic (seventeenth- and eighteenth-century) form the instrumental component may be just the one or two *basso continuo* instruments, playing a single chord between each of the singers' phrases; or it may be the whole orchestra playing anything from a single chord to a full, expressive phrase. But the orchestra does not get to sustain any rhythm or melody; that would deprive the singers of their autonomy of timing. Its role is to provide a tonal and expressive, but not exactly a rhythmic, ground against which the

singers' lines play. Recitative, dialogue that would be spoken if it were in a musical, is one of the main ingredients of opera.

A modern example of recitative with orchestra is found in Act 2 of George Gershwin's *Porgy and Bess* (1935). The beautiful Bess has taken up with Porgy, a crippled beggar, after escaping an abusive relationship with Crown. But Crown finds and rapes her, and has now turned up in the center of town to claim her for his own. She tells him, "You ain't my man!" and he mocks Porgy: "Ain' dere no whole ones left?" This line and Bess's response ("You keep yo' mouth off Porgy") both begin after a fresh chord from the orchestra. The orchestra sustains these chords, creating no beat pattern to control how the singers pace their lines. Crown's next line ("Woman, do you want to meet yo' Gawd!?") is more constrained: he needs to fit those syllables to the precise rhythms of an orchestral phrase that helps convey the "fierceness" of his threatening words. But that phrase breaks off at the end of his line, and the orchestra drops out to let him shout his next threatening words ("Come here!") in relatively free rhythm and barely sung pitch.

The orchestra replies for Bess before she does, as if she knows what she thinks but needs a moment to get up the courage to say it. In that moment the orchestra begins the melody that the audience remembers from the previous act as the theme of Porgy and Bess's love duet: "Bess, you is my woman now." When she is ready to speak, Bess joins in, adapting the words of the duet to her new situation: "Porgy my man now." Crown butts in, silencing Bess, but is unable to silence her melody, which he competes with by laughing, then mocking Porgy again in another barely sung line, then singing his own countermelody ("I got de forgivin' nature, an' I goin' take you back"). When all else fails, he resorts to violence against Bess, and only that stops the music of the love duet. The scene makes us doubt Bess's strength to stand up to Crown, and that tension is embodied musically in the play of the constantly changing orchestral part against the two characters' unpredictable outbursts.

In this recitative, where the singers exercise some control over the delivery of their lines, someone else is still needed to coordinate the orchestra and singers. The job falls to a musician who doesn't play at all, the **conductor**.

The Overture

Today the conductor's arrival in the pit sets off applause, providing one of a series of signals to the audience that the opera is starting. Other signals are the dimming of the house lights and the beginning of the

The Conductor

Today the conductor stands on a podium in the pit, waving a baton, but in earlier centuries the music was directed more by audible than by visual means. In eighteenth-century Italy the conducting function was often shared between two musicians, a harpsichord player (who might be the composer) and the first violinist. In France at the same time, choral and dance movements were coordinated by a time-beater "striking a large stick against a music stand or the front of the stage"[3] — by someone, that is, performing more like a percussionist in a traditional Asian drama than like a modern conductor. As conductors have been freed from playing any instrument, they have been placed on the podium, where not only the players but the singers and dancers can see them (most of the time), and the conducting function has grown from rhythmic leadership to a more general control over the interpretation of the music.

When Richard Wagner designed a "festival theater" in Bayreuth, Germany, for the performance of his operas (or music dramas, as he called them), one of the innovations in his design was to hide the orchestra from view by putting it under the lip of the stage. The sounds of the instruments, as a result, blend with each other before they reach the audience (or the singers). Here, the conductor Sebastian Weigle conducts a rehearsal of Wagner's *Parsifal*.
Enrico Nawrath

overture. But in the days when opera houses were lit by hundreds of candles, dimming the lights would have meant snuffing candles all over the house one by one. That wouldn't have served as much of a signal. And without the house lights being dimmed, the conductor's appearance in the pit would be hard to catch; it's hard enough even today, when at the start of the overture the pit gives off only dim light in the darkened house. If the opera began without *any* signal, the audience might miss some of the opening. People like to talk right up until the show starts, or even a little later, and presumably they always have. So it has always made sense to catch the public's attention and get them quiet.

Valery Gergiev

Valery Abisalovich Gergiev (b. 1953), one of the preeminent conductors working today, is the general director of the Mariinsky Theater, the revered home of opera and ballet in St. Petersburg, Russia. His remarks quoted in a 2001 study of his career reflect a modern view of the conductor's role in shaping a performance, a role far beyond time-beating. At the same time, Gergiev attributes a surprising importance to the timpani in the orchestra—also far beyond time-beating.

I know when an orchestra needs help from me rhythmically, but I also know when it needs help emotionally. Sometimes the players have to be driven—like passengers in a car. You say to them, "OK, we go." But they do not know where. The conductor must know, and he must tell them. He supplies energy, logic, and explanations—for a phrase, a strange interval, or why a composer has written this or that. He has to give reasons for all these, and in performance he must give his reasons with his hands and his eyes. . . .

This instrument we call the timpani is the foundation of the orchestra. It is not simply something that's beaten—it is a basic color in an orchestra's overall sound. A timpanist can give you a shock, a pleasure, can help you move from one section to another—from contrabassi to woodwinds—and it provides enormous support for a tuba or even a flute. This man—Sergei Antoshkin [timpanist of the Mariinsky Orchestra]—is my most interesting player.

John Ardoin, *Valery Gergiev and the Kirov: A Story of Survival* (Portland: Amadeus Press, 2001), pp. 217–18.

Especially in the candle-lit era, it might have required the loudest resources of the orchestra to catch the attention of a noisy audience. Many overtures from the seventeenth and eighteenth centuries in fact begin with a brass and drum fanfare, as in Claudio Monteverdi's *Orfeo* (1607), or with loud chords by the full orchestra, as in Wolfgang Amadeus Mozart's *Don Giovanni* (1787). What sense can we make, then, of the overture to another Mozart opera, *The Marriage of Figaro* (1786), which begins with a whispering bustle of strings? Maybe this was a trick, meant to catch the spectators unawares, some of them wondering if the show was beginning and all of them silenced when, about five seconds into the overture, the full orchestra was finally heard in the usual *fortissimo* (very loud) blast. A great many overtures of all periods, but most famously those by Gioachino Rossini to operas like *The Barber of Seville* (1816) and *William Tell* (1829), end with a ratcheting up of excitement that creates anticipation for the opera to follow. In the era of dimmable lighting and bowing conductors, composers have felt free to make a quiet opening, like a stage whisper, just as arresting as the loudest sound. Richard Wagner's overture to *Lohengrin* (1850), for instance, begins on a note mysteriously quiet and high, just as his overture to *Das Rheingold* (1876) begins on a note mysteriously quiet and low.

The overture also plays a decisive role in transporting the audience into the imaginary world of its opera. We are in an acoustically rich theater,

waiting for the audience chatter and the tuning of the instruments to die down, when we hear, out of the silence, the sound of the orchestra welling up from the pit. The whole dramatic experience of the opera can spring from the vivid first moment of being enveloped in that sound, before the curtain rises. Bizet's overture to *Carmen*, for example, is famous for its **local color** (its power to suggest a place and time), which transports its audiences to southern Spain, where the story is set. We could easily hear in this overture nothing more than a pair of colorful and highly charged dance pieces, followed by a melody that seems like the voice of doom. But if we know where the opera is set, we can associate that music with a certain image of Spain: a country of Gypsies and toreadors who live life for the moment and accept fate when it comes. Each theme, furthermore, reappears in the opera itself, where it gains a specific identity; one of those themes becomes the Toreador Song. As all the themes reappear in the course of the opera, accumulating dramatic and visual associations, an image of Spain comes into sharper focus.

There is neither local color nor a previewing of melodies in Mozart's overtures to *The Marriage of Figaro* and *Don Giovanni*. Both operas are set, like *Carmen*, in or near Seville, but their Spanish setting is a mask, a way of pretending that what happens "there" wouldn't happen "here" (which for Mozart's audiences was the Austrian Empire). These two overtures sound very different from each other because they are opening up different worlds of action, not different settings. The quiet bustle of the *Marriage of Figaro* overture leads us into a tale of domestic intrigue, while the overture to *Don Giovanni*, announced by two ominous chords, each with a creepy afterglow in the bass, leads us into a darker tale that ends with the protagonist dragged down to hell. Mozart seems to have followed the example of his older contemporary Christoph Willibald Gluck, whose preface to the score of *Alceste* (1769) advises that the overture should "alert the spectators to the action" and furthermore that it should "form, so to speak, [the opera's] argument." That is, it should set forth, in symphonic terms, the conflict at work in the drama.

Modest Musorgsky's overture to *Khovanshchina* (an opera he left unfinished at his death in 1881) is remarkable in that it prepares spectators for what is not to come. Musorgsky gave the overture the title "Dawn over the Moskva River." Built on what sounds like a Russian folk song (a symbol perhaps of humanity at its closest to nature), it depicts a world coming to life at the touch of sunlight. Yet the opera is a drama of city people locked together in a relentless cycle of rivalry, mistrust, betrayal, and violence. Not until the last scene does the action leave the city for a natural setting, a pine forest, but by then the characters have turned even the natural world into a site of death.

In retrospect the loveliness of this overture is a heartbreaking reminder of the innocence of nature that is lost on humanity. In general, the only way to appreciate how the overture opens up the world of its opera is to think back to it once the story is completed.

FURTHER READING

On the development of the Western orchestra, John Spitzer and Neal Zaslaw, *The Birth of the Orchestra: History of an Institution, 1650–1815* (Oxford and New York: Oxford University Press, 2004). On independent orchestral music within operas, Christopher Morris, *Reading Opera Between the Lines: Orchestral Interludes and Cultural Meaning from Wagner to Berg* (Cambridge: Cambridge University Press, 2002). On conducting, José Antonio Bowen, ed., *The Cambridge Companion to Conducting* (Cambridge: Cambridge University Press, 2003). In Hector Berlioz's *Evenings with the Orchestra*, trans. Jacques Barzun (Chicago: University of Chicago Press, 1956/1999), a great opera composer mocks operatic life in a collection of stories supposedly told in the orchestra pit during performances.

FOR RESEARCH AND REFLECTION

1. Watch a performance of an opera in English. Note moments when the orchestra seems to carry a singer along in its rhythm and moments when a singer seems to be in charge of the timing of her/his own thoughts and words. What is the difference in the way the vocal lines and the orchestral parts are coordinated at these two kinds of moment?

2. Watch an operatic scene in which instruments are played onstage (such as the finale to Act 1 of Mozart's *Don Giovanni*). Describe how seeing instruments as part of the action affects your consciousness of instrumental sound in the imagined world of that opera.

3. How does the sound of a particular instrument acquire significance in an opera? Study the role of the harp in Monteverdi's *Orfeo* or Gluck's *Orfeo ed Euridice*, the flute in the mad scene of Donizetti's *Lucia di Lammermoor*, the solo violin in Offenbach's *Orpheus in the Underworld*, or the harpsichord in Stravinsky's *The Rake's Progress*.

4. What does it mean for an overture to prefigure the argument or the nature of an opera? Try this idea out on an opera of Gluck, Beethoven, Wagner, or Debussy.

5. Listen to a medley overture in an opera of Verdi, Bizet, or Gilbert and Sullivan, or a Broadway musical like *Gypsy*. Which tunes does the composer choose to announce in the overture? How are they arranged, and what effect does it have when you hear them again in the course of the work?

 Additional resources are available at wwnorton.com/studyspace.

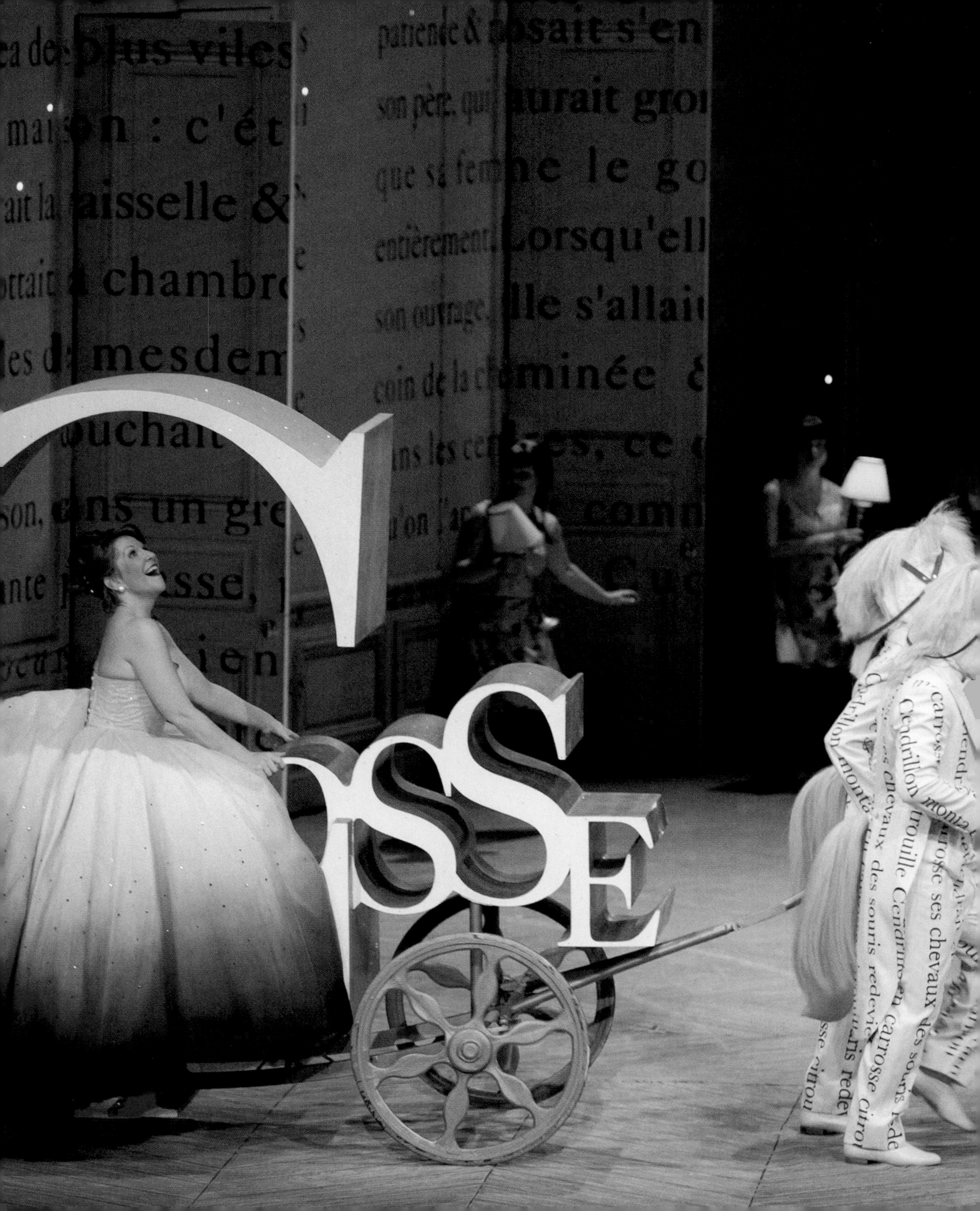

CHAPTER 3

The Cast Appears

Once the curtain goes up and the singers appear, the show belongs to them. Sets come and go, special effects dazzle us, and the orchestra keeps playing, but all those things are accessories to the people onstage, the performances they are giving and the fates of the characters they embody. Opera is a form of drama ruled to an extraordinary extent by singing. The singing furthers the dramatic action in that it conveys, times, colors, and shapes the characters' words. But if the words are going to make an impact on us, we have to understand them, and both the singing and its orchestral accompaniment can interfere with that. It may be hard for us to understand the words even if the singers are singing in English, and that is hardly the norm. Operas are most often sung in their original language. For centuries, opera texts were sold in little books (**libretti**) so that spectators could read the drama ahead of time or follow along. When the opera was sung in a language foreign to the audience, the libretto would also include a translation. Nowadays translations ("titles") are displayed on screens, usually over the stage.

But why aren't operas just sung in the audience's language, making the words and therefore their dramatic impact more immediate? The question has been debated long and passionately, and the arguments tell us a lot about the relationship of singing to drama. Those who advocate singing in translation argue that the sung words communicate meaning directly to the audience that way.

A singer making an operatic entry: Joyce DiDonato in the role of Cinderella (Cendrillon) arrives at the royal palace in her magical carriage. From Act 2 of Massenet's *Cendrillon* (1899), directed by Laurent Pelly at the Royal Opera House, Covent Garden, London.

Bill Cooper/Royal Opera House, London

Those who argue for the original language claim instead that the singers' notes are married so intimately to the rhythms and inflections of the original words that translating them obstructs the sense of the music. The collaboration of words and notes means more, dramatically, than the words by themselves.

Nevertheless, opera is widely enjoyed in circumstances that downplay the importance of the words and action. People listen to radio broadcasts or audio recordings or unstaged concert performances, availing themselves of plot summaries or librettos if they like, but certainly missing the stage action. It may be that these commonplace experiences are found satisfying because the soundtrack of opera—the singing and orchestral accompaniment—is the heart of the dramatic matter. The music characterizes every step in the unfolding story with a distinctive change; in Joseph Kerman's famous formulation, "music articulates the drama."[1] It is best, of course, when you can take in the words, music, and spectacle all together. But when you have followed an opera that way more than once, you may then be able to hear the soundtrack and feel that you are having the whole experience. For you, the music would now contain the unfolding of the story.

A different explanation is that the sound of the singers' voices is what really transports us to the opera's imagined realm. It may not even matter so much *where* the music takes us, simply that it takes us outside ourselves. In this way of thinking, it makes little difference whether we are experiencing the soundtrack alone or the whole spectacle: people turn to opera above all to be overwhelmed by the extraordinary voices of its singers.

Broadway performers are called *actors*; opera performers are called *opera singers*. They learn to act, but the acting they are really expected to master is with their voices. In Peking Opera the singers have to move with great skill and even perform acrobatics, but in Western opera dancing is done by a separate set of performers. A role like Carmen that calls for both singing and dancing is rare. It has always helped if the singers, especially in the lead roles, have the good looks of movie stars, especially now that opera is so often seen through the close-up lens of a video camera. But the right voice can still trump the right looks. The title characters in Wagner's *Tristan and Isolde* (1865) are young lovers, yet they are usually played by singers too old and hefty to look appealing or even plausible in the parts, because it takes sturdy singers with the stamina of middle age to deliver the music Wagner wrote for them.

Superhuman Voices in Human Roles

Through a combination of natural endowment and long, intense training, opera singers are capable of an arresting vocal power and beauty throughout an unusually wide range; a breathtaking clarity in fast, florid passages; and an irresistible personality in both joyous music and sad. These are not voices that could belong to the girl or boy next door. But their superhuman quality poses a problem for dramatic credibility. Though a singer's voice may need to be extraordinary enough to transport us to an imagined world outside our ordinary experience, at the same time it needs to make the character the singer is playing seem, if not like the boy or girl next door, then human enough to engage our interest. How can one voice serve both those purposes?

Nadir's Romance in *The Pearl Fishers*

Consider a number from another opera by Bizet, *The Pearl Fishers* (*Les Pêcheurs de perles*, 1863): "Je crois entendre encore" ("I think I hear once again"). The character who sings it is a young man named Nadir on the island now known as Sri Lanka. He is alone onstage, pouring out his feeling for a woman he fell in love with some time ago and swore he would forget. But now, having seen her again, he confesses to the night that he is ready to break his vow. Even before he begins to sing, the orchestral introduction to his song (or Romance, as it is called in the score) tells us that this is music designed to transport us to the realm of love. We can tell that from the quiet, wave-like figure that the cellos play over and over, and from the hypnotic way the English horn keeps pulling away from its first note, E, and returning to it. But the singer's lines are even more hypnotic, making an extraordinary voice sound unearthly. The song starts on the English horn's E, already a pretty high note for most men, and works its way up from there. What's more, it all has to be sung quietly—the hardest way to sing high notes.

Charles Castronovo, as Nadir, sings the Romance "Je crois entendre encore" in Act 1 of Bizet's *The Pearl Fishers*, in a production designed by Zandra Rhodes that premiered at the San Diego Opera in 2004.
© Ken Howard/San Diego Opera

Most hypnotic in its effect, and most superhuman in its demands, is the breath control required. In its leisurely tempo, this song spins out one long phrase after another, each one pausing several times to dwell on a note, without a breath, before moving on. The first two phrases (shown in Example 3.1), each of which can barely be sung in a single breath, form a long wave of almost unbroken vocal sound, leading up from the initial

3.1 Bizet, *The Pearl Fishers*: Act 1, "Je crois entendre encore"

note (E) and eventually down to the E an octave below it. And the number is just beginning. The guy next door would never make it through this song, and no one would want to hear him try. And yet the audience needs to feel connected to Nadir as he pours out his heart, or this opera would mean nothing to us. We are drawn into the spell of his yearning, and we know we are because we hang on the singer's every breath, almost literally. If he is really good, the whole audience will unconsciously match his breathing and find itself breathless in the process. This is not a painful experience, but a transforming one. One singer's remarkable breathing can take an auditorium full of people out of their boy-or-girl-next-door selves and transport them into the musical world of Nadir's rapture.

This may make it sound as if there is no tension between singing in its own right and singing for the sake of dramatic characterization. That would be misleading. From almost the beginning of opera, singers have been pulled one way by their creative bosses—the dramatist (librettist), the composer, the stage director, the conductor—and the other way by their fans. Fans go to the opera to hear their favorite singers deliver the solo numbers called **arias** (Nadir's Romance is an example), more than to see them lose themselves dramatically in those roles. The creative bosses, while not despising the appeal of star voices, want the singers to be in character, to put their vocal resources at the service of a dramatic and musical concept of the whole work, up until the moment when the curtain falls and they step out front to bow.

Singing Alone: Soloists

Today there is nothing surprising about finding men and women singing on the same stage, but opera was born into a world where civil and religious authorities sought to protect public morals by keeping women off

the stage. In the dramas of the ancient Greeks and Romans, male actors played all the roles, and the creators of the first operas, who were emulating those ancient dramas, knew it. In their own time (around 1600), men or boys specializing as female impersonators played the women's roles on stages from Japan and China to England. In 1629, when a visiting French acting company brought actresses to London, where women had long been banned from the stage, the company was "hissed, hooted, and pippin-pelted from the stage."[2]

The situation in Italy, as in France, was more mixed. In 1588 Pope Sextus V banned women from the stage, just as earlier popes had long banned them from singing in church. Because the pope was the secular as well as religious ruler of Rome, this ban kept women off the opera stages of Rome until 1798. But in other Italian cities, though women were not allowed to sing in church, they could perform in the princely courts, where most of the earliest operas were created. The rulers of those courts could draw from two sources of professional women singers: the performing forces of their own courts and the itinerant family theatrical troupes who presented partly improvised dramas called *commedia dell'arte*. Later, opera moved to public theaters in Venice, a city with a "curious mixture of freedom and suppression," according to Wendy Heller, and operas were performed there during carnival season, when Venice became "a veritable amusement park for Europe."[3] Women singers appeared there from the start, and once they were established in Venice, any other city (except Rome) that wanted opera expected to have it with women singers.

When opera became a commercial enterprise in seventeenth-century Venice, its first star was a woman, the soprano Anna Renzi. This portrait appeared in a publicity brochure, *Le glorie della signora Anna Renzi romana (The Glories of Madame Anna Renzi of Rome*; Venice, 1644).

The Gender of the Voice

Given that opera is drama centered on the singing voice, we might assume that women were cast in opera, in the face of deep-seated cultural resistance, because the contrast between men's and women's voices was needed to make the story dramatically viable. But before we make that assumption, we should take account of the complexity of operatic voices and casting. For one thing, in the first two centuries of opera many of the male roles, including the romantic, heroic leads, were played by **castrati**, male singers who had been castrated before puberty so that they would retain the high ranges of women when their voices matured. As a result, the difference between female and male characters was not consistently marked by a contrast of high and low

Singers on Expression

Baritone Manuel Patricio Rodríguez García (1805–1906), who belonged to the greatest family of singers in the nineteenth century, made his mark as a great voice teacher.

Nature attaches to every sentiment a characteristic accent. To threaten or entreat in other timbres and other modulations than those suitable to menace or prayer, far from exciting fear or compassion, would simply give occasion for mirth. Each individual has also a distinctive manner of expression, which alone is truthful and impressive. Age, habits, organization, surroundings, modify a similar sentiment in different people, and the artist must vary his colour accordingly.

Manuel García, *Hints on Singing*, translated from the French by Beata Garcia, new and revised edition (London: Ascherberg, Hopwood and Crew, 1894), p. 70.

Soprano Julianne Baird (b. 1952) has flourished as a singer, teacher, and scholar of opera and other vocal music of the seventeenth and eighteenth centuries.

Modern music teachers, and I am one, should respect the particular strengths and weaknesses of the singer standing before us to be taught. We must resist the pressure to fit the singer into some procrustean bed inimical to his talents. We must teach him the first principle: Know thyself. We must realize that there are important values—wit, ingenuity, feeling, for example—to strive for, other than the large voice and the plastic sameness in quality of sound for every note—other than the "beautiful pearl."

Bernard D. Sherman, *Inside Early Music: Conversations with Performers* (New York and Oxford: Oxford University Press, 1997), p. 241.

Soprano Dawn Upshaw (b. 1960) has sung a wide-ranging repertory, but is especially known for championing the operas and other works of contemporary composers.

With my students I talk a lot about being with the piece instead of projecting it. It's a wonderful thing to move away from just trying to give beautiful sound to an audience, and instead go in a completely different direction by trying to offer them a truth—one that may be beautiful but may also be very painful—yet in that way it connects with the world.

Interview by Jeremy Eichler, *Boston Globe*, May 3, 2009.

---

voices. At most there was a contrast in sound quality: castrati, though singing in the same range as women, could produce a more brilliant and powerful, but also a somehow unearthly, sound.

Meanwhile, there was no simple identification of the singer's gender with the gender of the role. As in other dramatic traditions, there were **drag roles** (women played by men) and **breeches roles** (men played by women). Many of these were comic secondary roles, but the role of a young male lover might be played by a woman. There were also roles that called for the character to be disguised, part of the time, in the costume of the other sex. Such gender mismatches and switches were visually comic, but also tantalizing. In an age when respectable women always wore full-length skirts, breeches roles and roles for women disguising themselves as men were created expressly so that men in the audience could see the shape of a woman's legs, and for that reason female singers were often unwilling to play them.[4]

Where there is cross-dressing, there is cross-voicing. Audiences that thrilled to the voices of men singing in women's ranges while playing men's roles also relished the vocal complications of drag and breeches casting and cross-gender disguises. In George Frideric Handel's *Alcina* (1735) the female character Bradamante, played by a female alto, disguises herself as her brother while retaining her womanly voice. In this ambiguous state she unintentionally captures the love of Morgana, a female character played by a female soprano, when what she is trying to do is win back the affections of her lover, the knight Ruggiero, who was originally played by an alto castrato. (The complications are not at all reduced these days when, there being no castrati, the role of Ruggiero may be sung by a female alto.) What we see may contradict what we hear: an exchange that looks straight may sound queer, and vice versa. Individual listeners, depending on their gender and sexual orientation, might be taken with this or that member of the cast, but the effect of this constant play of sexual ambiguities is not so much to provide objects for every sexual taste as to engage the audience as a whole in a game of discovering that sexual natures and relationships can't be resolved into simple categories.

The castrato voice was especially ambiguous. Neither male nor female, the product of castration, it was paradoxically found to be especially erotic. But all voices in opera can have that magical power by which, according to Michael Poizat, "all that is visual and all that tends toward signification fails and falls away."[5] Even the singer's identity may seem to drop away, especially as she or he reaches high notes that are beyond the range of most humans. As the human, gendered source of the sound dissolves from the listener's consciousness, the sound itself establishes a contact with the listener that is so direct and sensuous that it is easily confused with a sexual effect. This confusion stands behind much of the adoration of opera singers by their fans.

Early in the nineteenth century castrati disappeared from the operatic stage (though cross-gender casting and disguising did not), and a new ordering of voices has prevailed in works created since then: the sympathetic roles of the young lovers are usually sung by higher voices, and the older or less sympathetic roles by lower ones. Furthermore, the conventional associations are upheld often enough that audiences can sense something important about the story when the composer has toyed with the conventions. In *Carmen*, for instance, when the tenor falls for the mezzo-soprano, turning his back on the soprano, it is clear that things are heading for a bad end. Likewise, in Pyotr Il'yich Tchaikovsky's *Yevgeny Onegin* (1879) the title character, who commands center stage precisely by being an unconventional—and unsatisfactory—lover is played by a baritone, while the conventional lover Lensky, played by a tenor, doesn't live past the middle of the opera.

Vocal Ranges and Character Types

In opera since the early nineteenth century, the leading roles, usually those of the young lovers, are typically written for singers with the highest voices. The highest male voice in the ensemble is the **tenor** (like hypnotic-voiced Nadir in *The Pearl Fishers*). His high C is an octave lower than that of his leading lady (or his castrato predecessor), but from a tenor, that note sounds just as remarkable. The role of his rival or enemy or best friend is often written for a **baritone**. The baritone range is a more ordinary range for men, but like the tenor, the baritone achieves his great moments with high notes. On the other hand, the **bass**, who has the lowest voice on the operatic stage and is generally cast as a father or someone of considerable age and authority, makes his greatest effect with his lowest notes—notes that make us respect his power, but don't necessarily make us like him.

Among women singers, there is a parallel ordering. The **soprano**, with the extraordinarily high notes, generally plays the tenor's partner, or would-be partner (though the baritone may think he has a claim on her). Her rival or her confidante may be a singer of medium range, a **mezzo-soprano**, who has fairly high notes of her own, while the **contralto**, the lowest-voiced woman in the cast, is likely to play an older woman, perhaps a mother or a woman of evil character; she impresses with her extreme low notes.

Singing Together (1): Ensembles

The sound of combined voices is just as capable of transporting listeners into rapture as the sound of a single voice. And the combining of voices gives opera a dramatic resource unavailable to spoken drama. For two or more characters in a play to speak at the same time, even for a moment, is barely tolerable; in opera, two or three or a hundred can sing together for long stretches, and the way they join voices tells us everything about the moment we have reached in the action.

Duets: *The Marriage of Figaro*

Numbers in which two or more individual characters sing together are called **ensembles**. An ensemble of two is a **duet**. If the two characters are in love, the composer can represent the oneness of their love in a duet that dissolves the two voices into a single sound. The formula is irresistible and

inexhaustible; opera is full of **love duets**. Even Richard Wagner, who in theory despised the operatic convention of joining voices on the grounds that people don't usually speak at the same time, nevertheless resorted to it, if sparingly, at crucial stages in the love duet—actually a whole scene of secret and adulterous lovemaking—of *Tristan and Isolde*. In fact, even in more conventional love duets the lovers do not usually sing together all the time. Instead, the duet typically shows them coming together musically, through a progression that begins with the partners singing separately, then overlapping more and more, and finally singing the same words at the same time, mostly in sweet intervals of thirds or sixths, achieving and symbolizing a "perfect harmony."

This formula is an almost universal structure of duets in general, showing characters in all kinds of situations working their way in dialogue to some kind of unity. In musical terms there may be no way to tell a love duet from another kind of duet. In Mozart's *The Marriage of Figaro*, for instance, half a dozen numbers are duets, and duet passages occur in still other numbers, yet there is no love duet. Even the first two duets, between Figaro and Susanna (the lovers about to be married), just demonstrate how unready these two characters are for the challenges their love faces. Another duet, beginning "Via resti servita" ("Your humble servant"), is an insulting contest between Susanna and the aging governess Marcellina, who both want to marry Figaro. Their voices, at first answering each other hesitantly, begin to overlap more and more until they are singing whole phrases simultaneously. This may be the structure of the love duet, but it has a completely different spirit: their voices come together not from any warmth between them, but from warming to the game of putting each other down.

The closest approach to the spirit of a love duet comes in another number between two women, Susanna and her mistress, the Countess Almaviva. The Countess's husband is attempting to seduce Susanna, and the two women decide that Susanna should write the Count a letter in the form of a song lyric inviting him to a tryst, where his intentions will be exposed. In their conspiratorial duet ("Canzonetta sull'aria," or "Song to the tune of"—usually known by its opening words, "Sull'aria,") the Countess dictates the letter to Susanna, who repeats all the lines as she writes them.[6] The second half of the duet, in which they read back what Susanna has written, succinctly encapsulates all the musical stages of a love duet: the two voices are heard in different phrases, overlapping a little; then in the same phrases, still overlapping; and finally in shared phrases, mostly at an interval of a third. Even though writing the letter is an act of intrigue, the unguarded sound of their voices shows us that these two women, divided by class but free of competition with each other, enjoy the only trusting relationship in the opera.

Ensembles of Opposition: The *Rigoletto* Quartet

Two or more voices can also be brought together to create music of oppositions. The classic instance is the **quartet** (four-voice ensemble) "Bella figlia dell'amore" ("Pretty daughter of love") in Verdi's *Rigoletto* (1851). Gilda, daughter of Rigoletto, a court jester, has been seduced by Rigoletto's lord, the Duke of Mantua, and Rigoletto, wanting to cure her of her love for the seducer, brings her to an inn on a stormy night to witness the Duke seducing another woman. We hear the exchange inside the inn, in which the Duke plays up to the other woman, Maddalena, and she laughs him off; we also hear the exchange outside, where Gilda expresses her horror at discovering the Duke's nature and her father tells her to save her tears, keep quiet, and let him avenge her.

All of this could be done in a spoken play, and in fact it was. The opera is based on the play *Le Roi s'amuse* (*The King Enjoys Himself*) by Victor Hugo, and Verdi's scene closely replicates the comparable scene in that play. Since we can't understand two spoken conversations at the same time, in Hugo's scene Gilda's exchange with her father has to follow the Duke's exchange with Maddalena, so it is quite a while before Gilda lets us know how she is being affected. Music, on the other hand, allows Verdi to take us through the two conversations simultaneously. Verdi gives each of the four characters phrases of a distinctive cast and overlaps them in such a way that each singer can make a few telling words stand out, yet all four parts harmonize. And through this compressed music, in which the four singers express themselves simultaneously, the listener also feels how the fates of the four characters are locked together. Instead of the sound of individuals dissolving their individuality into union, we are left with the sound of a standoff. An opera can end with a love duet, but an ensemble like this quartet is by nature an unresolved stage before the end of the story.

Singing Together (2): The Chorus

In most operas there is a group of characters with no individual identities or names, but the identity — and the combined voices — of a group. This is the **chorus**. Not every opera has one, but ancient Greek tragedy, with its unforgettable choral episodes, provided an impetus for including a chorus in the

Two images of the quartet "Bella figlia dell'amore" in Act 3 of Verdi's *Rigoletto*, from productions 150 years apart, both at the Royal Opera House in London.
Above: the first British production, in 1853, just two years after the premiere in Venice, showing Gilda and her father Rigoletto, on the right, peering into the inn where the Duke is dallying with Maddalena.
Bettmann/Corbis

Below: in a production staged by David McVicar in 2001, Christine Schaefer as Gilda and Paolo Gavanelli as Rigoletto, on the left, listen in as Marcelo Álvarez (the Duke) takes Graciela Araya (Maddalena) into his arms.
Clive Barda/ArenaPal

earliest operas, and dramatic functions have been found for this group voice ever since. While the Greek chorus was made up of men, chanting their lines as they danced in front of the stage in a large outdoor amphitheater, the opera chorus throughout its history has included both men and women, singing in several parts, standing and moving (but usually not dancing) on the stage of an indoor theater.

At the time opera was invented, there was no single musical model for the sound of its chorus. The earliest composers were familiar with the great choral tradition of the Catholic Church and drew heavily on its part-writing techniques when writing choral numbers for their operas. The church choir, however, with boys singing the upper parts, had a very different sound from the opera chorus. A model that did mix women's with men's voices was immediately at hand at the princely courts where opera was born: the madrigal choir. Its sound can be heard in the choruses of early operas created for those courts, such as *Orfeo* (1607) by Claudio Monteverdi. But the delicate sound of the courtly madrigal choir did not persist long on the opera stage, and as opera houses grew larger, so too did the chorus until now in the major houses it may reach a hundred voices.

The sound of this large chorus depends on the dramatic role it is assigned. Unlike the chorus of men in a Greek tragedy, the opera chorus can represent the full diversity of a society, people of different classes, sexes, ages, occupations, and affiliations. The voices of those different groups can be posed against each other or brought together accordingly. The chorus can also represent an independent force, a mass character. In works like Musorgsky's *Boris Godunov* (1874) or Arnold Schoenberg's *Moses and Aaron* (first performed in 1957, six years after the composer's death), the chorus represents a people or nation that the individual characters push this way or that, but that cuts its own path toward its eventual destiny. The chorus can be cowed one minute and rebellious the next; it can turn from riotous disunity to hymnlike solidarity.

The Individual and the Mass: The Chorus in *Fidelio*

In some works the chorus, or some part of it, is identified with a particular character and serves to raise that character's plight to a more universal level. In Beethoven's *Fidelio* (1805; revised 1814), for instance, the plot revolves around the fate of the character Florestan, who is being held secretly and unjustly in solitary confinement by the vengeful governor of a Spanish prison. Before we meet him, we meet his fellow inmates when they are briefly let out into the prison courtyard. These men step out tentatively, letting their eyes adjust to the bright sunlight and their lungs to the fresh air,

to the accompaniment of slowly evolving orchestral harmonies. Then, just as tentatively, they begin to sing: "O what joy, to draw breath easily in the open air!" ("O welche Lust! In freier Luft den Athem leicht zu heben"). They sing in close harmony, their four vocal parts almost always staying within the interval of an octave. The sound of this men's chorus—close to the sound of a barbershop quartet—conveys a spirit of camaraderie, or brotherhood, that the prisoners keep alive in the face of oppression. Soon thereafter, when we meet Florestan in his lonely dungeon, this chorus has prepared us to consider him not as an isolated victim of some personal injustice, but as an individual whose prospects for freedom are tied to those of his fellow victims and to the restoration of justice in his society.

Florestan is liberated by his heroic wife Leonore, and in the final scene, as the unjust order is being overthrown, a new choral sound affirms the possibility of a just order taking its place. A crowd of townspeople rush into the prison, joining their voices to those of the prisoners, and for the first time in the opera we hear a mixed chorus of women and men, representing a society in which human relationships are restored to a fairer and more natural state. Then, as Leonore ceremoniously unlocks the chains that have long bound Florestan, the voices of soloists celebrating the moment as a triumph of divine justice are joined by that mixed chorus, overlapping with them in a hymnlike, four-part texture. That hymn style, borrowed from the congregational singing of Protestant churches, serves here—as in many opera choruses—to represent a community expressing its unity of sentiment and purpose.

The prisoners, under guard, are briefly allowed to soak in the light in Act 1 of Beethoven's *Fidelio*, as directed by Otto Schenk at the Vienna State Opera in 2011.
Wiener Staatsoper/Michael Poehn

The hymn derives much of its effect from the way the chorus mirrors the other mass of men and women in the opera house: the audience. The sing-ability of a hymn melody, in contrast to the elaborate and taxing melodies given to the solo singers, increases this effect, since members of the audience can almost feel it issuing from their own throats. Dramatically, then, the chorus possesses a unique power to grant the spectators a point of entry into the opera: it not only raises the conflicts of the individual characters to a more universal level, but also makes the audience feel a part of the multitude affected by those conflicts. If the sound of a solo voice in opera can transport us outside of ourselves, that of the chorus can make us feel at home.

Moving Together: The Ballet Corps

Dancers make up the other group of characters without individual identities in an opera. The **ballet corps**—the body of dancers—is often onstage at the same time as the chorus, and the two groups divide between them the functions of singing and dancing that the chorus in Greek tragedy performed together. Ballet developed in opera houses, and dance figures in many operas, but in an art form dominated by singing, the dancers play characters who are not only anonymous but voiceless. Their role can therefore seem marginal. They do their dancing at odd times, sometimes between acts or at the end. In French opera, in fact, sets of dance numbers are often called **divertissements**—that is, diversions. It is hardly surprising that composers have sometimes left it to others to write the ballet music for their operas and that critics describing an opera sometimes leave the dance completely out of account. So how can we make sense of the prominent place that dance has always had in opera?

Expressing the Music in Movement: *Carmen*

A first answer is that dancing takes up the energy of music and releases it in movement. In opera there is typically little rhythmic movement onstage for stretches of time, while the characters talk—that is, sing—through their problems. Even when this singing is done in music of a danceable rhythm, the singers do not usually move to it. It makes sense, therefore, that dance numbers tend to be provided at fairly regular intervals, increasing in their duration and prominence toward the end of the work. In the seventeenth and eighteenth centuries ballet **entr'actes** (separate dance entertainments) usually filled the time between acts, even when there were also danced

numbers within the acts. In the nineteenth century and later, when houses held intermissions between acts, operas often offered a substantial dance episode within one of the later acts.

In subtler ways too, an opera might first create and then fulfill a yearning to see the music danced. In the first act of *Carmen*, for instance, there is a lot of movement onstage that approaches dance — soldiers and boys marching, women factory workers flirting with male onlookers as they smoke, Carmen introducing herself to the same men in a tantalizing Habanera, Carmen with her hands bound promising, in seguidilla rhythm, to dance for Don José. All of this stepping and swaying and singing and promising gives way to the real thing in the second act, when Carmen and two friends dance a Gypsy dance. Then Carmen delivers on her promise to Don José, performing, for him alone, a dance that turns out not to be a seguidilla.

The capacity of the spectators to respond in kinetic sympathy to the dances onstage — that is, to feel their own nerves and muscles tense and relax in time with the movements — doesn't depend on the dancers performing dances the spectators know. But it doesn't hurt if they do, and composers have always known that. For three hundred years they wrote music that fit the social dances of the day, even if the dancers performed more elaborate steps than most members of the audience could imagine doing.[7] (In nineteenth-century opera, ballerinas began to dance on point — on the tips of their toes — a practice that was definitely not for spectators to try at home.)

Composers resorted to familiar dances even when they were inappropriate to the time or place of the work. The opera *Gustave III* (1833) by Daniel-François-Esprit Auber, set in the late eighteenth century, ends with a ball scene that included a galop, a dance that didn't exist at the time of the opera's setting, but was all the rage in the 1830s. This galop was such a sensation that sometimes audience members left their seats and tried to join in onstage.[8] Composers could even poke fun at the whole idea of appropriateness, as when Jacques Offenbach in his *Orphée aux enfers* (*Orpheus in the Underworld*, 1858), a parody of the Greek classical myth, made the Olympian gods dance a minuet — a dance that was "classical" in his day, though not in the sense of "ancient" — and then let it slip into something more contemporary and far more fun, a cancan. Today, however, composers of new operas hardly ever use the musical language of current popular dances.

Marking Differences: *Prince Igor*

A second reason for dance in opera is that it provides a means of marking cultural or social differences between groups within the drama, or between groups onstage and the audience. Dance scenes have often, for instance,

displayed peoples from faraway places as exotic. The Polovtsian Dances in Alexander Borodin's *Prince Igor* (first performed in 1890, three years after the composer's death) are a *divertissement* representing a night of feverish dancing by slaves of a nomadic tribe in medieval Russia. On the surface the opera tells of the moral triumph of a "civilized" people (the medieval Russians, with whom Borodin's Russian audience would presumably have identified) over a more "primitive" people (the Polovtsians and their slaves). But the fact that audiences have always awaited this scene more eagerly than any other suggests that there may be a different agenda at work: allowing the spectators a liberating trip into a culture that they can imagine as free of the restraints of their own culture. It is dance, not song, that takes them there.

Prompting Dramatic Action: *Yevgeny Onegin*

A third and last way that dance works in opera is to push the action forward. In a ball scene, for instance, the principal characters might come together for an important confrontation in the midst of the dancing, in which the ballet corps would naturally take the lead. Ball scenes are found in operas from Mozart's *Don Giovanni* (1787) to Sergey Prokofiev's *War and Peace* (1946) and Samuel Barber's *Vanessa* (1958). The two ball scenes in Tchaikovsky's *Yevgeny Onegin* (1879) show why composers have found them so useful dramatically.

The dance at the country house of the Larin family in Act 2 of Tchaikovsky's *Yevgeny Onegin*, in the production directed by Graham Vick at La Scala, Milan, in 2006. Here the music and dancing of the waltz fit with the relatively modest décor and costumes.

Marco Brescia/Teatro alla Scala

The first of these scenes is a dance at the country estate of a somewhat prosperous provincial lady. The opening music is a lovely waltz, danced by the principal characters — Olga and Tatyana (the two daughters of the house), Olga's suitor Lensky, and his best friend Onegin — along with the ballet corps, while members of the chorus sing pleasantries and gossip along with the music. In a break in the dancing, Lensky complains bitterly to Olga because she has promised a dance to Onegin. The jealous Lensky then challenges Onegin to a duel, which will end in his own death in the next scene. The dancing is no mere backdrop to the dramatic action, but actually precipitates the death of one character by another's hand.

Dance also serves the function here of marking class difference. In nineteenth-century society the waltz was the couples dance of the masses, and the waltz in this scene, however beautiful the music and elegant the dancing, signals to the audience that the main characters are not at the top of society. When we next meet Tatyana, years later, it is at another

The grand ball of the palace of Tatyana's husband, Prince Gremin, in the imperial capital of St. Petersburg, as performed in Act 3 of *Yevgeny Onegin*, in the same production at La Scala. Here the magnificence of Tchaikovsky's polonaise fits the aristocratic bearing and glamorous costumes of the dancers and the grandeur of the setting.

Marco Brescia/Teatro alla Scala

ball. This scene, by contrast, opens on a polonaise, a majestic processional dance performed by a glittering aristocratic company in a grand palace, and we sense immediately how high she has risen socially. She has married a prince, and Onegin, who has decided too late that he loves her, tries to rekindle her love for him in the face of everything the polonaise tells us, and should tell him, about his chances of prying her away from her new life.

Expressing, Marking, Prompting: *Nixon in China*

A concluding example of dance in opera embodies all three of the traditional uses, but with some novel twists. John Adams's *Nixon in China* (1987) dramatizes the state visit of President Richard Nixon, along with his wife Patricia and Secretary of State Henry Kissinger, to China in 1972, to meet with the Chinese leaders Mao Tse-tung, his wife Chiang Ch'ing, and Chou En-lai. In the course of the visit, Chiang Ch'ing takes the Nixons to see a "revolutionary ballet," *The Red Detachment of Women*. A dance performance is welcome for the kinetic release it provides in the middle of an opera about politicians who stand around in suits and uniforms, talking—especially since that static dramatic action is set, ironically, to music of endless, unrelieved motion.

The revolutionary ballet, watched by most of the principal characters, functions like a traditional *divertissement*. There is a sly take-off on the seventeenth-century tradition of monarchs dancing in the semi-operatic festivities performed at their courts: here the role of the villain in the ballet, Lao Szu, is played by the same singer who plays Henry Kissinger, causing Pat Nixon to turn to her husband and say, "Doesn't he look like you-know-who!" In a sense this *divertissement* even displays exoticism, and with a vengeance: *The Red Detachment of Women* was an actual Chinese revolutionary ballet, first performed in 1964. But an exotic ballet within an opera usually purports to represent the traditional arts of a foreign people, and a ballet created by Communist leaders to raise the revolutionary consciousness of the Chinese masses would not look traditional to anyone. Moreover, what the Nixons—and we—watch is not the actual *Red Detachment of Women*, but a hybrid. It retains the original story, as well as the format of narrative dance with interpolated songs, but its music and ballet movements (created in the original production by choreographer Mark Morris) are completely new, unmistakably Western, and fully integrated with the rest of the opera. In this version a Chinese revolutionary ballet is stripped of everything Chinese, the more starkly to reveal its revolutionary theme of struggle against oppression. To Pat Nixon, that is no exotic theme.

In John Adams's *Nixon in China*, James Maddalena as Richard Nixon and Janis Kelly as Pat Nixon intrude on the performance of the revolutionary ballet *Red Detachment of Women* in an attempt to comfort the victimized peasant girl (danced by Haruno Yamazaki). Looking to the side is Kathleen Kim as Chiang Ch'ing, the wife of Chairman Mao and creator of the ballet. A rehearsal of the production directed by Peter Sellars at the Metropolitan Opera, 2011.

Ken Howard/Metropolitan Opera

She can't stand to watch the scene in which a peasant girl is beaten sense-less. Dragging her husband onstage with her, she tries to stop the action. And Chiang Ch'ing, who had a role in the creation of the ballet, tries to take authorial control, shouting to one of the performers: "That is your cue." But she is mistaken, and the ballet is now held up as she sings in self-justification: "I am the wife of Mao Tse-tung." This ballet may start out as a *divertissement* staged for the American guests, but the characters watching it refuse to let it unfold apart from themselves. Each is on a different kind of power trip, and incapable of being a spectator. Like the dancing in *Yevgeny Onegin*, this ballet seems at first to be sidelining the main characters and the main action, but in the end it simply provides those characters with a new stage on which they continue to act out the larger drama.

FURTHER READING

On singers and singing in opera, John Rosselli, *Singers of Italian Opera: The History of a Profession* (Cambridge: Cambridge University Press, 1992); John Potter, ed., *The Cambridge Companion to Singing* (Cambridge: Cambridge University Press, 2000). On castrati, Roger Freitas, *Portrait of a Castrato: Politics, Patronage, and Music in the Life of Atto Melani* (Cambridge: Cambridge University Press, 2009).

On the dramatic functions of the chorus, especially in nineteenth-century opera, James Parakilas, "Political Representation and the Chorus in Nineteenth-Century Opera," *19th-Century Music* 16/2 (Fall 1992): 181–202.

On dance in and with opera, the special issue of *Cambridge Opera Journal* on opera and dance in seventeenth-century Venice: 15/3 (November 2003); Kathleen Kuzmick Hansell, "Theatrical Ballet and Italian Opera," in *Opera on Stage*, vol. 5 of *The History of Italian Opera*, ed. Lorenzo Bianconi and Giorgio Pestelli (Chicago and London: University of Chicago Press; original Italian ed., 1988), pp. 177–308; Marian Smith, *Ballet and Opera in the Age of Giselle* (Princeton: Princeton University Press, 2000).

FOR RESEARCH AND REFLECTION

1. How does a singer's voice allow her or him to create a dramatic personality? Take a major role in any opera, listen to all the different kinds of singing the singer does in that role, and consider how he or she uses that variety to create a rounded and developing portrayal of the character.

2. Listen to two or three different singers in the same scene of the same opera. How does the different sound of each singer's voice affect your understanding of that particular character?

3. Study the role of the chorus in any opera. To what extent does it embody a distinct character in the drama? Does it serve as an adjunct to one or more of the individual characters? Does it stand, like the chorus in a Greek tragedy, as an intermediary between the characters and the audience, helping the audience form judgments of the characters and their actions?

4. What does the act of dancing (or not dancing) tell us about the characters who dance in Bizet's *Carmen*, Richard Strauss's *Salome*, Alban Berg's *Wozzeck*, or Arnold Schoenberg's *Moses and Aaron*?

 Additional resources are available at wwnorton.com/studyspace.

CHAPTER 4

The Story Unfolds

Giuseppe Verdi's *La traviata* (*The Woman Gone Astray*, 1853) is another work, like *Nixon in China*, that brought contemporary life onto the operatic stage, though its subject matter was originally considered so shocking that the management of the house where it was first staged insisted that the opera be set a century and a half earlier, to blunt the shock. It too was based on a real story of real people, but their story came to Verdi transformed twice, first into a novel that in turn formed the basis of a play. The novel, *La Dame aux camélias* (*The Lady of the Camellias*, 1848), by the French novelist Alexandre Dumas the younger, was a fictional account of his own affair with the prostitute Marie Duplessis. Dumas made the novel into a play with the same title, produced in Paris in 1852. Verdi apparently saw the play there and decided to transform the story a third time. For that purpose he required the services of a **librettist**: a poet who writes a dramatic text (**libretto**) that is set to music. Verdi's librettist, Francesco Maria Piave, turned Dumas's French play into an Italian libretto, and just thirteen months after the premiere of the play in Paris, *La traviata* was produced in Venice.

In all three versions this is a story centered on the obstacles to happiness between a young man of respectable family and a high-society prostitute, despite their love for each other. Because it was impossible in those days to conceive of such a love leading to a happy ending—that is, marriage—the resolution had to be tragic. The prostitute dies, and audiences, believing in the lovers' mutual devotion while accepting the impossibility of happiness for them, wept all the more for both of them. As a novel, play, and opera this story

Camille-Joseph-Etienne Roqueplan, *Marie Du Plessis at the Theater*, Musée de la Ville de Paris, Musée Carnavalet, Paris. In his novel *La Dame aux camélias*, Alexandre Dumas the younger depicts his former mistress Du Plessis (1824–1847), as Roqueplan does in this watercolor, turning heads at the theater. That side of her Paris routine does not figure in Verdi's opera *La traviata*.
Bridgeman Art Library

Reading the Libretto and the Score

To get to know a play well, you will want to read its script as well as see it performed. This allows you to tell the playwright's contribution from the performers' and therefore to imagine new ways of performing the play. In opera the script is a **score**, containing the words and notes sung and played, as well as stage directions. A full (or orchestral, or conductor's) score includes all the vocal and instrumental parts, and it can be an eyeful to take in at once. A vocal (or piano-vocal) score, which reduces the orchestral parts to two staves, offers a more manageable text for most readers and rehearsal situations.

But the score is itself a kind of performance of the verbal script, the libretto. That is, the composer's music elaborates a certain interpretation, a certain delivery of the words. To distinguish the composer's contribution from the librettist's, you need to look at the libretto, the pre-script—the text in its literary form. If it is written in verse, seeing the verse form will help you hear that form, and with it the logic and force of the music, more clearly. Likewise, if there is a lot of repetition of lines in the music, the libretto will boil those down for you.

When you are listening to an audio performance in a language you don't know, it is worth the effort to follow along with a libretto that has both the original language and a translation, moving your eyes back and forth between them so that you can connect the words the singers are singing with their meanings. For that purpose it is best to avoid "singing translations" (like those in scores and some booklets of recordings), which sacrifice much of the meaning and order of the words to match the singability of the original. Look instead for "reading translations" (like those in this book), which aim for the closest correspondence to the order and meaning of the original. Better yet, learn to read and speak and sing the languages of your favorite operas for yourself.

swept over Europe and the Americas. For a century it retained its hold on the public in all three forms, and eventually in the form of movies as well. Today, although the other versions have faded in popularity, Verdi's opera has proved imperishable.

Studying how this tale unfolds in the opera, compared with the ways it unfolds in the novel and play, provides an illuminating lesson in the nature of the operatic medium. A novelist has hundreds of pages to flesh a story out; a playwright who adapts a novel must select just those episodes that can get the story enacted in a couple of hours. When a librettist adapts a play, the text has to be further shortened because singing slows the delivery of words, and lines are sometimes repeated when they are sung. And even when an opera uses the exact—if somewhat cut—language of an existing play (as do Claude Debussy's *Pelléas et Mélisande*, 1902, and Richard Strauss's *Salome*, 1905), the music transforms the audience's dramatic experience of the story.

From Novel to Play to Libretto:
La Dame aux camélias and *La traviata*

The novel of *La Dame aux camélias* has an elaborate narrating structure. After the death of the prostitute Marguerite Gautier (named Violetta Valéry in the opera), her lover Armand Duval (Alfredo Germont in the opera) tells another young, unattached, middle-class Parisian man, the narrator, the story of his relationship with her. This unnamed narrator conveys the story by relaying Armand's account, adding his own comments on Armand's state of mind. Given that the author, Dumas, is fictionalizing his own experience, we could say that the narrator is a literary device that allows him to distance himself from his past. This multiplicity of male narrating figures only reinforces our sense that while the lady who wears camellias may be the title character, this is the story of a man's experience of being her lover. We discover the precise feelings of a young middle-class man who falls in love with a woman "kept" by rich, powerful, older men and who demands an exclusive relationship with her that he, because he is middle class and just starting out in the world, can't afford, either morally or monetarily. But we have no access to the feelings of a lower-class girl who becomes a kept woman in high society and then falls in love with a young man of limited means. At the end, when she dies of the tuberculosis that drew his sympathy in the first place, he is not present, and since we are following the story through his experience of it, our sympathy is directed not to her, but to him in his grief.

Armand also misses another crucial event in the course of their relationship. After Marguerite has given up her grand apartment and her life in Paris to live in a humbler country home with him, she suddenly abandons him, without explanation, and returns to Paris and her former life. Her departure appears as a hole in his narrative. Then later, after Armand tells the narrator about Marguerite's death, he shows him—and us—the journal she left for him to read after her death. From this we finally learn that Armand's father visited her secretly and persuaded her to leave her lover for his own and his family's good. Since events are ordered in the novel as Armand becomes conscious of them, this unwelcome visit by his father appears not as a dramatic confrontation midway through the story, but as the retrospective explanation of the mystery at its center.

In the theater (both the play version of *La Dame aux camélias* and *La traviata*) the confrontation between the father and Marguerite/Violetta is enacted, not narrated—in its chronological sequence, after the two lovers have moved to the country and immediately before she returns to Paris. We therefore feel this scene as the event on which the whole drama turns. Whereas in the novel the story comes to us through Armand, on the stage he is absent

Giuseppe Verdi

In this letter of July 17, 1886, Verdi is writing to the librettist Arrigo Boito, with whom he has collaborated in turning Shakespeare's tragedy *Othello* into the opera *Otello*. He writes before the first production of the opera at La Scala in Milan, asking Boito's help with a problem about the libretto's publication: the grand ensemble near the end of Act 3 requires so many soloists and choral groups to be singing so many lines simultaneously that the lines will not fit onto two facing pages of the libretto. Verdi's unconventional solution, which he asks Boito to help him persuade the publisher Giulio Ricordi to carry out, is to print three pages' worth of text in the usual space of two. As the facsimiles from the published libretto on page 69 show, Ricordi complied exactly. The letter provides evidence of how deeply the composer cared about letting his audience understand the words, even when he had overlapped them so thickly that no one could possibly hear them all.

Dear Boito,

I too am a bit concerned about the printing of the third-act finale in the libretto, because I would really like the audience to be able to see and understand everything at a glance.

Turn this page over and you will see what I would propose. If something better can be found . . . so much the better. Obviously the page where there are the three columns should be complete in the middle of the libretto, with the stitching where there are the margins.

It is all right for Desdemona's solo to be printed at the bottom of the preceding page; in this way the audience will not be distracted, and would concentrate all its attention on her. Then, turning the page, they would find the whole hullabaloo of the ensemble laid out.

Giulio must not make objections about whether the edition is then less beautiful. The important thing is to let them understand . . . if they will want to understand!

Marcello Conati and Mario Medici, *The Verdi-Boito Correspondence*, trans. William Weaver (Chicago: University of Chicago Press, 1994), pp. 103–04.

from the scene that is the heart of the drama, though he is its main subject of discussion.

The transformation of this scene from novel to stage is part of a larger transformation of the story. Armand/Alfredo, instead of being the controlling character of the narrative, becomes a pawn in a struggle between his father, representing the claims of respectability, and Marguerite/Violetta, representing the claims of her victimhood. As they engage with each other and with Armand/Alfredo, we learn at least as much about the development of their attitudes as we do about his. In the opera we even hear Violetta thinking through her dilemma when she is alone. It could be argued that giving a prostitute a presence and a voice onstage challenged the conventional thinking of the day about sexual power. Yet while the stage versions may offer a deeper insight into the prostitute's suffering, it could also be argued that none of the versions is critical of a social order that left so many women of the underclass in such need of sympathy. Shedding tears for her might simply have been a way for audiences to acknowledge that the social order they believed in had its human cost.

The difference between a narrative and a dramatic medium is also manifest in the way the story moves from one location to another. The novel follows Armand in his incessant movement around Paris in pursuit of Marguerite, then

OTELLO

(rapidamente a Jago in segreto ed indicando Cassio)

(Vedi? non par che esulti
L' infame.

JAGO

No.)

OTELLO

(ad alta voce a tutti)

La ciurma e la coorte

(a Desdemona sottovoce e rapidissimo)

(Continua i tuoi singulti...)

(ad alta voce a tutti, senza più guardar Cassio)

E le navi e il castello
Lascio in poter del nuovo Duce.

LODOVICO

(a Otello, additando Desdemona che s' avvicina supplichevolmente)

Otello,
Per pietà la conforta o il cor le infrangi.

OTELLO

(a Lodovico e Desdemona)

Noi salperem domani.

(afferra Desdemona furiosamente)

A terra!... e piangi!...

(Desdemona cade. Emilia e Lodovico la raccolgono e la sollevano pietosamente)

DESDEMONA

A terra!... sì... nel livido
Fango... percossa... io giacio...
Piango... m' agghiaccia il brivido
Dell' anima che muor.
E un dì sul mio sorriso
Fioria la speme e il bacio
Ed or... l' angoscia in viso
E l' agonia nel cor.
Quel Sol sereno e vivido
Che allieta il cielo e il mare
Non può asciugar le amare
Stille del mio dolor.

The passage of overlapping utterances in *Otello*, published in the libretto of the opera exactly as Verdi proposed in his letter of July 17, 1886, to Boito. Operagoers would hear Desdemona sing the lines they read at the bottom of page 61 (above), then would turn the page and see, spread across three columns, the lines sung all at once by the other soloists and the ladies (Dame) and gentlemen (Cavalieri) of the chorus, while Desdemona repeated her lines. The trouble Verdi takes over this matter indicates the great stock he put in enabling his audience to understand all the words, especially when many were being sung at once. Arrigo Boito, *Otello* (Milan: Ricordi, 1887).

Harvard Theatre Collection, Houghton Library, Harvard University

EMILIA

(Quella innocente un fremito
D'odio non ha nè un gesto,
Trattiene in petto il gemito
Con doloroso fren.
La lagrima si frange
Muta sul volto mesto:
No, chi per lei non piange
Non ha pietade in sen.)

RODERIGO

(Per me s'oscura il mondo,
S'annuvola il destin;
L'angiol soave e biondo
Scompar dal mio cammin.)

CASSIO

(L'ora è fatal! un fulmine
Sul mio cammin l'addita.
Già di mia sorte il culmine
S'offre all' inerte man.
L'ebbra fortuna incalza
La fuga della vita.
Questa che al ciel m' innalza
È un'onda d'uragan.)

LODOVICO

(Egli la man funerea
Scuote anelando d' ira,
Essa la faccia eterea
Volge piangendo al ciel.
Nel contemplar quel pianto
La carità sospira,
E un tenero compianto
Stempra del core il gel.)

IL CORO

(a gruppi dialogando)

DAME

Pietà!

CAVALIERI

Mistero!

DAME

Ansia mortale, bieca,
Ne ingombra, anime assorte in lungo orror.

CAVALIERI

Quell'uomo nero è sepolcrale, e cieca
Un'ombra è in lui di morte e di terror.

DAME

Vista crudel!

CAVALIERI

Strazia coll'ugna l'orrido
Petto! Figge gli sguardi immoti al suol.
Poi sfida il ciel coll'atre pugna, l'ispido
Aspetto ergendo ai dardi alti del Sol.

DAME

Ei la colpì! quel viso santo, pallido,
Blando, si china e tace e piange e muor.
Piangon così nel ciel lor pianto gli angeli
Quando perduto giace il peccator.

JAGO (avvicinandosi a Otello che resterà accasciato su d'un sedile)
(Una parola.
OTELLO E che?
J. T'affretta! Rapido
Slancia la tua vendetta! Il tempo vola.
O. Ben parli.
J. È l'ira inutil ciancia. Scuotiti!
All'opra ergi tua mira! All'opra sola!
Io penso a Cassio. Ei le sue trame espia.
L' infame anima ria l'averno inghiotte!
O. Chi gliela svelle?
J. Io.
O. Tu?
J. Giurai.
O. Tal sia.
J. Tu avrai le sue novelle in questa notte...)
(abbandona Otello e si dirige verso Roderigo)
J. (ironicamente a Roderigo)
(I sogni tuoi saranno in mar domani
E tu sull'aspra terra!
RODERIGO Ahi triste!
J. Ahi stolto!
Stolto! Se vuoi tu puoi sperar; gli umani,
Orsù! cimenti afferra, e m'odi.
R. Ascolto.
J. Col primo albor salpa il vascello. Or Cassio
È il Duce. Eppur se avvien che a questi accada
(toccando la spada)
Sventura... allor qui resta Otello.
R. Lùgubre
Luce d'atro balen!
J. Mano alla spada!
A notte folta io la sua traccia vigilo,
E il varco e l'ora scruto, il resto a te.
Sarò tua scolta. A caccia! a caccia! Cingiti
L'arco!
R. Sì! t' ho venduto onore e fè.)
J. (Corri al miraggio! il fragile tuo senno
Ha già confuso un sogno menzogner.
Segui l'astuto ed agile mio cenno,
Amante illuso, io seguo il mio pensier.)
R. (Il dado è tratto! Impavido t'attendo
Ultima sorte, occulto mio destin.
Mi sprona amor, ma un avido, tremendo
Astro di morte infesta il mio cammin.)

back and forth between Paris and their suburban getaway, and finally—when she abandons him without explanation—between keeping away and trying to force her to take him back. We can understand his restlessness as standing for his inability to accept the place that society has ordained for him. The stage versions, by contrast, couldn't be constantly on the move, as that would have required constantly clearing the stage and setting up a new three-dimensional set with its own props and costumes. The staged versions call for just a few sets (five in the play, four in the opera): both versions open in Marguerite/Violetta's house in Paris, move to the house she rents in the suburbs, then to the house of another prostitute, and finally back to her house in Paris. If the novel takes place on the road with him, the play and opera unfold entirely on her ground.

Narrator's Voice, Characters' Voices

Armand's voice (filtered through the narrator) dominates the novel. Here, for instance, is a passage in which Armand, brought to meet Marguerite in her home, admits that he has long loved her from afar, and she warns him off:

> "You won't have much of a mistress; someone who is temperamental, ill, depressed, or gay in a way that is sadder than sorrow itself, someone who coughs blood and spends a hundred thousand francs a year—which is all very well for a rich old man like the Duke, but it's not much of a prospect for a young man like yourself. And, if it's proof you want, the fact is that all the young lovers I have ever had have never stayed around for very long."
>
> I did not answer: I listened. Her frankness, which seemed to verge on the confessional, and the dismal life which I half-glimpsed beneath the golden veil that covered its stark reality from which the poor girl sought escape in debauchery, drunkenness and sleepless nights, all made such an impression on me that I could not find a thing to say.
>
> "But come," Marguerite continued, "we're talking foolish nonsense."[1]

Armand doesn't have to find a thing to say to her. Through what he has said to us, he has made us observe the conversation through his eyes, and care about its impact on his feelings, not hers.

In the theater the more a character is onstage and taking part in the dialogue, the more claim that character has on our feelings. In the heyday of Greek tragedy there could be no more than two characters onstage at once, as there were only two actors available (aside from the choral interludes), but each could assume different roles by changing masks, and the action would progress through the successive confrontations of different pairs of characters. In traditions like opera (or soap opera), where more than two actors can appear at once, it is striking how much the story is still carried forward by exchanges between pairs of characters.

Striking but not surprising, if we consider that drama represents conflicts and that the essence of a conflict is dramatized by two people arguing two

sides of an issue. In *La traviata*, despite the cast of singers and dancers who fill the stage at times, every scene revolves around a dialogue between two characters. And here, unlike in the novel, it is Marguerite/Violetta who takes part in the crucial dialogue of each scene. In fact, she is the one character who is onstage for all but a few minutes of every scene. A look at the layout of scenes (the **scenario**) reveals how this remarkable shift of focus was achieved between the novel and the opera.

The Scenario of *La traviata*

The first act is set in a large room of Violetta's house in Paris, where a party is under way. Alfredo enters and is introduced to her as someone who asked after her every day for months, when she was confined to bed by her tuberculosis. At the sound of dance music, Violetta, feeling too weak to join in, asks her guests to go into the next room and dance. Alfredo stays behind to urge her to give up her life of pleasures and let him love and care for her. (This first important exchange of the two lovers is modeled on scenes in both the novel and the play.) After promising to let him be her lover, Violetta dismisses Alfredo and then, left alone, considers whether it is possible for her, a kept woman, to find true love; she tries to convince herself that it is not. (This monologue, Violetta's great reflective moment, has only sketchy precedent in either the novel or play.)

The second act consists of two scenes. The first is set in the suburban house where Violetta, having decided in the end to relinquish her fast life, is selling off the trappings of that life to sustain the love nest that she and Alfredo have made together. He is called away, and his father walks in, demanding that she give up Alfredo in order to save his family's reputation and Alfredo's chances of a respectable future. She gives in and agrees not to let Alfredo know that his father has prevailed on her to do so. Violetta then leaves, informing Alfredo in a note that she is returning to her former life in Paris.

The second scene is another party scene, this time at the home of Violetta's friend Flora. Alfredo comes to the party expecting to confront Violetta. He wins money at the gambling table, betting against the rich baron who is now Violetta's lover. She calls him to a private conversation, where she begs him to leave before the baron can challenge him to a duel. In order to prevent Alfredo from guessing the real reason she left him, she tells him she loves the baron, whereupon Alfredo turns their conversation into a public shaming. He calls all the guests in to watch as he throws his gambling winnings at her in payment, he says, for her past favors. (Some elements of this exchange can be found in the novel, but the whole scene comes from the play.)

The third act is set in Violetta's bedroom. She is dying, but takes heart when she receives a letter from Alfredo's father saying that his son now

Giuseppe Verdi in 1851, photographed by Adolphe Eugène Disderi. This portrait by a famous Paris photographer shows Verdi at about the time when he composed *La traviata*.
Hulton Archive/Getty Images

knows she has loved him all along and is rushing back from abroad to see her. Alfredo bursts into the room, and in their final encounter they fantasize about starting life over together, but she collapses and dies. (This exchange too comes from the play; it has no precedent in the novel, where Armand returns to Paris too late to see Marguerite before she dies.)

Whereas the opera is constructed differently from the novel, it is modeled fairly closely on the play. Nevertheless, the story makes a very different impression in the operatic version, not simply because it is sung, but also because the action unfolds in a sequence of discrete numbers. This traditional format is known as **number opera**: the librettist has arranged the text in sections that take various poetic forms, each one requiring the composer to create a number in a different musical form. Some of these numbers come to such a decisive close that the audience may break in with applause, even though that holds up the action. The layout of musical numbers in an opera is crucial to the dramatic layout (or **dramaturgy**) of the work, as a comparison of the first acts of the play and opera will show.

From Play to Opera (1): Dramaturgy in *La traviata*, Act 1

The opera begins with a quiet, slow **prelude** (a short overture), introducing a couple of melodies that will be heard later on. These tranquil melodies set us up to feel jolted when the curtain rises to reveal a grand party under way at Violetta's home, with bright music that sounds as if it is being played by a dance band. The play, by contrast, opens in Marguerite's bedroom, where two characters are talking, soon to be joined by a third. The odd thing is that these are one and the same scene, in the sense that they cover the same ground in the plot: the introduction of Armand/Alfredo to Marguerite/Violetta and the first steps in their relationship. If that is the essential action of the scene, what is gained in the opera by staging it at a large party?

Opera, with its choral and orchestral resources, can create a spectacle that suggests the world of lavish spending, constant socializing, and easy sexuality in which Violetta lives and from which Alfredo wants to rescue her. Dumas's play, lacking these resources, shows us the same world, but entirely by means of dialogue. Here a much smaller group of Marguerite's friends and would-be lovers has gathered at her house late in the evening, imposing on her ill health as they while away the night in witty, often cruel chitchat. Marguerite asks Armand if it is true that he came to ask after her every day when she was bedridden. He says yes; she thanks him for that, then turns to Arthur de Varville, a rich young man who is infatuated with her, and accuses

Alfredo bowing as he is introduced to Violetta (in black, wearing the red camellia). Alfie Boe as Alfredo and Myrtò Papatanasiu as Violetta in a production directed by David McVicar at the Welsh National Opera, Wales Millennium Centre, Cardiff, 2009.
© Richard Hubert Smith/Lebrecht Music & Arts

him of having failed to pay similar respects. Varville replies that he has known her for only a year. "And this gentleman," she says, indicating Armand, "has known me only five minutes."

Verdi's librettist, Piave, translated this little exchange verbatim into the opera, but in the play it is just one witticism in what seems like a whole evening of cutting banter. In the opera it stands almost alone, making a point about Violetta's sharp tongue, but not suggesting a life spent bantering. What goes on and on here is the diegetic party music, creating a festive spirit for the audience as well as the characters. Against the band music that never takes a breath, none of the characters gets in more than a short line at a time, and the audience, straining to hear what the characters are straining to say to each other over the music, understands instinctively the bashfulness of Alfredo, who feels out of place at the party and hardly gets in a single word, even while others are telling Violetta about him.

Alfredo's Toast in Song

The way he overcomes his bashfulness is to sing. The guests sit down to dinner; Gastone, the friend who brought Alfredo to the party, calls for someone to sing a toast (*brindisi* in Italian), and Alfredo answers the call. In the play too a song is called for at this point, but Gastone sings it. In the opera everything is sung, so it is not so clear how we can distinguish singing that represents the characters speaking (the normal case) from singing that represents singing. The libretto doesn't give a clue, since it is written entirely in verse. The passages we have heard so far, for instance, are in rhymed couplets, though the lines are broken up and distributed to the speakers in short phrases, so that our attention is not drawn to the verse structure.

The text of Alfredo's *brindisi* is at least easier to apprehend as a song lyric. It has shorter lines, some of which are rhymed in pairs ("infiora"/"ora"); they are united into a stanza by a periodic rhyme (a stressed final *a* on the fourth, eighth, and tenth lines); and one actor delivers the whole stanza.

Libiam ne' lieti calici	*Let's pour a drink in the merry cups*
Che la bellezza infiora;	*adorned by beauty;*
E la fuggevol ora	*and let the fleeting hour*
S'inebrii a voluttà.	*get drunk with voluptuous pleasure.*
Libiam ne' dolci fremiti	*Let's pour a drink in the sweet thrills*
Che suscita l'amore,	*that love excites,*
Poichè quell'occhio al core	*since his omnipotent eye*
Onnipotente va.	*goes straight to the heart.*
Libiamo, amor fra i calici	*Let's have a drink: love, in his cups,*
Più caldi baci avrà.	*will make our kisses all the hotter.*

Roberto Saccà (right) as Alfredo is joined by Corinna Mologni as Violetta and the chorus in singing the *brindisi* "Libiamo," in Act 1 of *La traviata*, in a production directed by Giancarlo del Monaco at the Finnish National Opera, Helsinki, in 2003.
Heikki Tuuli/Lebrecht Music & Arts

There is also an unmistakable change in the music when Alfredo begins to sing this text. Until now the orchestra has played its music and the singers have sung their phrases of chitchat independently. The characters appear to be too absorbed in talking to pay attention to the party music. But for Alfredo's *brindisi* the orchestra introduces his melody and then accompanies him with bass and chords and occasional melodic doubling as he sings it. The orchestra has become part of a character's utterance.

And the music, furthermore, helps us hear these ten lines as a stanza. The first two pairs of lines are sung to complementary melodic phrases, starting identically but ending differently, thus forming a musical **period**. The next two pairs of lines are sung to a different set of complementary melodic phrases, another period. Then there is only one pair of lines left, but Verdi has Alfredo sing it once and then has the chorus take it up, creating a refrain that rounds off the stanza. After this stanza Violetta supplies a second stanza to the same melody, and then the whole company joins with them to come up with a third.

Though this musical form—three stanzas of text, all sung to essentially the same music—helps us hear the *brindisi* as a song, form by itself is not a strong enough signal. Operas are full of numbers with stanzaic texts. The only unequivocal signal that the *brindisi* represents Alfredo (and then Violetta and the chorus) singing rather than speaking is verbal: just before he starts, the chorus sings, "Pay attention to the singer."

A Private Conversation Between Violetta and Alfredo

Now an offstage band strikes up a waltz, and Violetta sends her guests off to the next room to dance while she recovers from nearly fainting, Alfredo remaining behind with her. Their conversation starts like the chitchat at the beginning of the opera: a dialogue of short phrases delivered apparently without regard for the band music in the background. But this time the dialogue is too serious to remain in that format. Alfredo tells her she is killing herself; he offers to care for her, saying no one loves her as he does; but she laughs off his love. All of this comes from Dumas's play, where it is developed more elaborately. The opera compensates, though, with a musical effect that makes us (if not yet Violetta) take Alfredo seriously: as he begins his entreaty, the waltz music from the offstage band disappears. Instead, from the orchestra pit Alfredo gets his own accompaniment, a slower waltz beat in which he can pour out his account of how she changed his life:

Un dì felice, eterea,	*One happy day, like ethereal lightning*
Mi balenaste innante,	*you flashed before me,*
E da quel dì tremante	*and since that day, trembling,*
Vissi d'ignoto amor.	*I've lived by an unknown love.*

Alfredo pleads his case to Violetta, who is more interested than she supposed she could be. Anna Netrebko as Violetta and Jonas Kaufmann as Alfredo in a production directed by Richard Eyre at the Royal Opera House, Covent Garden, London, 2008.

Rob Moore/Lebrecht Music & Arts

Di quell'amor ch'è palpito	By that love that is the throbbing
Dell'universo intero,	of the entire universe,
Misterioso, altero,	mysterious, haughty,
Croce e delizia al cor.	torment and delight to the heart.

Alfredo needs to convince Violetta, and the audience, that his love is worthy of what he is asking: that she give up her way of life for him. In the novel his worthiness is not an issue, since he controls the narrative. In the play it is a potential issue, but we don't see it tested. In the opera, though, we will witness the crisis of conscience that Alfredo's declaration prompts in Violetta, and before we get there, we need to be shown that he can persuasively challenge her long-held belief that love is not for her. That is a task for music as well as words.

Alfredo's first musical phrase ("Un dì felice") moves slowly up a scale and retreats slowly from its peak. His second phrase ("E da quel dì") repeats the climb, but rises a step higher, coming to a pause just below the goal of the tonic (main) note of the scale. He then breaks through to that tonic note on the third phrase ("Di quell' amor"). As he specifies the nature of his love, his melody blossoms with the exultation and obsession of that love. The fourth phrase ("Misterioso") suggests its other sides: mystery (a feint at the minor mode) and a mixture of torment and delight (the dissonances of his notes against the bass and the resolutions of those dissonances).

The audience should be convinced by this performance, but Violetta is not carried away by it, at least not immediately, though we will soon find that he has planted a doubt in her mind about her loveless existence. For the time being she responds by insisting she is not cut out for his kind of love:

Ah se ciò è ver, fuggitemi!	Ah, if that is true, flee from me!
Solo amistade io v'offro:	I am offering you only friendship;
Amar non so, nè soffro	I don't know love, nor can I stand
Un così eroico amore.	such a heroic love.

The oom-pah-pah accompaniment to Alfredo's aria continues as Violetta begins her response. Hearing that continuation, we might suppose that she is going to sing a second verse to the same tune. In fact, although she does pick up the melodic outline with which Alfredo's melody has just finished, the style of her melody is as playful as his was earnest, as sparkling in its staccato (disconnected) notes as his was expressive in its legato (connected) notes, carefree in its melodic leaps where his was intense in each step it moved, and

colored by woodwind doubling where his was unadorned. Her melodic style, as much as her words, tells him that she is not the one for him.

As Violetta finishes her stanza, Alfredo returns to his, starting in the middle (on "Misterioso, altero"), as if he had been singing all along. But Violetta doesn't get out of his way; as he sings again of "torment and delight to the heart," she joins him in a descant, "You won't find it hard / then to forget me" ("Non arduo troverete / dimenticarmi allor"). In short, they are now singing in duet, but it is no love duet. Overall they maintain their contrasting melodic styles, though in order to sing together, they have to accommodate each other's styles somewhat, opening up intriguing opportunities for the performers. When the score says Violetta should make her melody "ever so sweet" (dolcissimo), should she act as if she is succumbing to his charms, or teasing him, or both? And when Alfredo in the shared **cadenza** (the wordless melodic flourish that suspends time just before the close) starts to match her brilliant vocalization, is he learning to be playful in love, or merely playing along to win her favor? The music allows for many interpretations that convey the ambiguity of this moment when love hangs in the balance.

When the two singers finish their duet, Gastone appears at the door to ask them what the devil they're doing. As he is speaking, we hear the dance band again from the next room, still playing its waltz. Gastone realizes he has interrupted something serious and withdraws, but the spell of their exchange has been broken. They keep talking, but the sound of the offstage band frames their conversation, suggesting that Alfredo's chance to draw Violetta away from her partying world is almost gone. Through wordless music the opera imparts this urgency to the audience, even while the relationship of the two characters continues to develop through their resumed conversation: Violetta takes a camellia from her bosom and gives it to Alfredo as a token that he may return the next day as her lover, and he rushes out in joy.

An Inner Debate: Violetta's "È strano"

The orchestra now replaces the offstage band, ushering in the chorus and other soloists, who thank Violetta for her hospitality and head off to more parties elsewhere. This return of the cast and music from the opening of the scene adds a second musical frame around the first and seems to isolate Alfredo's vision of love even further within the world of pleasures that Violetta lives in. Nevertheless, left alone, she now reflects on what Alfredo's offer could mean for her.

At the equivalent moment in the play, Dumas allows Marguerite not so much a reflection as a moment to let the audience know where she stands: "Why not? —What's the use? —My life is wearing itself out going between one answer and the other" (I, 13). For the opera, drawing on lines taken from

other scenes of the play, Piave turns this simple summation into a full-blown scene of self-examination, a crisis of conscience apparently leading to a decision. Since Violetta is the only character present now, the only way he could present her thinking through her dilemma was to construct this monologue as a debate she conducts with herself. Piave lets the two sides have the floor in turn, and each "speaker"—the voice that longs for love and the voice that clings to the life of pleasures—argues its case in two stages. This allows the poet and composer, using traditional alternations of forms, to articulate the contradictions in her thought with vivid and powerful contrasts.

Violetta is asking herself hard questions, which Piave constructs in largely unrhymed lines of varying length, forming no couplets or stanzas:

> È strano! . . . è strano! . . . in core
> Scolpiti ho quegli accenti!
> Saria per me sventura un serio amore?
> Che risolvi, o turbata anima mia?
> Null'uomo ancora t'accendeva . . . oh gioia
> Ch'io non conobbi, esser amata amando! . . .
> E sdegnarla poss'io
> Per l'aride follie del viver mio?

> It's strange! . . .
> I have those expressions carved into my heart!
> Would a serious love be a disaster for me?
> What are you deciding, my conflicted spirit?
> No man has ever inflamed you till now . . . O joy
> I never knew, to love and be loved! . . .
> And can I spurn that
> for the arid madness of my life?

By using this fluid verse form, representing a character voicing unformed thoughts, the librettist was obliging the composer to use a prosy style of music that gave the singer free rein in her delivery: recitative (see Chapter 2). In recitative—heard here for the first time in the opera—Violetta can entertain her thoughts as a series of short outbursts. These outbursts, unrelated to each other in the way phrases of a song would be, are kept separate by equally unrelated orchestral punctuations that often pull her abruptly into new keys. The style of her musical declamation gives us the impression that Violetta is letting her thoughts take her where they will.

The need to respond to her own questions, however, makes her take charge of her thoughts. This change is reflected in more orderly verse (rhymed stanzas) and more orderly music (formed like a song). In opera, as we have seen, a solo speech composed of such orderly verse and music is called an **aria**. Violetta's whole monologue will be an aria in two stages,

each introduced by its own recitative. We have now reached the first stage of the aria, in a slow tempo, the **cantabile** (songful):

Ah fors'è lui che l'anima	*Ah, perhaps he is the one whom my spirit,*
Solinga ne' tumulti	*alone in its confusion,*
Godea sovente pingere	*often enjoyed depicting*
De' suoi colori occulti!	*in esoteric colors!*
Lui che modesto e vigile	*The one who, modest and vigilant,*
All'egre soglie ascese,	*climbed up to my sickly threshold,*
E nuova febbre accese,	*and kindled a new fever,*
Destandomi all'amor.	*rousing me to love.*
A quell'amor ch'è palpito	*To that love that is the throbbing*
Dell'universo intero,	*of the entire universe,*
Misterioso, altero,	*mysterious, haughty,*
Croce e delizia al cor.	*torment and delight to the heart.*

An aria has the power to endow an entire speech with the character of a single image, drawn out of the text and realized musically in a controlling rhythm or figuration (pattern of notes) or instrumental color. In "Ah fors'è lui" the image is of a dream, realized in the rocking rhythms of a lullaby. As Violetta makes her way through the three **quatrains** (four-line sections) of the stanza given above, her dreaming moves from a vague image she has long cherished to a more fully realized one (she recalls Alfredo coming to her door when she was sick), and her voice grows higher and stronger on each line, as if she were about to wake. The moment of waking is marked dramatically in her music: she breaks through from the minor mode to the parallel major mode, as words and music that Alfredo sang to her in the previous scene break into her aria and become her own: "that love that is . . . torment and delight to the heart." We are beginning to understand what she meant a minute ago when she said, "I have those expressions carved into my heart." Her memory of Alfredo's words and music emerges so naturally within her own — with no change of rhythm or key — that we can readily believe what she is telling herself here: that his arrival in her life has simply activated the need and capacity for love that she has harbored all her life.

The Other Side of the Debate: "Follie!"

After a second stanza (often cut in performance) in which Violetta admits that she has experienced these thoughts since childhood, she pauses, and the second side of her debate begins, taking the same form as the first: a recitative, followed by the faster stage of the aria, called the **cabaletta**. In the recitative ("Follie!"/"Madness!") she reminds herself that she is in no position to look for love: "What should I do? Enjoy myself. Perish in the whirl of

sensuality!" This recitative is exceptionally florid, at the same time that it offers an exceptionally bleak view of enjoyment. But then, it is the view of a prostitute who knows she doesn't have long to live.

This thought leads her to the cabaletta, in which she describes her pursuit of pleasure as a life of freedom:

Sempre libera degg'io	*Always free, I must*
Folleggiar di gioia in gioia,	*frolic from joy to joy;*
Vo' che scorra il viver mio	*I want my life to flow*
Pei sentieri del piacer.	*along the paths of pleasure.*
Nasca il giorno, o il giorno muoia,	*At the birth or death of the day,*
Sempre lieta ne' ritrovi	*always merry at parties,*
A diletti sempre nuovi	*to delights ever new*
Dee volare il mio pensier.	*my thought should fly.*

This is the brilliant climax to Violetta's solo scene. Her music, expressing her need for "delights ever new," is itself full of the vocal delights of operatic showmanship: trills and other ornaments, breathtaking runs both legato and staccato, notes rhythmically displaced, spectacular leaps and high notes. This is the normal progression of a two-stage aria: a soulful cantabile followed by a dazzling concluding cabaletta, with a recitative before each stage to set the mood or explain its change.

Rosa Ponselle as Violetta in a production at the Metropolitan Opera, 1931.
© Metropolitan Opera Archives/Lebrecht Music & Arts

It is not altogether clear, though, whether we hear in the two stages of this aria a change of heart or the representation of her divided state of mind. Both possibilities are worth bearing in mind when we come to the end of the first stanza of "Sempre libera," because here, just as she reaches her cadence (stopping point), she hears Alfredo's voice, now from "under the balcony," once more singing his refrain (his words adjusted slightly to "Amor è palpito"). It seems like a genuine interruption and therefore an event in real time; he also sings in his own tempo, which is noticeably slower than hers. Alfredo is accompanied by a harp, which may suggest that he is serenading her with a guitar, or, as David Kimbell proposes, may sound "like a visitation from, or a vision of, a better world."[2] Violetta's comments over his phrases sound as if they are made in real time as well. At first she is surprised by his voice ("Oh!"), and then perhaps unsettled by his message ("Oh, love!").

She now returns to some of the vocal flourishes from her recitative ("Follie!"), and repeats the whole stanza of "Sempre libera" with an even more brilliant ending. At the cadence Alfredo sings "Amor è palpito" one

last time, again with the harp, but this time in Violetta's fast tempo. If he is really singing under her balcony and unaware of her monologue, why would he change tempo? Is he, as Kimbell says, "sounding only in her own mind" this time,[3] and would that mean that she has absorbed his message and so doesn't entirely believe her own, or that she has absorbed his message and no longer feels threatened by it? Or can we take these two intrusions into Violetta's musings together as a depiction of her uncertainty: at the first she seems to consider accepting his love, and at the second she seems to consider rejecting it?

The relationships of thought and word, the real and the imagined, are never represented straightforwardly in drama. In this scene mind games played with musical forms and musical recollection contribute to the ambiguity. We may think we have witnessed Violetta deciding to reject Alfredo, or we may think we have learned of her inability to decide. In either case she proves incapable of denying his love, because the next time we meet her, she has given up her Parisian life and gone away to live with him in quiet bliss.

From Play to Opera (2): Rhetoric in *La traviata*, Act 2, scene 1

At the beginning of the next scene (the first in Act 2) we find Alfredo alone in the country house he now shares with Violetta, reveling in her declarations of love and fidelity. By the end of this scene she will have given him a note telling him that she is leaving him forever. In between, while Alfredo is absent, an exchange between his father and Violetta that Julian Budden calls "the core of the opera" decides his fate.[4] Piave modeled this scene more exactly on the equivalent scene in Dumas's play than any other scene of the opera. We can't therefore learn much from it, as we did from the first act, about what is unique in operatic dramaturgy. And yet this operatic scene commands a different force from the equivalent scene in the play, mainly because they work with different kinds of **rhetoric**.

From the beginning of opera, musicians developed an art that would supply the effects of organization, style, and delivery that were prized in spoken rhetoric. In 1581 one of the earliest theorists of opera, Vincenzo Galilei — the father of the great physicist and astronomer Galileo Galilei — dared musicians to create music for singing actors that incorporated all the rhetorical skill that actors employed in the spoken theater.

> Let [musicians]. . . kindly observe in what manner the actors speak, in what range, high or low, how loudly or softly, how rapidly or slowly they enunciate their words, when one gentleman converses quietly with another. Let them

pay a little attention to the differences and contrasts that obtain when a gentleman speaks with one of his servants, or one of these with another. Let them consider how the prince converses with one of his subjects or vassals; again, how he speaks to a petitioner seeking a favor; how one speaks when infuriated or excited; how a married woman speaks, how a girl, a simple child, a witty wanton; how a lover speaks to his beloved seeking to persuade her to grant him his wish; how one speaks when lamenting, when crying out, when afraid, and when exulting with joy.[5]

Opera was created to give singing actors musical means to convey these differences, and almost three centuries later Verdi was occupied with the same project.

Violetta Meets the Elder Germont

The meeting of Violetta and Alfredo's father, Giorgio Germont (he is usually referred to simply as Germont), makes a perfect study of operatic rhetoric. It is a scene between two people from different social worlds who don't know each other and don't know at first how to talk to each other. They have to find rhetoric for that purpose. At the same time, there is nothing to their meeting but rhetoric. They both want something that the other is not willing to give. They use every argument they can muster. And in the end they both come out somewhere they never expected to be—even Germont, who holds all the cards. It is an astonishing manifestation of operatic persuasion.

As the scene opens, Violetta has learned to her surprise that Alfredo has gone to Paris for the day. She perhaps suspects that he is secretly intending to raise money for their expenses. She herself is secretly selling her possessions off for the same purpose. Her servant tells her there is a gentleman to see her. The gentleman enters and announces that he is Alfredo's father. "You?" she says, and offers him a chair. They are beginning stiffly, with routine gestures, singing in the plainest recitative. Germont starts right in, singing "forcefully":

> Sì, dell'incauto, che a ruina corre,
> Ammaliato da voi.

> Yes, whose son is running headlong to ruin,
> under your spell.

As he sings these lines, he accepts her invitation and sits down. The score doesn't need to indicate that she sits too; a gentleman would never sit while a woman was standing. But his lines bring her right back to her feet, "offended":

> Donna son io, signore, ed in mia casa;
> Ch'io vi lasci assentite,
> Più per voi, che per me.

> I am a lady, sir, and in my house;
> permit me to leave you,
> more for your sake than my own.

Rhetoric and Opera

Rhetoric is the art of argument, the use of language to persuade others to favor your position. In ancient Greece and Rome training in rhetoric was considered necessary for citizens, who needed to defend their interests in the courtroom and in political life. But people who knew how to deploy rhetoric also appreciated it as entertainment, and the dramatists of ancient Athens and Rome played to this taste by pitting their characters against each other as if they were arguing in court. As two scholars write of ancient Athens, "Oratory drew on the audience's experience of theater; drama drew on the audience's experience of political and legal speeches."[6]

Likewise in Europe from the Renaissance on, those who were going to need to speak persuasively in the public forum—that now meant lawyers and priests—were educated in classical rhetoric. Dramatists, including opera librettists, were generally men with this training: the most important opera librettists of every era—Philippe Quinault in the seventeenth century, Pietro Metastasio in the eighteenth, and Eugène Scribe in the nineteenth—were all trained for careers in the courtroom, and Piave, the librettist of *La traviata*, studied to be a priest.

She makes as if to leave. He has been too quick to insult her, and she has shown him she knows how to capitalize on his mistake. It is clear that this opera comes from an age and society with rules of social behavior different from ours. Even if we are not sure what they all signify, we can tell that knowing these rules confers power. Violetta knows. "What manners!" ("Quai modi!"), Germont says to himself. He realizes he is dealing with someone more formidable than he had expected. He may know that she came out of poverty, but seems not to have realized that her life as a kept woman has taught her how people at the highest level of society behave. She not only stays, but resumes her seat.

It is now Violetta's move. With a show of documents, she proves to Germont that she is sacrificing her possessions to support his son, not the other way around. He is impressed; again he has been proved wrong. But the knowledge that she is selling off items she was given by her rich patrons gives him a new way to attack her: "Ah il passato perchè v'accusa?" ("Ah, why is your past denouncing you?") This enrages her, and for the first time in this scene we hear a really expressive vocal phrase, as she climbs up to a high A, holds it strongly, and then curls her way down:

Più non esiste . . .	It exists no more . . .
Or amo Alfredo, e Dio	Now I love Alfredo, and God
Lo cancellò col pentimento mio!	expunged it, along with my repentance!

Under a continuous support of chords from the strings, Germont indicates that he takes her outburst to be sincere — "Nobili sensi invero!" ("Noble sentiments indeed!") — and she finds consolation in having proved herself to him:

Oh come dolce	*Ah, how sweet*
Mi suona il vostro accento!	*the sound of your words is to me!*

The orchestra is becoming more engaged in accompanying them, just as the two characters are finding terms on which to engage with each other.

Germont's Demand: "Pura siccome un angelo"

Violetta has won the first round, but for Germont, rising to his feet, this is just the moment to turn the conversation against her again:

Ed a tai sensi	*And from such sentiments*
Un sacrifizio chieggo.	*I ask a sacrifice.*

His music imitates hers, suggesting perhaps that he is trying to flatter her, so that she might let her guard down at the very moment he is going back on the offensive.

She is not disarmed, though, but chilled: as he finishes this ominous sentence, the strings make a jolting (deceptive) cadence and begin an uneasy tremolo (tremulous sound). It seems only reasonable to hear these disturbing moves in the orchestra as markers of the dread his words evoke in her. "Ah no!" she cries, rising to her feet too. She was expecting something like this. Now he announces that he is making his demand on behalf of his two children. "Two children!" Violetta exclaims. Alfredo seems not to have told her he has a sister. Germont explains in an aria:

Pura siccome un angelo	*Pure as an angel —*
Iddio mi diè una figlia;	*God gave me a daughter;*
Se Alfredo nega riedere	*if Alfredo refuses to return*
In seno alla famiglia,	*to the bosom of his family,*
L'amato e amante giovine,	*The beloved and devoted young man*
Cui sposa andar dovea,	*whom she should be marrying*
Or si ricusa al vincolo	*will now decline the marriage bonds*
Che lieti ne rendea.	*that would render them so happy.*

An aria, as we've seen, allows the composer to give an entire speech a single musical character, defined by an idea or image in the text. Here, Verdi, taking up the angel image, gives his music the character of a prayer. For the first two lines and again for the fifth and sixth, Germont sings almost entirely on a single note, the sweet third of the major chord that stays constant

beneath it. His words to this music sweetly but insistently let Violetta know how Alfredo's scandalous association with her could ruin his sister's hope of marriage. Then, as Germont moves into his plea to Violetta to make that marriage possible, his voice starts slowly up the scale, reaching a forceful E-flat on the word "prayers" ("prieghi"), as he gets to the point of his supplication:

Deh non mutate in triboli	*Oh, don't turn into thorns*
Le rose dell'amor,	*the roses of love:*
A' prieghi miei resistere	*may your heart be unwilling*
Non voglia il vostro cor.	*to resist my prayers.*

Germont hasn't come calling to inform Violetta about his "family values." He has come to persuade her to leave his family alone, and he has a cold rhetorical strategy to accomplish that. It is a prostitute he is beseeching, not God, and he is willing to use the shamefulness of her life against her. Not that he mentions her life in this speech; instead, he describes his daughter in a way that Violetta can only hear as a reproach to herself. Piave has made this even clearer in the libretto than Dumas did in his play. Where Dumas has the father say to Marguerite, "I have a daughter, young, beautiful, pure as an angel," Piave has him *begin* "Pure as an angel," establishing with his first word the right of his family not to be sullied by the impure Violetta. Likewise Verdi, by wrapping this speech in a halo of prayerful music, gives Germont's words a tone of righteousness, reminding Violetta that she does not belong with Alfredo's family in the company of the righteous. Sometimes, as every good trial lawyer knows, donning a halo can be a way of twisting the dagger.

Violetta's Resistance: "Non sapete quale affetto"

Violetta is too smart to be defeated by this hurtful speech. As soon as Germont is finished, she offers to get out of Alfredo's life for as long as it takes to get his sister married. But Germont interrupts her to say that's not enough. "What?" she says, "do you want me to renounce him forever?" "You must." "Oh no, never!" she cries. This rapid exchange might be set in recitative, but instead Verdi gives the singers recitative-like vocal lines that play out against an aria-like accompaniment (one with a constant rhythm that controls the singers' delivery and an occasional independent melody that backs up their melodies). This in-between style is called **arioso** (aria-like).

As the scene goes on, the dialogue continues in this style, with each new stage of the argument marked by dramatic changes to the rhythm and figuration. Sometimes one singer holds forth in tuneful, rounded melodic phrases, so that we think we are hearing the beginning of an aria. But it doesn't last. These two characters are locked together in a desperate battle of wills, and one of

them always cuts the other off or starts to sing while the other continues. Their confrontation needs more momentum now than a string of arias could give.

The actors are delivering lines that Piave has translated almost directly from Dumas's play, but their music shapes their interpretation of those lines. In the first part of this scene (set in recitative) verbal instructions tell the singers how to interpret their lines musically. In the rest of the scene the score is more sparing of verbal instructions, but now the vocal lines and their accompaniments always have a distinctive rhetoric built into the pattern of their notes—like the prayerful mode of expression in "Pura siccome un angelo." The notes, in other words, do just what Vincenzo Galilei asked music to do: convey the way a prince would speak to a petitioner or a lover would beg a favor of his beloved.

Violetta's response to Germont's extreme demand is to list the reasons it is impossible for her to give Alfredo up: first, she can't rely on anyone but Alfredo; and second, she is mortally ill. She puts this to Germont in the form of reproachful questions:

Non sapete quale affetto	*Don't you know what affection,*
Vivo, immenso m'arde il petto?	*alive and immense, inflames my heart?*
Che nè amici, nè parenti	*That neither friends nor relatives*
Io non conto tra' viventi?	*do I count among the living?*

Maria Callas as Violetta resists the arguments of the elder Germont, played by Ettore Bastianini, in Act 2 of a memorable production of *La traviata* directed by the film director Luchino Visconti at La Scala, Milan, in 1955. Callas was one of the first American singers to triumph at La Scala, the high temple of Italian opera.
Erio Piccagliani © Teatro alla Scala

Violetta delivers these lines in extraordinarily emphatic music. The rhythms of her phrases seem to make a drum of her voice, firing off a rat-a-tat on every downbeat, with the orchestra staying out of the way on those beats to allow her voice its full percussive effect. This energetic, even belligerent melodic rhythm may indicate that, outraged at the pressure Germont is putting her under, she is desperately looking for some strategy to reclaim the strong position she held at first. But it may equally well indicate that, recognizing how little power she has to stand up to Germont's demands, she is simply pouring out her anguish. However the actress negotiates between these possibilities, it is clear that Violetta has reached a breaking point. And her show of despair only increases as she declares—against a swooning background of descending chords, interrupting herself twice with screamed high notes—that she would rather die than suffer such torments. Then she abruptly comes to a stop.

Germont knows how to take advantage of her loss of control; if she wants to make herself the subject of their discussion, he can turn that against her. He picks up the tonic note of Violetta's cadence, C, and in a completely calm voice, without recourse to any harmonization from the orchestra, pushes into a new key, F minor:

È grave il sagrifizio,	It's a serious sacrifice,
Ma pur tranquilla uditemi.	but be still and hear me out.

The corresponding new direction of his argument is that even if she stayed with Alfredo, she would not be happy for long.

Germont barely starts in on this line of thought ("You are beautiful and young . . . In time . . .") when Violetta, guessing what he is going to say, interrupts to insist that she can love only Alfredo. But Germont is thinking of how long Alfredo's love, not hers, will last. This is his clinching argument, yet he sings as if tiptoeing into his subject. He delivers his words at a whisper, skipping from one clipped syllable to another, until he gets to a little flourish at the end of a line or a more sustained phrase at the end of each stanza, leaving the conclusion to her:

Un dì, quando le veneri	One day, when time will have
Il tempo avrà fugate,	sent lust packing,
Fia presto il tedio a sorgere . . .	tedium will be quick to arise . . .
Che sarà allor? Pensate!	What will happen then? Think about it!

Germont knows that he has resorted to the cruelest of arguments to gain the upper hand. By singing "with simplicity" (as the score indicates), is he hoping to bring his argument home without setting off another outburst? Is he trying to be delicate in discussing the betrayals of physical decay with a woman who depends on her youthful looks for everything? Are his little vocal

flourishes nevertheless slightly taunting, or scolding? The singer needs to find in the music an appropriate tone for Germont to be taking with Violetta at this crucial moment.

Whereas his previous demand brought a response of outrage, this whispered prediction brings the first words of concession from Violetta. As Germont warns that the lovers' mutual affection will be no balm to them since their relationship can't be blessed by holy matrimony, she quietly adds, "It's true, it's true!" For the first time, their voices are heard at the same time. They will continue to overlap. In opera, of course, it is nothing unusual for two characters to sing a duet. But in this dramatic situation, when the two characters have been arguing for so long, never mixing their voices together, the fact that they have begun to sing together signals that they are heading toward an agreement, even before Violetta announces her surrender. It is a kind of signaling possible only in opera.

Germont now advances in his argument from dire prediction to plea. With greater warmth, in sustained phrases, he urges her to become the "consoling angel of my family." Violetta then takes over, turning the mode from major to minor but maintaining the same rhythm, as she launches into a quiet and sorrowful yet soaring melody. But she is not responding to Germont; she is singing an **aside** — a thought directed to herself alone. (In a libretto or score, an aside is indicated by parentheses; in performance, usually by the speaker turning away from other characters.) She argues her own case for bowing to Germont's demand:

(Così alla misera, ch'è un dì caduta,	(So, to the miserable woman, once she has fallen,
Di più risorgere speranza è muta!	any hope of rising again is mum!
Se pur benefico le indulga Iddio,	Even if a charitable God is lenient with her,
L'uomo implacabile per lei sarà.)	man will show her no mercy.)

As she sings, Germont goes on repeating his plea. His growing insistence shows in a relentlessly syncopated phrase over an insistently unresolving bass (a dominant pedal). But as this long scene comes to a head, neither participant is listening to the other. They draw to a halt on a half cadence, a pause without resolution. Both singers are evidently ready for Violetta's answer.

Violetta's Concession: "Dite alla giovine"

She can hardly speak. She turns to Germont, crying, and gives the answer on which the whole story turns, yielding to him all her hope of happiness. Her solitary voice, leading into the resolution of the harmony, changes the mode from minor to major and in the process makes us feel her bravery in the

face of her tears. A slowly pulsing accompaniment tells us of her hesitation to speak. Above all, the painfully slow rise of her line, one step of the scale per long, slow, subdued measure, tells us how much it costs her to say these unbearable words, beginning as they do with her acceptance of Germont's own taunting description of his daughter:

Dite alla giovine sì bella e pura,	*Say to the young woman, so beautiful and pure,*
Ch'avvi una vittima della sventura,	*that there is a victim of misfortune*
Cui resta un unico raggio di bene . . .	*to whom there remains a single ray of blessing . . .*
Che a lei il sagrifica e che morrà.	*which she sacrifices to her, and that she is going to die.*

At the same time, that rising and then arching vocal line makes us feel how she is gathering her courage by speaking.

As she finishes, Germont acknowledges what a supreme sacrifice he is asking of her. He begins by acknowledging her tears: "Piangi, piangi, piangi, o misera" ("Weep, weep, weep, you poor woman!"). In the play Marguerite acknowledges *his* tears, and is grateful that he has taken her feelings seriously, despite her despised status. Germont's "Weep, weep," sung in musical sobs, reveals his sympathy, but also opens the act of sympathy out to the audience: he asks everyone to acknowledge the right she has earned to our respect as well as to her tears. In the opera, then, Germont briefly imposes himself on us as a narrator, asking us to see the action through his eyes even as he is conceding that Violetta has a worth he never imagined he would find in

Maria Callas and Ettore Bastianini in the same production of *La traviata* and only a few minutes later in the same scene, but showing the tremendous transformation that has come over both characters in the course of their meeting, to the point that Violetta in her desolation can call on Germont to "Embrace me as a daughter," and he is willing to do so.
Erio Piccagliani © Teatro alla Scala

her. Verdi builds on all of this: Violetta repeats her stanza of concession as Germont sings his consoling stanza beneath it. He has won, but now they are joined together, singing as fervent a duet as she sang with Alfredo in the first flush of love or will later, at its last gasp.

Violetta and Germont now have work to do, figuring out how to explain to Alfredo that she has left him, without revealing why. This requires still further strategizing, but now instead of using their strategies against each other, they are conspiring together. When the plotting hits a snag, Violetta says to Germont, "Embrace me as a daughter . . . then I will be strong," and they embrace. This is an amazing demand to make of the man who used the social gulf between her and his actual daughter only a few minutes earlier to pry her away from his son. That she can make him embrace her now as a daughter is a sign that she has seized the rhetorical initiative back from him: she has won sufficient respect from him that she can command him to disregard the social distinction on which his argument was based, though he will do so only because he has already won the argument. At the same time, her demand also shows how lonely she is making herself by giving up Alfredo. Altogether this tiny phrase teaches us the enormity of what this exchange has wrought, and it is Dumas's phrase, translated literally by Piave and set to the plainest recitative by Verdi. Sometimes, in opera, the characters' words have such a complex and crucial task to perform that the best the music can do is stand aside and let them do it.

By the time Violetta hears someone who may be Alfredo approaching, she has made Germont promise that after she is dead, he will explain to his son what a sacrifice she made for love of him. As Germont and Violetta sing a tender duet of farewell, wishing each other happiness, she reminds him of that promise. These words too come from the play, but through the musical device of the duet—unavailable in a spoken drama—the opera makes us feel how characters locked in struggle can slip into a bond of affectionate respect for each other.

This is the turning point of the story. The opera is far from over. But comparing the novel, the play, and the opera this far is enough to suggest what is distinctive about the dramaturgical and rhetorical resources of opera. This book now turns from a study of opera's resources to a chronological survey of its repertory. In that study we will return to *La traviata* and follow it to its heartbreaking conclusion.

Dumas's novel is translated into English as Alexandre Dumas fils, *La Dame aux Camélias*, trans. David Coward (Oxford and New York: Oxford University Press, 2000). His play is translated into English by Edith Reynolds and Nigel Playfair as *The Lady of the Camelias* (London, 1930; reprint Drama Books, 1957), and by Henriette Metcalf as *Camille: The Lady of the Camelias* (London and New York, 1931). On the transformation of Dumas's play into Verdi's opera, Julian Budden, *The Operas of Verdi*, vol. 2: *From "Il Trovatore" to "La Forza del Destino"* (New York: Oxford University Press, 1978), pp. 115–122. On verse forms and musical forms in Verdi's operas, chs. 4, 5, and 6 of Scott Balthazar, *Cambridge Companion to Verdi* (Cambridge: Cambridge University Press, 2004).

FOR RESEARCH AND REFLECTION

1. Take a favorite novel, story, play, or movie and imagine how you would convert it into an opera. Prepare a cast list, with vocal ranges for all the roles. Write a scenario and synopsis, indicating (or drawing) the stage set for each scene and outlining the action for each scene. Map out what parts of the dialogue you would arrange for recitative, arioso, aria, ensemble, and chorus, and when there would be dances.

2. Study another opera that is based on a novel, story, or play, and consider how the text of the original work was altered to suit the needs and strengths of the operatic medium.

3. Study the texts of several opera arias without listening to the music. Now listen to the music while following the lines of text. How does the music make you more or less conscious of the line structure and rhymes of that text?

 Additional resources are available at wwnorton.com/studyspace.

SEVENTEENTH-CENTURY MILESTONES

1598
Dafne, libretto by Ottavio Rinuccini and music by Jacopo Peri and Jacopo Corsi, performed in Florence.

1600
The oratorio or sacred opera *Rappresentatione di Anima, et di Corpo* (*Drama of the Soul and Body*), music by Emilio de' Cavalieri, performed and published in Rome.

Euridice, libretto by Ottavio Rinuccini, music by Jacopo Peri with insertions by Giulio Caccini, performed in Florence. This work and Caccini's own complete setting of the same libretto were both published in 1601.

1605
Johann Carolus begins publishing the first printed newspaper, *Relation*, in Strasbourg.

1607
Orfeo, libretto by Alessandro Striggio and music by Claudio Monteverdi, performed in Mantua.

1614
First opera performances outside the Italian-speaking lands given in Salzburg—including *Orfeo*, probably in Monteverdi's setting.

1618–48
Thirty Years' War, in part a conflict between Christian denominations, rages across Central and Western Europe, causing a staggering loss of life and devastating economies.

1631
Théophraste Renaudot begins publishing *La Gazette*, the first weekly newspaper in France.

1636
In New England, Roger Williams founds the colony later known as Rhode Island, where church and state are separated. In Europe and elsewhere in the Americas, established churches continue to use their authority to impose censorship on public theaters.

1637
The first public opera house, the San Cassiano Theater in Venice, opens with a production of *Andromeda*, libretto by Benedetto Ferrari, music by Francesco Manelli.

1642–60
Civil War and Puritan rule in England bring theatrical life there to a virtual standstill.

1643
Monteverdi's final opera, *L'incoronazione di Poppea* (*The Coronation of Poppea*), libretto by Giovanni Francesco Busenello, performed in Venice.

1645–62
Cardinal Jules Mazarin, the chief minister of France, brings seven Italian opera productions to France.

1649
Giasone (*Jason*), the most frequently produced opera of the seventeenth century, libretto by Giacinto Cicognini and music by Francesco Cavalli, performed in Venice.

1672
Jean Donneau de Visé begins publishing *Le Mercure gallant*, the first literary and cultural periodical in France.

1673
Cadmus et Hermione, the first of Jean-Baptiste Lully's *tragédies en musique* (operatic tragedies), libretto by Philippe Quinault, performed in Paris.

1686
Armide, the last of Lully's *tragedies en musique*, libretto by Philippe Quinault, performed in Paris.

1689
(perhaps first in 1687)
Dido and Aeneas, libretto by Nahum Tate, music by Henry Purcell, performed at a school near London.

PART II

Opera of the Seventeenth Century

Opera seems to stand apart from other forms of theater today, but it arose in Italian cities in the same era as the spoken theater of Shakespeare in London and Lope de Vega in Madrid: the late sixteenth and early seventeenth centuries. Opera did not develop in the church, where most drama of the preceding centuries was produced, but in princely courts, often as an entertainment at wedding festivities. It soon began a new life in public theaters in Venice, where troupes of performers made their living putting on operas day after day for a paying public, just as they did in the theaters of London and Madrid. Before the end of the seventeenth century, opera was performed in public theaters in cities across Europe. The birth of opera, then, was part of a larger, socially and economically important development: the birth of public theatrical life in modern Europe.

Francesco Cavalli, *Ercole amante* (*Hercules in Love*), Paris, 1662. Staged by David Alden at the Netherlands Opera, Amsterdam, 2009, with Wilke te Brummelstroete as Beauty and Luca Pisaroni as Hercules (icon for the French king, Louis XIV). The costumes playfully recall period dress, just as the backdrop evokes the perspective effects of period settings.
Ruth Walz

Though opera offered much the same set of stories and same kind of stagecraft as spoken theater, it operated through the medium of music. It was a laboratory in which musical practices were developed to animate all kinds of dramatic situations, and those practices were then transferred to other kinds of music. Opera thus belongs to the history of music as much as to the history of theater, just as both belong to the history of entertainment.

CHAPTER 5

Opera in Princely Courts: Florence and Mantua

Dramas of Identity, Drawn from Ovid

Religion, Identity, Autonomy

The development of modern drama, including opera, belongs to the history of consciousness as well as the history of entertainment. Earlier, in the centuries since the ascendancy of Christianity, drama in Western Europe had appeared largely in the form of religious plays, created under the auspices of the Catholic Church. This drama operated on principles so different from those of modern theater that historians debate whether to consider it theater at all. Church dramas were ritualistic reenactments of biblical stories, in which the roles of Jesus, Mary, and the disciples were often reserved for clergymen. These reenactments could be overwhelming events in the lives of spectators, but the performances were not judged on acting skills or stage effects; they were exercises in mass spiritual healing.

Theater in its modern form, including opera, evolved largely outside the churches. In the sixteenth and seventeenth centuries theater gave expression to what the literary historian Stephen Greenblatt has called "an increased self-consciousness about the fashioning of human identity as a manipulable, artful process."[1] People were still born into a particular religion, a particular social rank, even a particular profession, and with an attachment to a particular place. But

Bernardo Buontalenti, costume designs for female dancers in a Florentine interme- dio (performed between acts of a play), 1589. Victoria and Albert Museum, London.

now some were beginning to be conscious of their freedom at least potentially to change one or more of these markers of their identity, to define a new place for themselves in the universe, and to face the consequences of exercising this autonomy.

That sense of autonomy was often explored within religious contexts. Already in 1486 the Italian philosopher Giovanni Pico della Mirandola imagined the Creator saying to Adam:

> The nature of all other creatures is defined and restricted within laws which We have laid down; you, by contrast, impeded by no such restrictions, may by your own free will, to whose custody We have assigned you, trace for yourself the lineaments of your own nature. . . . We have made you a creature neither of heaven nor of earth, neither mortal nor immortal, in order that you may, as the free and proud shaper of your own being, fashion yourself in the form you may prefer.[2]

Pico was a humanist, a scholar steeped in classical Greek philosophy who developed a human-centered philosophy, but one that he believed was consonant with the theology of the Catholic Church (although he suffered papal condemnation for his work).

In the early sixteenth century religious reformers beginning with Martin Luther were challenging the authority of the church with the belief that individual Christians needed to build their own relationship to God rather than rely on the intermediary of the church to define that relationship. The Protestant Reformation that soon grew out of that belief created the largest rift in the Christian church in more than a millennium. Even though hardly any Christians were free as individuals to change their religious affiliation, Catholics as well as Protestants now became aware of the existence of other Christian denominations, which imparted alternative forms of Christian identity. In this changing world, theater provided a perfect cultural medium for testing and promoting new senses of autonomy. It is the nature of all theater to create identities: actors impersonate someone else. The dramas of the sixteenth and seventeenth centuries, including operas, also show people struggling to understand their proper place in the world.

In this age of religious wars every political jurisdiction of Europe had an established religious denomination, and the clergy had to approve even secular theatrical works before the civil authorities would allow them to be performed in public spaces. In many Protestant jurisdictions the clergy forbade theatrical performance outright, motivated by a wish to suppress sacrilegious or lewd behavior onstage or in the audience, but also in some cases by a belief that the illusion of the theater (the very act of pretending to be someone you weren't) was sacrilegious or idolatrous. By contrast, the theater flourished in countries that remained under Catholic rulers—especially the

Repertory, Canon, and History

For the first two centuries in the history of opera, almost every opera house commissioned new works for each season or borrowed recent ones from other houses. In the subsequent two centuries and more, by contrast, houses increasingly produced older works that had become classic; in other words, they drew their seasons largely from a **standard repertory** of works that audiences enjoyed seeing again and again. They also continued to produce some new works and to revive some forgotten ones that had never caught one. In this way the standard repertory has slowly evolved and grown. Though that repertory now consists of operas from several different centuries, opera houses present works from across that history on successive nights, all with virtually the same personnel, instruments, and staging resources, even though the works were created for quite varied performing means.

The study of opera, as opposed to the performance of opera, is concerned largely with the **canon** of works that historians and critics find of greatest historical importance, a list that does not entirely coincide with the standard repertory. The canon covers the entire history of opera, whereas the standard repertory—at least as it is represented in major houses—includes hardly any works from the seventeenth century and relatively few from the eighteenth. The canon is not the whole history of opera, but a set of works selected to help us think about opera in historical contexts. The remainder of this text surveys the canon in a way designed for exploring the interplay of cultural concerns, story types, and dramatic and musical practices in each relevant century.

Italian principalities, Spain, and France—as well as in England, when it became Protestant for political rather than doctrinal reasons.

The leaders of the Catholic Church embraced the idea of theater as a means of giving their flock models of how to take responsibility for their own identity. Not only did they tolerate secular drama in royal palaces and public theaters, they sponsored new forms of sacred drama, performed in church sanctuaries. A sung drama called *Rappresentatione di Anima, et di Corpo* (*Drama of the Soul and Body*), with music by Emilio de' Cavalieri, was performed in Rome, the seat of the Catholic Church, in 1600; it embodied a struggle of conscience in the debates of allegorical characters. Another type of sung drama, *Sant'Alessio* (*Saint Alexis*), with libretto by Giulio Rospigliosi (who was later Pope Clement IX) and music by Stefano Landi, performed in Rome in 1631 or 1632, follows a different dramatic model: it enacts the identity crisis of a Christian saint. By the middle of that century the Catholic Church reserved biblical and other sacred stories for its own quasi-operas, or **oratorios**, partly narrated and partly dramatized, presented during the Lenten season.

By then, secular opera had long been developing, largely in and around princely courts, above all the court of the Medici family, rulers of the Grand Duchy of Tuscany, in Florence. There, nobles, classical scholars, poets, musicians, and visual artists collaborated in dramatic and musical experiments over the course of the last decades of the sixteenth century. For a short period they worked under the sponsorship of Count Giovanni de' Bardi, in a group that became known as the Camerata. From time to time these collaborators would give their experiments prominence by producing works at large gatherings such as wedding celebrations of the Medici family.

Mythology and Ovid

Secular operas drew their subjects from classical mythology—as most operas would for the next two centuries. Much as the J. R. R. Tolkien or *Star Trek* stories do today, the classical myths provided people of that time with a widely shared, fully stocked world of characters and actions for their imaginations to play in. To the ancient Greeks and Romans these had been sacred stories, depicting humans like themselves encountering the gods and spirits of their world. But to sixteenth- and seventeenth-century Christians, classical mythology represented a world of gods and humans not associated with their own religious beliefs, yet offering plenty of material for moral reflection. Precisely because these myths were not their own religious stories, Christians could recast them with great freedom, using them to explore pressing questions of existence in their own society.

Given that the originators of opera sometimes claimed they were emulating Greek tragedy, we might expect them to have borrowed their plots from Greek tragedies—those grim stories of domestic and civic strife among legendary figures, especially from the times of the Trojan War. But the plots of the earliest secular

Apollo and Daphne, painted by the Florentine artist Antonio Pollaiuolo, probably in the 1470s, showing the moment of metamorphosis when Daphne turns into a laurel tree while fleeing the amorous Apollo. Little more than a century later, this story from Ovid would be the subject of the first opera, also created in Florence. National Gallery, London.

Art Archive/Eileen Tweedy

operas come instead from Ovid's *Metamorphoses*, the mythological storybook of ancient Roman literature. Ovid's mythological humans undergo magical transformations. *Dafne*, for instance, the earliest full-length opera to be performed, enacts the story of the chaste nymph (Daphne) who flees from the advances of the god Apollo and is saved by being transformed into a laurel tree. The opera, created by the poet Ottavio Rinuccini, the singer-composer Jacopo Peri, and the musician-banker Jacopo Corsi, was first performed in Florence in 1598.

Two years later Rinuccini produced another libretto, *Euridice*, based on Ovid's story of Orpheus and Eurydice; that was given two different musical settings, one by Peri and the other by Giulio Caccini. Ovid's story tells how Eurydice is bitten by a snake and dies on her wedding day; how her bridegroom, Orpheus, a superhumanly gifted singer, dares to venture down to the Underworld, where his heartfelt singing persuades the reigning god, Pluto, to let him lead Eurydice back to the world of the living; and how he nevertheless fails to fulfill the terms of Pluto's decree, which forbade him to look back at Eurydice before they left the Underworld, and thereby loses her a second time to death. Rinuccini's libretto omits this second terrible loss.

In 1607 a new opera on the Orpheus and Eurydice story was performed in Mantua, the seat of another Italian principality, with a new libretto by Alessandro Striggio and music by Claudio Monteverdi; this opera was called *Orfeo*. The following year *Dafne* was performed there, this time with new music by Marco da Gagliano; and a new Rinuccini libretto, *Arianna*, based on Ovid's Ariadne, was performed to music by Monteverdi. In one decade, then, six operas were created on three different stories of Ovid (see box at right). In the following two decades or so, these and other tales from Ovid would continue to provide the subjects of most new secular operas.[3] What could have made his stories so appealing as opera subjects?

> ## Early Court Operas
>
> ### FLORENCE, 1598: *DAFNE*
> - Libretto: Ottavio Rinuccini (after Ovid's *Metamorphoses*, Book 1)
> - Music: Jacopo Peri and Jacopo Corsi (now largely lost)
>
> ### FLORENCE, 1600: *EURIDICE*
> - Libretto: Rinuccini (after Ovid's *Metamorphoses*, Book 10)
> - Music: Peri (with insertions by Giulio Caccini)
>
> ### FLORENCE, 1602: *EURIDICE*
> - Libretto: Rinuccini
> - Music: Giulio Caccini
>
> ### MANTUA, 1607: *ORFEO*
> - Libretto: Alessandro Striggio (after Ovid's *Metamorphoses*, Book 10)
> - Music: Claudio Monteverdi
>
> ### MANTUA, 1608: *DAFNE*
> - Libretto: Rinuccini
> - Music: Marco da Gagliano
>
> ### MANTUA, 1608: *ARIANNA*
> - Libretto: Rinuccini (after Ovid's *Metamorphoses*, Book 8, and *Heroides*, 10)
> - Music: Claudio Monteverdi (largely lost)

The Story of Orpheus: Wedding Lessons

In the case of the three Orpheus operas, a number of writers have argued that this story about the power of song to overwhelm the ruler of the Underworld and to defeat death was chosen because it would dramatize

the power of the new sung medium.[4] It is true that Orpheus's plea to the guardians of the Underworld is the centerpiece of all three operas. But as we'll discover, the most impressive of these pleas, the one in the Striggio-Monteverdi *Orfeo*, can hardly have been designed straightforwardly as a symbol of the power of singing. Orpheus's song proves comically ineffective within the drama, failing to get him admitted into the Underworld.

A more general reason why Ovid's stories suit the medium of opera is that they are mythic: they depict a magical world in which humans and gods, animals and spirits intermingle, moving about in a vast and varied landscape, performing supernatural acts and undergoing supernatural transformations. These myths may have been thought perfect for the wonder-inducing resources of opera: the sounds of instruments filling the air, characters speaking in song, and a succession of colorful sets. The most specifically magical element of the stories, however, did not make it onto the stage. While Ovid's characters usually end by being transformed into a plant, animal, river, star, or other natural object, the operatic versions do not enact Ovid's metamorphoses; at most those are reported to the audience. At the end of Monteverdi's *Orfeo* (in the published score, at least) we do see the title character transported to heaven with his father, the god Apollo, in a stage machine. But it was the creators of the opera, not Ovid, who devised that metamorphosis.

In general, Ovid treats metamorphosis as a device for addressing the fear of mortality. His protagonists are often deprived of sexual fulfillment and therefore of the one form of immortality that Ovid's society believed in: having children. Metamorphosis plucks these characters out of a crisis of mortality and endows them with immortality, if not of a kind available to ordinary humans: they become something permanent in nature or the origin of something permanent (not just a laurel tree, but the species of the laurel tree). Furthermore, the stories immortalize the characters as literature. Ovid himself even boasts, at the conclusion of his work, that he has immortalized himself: "The better part of me will be carried up and fixed beyond the stars forever, and my name will never die."[5] The creators of the first operas, who lived with the Christian promise of a heavenly afterlife, found in Ovid ideas of mortality that their church did not teach. They seized on the idea that achievements made in this life could produce immortality in the form of everlasting fame. In that sense the conquest of death that they celebrated in the Orpheus and Eurydice story was not so much Eurydice's release from the Underworld as it was Orpheus's singing, making him the eternal symbol of musical eloquence.

In Rinuccini's *Euridice* Orpheus does not look back at Eurydice and lose her, but leads her in triumph back to the world of the living. By contrast,

in Striggio's *Orfeo*, as in Ovid's version, Eurydice is condemned by her husband's glance to return to the dead. The differences in these endings may in part be explained by the different occasions for which the operas were written: *Euridice* for the wedding of Maria de' Medici to the king of France, Henri IV, and *Orfeo* for an intellectual-artistic men's club in Mantua. But even *Euridice*, with its happy outcome, seems like a strange story to stage at a wedding, since it begins with the death of a bride on her wedding day. Further, Rinuccini and Gagliano's *Dafne*, about Apollo's attempted rape of Daphne, and Rinuccini and Monteverdi's *Arianna*, about a woman abandoned by her lover on an island, were both written to celebrate another ruling-class wedding.

Weddings are occasions on which individuals' identities, relationships, and place in the world are realigned. Royal weddings around 1600 did not give the bride or groom any say in those realignments; the decisive were made by their families and the church. The wedding operas for Florence and Mantua all show characters, at a moment in their lives when they have lost a sexual partner, confronting what it means to be on their own. It may have been paradoxical to stage such dramas of separation at the moment when bridal partners were being joined together. But at this period in history when the culture of autonomy was just being formed, staging so many of the earliest operas at wedding festivities may have served to acknowledge that even an arranged marriage could now be seen as a moment for the individuals involved, or at least the grooms, to consider their destinies as their own to shape.

In these operas the protagonists respond to the challenges that beset them by reflecting periodically on who they are and what they can make of themselves as they face these challenges. In the Striggio-Monteverdi *Orfeo* (1607), for instance, the title character's speeches of self-reflection dominate the whole opera. In the opening scenes of the lovers' wedding, he addresses one speech to the Sun and the other to the shady woods, establishing his happiness in his new identity as Eurydice's husband by contrast to his previous unhappy life as a bachelor. Then, just after he learns of Eurydice's death, he is already making up his mind to die, resolving that if he cannot bring her back with him from the Underworld, he will stay down there "in the company of death." Escorted to the border of the Underworld by Speranza, or Hope, he sings the plea of his life ("Possente spirto" / "Powerful spirit"), claiming that he is entitled to what other mortals are denied, simply because he is Orpheus. When he is allowed to take Eurydice back, he slips from praising his accomplishment to doubting himself even as he leads her away. And when he has lost her for the second time, he sings his longest reflection of all, "Questi i campi di Tracia" ("These are the plains of Thrace"). Here, in dialogue with his echo, he constructs a new identity for himself as Eurydice's survivor. Through Orpheus's endless reflections, the opera as a whole plots the course of this bridegroom's changing self-concept in changing circumstances.

Eurydice, meanwhile, gets no real opportunity for such reflections. Only in the Rinuccini-Monteverdi *Arianna* (created the following year, 1608) does a female protagonist first get that opportunity. In fact, the title character there, upon realizing that her lover Theseus has abandoned her, responds with a long, complex speech that became at the time the most famous number in any opera: Ariadne's Lament. But since society did not grant women the freedom men had to construct new identities for themselves, this magnificent lament, in the analysis of Suzanne Cusick, "dramatizes the struggle to die to the self"—any hope of a new identity dies here.[6]

The Acting Style of Music: Monteverdi, *Orfeo*

Speeches of reflection, forming the dramatic core of Florentine and Mantuan opera, were complex in language and argument, and yet they were sung. How, then, did music contribute to their dramatic effect? We saw earlier (Chapter 4) how Vincenzo Galilei had called for a musical declamation that would convey the distinctions that actors made in their delivery, reflecting what kind of character they were representing, whom they were speaking to,

and in what kind of exchange. Musicians like Peri, Caccini, Gagliano, and Monteverdi developed this kind of musical declamation for their operas, calling it **acting style** (*stile rappresentativo*) or **declamatory style** (*stile recitativo*, or recitative; see the discussion of recitative in Chapter 2). Peri, in his preface to *Euridice*, described the acting style as something midway between speaking and singing, the kind of delivery that he imagined the ancient Greeks used in tragedies—whose texts were composed in a meter between that of the most exalted poetry and the unmetrical "bounds of everyday discussion."[7]

In studying this style, therefore, we need to pay attention to the poetic form, especially the meter, of the texts. In the sixteenth and seventeenth centuries spoken dramas were normally written in verse. Meter and rhyme were believed to give beauty to the language in a play, and they were important aids to the actors in memorizing their lines. Italian drama was written in two different lengths of line (eleven and seven syllables), freely mixed together, and with a free use of rhyme. The line length and rhyme were thus unpredictable, and this helped actors keep their speeches from sounding singsong. When spoken language sounds too much like song, the meaning can get lulled out of it.

But what about opera? There all the words were sung, yet some represented the characters speaking to each other (or themselves) and others represented them singing songs. We have already come upon that kind of song-within-the-drama in the first act of *La traviata*: Alfredo's *brindisi*, "Libiamo" (see Chapter 4). In the earliest operas both individual characters and the chorus have songs of this sort. In this repertory, therefore, the acting style (the style when the characters are supposed to be speaking to each other) alternates with the **singing style** (the style when they are supposed to be singing). Examining the singing style first allows us to appreciate by contrast how extraordinary the acting style is.

Portrait of Claudio Monteverdi by Bernardo Strozzi, (c. 1640). Landesmuseum-Ferdinandeum, Innsbruck, Austria.
Erich Lessing/Art Resource, NY

The Singing Style

In early operas the songs are generally **strophic** (several verses sung to the same tune) and so require **strophic texts** (stanzas that are all identical in meter, number of lines, and usually patterns of rhyme). These strophic texts are easy to spot in the libretto because the other lines are ungrouped and of varying length and unpredictable rhyme (as in Italian spoken drama of the period).

An example of the singing style in Monteverdi's *Orfeo* is "Vi ricorda, o boschi ombrosi." Orpheus sings this song at his wedding feast (in Act 2), surrounded by his friends, telling how miserable he was before he

met Eurydice and how happy he is now to have found her. This is the first stanza:

Vi ricorda, o boschi ombrosi, Do you recall, O shady woods,
De' miei lungh' aspri tormenti, my long, harsh torments,
Quando i sassi ai miei lamenti when the very stones, turned compassionate,
Rispondean, fatti pietosi? would respond to my laments?

All four stanzas have the same poetic structure: four lines, each eight syllables long (adjacent vowels are counted as one), rhyming abba. Monteverdi identifies this as a song, even before Orpheus has begun to sing it, by having a group of string instruments introduce the tune in a **ritornello**, an instrumental refrain that returns after each stanza. In the opening ritornello we hear that the tune uses a catchy rhythm sometimes found in canzonettas (popular songs of the period), with a pleasing shift in the beat pattern within each line of text. The audience can already tell that the coming number is to be understood as a song.

5.1 **Monteverdi, *Orfeo*: Act 2, "Vi ricorda"**

The ritornello consists of four phrases. Though the song text also has four phrases, Orpheus takes seven phrases to sing it, since he sings the first line ("Vi ricorda, o boschi ombrosi") twice at the beginning and then twice more at the end (see Example 5.1). All the phrases have practically the same rhythmic structure, so that the line structure of the poetry is utterly clear in the phrase structure of the melody. Each phrase begins when the previous one ends, the singer snatching a breath whenever he can. The last two phrases are virtually identical to the first two in words and music, giving the whole stanza a feeling of coming around to where it began. The string group that plays in the ritornello drops out for the sung stanzas, leaving Orpheus with simply a **basso continuo** accompaniment—a part written as a bass line, which a bass instrument (like a gamba or cello or contrabass) might play, joined by a chord instrument (lute or organ or harpsichord) that adds harmonies above the line. In this song the bass part reinforces the catchy rhythms of the singer's melody, while lending harmonic clarity to the circuit that the singer's phrases make from beginning to end of the stanza. This is a tune that runs its course in such a gratifying way that we immediately want to go through the experience again. Orpheus and the string band oblige us with their additional ritornellos and stanzas.

The Acting Style

At the end of the song, however, the singing style almost immediately yields to the acting style, and the reason is the arrival of bad news that banishes the singing mood. Orpheus's bride, Eurydice, has been off gathering flowers with her friends, one of whom now returns to the banquet to report to Orpheus that Eurydice has been bitten by a snake and is dead. This is not a moment for the performers to sing in regular, rounded, predictable phrases. It is a moment when no one is prepared to speak and everyone has to think what to say. Orpheus in particular is so stunned that at first he can utter only a single word: "Ohimè" ("Woe is me"). But someone has to speak, so the witness relates how Eurydice was bitten and how she expired; then Orpheus's friends express their sympathy; and finally Orpheus himself manages to say something. In all of this, if we are to feel that we are living through the characters'

Andrea Mantegna, *Parnassus* (or *Mars and Venus*), 1497. This canvas, now in the Louvre in Paris, was painted for the ducal palace in Mantua, where Monteverdi's *Orfeo* was first performed more than a century later.
Erich Lessing/Art Resource, NY

Scene from Act 2 of Monteverdi's *Orfeo*, staged by Gilbert Deflo with scenery by William Orlandi and choreography by Veronica Endo, at the Edinburgh Festival, 2007. Furio Zanasi (with lyre) is Orpheus. The setting, costumes, and dance are evidently inspired by Mantegna's *Parnassus*, which hung nearby in the palace when the opera was first performed.
Douglas Robertson

experiences with them, they have to deliver their lines as if they are coming to terms with their feelings as they speak. We need to hear the gasps and plunging of their voices, the pauses and lurches of their thinking aloud. It was for dramatic moments of this sort that Peri and his contemporaries invented the acting style of music that Monteverdi uses here.

By the time his friends have expressed their sympathy, Orpheus has worked out a plan, and he addresses it in his imagination to Eurydice:

Tu se' morta, mia vita, ed io respiro?	You are dead, my life, and I am breathing?
Tu se' da me partita	You are parted from me,
Per mai più non tornare, ed io rimango?	never to return, and I am left?
No, che se i versi alcuna cosa ponno,	No, for if lyrics can do anything,
N'andrò sicuro a' più profondi abissi,	I will surely go to the deepest abysses
E intenerito il cor del Re de l'Ombre	and, having moved the heart of the King of the Dead,
Meco trarrotti a riveder le stelle,	I will carry you back with me to look on the stars again,
O se ciò negherammi empio destino	or if pitiless destiny refuses me this,
Rimarrò teco in compagnia di morte,	I will stay with you in the company of death.
A dio terra, a dio cielo, e sole, a dio.	Farewell earth, farewell sky, and sun, farewell.

This text has no stanzas; it is cast in the mostly long, unrhymed lines used in Italian spoken drama. But it does develop a progression of thought in clear

stages. Orpheus first dwells on the unbearable separation that Eurydice's death has created between them; then he promises to win her back from death or die trying; and finally he bids farewell to the world of the living as he sets out on his quest.

The original score of the opera (a published score, unusual for the period) tells us not only that the voice is accompanied by basso continuo, but even what instruments Monteverdi wanted to perform here: a flue-pipe organ and a *chitarrone* (theorbo, or large lute). Since this type of accompaniment is equally characteristic of the singing and acting styles, it is worth noticing how different the basso continuo part here is from the one in "Vi ricorda." It does not provide a catchy rhythm or even coordinate with the singer's melody; instead, it serves as a foil to his line (see Example 5.2). Its long, slow notes and harmonies change between the singer's phrases as often as they change within them, punctuating those phrases and marking the turns of his thought from one phrase to the next. At the same time, because they do not move with his notes, the singer has the rhythmic freedom to pace his delivery in an impulsive way that reflects Orpheus's distraught state of mind.

5.2 Monteverdi, *Orfeo*: Act 2, "Tu se' morta"

Orpheus, by Gerrit van Honthorst, around 1614–16. The Dutch painter, working within a decade of Monteverdi's opera, shows Orpheus playing not the lyre, as in Ovid's account and ancient depictions, but a modern instrument, the violin. Palazzo Reale di Capodimonte, Naples.

To some extent, an impulsive delivery is written into the notation. At the very opening of the speech, for instance, the notation tells Orpheus to sing the single word "Tu" ("you") and gasp. Then he is to sing "se' morta" ("are dead") and take a real breath. After that, he is to repeat those two words and go on: "se' morta, mia vita" ("are dead, my life"). The notes, in other words, prescribe that the actor sing these words like someone who can barely get a sentence out—exactly what we would expect from a character who has lost his wife on their wedding day. But thanks to the lack of a controlling rhythm from the accompanying instruments, the singer's exact timing, his exact calculation of how to create the dramatic effect, is up to him. The autonomy of the individual, a driving concern of seventeenth-century drama, finds a literal expression in the freedom of delivery that the acting style makes possible in opera.

As Orpheus is sputtering out those opening phrases, he is also colliding with the harmonies of the bass part. In his opening "Tu se' morta" the notes of "Tu" and "morta" fit with the bass note, G, but his F-sharp on "se'" is painfully dissonant with that G. Similar dissonances occur in the following phrases: on the next "se'" and then on the whole string of words "se' da me par-" both times he sings them. In each case the singer resolves the dissonant note into a consonant one on the next syllable. But he is stumbling into dissonance in every phrase, and into more and more pro-tracted dissonances as he proceeds, all while his voice is climbing slowly upward, reaching a climax of desperation on "rimango? No, no" ("I am left? No, no!") as his words lose contact with the bass part in both rhythm and harmony. His engagement with the bass allows the singer to portray a man staggering uncontrollably under his grief.

And then he gains a kind of control over it. The next part of his speech, af-ter all, depicts a more rational state of mind. Orpheus now proposes a plan to win Eurydice back and plots what he will do if he fails. Accordingly, the bro-ken delivery and wrenching dissonances of his opening disappear, replaced by a more controlled expression. One feature of that controlled expression is **word painting**, the use of a vivid musical image to illustrate a word or idea in the text. For example, Orpheus's voice sinks to its lowest pitch when he says he will go to the deepest abysses ("abissi") of the Underworld and again when he says he will stay in the company of death ("di morte"). He attains a still higher level of control in his last line, when he bids the world of the living farewell. Here his voice settles into what seemed impossible just a few moments before: a movingly dignified coordination with the bass, in almost a slow dance rhythm. The acting style takes a variety of forms because it dra-matizes the infinite—and often abrupt—changes of emotion and situation to which any human being is subject.

Song and Speech Combined: "Possente spirto"

In our day Monteverdi's Orfeo is considered the work in which opera came into its own. Unlike its predecessors, it has had many fully staged modern performances in opera houses; it was premiered, however, in a fairly small chamber of a princely palace, with just two sets, one of a meadow and the other of the Underworld. The cast was small: seven solo roles, shared among no more than five singers, and a chorus of unspecified size from which sing-ers were drawn to sing a few other solos.[8] The one resource used lavishly was instruments: the score names thirty-two. But Monteverdi never calls for

all of them to be playing at the same time, as in an orchestra, and so there could have been far fewer players than instruments.

For all that, *Orfeo* is a rich, colorful work, rich above all in the characterization of Orpheus. At almost every stage of the story, Monteverdi presents him as both an eloquent, self-conscious speaker (in numbers using the acting style) and a dazzling, overpowering singer (in numbers using the singing style). By this consistent pairing of song and speech numbers, he makes us consider that whatever crises of identity Orpheus endures, his identity as a singer is always part of the issue.

At his wedding, for instance, Orpheus expresses his joy at marrying Eurydice in acting style ("Rosa del ciel" / "Rose of heaven") as well as the song "Vi ricorda, o boschi ombrosi." It is only when he hears of her death that he loses his ability to sing; as we have seen, he can barely muster words for "Tu se' morta." It falls to the shepherds and nymphs of the wedding party to express his grief in a song that then becomes a magnificent choral ode, "Ahi caso acerbo!" ("O bitter turn of events!").

Once on the bank of the River Styx, Orpheus has to persuade the boatman Charon (Caronte) to ferry him across to the Underworld. He makes his appeal to Charon — "Possente spirto" ("Powerful spirit") — in an extremely elaborate singing style, while also accompanying himself most elaborately on his lyre. Charon is impressed, but doesn't allow himself to yield to pity. At that, Orpheus abandons the arts and structures of song and begins imploring the gods of the Underworld in raw acting style, ending with a nagging line that rises chromatically (by half steps) on words of sheer insistence: "Rendetemi il mio ben, tartarei Numi!" ("Give me back my beloved, gods of Hades!"). After that outburst some very quiet instrumental music puts Charon to sleep, and Orpheus rows himself across the Styx.

In the Underworld Pluto yields to his wife Proserpina, who has been affected by Orpheus's lamenting, and grants Orpheus permission to rescue Eurydice. As Orpheus begins to lead her away, he sings another strophic song with ritornellos, this one praising his lyre for the power it has demonstrated: "Qual onor di te fia degno" ("What honor would be worthy of you"). But as he completes the third stanza, he falls into questions — Why should he obey Pluto and not look back at Eurydice? How can he be sure she is following him? — switching back to the acting style. These thoughts, at once arrogant and self-doubting, lead him to turn toward Eurydice and lose her. In the last act, back home and alone, he examines himself once more in a magnificent reflection in acting style, "Questi i campi di Tracia" ("These are the plains of Thrace"). Now he decides that while there is no hope of regaining Eurydice a second time, he himself can go on living, but there can be no other woman worthy of his love. When Apollo then descends from the sky to offer him

Claudio Monteverdi

When he wrote this letter, on December 9, 1616, Monteverdi had been dismissed as court choirmaster to the Duke of Mantua and was established as music director at the Basilica of San Marco in Venice. Nevertheless he was still asked periodically to compose for the Mantuan court. The poet Alessandro Striggio, who had written the libretto of *Orfeo* for him nine years earlier and was still in the duke's service, conveyed a request to compose a work for the duke's wedding. Monteverdi's comments on the proposed text, Scipione Agnelli's *Le nozze di Tetide* (*The Wedding of Thetis*), indicate what kind of dramatic characters and situations it took to inspire operatic music from him.

In addition, I have noticed that the interlocutors are winds, Cupids, little Zephyrs, and Sirens: consequently many sopranos will be needed, and it can also be stated that the winds have to sing—that is, the Zephyrs and the Boreals. How, dear Sir, can I imitate the speech of the winds, if they do not speak? And how can I, by such means, move the passions? Ariadne moved us because she was a woman, and similarly Orpheus because he was a man, not a wind. Music can suggest, without any words, the noise of winds and the bleating of sheep, the neighing of horses, and so on and so forth; but it cannot imitate the speech of winds because no such thing exists.

And as to the story as a whole—as far as my no little ignorance is concerned—I do not feel that it moves me at all (moreover I find it hard to understand), nor do I feel that it carries me in a natural manner to an end that moves me. *Arianna* led me to a just lament, and *Orfeo* to a righteous prayer, but this fable leads me I don't know to what end. So what does Your Lordship want the music to be able to do? Nevertheless I shall always accept everything with due reverence and honour if by chance His Highness should so command and desire it, since he is my master without question.

The Letters of Claudio Monteverdi, trans. Denis Stevens, revised ed. (Oxford: Clarendon Press, 1995), p. 110.

a happy life in heaven instead of an unhappy one on earth, Orpheus gives up his mournful reflections in acting style for a joyfully songful duet with Apollo, "Saliam cantando al Ciel" ("Let us ascend, singing, to Heaven"). It is a very short song, but in its playful imitations, Apollo seems to prod Orpheus into taking up his role as singer once and for all.

Literary Form and Musical Style

Out of all these numbers, the one that most indelibly establishes Orpheus's identity as a singer is "Possente spirto"—despite the fact that it fails even to get his foot into the boat to the Underworld. Nevertheless, within the history of opera, it marks a momentous development. For this number, representing both a song and an elaborate argument, the librettist Alessandro Striggio had to decide whether to put the words into free verse (the normal form for acting style) or stanzaic verse (for singing style). He wrote "Possente spirto" in stanzaic verse and in doing so initiated a revolution. In Western drama stretching back to ancient Athens, stanzaic verse was not used for the complexly argued speeches by the principal characters that advanced the action of the drama; it was reserved for incidental or decorative or commenting speeches (often song-and-dance numbers) in the margins and interludes of the action.

Opening page of "Possente spirto" in the original published score of *Orfeo* (Venice: Ricciardo Amadino, 1609). The inscription at the top reads "Orpheus, to the sound of the flue-pipe organ and a theorbo, sings just one of the two parts." Each system on this page shows the two solo violin parts, the plain and embellished versions of Orpheus's lines, and the basso continuo line for organ and theorbo.

"Possente spirto" is the complexly argued principal speech of the main character, yet—representing that character singing—it is in stanzaic verse.

The specific form Striggio uses is called *terza rima*, a three-line stanza pattern with interlocking rhymes (aba bcb cdc . . .) that had been associated in Italian literature since the fourteenth century with Dante's narrative poem *Commedia* (*The Divine Comedy*). Striggio's six stanzas of *terza rima* in "Possente spirto," however, do not suggest a narration; they enunciate the six distinct stages of Orpheus's argument to Charon.

This created a dilemma for Monteverdi: whether to set each stanza to the same or different music. If he had used the same music, he would have

reinforced the impression that Orpheus was singing a song, because, then as now, songs commonly repeated their music stanza by stanza (**strophic repetition**). But that would have undercut the force of Orpheus's argument. Strophic repetition makes a song seem timeless: we feel that the singer could repeat it in different situations, to different listeners, any number of times. A dramatic character like Orpheus, on the other hand, pleading with Charon to row him to the Underworld, should make us feel he is choosing the right words for just that moment, to persuade just that listener. His music, no less than his words, needs to create that impression. For that purpose Monteverdi had at his disposal the acting style of music, which avoided repetitions and provided a fitting musical declamation for each line of text, so that we follow the character's discourse moment by moment. Yet for that very reason the acting style would not suggest a character singing.

Strophic Progression

In "Possente spirto," the first great show-stopper in the history of opera, Monteverdi found a way to make a musical "song" that was at the same time a musical argument, drawing with remarkable flexibility on both the song principle of strophic repetition and the rhetorical principle of the acting style. His solution was the revolutionary principle of **strophic progression**: the text stanzas, all identical in form, become musical units that are not identical to each other, but are equivalent in length, as clearly demarcated from each other as the stanzas of a strophic song, and related to each other in such a way that the whole sequence suggests a reasoned progression of thought.

Monteverdi demarcates the stanzas in "Possente spirto" with instrumental ritornellos, though only after the first three of the six stanzas. And even those ritornellos are not all the same, like those in Orpheus's earlier song, "Vi ricorda." Each is a new and magnificent fantasy played by a different set of instruments: a pair of violins, then a pair of cornetts (curved, wooden wind instruments), then a harp, joined in each case by the flue-pipe organ and theorbo as continuo instruments. The featured instruments play not just in their ritornellos, but also in the preceding stanza — more precisely, between the lines of that stanza (there the paired instruments mostly echo each other, whereas in the ritornellos they mostly move together in rhythm). Each of the remaining stanzas is also distinguished by its own instrumental combination, though those are heard only within the stanza itself: two violins and a large cello in the fourth strophe, basso continuo alone in the fifth, and three violins and contrabass in the sixth.

In all, Monteverdi uses distinctive instrumental colors and textures to impress on us the boundaries of each line and each stanza, and therefore the

stages of the argument, despite the wildly embellished styles of both sing-ing and playing. Listening to that variety of instrumental sounds, including winds as well as bowed and plucked strings, may make us wonder which of those sounds Orpheus is referring to when he describes the power of his fingers stroking the "soft strings" of his "golden lyre." We might want to consider John Whenham's suggestion that "Orpheus conjured up all the available forces of music to aid his plea to Charon."[9]

The style of Orpheus's singing in "Possente spirto" is as remarkable as the instrumental playing. Through most of it, Orpheus sings highly em-bellished lines. The score that Monteverdi published gives two versions of these vocal lines—an unusual procedure in itself. The more elaborate version (which performers in our day almost invariably choose) demands a **virtuoso** style of singing, a self-glorifying flood of notes. The plainer version follows the principles of Peri's acting style and invites the singer to add his own embellishments. To Nino Pirrotta the embellished version makes Orpheus's appeal sound like a mysterious religious rite, in which "a superhuman singer soothes and subdues the forces of darkness crossing his path."[10] Even an ecstatic performance of ritualistic song, however, can convey a rhetorical strategy.

The first stanza begins, like many a tactful plea, by flattering the listener, Charon, to dispose him to judge Orpheus's arguments favorably:

(1) *Possente spirto e formidabil nume,*   *Powerful spirit, formidable god, without*
    Senza cui far passaggio a l'altra riva   *whom a soul released from its body*
    Alma da corpo sciolta in van presume,   *presumes in vain to pass to the opposite*
    shore,

Ritornello: two violins

The arguments then follow. In the next two stanzas Orpheus counters the claim Charon has just made (that he can't let Orpheus into the Underworld because he is not yet dead) with the claim that nothing is as it seems: in a sense he is already dead (stanza 2), and in a sense this is not the Underworld (stanza 3):

(2) *Non viv'io, no, che poi di vita è priva*   *I'm not living, no, for since my dear wife*
    Mia cara sposa, il cor non è più meco,   *is deprived of life, my heart is gone from me.*
    E senza cor com'esser può ch'io viva?   *And without my heart how can I be alive?*

Ritornello: two cornetts

(3) *A lei volt'ho il cammin per l'aer cieco,*   *Toward her I have turned my path*
    through the sightless air,

    A l'Inferno non già, ch'ovunque stassi   *yet not to the Underworld, since wherever*
    Tanta bellezza il Paradiso ha seco.   *such beauty [as hers] is found, Paradise is*
    with it.

Ritornello: harp

Each of these three stanzas has its own magnificently embellished vocal lines, punctuated by equally magnificent instrumental passages, but the musical stanzas (like the instrumental ritornellos) are variations of each other: they all follow the same progression of bass and harmony, and even their elaborate melodies follow the same contours. So far, then, Orpheus's singing and playing, though dazzlingly inventive as the situation seems to require, also fit the orderly progression of the argument that his words make.

Orpheus (Furio Zanasi, right) singing "Possente spirto" to Charon (Antonio Abete) in the Edinburgh Festival production of *Orfeo*, 2007.
EFE Press Agency

The harp ritornello that follows the third stanza is the longest and—especially given that it is a duet played by a single player—most virtuosic instrumental passage of all, played on the instrument that's most like Orpheus's lyre. It prepares us to hear his next stanza as particularly important. When that new stanza comes, although Orpheus's singing is again elaborate, his argument is surprisingly simple: he tells Charon who he is. But when you are Orpheus, just revealing your identity (in lyre playing and then in words) can constitute an argument. Having already revealed what is exceptional about his condition, he now demands that Charon make an exception for him on the grounds that his identity too is exceptional. Other than that, there is no argument to this stanza:

(4) *Orfeo son io, che d'Euridice i passi*   I am Orpheus, who follow Eurydice's
   Seguo per queste tenebrose arene,   steps across these gloomy sands
   Ove già mai per uom mortal non vassi.   never before traversed by a mortal.

A new relationship develops here, however, between the singer's melodic lines and those played by the instruments: they begin to copy each other's melodic turns. To be precise, Orpheus's phrase on the word "seguo" ("follow") imitates what has just been played on the *basso da brazzo* (a predecessor of the cello). Eventually—also for the first time—the singer and the melody instruments begin to overlap and harmonize with each other. Orpheus is no longer showing off his claims to musical fame in an alternation of vocal and instrumental displays; now he self-confidently shows how the words "I am Orpheus" mean being able to put it all together.

After this stanza Monteverdi dispenses with the ritornello and plunges right into the fifth stanza, in which he discontinues the elaborate singing style (no longer giving the singer a choice of versions to perform). Instead he makes Orpheus perform in acting style, over a new bass line, with no interludes between phrases. And when he gets to the end, he repeats the third line, this

time with the bass line falling chromatically, so there is no mistaking that the musical pattern of the earlier stanzas has been broken in every possible respect. What occasions this utter change in the music? For one thing, Orpheus seems no longer to be speaking to Charon so much as thinking of Eurydice:

(5) *O de le luci mie luci serene,*
     S'un vostro sguardo può tornarmi
        in vita,
     Ahi, chi niega il conforto
        a le mie pene?

O clear eyes that light my eyes,
if a look from you can restore
   my life,
oh, would deny me relief
   from my suffering?

Joseph Kerman assumes that in forsaking the musical pattern he has maintained up to this point, Monteverdi is indicating that Orpheus, noticing that nothing he has done so far impresses Charon, "forgets himself abruptly."[11] That fits with his appearing to address Eurydice instead of Charon. But it ignores the challenge that Orpheus is laying down to Charon here. Who is Charon, he is saying, to deny relief to the suffering of one whose wife has the power, through the supernatural glance of her light-giving eyes, to bring him back from death? So far from forgetting what he is doing or whom he is addressing, Orpheus is raising the stakes in his argument. No longer demonstrating his musical powers, he is now associating himself with the power to restore life, in the unadorned musical prose of the acting style. His time to "forget himself" will come in his uncontrolled expression after he has finished this speech and Charon has turned him down.

For now, though, he completes his case. Again he moves into a new stanza (the sixth) without pause or ritornello, again shifting his argument. The final argument takes four lines of text instead of the usual three, the extension creating a stanza in which alternate lines rhyme. The open-endedness of the *terza rima* structure is therefore brought to a close. But the extra line also gives Orpheus time to move from flattery and supplication (line 1) to the assertion that as a musician he is no threat (lines 2 and 3) and yet irresistible (line 4). This final stanza, then, is not so much a new argument as a summary of all the previous ones:

(6) *Sol tu, nobile Dio, puoi darmi aita,*
     Ne temer dei che sopra un'aurea cetra
     Sol di corde soavi armo le dita
     Contra cui rigid'alma in van s'impetra.

You alone, noble god, can help me,
nor should you fear me arming my fingers
with only soft strings on a golden lyre,
against which a rigid spirit has no resort.

What musical means could Monteverdi use to support the different arguments compressed into those four short lines? In a sense he chooses, like Striggio, to summarize and synthesize all his previous strategies. He returns to the bass line, chord progression, and melodic contour of the first four stanzas. At the same time, the melodic line continues in the acting style of

the fifth (again he offers no embellished version of the vocal line). Yet there is also a new tone in the music of this stanza. As in the first four, Monteverdi introduces a new set of melody instruments (this time three violins and a contrabass); but here, rather than playing elaborate passages between the singer's phrases to impress Charon, they provide a continuous warm harmonization of Orpheus's phrases, lending self-assurance and purposefulness to his singing voice. In fact, the musical warmth and effect of self-confidence increase right up to the end, thanks to the change from minor to major mode that Monteverdi introduces for the fourth line and to the striding rhythm of the melody against the bass on the last three words. By the time Orpheus finishes his speech-song, then, it is as if, in trying to persuade Charon to take him where he wants to go, he finds his own voice and his own stride. His pursuit of his dead wife has led him to a discovery of himself.

Pieter Breughel the Elder, *Orpheus in the Underworld*, 1594. In the lower left corner of this densely populated landscape of Hell, the Flemish painter shows the scene that begins Act 4 of Monteverdi's *Orfeo*: the rulers of the Underworld, Pluto and Proserpina, consider Orpheus's plea that they release Eurydice from the dead. This Orpheus plays the harp. Galleria Palatina, Palazzo Pitti, Florence.

Scala/Art Resource, NY

"Possente spirto" in Historical Context

"Possente spirto" is a musical speech-song like no other in early opera, containing and extending the whole expressive range of the new operatic medium. If it had no true precedent, it also produced few if any imitations, especially not of its text in *terza rima* or its music in variation form that gets broken and then restored. But the general strophic principles that it pioneered proved prophetic. Within the first century of opera, it became routine for characters to deliver important speeches in stanzaic verse and for the stanzas to be delivered in a corresponding strophic progression of music. A speech of this sort would come to be called an **aria** (Italian for "air"), and for the next couple of centuries—and that means for most of the works that form the standard repertory today—the aria was the central kind of dramatic utterance in opera. The strophic principles of the aria, consequently, had to cover many kinds of speeches, not just arguments, and certainly not just arguments in the form of songs.

Furthermore, the principles could be applied in ways that Striggio and Monteverdi never imagined. Later in the seventeenth century aria texts would often consist of inconsistent stanzas (sometimes an alternation of rhymed stanzas with stretches of spoken-drama verse), set to an alternation of singing-style and acting-style music. In eighteenth-century opera those styles became more segregated into separate numbers, and aria texts generally consisted of formally identical stanzas; from as few as two short stanzas, the composer might create the impression of an elaborate progression by using one of those stanzas over and over. What always marked the aria was the idea of a character thinking and speaking in coherent stages of thought, each stage represented by a distinct poetic and musical stanza.

Opera composers, then, had to make music think in stanzas. They learned to apply their arts of melodic declamation, rhythmic articulation, harmonic modulation, accompanimental figuration, and instrumental coloration to this problem. We will explore the results of their efforts throughout this book. But the challenge was not confined to dramatic music, or even to music with texts. Borrowing opera's principle of strophic progression, Western composers also turned their attention to instrumental music in complex forms. Arias provided a rough model for instrumental movements that flowed in a succession of related stages, similar to each other in extent: the alternating orchestral ritornellos and solo sections of the concerto, the statements and transformations of stanza-like themes in the sonata and symphony. Since the birth of opera, or more precisely since "Possente spirto," thinking in progressions of differentiated musical "stanzas" has been the story of Western classical music.

FURTHER READING

On the development of drama, including church drama, in the centuries up to and including the time when opera arose, William Egginton, *How the World Became a Stage: Presence, Theatricality, and the Question of Modernity* (Albany: State University of New York Press, 2003).

On the development of courtly opera, chs. 19 and 20 of Lorenzo Bianconi, *Music in the Seventeenth Century*, trans. David Bryant (Cambridge and New York: Cambridge University Press, 1987); documents by composers and others involved in that creative process in Piero Weiss, *Opera: A History in Documents* (New York and Oxford: Oxford University Press, 2002).

On Monteverdi's life and career, Paolo Fabbri, *Monteverdi*, trans. Tim Carter (Cambridge and New York: Cambridge University Press, 1994). On *Orfeo*, Tim Carter, *Monteverdi's Musical Theater* (New Haven: Yale University Press, 2002); John Whenham, ed., *Claudio Monteverdi: "Orfeo"* (Cambridge and

New York: Cambridge University Press, 1986); Joachim Steinheuer, "Orfeo (1607)," in *Cambridge Companion to Monteverdi*, ed. John Whenham and Richard Wistreich (Cambridge and New York: Cambridge University Press, 2007), pp. 119–40.

FOR RESEARCH AND REFLECTION

1. Compare the dramatization of the theme of autonomy—an individual's freedom to define his or her own identity or allegiances—in *Orfeo* with the dramatization of that theme in any tragedy or history play by Monteverdi's English contemporary William Shakespeare.

2. Nowadays *Orfeo* is sometimes produced in relatively small opera houses, sometimes at special festivals devoted to the performance of music from Monteverdi's era, but seldom in the biggest opera houses, like the Metropolitan in New York. Why might the resources of such a great opera house be considered a liability rather than an advantage in performing this first great masterpiece of the opera repertory?

3. Study the middle of Act 2 of *Orfeo*, from the arrival of Eurydice's companion, bringing news of her death, through Orpheus's response to that news in "Tu se' morta." Consider how Monteverdi allows each speech in this sequence its own dramatic effect through a distinct use of the acting style. Then consider the dramatic effect of framing this supremely painful and unguarded dialogue with much more formal musical numbers bearing the commentary of Orpheus's companions.

4. Monteverdi's score for *Orfeo* is remarkable among seventeenth-century opera scores in its thoroughgoing specification of instrumentation: not only the different kinds of ensembles to play the various preludes, ritornellos, and dances, but frequent changes in the plucked string and keyboard instruments used to accompany the acting-style dialogue. Study some of these specifications; what dramatic sense can you make of the composer's choices?

5. How does the virtuosity of Orpheus's singing and the instrumental playing in "Possente spirto" compare with other kinds of musical virtuosity you know? In what kinds of music is virtuosity apt to be found, and what relationships can it create between the performer and the audience?

 Additional resources are available at wwnorton.com/studyspace.

CHAPTER 6

Opera in Commercial Opera Houses: Venice

In 1637, three decades after the creation of *Orfeo*, an opera was staged for the first time in a commercial theater. The work, performed in the San Cassiano Theater in Venice, was *Andromeda*, with a libretto by Benedetto Ferrari and music by Francesco Manelli. Soon Venice had numerous commercial opera houses, and the system of opera production that we know today was launched. Here, an opera was performed not once or twice at a special event, but night after night within the carnival season. After that, a touring company might take it to other Italian cities. As opera companies were formed in other cities, the score of a work premiered in Venice might be acquired by some of those companies. Audiences were no longer made up of the invited guests of a princely patron, but of people who leased a box for the season or bought a single ticket for one performance.

The operas themselves were of a very different sort from the ones created for the courts of Florence and Mantua. Their staging was far more spectacular. Whereas the court operas *Euridice* and *Orfeo* made do with two sets each, a Venetian opera could easily require ten or twelve. *Bellerofonte*, with music by Francesco Sacrati, was produced at the Novissimo Theater in 1642 with eight sets and many special effects. In its Prologue alone, set by a harbor, Justice descends to the stage in

Lucia Cirillo as Minerva and Magnus Staveland as Telemaco in the 2011 Vlaamse (Belgium) Opera production of Monteverdi's *Il ritorno d'Ulisse in patria* (*Ulysses' Return to His Homeland*), which premiered in Venice in 1640. In this staging by Michael Hampe, the goddess Minerva enters, like any divinity in a seventeenth-century opera, by descending from the rafters.

Vlaamse Opera/Annemie Augustijns

a cloud, Neptune arrives in a seashell-shaped chariot, and when the city of Venice comes in for praise, a model of the city rises up out of the waves in the distance. Later in the opera the hero Bellerophon flies in on his winged horse Pegasus to attack and kill the monstrous Chimaera. Venetian opera was also enriched with dance spectacle, sometimes involving dancing animals, represented by costumed stagehands or dancers or mechanical animals. By the end of the seventeenth century, even live horses and camels had appeared on the opera stage, and by one account live deer, bears, and wild boars had been hunted down onstage.[1]

Sebastiano Mazzoni, *The Annunziation*, painted around 1650. Older depictions of the Archangel Gabriel's announcement to the Virgin Mary that she would become the mother of Jesus tended to show the archangel standing or kneeling on the ground or on a low-hovering cloud. Mazzoni's version, painted soon after he moved to Venice, has him descending from the rafters like a deity in a Venetian opera of the period. Gallerie dell'Accademia, Venice.

The Venetian operas also differed in the stories they presented. Many sources besides Ovid's *Metamorphoses* were now used, from classical epics and tragedies and the histories of Roman and Middle Eastern generals and emperors to popular fictions of the Crusades. From these sources librettists produced plots focused not so much on one central character's identity problems as on the interlocking relationships of several characters. Above all, they are love stories, in which characters throw themselves into the wrong relationships before discovering the partners who are right for them. Though the Bellerophon of classical mythology is an action hero, in Sacrati's opera his exploits as a fighter take a back seat to his search for the right wife from among the three women who court him.

Gods and mortals, rulers and servants, lovers and clowns mingle with each other onstage, and in place of the generally lofty tone of the earlier court operas, there is an endless interplay of serious and comic tones. In *Calisto* (1651), composed by Francesco Cavalli to a libretto by Giovanni Faustini on a subject from Ovid, Jupiter, the lecherous king of the gods, finds his advances spurned by the nymph Calisto. Calisto has made a vow of chastity as a follower of the virgin goddess Diana, an obstacle that Jupiter circumvents by disguising himself as Diana. Calisto, trusting in Diana, allows the disguised Jupiter to seduce her. After sacrificing his dignity as king of the gods in this comic disguise, Jupiter has no trouble reclaiming that dignity once he reveals himself to Calisto. His bass voice now rings out in regal music, supported by a churchly choir of celestial spirits.

The music distinguishes Venetian opera from earlier court opera just as clearly as the spectacle and the plots do. The singing style—with its instrumental ritornellos, steady rhythms, and rounded forms—is no longer so confined to numbers that represent characters singing or dancing; it is also used when characters speak to others or to themselves. In these dramatic scenes a single speech may be built of an alternation of acting-style and singing-style sections (or, as they would come to be called, recitatives and arias); there may also be sections in an in-between style (eventually called **arioso**). This mixture of styles allowed a speech to be delivered partly in a plain musical declamation and partly with characterizing music: a joyful speech in a lively dance spirit, a soothing speech in the rhythm of a lullaby. Another musical difference in this repertory is the increasing centrality of duets and other small ensembles—a fitting development, given that opera had become more concerned with portraying social, especially amorous, relationships. The mid-seventeenth century in Venice was the great age of the love duet in opera.

All of these changes in the nature of the operatic show can be connected to the commercial nature of the operatic enterprise in Venice. The paying audience was a novelty in its autonomy and diversity, and the system of

Peter Paul Rubens, *Jupiter and Callisto*, 1613. A painter could show Jupiter transformed into Diana, goddess of the hunt, by depicting Diana (here caressing the nymph Callisto) with Jupiter's emblematic eagle hiding behind a bush. How Francesco Cavalli disguised the bass singing Jupiter as the soprano Diana in his opera *Calisto* (1651) is not clear. Gemäldegalerie Alte Meister, Kassel, Germany.
Art Resource, NY

production was novel in that a company performed one or at most two works throughout its season. Each of these new conditions contributed to the form of the operas themselves.

Producing Opera for the Public

Autonomy of Audiences

Venetian audiences were autonomous in two senses. The spectators were there on their own account—not, like the spectators of court operas, at the invitation (the command) of their prince. And they were there to see an opera on its own account, not in conjunction with a wedding in the prince's family. Opera in Venice, in other words, filled the theater only when people were persuaded that it was worth spending their time and money on. To persuade people of that, the theaters relied on word-of-mouth, but also on advertising—in itself a fairly new practice at the time. Starting in 1638 (when a second opera house set up in competition with the first), the production of a new opera was apt to be advertised by publishing its scenario, a scene-by-scene description of the action, along with puffs about the work, theater, composer, set designer, and performers. After a few years this practice was replaced by the publication of the libretto to build anticipation in a different way: it allowed patrons to read and appreciate the opera as a literary work before seeing it as a musical-dramatic spectacle.

The managers, creators, and performers had to see to it that the show did not disappoint the audience. That may seem obvious, but it is nevertheless part of the difference between a commercial entertainment and a courtly one. If a prince had any kind of spectacle put on at his court, it did not matter whether the audience liked it. "The production was—officially at any rate—a success," as the musicologist Franco Piperno puts it. Furthermore, a court spectacle, especially at a wedding, was a demonstration of the prince's extravagance; a good part of its value lay in being more costly than others could afford. But at a commercial opera house the cost of productions had to stay in line with receipts. "Opera at court," Piperno adds, "was like a book printed privately in a very limited edition; in a public theater, opera became like a paperback."[2]

One of the great attractions of Venetian opera was the stage wizardry of Giacomo Torelli. At the Novissimo Theater he not only designed sets (such as those for *Bellerofonte*) that dazzled the Venetians; he also devised machinery that changed the whole set at once, before the eyes of the audience—with ropes connected to a single drum, so that the whole change could be performed "by a boy of fifteen," as an advertisement bragged.[3] This last marvel held down labor costs enormously, since in courtly spectacles it would often take sixteen people to change a set. An industrial-age model of efficiency in production was already being practiced in the seventeenth-century opera house.

Diversity of Audiences

The autonomy of the house produced diversity in its audience: whereas the audience members at a court opera were united by bonds to the prince, those at a commercial house were united simply by their decision to attend. In fact, Venetians had no bond to any prince. Venice, calling itself a republic, was an oligarchy, ruled by noble families from whose members the doge, or duke, was elected for life. These noble families held sway at the opera house. Each house was built or at least backed financially by a noble family or a consortium, and noble families leased most of the boxes that lined the house, occupying them night after night. Commoners who were rich enough also leased boxes. Space or benches in less desirable parts of the house were occupied by poorer people: soldiers who were brought in to keep order; the nobles' servants, who accompanied their masters; and opera lovers from various walks of life.

Given that soldiers and servants didn't pay to attend, the lower-class part of the audience made a negligible contribution to opera-house revenues.[4] The success of an opera depended on the pleasure that the audience demonstrated, and the wealthy patrons who kept the house in business were no doubt the most vociferous in expressing their pleasure and displeasure at

individual singers or entire productions. Nevertheless, every part of an audience has some effect on the atmosphere in a theater, and the Venetian houses must in some way have taken account of every element of their audience: the educated and the uneducated, the operatically experienced and the novices, the refined of taste and the crude, the military and the clergy, women and men, those who would identify with stage rulers and those who would identify with stage servants.

One element of the audience deserves special consideration: foreigners. Venice had long been the most cosmopolitan city in Europe, thanks to its activity as a trading center, connecting goods and people from three continents. Tourism made it even more cosmopolitan: royalty, nobles, and wealthy people from all over Europe flocked to Venice in the carnival season for masked balls, gambling, and opera. As Cristoforo Ivanovich, a Venetian librettist, wrote in his chronicle of Venetian opera in 1681, "The entertainments produced during Carnival-tide in Venice are as curious as the Bacchanalia of ancient Rome used to be, for which reason — today as in ancient times — the world converges in pilgrimage to watch the aforesaid displays" (see box on p. 133).[5]

In the last quarter of the seventeenth century, certain rulers of German principalities who supplied mercenary troops to Venice so that it could wage war against the Turkish empire were frequent visitors to the Venetian opera houses. The managers of the houses, doing their part to support the alliance, entertained these princes with operas dedicated to them, some on themes of legendary German heroes or historical Crusades against the Turks.[6]

Attention to foreign tourists took subtler, more pervasive forms as well. If the Venetian houses had put on operas like Peri's *Euridice* or Monteverdi's *Orfeo*, which relied for all their effect on the listener's unflagging attention to the interplay of music with poetic Italian, it is hard to imagine that many tourists with a less than perfect understanding of Italian would have been interested. Venetian librettos were still highly poetic and full of learned classical references that only the educated members of the audience would have understood. But since that poetic dialogue was set in an alternation of acting and singing styles, the singing-style sections, at least, would have conveyed the singers' situations even to those who didn't understand every word. And the operas

also provided other pleasures: the visual spectacle of sets, costumes, special effects, and dance, along with the singing of star singers. These were pleasures that could be shared by all sorts of people in those diverse Venetian audiences, the way special effects and panoramic vistas are in movies today.

Foreign rulers who had been to the opera in Venice created their own opera houses at home, and in some cases hired singers and composers and set designers away from Venice. Tourists who were not in a position to do that could at least spread the word about what they had heard in Venice. Opera provided these tourists with an artistic experience that grabbed them on several levels, despite the language barrier, and their enthusiasm encouraged the building of theaters all across Europe for the performance of opera, usually in Italian. From that development it has followed that millions of people around the world are still going to opera houses three and a half centuries later for the astonishing purpose of hearing dramatic performances in languages most of them don't understand.

Drawing of a spectacular stage effect, complete with a "glory" (a machine representing a wreath of clouds that could be lowered and raised, bearing actors), created in the opera *Germanico sul Reno* (*Germanicus on the Rhine*), with music by Giovanni Legrenzi, performed at the San Salvatore Theater in Venice, 1676. The subject, the exploits of the Roman emperor Germanicus, was of special interest to visiting German princes being cultivated by the Venetian state. Bibliothèque-Musée de l'Opéra, Paris.

Archives Charmet

Opera Seasons

The other new commercial condition in Venice was the long run of a single opera. A court opera like *Euridice* or *Orfeo* was designed to be performed once or twice, even when it was not created to celebrate a wedding. A commercial opera house in Venice by contrast gave performances several times a week, during a season that lasted a couple of months. Nowadays the major houses are repertory theaters, performing from a half dozen to two dozen works in a complex nightly rotation, over a season that lasts most of the year. The Venetian house was more like a Broadway theater, playing the same work night after night for weeks, after which another new production might replace it. But Broadway regulars tend to see different shows, or take turns going to the theater, movies, sports events, and concerts. During opera season many boxholders in Venice (and elsewhere in Europe) lived in their opera boxes practically every evening. In that season, then, they heard one opera performed many times by a largely unchanging cast.

The operas therefore had to bear up under repeated viewing. A work like *Euridice*, designed to be seen once, could be short and intense, requiring

concentrated attention on a single plot line from beginning to end. An opera for Venice needed to be hours long because operagoers were spending the whole evening in their boxes, but by the same token it couldn't demand their full attention every moment. Furthermore, it couldn't be focused on a single character or a single relationship, because that would require one or two singers to be onstage all evening, singing at full throttle much of the time—and then to do so again the next night and the next. Accordingly, Venetian operas have diffuse plots, involving a fair number of characters in a complex web of relationships, so that the singers were always appearing in different combinations and no one was onstage for very long at a stretch. If you didn't much like one of the singers, he or she wouldn't put you off the whole show. The powerful declamation of the acting style alternated with the memorable melodies of the arias: people never tire of a favorite tune. The elements of entertainment—song, dance, spectacle, comic antics, moments of high tension and heartbreak—were likewise alternated so that each spectator got a regular dose of what she or he liked best. Everything was geared to keeping people from being worn out by the show and keeping them coming back. Venetian opera also brought people back for more by raising human issues that mattered to them. But it did so within the structures that kept them entertained.

Resistance and Surrender to Love: Cavalli, *Giasone*

Each character in a Venetian opera typically has his or her own dramatic and musical personality. The singers of the smallest roles, especially the gods and goddesses who drop in to help out their favorite humans, are sometimes given the most dazzling music to sing. All of them are capable of holding our interest when they take the stage, just as figures in a crowded fresco who are drawn with equal force and bathed in the same light are all capable of holding our eye. Most striking is the degree of moral credibility the characters possess, so that they can make at least a momentary claim to our sympathy, however foolish or wicked they might be. They do this because their words and music make us feel their situation the way they themselves do.

A characteristic Venetian opera in this respect is *Giasone*, with a libretto by Giacinto Andrea Cicognini and music by Francesco Cavalli. Cavalli, a follower of Monteverdi, became the most important opera composer in mid-seventeenth-century Venice. In fact, *Giasone*, premiered there in 1649, was the most widely produced opera of the seventeenth century. Its title character is Jason, the mythological Greek hero who steals the Golden Fleece from the monsters guarding it, but like *Bellerofonte*, this opera is concerned only momentarily (if spectacularly) with the hero's battles and almost entirely with

love entanglements. One of the two women competing for Jason's love is Hypsipyle (Isifile in Italian), Queen of Lemnos, who has twins by Jason, but whom he has abandoned to go on his quest for the Golden Fleece. She has sent her servant Orestes to find out if Jason is still faithful to her, and in the scene we will consider first, Orestes returns to find her asleep. Mistaking him, in her dreamy haze, for Jason, she asks him if he has returned to her. Orestes, seeing the possibility of taking advantage of her so long as she doesn't wake up, plays along. He declares that he is faithful to her, and she encourages him to approach her bed, which he does, telling himself that since she is no longer a virgin, she has nothing left to lose. As he prepares to kiss her, she wakes up and recognizes him, to the annoyance of both.

Hypsipyle is the betrayed woman of this opera. But she puts her dignity at risk by displaying her lust, especially by displaying it, even if unwittingly, toward her servant. Orestes, meanwhile, has no dignity to risk in this situation because he is the servant. He might well lose everything else, though, if he were to let his lust carry him too far with his mistress and queen. The audience is therefore caught between wanting to see how far this farcical love scene can go and dreading the consequences if it goes too far. It goes only far enough to reveal Orestes' willingness to go further. Even that might lead Hypsipyle, once she awakens, to condemn Orestes for trying to take advantage of her. But such a reaction would only make her seem hypocritical, and it is characteristic of the moral sophistication of Venetian operas that instead of condemning him, she sets about restoring her dignity. She turns immediately to asking Orestes what he has found out about Jason. He informs her that Jason has taken up with another woman, and then he departs, leaving her to bid a moving farewell to her hopes of love. Like Jupiter in the opera *Calisto* (also by Cavalli), she shows how the foolish and the noble can alternate in a single character, how they can be portrayed as two sides of human nature. The amazing thing in this scene is how Hypsipyle can switch from one role to the other right before our eyes and be convincing in both.

Stefano della Bella, costume drawing for Venus in Cavalli's *Hipermestra*, Teatro della Pergola, Florence, 1658. This beautiful drawing by a major artist, part of a set of costume drawings for one of Cavalli's few operas written for theaters outside Venice, gives a rare sense of costuming and bearing on the mid-century Venetian operatic stage. British Museum, London.

The Lament

Hypsipyle's soliloquy, beginning "E che sperar poss'io" ("And what can I hope for?"), is called a **lament**, but it progresses through several conflicting thoughts, not all in a lamenting spirit. Hypsipyle declares that she can hope for nothing because she has been wounded too often; she tells hopes to be gone, since her heart is dead and can't be comforted by hope; then she wonders whether Jason still might return to her; she lashes out against that hope; she decries the torments to which she is subjected; once more she urges hopes to be gone; and finally she decides that though desperate, she is still a queen, and vows to find Jason and kill him.

All of this text is written in nonstrophic verse and set in recitative, except for a short strophic section that appears twice and is set in singing style. This is the stanza in which Hypsipyle pushes hope away:

Speranze, fuggite,	Hopes, be gone!
Sparite da me;	Vanish from me!
Il cor, ch'è già morto,	My heart, dead already,
Del vostro conforto	cannot bear
Capace non è.	your comfort.

Cavalli's music to this stanza, unlike his acting-style music for the rest of the speech, has a steady dance rhythm—a slow three-beat rhythm that at first seems to draw to a halt every time on the second beat. Against that rhythm the singer makes a steady progression. She begins in one-word phrases, singing each one a step higher than the last, as if demonstrating the effort it takes her to push away the hopes that plague her (see Example 6.1). Then the halting step in the bass ceases, and she collapses into a despairing monotone on the line "My heart, dead already." As if unable to move on from this thought, she now repeats the whole passage, this time returning it to the minor key in which it began.

Hypsipyle's speech as a whole demonstrates the difficulty she has in admitting to herself that she has lost Jason, and nothing shows that difficulty more powerfully than the fact that this heartbreaking song of despair appears at two different times—exactly the same both times—in the midst of her acting-style debate with herself about what she should do. In one sense "Speranze, fuggite" represents only one side of that debate, and not even the side she ends on. But though she ends by rushing off to avenge herself, it is this recurring moment of song—the true lament in her lament—that remains in our memory as the emblem of Hypsipyle's lost love.

Even with its changing thoughts and expressions, this solo distinguishes Hypsipyle from her rival—the sorceress Medea, who has stolen Jason away from Hypsipyle and who, like her, has borne him twins. For most of the

6.1 Cavalli, *Giasone*: Act 2, "Speranze, fuggite"

opera Hypsipyle tries to win Jason back, but he remains in the arms of Medea (who for his sake has rejected her devoted suitor Aegeus). Repeatedly we hear Hypsipyle grieving over her loss in solo laments, while Medea enjoys Jason's love in a series of love duets. This musical contrast in the two characters' modes of expression comes to seem like a fixed condition in the opera, reflecting the contrast between two kinds of women—the faithful and the bewitching—as well as between two possible fates of women, the betrayed and the satisfied. The faithful woman seems destined to be betrayed, while the bewitching sorceress possesses the power to have whatever man she chooses, displaying her magical powers in her one soliloquy, "Dell'antro magico" ("Of the magic cave"). The audience can weigh these differences as it indulges itself in both the heartbreak of the laments and the rapture of the love duets.

The Love Duet

Near the beginning of the third act of *Giasone*, Medea and Jason sing the fourth and last of their love duets at a moment of peace in the action, when they lie down amid leaves and flowers to sleep. This number illustrates the characteristic sequence of love duets, from an exchange of comments between the two lovers to a joining of their two voices in shared words. In fact, this duet makes that progression twice. In the lines they exchange with each other, the characters develop poetic imagery; in the lines they share, the sense of the words is overwhelmed by the sheer sound of two voices luxuriating in close harmony (Medea is sung by a soprano, Jason by an alto, originally an alto castrato). In the second sequence, for instance, Medea invites Jason to sleep in her arms ("Dormi, stanco Giasone"/"Sleep, weary Jason"), and he replies in kind. While their poetry develops images of lovers capturing each other, their music develops the metaphor of sleep in musical terms. With its

Cristoforo Ivanovich

Ivanovich, a librettist who worked in Venice and other cities, published in 1681 a catalogue of operas that had been produced in Venice, *Le memorie teatrali di Venezia* (*Theatrical Memoirs of Venice*). Included in the volume is his invaluable description of how opera houses were organized and run.

The most secure income of every theatre is provided by the leasing of boxes. There are at least one hundred of these, besides the various orders of galleries; not all are equal in price, the latter being calculated on the basis of the order and number (i.e., the excellence of position) of each box. . . . From the very beginning, theatre proprietors have customarily practised two types of charges: first, a cash payment for each box (this serves largely to cover construction costs, and is the principal reason for the ease and rapidity with which the construction of a number of theatres has been possible); second, an agreed annual rent, paid every year in which there is an opera season (only in this way does the said payment correspond both to the expenses incurred by the theatre and the comfort and convenience enjoyed by the occupation of the box). The right acquired by the possessor of the box is that of retaining it on his own account, without the option of reletting it to others; he may make use of it for his own purposes and lend it out as he likes.

Lorenzo Bianconi, *Music in the Seventeenth Century,* trans. David Bryant (Cambridge: Cambridge University Press, 1987), p. 308.

---

lilting triple rhythm, its sinking ground bass (a bass line that descends in slow, regular steps, repeating a number of times), many repetitions of the word "dormi" ("sleep"), and an instrumental refrain that simply repeats the sung refrain, this is a lullaby. The lovers then end the duet with shared thoughts of dreaming about each other. They begin in dialogue — "What will you dream about?" "Your heavenly rays." Then they join their voices in a phrase of ravishing and seemingly motionless harmony:

Placidissimo sonno,	*Peaceful, peaceful sleep,*
Che in grembo delle larve	*that spirits me to heaven*
al ciel m'invia!	*in the embrace of fantasies!*

Finally, their voices intertwine in repetitions of a single phrase: "Let us adore each other in our dreams, my soul!" ("Adoriamoci in sogno, anima mia!").

This duet is typical of love duets in Venetian opera in that a different texture or rhythm in each section — sometimes each line — creates a different musical metaphor for love. The lullaby rhythm of "Dormi, stanco Giasone," for instance, represents the obliviousness of lovers to anything outside themselves. The joining of the singers' voices on "Placidissimo sonno" represents the joining of the lovers' bodies and spirits. And the intertwining of their voices on "Adoriamoci in sogno" represents the intertwining of their limbs and lives. In opera of later centuries there is often just a single love duet between the principal lovers — why should

there be four between the same couple here? The most obvious hypothesis seems to be that Venetian audiences couldn't get enough of the pleasure of imagining a couple's pleasure. There is also a dramatic effect, however, in hearing all these love duets: we come to think of Jason and Medea as two people who are made for each other, whatever misery their love causes other characters.

But then, how dramatic would it be for the leading couple to stay blissfully together, their love never disturbed, all through the opera? In the end they do not stay together. Jason, trying to satisfy Medea's demand that he do away with Hypsipyle, sets up a plot to drown her, but the plot goes awry, and it is Medea who is thrown into the sea by mistake. Rescued by her devoted suitor Aegeus, she realizes his worth and tells Jason to return to the woman he belongs to. But though Hypsipyle is ready to have him back, despite knowing that he just tried to have her drowned, Jason is still entranced by Medea. Even though it would resolve everything neatly if he returned willingly to Hypsipyle, making that return dramatically convincing is the greatest challenge that the librettist and composer faced. So far Hypsipyle has not gotten anywhere presenting herself to Jason as the wronged woman, yet she doesn't seem capable of playing the seductress, a role we know he falls for. So now she plays the wronged woman once more, pulling out all the stops.

Hypsipyle, holding her twins, sings her plea "Infelice, che ascolto?" in Act 3 of Cavalli's *Giasone*. Staging by Toni Dorfman, with Lucy Fitz Gibbon as Hypsipyle, Yale Baroque Opera Project, New Haven, Connecticut, 2009.

Harold Shapiro

In the final scene she sings one last lament, "Infelice, che ascolto?" ("Unhappy me, what am I hearing?"). This one is addressed mostly to Jason, and it is a shocker. Hypsipyle invites Jason, since he has failed to kill her quickly by drowning, to hack her slowly to pieces:

E'l mio lento morire	*And may my slow dying*
Prolunghi a me il tormento,	*prolong the torment for me,*
a te'l gioire.	*the pleasure for you.*

She reminds him that he is the father of her children and asks him not to let them starve. As in her earlier lament, there is one section here that stands apart in its songful rhythm (the rest is in an alternately frantic and tortured acting style). In this section Hypsipyle calls on Medea and Aegeus to intercede with Jason so that he will allow her children to watch him kill her and allow them to drink her blood and thus imbibe her innocence. Finally, she tells her children that she is entrusting them to Jason, "my executioner and your father," and tells Jason that though he is her murderer, she adores him. This is all so gruesomely self-abasing, so grotesquely masochistic,

that it is hard to know whether to take it as a pathological display or an over-the-top ploy to shame Jason. It is hard to guess how the original audiences, living in a very different age and culture, would have been expected to respond. But within the drama it does the trick. Jason declares that he is vanquished and shamed by her, he wishes Medea and Aegeus well, he throws himself on Hypsipyle's mercy, and she accepts him. They sing a love duet, and the opera is over.

The Dénouement: Surrendering to Love

Jason's shamed response to Hypsipyle's speech constitutes the **dénouement**, the unknotting of the plot that allows the opera to come to an end. It is an action by one character that allows all the principal characters to be paired in acceptable, perhaps even inevitable, couples. In a sense all Jason does here is to drop the resistance he has maintained all along to the love of Hypsipyle, who as a queen and the first woman to bear children by him has the first and strongest claim to his love. But by dropping his resistance, Jason not only sets things right between himself and her; he releases Medea to set things right with Aegeus. By singing a love duet now with Hypsipyle, even a relatively plain and simple one, he in effect cancels all those gorgeous, longer ones he sang earlier with Medea. If the diverse and sporadically attentive Venetian audiences required clear musical signs — the distinction between a lament and a love duet, for instance — to guide them through the opera and keep them interested, then the resolution above all needed to be signaled musically. A love duet in which Jason's voice joined with Hypsipyle's instead of Medea's served that purpose, affirming in sound the coupling that had been resisted until then.[7]

This particular battle of love duets may even hold a key to the exceptional popularity of *Giasone* in its day. For most of the opera the spectators have the pleasure of relishing the sensuous love music of Jason and Medea — a guilty pleasure in the sense that Hypsipyle is reminding them all the while of how heartlessly Jason has abandoned her for Medea's love nest. Then at the end, the spectators have the satisfaction of seeing the characters rearranged in couples that answer everyone's moral claims and emotional needs. The opera is both titillating and conventionally moral; the audience has it both ways. But if *Giasone* was exceptionally popular, its basic plot mechanism is utterly characteristic of Venetian opera: one character finally surrenders to the partner he or she has been resisting all along, causing the rearranging of all the other partnerings. Compared with other dramatic traditions (and for that matter with real life in European society at the time), it is striking how much freedom the characters

in this repertory have to choose their own partners. On the whole, these are not Romeo and Juliet stories of lovers with external obstacles to their love. The characters are themselves the obstacles to their own happiness.

Pleasure and Moral Judgment: Monteverdi, *L'incoronazione di Poppea*

Earlier in the decade of the 1640s, Claudio Monteverdi, now in his seventies, adapted his operatic art to the new, commercial brand of opera in three new works for Venetian theaters. Only two of these works survive, one of which has become the most celebrated opera of the seventeenth-century Venetian repertory: *L'incoronazione di Poppea* (*The Coronation of Poppea*), with libretto by Giovanni Francesco Busenello, premiered in 1643. *Poppea* is a historical opera about the decadence of the Roman Empire and its most notorious emperor, Nero (Nerone).

In the course of the opera Nero forces his former tutor, the philosopher Seneca, to commit suicide and exiles his wife—the Empress Ottavia—and two other important characters, all so that he will be free to marry his high-born mistress, Poppea, and crown her empress. But since most of these victims are themselves engaged in murderous conspiracies against Nero and Poppea, the spectators have a hard time finding characters who are worthy of their sympathy. Instead, they are invited to feel things the way the characters feel them, whatever their moral failings—to enjoy, for instance, the gorgeously sensuous love music of Nero and Poppea, despite the suffering their love causes others.

As the action begins, Nero has been spending the night in Poppea's bed, but we discover their affair through the eyes of the man who thinks he is going to marry Poppea, Ottone. Returning to Rome after some time away, Ottone approaches Poppea's palace at dawn in search of her embrace, only to find the emperor's guards posted outside. He departs in despair, and when we then meet Nero and Poppea rejoicing after their night of love, we already understand that in loving each other, they are betraying her fiancé Ottone and Nero's wife Ottavia. Their tender duet of leave-taking, tainted by this betrayal, devolves into tension between them, as Poppea—ambitious to replace Ottavia on the throne—artfully and persistently extracts a promise from him that he will keep returning to her bed. In this love scene we feel the lovers' passion for each other, their betrayal of others, and their self-promoting schemes all at work together.

L'incoronazione di Poppea
PRINCIPAL CHARACTERS

- **Nero** (**Nerone**), Emperor of Rome, married to the Empress **Ottavia**.
- **Poppea**, his high-born mistress, wants to replace Ottavia as Nero's wife.
- The philosopher **Seneca**, Nero's old tutor, fails to thwart their union.
- **Ottone**, Poppea's rejected fiancé, clings to her, but eventually accepts the love of **Drusilla**.

Virtually all the scenes of *L'incoronazione di Poppea* are emotionally and morally complicated in this way. There are love duets and laments, disputes and celebrations—all the musical forms that Venetian audiences relied on to guide them through an opera's dramatic progression—but the world in which these characters live is such a morally compromised place that we can respond to the power and beauty of their music only if we resist passing judgment on them and instead give ourselves over to appreciating how they negotiate through that world.

Suspending Judgment

We already find our ability to suspend judgment challenged in this first scene with Nero and Poppea, but it is far more seriously tested after the death of Seneca. That man of principle attempts to dissuade Nero from repudiating Ottavia in order to indulge his lust for Poppea. At Poppea's insistence, Nero orders Seneca to poison himself. Seneca does so in a scene of immense dignity, surrounded by his inconsolable disciples. When we encounter Nero afterward, he evades responsibility for Seneca's death. Saying, "Now that Seneca is dead, let's sing songs of love," he makes the young poet Lucan join him in a virtuosic and rapturous duet, a madrigal in tribute to Poppea. Absorbed into the ecstasies of love that their duet evokes, we can hardly think about Nero's guilt. Likewise, when we next encounter Poppea, she too begins, "Now that Seneca is dead," and launches into a song of love, indulging in the seductive style she exhibits from beginning to end of the opera. In her case her love is indistinguishable from her ambition to be empress, and she can even remind us of that without allowing us to give another thought to Seneca. On finishing her song, she is so relieved to have Seneca out of her way that she lies down for a nap.

In these songs the two lovers seem to obliterate their responsibility for Seneca's death by obliterating any memory of him. Viewers, however, have not always been able to countenance this behavior without finding the work itself morally suspect. *L'incoronazione di Poppea* was criticized on moral grounds in its own day and has been again in ours, though the grounds have changed. When it was produced in Naples, eight years after the Venetian premiere, papal censors ordered the depiction of Seneca's suicide removed because the Catholic Church condemned suicide as a sin. To viewers today it may seem that the censors were cutting short the one voice of morality in the work.[8] They are more apt to be troubled by what Richard Taruskin calls "this most unedifying—and in places virtually obscene—entertainment,"[9] not so much because of Nero and Poppea's erotic music but by the use of that music to make the audience accept the freedom with which Nero and Poppea enjoy their passion without paying any price for trampling on others.

Monteverdi and librettist Busenello filled the stage with characters from the notoriously decadent world of the Roman Empire and then asked their audience to take these characters as they found them. In this they exemplify the moral sophistication of seventeenth-century Venice, an island of refuge and recreation for tourists from a European-Mediterranean world tearing itself apart in wars fueled by religious intolerance. To the most cosmopolitan city of this era we owe one of the most urbane forms of entertainment ever devised. To sit through *Poppea* and allow it to speak to us about the moral complexity of life is to treat ourselves to an incomparable artistic pleasure. In practically every scene we can be surprised not only by the mixture of the appealing and the unforgivable in the characters, but also by the complexity of our own response to them. Comparing how the characters' words and actions appear to themselves, to others, and to us, we can feel an indescribable friction caused by our contradictory responses. This confusion of response may be delicious or disturbing or illuminating, or all three at once.

Plotting Murder

Later in the opera, for example, it is both chilling and hilarious when the Empress Ottavia, deciding to have her rival Poppea killed, calls on Ottone to do the deed. He is an obvious ally, since Poppea's affair with Nero has betrayed Ottone's love just as it has betrayed Ottavia's marriage. Ottavia commands Ottone in imperious language, set to imperious recitative. He seems taken aback. "To kill whom?" he asks, though his apparent innocence is undercut by the fact that in an earlier scene, in his rage at Poppea, he considered the same idea himself. "Poppea," Ottavia repeats. Ottone quails: "Poppea? Poppea? that I kill Poppea?" The more he squirms and stalls, the more indignant Ottavia becomes, frightening him into saying one thing to himself and another to her. But if we can feel how frightened he is of her, she comes across to us as pompous, and she makes her scheme seem ridiculous by telling him to disguise himself as a woman to escape recognition. In effect she is treating Ottone as nothing more than an actor she is hiring to execute a piece of stage business.

Still, she is the empress, and he has to take her seriously when she says that unless he obeys her, she will falsely accuse him of assaulting her and will have him tortured. We cannot be surprised that at this point he agrees to do the deed, though we also cannot be sure that he is capable of pulling it off. Because Busenello's text shows one human being ruthlessly exploiting the weakness of another, Monteverdi's music explores powers of the acting style that went untested in the high-toned dialogue of earlier court opera, even his own *Orfeo.* The fits and starts and rises and falls of these singers' lines allow them to play up—comically as well as seriously—the mismatch of power and will that is expressed in their words. And we as listeners, prevented by that half-comic, half-serious effect from siding emotionally with one character over the other, can observe the dynamics of their interaction more dispassionately and therefore perhaps more fully than we would if we did take sides.

Resisting Love

Ottone goes off to find a woman's cloak for his disguise, and that brings him to Drusilla, the woman whose love he has been resisting all through the opera, in his pursuit of the faithless Poppea. Ottone's relationship with Drusilla, though apparently a subplot, actually provides the opera with the crucial (and characteristically Venetian) plot mechanism of resistance followed by surrender to the right lover. After all, Nero and Poppea never resist their love for each other, as Cavalli's Jason resists the love of Hypsipyle, and so the resolution of their drama cannot come from surrender. We find them in each other's arms at the beginning, clinging to each other throughout, and reigning together at the end. In the sense that Ottone gives this opera not only its murder plot, instigated by

Anonymous seventeenth-century Italian bust of the Roman emperor Salvius Otho (32–69 CE). Early audiences at *L'incoronazione di Poppea* would have recognized Poppea's jilted fiancé Ottone as Otho, who eventually succeeded Nero as emperor. Chateaux de Versailles et de Trianon, Versailles, France.
Gérard Blot/Réunion des Musées Nationaux/Art Resource, NY

Ottavia, but also its love mechanism, he is the central character, just as he is the one who appears most onstage. On his way to murder Poppea while still in love with her, he comes upon Drusilla, whom he does not love, but he is willing to prevail on her to lend him her cloak as his disguise. The apparently sweet Drusilla, recognising an opportunity to win his loyalty, agrees, proving that she is no more innocent than anyone else in this story.

Ottone, dressed as Drusilla but armed with a sword, now enters the garden where Poppea is sleeping. He sings a long monologue, debating whether he can conquer his love and carry out his mission to kill her. He appears to persuade himself that he can, but Cupid—that is, his love for Poppea—stays his hand until she wakes up, her nurse rushes in, and Ottone flees. What now breaks his resistance to loving Drusilla instead of Poppea

Gillian Keith as Poppea and Marcus Ullmann as Nero in a neoclassical staging of *L'incoronazione di Poppea* by Gilbert Blin at the Boston Early Music Festival, 2009.
Frank Siteman/Courtesy of Boston Early Music Festival

is his conscience. Since he was disguised as Drusilla when he was seen preparing to murder Poppea, it is Drusilla who is arrested for the attempt and taken before Nero. At first she proclaims her innocence, but when Nero threatens to torture her into revealing her accomplices, she worries that under torture she might name Ottone. Declaring that she finds herself caught between "love and innocence," she decides to protect Ottone by taking the blame as sole perpetrator of the deed. (We know that she is not so innocent of the attempt on Poppea's life, but here again we see things through the character's own eyes and disregard her false claim.)

Surrendering to Love

Ottone, struck by remorse, now announces to Nero that Drusilla is innocent and he is guilty. A contest ensues in which each tries to protect the other by claiming sole responsibility for the attempted crime. Eventually the contest dissolves into a shouting match:

Ottone:	*Il patibolo orrendo a me s'aspetta.*	*The horrible gallows await me.*
Drusilla:	*A me s'aspetta.*	*Await me.*
Ottone:	*A me s'aspetta.*	*Await me.*
Drusilla:	*A me*	*Me.*
Ottone:	*A me*	*Me.*
Drusilla:	*A me*	*Me.*

Though the two characters are trying to distinguish themselves from each other, they are settling into identical language, into meaningless sameness,

as people often do in shouting matches. We could be forgiven for hearing in this contest of wills the sweet nothings of a love duet, and Ottone seems to hear it that way too.

In any case his resistance to Drusilla now disappears. Nero decrees that Ottone shall live but be exiled and Drusilla shall suffer no punishment but "live in the fame of my clemency" (Seneca's ghost might have something to say about that!). Drusilla decides to go into exile with Ottone, and they both declare that if they have each other, they have all they could wish for. The union of these two characters, by dissolving Poppea's betrothal to Ottone, frees her to marry Nero, just as the revelation that Ottavia instigated the murder plot frees Nero to banish her and marry Poppea. Ottavia, wronged yet guilty, makes us forget her guilt in her heartbreaking farewell to Rome and friends ("A . . . dio Roma"), which uses the comic device of stuttering to suggest a grief so complete as to leave her speechless. This is an opera in which we hear every kind of human speech and human interaction set to music, and here in Ottavia's farewell even the loss of speech and interaction turns into music.

Ottone's change of heart, like Jason's in *Giasone*, realigns all the relationships and thereby resolves the plot. Because Ottone and Drusilla, despite participating in a murder attempt, are willing to die to protect each other, the opera has at least been resolved by admirable behavior. But this is still Venetian opera at its most morally complex, and before we can invest too much satisfaction in the self-sacrificing behavior of Drusilla and Ottone, or hear them sing a true love duet, they are whisked out of the way. After that, our attention is focused primarily on Poppea and Nero, who have triumphed through their cold-blooded exploitation of others' weaknesses and mistakes. From them we now hear even more gorgeous love duets than before. Their closing duet, "Pur ti miro" ("I just look at you"), was apparently composed not for the original production of *Poppea*, but for a later production and by someone other than Monteverdi. Nevertheless, with its lulling ground bass in lilting triple rhythm and its piercing sweet dissonances between the two voices, it ends the opera on a fitting note of ecstatic oblivion.

The pleasure these duets give us would be disturbing if we expected an opera, or any work

Ottone, wearing Drusilla's dress, tries to kill Poppea but is restrained by Amore, in Act 2 of *L'incoronazione di Poppea*. Staged by Robert Carsen at the Theater an der Wien, Vienna, 2010, with Trine Wilsberg Lund as Amore, Lawrence Zazzo as Ottone, and Juanita Lascarro as Poppea.
Herwig Prammer/RTR/Newscom

of art, to make us believe that people always get their just deserts. But even if we believe otherwise, we may still wonder at the relationship Busenello and Monteverdi created between pleasure and morality. In a drama where all the characters seem to be pursuing their own happiness without much regard for others, this dénouement comes from a moral breakthrough, from Ottone learning to pay heed to someone else's happiness. Fine, we might say, but Poppea and Nero never learn to do that. For that matter, in *Giasone* the title character may eventually consider Hypsipyle's happiness, but the opera as a whole does not condemn the heedless pleasure that occupies Jason and Medea for most of its duration, any more than *Poppea* condemns such pleasure. Instead, these works show us how haphazard the relationship of happiness to morality is. That can be a morally serious premise for a work of art, though it can also be an easy and self-satisfied one.

Where Venetian opera is most serious—and *Poppea* perhaps most of all—is in asking the audience to take responsibility for enjoying the work. This kind of opera spreads a rich array of pleasures in front of us, not just those of music and dance and visual spectacle, but also that of involving ourselves in the actions of the characters, whatever they are like. When we get to the end of *L'incoronazione di Poppea*, we may realize that we are just as capable of enjoying the triumphant passion of Poppea and Nero, for all her ambition and his cruelty, as we are the moral triumph of Drusilla and Ottone. Surprised at our own responses, we may discover something not just about the moral ambiguity of life, but also about the relationship of morality and pleasure in ourselves. It is the specialty of Venetian opera to give pleasure in a way that prompts that kind of self-consciousness.

FURTHER READING

On opera production in seventeenth-century Italy, Lorenzo Bianconi and Thomas Walker, "Production, Consumption and Political Function of Seventeenth-Century Opera," *Early Music History* 4: *Studies in Medieval and Early Modern Music*, ed. Iain Fenlon (Cambridge: Cambridge University Press, 1984), pp. 209–96; the opening sections of Franco Piperno, "Opera Production to 1780," in Lorenzo Bianconi and Giorgio Pestelli, eds., *Opera Production and Its Resources*, trans. Lydia Cochrane (Chicago and London: University of Chicago Press, 1998), vol. 4 of their *History of Italian Opera*; Ruth L. Glixon and Jonathan E. Glixon, *Inventing the Business of Opera: The Impresario and His World in Seventeenth-Century Venice* (Oxford: Oxford University Press, 2006).

On the repertory of seventeenth-century Venetian opera, Ellen Rosand, *Opera in Seventeenth-Century Venice* (Berkeley and Los Angeles: University

of California Press, 1991); Wendy Heller, *Emblems of Eloquence: Opera and Women's Voices in Seventeenth-Century Venice* (Berkeley and Los Angeles: University of California Press, 2003).

On Cavalli's music, the introduction to Jennifer Williams Brown's edition of the score of *La Calisto* (Middleton, Wis.: A-R Editions, 2007). On Monteverdi's *Poppea*, Iain Fenlon and Peter N. Miller, *The Song of the Soul: Understanding "Poppea"* (London: Royal Musical Association, 1992); Ellen Rosand, *Monteverdi's Last Operas: A Venetian Trilogy* (Berkeley and Los Angeles: University of California Press, 2007).

FOR RESEARCH AND REFLECTION

1. Watch at least one scene of an unfamiliar opera three times. How do you change what you focus on as you become more used to it?

2. Watch a scene of an opera in a language you don't understand. Prepare by reading a plot synopsis. Watch the scene without subtitles. How well can you follow the action? What do you feel you are missing? What can you enjoy?

3. How do the special effects in a seventeenth-century Venetian opera, such as Monteverdi's *Il ritorno d'Ulisse in patria* (*Ulysses' Return to His Homeland*) — the abrupt changes of scene, the descent of gods out of the sky — color your experience of the work? Are they a silly distraction from the story, or do they help make it compelling? Do they contribute to the magic of the work, along with the music, dance, costumes, and sets, or are they in a realm of their own? Do they work like special effects in a Hollywood movie?

4. In Cavalli's *Giasone* how does the beauty of the love duets between Jason and Medea affect your feelings at the end, when they both switch to different lovers?

5. Does *L'incoronazione di Poppea* strike you as a comedy in which you just have to accept that some characters come to a bad end, whether they deserve it or not, or a serious work in which you just have to accept that some ruthlessly selfish characters are allowed to enjoy the fruits of their ruthlessness, and in fact get applauded for it in the end? What is the moral tone of this work, and how is it established?

 Additional resources are available at wwnorton.com/studyspace.

CHAPTER 7

National Opera: Paris and London

Opera might very well have remained an exclusively Italian art. Elsewhere there were other forms of courtly entertainment with song and dance, and other forms of commercial theater. But almost from its earliest days, opera took to the road. Italian performers took their productions to cities outside Italy—including Salzburg, Vienna, and Warsaw—even before the first commercial opera house opened in Venice in 1637. A lot of money was needed to bring opera to these places. Not only did singers have to make the trip, but stage designers needed to go and supervise the building or outfitting of a theater with the machinery required for stage effects that were hardly known in other theatical traditions. It took a monarch, not a commercial theater, to spend that kind of money to keep up with foreign fashion.

The Enterprise of Opera in France

In France a stand-in for the monarch played that role. The death of King Louis XIII in 1643 left France with a four-year-old king, Louis XIV. In the ensuing eighteen years of regency the country's most powerful political figure was Cardinal Mazarin, an Italian (born Giulio Mazzarini). Between 1645 and 1662 he brought Italian singers, stage designers, and composers to France to produce seven different operas.[1] That magician of Venetian operatic staging, Giacomo Torelli, and a family of theater architects named Vigarani refitted

Jean Berain, drawing of an infernal scene, probably for a revival of Lully's *Thésée* (which premiered in 1675) at the Paris Opera. Victoria and Albert Museum, London.
Eileen Tweedy/The Art Archive

or built several theaters in Paris for the staging of these spectacular operas. Cavalli came from Venice to write an opera, *Ercole amante (Hercules as Lover)*, for the celebrations marking the marriage of Louis XIV to the Spanish princess Maria Theresa, though by the time the new theater was finished, in 1662, the wedding was long over and Cardinal Mazarin was dead.

A royal patent Mazarin's death seemed to spell the end of opera in France, but in 1669 a fresh initiative brought it back on new terms. The king granted a patent, or permit, to the poet Pierre Perrin to establish an "academy"—a commercial opera house—for the performance of opera in French. Working with the composer Robert Cambert, Perrin produced the opera *Pomone* in 1671. But the next year composer Jean-Baptiste Lully persuaded the king

Premiere Journée.
Alceste, Tragedie en musique, ornée d'entrées de Ballet, representée à Versailles dans la cour de marbre du Chasteau éclairé depuis le haut jusqu'en bas d'une infinité de lumieres.

Dies primus.
Alcestis Tragædia, perpetuo cantu et variis Saltationibus decorata, in marmoreo Palatij Versaliarum cavædio, undequaque facibus accensis illuminati, acta.

Night performance of Lully's *Alceste* in the Marble Court of the royal chateau at Versailles, July 4, 1674, in an engraving of 1676 by Jean le Pautre. Note the extraordinary lighting system of torches set all around the building, and the orchestra divided on the sides of the stage, affording the king an unimpeded view of the action. Bibliothèque Nationale, Paris.
Giraudon/Bridgeman Art Library

to transfer the patent to him, and it was Lully who created both the lasting operatic institution in Paris (known as the Académie Royale de Musique) and the founding repertory of French opera. Lully, an Italian (born Giovanni Battista Lulli), had been taken at age fourteen to Paris, where he served as a violinist and dancer at court. Later he composed court ballets, collaborated with the playwright Molière in works that mixed comedy with dance, and became the director of music for the royal household. From 1672 until 1687 (the year of his death) he created an opera every year but one. Almost all of them were performed, as the royal patent specified, both at court (which meant at one of the royal palaces outside Paris) and at the public Académie in Paris. He composed all but a few of these works to texts by the playwright Philippe Quinault.

Unlike the Venetian opera houses, Lully's Académie was both a court-sponsored and a commercial enterprise. He received a kind of financial help from the king: he would have the sets and machines for an opera built at the king's expense for the court production and then brought to the opera house in Paris for its public run. But the financial risk and profit of that public run was Lully's, and he made a fortune from the Académie. The king took a hand in choosing the subjects that Quinault and Lully were to set, and he concerned himself occasionally with the workings of the house, determining the seating arrangements and attempting to suppress whistling (the seventeenth-century form of booing) and other disorderly behavior by the public.[2]

In turn, Lully recognized the dependence of his enterprise on the king's good will, and his works bear the marks of that recognition. Each opera opens with a substantial prologue extolling the greatness of Louis XIV (who is usually referred to simply as "a hero"). The action then centers on a mythological or legendary hero who, as Lois Rosow writes, could be understood as a symbol for the king.[3] But it wasn't in the king's power to suppress whistling, or in a larger sense to determine the success of a given work or performer. That power was exercised by the public.

From monopoly to repertory What is most remarkable about Lully's patent from the king is that it gave one composer a lifetime monopoly on the creation of operas in France. And because Lully ran the Opéra (as the Académie came to be called), he controlled every aspect of production. A dancer, singer, and violinist as well as a composer, he supervised the movements and gestures of the singers and dancers, along with the phrasing and expression of the singers and players, in minute detail. The repertory, like the performance, was entirely his. Besides the new opera he wrote every year, the only other works performed were revivals of his own earlier operas. So whereas in Italy an opera produced one year at a certain house was unlikely

to be performed there again, in Paris the same Lully operas appeared time and again in a steadily accumulating repertory. *Thésée*, for instance, which premiered in 1675, reappeared in three revivals in the remaining twelve years of his career and many more in the century following his death.[4] Not until Richard Wagner had his own theater built in Bayreuth, Germany, two centuries later would any musician dominate an opera house and its repertory as Lully did.

The effect of this endless recirculation of the same few works was that France quickly came to acquire an operatic culture unique for the seventeenth century. The audience at a revival in Paris was apt to be filled with people who had seen the work many times before, who knew much of it by heart, who compared the singers in front of them with their predecessors in the same roles, and who often sang along in their favorite numbers. The English poet John Dryden, in a poem of 1685, described the Paris audience joining in with a chorus of Lully:

> In France, the oldest Man is always young,
> Sees Operas daily, learns the Tunes so long,
> Till Foot, Hand, Head, keep time with ev'ry Song.
> Each sings his part echoing from Pit and Box,
> With his hoarse Voice, half Harmony, half Pox.[5]

It is worth noting that Dryden describes someone seeing opera "daily" (performances were given at least three times a week during the season). And it wasn't just by going to the Opéra daily that people learned "the Tunes" well enough to sing along, but also by practicing the music at home. While Italian operagoers could usually buy only librettos of their favorite operas, the French could buy scores as well. By this means even people who never attended operas could nevertheless learn songs from them.

Public opinion The management of the Opéra, as of theaters elsewhere, could judge public opinion from box-office receipts. But in Paris there were also journals and other publications (no daily newspapers yet) providing new means of invoking, shaping, and assessing what people thought about opera. And as publications on opera proliferated, the belief grew that people's opinion of opera mattered—even as the king was presuming to tell his subjects whether or not they could whistle their disapproval. Seventeenth-century Paris therefore offers us the first opportunity to learn how public opinion was brought to bear on the development of the genre, as well as to witness the birth of the media of public opinion that still operate in the life of the arts today.

A monthly journal, the *Mercure galant*, devoted largely to political and literary matters, was founded in 1672, the same year that Lully began producing operas. It provided information and commentaries on the productions at

The Making of a Hit Song

The critic Jean-Laurent Lecerf de la Viéville deduced something about the beauty of certain numbers by Lully from the very fact that they were popular among people who could not have heard them at the Opéra. Here, in a dialogue-essay published in 1705, he lets one of his characters describe what it means for an aria (*air* in French) first heard twenty years earlier to have spread throughout French society:

> When I heard, for example, the air from *Amadis*, "Amour, que veux-tu de moi," etc., sung by all the *cuisinières* [kitchen maids] of France, I was right in thinking that this air was already certain to have won over everybody in France, from the rank of princess to that of *cuisinière*; . . . and remarking that it . . . pleased equally the learned and the ignorant, the intelligences of the highest order and of the lowest, I concluded that it must be very beautiful, very natural, very full of true expression, to have moved so many different hearts and soothed so many different ears."[6]

Lecerf de la Viéville found in this air musical qualities that could overcome socially determined differences and create a national musical consciousness. Lully certainly constructed it with enough internal repetitions that listeners could remember its essential melody and words and begin repeating them as they left the theater. In the first place, the orchestra plays the whole air through before the singer begins. Then the melody itself is constructed around a refrain heard at the beginning and end, to these words:

Amour, que veux-tu de moi?   Love, what do you want of me?
Mon coeur n'est pas fait   My heart is not made
  pour toi.   for you.

Its arresting opening phrase is also heard in the middle of the air, while the second line of text, containing the crucial idea of a heart not made for love, is repeated (see Example 7.1).

The presentation of the air is dramatically arresting: it comes at the beginning of an act, when the sorceress Arcabonne makes her defiant entrance into the drama. Hers is a stance that anyone in the audience, from a princess to a kitchen maid, might like to imagine trying out. This air may be an early case, then, of a phenomenon that has continued in opera and more recently in Broadway shows: a song that is designed as much for an independent existence beyond the show as for dramatic effect within it. Detachable airs like this appear only in the last of Lully's operas, when his system for re-circulating his works, including revivals and the publication of scores, was well established.

7.1 Lully, *Amadis*: Act 2, "Amour, que veux-tu de moi?"

the Opéra, in effect serving the same purpose the press does today: sparking people's interest in going to the opera and sustaining their interest afterward in what they had seen.

Paris was also a center for the publication of pamphlets (separately published essays) on all kinds of subjects, including opera. This was not in itself new. At the time opera was created, Florentine musicians and intellectuals had discussed their ideas in pamphlets and in the dedications of scores. But once opera was launched and found a public that accepted its premises, there was much less public discussion of its nature in Italy for another century and a half. In France, by contrast, opera was subject to a public debate that never let the presses rest. The difference may be explained partly by the fact that in France opera was a foreign import, and when the Italian Lully began writing operas in French, opinion among the French was divided over whether the genre was suited to their language, their musical and dramatic traditions, or the spirit (what writers called the *genius*) of the nation.

When prominent intellectuals judged French opera by the standard of spoken drama, they generated a public controversy that the creative team of the Opéra and its public could not altogether ignore. Quinault and Lully modeled their operas on the spectacular, fantastic, dance-and-comedy-filled Italian works that Cardinal Mazarin imported from Rome and Venice. They built on the composer's experience writing music for ballet spectacles. Still, they called their operas "musical tragedies" (*tragédies en musique*), and much of the Parisian literary establishment judged them against the somber neoclassical tragedies of Pierre Corneille and Jean Racine. In 1674, when Quinault and Lully brought out their *Alceste*, based on a tragedy by Euripides, critics (including Nicolas Boileau and Racine himself) denounced it for its extravagant spectacle, comic subplot, and lack of tragic realism.[7] The public loved it. The king loved it. It has been considered a masterpiece ever since. But Quinault and Lully never based an opera on a classical tragedy again.

Literary critics often treated opera librettos as if they were the scripts for spoken plays. All they asked of the music was that it not interfere with the clarity of the words. In this respect too they seem to have had an effect. Quinault wrote lines that could be understood even when sung, and at a time when Italian composers were cultivating an increasingly florid style (such that the flow of

Jean Berain, design for the suspended chariot of the sun from which the intemperate Phaëton, struck by a thunderbolt from Jupiter, plunges to the stage in the final scene of Lully's *Phaëton*, 1683. Centre Historique des Archives Nationales, Paris.
Archives Charmet/Bridgeman Art Library

words, especially in arias, would often be suspended while the singer let loose a torrent of notes on a single syllable), Lully set Quinault's lines soberly. Even in **airs**, the French version of arias, he seldom gave any syllable more than one or two notes. The result is that in the history of opera, there is hardly any body of works, in any language, in which the musical setting lets the singers deliver the words so clearly as the operas of Quinault and Lully.

But poets and literary critics were not the only members of the audience Quinault and Lully needed to take into account. One anecdote from their time features a very different kind of spectator: the star-worshipping fan. In the top balcony of the Opéra at one performance, two elderly women began insulting each other because one adored the dancer who was performing, and the other preferred another dancer. Eventually they drew in the elderly man sitting between them, who told them they were crazy to get so excited over "peasant dancers" when "the only reason for going to the Opéra was to hear and admire Mlle. Le Rochois" (a singer). The exchange became so heated (the man's wig and the women's hair combs were thrown to the auditorium floor far below) that the opera was brought to a stop and Lully himself had to bring all three favorite performers up to the balcony to make peace among their fans.[8]

We may take this anecdote with a grain of salt and still value it for alerting us to the advent of operatic fans, for whom the story, the words, the music, the choreography, the spectacle, the Opéra itself mattered only as means of bringing the beloved performer before them. Lully's action suggests that he recognized the importance of treating even outrageous fandom with a kind of respect. And the publication of this anecdote (after his death) tells us that somebody other than Lully — somebody not profiting from this fandom — noticed it, if only to laugh at it.

Reporting the operagoer's experience The rich and aristocratic operagoers who occupied the boxes rather than the top balcony no doubt behaved

The scene of Phaëton's fall, as the audience saw it, captured in an engraving by Henri de Baussen in the second edition of the score of *Phaëton*, Paris, 1709.
Harvard Theatre Collection, Houghton Library, Harvard University

differently. They often bought the libretto and read it ahead of time. They were generally more restrained in expressing their opinions, some of them even withholding their judgment of a work until they had experienced it several times.[9] But that does not mean that their attention was completely fixed on the words and music. Evrard Titon du Tillet, a highly placed courtier, published a book in which he recorded his own response to Marie Le Rochois, the singer so loved by the man in the top balcony. While Titon du Tillet concedes the beauty of her singing, he seems most captivated by her acting:

> If she surpassed herself in any one thing, it was, in my opinion, in her acting and in her expressive and striking *tableaux* in the roles she played, with which she delighted all her spectators. . . . She had the air of a queen and of a divinity, the head nobly placed, an admirable carriage, with all her movements beautiful, appropriate and natural. She understood marvelously well that which is called the *ritournelle*, which is played while the actress enters and presents herself to the audience, as in pantomime; in the silence, all the feelings and passions should be painted on the performer's face and be seen in her movements, something that great actors and actresses have not often understood. When she would become passionate and sing, one would notice only her on the stage.[10]

This kind of description is commonplace today, but back then such accounts were helping create a revolution in criticism—and therefore in the life of the performing arts. The literary critics who either attacked or defended Quinault and Lully, following a long-established path, dwelled on analysis of the published text of a work. Writers like Titon du Tillet, on the other hand, recorded an operagoer's experience of seeing it performed.

The critic Jean-Laurent Lecerf de la Viéville turned this kind of observation into a system. Any true criticism of a work, he argued, required taking account of three different categories of spectator, each of which had its own basis for judgment and therefore its own taste: "We must listen to the reasoning of the learned, defer to the feeling of the connoisseurs, and study how the people are moved." In defiance of critical tradition, he counted the judgment of "the people" (the untrained spectators) as the surest and most genuine and therefore ranked the operatic scenes that pleased them the most above those that pleased the learned and the connoisseurs. In particular, he treasured those scenes to which the audience responded with such unanimity that "the people" seems to enclose within it all other categories of spectator as well. At one such moment in Marie Le Rochois's performance of the title role in *Armide*, when

> Armide works herself up to stab Renaud, in that last scene of the second act, I have twenty times seen everybody seized by terror, not breathing, motionless, their souls gone entirely to their ears and eyes, until the violin melody that ends the scene gave them permission to breathe; then they took a breath once more with a hum of joy and admiration. I had no need to reason. That unanimous response of the people told me with complete certainty that the scene is ravishing.[11]

Louis XIV

In a royal patent of 1672, King Louis XIV gave Lully the exclusive right to produce opera in France. The following passages from that document vividly suggest how that royally sanctioned monopoly conveyed the opportunity not only to make a profitable career of composing, but also to dominate the musical culture of the nation.

We have permitted and granted to the said sieur Lully and do permit and grant to him by these presents, signed in our hand, to establish a Royal Academy of Music in our good city of Paris, which shall be composed of the number and quality of persons which he shall deem suitable, whom We will choose and engage on the strength of the report he shall present to Us, in order that they may perform before Us, whenever it shall please Us, musical pieces which shall be composed both in French verses and in foreign languages, equal and similar to the Academies of Italy; to be held and enjoyed by him throughout his life, and after him by that child of his who shall be endowed with and chosen for the inheritance of the said charge of Superintendent of the music of our chamber; with the power to take as associate any person he shall see fit for the establishment of the said Academy;

and in order to defray the great expenses that will be necessary for the said performances, both on account of the theaters, machines, scenery, and costumes, as well as for other necessities, We permit him to present to the public all the pieces he shall have composed, even those which shall have been performed before Us, without, however, the right to use musicians in our employ for the production of said pieces. . . . While we prohibit and forbid very expressly all persons, even the officers of our household, to enter without paying; as also to have any musical piece sung throughout its entirety, whether in French verses or any other language, without the written permission of the said sieur Lully, on pain of a fine of ten thousand livres and confiscation of the theaters, machines, scenery, costumes, and other things thereto pertaining, one third payable to Us, one third to the General Hospital, and the other third to the said sieur Lully.

Translation by Piero Weiss in his Opera: A History in Documents *(New York and Oxford: Oxford University Press, 2002), p. 41.*

Better than any other writer of his time, Lecerf de la Viéville makes explicit what many people must have recognized about the experience offered in an opera house that was part royal showplace, part national academy of musical drama, and part operatic fan club: that there were different ways of responding to opera and that a successful work had to accommodate the constituencies who responded in all those ways. Lully has often been decried as the autocrat—the Louis XIV—of the Opéra, but in fact he maintained his power over the development of French opera by adroitly satisfying the competing needs of his various constituencies.

The Operas of Lully

Both the subject and libretto of an opera were the products of multisided negotiation. The king sometimes approved or even chose the subject, and at times he may have taken an interest in the production down to the costumes. Quinault had to submit his libretto to both Lully and the Académie des Inscriptions (a bastion of the literary establishment) and often had to revise

Bust of Lully by Gaspard Collignon (d. 1702). The sculptor, working in a monumentalizing medium, nevertheless shows Lully as an intensely focused artist. Church of Notre-Dame-des-Victoires, Paris.

Giraudon

it repeatedly until both were satisfied.[12] The subjects, especially in the first ten years of collaboration between Quinault and Lully, were most often taken from Ovid, especially the *Metamorphoses*. At the king's instigation, however, three of their last operas were based on Spanish or Italian neo-chivalric epics that were immensely popular in France: *Amadis* (1684), *Roland* (1685), and *Armide* (1686).

All these subjects involved fantastic changes of setting and divine interventions or magical enchantments, and thus offered scope for the marvels of scenic display and stage machinery that French opera learned from its Italian models and for the dance and pantomime that were the specialty of the French stage. But even when the operas are based on stories from the *Metamorphoses*, they are not focused on the protagonists' identity crises, as the earliest Florentine and Mantuan operas were. Moreover, though they do typically involve triangles of mismatched and competing lovers like many Venetian works, the plots of French operas are less apt to be resolved into a satisfactory pairing off of lovers (as *Giasone is*, for instance, or even *Poppea* to a degree). They more often depict love as a battlefield in which there are losers as well as winners.

The Battlefield of Love: *Alceste*

One way to understand the model of operatic drama that Quinault and Lully had in mind is to study the way they adapted a source that did not fit that model. An example is the opera so criticized by the literary establishment in 1674: *Alceste*, based on a tragedy by Euripides. The story concerns a happily married couple, not young lovers looking for mates. The husband is a dying king who can be saved from death only if someone will agree to die in his place. His wife, Alceste, makes that sacrifice, but the hero Hercules ventures into the Underworld to rescue her and restores her to her husband. What Quinault's libretto added to Euripides' story is that Hercules' desire to restore Alceste to life is driven by his own love for her, a love that he renounces when he sees how devoted she and her husband are. At the end of the opera his "triumph" in overcoming his own love is celebrated equally with the bliss of the married couple, and this is what gives the work its subtitle: *The Triumph of Alcides* (another name for Hercules).

Quinault's libretto not only creates a love triangle where there was none in the original tragedy, but in the process allows one member of that triangle, Hercules, to discover a virtue that was not so prominent in Venetian opera: self-denial. Several other Quinault and Lully heroes exhibit it as well: Renaud

in *Armide* and the title character in *Roland*, among them. Love and the path of military glory are often presented as incompatible pursuits, and a male protagonist who ends up loveless on the path of duty is praised to the skies.

A sexist distinction rules these plots, however. While a male character who is left loveless at the end may be glorified, a female character in the same situation withdraws in disgrace. In fact, a woman is more often the one left out in the cold, and she is usually marked for a bad end from the start: she has generally used sorcery or divine power or a monster to advance her own love or to sideline her rival. This is the case in *Thésée* (Theseus, 1675), *Atys* (1676), *Bellérophon* (1679), *Armide*, and *Amadis*. Still, a few of these women are depicted with great sympathy, especially the goddess Cybèle in *Atys*, whose mourning for Atys when she has driven him to suicide makes the ending of that opera affecting; and Armide, a sorceress whose struggle with love, which is to say with her own humanity, makes the failure of her magic powers a tragic dénouement. In its day, Lecerf de la Viéville tells us, *Armide* was referred to as "the ladies' opera."[13]

Even though French operas of the late seventeenth century tell a different kind of story from Italian operas, they owed many of their representational resources to Italian works of the same period or earlier. The Italian designer Carlo Vigarani outfitted the theater used by the Opéra and designed its stagings for some years. A chorus and ballet corps frequently joined the solo singers onstage, as they had in the earliest Italian operas, so that the love entanglements were played out not on private battlegrounds, but within "on-stage societies."[14] The singers mixed the acting, or recitative, style with the singing style of the *air*, and they mixed solo singing with duets, trios, and other ensembles. Finally, though the string section of Lully's orchestra produced a massed sound that was hardly known in Italian opera, he followed Italian practice in using simple continuo accompaniment for most of the dialogue and a more colorful blend of sounds in the overture, ritornellos, and music for pantomime, dance, and chorus.

The Spell of Rhythm in Speech: *Alceste* and *Atys*

Despite their similarities of means, the operas of Lully sound completely unlike any Italian opera of the same period. There is hardly a phrase by Lully that wouldn't sound jarringly out of place in an Italian work (even disregarding the different languages). What makes that difference? It is partly a matter of the voices. Lully's operas had no roles for castratos; instead he launched the tradition, now common in all opera, of assigning the roles of heroic young lovers to high tenors.[15] But a more pervasive difference is that Lully's music casts a rhythmic spell unique to the French tradition he founded. It does so from the first chord of the overture, which always begins in a majestic processional mode.

Jean Berain, costume drawing for Prince Thésée (left) and the High Priestess of Minerva in Lully's *Thésée*, 1675. Like other costume drawings by Berain, the master scenic and costume designer of Lully's operatic establishment, these show not only the actors' costumes in all their elegance but also the stylized and eloquent poses and gestures demanded of those actors. Louvre, Paris.

Réunion des Musées Nationaux/Art Resource, NY

It is not simply a matter of dance rhythms, though Lully was a professional dancer—a rare background for a composer—and his operas are full of irresistible dance numbers. But they are also full of dialogue music, which manages to change its melodic rhythms and even its meters frequently and unpredictably without losing its rhythmic power. Costume designs from the period give a sense of how the singers, no less than the dancers, evoked the power of dance even in the poses they assumed when still. Once you get into the swing of this music, once you have seen it performed by singers who recreate the movements characteristic of this tradition, you can feel your body involuntarily lift and your arms spread into those poses even during the most irregularly paced passages of dialogue. The dialogue music therefore makes an intriguing place to begin an investigation of Lully's rhythmic effects.

Music usually casts its spell by means of repetition. We have already encountered a spellbinding dance number with solos and chorus that Lully generated out of endlessly varied repetitions of a short phrase: the passacaille from the fifth act of *Armide* (see Chapter 2). In his dialogue scenes, the spell comes instead from the unceasing flow of relatively short poetic and musical lines. In each musical phrase a singer delivers one or two lines of verse, conveying a full clause or sentence of text. Though phrases may differ in their length or rhythm, they chime with each other, both verbally and musically,

as they end. The verses rhyme, either in pairs (aa) or in alternating pairs (abab), and the musical phrases tend to end in cadences, usually marked by the singer with a short ornament—this could be a trill or an **appoggiatura** (a slide into the final note from an adjoining note), either written in or expected of the singer. In French opera, ornaments do not take over the singing line the way they can in Italian (in Orfeo's "Possente spirto," for example). Lully's simple ornaments, routinely crowning phrases at their cadence, create a hypnotic declamation in phrases that succeed each other like so many waves of sound and sense.

A maxim air in *Alceste* An air from the fourth act of *Alceste* exemplifies the rhythmic nature of Lully's dialogue music. Hercules has descended to the Underworld to plead with Pluto, who rules there, to allow Alceste to return to the living. Proserpina, Pluto's wife, is sympathetic to Hercules' case and seconds it in her own plea to Pluto. Her clinching lines are these:

<table>
<tr><td>C'est un arrêt du sort,</td><td>It's a decree of fate:</td></tr>
<tr><td>Il faut que l'amour extrême</td><td>a supreme love will always be</td></tr>
<tr><td>Soit plus fort que la mort.</td><td>stronger than death.</td></tr>
</table>

Lully sets the first line in one melodic phrase and the next two in another (see Example 7.2). The second phrase ("Il faut que l'amour extrême") begins in the same rhythms as the first, but then continues ("Soit plus fort que la mort") to its cadence in new rhythms. The two phrases are united by their cadences, the first making a weak cadence on a G minor chord, the second a full cadence on G major. But in the first phrase (line 1) Proserpina simply asserts the importance of what her second phrase says about the power of love. Once she sings the second phrase, she repeats it, in the same rhythm though in different

7.2 Lully, *Alceste*: Act 4, "C'est un arret du sort"

pitches, leading to a different cadence. Her strategy is to persuade her husband by insistence, and her insistent rhythms support her repeated words.

The strategy works. Pluto's response is not just to announce his agreement, but then to repeat for himself Proserpina's message, again using the same rhythms in different notes:

Les enfers, Pluton lui-même,
Tout doit en être d'accord:
Il faut que l'amour extrême
Soit plus fort que la mort.

The Underworld and Pluto himself
should all agree:
a supreme love will always be
stronger than death.

Finally, Proserpina and Pluto are joined by Alecto (one of the Furies) in one last version, still in the same rhythmic pattern, turning Proserpina's assertion into an acclamation of the power of love by the forces of the Underworld.

Verbal and rhythmic repetition has given these words an accumulating force within the scene and a hypnotic power over listeners. The words themselves are formulated to bear repeating and to deserve remembering. They form a **maxim** — a pithy saying or general statement of a human truth, a principle from which a particular course of action (in this case, the freeing of Alceste) can be deduced. Maxims are uttered so regularly in French opera (starting with Lully) that the numbers in which they are heard have been designated "maxim airs."[16] In fact, maxims were a pervasive form of expression in all kinds of French writing at the time, and several of the very writers who came down hardest on the idea of opera as a plausible form of drama — Boileau and Racine, for example — were famous for their own maxims. In the face of that criticism, it was no doubt wise for Quinault to fill his libretto texts with maxims and for Lully to emphasize them through

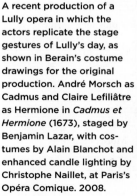

A recent production of a Lully opera in which the actors replicate the stage gestures of Lully's day, as shown in Berain's costume drawings for the original production. André Morsch as Cadmus and Claire Lefiliâtre as Hermione in *Cadmus et Hermione* (1673), staged by Benjamin Lazar, with costumes by Alain Blanchot and enhanced candle lighting by Christophe Naillet, at Paris's Opéra Comique. 2008.

Éric Mahoudeau/Lebrecht Music & Arts

repetition; those were in any case the lines it would be most plausible dramatically to repeat. In repeating them, however, he was also creating musical structures of an enchanting rhythmic power.

Dance rhythm in an air in *Atys* Many of Lully's airs are in dance rhythms, as are virtually all the choruses, instrumental pieces, and dance numbers. Even those dance rhythms, though, are closely connected to the rhythms of sung verse. An extreme (though by no means unusual) case is the air "Que l'on chante" in the fourth act of *Atys*. It is sung by the river god Sangar and then taken up by the chorus of other water deities. Here the case is extreme because, in what has been called a "doubled continuo air,"[17] the singer's melody doubles the orchestral bass line. This melody mixes just four different rhythmic motives (short-long, long-short, one very long, and three short), each a half measure long, in an ever-changing combination that was used to dance a type of minuet (see Example 7.3). At the same time, each motive is chosen to suit the rhythm of the words that go with it. What comes out as a captivating dance rhythm, then, issues from apt text setting. Fittingly the song, addressed to those gathered for what Sangar thinks is to be his daughter's wedding, is an invitation to both singing and dancing:

Que l'on chante, que l'on danse,   Let's sing, let's dance,
Rions tous lorsqu'il le faut.   let's all laugh when we need to.
Ce n'est jamais trop tôt   It's never too soon
Que le plaisir commence.   for pleasure to begin.

7.3 Lully, *Atys*: Act 4, "Que l'on chante"

Here again we encounter a couplet that expresses a maxim: "It's never too soon / For pleasure to begin." In this repertory there are plenty of airs built around maxims that promote the pursuit of pleasure in this sprightly (the French might have called it *galant*) way. They are a specialty of minor characters like Sangar, who are most often servants or confidants to the principal characters, though Sangar is a deity and the father of a principal. Such airs scandalized some French operagoers, including the king's mistress, Madame de Maintenon, whom he later married. Even Quinault himself, when he gave up composing librettos, wrote an apology for having "sung too much of games and loves."[18]

It could be argued — and before his renunciation Quinault himself would presumably have argued — that the sentiments expressed by this or that character, and especially by minor characters, are hardly to be taken as the moral message of the work as a whole. A drama enacts a conflict between different moral attitudes, at least some of which are surely questionable, and it would be difficult to claim that the pleasure-seeking attitude promoted by a minor character is the attitude that triumphs in the tragic ending of *Atys*. Nevertheless, when any questionable moral claim is put into the form of a musical maxim, we cannot necessarily dispose of all objections simply by invoking the dramatic context. Maxims are by nature detached from particular cases, and musical maxims may live on in our memory as song, released from whatever we thought of the characters who sang them. An opera, like a dramatic work of any sort, may transmit something more complicated than a single moral message to its audience.

In *Atys* the call to pleasure is both heard and rejected. When Sangar has completed "Que l'on chante," the chorus of water deities takes it up and sings its own four-part version. This invitation to sing and dance introduces a *divertissement* in which dances and songs are interspersed. At the end of the sequence, the hero of the opera, Atys, comes on to announce that the wedding of Sangar's daughter that everyone has been celebrating is not to take place. Sangar and his fellow deities resist this news, providing an opportunity to hear the chorus sing in a speech rhythm rather than a dance rhythm. They spit out their challenge to Atys in determined, rhythmically unified interjections:

Opposons nous à ce dessein barbare!　　　Let us oppose this barbarous plan!

The Spell of Rhythm in Movement: *Alceste* and *Armide*

The battle scene in *Alceste* Choral music, along with music for orchestra alone, provides crucial support for **pantomime** scenes (where characters carry out action through wordless gesture and movement). An examination of four pantomime scenes (three for chorus and one for a soloist)

will demonstrate how Lully's music animates as great a range of stage movement as it does of speech. The first of these is the battle scene in the second act of *Alceste*. The battle provides the pretext for Alceste's husband Admète to be mortally wounded, so that she can sacrifice her own life to restore his. The scene is dominated musically by marches, performed by the orchestra, dancers, and chorus. A battle complete with siege engines (like catapults) is then mimed by dancers, while the chorus, divided to represent the opposing sides, sings the calls to battle and the cry of surrender.

The lamentation scene in *Alceste*

The following act presents a second type of pantomime scene, the lamentation. The people of Admète's kingdom (embodied in both the chorus and the dancers, who process bearing flowers and ornaments) lament his approaching death. Then after rejoicing at his unexpected recovery, they lament again upon discovering that Alceste has sacrificed her life for his. Here the operatic chorus plays a role modeled on that of a Greek chorus: they take up the feelings of the principal characters and express them as the feelings of the whole community.

Because of the pressure Lully felt to make the words clearly understandable, he almost always has his chorus sing in rhythmic unison, though in full harmony. In this lamentation scene he does so even when the choral grieving for Admète consists of nothing but repetitions of the word "Hélas!" ("Alas!"). Later, when Alceste becomes the object of the grieving and Admète can do nothing but endlessly repeat the words "Alceste is dead," the chorus echoes his phrase, this time in overlapping phrases that imitate each other, suggesting that their grief is individual as well as communal. Yet even here the singers come to a rhythmically unified cadence on those words. In the scene as a whole, the chorus is in a sense

The frontispiece of the original libretto of Lully's *Armide* (Paris: Ballard, 1686) shows two events at the end of the opera. In the front Renaud, abandoning Armide to pursue glory, departs in a boat in which Glory sits; behind, at the order of the disconsolate Armide, her demons destroy the magic palace that was the temple of her love for Renaud. The destruction is depicted here as it was staged by Jean Berain in one of the most famous spectacles of seventeenth-century opera.

Hulton Archive/Getty Images

no more than a witness to the action and a sharer in the grief. But especially since Admète turns from the object of grief into the chief mourner in the course of the act, the chorus provides the real continuity. It shapes the whole act into a communal ritual, within which individuals—both principals and representatives of the people—express themselves in lamenting and procession.

The sleep scene in *Armide* A third type of pantomime scene that regularly involves the chorus is known in French as the *sommeil* (sleep scene), a scene of enchantment in which a sorceress or goddess has the hero lulled to sleep, making him vulnerable to magic spells or attack or a dream that the enchantress visits upon him. Lully makes this scene in *Armide* (scenes 3 and 4 of Act 2) a substantial *divertissement* of numbers involving solo and choral singing and dancers miming and dancing. A lulling character rules all this song and movement: the orchestral lines keep returning to the note or chord they have just left, creating an undulating or eddying rhythm. In fact, Lully's use of a single kind of rhythm—march rhythm in battle scenes, processional rhythm in lamentations, sleep rhythm in sleep scenes—to imbue a long and diverse scene with a single musical character represents one of his lasting contributions to opera.

As the sleep scene begins, the protagonist Renaud lies down on a grassy riverbank to rest and, to the undulating accompaniment of the muted strings, which imitate the soporific waves of the river, he falls asleep. A nymph emerges from the river, accompanied by other nymphs, shepherds, and shepherdesses, and sings of how much better it is to enjoy love than to pursue military glory. A new undulating phrase emerges from the muted strings, playing in an airy register (that is, without a low bass part). This ungrounded sound suggests that we have entered into Renaud's dreams. A chorus without low voices sings a maxim on a familiar, morally seductive theme:

Ah! quelle erreur! quelle folie!	*Oh, what a mistake! what madness!*
De ne pas jouir de la vie!	*Not to enjoy life!*

These singers' phrases have the rhythms of speech, not the continuously eddying flow of the orchestral music that introduces them. Still, they stay within the tempo and meter and high register of that music and so within the dream mode that it establishes. Further numbers make clear that the singers and dancers filling Renaud's head with dreams of love are demons sent by the sorceress Armide to keep him enchanted so that she can slay him.

Nicolas Poussin, *Rinaldo and Armida*, 1629. The episode of Armida caught by love as she attempts to slay Rinaldo was a favorite passage in Torquato Tasso's poem *Gerusalemme liberata (Jerusalem Freed)* long before Quinault and Lully made a sensational operatic moment of it. Dulwich Picture Gallery, London.
Bridgeman Art Library

Then the chorus "Ah! quelle erreur!" returns, rounding off the sleep scene with its dreamiest, most tender, most innocent-sounding music.

A monologue in *Armide*   That tender music is chased offstage by a crash—a blast from the full orchestra, switching harmony to minor and switching rhythm to the most jagged, least dreamy style in Lully's vocabulary. This is the moment when Armide enters, dagger in hand, to stab Renaud, the knight who has resisted both her charms and her magic power. When Marie Le Rochois performed this role, she was praised by Titon du Tillet, as we learned, for "her expressive and striking *tableaux*," for understanding that in this long prelude, or *ritournelle* (twenty measures in all), "all the feelings and passions should be painted on the performer's face and be seen in her movements." The music, in other words, does not simply express Armide's murderous mood; it animates the movements and expressions by which the actress displays that mood. Written in the style of an overture (what is called "French overture" style when Bach or Handel uses it), this is literally processional music. But Armide is not making a stately procession onto the stage; she is making a deadly advance toward the sleeping Renaud, displaying her contradictory feelings even before she gives voice to them.

Marie Le Rochois in the role of *Armide* at the premiere in 1686. The anonymous artist here, like Poussin, depicts her holding the knife with which she nearly kills Renaud.
© DeA Picture Library/Art Resource, NY

7.4 Lully, *Armide:* Act 2, "Qu'il éprouve"

She then begins the recitative in which, for all its length, Mlle. Le Rochois could evidently make an audience afraid to take a breath. At first her sentiment is clear:

Enfin, il est en ma puissance,
Ce fatal ennemi, ce superbe vainqueur.
Le charme du sommeil le livre à ma vengeance.
Je vais percer son invincible coeur.

Finally he is in my power,
this mortal enemy, this proud conqueror.
The spell of sleep delivers him to me for revenge.
I am going to pierce his invincible heart.

Stéphanie d'Oustrac, arm
poised to kill, as Armide and
Paul Agnew as Renaud in
Act 2 of *Armide*. Staging by
Robert Carsen at the Théâtre
des Champs-Elysées, Paris,
2008.

Stephane De Sakutin/Afp/Getty Images

But in raising her dagger, swearing (on a rising vocal line) that he will feel her rage, she loses her nerve. Her voice suddenly dipping low, the bass line slipping down from under its chord, she asks herself what is disturbing her (see Example 7.4):

> Qu'il *éprouve toute ma rage* . . .
> *Quel trouble me saisit? Qui me fait hésiter?*
> *Qu'est-ce qu'en sa faveur la pitié me veut dire?*

> Let him feel my full rage . . .
> *What disturbance is taking hold of me? Who is making me hesitate?*
> *What does pity want to say to me in his favor?*

Her doubts now lead her into a struggle with herself, in which she eventually admits that what is holding her back is love: she sighs for him. She reaches that realization by exploring both sides of her feelings, the urge to strike Renaud and the urge to resist that urge. We have met such a trial of conscience before: in *L'incoronazione di Poppea* Ottone stands over a sleeping Poppea with a dagger and undergoes exactly the same struggle that Armide does here. But Armide's dilemma takes a different verbal form, as she pits one position against the other in tiny, telegraphic phrases:

> *Frappons* . . . *Ciel! qui peut m'arrêter?*
> *Achevons* . . . *je frémis! Vengeons-nous* . . . *je soupire!*

> Let's strike . . . Heavens! Who can be stopping me?
> Let's be done with it . . . I'm trembling! Let's be avenged . . . I'm sighing!

From this alternation of verbal phrases Lully constructs a contrast of musical phrases, the murderous ones ("Achevons," "vengeons-nous") in the singer's upper register, the self-restraining ones ("je frémis," "je soupire") in her lower register. At the same time, the contrasted phrases mirror each other musically — "je frémis" almost an inversion of "Achevons," "je soupire" an exact transposition of "vengeons-nous" — so that we can hear the warring impulses as opposing manifestations of her obsession with Renaud. Furthermore, the quick succession of these tiny phrases, both contrasted and related, challenges the performer to enact Armide's dilemma in a rapid, stark, obsessive alternation of tones of voice, facial expressions, and bodily gestures.

This passage must have been in the forefront of Titon du Tillet's memory when he wrote of Le Rochois's performance, "Fury animated her face; love seized her heart. Now one, now the other agitated her in turn; pity and tenderness succeeded them in the end, and love finished the victor. What beautiful and true bearing! What movements and different expressions in her eyes and on her face during this monologue of twenty-nine lines."[19]

Lully's greatest gift to opera lies in the spellbinding connections he makes between the movement of music and the movements of the performers onstage. Knowing that he was a dancer, we might expect to find those connections at their strongest in the divertissements and other danced numbers, as well perhaps as in certain airs and choruses that he composed on dance rhythms. But even in this long recitative, what moved his contemporaries was clearly the connection of bearing and movement and facial expressions to the declamation of words, and their testimony tells us how pervasive the spell of movement is in his concept of opera.

National Opera Elsewhere: London

French was not the only new language in which opera began to be sung in the late seventeenth century. Opera in German and in English began to establish itself at the same time, although England had to wait for the reopening of the public theaters, which were shut in the 1640s and 1650s under the revolutionary Puritan regime. With the monarchy restored in 1660, even under a king who eagerly supported opera (Charles II), the London public was hostile to it. Theaters commissioned composers like Henry Purcell to write semi-operas or to provide incidental music for spoken plays. The only fully sung stage works in English were small-scale, created for court or for other private venues.

The creation of operas in English and other languages in the late seventeenth century did not lead to sustained traditions like those of Italian and French opera. Yet a single English opera from this period was so frequently staged and recorded through much of the twentieth century (much more so

than operas of Monteverdi, Cavalli, or Lully) that that work became the primary means for audiences to learn what opera was like in its first century. Today, when performances as well as audio and video recordings of many seventeenth-century operas are abundant, this work still holds a special place, especially for English speakers, because it allows us to experience with the immediacy of our own language the techniques that Italian and French composers developed for matching notes to words and movement. Besides, it is a work that despite its unusual brevity demonstrates the enormous dramatic and musical range of seventeenth-century opera. This work is Henry Purcell's *Dido and Aeneas*.

Dido and Aeneas, Act 3, scene 2, staged by Deborah Warner at the Netherlands Opera, Amsterdam, 2009. Luca Pisaroni as Aeneas, Malena Ernman as Dido, and Judith van Wanroij as Belinda.
Ruth Walz

Purcell, *Dido and Aeneas*

The story of Dido is the romantic episode in the ancient Roman epic poem of the founding of Rome, Vergil's *Aeneid*. Dido, the widowed queen of Carthage, falls in love with Aeneas, a hero of the Trojan War; when the gods command him to found the city of Rome, he abandons her and she kills herself. The episode had been used as an opera plot in Italy many times, beginning with Cavalli's *Didone* of 1641, by the time Nahum Tate, Purcell's librettist, got to it. Tate's version is not only compressed, compared with the full-length Italian operas on the subject, but odd in its presentation of the story. His Aeneas, for instance, is not just a cad (even Vergil's Aeneas is that); he is a cad who barely cuts any figure in the opera. As soon as he is a couple of lines into his declaration of love to Dido, for instance, her confidante Belinda takes over the promotion of his suit for him with an extended aria ("Pursue thy conquest, Love"), and he never resumes it. Further, we never hear Dido utter a word of love to him. They sing no love duet—an almost unheard-of omission in a seventeenth-century opera. It is curious to find the stages in their relationship so incompletely marked, especially since endless room is made for choruses and dances.

Some of the opera's oddness may be explained by the performing circumstance for which it was created. The first known performance was given in 1689 by students at a boarding school for "young gentlewomen" run by a noted dancer. Assuming that the opera was conceived for those performers at their school, it is easy for us to understand why it is short, with heavy emphasis on group singing and dancing and less on the love relationship of

the soloists, and on the male lead in particular. But then, why pick the story of Dido and Aeneas for performance by schoolgirls, and why create for male singers not just the role of Aeneas, but also one or two subsidiary roles as well as three of the four choral parts? There is actually almost nothing that can safely be assumed about the creation of this opera, and the earliest surviving score, dating from almost a century after the first performance, departs significantly from the libretto, which comes from the boarding school production. In other words, some of what seems odd about the work may derive from changes made in its early history, but we don't know who made what changes, or when, or why.

Yet for all its oddness in representing its story, *Dido and Aeneas* displays the full dramatic, musical, choreographic, and scenic range of seventeenth-century opera. It mixes the tragedy of the abandoned Dido with the comedy of a sorceress and her coven of witches—who substitute for Vergil's Olympian gods in disrupting the lovers' romance. It mixes musical and dance styles from the Italian and French traditions of opera with some distinctively English numbers. The French influence can be heard from the processional opening of the overture to the dance rhythms in both dance and vocal numbers. The Venetian influence can be heard above all in the slow triple rhythm and ground-bass structure of Dido's dying Lament, "When I am laid in earth." The distinctively English numbers include a sailor's song and dance, or hornpipe, and several choruses in the imitative styles of English madrigals and anthems. These styles, each with its own dramatic tone, make striking contrasts because they are pressed against each other in such a compact work. A dramatic progression driven by contrasts is characteristic of seventeenth-century opera of all nations; in the decades after *Dido and Aeneas* that taste was replaced by a concern for dramatic consistency, or decorum.

Operatic word-setting in English Two examples show how the techniques developed by Italian and French opera composers for setting words to music operate in English. In the first-act duet and chorus "Fear no danger to ensue," the singers and instruments all move in rhythmic unison, creating a minuet step. And as in Sangar's air with chorus "Que l'on chante" in *Atys*, the concatenation of long-short and short-long motives, determined by the words, creates the music's enchanting rhythm (Example 7.5 shows the upper voice in the opening of the duet). In the first line, for instance, the short-long motive suits "Fear no" because it gives equal weight to both words, the downbeat accent on "Fear" balancing the length and rise in pitch on "no." Of the three two-syllable words in the line, the two that are stressed on the first syllable ("danger" and "hero") both start on a downbeat, and the one stressed on the second syllable ("ensue") goes from upbeat to downbeat. But "danger" and "hero" are also distinguished

7.5 Purcell, *Dido and Aeneas*: Act 1, "Fear no danger"

from each other, "danger" set as a long-short motive, its initial half note giving the singers time to slide into the n, while the short-long motive on "hero" saves them from distorting the first syllable by losing the connection he- has to r in spoken English. Sing this line to Purcell's rhythms, then alter those rhythms in any way, and you will discover how the charm of his melody grows out of his minute attention to the flow of words.

A more impassioned speech, but just as artful in its word setting, is the final exchange, in recitative, between Aeneas and Dido. When the departing Aeneas, withering under Dido's outrage at his perfidy, offers to stay with her after all, she spurns his offer:

No repentance shall reclaim
The injur'd Dido's slighted flame;
For, 'tis enough, whate'er you now decree,
That you had once a thought of leaving me.

The first of these couplets is in shorter lines (of four iambic feet each), which Purcell pushes along in steady beats (see Example 7.6). The second, in which Dido explains to Aeneas why he can expect no second chance from her, is in longer lines (of five iambic feet), which Purcell draws out further, stretching certain syllables into a second beat,

7.6 Purcell, *Dido and Aeneas*: Act 3, "No repentance shall reclaim"

Malena Ernman sings Dido's Lament in the final scene of *Dido and Aeneas*. Staging by Deborah Warner at the Netherlands Opera, Amsterdam, 2009.
Ruth Walz

allowing Dido to bear down on Aeneas with these words. The first line of this couplet — "For 'tis enough, whate'er you now decree" — ends with the final syllable of "decree" on a downbeat, giving emphasis to his present plea, in order to dismiss it. But on the rhyming line that follows — "That you had once a thought of leaving me" — Dido does not end with a corresponding emphasis on its final word, "me." Instead Purcell stretches her line so that her emphatic downbeat falls on the word that describes Aeneas's crime: "leaving." What feels like the willful avoidance of an obvious correspondence between the two lines in fact makes us focus on Dido's point.

Dido's Lament   Their confrontation concludes with the one bit of duet allowed the two lovers: a shouting match. After that the opera ends with Dido's death scene, which consists of her Lament, sung between two mournful choruses. It is amazing that a scene of such grave beauty could arise within such a modest and motley dramatic frame. Yet it is in coming to terms with this finale that a study of the Italian and French operatic repertories standing behind Purcell is most helpful. The two choruses are closely related to each other in dramatic tone, in key and melodic motives, and in their alternation of two styles: a Lullian style that speaks the words with one voice and a madrigalistic style that interweaves the voices. But the choruses serve very different dramatic functions.

The first, modeled on Greek tragedy, is a commentary on what has happened, sung by the people of Dido's kingdom. Its text is a maxim: "Great minds against themselves conspire / And shun the cure they most desire." It is an observation by those capable of standing back from the events. But it is also an act of participation by Dido's subjects in her destiny, sung — like many French operatic choruses and unlike Greek tragic ones — in the middle of a scene, in this case before Dido has delivered her final words. The second chorus, "With drooping wings ye Cupids come," is sung after those final words and is therefore placed like a Greek tragic chorus. It is also accompanied by the appearance of cupids over Dido's tomb and is therefore the musical component of an operatic stage-machine effect. So while we are hearing the lament of Dido's subjects, like that of Orpheus's friends at the

death of Eurydice or of Admète's subjects at the death of Alceste, the action of the opera is brought to an end by the arrival of characters from outside the world of that action.

Dido's Lament, "When I am laid in earth," not only features the ground-bass structure and rhythm of a Cavalli lament, but is worthy of Cavalli in its heartbreaking beauty. Against the relentless sinking of the chromatic bass line, Dido's voice constantly struggles upward and just as constantly tumbles down. She struggles against letting the "fate" of the bass line bring her words and voice down, yet in the end it does. Her situation is heartrending because at the moment when she is giving up on life, she still feels torn between two identities. One is the widowed queen whom she asks her listener to remember (whether we think of that listener as her confidante who is standing right there or her people or Aeneas or ourselves); the other is the spurned lover whose "wrongs" in yielding to Aeneas's love she asks her listener to forget: "When I am laid in earth, may my wrongs create / No trouble in thy breast. / Remember me! But ah! forget my fate."

Purcell dramatizes the conflict between those two identities by a simple musical superimposition. In the second half of the Lament Dido's desperate monotone on "Remember me!" calls for her identity as the widowed queen to be kept alive. Meanwhile the violins play the appoggiatura (the tugging dissonance resolving into consonance) to which Dido has just sung "laid" (see Example 7.7). This motive wordlessly keeps alive the very memory, the very side of her life, that her words say she wants buried

7.7 Purcell, *Dido and Aeneas:* Act 3, Dido's Lament

and forgotten. Though she sings a lament in the style of Cavalli, this Dido is no Venetian opera heroine. In fact, the heroine of Cavalli's Dido opera exemplifies that tradition by turning from Aeneas, once he has abandoned her, to recognize another prince as her true lover and ending the opera in a love duet with him. Purcell's Dido, in her dramatic nature if not her musical style, is more a throwback to the early court operas: in her state of loveless abandonment she struggles through her earlier assumptions and comes to terms with her conflicted identity.

FURTHER READING

Documents and commentary relating to seventeenth-century French opera in Caroline Wood and Graham Sadler, eds., *French Baroque Opera: A Reader* (Aldershot, Eng.: Ashgate, 2000); Piero Weiss, *Opera: A History in Documents* (New York and Oxford: Oxford University Press, 2002); Georgia Cowart, *The Origins of Modern Musical Criticism: French and Italian Music, 1600–1750* (Ann Arbor: UMI Research Press, 1981).

On the various genres of dance and musical spectacle at the court of Louis XIV, Georgia Cowart, *The Triumph of Pleasure: Louis XIV and the Politics of Spectacle* (Chicago: University of Chicago Press, 2008). Period set and costume designs for Lully operas are reproduced in Jérôme de La Gorce, *Féeries d'opéra: Décor, machines et costumes en France, 1645–1765* (Paris: Editions du patrimoine, 1997); and La Gorce, *Berain: Dessinateur du Roi Soleil* (Paris: Herscher, 1986).

On Purcell's life and work, Peter Holman, *Henry Purcell* (Oxford and New York: Oxford University Press, 1994). On *Dido and Aeneas*, the Norton Critical Score, ed. Curtis Price (New York: Norton, 1986); Ellen T. Harris, *Henry Purcell's "Dido and Aeneas"* (Oxford: Clarendon Press, 1987); *Performing the Music of Henry Purcell*, ed. Michael Burden (Oxford: Clarendon Press, 1996); Bryan White, "Letter from Aleppo: Dating the Chelsea School Performance of *Dido and Aeneas*," *Early Music* 37 (2009): 417–28.

FOR RESEARCH AND REFLECTION

1. Explore the different kinds of writing about opera published nowadays: opera star profiles and interviews in fan magazines like *Opera News*; customer reviews of CDs and DVDs on Amazon.com; professional reviews

of productions in newspapers and in magazines like *The New Yorker*; blogs by opera lovers of all sorts; scholarly books and articles like the ones cited throughout this book. Consider how differently the subject of opera is treated in each of these kinds of publications and what different assumptions the writers make about their readers.

2. Culinary workers in France no longer sing "Amour, que veux-tu de moi." What operatic numbers can people today who are not fans nevertheless recognize or hum along with, or use as ringtones? What might they know about the source of those melodies or their original dramatic significance? How can you find out?

3. What features of Lully's music give it its verve? In the last few decades specialist performers have brought it to life in extraordinary ways, interpreting it in ways that are not obvious readings of the notes. What kinds of performance practices of seventeenth-century France might have driven their experiments?

4. In any Lully opera a kernel of dramatic action is wrapped in a large amount of allegorical speech, dance, and ritualized action. Does this dramatic kernel nonetheless animate the whole work? If so, how? If not, what does?

5. Read the story of Dido and Aeneas as told by Vergil in Book 4 of *The Aeneid*. To what extent does Purcell's opera capture the spirit of Vergil's tale, despite the change of medium from epic poem to opera? In what ways does the opera give the story a new twist and a new spirit?

6. How does the experience of hearing *Dido and Aeneas* in English, without seeing the words, compare with the experience of hearing a seventeenth-century opera in Italian or French while following subtitles that translate the words into English?

 Additional resources available at wwnorton.com/studyspace.

EIGHTEENTH-CENTURY MILESTONES

1709

The first public performance of a comic opera in Neapolitan dialect, *Patrò Calienno de la Costa*, with music by Antonio Orefice, at the Fiorentini Theater in Naples, begins the eighteenth-century tradition of comic opera.

1711

George Frideric Handel's career presenting Italian opera in London begins with the production of *Rinaldo*, libretto by Giacomo Rossi, at the Queen's Theatre.

1715

Death of Louis XIV of France.

1724

Giulio Cesare in Egitto (Julius Caesar in Egypt), libretto by Nicola Haym and music by Handel, performed in London.

1727

Partisan fans of the sopranos Francesca Cuzzoni and Faustina Bordoni, playing rivals in a London production of *Astianatte* (libretto by Nicola Haym, music by Giovanni Bononcini), cause a notorious disruption of a performance.

The Beggar's Opera, play by John Gay featuring popular tunes of the day and mocking the Cuzzoni-Bordoni fiasco, initiates the genre of the ballad opera.

1733

La serva padrona (The Servant-Girl Mistress), libretto by Gennaro Antonio Federico and music by Giovanni Battista Pergolesi, premieres in Naples.

Hippolyte et Aricie, libretto by Simon-Joseph Pellegrin and music by Jean-Philippe Rameau, premieres in Paris.

1752

Performance of Pergolesi's two-decade-old comic opera *La serva padrona* in Paris touches off a political-cultural storm, known as the "Querelle des bouffons" ("Dispute over the actors").

1756–63

Seven Years' War brings death and destruction across Europe, the Americas, and Asia.

1762

Orfeo ed Euridice, libretto by Ranieri de' Calzabigi and music by Christoph Willibald Gluck, the first of Gluck's "reform" operas, performed in Vienna.

1769

The score of *Alceste*, libretto by Ranieri de' Calzabigi and music by Gluck, is published.

1774

Gluck's career as a composer of French classical operas begins with the premiere of *Iphigénie en Aulide (Iphigenia in Aulis)*, libretto by M. F. Roullet, in Paris.

1775–83

The American Revolution, together with the Haitian Revolution (1791–1804), begins the long process through which the Western Hemisphere is freed from European control.

1783

The Hapsburg emperor Joseph II, having dismissed the Italian opera troupe from the Viennese court theater in the mid-1770s, establishes a new Italian comic opera troupe in Vienna.

1784

Richard Coeur-de-lion (Richard the Lion-Hearted), libretto by Michel-Jean Sedaine and music by Ernest-Modest Grétry, premieres at the Comédie-Italienne, Paris.

1786

The Marriage of Figaro, the first of Wolfgang Amadeus Mozart's three comic-opera collaborations with the librettist Lorenzo Da Ponte, performed by the Italian troupe in Vienna.

1791

The Revolutionary government in France abolishes state and church censorship of theater (including opera). The French example was not imitated elsewhere in Europe, nor did it last long in France.

PART III

Opera of the Eighteenth Century

In the eighteenth century opera was dominated by extraordinary singing. Italian conservatories, the only institutions in Europe devoted to the training of opera singers, produced singers who were in demand—and who created demand for Italian opera—all across Europe. Even in France, where Italian operas had failed earlier to gain a foothold, their appearance now created furious debate about whether native singers and operas could withstand the competition.

As singers held audiences captive with ever more spectacular vocal display, critics and librettists aimed to reform opera by turning it into a more dignified form of drama. This reforming impulse achieved its earliest success by excluding comic characters and episodes from serious (or tragic) opera plots. That did not mean that comedy lost its place in opera; rather, it developed a separate place. Sometimes brief comic operas, called **intermezzi**, were

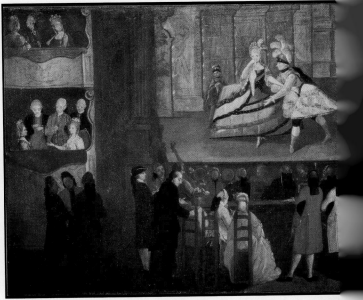

School of Pietro Longhi, painting of a mid-eighteenth-century Italian opera performance. Most images of performances from the first two centuries of opera commemorate special events: a royal wedding or saint's day or the hosting of a royal visitor. This exceptional painting records an ordinary night at the opera. Museo Teatrale alla Scala, Milan.
Art Resource, NY

performed between the acts of serious operas (dance sequences could also be inserted there). Eventually, full-length comic operas were performed on their own evenings or even in their own opera houses. Now there were two species of opera: serious opera (often known in retrospect as **opera seria**), usually on classical Greek or Roman subjects; and comic operas on mundane and often contemporary subjects.

CHAPTER 8

Opera on Classical Subjects

Handel and Italian Opera

Opera across Europe changed drastically in the few decades from the 1680s, when Purcell's *Dido and Aeneas* was produced in London, to the 1720s, when George Frideric Handel's operas held the stage there. We can sort out what was new by looking closely at a single number from a Handel opera: Sesto's aria "L'angue offeso mai riposa" ("The offended serpent never rests"), from *Giulio Cesare in Egitto* (*Julius Caesar in Egypt*), which premiered in 1724.

The Rhetoric of Repetition: "L'angue offeso"

This aria has the obsessive character that generally sets eighteenth-century opera apart from seventeenth-century. The obsessive effect derives to a great extent from a highly repetitive rhythm, in 3/4, within relatively static harmonies. The instrumental bass line is particularly compulsive, marching in continuous quick steps—six eighth notes per measure—throughout the whole long aria; and those notes often outline the same chord for measure after measure. In the opening orchestral ritornello, for instance, the bass sticks to a C minor sonority for more than two measures, then an E-flat sonority for most of another four. (In much seventeenth-century music, by contrast, practically every new bass note bears a change of chord.) All the while, the melodic line of the violins and oboes has its own repetitious rhythm: static on the first two beats of a measure, then lashing out suddenly from the third beat to the

The Meeting of Mark Antony and Cleopatra is part of a fresco series that Giambattista Tiepolo painted in the Palazzo Labia, Venice, 1747–50. The series tells episodes from the Egyptian queen's conquest of the Roman general's heart; her earlier conquest of another Roman general, Julius Caesar, is the story of Handel's opera *Giulio Cesare* (1724). But Tiepolo's painting is operatic in its own way: between two doorways of the Labia Palace we see figures costumed and posed like singers of this period in an opera set in ancient Rome.

Palazzo Labia, Venice/Alinari/Bridgeman Art Library

next downbeat (see Example 8.1). Winton Dean and John Merrill Knapp hear in these "contours of the main theme the coil and spring of the angry serpent to which Sesto compares himself."[1] As the ritornello continues, the "coil" of static harmony and restless rhythms takes new forms, until the violins and oboes, as if bottled up too long, "spring" in an outburst of quick notes to a cadence.

8.1   Handel, *Giulio Cesare in Egitto*: "L' angue offeso," orchestral ritornello

Now the singer enters, but the violins and oboes do not get out of the way, leaving just the basso continuo instruments to provide support, as would generally happen in a seventeenth-century aria. Instead they double the voice, which has taken up the melody that opened the ritornello. Soon they are playing attention-grabbing lines of their own, full of continuous quick notes and breathtaking leaps, against the equally florid lines of the singer in the same soprano range. Much more than in earlier opera, singers in a Handel opera have to hold their own against instruments that compete with them on their own terms. Four times in the course of the aria, Sesto needs the agility and long-held breath to deliver phrases eight measures long (in a moderate tempo), of which half the length is made up of continuous quick (sixteenth) notes. Furthermore, the range required of the singer, an octave and a half, rivals that of the violins—and outdoes that of even such a show-stopping seventeenth-century aria as Monteverdi's "Possente spirto." Clearly "L'angue offeso" calls for a singer of exceptional powers. And yet Sesto is not by any means the starring role in this opera.

Sesto is a male character, but while Handel composed several of the other male roles, including Julius Caesar, for castrati, he composed the role of Sesto for a woman; the character is a boy and so could be imagined having a voice that is high but lacking the heroic ring of a castrato. The formidable singer for whom Handel wrote this role, Margherita Durastanti, had sung leading roles in the greatest opera houses of Europe, and the fact that he could hire her to sing a secondary part tells us something about the state of opera in London.

For three decades Handel made his career in London, composing and producing operas, almost all of them in Italian, a language his audience needed bilingual librettos to follow. He composed them in Italian so that they could be sung by Italian singers, whom he brought to London because they were just about the only singers then who had the vocal training (and in the case of the castrati, the kind of voice) to do justice to arias like "L'angue offeso." For male singers, that training was available mostly in the conservatories of Naples and other Italian cities. For female singers, who were not admitted to conservatories, it was available from private teachers, who were often family members, or clerics.[2] The agility, range, breath control, style, vocal coloring, and embellishing skills of these singers made Italian opera the favorite entertainment of those who could afford it everywhere in eighteenth-century Europe except France. And in London, the wealthiest European city, opera lovers provided Handel sufficient means to bring a half dozen great Italian singers (including, in the case of *Giulio Cesare*, three famous castrati) to perform both principal and secondary roles in a single work.

Text: The simile aria An aria was more than a display of musical skills, however, and in order to understand what was novel about an aria like "L'angue offeso," we need to turn to Sesto's text and its place in the drama. The opera is set in Egypt (first century BCE), where the rival Roman generals Pompey and Julius Caesar have been leading their armies in battle with each other. At the beginning of the opera Ptolemy, the young king of Egypt, has had Pompey killed, presumably to win favor with Caesar, and has made Pompey's widow Cornelia and son Sesto his prisoners. For the first half of the opera Sesto seethes with a passion to avenge his father's death, and at a moment when Romans and Egyptians are taking up arms against each other, he is advised that he might now find the opportunity to kill Ptolemy. Left alone onstage, he expresses his obsession with revenge:

> ## Giulio Cesare
> ### PRINCIPAL CHARACTERS
>
> - Two rival Roman generals, Pompey
> - and **Julius Caesar** (Giulio Cesare), entering Egypt with their armies, become pawns in the power struggle of the Egyptian would-be
> - king **Ptolemy** (Tolomeo) with his
> - older sister, the queen **Cleopatra**. Tolomeo beheads Pompey, and
> - holds Pompey's widow **Cornelia**
> - and son **Sesto** prisoner, while Cleopatra seduces Caesar to win his support.

L'angue offeso mai riposa *Se il veleno pria non spande* *Dentro il sangue all'offensor.*	*The offended serpent never rests* *until its poison seeps* *into the blood of the offender.*
Così l'alma mia non osa *Di mostrarsi altera e grande* *Se non svelle l'empio cor.*	*So too my spirit dares not* *show how proud and great it is* *until it plucks out the wicked heart.*

Sesto is reaching for a poetic comparison to convey his readiness to commit this violent act. Italians in fact call an aria with a text of this kind a "comparison aria" (*aria di paragone*). In English it is generally known as a **simile aria**.

Like a maxim air, a simile aria invites the audience to see the dramatic situation onstage as one instance of a more universal experience. But whereas a maxim formulates advice for the present situation, a simile text illuminates that situation by comparing it to a fictional one, either natural or human. In "L'angue offeso" the librettist Nicola Haym makes the image of the wounded snake a vivid analogy to human vengefulness: the venomous purpose, the restless watchfulness, and the lightning attack. Of these elements, Handel's music—with its ceaseless rhythms bottled up by static harmonies—expresses the restless watchfulness most strongly. And that precisely captures Sesto's state of mind at this moment, still awaiting his chance to strike Ptolemy down.

The text, with its two short stanzas, is quite compact—more like the text of a Lully air than one of the long solo numbers in a Cavalli opera. Furthermore, the two stanzas are closely tied to each other in both sense and form: sense in that the first stanza proposes the analogy of the snake and the second explains how Sesto considers his spirit comparable; form in that each line of the first stanza rhymes with the corresponding line of the second.

Musical form: The da capo aria When the text is performed to Handel's music, however, the aria lasts much longer than a Lully air, in fact every bit as long as a Cavalli solo with six or seven large stanzas. The main reason is that Handel repeats words, lines, and stanzas far more than a seventeenth-century composer would. What's more, he does this according to a pattern that turns his two tiny stanzas of text into five substantial musical strophes, marked off from each other by orchestral ritornellos:

Angelika Kirchschlager in the role of Sesto, singing the aria "L'angue offeso" in *Giulio Cesare* at the Glyndebourne Festival in England, 2005. The staging by David McVicar casts the invading Romans as nineteenth-century British imperialists, allowing Sesto to express his vengeful thoughts with a pistol.

Robbie Jack/Corbis

Musical strophe 1:	stanza 1
Strophe 2:	stanza 1
Strophe 3:	stanza 2
Strophe 4 (=1):	stanza 1
Strophe 5 (=2):	stanza 1

An aria with that kind of reprise of the first musical strophes is known as a **da capo aria**, because instead of writing out the reprise, the composer would simply write *da capo* (from the top) at the end of the third strophe. In almost any Italian opera from the first half of the eighteenth century, the great majority of the arias take this form, which is put to a multitude of dramatic purposes.

The singer's first two phrases in this aria are striking for presenting the whole first stanza, about the serpent, so straightforwardly that an

Italian speaker can understand that whole sentence at once. Then, after the violins and oboe give the singer a break, she starts in on the same words again (still in the first musical strophe). But this time she repeats phrases of her text more often along the way, and she has to take more breaks to do so. Then she gets carried away with passagework on a single syllable (the "a" of "spande"), so that by the time she finishes both the textual stanza and the musical strophe, she has produced the first of those eight-measure-long phrases (see Example 8.2). From a rhetorical perspective her plain musical delivery has given way to an eloquence in which the words can now be taken for granted.

8.2   Handel, "L'angue offeso," first musical strophe

The second musical strophe begins with a new version of the opening ritornello, shorter than before, but more brilliant because Handel takes the high instruments higher and the low instruments lower. The singer then begins the second stage of her argument—with not only the same words as before, but the same musical material in a similar progression. The big difference this time is that the singer and orchestra make a much bigger deal about ending. In the eight-measure vocal phrase of this strophe, the singer holds on unexpectedly long to the final note and sings past it to a nonfinal chord, then takes a breath and sings the cadence all over again; a final version of the orchestral ritornello follows. When the first two musical strophes are reprised at the end, this strophe will end the whole aria, and then its emphatic finality will be especially appropriate.

For now, it leads into a third musical strophe, in which Sesto finally delivers the second stanza of text, bringing the serpent simile to bear on his own vengeance-seeking situation. Since this stanza gives the simile its point and this third musical strophe is our one chance to hear it, Handel gives it the plainest music of all. The singer goes just once through the first two lines, accompanied by just the continuo instruments, and then through the last line with several repetitions, with more competition from the violins and oboes. This plain music allows listeners to comprehend the words, but it also denies the words the musical force to clinch Sesto's argument.

We now hear the reprise of the first and second strophes. Singers in Handel's day were expected to improvise embellishments in such a reprise, even when the vocal lines were florid to start with, and to elaborate the cadences, especially the final cadences, with their own cadenzas. Italian singers, who surpassed all others in the art of embellishment, could turn the lengthy reprise of a da capo aria into something more than simple repetition by investing it with their most expressive, dazzling, and applause-inspiring effects.

The dramatic nature of the da capo aria The five clearly articulated musical strophes of "L'angue offeso" build to a brilliant conclusion, especially when embellished, like stages of an orator's argument. But there is no linear progression of argument or thought here, such as Monteverdi produced in "Possente spirto" and Cavalli in "Infelice, che ascolto." The da capo form creates a circular progression: the words are the same in all but one of the five strophes, and even the music has run its course by the end of the third.

In fact, some writers in Handel's day and many in ours have considered arias of this sort inherently undramatic. Charles de Brosses, a French tourist in Rome in 1739, complained that in Italian opera the arias were "not always sufficiently connected to the subject." However "exquisite," they had the "effect of distracting, of letting the interest cool off while charming the ears."[3] A modern historian of opera, Donald Grout, judged the arias undramatic by nature: the singer is "expressing his emotions or conveying some general sentiments or reflections appropriate to the current situation—not to his fellows on the stage but to the audience. While this goes on, the progress of the drama usually comes to a complete stop."[4]

In singing "L'angue offeso," Sesto certainly seems to delay executing his plan to kill Ptolemy. By standing on the empty stage for five minutes, declaring in song that he is ready for action, he could give us the impression that he is anything but ready. Whatever his words say, the obsessive style of his music—the unchanging flow of bass notes, slow harmonic pace, and melodies all formed around the same rhythmic waiting and lunging—could suggest he is really ruled by indecision. The circularity of the da capo form could reinforce that impression. On the other hand, the character of the music, established in the opening ritornello before Sesto sings a word, draws the listeners into Sesto's zone, and its persistence through the da capo reprise helps the audience stay in that zone as he asserts his snakelike vengefulness. The form in itself expresses obsession, and when characters sing these arias, whether they are addressing an argument to someone else or, like Sesto, thinking aloud, they are usually expressing their obsession of the moment. Da capo form may actually help arias move the dramatic action forward by taking the audience inside the circles of thought that drive the characters to act. The advent of this aria form, then, made possible a new kind of operatic drama.

The Testing of Love

The rise of the da capo aria was just one part of the change that came over Italian opera early in the eighteenth century. Reform-minded librettists were focusing more exclusively on the interactions of the principal characters by providing fewer subplots with comic characters and fewer opportunities for visual spectacle, choral pomp, and dancing. They accustomed audiences to the idea that serious and comic effects did not belong in the same drama. Nicola Haym created the libretto of *Giulio Cesare* by reworking a libretto of the same title written in 1677 by Giacomo Francesco Bussani (for music by Antonio Sartorio), and though he left in some spectacle, he removed the one entirely comic character as well as a lot of humorous disguises that even the noble Roman characters had assumed.

The dominance of the singer As Italian librettists gradually pared down the occasions for diverting and bawdy spectacle, they perhaps unwittingly cleared the stage for another kind of spectacle: the extreme vocal virtuosity that singers were developing at that moment. The more librettists constructed sober dramas of dialogue, the more the audiences craved a performance that included not-at-all sober displays of singing. And because the singers were stars, the librettists learned to accommodate their demands. In a treatise of 1715 the librettist and critic Pier Jacopo Martello advises fellow librettists to calculate the number of arias for singers based on their relative star power. He even suggests, not altogether tongue-in-cheek, that they surrender any hope of dramatic coherence:

> Be prepared cheerfully to change tolerable arias into bad ones if a singer or songstress should wish to tag onto your recitative something that earned them applause in Milan, Venice, Genoa, or elsewhere; and if its sentiment is the very opposite of what you had at that point—what then? Let them have their way, or they will swarm all over you and pierce your ear with soprano and contralto rebukes.[5]

By now, composers were distinguishing the acting style from the singing style more clearly than ever before. Most of the dialogue was set in a business-like version of the acting style: talky vocal lines in a fluid rhythm, following the rise and fall of spoken declamation rather than any songful course, hardly repeating any words, with a simple continuo accompaniment. This was called *recitativo semplice* (**simple recitative**) or, later, *recitativo secco* (dry recitative). After this conversation went on a while, one character took control by launching into an aria, often elaborate both vocally and instrumentally and often in da capo form. When the aria was finished (and applauded), the character who sang it usually left the stage. As this scheme took hold, arias

Portrait of Senesino (stage name of Francesco Bernardi), the alto castrato who played the title role in Handel's *Giulio Cesare*. This engraving, based on a painting by Thomas Hudson, shows the singer with the score.
© City of Westminster Archive Centre, London/Bridgeman Art Library

naturally grew longer, but also fewer: Haym and Handel's *Giulio Cesare* has half as many as Bussani and Sartorio's *Giulio Cesare* of half a century earlier.

The recitative now provided a musically neutral background against which the arias stood out in sharp relief. Pier Jacopo Martello compared their alternation to *chiaroscuro*—the highlighting of characters in painting by placing them against dark backgrounds.[6] In an Italian opera of this period there was always an alternation of recitative and aria, along with a few vocal ensembles and instrumental numbers, and yet the dramatic progression of the opera as a whole can be felt largely in terms of the cumulative effect of the arias—the musically forceful units. Because each one has a single, sharply etched profile, because it creates its own zone, the power of the drama can be felt in the progression of the arias that each character sings and in the contrasts between one character's arias and another's.

Duty, love, and self-sacrifice By the late seventeenth century Italian librettos were leaving behind the old themes of discovering one's identity or soul mate for a new theme of responsibility. Already in the libretto of 1677 that was reworked for Handel's *Giulio Cesare* in 1724, Caesar is a general responsible for his troops, and Cleopatra is a queen responsible for the fate of her people. Their challenge is to reconcile those responsibilities with the desires of their hearts, to survive tests of their devotion to each other without betraying their people.

Such tests typically emerge from political ambition, sexual competition, and perceived betrayals within a circle of half a dozen characters who are locked in a web of obligations and contentions. Eighteenth-century classical opera is a drama of court intrigue. Usually blame is not spread evenly: there is one, usually a tyrannical ruler, who is most guilty of subjecting others to cruel tests of their devotion. In *Giulio Cesare* it is the Egyptian king Ptolemy, who is struggling with his sister Cleopatra for the power to rule Egypt and who, besides decapitating Pompey and subjugating his widow and son, makes war on Cleopatra and her lover, Julius Caesar.

The sympathetic characters in these operas, bending under the testing, generally decide to sacrifice themselves in some way for the sake of their honor, their lover, or their country, in any case for what Piero Weiss calls "a Higher Cause." The "ethical underpinning" of this repertory, he writes, is "instruction through admirable examples of self-sacrifice."[7] Here, both Caesar and Cleopatra show their willingness to sacrifice themselves for each other by taking up arms in what seems a hopeless battle against Ptolemy. Other characters propose to commit suicide. Pompey's widow Cornelia, for instance, twice threatens to kill herself in the face of Ptolemy's or his general's unwanted advances; her son Sesto threatens to kill himself when he fails to avenge himself on Ptolemy for his father's death. Rarely does a character actually carry out a threat of suicide.

It was a great convenience for the librettists to set these operas in ancient Rome or other societies that were famous for considering suicide an honor-saving act. If they had taken place in contemporary Europe, where the church taught that suicide was a sin, even a threat of suicide would have jeopardized the sympathy of the audience. But on the understanding that different rules applied in the ancient world, the librettists could achieve a doubly sentimental resolution with a suicide threat by a Roman like Cornelia. She would win sympathy by being willing to die to save her honor, and when the need for self-sacrifice was unexpectedly removed, as is usual in operas of this period, the audience could feel both inspired by her honorable gesture and relieved that she survived. By means of this irresistible device, Italian opera on classical subjects touched the hearts of audiences all across Europe, providing them an unattainable ideal of lovers' devotion in a bygone world.

Giulio Cesare in Egitto

To study how this theme of testing and self-sacrifice is dramatized, it is necessary to follow the sequence of arias, observing which characters sing how many, of what kind, and in what order, and how these sequences build up an impression of the characters' differences and relationships. In *Giulio Cesare* Handel wrote the roles of Caesar and Cleopatra for two of the greatest singers of the eighteenth century, the alto castrato Senesino (the stage name of Francesco Bernardi) and the soprano Francesca Cuzzoni. True to Pier Jacopo Martello's formula, these roles include an equal number of arias, eight, plus a duet at the end of the opera, while none of the other six roles has nearly so many.

Caesar, fresh from defeating his rival Pompey, gets the first solo word. After arriving in Egypt to a chorus of well-wishers, he sings two arias that establish his heroic character. The first, "Presti omai l'egizia terra" ("Render at last the land of Egypt"), simply returns their greeting to the Egyptian people. But then Ptolemy's general delivers the severed head of Pompey to Caesar, and his second aria, "Empio, dirò, tu sei" ("You are wicked, I'll tell him"), displays righteous fury toward the absent Ptolemy. Both arias test the singer's virtuosity by making him compete with the agility of the violins. In the second, he expresses his rage in long, sustained explosions of notes, some full of words and others **melismatic** (flowing quickly on a single vowel). His phrases do not translate a spoken declamation of the lines into musical pitches and rhythms, as the acting style in the earliest operas did. Rather, like Sesto's phrases in "L'angue offeso," they provide a musically expressive emblem of the character of Caesar's thought at this moment.

This aria is followed by one from Cornelia: "Priva son d'ogni conforto" ("I am bereft of any comfort"). Having just learned of her husband's death by being shown his head, she responds to this horror with the superhuman

François Lemoyne's painting *Cleopatra* (ca. 1725), showing the queen dissolving a priceless pearl in vinegar to win a bet with the Roman general Mark Antony, is precisely contemporary with Handel's opera about Cleopatra's earlier affair with the Roman general Julius Caesar. Minneapolis Institute of Art.

William Hood Dunwoody Fund

self-control we might expect of a noble Roman wife. She begins her aria without introduction by the orchestra, a move so unusual in this repertory that it marks the directness of her expression. Likewise, she does not compete with the instruments; rather, they double and harmonize her lines. The lines themselves are completely unadorned, providing a natural declamation for her words. Her aria, not designed to impress any other character, is a picture of the sincerity and depth of her grief. Like Sesto, Cornelia is a secondary figure in the story, and the singer for whom Handel composed the role, Anastasia Robinson, was known as an expressive singer but not a virtuosic one. Nevertheless, when she holds the stage to sing, she presents herself not as a minor character but as a human being utterly capable of drawing us into her plight through her music.

Both Caesar and Cornelia have now given themselves over to their very different feelings at the murder of Pompey. When we first meet Cleopatra, by contrast, she is too busy calculating her advantage to indulge her feelings. Her brother Ptolemy intrudes and, hearing her boast that she can handle both Caesar and him, tries to put her in her place as a woman. Her reply is an elder-sisterly putdown, mocking his threats with a display of feminine insouciance and mocking his claims to the throne they share by insisting on his inexperience in both politics and love:

Non disperar: chi sa?	*Don't despair: who knows?*
Se al regno non l'avrai,	*If you're not lucky at ruling,*
Avrai sorte in amor.	*you'll be lucky in love.*

The mordents (quick, biting ornaments) on the repeated violin notes at the beginning of the aria set the mordant, teasing tone. She sings her own string of (written-out) mordents when she has first sung "amor." If Cleopatra has any worry about her power, she is certainly not letting her brother, or us, know about it yet. In the rest of this act her self-assurance only increases as she finds that Caesar is susceptible to her beauty and therefore might be willing to serve her political plans. At this point, in other words, her seduction of Caesar is a matter of ambition; her heart isn't yet in it, or in her music. There is no sign here of a character with Cornelia's depth.

Then we receive our first impression of Ptolemy. He is the tyrant who tests the steadfastness of all the others, and he seems all the more dangerous for being young and green. The aria "L'empio, sleale, indegno" ("The wicked, treacherous, contemptible one") expresses his determination to have Caesar

killed as an obstacle to his ambition to rule Egypt. His spiteful tone is rendered by the clipped phrases and staccato articulation of the music. Hearing this petulant fury so soon after the noble fury of that other male alto, Caesar, gives us a fix on both characters.

Accompanied recitative and the act of reflection The scene changes from the Egyptian court to Caesar's camp, where Pompey's ashes are displayed in an urn. Caesar delivers a monologue in recitative, introduced and accompanied by the full string section. This sort of recitative is known as *recitativo accompagnato* (**accompanied recitative**) or *recitativo obbligato*. It is used to give special weight and character to a speech—generally in monologue—that is too momentous to be conveyed in simple recitative, yet too long and complex to be subjected to the endless repetitions of an aria. In this accompanied recitative, "Alma del gran Pompeo" ("Soul of the great Pompey"), Caesar contemplates not only the sorry fate of Pompey, but the frailty of all human existence, and the halo of string chords that sustains his simple, dignified phrases through some startling modulations gives his thoughts the aura of a philosophical quest.

Caesar's monologue is succeeded by the appearance of Cleopatra, who throws herself at his feet and captures his heart. The next aria, then, has Caesar friskily telling Cleopatra she is prettier than a flower, "Non è si vago e bello" ("Not so pleasing and pretty"). When Ptolemy then invites him into the royal palace, he suspects that Ptolemy means to treat him as he treated

Sarah Connolly as Julius Caesar and Danielle de Niese as Cleopatra in a 2005 Glyndebourne (England) production of *Giulio Cesare*.
Robbie Jack/Corbis

Pompey. He expresses that suspicion in the simile aria "Va tacito e nascosto," comparing himself to a hunted animal, with the sound of the hunting horn providing the musical sign of the hunter:

Va tacito e nascosto,	Quietly and stealthily,
Quand'avido è di preda,	when he is avid for prey,
L'astuto cacciator.	moves the wily hunter.

The horn's soft, repeated eighth notes seem to describe the hunter's creeping step, while the imitation of that creeping figure between bass and horn (and later between bass and voice) increases the sense of a conspiracy hidden in all this stealthy movement. Already in the first act, a series of arias and one accompanied recitative have introduced Caesar to us in turn as heroic general, mournful philosopher, headlong lover, and wary politician.

In the second act the bond between Caesar and Cleopatra, created by calculation on her part and infatuation on his, turns into devotion. As Ptolemy tests that devotion by trying to get them both out of his way, Handel expands his palette of sounds, styles, and forms. Cleopatra invites Caesar to a lavishly staged seduction in a cedar grove, a spectacle in which scenery representing Mount Parnassus (home of the Muses) opens up to reveal Cleopatra enthroned as Virtue (!) in the midst of the nine Muses. The unveiling of this vision occurs to the most sumptuous music in the opera: an orchestral number (or **sinfonia**) in which nine instruments (including oboe, viola da gamba, harps, and theorbo) that stand in for ancient instruments are played onstage, reinforced by the full orchestra in the pit. Their music, a languorous dance, matches the music of the aria Cleopatra then sings, "V'adoro, pupille" ("I adore you, pupils").

Here, the aria is not a self-contained musical speech, but part of a larger musical sequence and stage spectacle. Caesar holds it up for a moment, just before the da capo, with a line of recitative that lets us know what an effect this spectacle is having on him. But when Cleopatra finishes the aria, the mountain closes around her, leaving her servant to invite Caesar to join Cleopatra in her bedchamber. He expresses his anticipation in an **obbligato aria** (in which a solo instrument creates an elaborate duet with the singer). In this case, "Se in fiorito ameno prato" ("If in a pleasing, flowery meadow"), the instrument is a violin, and its playful phrases, often completely unaccompanied, suggest the image of Cleopatra tantalizing Caesar and drawing him toward her.

Before he reaches her, however, we watch scenes of Cornelia repelling the advances of Ptolemy's general and of Ptolemy himself, after which Sesto saves her from suicide. Left to himself, Sesto, resolving to kill Ptolemy, sings "L'angue offeso." This violent world of political and sexual plotting is bound to disturb the love of Cleopatra and Caesar as well. In fact, when we return to them, just as she is offering herself to him, an officer rushes in to warn him

that Ptolemy has sent assassins to kill him. At this, Caesar returns to his heroic mode, in the aria "Al lampo dell'armi" ("To the flash of weapons"), and hurries off, leaving Cleopatra to confront what this threat to Caesar's life reveals to her: having seduced him in the first place in order to enlist his support in her political struggle against her brother, she has fallen so deeply in love that she now puts aside her political ambition in her desperation to save his life. This moment of self-examination is shaped into another accompanied recitative, the medium in eighteenth-century opera that, lacking the circularity of the da capo aria, conveys the progression of a character's thought, leading to a determination. Cleopatra's reflection forms the moral turning point of the opera.

The lovers' devotion Hearing the voices of the assassins calling "Let Caesar die!" as Caesar finishes his aria and rushes offstage, Cleopatra gives voice to panic in a short outburst accompanied by sustained string chords:

Che sento? Oh Dio!	*What am I hearing? Oh God!*
Morrà Cleopatra ancora.	*Then Cleopatra will die too.*

A decision-making scene like this is usually constructed as a debate. To project this inner debate, the librettist will present the character's thought process as a kind of ventriloquy, in which two sides of the person argue with each other. Here the regal side of Cleopatra silences the panic-stricken side as she tries to persuade herself she can defeat her brother's forces on her own:

Anima vil, che parli mai? Deh taci,
Avrò per vendicarmi
In bellicosa parte
Di Bellona in sembianza un cor di Marte.

You cowardly soul, what are you saying? Be quiet.
To avenge myself in combat,
appearing like [the war goddess] Bellona,
I will have the courage of Mars.

The orchestra announces this new stage of her debate by an agitated scrubbing on a single chord, and this continues on a series of different chords until she has finished portraying her bellicose side. Quieter, sustained chords follow, marking a return to her less self-assured side. No longer panicked, she recognizes her dependence on Caesar's well-being and prays to her gods to protect him:

Intanto, O Numi, voi che il ciel reggete,	*Meanwhile, gods who rule heaven,*
Difendete il mio bene,	*protect my beloved, for he is*
Ch'egli è del seno mio conforto e speme.	*the comfort and hope of my heart.*

In the three stages of this speech Cleopatra moves from helplessness to self-assurance and then resorts to prayer as her helplessness returns. But does she come to a decision in the third and final stage? She does in the sense that she rejects

Natalie Dessay as Cleopatra in Laurent Pelly's staging of *Giulio Cesare* at the Paris Opera, 2011. Sitting beside a plastic-wrapped bust of Caesar in an imaginary Museum of Egyptology, this Cleopatra is clearly thinking of her beloved as either doomed or dead.

© Marion Kalter/Lebrecht Music & Arts

what she considered in the second stage: the possibility that she can accomplish anything by her own might. Throwing herself on the mercy of the gods is her recognition that she is no longer a powerful queen, but a woman who can't survive emotionally or politically without a man she is helpless to save.

Furthermore, she now affirms that recognition by turning her prayer into an aria:

Se pietà di me non senti,	*If you feel no pity for me,*
Giusto ciel, io morirò.	*just heaven, I will die.*
Tu dà pace a miei tormenti	*Lay my torments to rest*
O quest'alma spirerò.	*or I will give up my spirit.*

Few of the numbers we have heard to this point can compare with this one for heartfelt expression—probably only Cornelia's aria, along with Caesar's accompanied recitative "Alma del gran Pompeo." And this is far more wrenching, partly because its texture is more dense, with pulsing chords in eighth notes, against which the violins play incessant, twisted, sigh-like phrases. The singer enters with the same four pitches as the first violin phrase but in her own eloquent configuration: each of her short phrases starts after the downbeat on which the preceding sigh of the violins landed, so that she seems to be gasping out her thoughts through her sighs. The aria is also more wrenching because of its recurring bass suspensions (bass notes that become dissonant when the harmony above them shifts); its chromatic sequences (phrases that rise step by painful step as they repeat); and its deceptive cadences (dodged—sometimes

hair-raisingly dodged—phrase endings that extend her grieving whenever she seems ready to let it rest). Finally, it is more powerful because it lasts much longer—dwells in its zone much longer—than those earlier numbers.

In this aria, along with the preceding accompanied recitative, Cleopatra needs to show her vulnerability in love—exactly what we wouldn't have suspected in the first act—if the testing of that love is to mean anything to us. Her aria serves that dramatic purpose in that it movingly displays her loyalty to a love that seems hopeless. Once she has finished, we next need to discover whether Caesar feels just as deeply about her. We don't have long to wait. At the beginning of the third act, a battle between Cleopatra's soldiers and Ptolemy's ends in her defeat and imprisonment. She sings yet another lament, "Piangerò la sorte mia" ("I'll bewail my fate"), this one alternately heartbroken and (in a highly contrasting middle strophe) furious. Then in a new scene we discover Caesar, who had thrown himself into the sea to escape Ptolemy's forces, standing alone on the shore, examining his situation.

His monologue begins with a surprisingly sweet orchestral sinfonia, leading into an accompanied recitative: He tells us how fate spared him from drowning, and how bereft he feels to be "the monarch of the world" with no troops to lead. When he begins an aria, accompanied by the sweet music of the earlier sinfonia, his words explain that sweetness: he is speaking to the gentle breezes, and the soft stirring of the violins in thirds represents the billowing of the breezes around him. Talking to the breezes was a conventional poetic conceit in that day for lovers communicating to their distant loved ones. In this way Caesar is asking us to look at him as a lover, not as a soldier.

Aure, deh, per pietà	Breezes, for mercy's sake,
Spirate al petto mio,	breathe into my breast
Per dar conforto, oh Dio!	to bring comfort, O God,
Al mio dolor.	to my sorrow.

In the second stanza, as the violins continue billowing, Caesar asks the breezes where his beloved is:

Dite: dov'è, che fa	Tell me, where is
L'idolo del mio sen,	the idol of my bosom,
L'amato e dolce ben	the beloved, sweet boon
Di questo cor.	of this heart, and what is she doing.

But apparently the sight of his destroyed army around him distracts him from completing the aria—he breaks it off just at the point of returning to the top and launches into more accompanied recitative:

Ma d'ogni intorno i' veggio	But all around I see
Sparse d'arme e d'estinti	the unfortunate sands
L'infortunate arene,	strewn with weapons and corpses:
Segno d'infausto annunzio al fin sarà.	an omen foretelling a bad ending.

This is not a thought to tell to the breezes, and so it makes sense that Handel sets it to separate music from the aria, after which Caesar returns to the aria and completes it.

This interruption, taking us out of the character's zone, is an extraordinary occurrence in a da capo aria. And because it is extraordinary, it prompts us to realize that although the Egyptian queen may forget her royal status under the spell of desperate love, the Roman general, even while playing the blushing lover, never forgets that he is destined to be "monarch of the world." We cannot reconcile these two sides of his identity the way eighteenth-century audiences could: the sweetness of the poetic conceit and the music, to say nothing of the singer's alto range, do not fit readily with modern ideas of a heroic lover. But it is possible for us to appreciate this as Caesar's moment of truth, just as crucial to the drama as Cleopatra's prayer. For us to believe in the strength of their love, we need to feel that they have both been transformed by that love. In "Se pietà di me non senti" we find the calculating Cleopatra overwhelmed by love; in "Aure, deh, per pietà" we find the proud soldier Caesar softened by it.

It is striking that at this point of greatest tension in the plot, the moment when Caesar and Cleopatra are in the greatest danger, their feelings are not represented by a love duet. In fact, they sang no love duet earlier when they first fell in love (as they do in Sartorio's opera of 1677 and as lovers in Cavalli or Lully normally do). And now, from the moment in the second act when Caesar flees assassination until the moment late in the third when he rescues Cleopatra from captivity, they are never together onstage. But at the end, when they are reunited and triumphant, they sing one full love duet as well as a love-duet passage in the middle of the final chorus of general celebration.

A drama of interchangeable parts It is characteristic of eighteenth-century opera to isolate the lovers from each other, keeping each from knowing whether the other is still faithful, or even alive. Their love is tested by the intrigues of others right up to the dénouement. In *Giulio Cesare*, as in many other operas by Handel and his contemporaries, the heroine and hero express their desperate devotion to each other in separate monologue recitatives and arias, almost always near the middle of the work. This is not to say that all Handel operas—let alone all eighteenth-century operas on classical subjects—are the same, either in plot or layout of arias. But a common general plot structure, built around the theme of the testing of love, determined that certain kinds of musical numbers were apt to occur only at the beginning, middle, or end of the work.

Because the kinds of situations that characters would find themselves in were generic, many of the numbers they sang could be freely exchanged. Composers recycled arias from earlier operas or shuffled them around in the course of rehearsals and revivals: Handel wrote Caesar's simile aria of

the stealthy hunter, "Va tacito e nascosto," in the first place for Cleopatra's confidante to sing, but reassigned it to Caesar by the time the opera opened.[8] Star singers, as Martello told us, would introduce their favorite arias from other operas into a new work. Librettists and composers often created a whole work, called a *pasticcio* (pastry), out of numbers recycled from earlier works. As Barry Emslie writes, in this world of operatic composition, "productivity—operatic carpentry—was everything."[9] That produced a particular experience of the dramatic characters. Handel and his contemporaries created their characters "facet by facet,"[10] through the sequence of arias and other numbers they gave those characters to sing as they interact with each other. As a result, we perceive each character as if in a series of snapshots, taken at different moments of crisis. The snapshots are not connected for us by a distinctive personality so much as by the character's capacity to perform appropriately and eloquently in every situation, no matter how daunting.

In *Giulio Cesare* all the characters are locked together in a power struggle, constantly turning the tables on each other and facing new dilemmas. In the course of the struggle Caesar and Cleopatra engage us more fully than any of the other characters. They are not more noble or sympathetic than Cornelia or Sesto, but they sing more solos, in a greater variety of situations, and therefore display a wider range of expression. Beyond that, they are the two characters in whom love and political aspiration combine, so that we come to care about their relationship, not just about them as individuals, and about the relationship between their love and their political fortunes. The variety and virtuosity of their music come to seem a sign of their capacity to withstand the testing of their love in the crucible of political struggle.

Like the Hollywood Western or the detective novel, eighteenth-century opera on classical subjects taught its audience much the same lesson over and over, drawing on much the same stock of characters, situations, musical conventions, and plot progressions. And as in the Western and detective novel, the formulas allowed audiences to appreciate the highlights of an individual work and to keep their bearings, without even paying strict attention from beginning to end. The fact that the story was formulaic doesn't mean that it didn't matter. On the contrary, it indicates that eighteenth-century audiences had an insatiable need to keep witnessing a love that could be tested, deceived, tortured, driven to the point of suicide, and yet survive.

Rameau and French Opera

Change did not come so readily to French opera as to Italian in the early eighteenth century. One reason was that for decades after the death of Lully in 1687, his operas (called **tragédies en musique** in France) continued to be

performed and to set the standard for any new works. Innovation was more acceptable when it took place within a somewhat new genre like the *opéra-ballet*, in which each act had its own dramatic subject. In the *tragédie en musique* Lully was not challenged until 1733, half a century after his death, when Jean-Philippe Rameau wrote *Hippolyte et Aricie* (*Hippolytus and Aricia*). At the time of Rameau's death an obituary writer looked back at the premiere of *Hippolyte* as "the starting point of the revolution that has occurred in French music and of its new advances."[11] Yet if, like the original listeners, we measure *Hippolyte* against the tradition of Lully, we may be disconcerted to find ourselves thinking that it is like a Lully opera, only more so.

The scenic spectacle in *Hippolyte* and other Rameau operas—scenes in Hell, natural disasters, magnificent temple rituals, gods descending from heaven—is just as prominent as in Lully's operas and accompanied by more spectacular music. While a Lully work might include over a dozen dance numbers, Rameau's *Dardanus* has thirty.[12] He used the chorus just as frequently as Lully and made it perform more complex and varied music. Rameau's solo vocal lines, in both recitatives and airs, are in the distinctive French style of Lully's—generally syllabic, but full of appoggiaturas and other graces, especially at cadences, and frequently changing in meter. Rameau just wrote more accompanied recitatives and more long, elaborately accompanied airs, including some in the da capo form borrowed from the Italian practice of his day. So what are the points that led people of Rameau's time to say that *Hippolyte et Aricie* was the starting point of a revolution?

Accompaniment as Soundtrack: An Air in *Dardanus*

The next sentence of that same obituary reads, "At first people were astonished at music so much more laden and more fertile in images than they were accustomed to hear in the theater." What the writer meant by "laden" (the French is "chargée") we can guess from other comments of the time, many of which dwell on Rameau's almost continuous use of the whole orchestra. French listeners, after all, were accustomed by Lully and the whole French tradition to hearing singers deliver their words in an unfailingly clear musical declamation: melodies that stuck close to a spoken delivery of the lines, basso continuo accompaniments that gave a discreet underpinning, choruses sung in rhythmic unison, and in all the vocal numbers few repetitions of words to hold up the dramatic dialogue. Rameau pushed against all that. His choral writing, for instance, is far more complex than Lully's, the interplay of melodic lines obscuring the words. But it was above all the rich orchestral accompaniments he composed to the solo vocal numbers that angered his critics. They were "insolent," one wrote, "making a mockery of their subject." To Jean-Jacques Rousseau, Rameau "made his accompaniments so confused,

Painted model by Piero Bonifazio Algieri for the stage set of Act 5, scene 3, of Rameau's *Dardanus*, probably in its 1760 revival at the Paris Opera. Models like this one in the collection of the Château de Chambord provide a vivid impression of the glories of the eighteenth-century French operatic stage.

Akg-images

so laden, so frequent, that the head has difficulty in following the continual racket of the various instruments during the performance of those operas, which would be quite pleasant to hear if they deafened the ears a little less."

Yet Rameau's accompaniments are crucial to his highly original conception of opera, one that might have perplexed his earliest audiences, but that he never compromised. His operas are dramas of conflicting atmospheres that are tied to moral conditions and identified with the natural setting in which the characters find themselves. The orchestral accompaniments, especially for the soul-baring monologues of the principal characters, can't be understood as simply a harmonic and rhythmic ground against which the singers' musical rhetoric plays, the way they could in almost all seventeenth-century opera. Nor do they really collaborate with the vocal melody in expressing the character's emotional state, as the accompaniments do in most eighteenth-century Italian arias, including Handel's. Instead, they create an atmosphere of thought and feeling from which the singer draws the capacity to express her- or himself. This instrumental texture has its own presence and force in the drama, sometimes independent of the character who partakes of it.

It is hardly surprising, then, that in Rameau's operas the important monologues tend to come at the beginning of an act or scene that introduces a change of setting. This device ties the character's reflections to the new place, time of day, or moment in the action. The orchestral introduction, or ritornello, to the air establishes a musical atmosphere fitting both the setting and the character's mood, whereupon the singer's words connect the two explicitly.

"O jour affreux" At the beginning of the third act of *Dardanus*, the princess Iphise connects the misery she feels to a sense of time: her opening words, "O jour affreux" ("O frightful day"), convey her realization that she has reached a terrible moment in her life. Dardanus, whom she loves, has been captured, and (since he is her father's enemy) she feels both horror at his certain death and remorse for loving him. It is the long orchestral introduction, however, that really makes us feel what this day is like for her. This ritornello is twenty-eight measures of continuous movement in quarter-note chords, restlessly pressing forward by step, now upward and now downward, stumbling on almost every downbeat (often the top voices pause while the bass keeps moving, creating a suspension) and then pressing forward again, never coming to a rest until the whole passage ends (see Example 8.3). It is a remarkable musical picture of an agitated soul, trapped by conflicting loyalties, forever tugged by one as she yearns toward the other.

8.3 Rameau, *Dardanus*: Act 3, scene 1, "O jour affreux"

This is the ritornello to Iphise's air, but it clearly isn't laying down her melody for her, the way most operatic ritornellos do. No singer could sing the continuous melody that the violins play here without breaking the phrases to breathe. Instead, Rameau gives Iphise her own melody in discrete, fairly short phrases, while continuing the orchestra's atmospheric accompaniment. But he no longer maintains it so relentlessly. At Iphise's opening words, the orchestra suspends its climbing quarter-note motion, then resumes it, only to suspend it again, even allowing her to switch from duple to triple meter as she completes the first line of her text: "O jour affreux! Le ciel met le comble à mes maux" ("O frightful day! Heaven has topped up my troubles"). The motion resumes as she begins her second line: "Dardanus est captif! Dieux! sa perte est certaine" ("Dardanus is a captive! Gods, his doom is certain"). But that motion is suspended again when she sings "sa perte est certaine," and the triple meter returns when she repeats it.

Given that the ritornello derives its powerful atmosphere from the relentless repetition of a rhythmic motive, why would Rameau use the motive less repetitively once Iphise began to sing? The rhythm of her words does not require any switch in musical meter—words of any poetic meter can be set to any musical meter. Instead, Rameau seems to change the musical meter as a way of imparting seriousness to the character's expression. French composers thought that a character in a taut dramatic situation, like Iphise, should express herself in rhythmically unpredictable and therefore edgy-sounding outbursts, not in the singsong of a regular meter.

French composers since Lully had used this device of metrical variety in the sung portions of their dramatic airs. The difference with Rameau is that he was yoking together in one number two kinds of music—atmospheric music for the orchestra and rhetorically expressive melody for the singer—that worked on seemingly incompatible rhythmic principles. As the air proceeds, it seems as if Rameau gradually gives up the atmosphere in favor of the rhetoric. In the second vocal strophe the ritornello motive continues, but in the orchestral break after that strophe, Rameau turns to a new ritornello in triple meter. In the third vocal strophe, which alternates between three different meters, the original ritornello music is not heard at all. But when the singer is finished, that music returns to conclude the air, and it feels as if the ritornello music was present, if often unheard, all along. Its return in effect encloses Iphise's whole outpouring of thoughts in the persisting atmosphere of her despair.

This subtle accommodation of two different rhythmic concepts—one necessarily unvarying and the other necessarily varying—within a single air is by no means unique to "O jour affreux." It is found over and over in Rameau's monologue airs, including Dardanus's "Lieux funestes" ("Funereal spot") in the 1744 revision of *Dardanus*, and Télaïre's "Tristes apprêts" ("Sad preparations") in *Castor et Pollux* (1737). Recall the first scene of Verdi's *La traviata* (see Chapter 4), where a dance band is playing music in the next room that the characters onstage—Violetta and Alfredo—can presumably hear, but are ignoring. In the Rameau monologue airs, by contrast, the orchestral music represents something more like a movie soundtrack. We don't imagine that the character onstage hears it. We hear it as addressed directly to us, feeding us a way to take in the scene, the moment, the character's dilemma. In a movie the soundtrack music and the dialogue come at us from different tracks, and because the characters are speaking rather than singing, we have no trouble apprehending the two tracks separately while feeling their effect jointly. But in an operatic air the orchestral and vocal tracks belong to a single musical texture. Even when we hear the orchestral music as "soundtrack" to the singer's melody, they both have to fit rhythmically and tonally into a single musical frame. That is what Rameau achieved.

Denis Diderot

Diderot (1713–1784), philosopher, novelist, dramatist, arts critic, and editor of the *Encyclopédie*, was a central figure of the French Enlightenment. He wrote his satire *Rameau's Nephew (Le Neveu de Rameau)* sometime in the 1760s or 1770s, a time of enormous interest in reforming opera to make it truer to the nature of human feeling and expression. Diderot's satire exerted no influence at the time (as the dedication to Gluck's *Alceste* did) because it was not published for several decades. But the thoughts spoken by the character "Him" (modeled on a nephew of the composer Rameau) represent better than any other text of the time a longing for opera to express passion at its most extreme.

Declamation should be pictured as a line, and melody as another line that snakes up and down above it. The more powerful and true the declamation—the model for the song—the more the song mirroring it will break it into separate phrases; then the truer the song, and the more beautiful. And that's what our young musicians have understood so well.

The animal cry of passion should be what determines the melodic line. Expressions of passion should come fast one upon another; they should be brief and their meaning fragmented, suspenseful, so that the musician can use the whole as well as each part, omit a word or repeat it, add a word that's missing, turn the phrase upside-down and inside-out like a polyp, without destroying its meaning.

The passions must be intense and the sensibility of the musician and lyric poet extreme. Almost always, the aria is the culminating point of the scene: we need exclamations, interjections, pauses, interruptions, affirmations, denials; we call out, invoke, shout, moan, weep, laugh openly. No wit, no epigrams, none of those pretty conceits. They're too remote from simple nature.

Rameau's Nephew, 1760s or 70s. Translation by Margaret Mauldon, in Diderot, *Rameau's Nephew and First Satire* (Oxford: Oxford University Press, 2006), pp. 63–64, 70–71.

In fact, Rameau can be credited with creating the modern concept of soundtrack music—music to be heard against words rather than music to sing words with—long before there were movies. More than any Western composer before him and more than any other of the eighteenth century, he devoted his music to the functions of background: conjuring up a musical atmosphere to suit the setting, action, and mood of a dramatic scene; sustaining or altering it, as the action required; and guiding the movements of dancers and actors onstage with musical gestures. Called by one biographer "a poet and a magician" in music,[13] Rameau shows his atmospheric wizardry with voices as well as instruments, in dance music and choruses as well as airs, in abrupt changes of musical character as well as in his systematic musical coloring of whole scenes or acts.

Disruption and Authority: *Hippolyte et Aricie*

In *Hippolyte et Aricie* Rameau gives the whole second act, set in the Underworld, his characteristic musical coloring. In a sense the act is a diversion: a principal character, the Athenian king Theseus, is sidetracked on his way home from war by a fruitless attempt to rescue a friend from the Underworld. His family, learning that he has gone there, naturally assumes that he is dead—and that is

the only thing that has consequences for the drama as a whole. But this diversion allows Rameau to paint in consistently dark musical colors. For one thing, he and his librettist, Simon-Joseph Pellegrin, allowed only male characters in this act and therefore (because French opera didn't use castratos) only low voices. We hear Theseus (a bass), the gatekeeper Tisiphone (tenor) — who answers Theseus's pleas for admittance by echoing those pleas in his face — Pluto (bass), Mercury (tenor), a male chorus of Infernal Divinities, and strangest of all, three male singers representing the Parcae, or Goddesses of Fate. Since their grim message to Theseus at the end of the act is, as we'll see, what draws the attention of the audience back to the main action, it makes a disconcerting effect for that message to be delivered by male actors dressed as goddesses. But their low voices also help keep the sound of the whole act dark.

The orchestra, meanwhile, maintains its own variety of hellish tones through most of the act. Pluto responds to Theseus's pleas by calling on the rivers of the Underworld to avenge him on Theseus (in the air "Qu'à servir mon courroux tout l'Enfer se prépare" / "Let all of Hell prepare to serve my anger"), the threatening rivers represented by a demonically swirling figuration in the violins. This is followed by diabolical dances and choral music in spiky or frenzied rhythms. In the middle of this come the only calm

Stéphane Degout as Theseus, with the three Goddesses of Fate in Act 2 of Rameau's *Hippolyte et Aricie*, staging by Ivan Alexandre. Théâtre du Capitole, Toulouse, France, 2009.
Patrice Nin

numbers in the act: an anthem-like pronouncement by the Goddesses of Fate that only Destiny can determine when Theseus will die ("Du Destin le vouloir suprême" / "The supreme will of destiny") and a prayer by Theseus to his father Neptune to get him released from this Underworld that he was previously so ready to enter ("Puisque Pluton est inflexible" / "Since Pluto is unyielding"). The tone of this air is set by its measured, wave-like accompaniment, which almost makes us forget we are in Hell. This is a prayer by a character who knows just what he wants, unlike Iphise in her monologue. Accordingly, his melodic lines here are so purposeful that, unlike hers, they create no metrical disruption to the steady rhythm of his accompanying waves.

After more negotiations, set to more demonic music, Theseus is told he may leave the Underworld. But the Goddesses of Fate get in one last dig before he goes. To violin flourishes of furious energy they proclaim, "What sudden horror your fate inspires in us!" ("Quelle soudaine horreur ton destin nous inspire!"). In a creepy passage of chromatic sliding (so difficult for the original singers that Rameau had to rewrite it), they tease him for leaving: "Where are you running to, you unlucky man? Tremble with fright!" ("Où cours-tu, malheureux? Tremble! Frémis d'effroi!"). And to a phrase of schoolmarmish musical imitation they shake their fingers at him, delivering their gloating lesson: "You are leaving the realm of Hell only to find a Hell at home" ("Tu quittes l'infernal empire, pour trouver les enfers chez toi"). All the thundering threats of Pluto and his chorus of devils are nothing for Theseus to bear, compared with the cruelty of this news, delivered in mocking tones by a male trio in drag—a cast that in itself mocks the classical personification of fate. It is no joke that Theseus is mocked at his entrance to the Underworld (by Tisiphone) and at his departure (by the Fates): mockery is one of Hell's surest weapons.

Disrupting the musical texture A number sung by Theseus later in the opera shows another important side of Rameau's originality. Theseus returns home at the climax of a powerful scene between his wife Phaedra and his son by a previous marriage, Hippolytus. Phaedra, thinking Theseus dead, has confessed to a guilty passion for Hippolytus, and when he then spurns her, she seizes his sword in order to kill herself. Theseus arrives at the moment when Hippolytus is taking the sword away from her and mistakenly assumes that Hippolytus is attempting to rape her. Left alone, Theseus wrestles briefly and affectingly with his conscience as a father, but decides that Hippolytus must pay with his life. Standing on the seashore, Theseus invokes Neptune one more time, in the air "Puissant maître des flots" ("Powerful master of the waves"), and then in recitative asks him to bring death to Hippolytus. Neptune's response is immediate: the sea begins to foam.

Rameau renders this turbulence almost palpable in a virtuosic piece of orchestral nature painting (see Example 8.4). This number turns out not to be an independent orchestral number, but the introduction to an air. As it continues, Theseus exults that his wish to punish his son is working:

Mais, de courroux, l'onde s'agite;
Tremble, tu vas périr, trop coupable Hippolyte.

But the waves are agitated with anger;
tremble — you are going to perish, most culpable Hippolytus.

8.4   Rameau, *Hippolyte et Aricie:* Act 3, scene 7, Foaming of the Waves

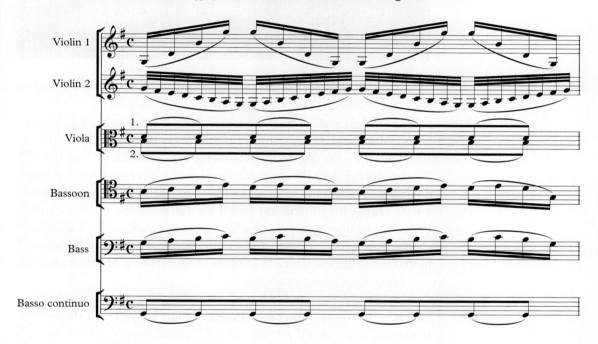

Just then, when Theseus is in the middle of speaking the name of Hippolytus, Rameau stops the music abruptly in its tracks. In a new meter, to a completely new orchestral figuration, Theseus announces that he has overcome any lingering hesitation he had about wishing death on his son:

Le sang a beau crier; je n'entends plus sa voix:

The tie of blood has cried out in vain; I no longer hear its voice.

The abrupt break suggests that in speaking his son's name, Theseus finds the unholy strength to deny the tug of fatherly love and therefore no longer needs to displace the guilt for killing Hippolytus onto his own father, Neptune.

The Foaming of the Waves in Act 3 of *Hippolyte et Aricie*, with Stéphane Degout in the front as Theseus and Jérôme Varnier behind as Neptune. Théâtre du Capitole, Toulouse, France, 2009.

Patrice Nin

At the very moment when Theseus no longer needs to hear the sound of Neptune's foaming waves, then, Rameau removes them.

This shattering of the musical pattern, while startling, is perfectly characteristic of Rameau. He establishes an atmosphere for an air with a strongly rhythmic ritornello, only to have the singer stray from that rhythm (Iphise's "O jour affreux") or the orchestra abandon it (the present case). A dance number will sometimes establish a strong bass line or pattern of figuration, only to change the pattern, and with it the dancers' steps, without warning. In *Dardanus* he interrupts a dialogue between two characters with an offstage chorus singing in a jarringly different mood. These effects are not signs of quirkiness on Rameau's part. In an opera of atmospheres, drama comes from disrupting the reigning atmosphere.

Even Theseus's revenge on his son is disrupted. A sea monster sent by Neptune kills Hippolytus, whereupon Phaedra admits her guilt and Hippolytus's innocence, then goes off and kills herself. Theseus, overcome by remorse, is getting ready to drown himself when Neptune tells him that the goddess Diana has restored Hippolytus to life, but that Destiny has forbidden him ever to see his son again. Theseus's two great airs in this scene give the opera its moral resolution. In one he grapples with his guilt ("Grands dieux! de quel remords" / "Great gods! With what remorse"); in the other he accepts the penalty imposed on him and wishes his son happiness ("Je ne te verrai plus!" / "I will never see you again!"). Though the work is named for Hippolytus and his lover Aricia, their joyful reunion in the succeeding scene seems by comparison an almost perfunctory tying up of loose threads. Much more than in the older versions of the story on which it was modeled—the plays of Euripides and Racine—the center of gravity in this opera turns out to be Theseus.

Disrupting parental authority A father who suffers remorse for the harm he has inflicted on the younger generation was a novel figure on the operatic stage in 1733. After *Hippolyte*, Rameau went on to feature similar father figures in later operas: Teucer in *Dardanus*, who allows his daughter to marry his enemy at the command of Venus; and Boréas in *Les Boréades* (composed by 1763), who has to admit that his daughter's suitor is more suitable than he believed. Evidently characters like these struck a chord with eighteenth-century audiences.

After Rameau, remorseful and abdicating fathers continued to appear in tragic operas, challenging traditional ideas of authority within the family and the state. Among these were both Italian and French settings of Euripides' story of Iphigenia in Aulis (a French setting by Gluck appeared in 1774) and Mozart's *Idomeneo* (1781). At the same time, comic operas were offering tales of remorseful rulers (figurative father figures) that challenged traditional ideas of authority in the political arena. These included Mozart's *Marriage of Figaro* (1786) and operas on the theme of the "generous Turk" (such as Mozart's *Abduction from the Seraglio*, 1782). The issue of authority, in its widest sense, was becoming supremely urgent in eighteenth-century society, and if Rameau was forced in some respects to follow in the footsteps of Lully, he nevertheless led the way in showing how powerfully opera could speak to this pressing new issue.

Gluck and the Late Eighteenth Century

In the years before Rameau's death in 1764, a creative team assembled by the director of theaters in Vienna, Count Giacomo Durazzo, was experimenting with ways to challenge the formulas of Italian opera on classical subjects. The team included the librettist Ranieri de' Calzabigi, the choreographer Gasparo Angiolini, and the composer Christoph Willibald Gluck. They collaborated on an innovative pantomime ballet about Don Juan in 1761 and an opera on the Orpheus story, *Orfeo ed Euridice* (which featured a large role for ballet), in 1762. Calzabigi had paid attention to the French operatic tradition, including Rameau, during a long sojourn in Paris and had written a treatise in which he advocated the reintroduction of some features of French opera—chorus, ballet, and spectacular scenic effects—into Italian opera.[14]

By the time of his second operatic collaboration with Gluck, *Alceste* (produced in Vienna in 1767), Calzabigi had developed his ideas into an extraordinary essay, which he wrote from the composer's perspective, so that Gluck would sign it and would seem to have written it. In this essay, which appeared as the dedication of the published score, Calzabigi makes no reference to French opera; his case is worded as an attack on the conventions of Italian opera—conventions that both he and Gluck knew well because they had lived with them in their own work for decades. It is striking that

he describes the novelty of *Alceste* almost entirely in terms of what they left out: "When I undertook to write the music of *Alceste*, I decided to divest it wholly of all the abuses which, introduced either by the ill-considered vanity of the singers or by the excessive indulgence of the composers, have for so long disfigured Italian opera." The list of divestments includes vocal ornaments and display, especially at dramatically inappropriate moments; any "tedious instrumental introduction" that would "stop an actor in the heat of the dialogue"; the endless text repetitions and circularity of the da capo aria; and the "divisive split in the dialogue caused by aria and recitative." The one positive description he allows of the music of *Alceste* is that it strives for "a simple beauty." As to the libretto (it was, after all, the librettist who wrote this, even if the composer signed it), the dedication claims that *Alceste* represents "a new plan for the drama," replacing "flowery descriptions, superfluous similes, cold, sententious morals with the language of the heart, vehement passions, interesting situations, and an ever-changing spectacle."[15]

Obsession and Amplification: *Orfeo ed Euridice* and *Alceste*

Calzabigi could have mentioned many more conventions, especially dramatic ones, that he and Gluck avoided. But since they chose to write their first two experimental operas on two of the oldest and best-known operatic subjects, we—like their contemporaries—can discover for ourselves, by comparison with earlier settings, how unconventional their treatment was. In both works they stripped the plot, as it had traditionally been presented, of most of its basic action, to say nothing of subplots and intrigue, and of some minor and even major characters. Both operas begin relatively late in the story. In *Orfeo ed Euridice* we don't get to meet Eurydice at her wedding, as we do in the early court operas; she is already dead when the opera begins. In *Alceste* we don't get to see the king, Admetus, being wounded in the battle to rescue Alceste, as we do in Lully's opera. This Admetus is already dying at the opening, and the audience isn't told why, any more than his wife and subjects are.

In both cases we are simply presented with a grievous situation and invited to contemplate the mourners in their struggle with a loss. Sad choruses fill us with sympathy for the principals, who elicit that feeling simply by posing in front of us. The opening number of *Orfeo ed Euridice* is a chorus over which Orpheus sings the name Euridice three times and nothing more. Alceste too enters during a chorus, not even singing, but clutching her two children. Whereas Lully's Alceste was a bride, Gluck's Alceste and children make a pitiable spectacle as widow-and-orphans-to-be.

The "simple beauty" of these two opening scenes is that they leave us ready to shed tears for characters before those characters have even told us about themselves. In the course of the drama the characters hardly seem to operate in a world of other people and external events. The action we follow is the interior history of someone dealing with loss. It is a psychological progression, a largely unverbalized contention between opposing sides of someone's soul — sides that are often represented in the mute, symbolic figures of dancers.

When this Orpheus wants to enter the Underworld, he doesn't plead his special circumstance to Charon by elaborate singing and playing, as Monteverdi's Orpheus does. He faces a mob of singing and dancing furies and specters and wears down their resistance — that is, his own fear — by persistent strumming (his lyre is an offstage band of harp and pizzicato strings) and by repeating a simple plea for pity. Once the furies yield, he finds himself in the Elysian Fields, the part of the Underworld reserved for the shades of heroes. There the delectable garden scenery, an enchanting minuet (the Dance of the Blessed Spirits), and the breathtaking mood music to which he sings "Che puro ciel" ("What pure heaven") while contemplating this vision of paradise make us feel that he has reached his goal. He just needs to find Eurydice, and they can leave. There has been no Pluto to persuade, no Proserpine to help Orpheus plead his case. In fact, the only solo character in the opera other than Orpheus and Eurydice is Cupid (Amore) — the spirit of love necessary to sustain his faith that he can win Eurydice back. In this Orpheus opera the battle is all in his head.

Likewise, in Gluck's *Alceste* the battle the title character fights is with herself, once she learns that Admetus can be brought back to life only if someone else is willing to die in his place. At this point in Lully's version, Admetus's father and others who ought to be willing to sacrifice themselves give their reasons for declining the honor. But in Gluck's opera, when the oracle of Apollo announces what it would take to save Admetus, the whole chorus that fills the stage suddenly takes flight. Alceste is left alone with her small children, and there is no question who is going to die. Her struggle is nonetheless long and tortuous. In the accompanied recitative "Ove son?" ("Where am I?") she resolves to be the one to sacrifice herself. In the aria "Ombre, larve," her voice bolstered by trombones and other winds, she draws on an "unknown force" within herself to prove to the infernal gods, and herself, that she has the strength to face death:

Joseph Siffred Duplessis, *Christoph Willibald Gluck at the Spinet*, 1775. This portrait of Gluck as a model of creative inspiration was painted shortly after he began composing operas for Paris. Kunsthistorischesmuseum, Vienna.
Erich Lessing/Art Resource, NY

| Ombre, larve, compagne di morte, | Ghosts, phantoms, comrades in death, |
| Non vi chiedo, non voglio pietà. | I don't seek, don't want your pity. |

But she protests so much because she is still not ready to die. In another scene she goes alone into a thick, dark forest sacred to the infernal gods, where she symbolically faces her fear of death. In the scenic monologue "Partì. Sola restai" ("She is gone, and I've stayed here alone") she calls up the Lord of the Abyss, and when his voice sounds and "luminous spectres" appear out of the woods, she passes out. When she comes to, a chorus of invisible demons engages her in a many-against-one dialogue (like the one Orpheus has at the gates of the Underworld), warning her of the finality of what she is proposing to do. In the course of this confrontation she discovers the real resolve to go forward — and even to wangle from the demons a short delay while she bids farewell to her husband and children. This demonstration of how Alceste comes to terms with her fear, stretched over two scenes, is the heart of Gluck's opera. In Lully's, by contrast, Alceste is offstage while the other characters explain why they decline to sacrifice themselves, and when they are finished, she has done the deed and Admetus has come back from the dead. Lully's opera isn't about what it takes for Alceste to give up her life; Gluck's is barely about anything else.

Simple beauty This is the kind of "simple beauty" Calzabigi gave his plots. But the dedication, signed if not written by Gluck, directs attention more explicitly to the simple beauty of the music. And indeed, Gluck's music in both *Orfeo ed Euridice* and *Alceste* represents as radical a simplification as Calzabigi's librettos, when it is compared with the music of Handel and Rameau and others of the previous generation. For one thing, in his dance numbers Gluck embraced the trend of his day for plainness of style and regularity of form: songful melodies, with relaxed harmonic movement, in **periodic phrases** (long complementary phrases with clearly articulated smaller phrases within them, as in the verse or refrain of "Jingle Bells"). Those features can be found, for instance, in the Dance of the Blessed Spirits (Act 2, scene 2) of *Orfeo ed Euridice*, where the melodic phrases, rising and falling with the regularity of steady breaths, give the music a feeling much prized in Gluck's day: naturalness.

Gluck provides even more regularity of this sort in the processional *ballo* (or dance, but we would call it a march) that opens the scene at the Temple of Apollo (Act 1, scene 3) in *Alceste*. Priests are leading animals to the temple to be sacrificed, in preparation for the pronouncement by Apollo's oracle that Admetus is doomed unless someone comes forward to die in his place. The phrases are built up in pairs within pairs: two-measure pairs within four-measure pairs within eight-measure pairs. The bass and chords change like clockwork on every beat. The melody seems more fluid, but it too is extraordinarily regular in its rhythm: almost every measure contains either two half notes

or a half note followed by two quarters. This music, because it is so radically restricted, not only regulates the movements of the priests, but casts a spell of what seems like supernatural control over this scene of ritual without rising above a whisper. Nevertheless it seems natural, with a structure of breathing built into its phrases, all of equal length, each one smoothly rising and just as smoothly falling. It has the four-part texture of a hymn and is just as memorable and singable. In fact, the flutes and strings sound uncannily as if there are human voices mixed in with them. Gluck's operas are filled with ritual scenes of humans in contact with divinities. For such scenes he always called on this musical language both superhumanly formal and naturally expressive.

"Che farò senza Euridice?" It's easy to understand how music that is so regular in its rhythms and periodic in its phrasing would be suitable for dancing or ritual procession. But can it be appropriate for the vocal numbers? Throughout the history of opera (a century and a half, by Gluck's day), composers had balanced acting styles of vocal music (tending to irregularity in phrasing) with singing styles (tending to regularity). And Gluck did the same; there are still both arias and recitatives in *Orfeo ed Euridice* and *Alceste*. Where he departed from tradition was in favoring a highly periodic singing style in arias created for moments of the highest dramatic tension.

One aria of this type is heard in the third act of *Orfeo ed Euridice*. The attempt by Orpheus to lead Eurydice out of the Underworld without looking back at her is an action that is accomplished quickly in Peri's *Euridice*

Details of the statues of Eurydice and Orpheus by Antonio Canova, 1776, when Gluck's opera was a sensation across Europe. The statues are free-standing, but designed to dramatize the instant when Eurydice is about to be dragged back to Hades (by the infernal hand that is shown seizing hers), while Orpheus's face registers the shock of realizing that in turning back, he has condemned her to that fate. Museo Correr, Venice.
Mimmo Jodice/Corbis

and Monteverdi's *Orfeo*. Once he *has* looked back and she is condemned to return to the Underworld, both Peri and Monteverdi give Orpheus long recitatives of reflection and decision. Their versions, after all, focus on Orpheus's struggle over his identity. In Gluck's opera, by contrast, where the focus is on the psychology of love, the approach to the fatal glance is prolonged. An extended sequence of recitatives mixed with a duet and an aria dramatize Eurydice's misreading of Orpheus's behavior and his response to her misreading. Then, when he has looked back and she has disappeared, Gluck gives Orpheus just a short aria demonstrating his disorientation:

Che farò senza Euridice?	*What will I do without Eurydice?*
Dove andrò senza il mio ben?	*Where will I go without my treasure?*

The melody of this aria (which has been Gluck's most celebrated number ever since his day) is full of pairs of tiny phrases, either complementary (periodic) or identical, creating a singsong effect: in the first strophe the first phrase of each pair begins "Che farò" and the second begins "Dove andrò" (see Example 8.5). There is no rhetorical fire in these phrases, but then Orpheus is not trying to argue with anyone here. The one scene of confrontation between two characters in this opera has just finished, and in that scene Orpheus was not at liberty to tell Eurydice the only thing he cared to say: that he was avoiding looking at her because that was the condition of her release from the Underworld. Now he is beyond reasoning, and the singsong phrase repetitions of "Che farò senza Euridice?" suggest that his sense of loss is obsessing him like a tune he can't get out of his head.

8.5   Gluck, *Orfeo ed Euridice*: Act 3, scene 1, "Che farò senza Euridice?"

Doubling the voice   Orpheus's sense of obsession is reinforced by the texture of his aria, in which the first violins constantly double his lines, mostly an octave higher (the part was written for an alto castrato). The device of doubling the singer's voice in arias was used sparingly in earlier

David Daniels as Orpheus and Isabel Bayrakdarian as Eurydice in the Chicago Lyric Opera production of *Orfeo ed Euridice*, 2006. The staging by Robert Carsen shows the prolonged moment of misunderstanding and tension between the lovers as a moment under social scrutiny.

Dan Rest/Lyric Opera of Chicago

opera, as a special effect. Gluck made it a standard procedure, and it has remained one in opera (as well as in Broadway shows and a great deal of other vocal music) ever since. The effect is to make the soloist's voice sound bigger than life, a pre-electric form of amplification. And like electrical amplification, it changes the quality of the singer's voice as well as the relationship of that voice to the sound of the orchestra. The vocal sound becomes less distinguishable from that of the orchestra as a whole. The singer seems less like a single person onstage and more like a presence filling the whole interior of the opera house. Thus, in an opera focused on the inner life of the central character, the simple device of doubling the character's voice with instruments—like a close-up shot in a movie—contributes subtly but powerfully to the audience's sense of being drawn inside that inner life.

The rest of the texture of this aria looks dull on the page: the bass instruments provide unobtrusive harmonic and rhythmic support, while the second violins and violas saw away in endless paired eighth notes, providing harmonic filler. These filler parts create what in pop music two centuries later would be called a "wall of sound." The singer breathes at regular intervals, but the music as a whole never does, except at a few cadence points. The sawing pairs of eighth notes do not add to the character or atmosphere of his expression, the way accompanying parts in Handel or Rameau arias do. Instead, they provide a relentless, motoric drive that lasts for the whole length of the aria.

Similarly relentless figures are the harp arpeggios, representing Orpheus's lyre, in the music by which he gains entry into the Underworld, and the figuration of the first violins in the scene in the Elysian Fields ("Che puro ciel").

The latter, the breathless element in a texture rich in nature sounds, provides a means of holding listeners' attention captive. And likewise in "Che farò senza Euridice?" Orpheus may take breaths in order to keep singing, but his accompaniment seems to tell us that we don't dare breathe until it is over.

Weeping at the opera There is considerable evidence about how listeners in Gluck's day responded to his operas. It comes not so much from Vienna as Paris, where in the 1770s Gluck produced revampings in French of both *Orfeo ed Euridice* and *Alceste*, as well as several original French operas. As we've seen, Parisian audiences in Lully's day paid rapt, breathless attention to crucial scenes, and Gluck's operas seem to have benefited not just from that selective kind of attention but from a new, more self-conscious attitude that audiences should pay attention throughout a whole opera. A Parisian journalist, for instance, reported that "one sees for the first time a musical tragedy heard with sustained attention from start to finish."[16] Paris audiences, it seems, were prepared to listen exactly the way Gluck's music encouraged them to listen.

Likewise, they were prepared to weep as his operas invited them to weep. It was an age of sensibility, when cultivated people trained themselves to display their sympathies in public, while novels and dramas were judged by their success in drawing tears, and actors were expected to be able to cry so as to

Pierre Peyron, *Alceste Sacrificing Herself to Save Her Husband Admetus*, 1785. Painted within a decade of the Paris premiere of Gluck's *Alceste* in its French version (1776), the work shows a scene that does not occur in the opera but that does, like the opera, use the sight of Alceste's children to increase the audience's pity for her. Louvre, Paris.

Erich Lessing/Art Resource, NY

induce the same in the audience. A French actress created a stir by bringing her young children onstage to increase the sympathetic response to her character's plight, a ploy replicated in Gluck's *Alceste*.[17] Evidence suggests that Gluck's operas, exploring through music the inner experience of loss, drew from the public an extraordinary outpouring of emotion at certain moments. It is no surprise that one such moment was "Che farò senza Euridice?," Orpheus's aria of psychic meltdown at losing Eurydice for the second time. (In the French version it is "J'ai perdu mon Eurydice" / "I have lost my Eurydice.") Jean-Jacques Rousseau, whose novel *La nouvelle Héloïse* had itself been, in the words of Anne Vincent-Buffault, "a key event in the history of tears," was reported to have emerged weeping from a performance of the French version of *Orfeo ed Euridice* and, when questioned about it, to have explained, "J'ai perdu mon Eurydice!"[18]

Such testimonials of intense response may be hard for modern listeners to fathom. Here is another one, from a letter written by a young woman to the Paris *Correspondence of Amateur Musicians* describing the effect of that quiet march in *Alceste*:

> I took care to close myself up within my box. I listened to this new work with profound attention. Soon they came to the beautiful march of the priests of Apollo in the first act. From the first measures I was seized by such a strong feeling of awe, and felt within me so intensely that religious impulse that penetrates those who attend the ceremonies of a revered and august religion, that without even knowing it I fell to my knees in my box and stayed in this position, suppliant and with my hands clasped, until the end of the piece.[19]

This is not a kind of behavior we expect to see at the opera house today, however awe-inspiring we might find *Alceste* to be. What have we lost? Is it the capacity to feel what this listener felt or the social climate that allowed her to respond with such behavior? Was her feeling of religious awe heightened by her dread of what she knew the ceremony was going to bring Alceste, or was it purely a reaction to the sights and sounds of the ceremony (intensified by the smoke-filled air of the opera house)? And did those sights and sounds fill her with awe because they reminded her of the ceremonies of her own religion or because they opened up different possibilities of religious experience? Her testimonial doesn't allow us to answer these questions, but it is valuable because it lets us realize how little we can comprehend, let alone share, the experience an artwork of another age gave people in that age—even one we might still find moving.

Visions and Self-Sacrifice: The Iphigenia Operas

The new works Gluck created for the Paris Opera are not as radically innovative as *Orfeo ed Euridice* and *Alceste*; he didn't try to remake the *tragédie en musique* the way he remade Italian opera. His two major new works for Paris are dramas in

which the principal characters wrestle with real-life opponents, not just with their own demons. Both derive from tragedies by Euripides about the same character, Iphigenia, from the legends of the Trojan War. In the first, *Iphigénie en Aulide* (*Iphigenia in Aulis*, 1774), King Agamemnon, leader of the Greek expedition against Troy, is ordered by the angered goddess Diana to sacrifice his daughter Iphigenia as the price for granting the Greeks the wind they need to launch their ships. The second, *Iphigénie en Tauride* (*Iphigenia in Tauris*, 1779), takes place years later in the remote land of Tauris, where Iphigenia, now a captive priestess, is required to choose one of two captured Greek soldiers to sacrifice, not knowing that one of them is her brother Orestes.

These two operas, then, tell classic stories of family contentions acted out in the political arena. If as a result Gluck couldn't focus so exclusively on the character's inner drama as he had with Orpheus and Alceste, the librettists gave him a more concentrated dramatic device for achieving that exploration: the vision, or dream, sequence. In a character's vision we come to understand the guilt or dread that shapes his or her actions. In *Iphigénie en Tauride* the vision, presented in pantomime and choral song, comes to Orestes in a dream. It displays his remorse at having killed his mother Clytemnestra, for her role in slaying his father Agamemnon upon his return from the Trojan War. Dancers and choristers representing the Eumenides (the Avenging Goddesses) torment him with the guilty thought he can never escape: "No mercy: he killed his mother" ("Point de grâce, il a tué sa mère"). In this state of delirium he utters inarticulate cries: "Oh, what torments!" ("Ah! quels tourments!"). The vision sequence then

reveals a cryptic truth. Orestes wakes as Iphigenia enters the room and, still lost in his delirium, he mistakenly calls "Mother!" ("Ma mère!"). Since the siblings Orestes and Iphigenia have still not recognized each other at this point, neither understands—as the audience does—that he is close: Iphigenia is not his murdered mother, but her daughter.

Visions like this reveal to us what drives Gluck's characters. And most often they are driven to self-sacrifice. Alceste, exchanging her own life for her husband's, is the classic exemplar. But the theme of self-sacrifice—not simple suicide, of the sort that was so favored in Italian opera of Handel's day, but Alceste-like sacrifice to save someone else—seems unfailingly to have inspired Gluck. In *Iphigénie en Tauride* the practice of human sacrifice hangs as a threat over the characters, and though it is not fulfilled in the end, the threat creates in Orestes and his comrade-in-arms, Pylades, a self-sacrificing competition. Under the threat that one of them must die, Orestes insists all through the opera that he be the one, since he killed his mother and led Pylades to this place of death, while Pylades claims the right to die to save his friend's life.

The germ of the impulse for self-sacrifice may come from the tragedies of Euripides, but only in Gluck's operas does it spread from character to character like an epidemic. What was there in eighteenth-century culture that made such fatal generosity a gesture that Gluck and his librettists could count on their audiences to respond to, time after time within a single drama and then from one drama to another? We begin to see when we compare Gluck's

Orestes' Vision in Act 2 of Gluck's *Iphigénie en Tauride*, staged by Toresten Fischer at the Theater an der Wien, Vienna, 2010. In this production the mute figure of Orestes' dead mother, Clytemnestra (played by Anna Franziska Sma), appears above the stage to haunt the sleeping Orestes (Stéphane Degout).
Armin Bardel

Orpheus with Peri's or Monteverdi's from a century and a half earlier. His Orpheus does not, like theirs, turn the loss of his wife into an opportunity to pursue a Renaissance quest for identity. On the contrary, he believes that by sacrificing himself he can save her life, and by losing himself in that commitment to her, he miraculously finds her again.

Gluck's Orpheus, Alceste, Iphigenia, Orestes, Pylades, and others are all products of the eighteenth-century cult of sensibility. Like Rousseau weeping at Orpheus's loss, like the young woman who fell to her knees on hearing the march in *Alceste*, these characters lose themselves—that is, lose their sense of distinctness from others—in their devotion to someone else. In Gluck's day they elicited extraordinary depths of sympathy from their audiences precisely because they modeled sympathy in such an extreme form. All the originality of Gluck's operas—all the dramatic and musical techniques by which he concentrates our attention on a character's inner conflict—seems designed to promote this beautifully simple correspondence between sympathy in the characters and sympathy in the audience. Self-sacrifice, then, is not just a theme that Gluck favored in his operas; it is the theme that he found would connect his creations most strongly to the emotional susceptibilities of listeners in his day.

FURTHER READING

On eighteenth-century Italian opera on classical subjects, Reinhard Strohm, *Dramma per Musica: Italian Opera Seria of the Eighteenth Century* (New Haven and London: Yale University Press, 1997); and Martha Feldman, *Opera and Sovereignty: Transforming Myths in Eighteenth-Century Italy* (Chicago: University of Chicago Press, 2007). On the early eighteenth-century reformers of the Italian libretto and their concerns, Renato Di Benedetto, "Poetics and Polemics," trans. Kenneth Chalmers, in *Opera in Theory and Practice, Image and Myth* (Chicago and London: University of Chicago Press, 2003), vol. 6 of Bianconi and Pestelli, eds., *The History of Italian Opera*, esp. pp. 13–38; and Strohm, *Dramma per Musica*, esp. pp. 19–29.

On Handel's life and career, Donald Burows, *Handel* (New York: Schirmer, 1994). On *Giulio Cesare*, ch. 22 of Winton Dean and John Merrill Knapp, *Handel's Operas, 1704–1726*, rev. ed. (Oxford: Clarendon Press, 1995). On Rameau's composition and revision of his operas, Charles Dill, *Monstrous Opera: Rameau and the Tragic Tradition* (Princeton: Princeton University Press, 1998). On Gluck's life and career, Patricia Howard, *Gluck: An Eighteenth-Century Portrait in Letters and Documents* (Oxford and New York: Clarendon Press, 1995).

1. Listen carefully to a singer who specializes in eighteenth-century opera perform a da capo aria by Handel, especially a slow one. What embellishments does the singer add when repeating the opening section of the aria, and in what kinds of phrases does she or he add the most? Is the effect of the embellishment to intensify the dramatic characterization or to draw your attention away from the drama to the singing itself?

2. Go through a Handel opera and find all the arias that are not in da capo form. Can you discover in each case why it made sense for the librettist and composer to take a different course from the usual?

3. Examine several arias from a Handel opera, and determine whether each one is built on a single musical figure (in the accompaniment or the vocal part or both). If so, how is that figure related to the text of the aria or the situation of the character?

4. A Rameau opera typically employs a much richer variety of musical numbers—choruses, dances, pantomimes, ensembles, and choruses, as well as solo numbers—than a Handel opera. How does that richer variety make for a different dramatic experience?

5. What skills do the roles in a Rameau opera particularly call for, as compared with a Handel opera?

6. Gluck's operas starting with *Orfeo ed Euridice* display the simplicity of dramatic action, language, and musical style that he advertised in his dedication to *Alceste*. Watch a performance of one of them, and consider whether all those self-consciously simple means produce a dramatically simple effect.

7. What kind of place is the classical world presented to audiences in the operas of Handel, Rameau, and Gluck?

 Additional resources are available at wwnorton.com/studyspace.

CHAPTER 9

Opera on Comic Subjects

O nce comic characters were largely excluded from operas on classical subjects, as they were at the beginning of the eighteenth century, they made themselves another home. Another home often meant another theater, where singers specializing in comic performance appeared in operas that capitalized on their skills. People then began to divide opera into two distinct types, each identified by its venue. We think about types of music in the same way today. Music played in a jazz club is called jazz, and music played in a concert hall is apt to be called classical music. The musicians in these venues tend to differ in their training and skills, and so did opera singers in the eighteenth century. In fact, that difference in performing skills is the surest guide to the difference between comic opera and classical opera (opera on classical subjects) in that century. A surer guide, certainly, than the terms people then used to distinguish one from another (see "What's in a Term?," p. 219).

A house focusing on comic opera might feature a few highly trained singers, capable of singing the most virtuosic music of the day (and perhaps dividing their time between comic and classical opera houses); others less highly trained in vocal technique, but skilled at getting a laugh with their singing as well as their acting; and still others who could tug at heartstrings with their singing and good looks. The roster usually did not include castratos.

Comic opera dealt in the here and now. Its characters came from every walk of life. Upper-class characters expressed themselves in the literary and musical styles of classical opera (sometimes exposing themselves to ridicule), and lower-class characters, living by their

Detail of a watercolor of a comic opera performance in the late eighteenth century. The arrangement of the instrumentalists, who are led from the harpsichord (bottom left), is typical for the time. Deutsches Theatermuseum, Munich.
Bridgeman Art Library

wits, expressed themselves in witty words and songs. In Italian comic opera all the words were sung, in the same frame of recitative, aria, and ensemble that was used in opera on classical themes. New styles of aria and ensemble, however, were developed to display the characters' wit as well as the dynamics of humorous situations. In French comic opera the characters spoke most of their dialogue and therefore displayed much of their verbal wit without benefit of music. In other countries native forms of comic opera, also using spoken dialogue, developed alongside the imported Italian or French kinds.

Opera on classical subjects was left with characters who were all noble in status (whether noble or ignoble in nature), while comic opera put humorous characters up against serious ones, servants up against masters, country bumpkins up against the urbane rich. Likewise it put lowly styles of vocal music up against affecting or virtuosic styles. Like classical opera, comic opera overwhelmingly told stories about the struggles of young adults to overcome the obstacles to their love. But it was only in comic opera that characters from different social worlds met on the stage, and so it was only there that the obstacles were apt to be caused by differences in social standing. When characters use the universal tricks of comic plots, such as disguise, they most often use them to cross social boundaries: a countess disguises herself as a servant or a servant as a countess. In the midst of the confusion this boundary-crossing creates, the relationship between two social worlds becomes transparent.

The other line that comic opera regularly crosses is the gender boundary. A character may be disguised as a person of the other sex or may behave like one, in either case making the audience conscious of its own gender expectations. Of course, gender boundaries are also explored in classical opera, which plays with the ambiguous gender identities of singers as well. But comic opera stands apart in treating gender or class as a subject to laugh about and in making an explicit issue of the stereotypes involved. It is only comic operas that have titles like *La serva padrona* (*The Servant-Girl [Who Becomes] Mistress*) or *Così fan tutte* (*All Women Do the Same*).

Seeing and Hearing Double

Eighteenth-century comic opera exposes social and gender distinctions by the age-old device of letting the audience see double. Through the transparency of a disguise, for instance, the audience sees a character as both a servant and his master. By other means, such as his asides to the audience, the spectators see him as both a character in the action and a fellow spectator confiding in them. Classical opera maintains the illusion of the drama so that

What's in a Term?

The term "comic opera," or its equivalent in other languages, was by no means the universal term in the eighteenth century for an opera on a comic subject. Mozart's Italian opera *Don Giovanni*, for instance, is called a **dramma giocosa** (humorous play) in its libretto and an **opera buffa** (opera played by comic actors) in its score. The French **vaudeville** and the English **ballad opera** were dramas in which well-known songs were given new words for satiric effect. But just as we don't expect a musical comedy necessarily to be funny all the way through or have a happy ending, the terms used in the eighteenth century did not carry such implications either. *Don Giovanni* has a happy enough ending once its protagonist has been dragged down to Hell. In France *opéra comique* meant a work performed at an opera house that used spoken dialogue between the musical numbers. An *opéra comique* could actually be more serious in subject and tone than a *tragédie en musique* (tragedy in music) — something that almost never ended tragically.

the audience can never detach itself from the characters' plight; comic opera repeatedly exposes the illusion of the drama, so that the audience feels that it is also looking critically at the characters and their world.

Comic opera also lets us hear double. The original audiences sometimes heard songs they knew well, sung to new and disconcerting words, the way audiences hear songs by the Capitol Steps today. At other times they heard arias

The trio "Ah taci, ingiusto core," from Act 2 of Mozart's *Don Giovanni*, as performed at Her Majesty's Theatre, London, in 1846. This etching, originally published in the *Illustrated London News*, April 25, 1846, shows one form of exchanged identity between master and servant: Leporello wears Don Giovanni's hat and cloak to impersonate him singing to Donna Elvira, while the crouching Don Giovanni actually does his own singing.
Hulton Archive/Getty Images

in grave styles that they associated with classical opera, now sung in farcical situations. In both ways music could act like a disguise in holding social hypocrisy up to ridicule. Two of the most successful comic operas of the eighteenth century can help demonstrate the processes of seeing and hearing double.

The Beggar's Opera

The Beggar's Opera, a spoof of Italian opera, took London by storm in 1728, when Italian operas by Handel and others had dominated the theatrical scene for almost two decades. With this work the poet John Gay created a new theatrical genre, the **ballad opera**. The Beggar's Opera, presenting itself as the creation of a London beggar who introduces and concludes the action, is a story of London thieves and molls and corrupt jailers. Its dialogue is spoken, and the music consists of simple ballads and other English popular songs of the day, outfitted with new words. In spite of this unoperatic music, the work satirized Italian opera, according to Roger Fiske, "in the main by upending both its musical style and its moral flavour."[1]

Gay makes sure his audience notices his upending of operatic conventions. In the Introduction, for instance, the Beggar, pretending to be the author, tells the audience:

> I have introduced the similes that are in all your celebrated opera: the swallow, the moth, the bee, the ship, the flower, etc. Besides, I have a prison scene, which the ladies always reckon charmingly pathetic. As to the parts, I have observed such a nice impartiality to our two ladies, that it is impossible for either of them to take offence. I hope I may be forgiven, that I have not made my opera throughout unnatural, like those in vogue; for I have no recitative: excepting this, as I have consented to have neither prologue nor epilogue, it must be allowed an opera in all its forms.

The Beggar's line about being impartial to the two ladies, for instance, is a reference to the notorious rivalry of two Italian sopranos, Francesca Cuzzoni (Handel's Cleopatra) and Faustina Bordoni, who demanded equally show-stopping arias when they were to appear in the same opera. Their competing fans set off a riot in the King's Theatre eight months before the premiere of The Beggar's Opera when they played the roles of rivals for the hand of King Pyrrhus in Giovanni Bononcini's Astianatte.[2] In Gay's work, accordingly, the two main women characters, Polly Peachum and Lucy Lockit, rivals for the affection of the thief Macheath, sing duets in which they are equally matched, line for line. They act not only like the two Italian singers, but also like the characters those singers played: in Astianatte one of the rivals tries to have Pyrrhus killed rather than lose him to the other, and in The Beggar's Opera Lucy tries to get Polly to drink poison. And when Macheath is about to be executed for his crimes,

they display their grief in a trio with him, outdoing each other (in matching phrases) in their willingness to be hanged alongside him (see Example 9.1).

9.1 Gay, *The Beggar's Opera*: Act 3, scene 5, "Would I might be hang'd!"

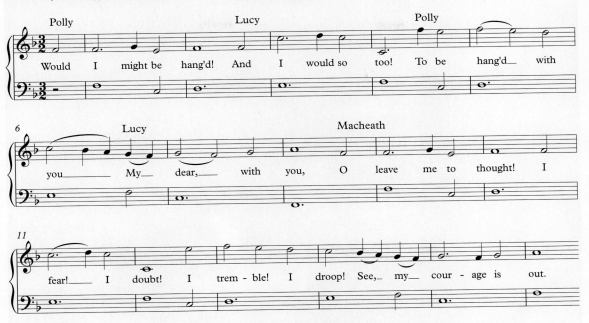

Neither the words nor the music of the trio is funny in itself. The melody was taken from a ballad of the time, "A Hymn upon the Execution of Two Criminals." Spectators who knew the ballad heard the ostensibly serious new words ("Would I might be hang'd!") against the undoubtedly serious first-person narrative of the familiar ballad:

All you that must take a leap in the dark,
Pity the fate of Lawson and Clark;
Cheated by hope, by mercy amus'd,
Betray'd by the sinful ways we use'd:
Cropp'd in our prime of strength and youth,
Who can but weep at so sad a truth.

Hearing the song double may not make it funny, but hearing it double while seeing it double does. The two molls, Polly and Lucy, acting like prima donnas, alternately murderous and self-sacrificing, show how ludicrous the noble behavior of classical heroines and the noble manner of prima donnas are when they are brought down to the level of humble human existence.

Over and over, in fact, it appears that the real object of mockery here is not the noble ideals celebrated in Italian opera so much as the hypocrisy of the

Scene in Newgate prison from Act 3 of *The Beggar's Opera*, by William Hogarth, 1731. The painting shows the shackled prisoner Macheath standing between Lucy Lockit (kneeling on the left, pleading on Macheath's behalf with her father, the jailer) and Polly Peachum (kneeling on the right, pleading on his behalf with *her* father, the master criminal). Tate Gallery, London.
Art Resource, NY

English aristocrats who in patronizing that kind of opera pretended that they aspired to live by those ideals. Polly's mother is scandalized when she learns that Polly has married the thief Macheath: "If you must be married, could you introduce nobody into our family but a highwayman? Why, thou foolish jade, thou wilt be as ill used, and as much neglected, as if thou hadst married a Lord!"

Polly protests that she didn't marry "for honour or money. But I love him." "Love him! Worse and worse!" cries her mother. "I thought the girl had been better bred." There are no upper-class characters, but the aristocracy is present throughout as the butt of language like this that upends its social standing, as well as of songs and dramatic structures that mock its taste for Italian opera. The audience senses the aristocracy as the double of the lower-class characters embodied onstage.

At the end of the work the Beggar returns to the stage, like an operatic god descending from the clouds, to announce that Macheath will be spared execution for no better reason than that "an opera must end happily . . . no matter how absurdly things are brought about." Invariably at that moment in the initial run, "the gallery cheered hysterically."[3] For these least privileged members of the audience, it may have been worth a lot to witness the upending spectacle of an "opera" in which someone quite the opposite of noble got a break for once.

The Beggar's Opera was a tremendous cultural phenomenon in London, where it was performed every year for the rest of the eighteenth century, and around the English-speaking world. At its bicentennial in 1928 the dramatist Bertolt Brecht and the composer Kurt Weill—one of the great musical-theater teams of the twentieth century—used it as the basis of their Dreigroschenoper, which in turn enjoyed record-breaking runs in both German and (as The Threepenny Opera) English. Our second example of a comic opera exerted extraordinary power in a different way.

Pergolesi, *La serva padrona*

In Naples, where it was created in 1733, Giovanni Battista Pergolesi's La serva padrona (The Servant-Girl [Who Becomes] Mistress) was a typical **intermezzo**, a tiny comic opera for a cast of three, its two parts performed between the acts of a classical opera, also by Pergolesi. But when an Italian troupe under Eustachio Bambini played at the Paris Opera from 1752 to 1754, their performances of La serva padrona made that work the central exhibit in what is known as the "Querelle des bouffons," or "Dispute over the actors": a furious public debate about the claims of French and Italian opera that disguised a battle over political culture.[4] La serva padrona turned out to be inspirational in the development of comic opera in France.

The characters are petty and quarrelsome representatives of contemporary society, like characters in a television sitcom, but not disreputable like those in The Beggar's Opera. In fact, though there are just two singing roles (and one silent), those two provide a contrast in social class, while the dozens of characters in The Beggar's Opera all represent a single class. The action is a struggle between an elderly gentleman, Uberto, and his servant, Serpina, who enrages him by ignoring his orders even though he has been her guardian since she was young. She is after his money and social standing, and her disobedience is just part of her plot to get him to marry her.

La serva padrona is sung throughout (in recitatives and arias), but in its first part both characters use the same comic style of music, scrappy of thought

Pergolesi, *La serva padrona*, staged by Désiré Defrère at the Metropolitan Opera in 1935. Editha Fleischer as Serpina taunts the proud Uberto (Louis D'Angelo) with the news that she intends to marry the silent, mustached Vespone (Angelo Badà).

Carlo Edwards/Metropolitan Opera Archives

and manic in momentum. The scrappy thoughts are conveyed in tiny syllabic phrases, often in an inflexible rhythm, built on simple, cadencing harmonies. The manic momentum comes from incessant repetition of those phrases and cadences, the phrases progressively reduced in length and complexity, new words giving way to the same ones heard over and over. The impression is of a buildup of verbal energy without a buildup in rhetorical power, as if the need to speak has outrun what the character has to say.

Comic characters in the theater were always more apt to be servants than masters, and in eighteenth-century comic opera this manic style of singing typically marked servants apart from their masters. But in *La serva padrona*, because Uberto uses the style, it appears to mark some kind of parity between master and servant. And when there is finally a change, the new style, slower and more dignified, is sung by Serpina. This aria, the only instance of a serious style in the whole work, marks the moment when she gains the upper hand over her social superior.

The aria comes in the work's second part. Uberto has announced to Serpina that he is going to find himself a wife, who will not be Serpina. She replies that she has already found herself a husband, an ill-tempered Captain Tempest. This draws from Uberto the first expression of sympathy we have heard from him. In her slow aria she plays on that sympathy:

A Serpina penserete	You will think of Serpina
Qualche volta in qualche dì,	sometimes on some days
E direte: Ah! poverina,	and you'll say: Oh, poor thing,
Cara un tempo ella mi fu.	she was once so dear to me.

Not only is this aria much slower than any number in the first part, but its phrases are constructed to give, for the first time, an impression of thoughtfulness. The vocal lines are longer, and though phrases are repeated, Serpina doesn't appear to get stuck but keeps moving through the long sentence that constitutes the stanza. Likewise, a harmonic modulation in the course of the stanza gives the effect of a thought progression, not a manic repetition. Serpina's music tells Uberto that she is being serious for once, that she is no longer playing mind games with him now but is concerned about how he will remember her.

No sooner is that sentence out of her mouth than she turns and admits to the audience that she is indeed playing another mind game with Uberto. An abrupt return to the comic style of music marks those words as an aside:

(Ei mi par che già pian piano	(It seems to me that little by little
S'incomincia a intenerir!)	he's starting to soften.)

Since this is the classic style of scheming servants, we can tell before we even hear her words that Serpina's seriousness was an act, a disguise. Before the aria is done, she will have changed in and out of the disguise several times, switching back and forth between her ongoing appeal to Uberto and her ongoing appraisal of how she is doing. In the process we see and hear double. Whenever she is singing to Uberto, her pretense of seriousness betrays to us that she is a scheming servant. And whenever she addresses us in her asides, her admission that she is scheming comes across as honest. In the end, as we can tell from her virtuosic display of styles and actions (while Uberto is locked into one style and no action), she will get him to marry her, and the servant will become, as the title promises, the mistress of her master.

Both dramatically and musically, comic opera in the eighteenth century followed the model of La serva padrona much more than that of The Beggar's Opera. Most comic operas relied for their musical effect on contrasts and blendings of styles from many sources, high and low, to produce a complex characterization of individuals and situations that could be comic and affecting at the same time. Likewise, the explicit political and class satire found in The Beggar's Opera, which risked government censorship even in England,[5] would certainly not have been allowed on the stage in other European jurisdictions. By contrast, censorship would have found no easy target in La serva padrona: Serpina doesn't insult the class Uberto belongs to, the way Mrs. Peachum insults the English nobility; she simply insults Uberto. Nevertheless, the audience laughs with her at his expense, and eighteenth-century theorists of drama were fond of saying that comedy instructed by holding negative examples up to ridicule. Did audiences in those days laugh at Serpina's triumph over Uberto because they approved of a foolish and arrogant master getting his comeuppance, or because they found an ambitious serving girl a ludicrous paradox, or because they found both characters so far beyond the pale that they deserved each other? Did comic opera help them to question the inequalities of class and gender on which their society was built, or help them feel comfortable with those inequalities? We can't necessarily extrapolate eighteenth-century responses from our own. But we can ask similar questions of the three great masterpieces in this tradition created late in the eighteenth century by the Italian librettist Lorenzo Da Ponte and the Austrian composer Wolfgang Amadeus Mozart.

The Comedy of Class and Gender Conflict: Three Mozart Operas

The Predatory Noble at Home: *The Marriage of Figaro*

The Marriage of Figaro (*Le nozze di Figaro,* 1786) is based on a French comedy of 1778 by Pierre-Augustin Beaumarchais, a comedy that King Louis XVI of France first banned as too dangerous, then allowed to be performed publicly in 1784. The Austrian emperor Joseph II likewise banned its performance in Vienna. Da Ponte reported that the emperor banned the play because it was written "with too much license for a well-mannered audience," but that later (in 1786) he agreed to allow the performance of the opera because the libretto "omitted and shortened anything that could offend the sensibility and decency of a spectacle at which His Sovereign Majesty presides." Modern scholars take Da Ponte's account with a grain of salt.[6] It is never easy to tell why a censoring authority really decides whether to ban a work of art. But it is worth considering the relationship of this opera to the original play as a way of understanding the social and political issues that animate it.

The opera, like the play, has at its core an exercise of aristocratic privilege that a monarch in France, Austria, or anywhere in Europe in the 1780s might well have been reluctant to allow theaters to show. A Spanish aristocrat, Count Almaviva, has officially forsworn the feudal privilege known in French as the *droit du Seigneur*, the supposed right of a lord to have sex with a bride of the lower estates in his realm before she and her husband consummate their marriage. Nevertheless, the Count is using the promise of a dowry to demand sexual favors from his servant Susanna, who is about to marry his servant Figaro. The Count is a predator three times over. In preying on Susanna (who is his subordinate in both rank and gender), he humiliates Figaro (his subordinate in rank but his double in gender) and wounds his wife (his double in rank but his subordinate in gender). The Countess, heartsick at her husband's constant infidelities as well as his unjust questioning of *her* fidelity, joins forces with Susanna and Figaro. Through their intrigues they shame the Count: he is caught trying to seduce a woman he thinks is Susanna (but who turns out to be the Countess in disguise) and venting his rage at Figaro for carrying on with a woman he thinks is the Countess (but who turns out to be Susanna in disguise).

For Beaumarchais to frame an aristocrat's sexual harassment of his servant against the background of the *droit du Seigneur* was bold. This was a time in European history when noble privileges increasingly grated against the intellectual and social ambitions

---

The Marriage of Figaro

PRINCIPAL CHARACTERS

- The **Count** and **Countess Almaviva**, Spanish aristocrats
- **Figaro** (the Count's valet) and **Susanna** (the Countess's maid), betrothed to each other
- Other members of the household: **Cherubino** (the Count's page); **Don Basilio** (the music master); **Antonio** (the gardener and Susanna's uncle) and his daughter **Barbarina**
- Hangers-on: **Bartolo** (a doctor); **Marcellina** (his housekeeper); **Don Curzio** (a judge)

of the unprivileged classes and even embarrassed many nobles. When Da Ponte shortened the play for Mozart, he stripped away denunciations of the nobility that Beaumarchais had put into Figaro's mouth, but he did not reduce the Count's assertion of a nobleman's right to sexual license. And he did not change the ending, in which the Count is literally brought to his knees by the conspiracy of his servants and his wife—and that, we might suppose, is the action that most forcefully celebrates the resistance of the lower orders and the supposedly subservient sex.

Yet in another light, this ending is just what was expected from any comic opera. In fact, Northrop Frye's general theory of comedy stipulates that it is the most powerful figures, not the powerless, who initiate the action of comedies through some "blocking" motion, just as they allow it to come to a resolution. The musicologist Mary Hunter, applying this model to *The Marriage of Figaro*, writes, "It is the Count's desire for Susanna which sets off Figaro's series of stratagems, and at the end it is the reconciliation between the Count and Countess that permits the formal (though not the emotional) union between Figaro and Susanna."[7] This ending, which has struck many critics besides the French king and Austrian emperor as an endorsement of revolutionary discontent, might equally well be regarded, it seems, as a sign that the opera was simply performing the traditional comic function of helping spectators let off steam about social inequities.

Portrait of Wolfgang Amadeus Mozart in 1789 (between the premieres of *Don Giovanni* and *Così fan tutte*). Engraving after a drawing by Dora Stock in the Mozarteum, Salzburg, Austria.

Figaro's aria "Se vuol ballare" The opera features eleven characters: the Count and Countess Almaviva, their servants, and hangers-on in their household. Almost everyone sings at least one aria, and most of these are soliloquies, opportunities for the characters to express their resentment at the way other characters are treating them. In the earliest of these arias, for example, Figaro sings with barely suppressed rage because he has just learned that the Count is using Figaro's imminent marriage to Susanna to pursue his own sexual designs on her. Figaro's music alternates between two different dance rhythms, as if his words were suddenly dancing to a new step. Though there may not be a lot of literal dancing in eighteenth-century comic opera, the dance element has "gone underground," as Wye Allanbrook writes. New stages in the thought progression of an aria, as well as in the dramatic progression of a whole scene, are apt to be marked by changes from one dance-music style to another, providing "choreographies for the motion of character."[8]

Dancing is in fact the image Figaro uses in this aria to express his desire to take revenge on the Count:

Se vuol ballare,	*If you want to dance,*
Signor Contino,	*my dear little Count,*
Il chitarrino	*I'll play the guitar for you.*
Le suonerò.	

He sings this in the strong triple rhythm of a minuet, the social dance most associated with the aristocracy, thereby asserting his determination to take

control of his master's world. But later in the aria, when he is enumerating the ways in which he "will overturn all the machinations," he switches into the quick duple rhythm of the *contradanza*, a less elegant dance performed more in bourgeois dance halls than in aristocratic ballrooms. This striking change in musical style could dramatize his power as a servant to dominate his master—or his fantasy of that power—because he can move more easily than the master can between their two different social worlds.

An aria that is prone, as this one is, to sudden switches in theme, rhythm, style, and character depicts a very different progression of thought from, say, a da capo aria, where any strong changes are contained within a predictable, circular scheme. On the whole, comic-opera arias proceed through discrete musical stages, each one presenting a stanza of text. A decisive change in the music is generally made at the beginning of a new stanza. But compared with a da capo aria by Handel or a variation-form aria like Monteverdi's "Possente spirto," a comic aria by Mozart is more apt to seem ruled by impulsive contrast and to come out somewhere different from where it started.

Ensembles in comic opera Ensembles are even more prone to come out somewhere unforeseen: they express a group-dynamic process, often resulting in changed relationships among the characters. Though ensembles are infrequent in classical operas like *Giulio Cesare*, they are almost as numerous as arias in *The Marriage of Figaro*. In the course of the eighteenth century they came to occupy a greater portion of the time in comic operas, often filling the beginnings and endings of acts and much of the action in between. More and more of the intrigues, interactions, and stage business came within ensembles and therefore played itself out not in recitative or spoken dialogue, but in music of controlled rhythms and sustained orchestral textures. Whereas an aria like "Se vuol ballare" may be serious in tone, because Figaro takes his situation seriously, ensembles tend to create the funniest moments, because the characters are singing at cross purposes to each other.

An ensemble at the beginning of an act (**introduzione**) or at the end of one (**finale**) might be far and away the longest stretch of music uninterrupted by recitative in an opera. The finale to the second act of *The Marriage of Figaro*, admittedly an extreme case, takes well over twenty minutes to perform. The endless twists in the action that occur along the way—at its center the Count's disturbing questioning of the Countess's fidelity—leave the spectator's mind spinning. The opera's six duets are no love fests; all except for the Letter Duet of Susanna and the Countess (examined in Chapter 3) are contentious. And one trio is an indestructible piece of situation comedy.

The trio "Cosa sento!" The scene containing this "armchair" trio, "Cosa sento! Tosto andate" ("What am I hearing? Go at once," Act 1, scene 6), begins with an adolescent page, Cherubino, visiting Susanna in her room.

He has a crush on all the women in the castle, especially the Countess, and is therefore in danger of arousing the jealousy of the Count. Cherubino doesn't want the Count to see him hanging out with Susanna either, since the Count expects to take her as his mistress. So when the Count unexpectedly approaches her room, Cherubino hides behind a chair. The Count enters and promises Susanna whatever she wants if she will meet him in the garden that night, but at the approach of the music master Basilio, who has been serving as his go-between with Susanna, the Count too decides to hide, not wanting to be seen with Susanna. As Cherubino sneaks around to the front of the chair, climbs into it, and is covered with a dress by Susanna, the Count hides behind it. Basilio enters and describes to Susanna Cherubino's crush on the Countess, which he says everyone is talking about. The Count emerges from his hiding place in a fury, and the trio begins.

This number is in a lively four-beat rhythm. According to Tim Carter, the "kinetic energy" of the orchestral part, with its undertow of quick-pulsed notes, "maintains the momentum."[9] Against this momentum the Count can express his rage, Susanna her consternation, and Basilio his unholy glee, all in short-breathed scraps of sentences. At the opening, for instance, the Count takes four disconnected phrases to get out his two short lines of text, ordering Basilio to send Cherubino away:

Cosa sento! tosto andate   What am I hearing! Go at once
E scacciate il seduttor.   and drive away that seducer.

Basilio replies with a transparently insincere apology:

In mal punto son qui giunto.   I have come here at a bad moment;
Perdonate, oh mio signor.   forgive me, my lord.

His melody, like the Count's, takes four disconnected phrases, but these are all in the same "oily and sanctimonious" rhythm, as Wye Allanbrook calls it: two half notes, two quarter notes, and a rest.[10] And now the orchestra, instead of carrying the singer along with bustling energy, unites rhythmically with Basilio's words, so that the music altogether steps and halts, steps and halts. As soon as he finishes the lines, the orchestral momentum returns.

A long passage of absolutely continuous motion by the strings carries through the first episode of stage business: Susanna becomes faint; Basilio and the Count carry her over to the chair; she recovers in time to avoid disturbing the hidden Cherubino. Although the movements and the singing of the three characters through this business may be discontinuous and jerky, the "kinetic energy" of the orchestra seems like a power greater than any of them, pushing events forward at its own tempo and determining for itself whether Cherubino will be discovered. At this point Basilio returns to the subject of Cherubino, claiming disingenuously, in his "sanctimonious" theme, that what he had reported

Count Almaviva discovers Chérubin hiding in the armchair in Beaumarchais's play *The Marriage of Figaro*, as he does in the trio "Cosa sento!" of Mozart's opera. This is an illustration by Jacques Philippe Joseph de Saint-Quentin from the published text of the play, 1785. Bibliothèque-Musée de la Comédie-Française, Paris.

Giraudon/Bridgeman Art Library

The armchair scene in Mozart's *The Marriage of Figaro*, just before the arrival of Don Basilio and the beginning of the trio "Cosa sento!" Joyce DiDonato as Cherubino, Mariusz Kwiecień as Count Almaviva, and Danielle de Niese as Susanna in a production by Peter Hall and Herbert Kellner at the Chicago Lyric Opera, 2010.

Dan Rest/Lyric Opera of Chicago

about Cherubino and the Countess "was only my suspicion." That in turn leads the Count to call again for Cherubino's dismissal and to offer further evidence against him. The evidence is a story, and to take command of the situation, he needs to shake off the commanding energy of the orchestra. Accordingly, its steady momentum disappears, and he begins his story in accompanied recitative.

The Count tells of going that morning to the room of Barbarina, the pre-adolescent daughter of his gardener, to find her flustered. He searched the room, he says, and as he begins to reenact his search, he drops the recitative in favor of Basilio's sanctimonious theme, which has just the step-and-halt rhythm he needs to accompany his movements (see Example 9.2).

9.2 Mozart, *The Marriage of Figaro*: Act 1, scene 7, "Cosa sento!"

His narration is turning into more stage business:

Ed alzando pian pianino	*And very gently lifting*
Il tappeto al tavolino,	*the tablecloth from the table,*
Vedo il paggio . . .	*I see the page . . .*

The tension the audience feels from watching the Count step toward the chair is increased by hearing the inexorable downward stepping of his narrating phrases. When the Count pauses on "I see the page," he lifts the dress on the chair to reveal to his astonishment exactly what he is describing: Cherubino hiding from him.

The Count's narration is stopped in its tracks, and the orchestra, embodying the power of the situation over everyone present, continues the sanctimonious theme without him, leading it back upward. At the same time, an impatient sustained note (dominant pedal) holds time still as the three singers (for Cherubino sings not a note in this number) make their three scrappy responses to this revelation:

The Count (*surprised*):
Ah! cosa veggio!   *Oh, what do I see!*

Susanna (*fearfully*):
Ah! crude stelle!   *Oh, cruel stars!*

Basilio (*with a laugh*):
Ah! meglio ancora!   *Oh, even better!*

After this point, only two-thirds of the way through the trio, there is no more stage business, and although the characters now have more trouble than ever to sort out, that will wait until the trio is done. The final third is taken up with the Count's reproaches, Susanna's despair, and Basilio's glee at eveyone's trouble, all expressed simultaneously for the most part. The momentum of the orchestral music is as important as ever, carrying all three singers along together, even though each is isolated in her or his thoughts. The number even ends like a machine winding down, growing softer and slower as both the vocal lines and the string parts descend in range. The dramatic tension of Cherubino and the Count hiding is not resolved when they are discovered, but turns into shame for them and Susanna; the kinetic energy in the music, accordingly, does not resolve, but simply drains away.

Sounding natural: "L'ho perduta" The armchair trio gives us a sense of characters trapped in the complexity of their relationships to everyone around them, and as the opera proceeds, that sense never relents. The Count's plot to shame his wife and to have his way with Susanna is countered by the plotting of the Countess, Susanna, and Figaro to foil him. By the last act, when these

plots run into each other, in the confusion of a dark garden where Susanna and the Countess are disguised as each other, the audience is apt to be as bewildered as any of the characters, and that effect in itself makes a point about the craziness of lives in which everything is dissimulation and double-dealing. Within this act of bewildering artifice, Da Ponte and Mozart placed several numbers of breathtaking simplicity and naturalness. The stratagem is characteristic of thinking in the eighteenth century, when the idea of the state of nature was used in every cultural medium to expose by contrast the artifices and ills of society. It appears perhaps most powerfully in the writings of Jean-Jacques Rousseau and in his little operatic depiction of rustic innocence, *Le Devin du village* (*The Village Soothsayer*), premiered before the French royal court in 1752. Three numbers from the fourth act of *The Marriage of Figaro* partake of that spirit.

As the act begins, the youngest character in the opera, Barbarina, enters looking for a pin that she is supposed to deliver from the Count to Susanna, but that she has lost. The Count has presumably entrusted the mission to this child because he considers her the one person in his household too young to understand what it signifies: that he accepts Susanna's invitation to meet him in the garden that evening. Barbarina is distraught because she is afraid that the loss of the pin will anger Susanna (who is her cousin) and the Count ("the master"):

L'ho perduta . . . me meschina . . .	I've lost it . . . miserable me . . .
Ah, chi sa dove sarà?	Oh, who knows where it is?
Non la trovo . . . E mia cugina . . .	I don't see it . . . And my cousin . . .
E il padron . . . cosa dirà?	And the master . . . what will he say?

Her music conveys what Allanbrook calls "her little-girl anguish." The gently rocking 6/8 rhythm of her accompaniment comes from the *pastorale*, music associated with the dancing of make-believe shepherds and shepherdesses. The whispering of the muted violins matches her "wavering child's voice" (Mozart wrote the role for a twelve-year-old). Above all, her childlike un-selfconsciousness appears in "the nursery-rhyme simplicity of the phrase structure": her unguarded thoughts spill out in tiny phrases, sometimes getting stuck in their repetitions, never really getting anywhere.[11] In fact, her aria pauses on a question, never to finish, when Figaro walks in and asks her what's wrong.

The serenade: "Deh vieni, non tardar" Several numbers later we hear an aria equally straightforward and natural, if not quite so simple. But in this case the naturalness is deceptive because the singer is deceiving. And the musical genre, the **serenade**, is traditionally straightforward yet deceiving. As staged in opera, a serenade is a wooing song that a young man, usually noble

in birth, sings to his beloved at night while standing in the street or the garden of her house, under her window. Under the cloak of night he often keeps his identity hidden from her, playing the secret admirer, and invariably tries to keep it hidden from her father or guardian. The lover accompanies himself on a guitar or mandolin (which may be represented by a dummy instrument in the actor's hands, while an actual guitar or mandolin is played in the pit or the string section plays pizzicato to sound like one). The song is usually simple, tuneful, and strophic, like a popular song of the day, often in an easygoing 6/8 rhythm.

The serenade in *Figaro* fulfills most of these conventions. It is sung at night, in the garden of the Count's castle. The singer is in disguise. The song is in 6/8, the melody all (until the end) in phrases of identical length, the accompaniment pizzicato string chords, with lovely punctuations of woodwind color suggesting the sounds of the garden at night. The text is not in stanzas and the music accordingly is not in strophes, but the words bear the message of all serenades: Come to me, my beloved.

Deh vieni, non tardar, o gioia bella,	*Come, don't delay, O my lovely joy,*
Vieni ove amore per goder t'appella.	*come to where love calls you to pleasure.*

But there is one crucial twist: here the woman is serenading the man.

The singer is Susanna, disguised as the Countess, apparently singing to the Count. The fact that a female servant is serenading a nobleman is a sign that she is turning the tables on him. And the situation is even more complicated than that. Susanna has learned that Figaro thinks she is actually planning to offer herself to the Count, and she knows that Figaro is hiding in the garden to keep an eye on her. Her serenade is therefore really directed at him: it is a trick to tweak him for his jealousy, while she waits for the trick on the Count to begin. She knows that Figaro will recognize her voice. And the serenade

has the effect she expects: Figaro is outraged that she seems not only willing to give herself to the Count, but impatient for his arrival.

Impatience for love is the sentiment serenades normally express. But a serenade is normally meant to be heard only by the beloved, while this one is meant only to be overheard by the "wrong" person. In addition, though the strings mostly play pizzicato, Susanna doesn't appear to play a guitar; she doesn't, in other words, altogether assume the figure of the serenader. For that matter, while the conventional male serenader sings of his unfulfilled sexual longing, Susanna barely mentions herself. At the beginning of the aria she calls her lover to the pleasures of love; for most of the rest she describes the alluring beauties of the garden at night; and at the end she combines the two themes:

Vieni, ben mio, tra queste piante ascose
Ti vo' la fronte incoronar di rose.

Come, my beloved, among these concealing plants
I'm going to crown your brow with roses.

She makes herself part of the allure of the night by blending her voice with the sounds of the orchestra, and particularly by taking up in her final phrases the rising scale that has been the night sound of the woodwinds all along.

Instead of drawing attention to her longing in the traditionally masculine way of the serenader, then, she draws attention in a traditionally feminine way, displaying the beauty of her voice as a reminder of the beauty of her appearance. She succeeds in enraging Figaro with this display; she makes him realize how enticing she would be to the Count, by making him feel her enticing effect on himself. And since she actually is being faithful to Figaro and wants him to love her, that effect is ultimately more important to her than enraging him.

The complexity of this dramatic situation is characteristic of *The Marriage of Figaro*. A third number of musical simplicity at the end of this act—the dénouement of the opera, in fact—is powerful because, in contrast to everything that has come before, its simplicity discharges the duplicities that all the characters have engaged in. The Count's advances on the woman he supposes to be Susanna are foiled when she drops her disguise and shows herself—not just to the Count, but to his servants as well—to be the woman he has falsely accused of infidelity: his wife. In a simple musical prayer he begs her forgiveness, which she grants, bringing that simple melody to its conclusion.

The Predatory Noble at Large: *Don Giovanni*

In their next collaboration (1787) Da Ponte and Mozart chose another story of an aristocrat's abuse of his privilege for sexual purposes. In this case, though, there was no issue of censorship, perhaps because the tale was so

old and familiar that it was hard for anyone to imagine one more setting posing a threat to public morals or political tranquility. This was the story of Don Giovanni. (Don Juan, the character's original Spanish name, is still used in English to refer to an inveterate seducer.) In the opera Don Giovanni uses his rank differently according to whether he is taking advantage of a noble woman or a commoner. He also mistreats his servant Leporello, who has to act as his sentinel, messenger, and decoy, procuring pleasures for his master while enduring danger and humiliation. Like the Count in *The Marriage of Figaro*, Don Giovanni humiliates his servant—his lower-order double—as he preys on women of both the upper and lower ranks.

Here too the predatory behavior of the aristocratic lead character initiates the action, but since Don Giovanni is a serial seducer, he gets his opera going by making attempts on two women, one aristocratic (Donna Anna) and one a peasant bride (Zerlina). In the meantime a third (Donna Elvira), whom he has seduced and abandoned before the action begins, inconveniently turns up to haunt him. Despite his past record of conquests, Don Giovanni doesn't in fact get anywhere with any woman in the course of the opera. He complains to Leporello that the devil seems to be "amusing himself by blocking my pleasurable pastimes today" (Act 1, scene 11). In that frustration he is like the Count. What is different in this case is that though here too the predator's sexual targets and his servant join forces against him, they are ineffectual. In evading their fury, Don Giovanni seems to prove that the real privilege of noble rank is escaping punishment when no one else would.

Don Giovanni does get punished in the end, however, dragged to Hell by the ghost (more precisely, the funerary statue) of Donna Anna's father, whom he killed at the beginning when that nobleman, called the Commendatore (Commander), tried to defend his daughter's honor against Don Giovanni's assault. In one sense this is a classical-opera ending, an unexpected intervention by a visitor from another world that resolves the action when the characters reach a stalemate. But on Frye's model it is a typical comic-opera ending, achieved by the action of the noble character who initiated all the trouble in the first place: Don Giovanni accepts an invitation from that statue to dine with him in Hell. By either model the crucial resolution is not so much the fate of Don Giovanni as his removal from the scene, freeing the others to go about their lives as they please.

Introduzione The opera opens with Leporello's solo "Notte e giorno faticar" ("Toiling night and day"), like Figaro's "Se vuol ballare" a servant's complaint about his master. But Leporello,

Don Giovanni
PRINCIPAL CHARACTERS

- **Don Giovanni**, nobleman
- **Leporello**, his servant
- **Donna Anna**, noblewoman
- **Commendatore**, her father
- **Don Ottavio**, her fiancé
- **Donna Elvira**, noblewoman from a distant city
- **Zerlina**, peasant bride
- **Masetto**, her peasant bridegroom

as we will gradually realize, has no real ambition to revenge himself or improve his condition. The action begins when he finishes and Don Giovanni enters with Donna Anna, whose bedroom he has entered in order to force himself on her. She, having resisted his assault, is now struggling to keep him from escaping. A long, evolving ensemble ensues: she calls for help; her father arrives and draws his sword to defend her; Don Giovanni kills him; and Donna Anna, who has hurried off to fetch her fiancé Don Ottavio and returned with him to discover her father lying dead, makes Don Ottavio pledge to avenge the death. This ensemble is a chain of movements, each with its own rhythm, key, texture, and musical character. The movements follow each other seamlessly, without pause, without room for applause, but with changing participants as characters rush on- and offstage. There are moments of reflection—like the eerie trio of three basses (the Commendatore, Don Giovanni, and Leporello) as the wounded Commendatore dies—as well as plenty of action. The full expressive range of the drama is present in microcosm.

A recent (2011) version of Leporello impersonating his master in the trio "Ah taci, ingiusto core." (Compare p. 219.) Staged by Pier Luigi Pizzi in a production at the Teatro Comunale in Bologna, Italy, with Carmela Remigio as Donna Elvira, Andrea Concetti as Leporello (wearing his master's cloak and shielding his face with his master's hat), and Nmon Ford as Don Giovanni.
Rocco Casaluci

The opera continues to unfold with expressions of resentment by Don Giovanni's victims, his further attempts at seduction, and his narrow escapes whenever his victims figure out what he is up to. All of these elements are brought into remarkable compression in another extended ensemble, the finale to the first act.

Finale to Act 1 Finales (which can come at the end of any act) have the same structure of compressed movements as the Introduzione. But since it is often only in the finales that the whole cast is onstage, they make clear what it would take to resolve matters for everyone and therefore what is at issue in the drama. In a mid-point finale (as this is because the opera has only two acts) the characters reach a standoff, resolving nothing. In the last-act finale an intervention or concession, often by one character in a position of power, initiates the resolution.

The first-act finale of *Don Giovanni* is an exceptional creation in that its action is played against a complex background of interlocking dances, but in other ways it makes a characteristic example of a mid-act finale. It includes all the characters (except the dead Commendatore), and it brings up at full force the class and gender issues that sustain the whole opera. Don Giovanni is giving a dance party, to which he invites guests ranging socially from aristocrats to peasants. But he keeps them segregated by class, each class dancing to its own kind of music in a space of its own, with the result that the guests

who are trying to take revenge on him have trouble uniting against him. This finale also provides an encyclopedic example of the workings of disguise, deceit, and distrust in comic opera. The party creates a stage on which both honest feelings and games of deceit are played out, couples form and reform, and characters mask and reveal themselves, all under the convivial cover of music and dancing.

The finale proper (that is, the stretch of musical numbers, uninterrupted by recitative, leading up to the end of the act) begins before the party, in the garden of Don Giovanni's house. There the peasant bride and bridegroom Zerlina and Masetto, whose wedding plans have been threatened by Don Giovanni's flirtation with Zerlina, are quarreling: Masetto is suspicious that Zerlina is succumbing to Don Giovanni's attentions, and she is resentful of his suspicion. Don Giovanni enters, accompanied by four "nobly clad" servants. Stepping to the commanding sound of full orchestra with timpani in processional mode, he trumpets a general invitation for people to come and enjoy themselves, and his servants second him in chorus. He is flaunting his power and wealth as a nobleman, using his generosity as a host to compel, wielding the irresistible rhythms of the dance to melt his guests' resistance, so that they forget who they are and where their real affections lie.

Zerlina, having just objected as Masetto took up a hiding place in the garden to keep an eye on her, now tries to hide there from Don Giovanni ("Tra quest'arbori celata" / "Hidden among these trees"). He spots her and draws her toward an alcove, where she will be "fortunate," he says, to receive his love. But that is where Masetto is hiding, and Don Giovanni is taken aback to find him there. Quickly recovering his lordly self-confidence, he mocks Masetto to his face, and when one of the party bands is heard striking up a tune, he insists that the couple come into his house with him. They don't resist. They even pretend to be willing: "Andiamo tutti tre" ("Let's go, all three of us").

By the end of this conversation, Don Giovanni has joined Zerlina and Masetto in their chattering style of sung dialogue. He can assume the conversational style of the lower orders while bending them to his will. As the three leave the stage, another three take their place: Donna Elvira, whom Don Giovanni abandoned; Donna Anna, whom he tried to rape; and Don Ottavio, her fiancé. These three are masked, hiding their identities so that they can expose Don Giovanni's sins. But being masked was also an upper-class mode of party-going, and when Leporello spots them from the window, his master tells him to invite them to his party. Meanwhile the onstage band is striking up a new dance: a minuet, considered at the time "the epitome of choreographic elegance and refinement."[12] It sets a tone for the politely guarded exchange within which these masked aristocratic characters pursue their secret designs. Leporello, though appearing as himself, acts here as his master's mask, not for

Pietro Longhi, *Conversation Among Dominos*, 1750s. Since the eighteenth century, the domino (a hooded cape with a mask) has been worn in Venice during the Carnival season, especially by people of the upper classes. In *Don Giovanni* the three aristocratic visitors to Giovanni's ball take advantage of the practice to hide their identities. Ca' Rezzonico, Museum of the Venetian Eighteenth Century, Venice.

Cameraphoto Arte, Venice/ Art Resource, NY

In this staging of the Act 1 finale of *Don Giovanni*, the three party guests mark themselves as aristocrats (even as they disguise their identities) in an outlandish version of the domino, while Don Giovanni's shades make him inscrutable without disguising him. From the left, Shawn Mathey as Don Ottavio, Serena Farnocchia as Donna Elvira, Lucas Meachem as Don Giovanni, and Ellie Dehn as Donna Anna in a 2011 staging by Gabriele Lavia at the San Francisco Opera.

Cory Weaver/San Francisco Opera

the first or last time. Nevertheless, from Don Giovanni's peek out the window at them and his one answer to Leporello, the masqueraders recognize their prey: "(Al volto ed alla voce si scopre il traditore.)" / "(His face and his voice give the traitor away.)"

When the minuet comes to a close, Leporello withdraws from the window into the house, and the three masqueraders are left in the street, ready to enter. They pause to pray for success in their mission. In this prayer they stand not only poised at the door, but totally removed from the delirious and deceitful party world they are about to invade. On the heels of the minuet music that has issued from the house, they sing music so ethereal that it never touches the ground. We hear their voices at first completely unaccompanied, then lightly punctuated by the woodwinds, and later colored by the fluttering of a clarinet. Their billowing lines rise and fall in complex coordination with each other, never in rhythmic unison. Nor do the three characters sing exactly the same words. Donna Elvira's seek revenge more openly than the others':

Donna Anna, Don Ottavio:
Protegga il giusto cielo   May a just heaven protect
Il zelo del mio cor.   the zeal of my heart.

Donna Elvira:
Vendichi il giusto cielo   May a just heaven avenge
Il mio tradito amor.   my betrayed love.

Nevertheless, their lines and words harmonize with spellbinding effect.

This moment of stillness is an example of what John Platoff, in his analysis of comic-opera finale structures, calls a "self-contained expressive passage."[13] The music here has an extraordinary poise, suiting a group of characters who are poised to act yet hesitant to face what lies ahead. They are not just united in purpose, but held transfixed by their shared feeling while this moment lasts. The genius of late eighteenth-century comic opera is most fully realized in its ensembles because they not only carry much of the hilarious stage business (formerly the preserve of recitative or spoken dialogue), but also provide, as in this case, a means for moments of reflection (formerly the preserve of solo numbers).

At this point the scene changes to Don Giovanni's ballroom. There is no break in the music, however. In eighteenth-century theaters scene changes within an act could be carried out mechanically and instantaneously without lowering any curtain. We hear party music as Leporello and Don Giovanni, acting as if there were no difference between master and servant, entertain a ballroom full of peasant guests. Leporello welcomes the three noble masqueraders, the music turning suddenly pompous and courtly ("Venite pur avanti" / "Come right in!"), and Don Giovanni leads them in a salute to

Don Giovanni, assuming he can take advantage of the confusion at his party, grabs Leporello in an attempt to blame him for his own assault on Zerlina, but Don Ottavio, pulling a pistol to halt this deceit, also unmasks himself, revealing that he knows even more about Don Giovanni's crimes. Saimir Pirgu as Don Ottavio, Ildebrando D'Arcangelo as Don Giovanni, and Alex Esposito as Leporello in a production at the Vienna State Opera in 2010.
Leonhard Foeger/Reuters/Newscom

liberty ("Viva la libertà!"), a word that to him could mean simply sexual license.[14] Now begins the main dance sequence, in which three different on-stage bands successively strike up three different dances, all coordinated with each other: a minuet in 3/4, a *contradanza* in 2/4, and a *Teitsch* (or "German") in 3/8. The main characters join in one dance or another, while keeping a suspicious eye on each other and conversing against the music.

The three dances keep the guests separated from each other by class, making them easier for Don Giovanni to control. He hasn't recognized his masked guests, but he can tell that they are aristocrats. When the first band strikes up the minuet, Donna Anna and Don Ottavio obligingly dance to that, effectively isolating themselves from everyone else. Donna Elvira recognizes Zerlina as a fellow victim of Don Giovanni, but it is all Donna Anna can do to keep dancing and, at Don Ottavio's urging, keep pretending that she doesn't know what is going on.

What is going on is that Don Giovanni is preparing an assault on Zerlina. As the second band tunes up, he leads her in dancing the *contradanza*, a

favorite middle-class dance, which presumably offered a middle ground on which a lecherous aristocrat could seduce a temptable peasant. But Masetto's presence is a threat to the seduction. So, as the third band strikes up the *Teitsch*, Leporello takes it upon himself to confine Masetto in his powerless social position by dancing this peasant dance with him. The device of isolating the classes works at first. Don Giovanni drags Zerlina to an offstage room. She cries, "Oh gods, I'm betrayed!" ("Oh Numi! son tradita!"), and Masetto, busy with Leporello, doesn't notice. The three masqueraders across the room, caught up in their minuet, do notice, but comment as if Zerlina is their pawn and Don Giovanni is in their control: "L'iniquo da se stesso nel laccio se ne và" ("The villain is leading himself into the snare").

Two actions now reconfigure the social and sexual forces of this scene. The first is Zerlina's renewed cry for help, abruptly cutting off the dance bands (the minuet stops just short of its last phrase) and bringing the pit orchestra back in at a furious new tempo and in a radically new key. Suddenly everyone is heading for a door. All the guests except the principals flee, and the masqueraders force open the door through which they heard Zerlina's cries, while she enters from another door. For a moment nothing happens, and then as the music switches to another unexpected key and a less frantic tempo, Don Giovanni, sword in hand, leads Leporello in and accuses him of the assault on Zerlina, displacing blame and danger onto his convenient lower-class double. But this is answered by the second reconfiguring action: Don Ottavio, drawing a pistol, forces him to release Leporello as he, Donna Elvira, and Donna Anna unmask themselves.

Don Giovanni is stupefied to discover who these guests are, to find three of his victims and their two male defenders now united against him, all calling him "traitor" ("traditore"). His stupefaction seems to infect them as well, producing what Platoff calls a "shock tutti"—"an astonished [group] response to some unexpected event in the story."[15] In this case what astonishes the victims is that they have caught Don Giovanni together, proving that what he has done to each of them he has done to all of them. Taking strength from each other, they repeat: "Everything is now known . . . everything . . . everything" ("Tutto, tutto già si sa . . . tutto . . . tutto").

The stillness of the "shock tutti" gives way to the fury of a *stretta* (a speeded-up final passage), in which the five members of the victim party denounce Don Giovanni ("Trema, trema, scellerato" / "Tremble, you scoundrel"). Don Giovanni, in answering them, is reinforced by Leporello, who in this scene has been his master's accomplice, deceiving double, lower-class mirror, and dupe, and now again his accomplice. At first, singing when the others are taking a breath between phrases, these two simply, softly admit that Don Giovanni has been caught off guard: "È confusa la mia/sua testa" ("My/his head is confused"). Then, faced with further denunciations, they find a

stronger voice: "Ma non manca in me/lui coraggio" ("But I don't/he doesn't lack courage"). Eventually, as the two parties continue to face off with their words and body gestures, their voices join together in an endless cadence. Neither side can make the other budge. Neither gets the last word or the last note. The standoff is reached in both sight and sound, and the act is over.

Donna Anna's aria "Non mi dir" The principal characters are never united onstage again. But they go on pursuing each other, Don Giovanni seeking sexual adventure and his victims seeking revenge. Though they are endlessly frustrated in that effort, they begin to mend their own lives and relationships. Zerlina and Masetto make peace with each other. And while Don Giovanni is taking refuge from his pursuers in a cemetery, where he makes the fatal mistake of jokingly inviting the statue of the Commendatore home for dinner, Don Ottavio and Donna Anna discuss their future. He assures her that her father's death will soon be avenged, and he asks her to marry him immediately. Donna Anna recoils at the suggestion that she could do that while still grieving, and he loses patience, calling her cruel. Her response is a recitative and aria of a dignity and splendor given to no other character in the opera.

Donna Anna, along with Don Ottavio, seems like a visitor from the world of classical opera. Whereas comic characters were considered disruptive and undesirable in eighteenth-century classical operas, classical characters were welcome in comic opera, where they could enrich the expressive range of the whole. Donna Anna enriches it here with what Mary Hunter calls a "sentimental statement,"[16] a number expressing her upper-class sensibility naturally, nobly, and honestly, free of the disguises, dupings, and betrayals in which she has become embroiled. The Countess, in *Figaro*, finds that freedom only when she is alone; Donna Anna finds it here in the company of Don Ottavio, her companion in classical-opera sensibility.

Donna Anna begins with an accompanied recitative, ("Crudele! Ah no, mio bene!" / "Cruel! Oh no, my beloved!") that deserves to be considered as part of her aria, "Non mi dir" ("Don't tell me"), not only because it begins her self-defense, but also because it previews two orchestral phrases that figure prominently in the aria. In the recitative Donna Anna explains to her lover that though she longs to marry him, neither propriety (what "the world" will say) nor her grieving heart will permit her yet.

Her aria takes the form developed for the "sentimental statement": the **rondò**, a nobly simple slow movement followed by a nobly virtuosic faster one. In the *Larghetto* (slow movement) she answers Don Ottavio's charge of cruelty in

Anonymous oil portrait of Henriette Sontag (1806–1854) as Donna Anna, dressed in mourning for her father. Sontag was one of the greatest singers of her day, renowned for roles in operas of Mozart, Weber, Rossini, and Donizetti, as well as for having sung the soprano solo in the premiere of Beethoven's Ninth Symphony at age eighteen.
Archives Charmet/Bridgeman Art Library

a three-stage argument, each stage taking two lines of poetic text. The first couplet simply denies the charge; the second reminds Don Ottavio that she loves him; and the third tells him to stop tormenting her if he doesn't want to kill her with grief. Mozart has Donna Anna sing these three couplets straight through with hardly any repetitions and only the briefest interruptions, yet he gives each couplet a completely different melody, accompaniment, and relationship between the voice and the orchestra. The first is set to a slowly unfolding, soulful melody, doubled by the first violins and animated by the steady accompaniment of other strings:

Non mi dir, bell'idol mio,	Don't tell me, my beautiful idol,
Che son io crudel con te;	that I am cruel to you —

A new and livelier orchestral phrase sets up Donna Anna's next couplet, sung to a new melody that's intertwined with the orchestra's line instead of doubled by it:

Tu ben sai quant'io t'amai,	You know very well how much I loved you;
Tu conosci la mia fè.	you are aware of my fidelity.

Her third couplet is introduced by yet another new phrase, in a new instrumental color (a pair of clarinets answered by flute and bassoon). She sings each line to one of these woodwind phrases:

Calma, calma il tuo tormento	Calm your tormenting
Se di duol non vuoi ch'io mora.	unless you want me to die of grief.

The changing of musical materials from one couplet to the next clearly marks the stages of her argument off from each other. That rhetorical design bespeaks a simplicity that is noble in the sense of cultivated, not artless. And when she pauses on a half cadence and starts the progression again, Donna Anna soon reveals her artfulness by treating the musical phrases as interchangeable: she omits the second couplet of her text and sings the third ("Calma, calma") to the musical phrase that went with the second. That transfer works because her phrases all express the same bleak mood, the heavy-heartedness that Don Ottavio has aroused in her by calling her cruel. This slow part of Donna Anna's aria comes across as natural, despite its complexity, because in a world of dissimulation she doesn't seem to be able to hide her feelings.

Nor is she able to keep them from changing, even as she speaks. As she continues this third couplet, we can hear a change come over her. The music switches mode from major to minor, and the repeating violin phrase intertwined with the vocal line begins to step down by the interval of a third at each repetition. The incessant modulation of the music suggests that her mind is in turmoil, which is to say that while her words are still addressed to Don Ottavio, her thoughts are becoming fixed on her own despair. She

Victor Maurel

The French baritone Victor Maurel (1848–1923), who created the role of Iago in Verdi's *Otello* (1887) and the title role in his *Falstaff* (1893), was also one of the outstanding Don Giovannis of his age. The following excerpt from his memoir *Dix Ans de carrière, 1887–1897* (*A Decade in a Career,* 1897) tells how he discovered the performing conditions on which *Don Giovanni* depends for its best effect. For this, Maurel should count as one of the founders of the early music, or historically informed performance, movement in music. His account begins in 1871, when he was in Naples to perform Verdi at the San Carlo, the city's major opera house, and decided on a lark to drop in on a production of *Don Giovanni* at a smaller house, the Teatro del Fondo.

I entered; the hall was of moderate dimensions, not at all luxurious in appearance, but already filled with a considerable crowd. The orchestra was in place; I was struck by the small number of players, barely thirty. Under the direction of Maestro Serrao they attacked the overture, and from the first measures I was surprised by sonorities and musical patterns that I didn't remember noticing before.

I became less inclined to scoff. The performance began; the scenery seemed to me miserable; the protagonist, [Francesco] Steller, with his beautiful voice and fine appearance, was the only artist of merit in the company: the others were third- or fourth-rate.

Still, despite these defective conditions, I experienced something very special: I noticed for the first time that there was a really interesting plot, and I took pleasure in following it. Upon leaving, I was satisfied and at the same time discontented: satisfied at having spent a pleasant evening and discontented at not being able to give myself an exact account of what had given me pleasure.

After that, Maurel was dissatisfied every time he played Don Giovanni in a great opera house. He gave up the role for many years, until he felt ready to conquer this "inexplicable obstacle."

But the obstacle wasn't in me, as I'd thought; from the first stage rehearsal, in the immense hall of the Metropolitan Opera, I understood that it lay outside me. Here it is: *Don Giovanni* wasn't made for the grand stage. In fact, the work abounds in details that are the delight of delicate spirits, and these details can't be given their full value except when the theatrical conditions are visually and acoustically special, conditions impossible to realize when the work is presented in too large a frame.

Dix Ans de Carriere, 1887–1897 (Paris: P. Dupont, 1897; reprint New York: Arno Press, 1977), author's translation, pp. 317–18 and 332.

---

doesn't stew for long. At the end of this phrase a new theme introduces the tempo of the fast movement (*Allegretto moderato*), and her words suggest that she is turning her thoughts to the future:

Forse un giorno il cielo ancora	Perhaps one day heaven will again
Sentirà pietà di me.	feel pity for me.

These words of hope seem to float in the air: the bass range suddenly goes silent, and Donna Anna's voice is supported by only the fluttering of the second violins, creating ungrounded harmonies under the notes of her melody. Imagining what it would be like to be released from everything oppressing her (Don Giovanni's assault, his killing of her father, even Don Ottavio's overbearing solicitousness), she is discharging all the energy that those oppressions have pent up within her in a flood of high spirits. While endlessly repeating the words of her one new couplet, she pours out one new phrase after another. Some of them race; some are high-flying; some barely contain their energy in offbeat note repetitions; some crowd in on each other so that

she can barely breathe between them. She never returns to any of them, but always presses on to something new. It is an expression of hope unbounded.

Don Ottavio is still standing there, but this last couplet is not evidently addressed to him, and the all-consuming spirit of her music leaves little room for him. His continuing presence may in fact serve as a measure of how completely her mind turns inward. In that sense this part of her aria might be considered an example of what Mary Hunter calls "the performance of absorption," an outpouring of feelings that is believable and affecting because of the singer's "apparent unawareness of an audience"—in this case Don Ottavio, as well as the audience on the other side of the footlights.[17] Donna Anna's breakthrough into a rapture of hopefulness, in other words, touches us insofar as we feel that she is not trying to put something over on someone else, but is letting us hear what she is feeling inside. This is a form of expression that seems natural not because it is innocent or simple (like Barbarina's), but because the singer is expressing herself in what is (or might as well be) complete privacy.

Furthermore, "Non mi dir" is especially powerful because we don't discover Donna Anna in a self-absorbed state, but watch and listen as she falls into that state in the course of the aria. We follow her through a psychological process, from defending herself with a heavy heart against Don Ottavio to discovering that there is room for joy to return to her life. This mapping of an inner process is the unique form of expression that "Non mi dir" and other *rondò* arias provide in comic operas. It is accomplished musically by the dramatic transformation of tempo and character between the somber *Larghetto* and the rapturous *Allegro*.

Momentous as this aria may be for Donna Anna, it doesn't determine the outcome of the opera. What it contributes is an inkling of gravity that colors the whole drama. In an opera largely made up of deceptions and shenanigans, "Non mi dir" gives spectators a moral touchstone, allowing them to feel that this is one character they can trust because she has displayed the processes of her heart at a moment when her social guard was down. Trusting her, taking her to heart, they can then take seriously the games of dissimulation that occupy the rest of the opera because they realize the power those games have to affect her happiness.

The Male Prerogative of Testing Love: *Così fan tutte*

The third Da Ponte/Mozart collaboration, *Così fan tutte* (*All Women Do the Same*, 1790), is about two young men, best friends, who are so confident in the affections of their fiancées (two sisters) that they allow themselves to be drawn into a wager testing the women's faithfulness. This is not a story about class inequities. It is true that the old cynic who proposes the wager to them, Don Alfonso, is the only character with an honorific title, but that may be a

mark of respect for his greater age. He initiates and resolves the action, but he also collaborates with a serving woman, Despina, in the succeeding intrigue: they manage the test of fidelity together.

Inequities of gender, however, do drive the plot. In many classical and comic operas the love of a young couple is tested by a third party, typically a powerful male character who wants the woman for himself. But in *Così fan tutte* it is the young male lovers themselves who test the constancy of their fiancées, for no better reason than to win the money offered in a wager by a cynical old man to whom they bragged about their loves. This plot has antecedents: in stories by Ovid and the Italian storytellers Boccaccio and Ariosto, it is the man who decides to test the woman's constancy, not in response to outside provocation, but because he is, in Miguel de Cervantes' phrase, "recklessly curious."[18] In societies where men customarily asserted that women were incapable of faithfulness (the meaning of the title *Così fan tutte*), there was endless room for comedy around a man who believed that his own lover was the exception.

The comedy comes when he learns that in testing her devotion, he is testing his own. In *Così fan tutte* this doubling is itself doubled because there are two pairs of lovers: the two men conduct their tests by pretending to go off to war, returning in disguise, and pretending to fall in love with each other's fiancée. The two women at first double each other in their shared resistance to these unwelcome suitors. But then they decide to have some fun with these suitors, and from that point on, the pairs of men and women mirror each other. The women, not knowing that the men are playing a game with them, play a game with the men. The men, caught in it, feel the rejection and jealousy that they have brought on themselves. And the revelation of their deceit in the final scene brings shame to the sisters for having abandoned their men. Though this operatic farce, created when the French Revolution was beginning, pays no attention to the weighty social and political crises of its day, it opens up the utterly serious subject of how we deceive ourselves in deceiving others.

Pairing and differentiating voices The two male lovers, Guglielmo and Ferrando, play the game together onstage through most of the opera, as do the sisters, Fiordiligi and Dorabella. The result is any number of ensembles in which the two men's voices are heard as a pair, singing the same phrases in harmony, or the two women's are, or both pairs sing together, or one or both sing with Don Alfonso or the sisters' maid, Despina. From beginning to end, then, we hear the most ravishingly harmonious succession of duets, trios, quartets, and quintets imaginable. But these ensembles, constructed on the

> ## Così fan tutte
> ### PRINCIPAL CHARACTERS
>
> - **Fiordiligi** and **Dorabella**, well-born sisters
> - **Despina**, their maid
> - **Guglielmo**, an officer in love with Fiordiligi
> - **Ferrando**, an officer in love with Dorabella
> - **Don Alfonso**, an elderly cynic

whole to display how interchangeable each pair is, cannot provide the audience with much sense of what distinguishes one member of a pair from the other. That job is given to the arias.

In the first act, for instance, when the men have made their wager, told the sisters that they are leaving for war, bidden them a farewell of faked tears, and left the women to bestow a touching and sincere blessing, one of the sisters — Dorabella — steps forward to express the anguish both of them feel. But since she is singing a solo, her expression characterizes her alone. Beginning with an accompanied recitative in which she rails at Despina (who has no idea what has happened) to leave her alone, Dorabella launches into an aria that is a picture of hysteria: "Smanie implacabili" ("Implacable frenzies"). The violins endlessly spin out tiny whirling phrases, and Dorabella delivers a gasping but relentless rant, in words describing how her love has turned to a fatal agony.

Fiordiligi sings her first aria a couple of scenes later, when the men have returned in ridiculous disguise as turbaned Albanians. She too speaks for both the sisters, telling the men to be gone. But her self-characterization could not be more different from Dorabella's. Instead of a portrait of hysteria, she presents herself as the strong and reliable one. "Come scoglio immota resta," her aria begins: "Just as a rock remains unmoved by winds and storms, so this soul is ever strong in its devotion and love." And her music matches those words, displaying her power and control as a singer. Sure enough, it will turn out to be Fiordiligi whose devotion to her fiancé outlasts Dorabella's.

Despina's aria "In uomini, in soldati" Between these two arias, the maid Despina establishes her own profile in an aria. But the way she distinguishes herself is not simply a matter of temperament; she is displaying her character as a servant. In drama of all sorts there was a long tradition of servants who presume to lecture their masters about love, generally by posing their perspective of bitter experience and deep cynicism against the naïve idealism that is the luxury of the ruling class. The servant gets to speak, but not necessarily to be taken seriously. The sisters hear Despina out, but don't heed her. She expects that and compensates with an unstoppable outpouring of words. Whereas the powerful derive eloquence from outpourings of notes on a few well-chosen words organized into arguments, their powerless servants derive eloquence from their energy in generating words and images on a single subject, piling them up into long rhymed lists.[19] They are the rap singers of opera.

When Despina learns that the sisters' lovers have gone off to war, leaving them distraught, she sings "In uomini, in soldati," a response to the idea that their lovers are "examples of fidelity." In fact, she begins by throwing that idea back at them as a taunt:

In uomini, in soldati,	In men, in soldiers,
Sperare fedeltà?	you hope for fidelity?
Non vi fate sentir per carità!	Just listen to you, for pity's sake!

After she repeats each phrase insistently, the rest of her aria forms an answer to her own question. Three woodwind instruments ring out like bells calling attention to an important announcement. With this announcement Despina switches into a swaggering new triple rhythm that will last for the rest of the aria. In effect she is really starting the aria with these words: "Di pasta simile son tutti quanti" ("They're all cut from the same dough"). Men, that is, are all incapable of being faithful. It is Despina's answer not just to her mistresses, but to the men who say the same about women.

Now that she has announced her principle, she begins listing the corroborative detail. Here she has no real melody, but recites breathlessly, without repeating a word, all on one note (with an octave drop at the end of almost every phrase). In this too she is like a rap singer, a virtuoso at delivering rhythmicized words. As her recitation continues, growing slightly more melodic, she draws a lesson after every four lines. There are three:

. . . son le primarie	These are their primary
Lor qualità.	qualities.

. . . Nè val da' barbari	From such barbarians
Chieder pietà.	it's not worth asking for pity.

. . . Amiam per comodo,	Let us love as it suits us,
Per vanità.	for the sake of our vanity.

Nuccia Focile (in red) as Despina, singing "In uomini, in soldati" to Magdalena Kožená (left) as Dorabella and Barbara Frittoli (right) as Fiordiligi, in Act 1 of *Così fan tutte*, staged by Robin Guarino at the Metropolitan Opera, 2005.
Marty Sohl/Metropolitan Opera

The aria as a whole moves from shock ("Just listen to you!") to diagnosis ("Men are all cut from the same dough") to a proposed remedy ("Let us love as it suits us"). Despina seems more and more confident as she holds the attention of her mistresses with her verbal energy, until at the end she lets go of words altogether. When something like the main theme of the aria (heard first to the words "Di pasta simile son tutti quanti") comes back for the third and last time, she simply trills her way nonchalantly down the phrase: "La ra la, la ra la, la ra la la." Despina hasn't exactly challenged her mistresses' authority, but under the guise of offering them advice, she has had the audacity—which Figaro lacks—to contradict them to their faces. In the end, what she is really offering them is what rappers call "attitude."

The duet "Fra gli amplessi" The ensembles in *Così fan tutte* generally depict characters as interchangeable. Near the end, however, there is one ensemble that enacts a betrayal, in which consequently it matters who is singing what to whom. This is the duet "Fra gli amplessi" (Act 2, scene 12), which pushes the drama to its dénouement. When it begins, Fiordiligi has held out longer than Dorabella, but she is finding it harder and harder to resist her sister's "Albanian" fiancé Ferrando. In her despair she decides to don a soldier's uniform (Ferrando's, actually) and run off to the battlefield to find Guglielmo. Meanwhile, though, Ferrando, enraged by the news that Dorabella has forsaken him for the disguised Guglielmo, resolves to have his revenge by getting Fiordiligi to forsake Guglielmo for him. At the beginning of the scene Fiordiligi is putting on the uniform, not realizing that Guglielmo and Ferrando as well as Don Alfonso are all in hiding, watching her.

The number that she begins to sing can only be an aria, it seems. She describes the pleasure it will give her and Guglielmo to see each other again. But just at that point Ferrando walks in and, without missing a beat in her music, answers her phrase about Guglielmo's anticipated pleasure with one about his own anticipated death if she goes, turning her joyful E major chord into his own mournful E minor one:

Miah Persson as Fiordiligi at the moment of her surrender to Ferrando (Topi Lehtipuu) in the duet "Fra gli amplessi," from Act 2 of *Così fan tutte*, staged by Claus Guth at the Salzburg (Austria) Festival, 2009.

Calle Toernstroem/Reuters/Newscom

Fiordiligi:
Oh che gioia il suo bel core   Oh what joy his fine heart
Proverà nel ravvisarmi!   will feel on recognizing me!

Ferrando:
Ed intanto di dolore   While I shall die,
Meschinello io mi morrò!   miserable, from grief!

This moment, in which the two characters are so starkly contrasted in word and musical mode, yet so smoothly

matched, sets the tone of their engagement. They resort to histrionic gestures—she orders him to leave, he asks her to stab him with a sword—yet they constantly answer one another in each other's musical phrases. They even sing in parallel harmony, both observing that her constancy is starting to vacillate. Nevertheless, it seems that on these terms he could go on pleading indefinitely and she could go on vacillating without yielding. Apparently it will take a change in their verbal and musical terms of engagement before they can resolve anything. That change comes when Ferrando takes the floor by himself and sings—in a new key, tempo, and rhythm and with simple violin doubling—a serene prayer for Fiordiligi's love:

Volgi a me pietoso il ciglio!	Turn a merciful look on me!
In me sol trovar tu puoi	In me alone you can find
Sposo, amante, e più se vuoi.	a husband, lover, and more if you want.
Idol mio, più non tardar.	My idol, delay no longer.

As Ferrando repeats his last two lines, a word or phrase at a time, she inserts words of her own that gradually concede her surrender to him:

Giusto ciel! . . . crudel . . . hai vinto.	Just heaven! . . . cruel one . . . you have won.
Fa di me quel che ti par.	Do with me as you will.

But before indicating her surrender in words, she joins with Ferrando in a project of musical cooperation (or is it one-upmanship?). As the bass line moves slowly up the scale from C-sharp to F-sharp, the singers interweave their tiny phrases, picking up on each other's notes and moving them up by successive steps, the top notes of the tiny phrases forming one slowly rising scale and the bottom notes another (see Example 9.3). It is like a duet in which both singers sing both parts. The bass then steps chromatically down from F-sharp to E and hovers around E in preparation for a cadence on A. If it seems to take forever for that cadence to arrive, the anticipation is double: we can feel in the prolonging of the phrase that Fiordiligi will announce her surrender at the cadence. But meanwhile the constructing of lines continues, joined by the oboe. Fiordiligi sings her words of surrender ("Do with me as you will") in a scale that rises to E and plunges to A just as the oboe completes a descending scale to A and the bass finally makes its cadence, also on A. The force of this convergence of cadencing lines and surrendering words is overwhelming.

The dramatic and musical satisfaction of the moment is disturbed by someone whose feelings in the matter we may have forgotten. Guglielmo, seeing his fiancée surrender to his best friend—and seeing his wager lost—has to be restrained by Don Alfonso from rushing forward out of their hiding place.

9.3 Mozart, *Così fan tutte:* Act 2, scene 12, "Fra gli amplessi"

Meanwhile, Fiordiligi and Ferrando embrace, singing the joyous passage of parallel and intertwining harmonies that define a love duet. In this case the heart of the duet lies in what is accomplished already: the strenuous process by which these two characters, one furiously resisting and the other courting for revenge, accommodate each other. Yet the accommodation doesn't mean they are in love with each other, and the concluding passage of what sounds like love-duet music may not be sufficient to convince an audience that they are. In fact, at this point in the opera the game of love has not yet been played out, and while these two lovers may now have felt the bitterness of betrayal and guilt, they have further innocence to shed about the nature of love before the game is over.

Resolutions

In some respects the finale that ends a Mozart comic opera is like the performance for which the mid-point finale was the rehearsal. In the mid-point finale nothing is resolved and the cast is left divided against itself, while in the end-point finale a figure of power permits the issues that divided the cast to be resolved, and the characters join together to sing the moral they draw from their experience.

In *Così fan tutte* Don Alfonso brings resolution by exposing the test of love that he initiated. The two young men drop their disguises, and all four lovers are revealed to have betrayed their partners and—just as discomfortingly, since it was the subject of the bet—to have been thoroughly naïve about love. They join with Don Alfonso and Despina in singing about the calm with which you can face life if you temper your expectations with reason.

In *Don Giovanni* the title character has no power to resolve the plot, but neither do his victims have the power to liberate themselves from his predatory spell. Only the spirit of a dead man—in fact, of a dead nobleman of high military standing—can achieve that. The Commendatore drags Don Giovanni down to Hell, and the others, in the epilogue, can then sing individually about getting on with their lives and together about evildoers getting their just deserts.

In *The Marriage of Figaro* the figure of power, Count Almaviva, does not get so radically out of the others' way, but he does get down on his knees when

In *Così fan tutte* the two sisters and their fiancés make dangerously interchangeable pairs. In this 2001 production at the Theatre de la Jeune Lune in Minneapolis, it helped that the two sisters, Fiordiligi and Dorabella, were played by two real sisters, Jennifer Baldwin Peden (left) and Christina Baldwin. Marshall Urban (left) played Guglielmo, and Sean Fallen Ferrando.

Michal Daniel/Minnesota Opera, Minneapolis

he is revealed to be the would-be adulterer that he is wrongly accusing his wife of being. She can then forgive him, and the whole cast sings in praise of the healing power of love.

These are all pretty mundane lessons, which Mozart set to appropriately trite tunes, as if the hard-won lessons of the drama were obvious truths staring the characters in the face all along. But then, comic operas like Mozart's were the sitcoms of their day: stories of ordinary people who learn to cope with duplicities defined by traditional inequities of class and gender, and who emerge capable of loving with their eyes open. That's all. They don't have the fates of nations depending on them, and they don't need gods descending from the clouds to rescue them. Even the finale of *Don Giovanni*, a stupendous gothic whirlwind of sound in which a supernatural being triumphs over the previously untouchable protagonist, has no transforming effect on anyone else in the cast. When it is over, Leporello, who has watched it all from a hiding place under the table, brushes himself off and heads for the nearest inn to look for a new boss.

But then, what becomes of the idea, proposed earlier in this book, that opera is a form of drama particularly suited to fantastic themes and settings because its aura of continuous musical sound carries spectators off to another world and holds them there? And how have these three Mozart operas on such mundane subjects secured a firmer place in the repertory than all the operas on mythological and remote historical subjects written in the two centuries before them?

Perhaps comic opera can be considered an eighteenth-century experiment in which the aura of music helped transform the everyday into the otherworldly, or unlock the poetry of the prosaic. Already early in the century, works like *La serva padrona* allowed spectators to absorb a dramatic situation simultaneously from conflicting perspectives, hearing in a character's music that she intends another character to take her seriously, but also realizing that she is putting him on. For the rest of the century librettists like Da Ponte and composers like Mozart developed this concept into a method for comprehending the most complex dramatic situations in what feel like natural means of musical expression. They created comic characters (comic even if they are countesses) who cope resourcefully with the duplicities and ambiguities, the bruising and absurdity, that any spectator will recognize as natural to social life. The dramatic predicaments, even more than the here-and-now settings, make the characters seem all too human. But the grace of the language and music in which they express themselves as they negotiate those all-too-human predicaments makes them seem like creatures from a different world.

FURTHER READING

On Mozart's life and career, *Mozart's Letters, Mozart's Life: Selected Letters*, ed. and trans. Robert Spaethling (New York: Norton, 2000). On his comic operas, Wye Jamison Allanbrook, *Rhythmic Gesture in Mozart: "Le nozze di Figaro"* & *"Don Giovanni"* (Chicago and London: University of Chicago Press, 1983); Jessica Waldoff, *Recognition in Mozart's Operas* (Oxford: Oxford University Press, 2006); Mary Hunter, *Mozart's Operas: A Companion* (New Haven and London: Yale University Press, 2008). On the three Da Ponte operas, all from Cambridge University Press (Cambridge and New York): Tim Carter, *W. A. Mozart: "Le nozze di Figaro"* (1987); Julian Rushton, *W. A. Mozart: "Don Giovanni"* (1981); Bruce Alan Brown, *W. A. Mozart: "Così fan tutte"* (1995).

FOR RESEARCH AND REFLECTION

1. In their day the comic operas of Mozart and other eighteenth-century composers presented recognizable, if absurd, portrayals of contemporary life. When we watch them today, in what ways do they still represent the lives of recognizable people, and in what ways do they represent people of another age and world?

2. Compare *The Beggar's Opera* with its twentieth-century German remake, *The Threepenny Opera* (*Die Dreigroschenoper*), composed by Kurt Weill to a text by Bertolt Brecht. In what ways does the remake update the original, and in what ways does it retain connections to the eighteenth-century world of the original?

3. To what extent does *La serva padrona* contain the essential dramatic matter, as well as the essential musical means, of Mozart's comic operas?

4. Don Giovanni's victims—all the other characters in the opera—unite to resist him, and we hear their union in a series of ensembles. How do the other characters in *The Marriage of Figaro* come together to resist the Count, and what musical forms does their unity take?

5. When Don Giovanni and his servant Leporello trade identities, do they keep their own musical identities or take on each other's? What are the signs of those musical identities?

6. In *Così fan tutte* all the characters get involved in a game of switching partners, and all four at one point or another become more serious about it than they meant to be. How can you judge where game playing ends and seriousness begins in this work?

 Additional resources are available at wwnorton.com/studyspace.

NINETEENTH-CENTURY MILESTONES

1795
National Conservatory of Music (the Paris Conservatory) created by the French revolutionary government, leading to a new system of training for singers and other musicians.

1805
Fidelio, libretto by Josef von Sonnleithner from the opera by Jean-Nicolas Bouilly, music by Ludwig van Beethoven, performed in Vienna.

1814–15
Congress of Vienna remakes the boundaries and power arrangements of Europe after the final defeat of Napoleonic France.

1816
The Barber of Seville, libretto by Cesare Sterbini from the play by Beaumarchais, music by Gioachino Rossini, performed in Rome.

1828
La Muette de Portici (*The Mute Woman of Portici*), the first work in the grand opera tradition, libretto by Eugène Scribe and Germain Delavigne, music by Daniel-François-Esprit Auber, performed in Paris.

1836
Les Huguenots, libretto by Eugène Scribe and Emile Deschamps, music by Giacomo Meyerbeer, performed in Paris.

1842
Ruslan and Lyudmila, libretto by Valerian Shirkov and others after a poem by Alexander Pushkin, music by Mikhail Glinka, performed in St. Petersburg.

1843
Der fliegende Holländer (*The Flying Dutchman*), libretto and music by Richard Wagner, performed in Dresden.

1853
La traviata (*The Woman Gone Astray*), libretto by Francesco Maria Piave after the novel and play by Alexandre Dumas the son, music by Giuseppe Verdi, performed in Venice.

1859
Bolshoi Theater inaugurated in Moscow. Other grand new state opera houses inaugurated in St. Petersburg (Mariinsky) in 1860, Vienna (Court Opera, later State Opera) in 1869, and Paris (Opéra) in 1875.

1870
Italy unified as a kingdom after decades of struggle to drive out foreign forces.

1871
End of the Franco-Prussian War, resulting in the creation of the German Empire and the Third Republic in France, replacing the imperial rule of Napoléon III.

Aida, libretto by Antonio Ghislanzoni and music by Giuseppe Verdi, performed at the recently opened Opera House in Cairo.

1874
Boris Godunov, libretto and music by Modest Musorgsky after a play by Alexander Pushkin, performed in St. Petersburg.

1875
Carmen, libretto by Henri Meilhac and Ludovic Halévy after a novella by Prosper Mérimée, music by Georges Bizet, performed in Paris.

1876
First complete performance of *Der Ring des Nibelungen* (*The Ring of the Nibelung*), words and music by Richard Wagner, based on German and Scandinavian epic poetry, given at the Bayreuth Festival Theater, built for that work in Bayreuth, Germany.

1887
Otello, libretto by Arrigo Boito after the play by Shakespeare, music by Giuseppe Verdi, performed in Milan.

1890
Cavalleria rusticana (*Rustic Chivalry*), an early landmark of human-interest opera, libretto by Giovanni Targioni-Tozzetti and Guido Menasci after a play by Giovanni Verga, music by Pietro Mascagni, performed in Rome.

1896
La bohème (*Bohemian Life*), libretto by Giuseppe Giacosa and Luigi Illica after a novel by Henri Murger, music by Giacomo Puccini, performed in Turin, Italy.

PART IV

Opera of the Nineteenth Century

Nowadays the nineteenth-century repertory stands for opera as a whole. Opera houses advertise their offerings and cartoonists make fun of opera by choosing characters from nineteenth-century works to stand for the whole enterprise: the Spanish Gypsy Carmen with a rose between her teeth, the Norse heroine Brünnhilde with her horned helmet and spear, or the ancient Ethiopian princess Aida enslaved in the shadow of the pyramids. In major opera houses today, one century out of the four of operatic history often occupies a full half of the repertory. How can opera in our culture be so overwhelmingly identified with just that one century? What features of nineteenth-century operas allowed them to chase the repertories of the previous two centuries off the stage without being chased off in turn by twentieth-century works?

For one thing, these operas introduced significantly new subject matter, which

Scene design by Charles Séchan and others for a clerical-military procession at the fifteenth-century Council of Konstanz, in Halévy's *La Juive* (*The Jewish Woman*), Paris Opera, 1835. This historically inspired staging, which exerted a lasting influence on opera, is not spectacle for its own sake: the power displayed here turns ugly when the Christian majority discover that Jewish craftsmen are not participating in their celebration. Bibliothèque de l'Opera Garnier, Paris.
Archives Charmet/Bridgeman Art Library

not only suited the sensibility of nineteenth-century audiences but has continued to resonate with audiences into the twenty-first. When they deal with political power, for instance, they may be set in an age of kings centuries earlier, but they portray relationships between leaders and their people as experienced in modern states. Likewise, when the stories deal with domestic conflict, whether in contemporary or legendary settings, they explore family and psychological dynamics in terms that remain largely recognizable today.

CHAPTER 10

Opera on Themes of Political Conflict

A New Scale of Action and Sound

The stories of nineteenth-century opera, in particular stories about the fate of nations, required large masses of singers, dancers, and extras, together with masses of instrumentalists and backstage hands to support them. These numbers in turn required larger audiences than before to pay for them all. A new concept of staging permitted that growth. In earlier operas everyone onstage had to stay close to the front; otherwise they would have shattered the illusion of space created by the staggered wing flats of the scenery. Nineteenth-century staging, by contrast, relied on three-dimensional sets, which divided the stage into distinct zones, all equally inhabitable.

In some cases the spaces themselves were also increased. When opera houses were replaced in the nineteenth century, they were often built on a larger scale than before. The opening of a new theater for the Paris Opera in 1821, with a greatly enlarged stage and proscenium as well as a slightly greater seating capacity than its predecessor, facilitated the creation in subsequent decades of the most spectacular operas ever designed for regular production. This repertory, fittingly known

The final scene of Verdi's *Aida*, represented on the cover of the score published by Ricordi in Milan in 1872. The scene shows the Ethiopian princess Aida and her lover, the Egyptian general Radamès, being buried alive together under the Temple of Vulcan. New print technologies developed in the nineteenth century put vastly more opera images, and more colorful ones, in the public eye than ever before.

Leemage/Lebrecht Music & Arts

as **grand opera**, spread its influence across the whole operatic world, to the extent that the nineteenth century can be considered the age of grand opera.

Between the mid-eighteenth and mid-nineteenth century, the orchestra and chorus more or less doubled in size at many houses, becoming more capable of overwhelming listeners with sound. Hector Berlioz, famous for composing for gargantuan forces, described how Gioachino Rossini upped the sonic ante in *Le Siège de Corinthe* (*The Siege of Corinth*), which was produced in Paris in 1826:

> [Rossini] put the bass drum everywhere—and the cymbals and the triangle, and the trombones and the ophicleide [a bass brass instrument], making them blare out clumps of chords and play headlong rhythms with all their might. He brought out of the orchestra such brilliant clusters of sounds, if not of harmony, and created such thunderclaps that the audience, rubbing their eyes, enjoyed this new sensation, the most vivid if not the most musical that they had ever experienced.[1]

As a result of these changes, the solo singers shrank in relation to the spaces they were expected to fill and the masses of singers and players assembled to "reinforce" them. The soloists were being asked to sing for long stretches in the highest parts of their range and at their peak volume. They needed a brilliant vocal production to command attention in the crowd scenes and a superhuman presence to impose a hush on the huge auditorium in intimate scenes. In response, they developed an extraordinarily powerful, open sound that they could sustain throughout an entire role. This is the sound that still characterizes operatic singing today. The capacity of opera singers to fill large halls by the sheer power of their voices has thrilled audiences for almost two centuries, enduring even in our age of amplification.

As opera singers adopted this new technique in the nineteenth century, they gradually sacrificed the technique that had given them an easy intimacy with their audiences when houses and casts were relatively small. They surrendered their conversational tone, especially in recitative; their flexible vocal characterization, or impersonation, especially in comic opera; and the florid embellishments of eighteenth-century style. Today the seventeenth- and eighteenth-century repertories have largely become the province of specialist singers, dancers, and players, often performing away from the biggest houses to audiences of early-opera enthusiasts.

Meanwhile, the major houses, even those built recently, have been kept mostly to the size and configuration of those from the nineteenth century, and they continue to use essentially the same resources: sets moved by rollers and ropes; a large orchestra, chorus, and ballet corps; and soloists with nineteenth-century vocal techniques. Amplification is done modestly and surreptitiously, if at all. The only really modern resources generally used in

the opera house today are visual: the equipment for lighting, visual projection, and supertitles. And operas written since the nineteenth century have by and large been required to stick to these resources.

A Musical Language for Themes of Tragic Destiny

Not all operas composed in the nineteenth or twentieth century relate stories that require big-theater resources. Many are tales of love and family relationships between a very few characters. But even these stories often suit the vehement operatic sound of the last two centuries because they partake in the general turn to tragic endings. In the seventeenth and eighteenth centuries even operas on tragic stories were generally resolved happily: a timely discovery or a goddess or god descending from the clouds rescues the protagonists from a catastrophic fate. In the course of the nineteenth century this tradition gave way to a pattern of inexorably unhappy endings (except in comic opera, which became increasingly marginalized after Mozart). Not only do Carmen, Brünnhilde, and Aida all bring down the curtain with their deaths; so do the heroines of domestic dramas in contemporary settings (the settings reserved for comedy in the eighteenth century), heroines like Violetta in Verdi's La traviata and Mimì in Puccini's La bohème.

The sense of inescapable tragic destiny that pervades these operas comes as much from the music as from the plots. The powerful styles of singing and playing convey to the audience the sound of people struggling hopelessly against the fates in which they feel trapped. The audience also hears the march of destiny in the repetition of threatening musical motives. In Carmen we hear a motive of foreboding that dogs the title character every time she appears, warning us of her doom. In Wagner's Der Ring des Niebelungen (in which Brünnhilde appears) every motive in the orchestra seems to recur endlessly, taking on a dramatic significance of its own and weaving together with others, until we feel that the characters live in a musical web from which no one could escape.

At the same time, major opera houses in this period were moving away from the **stagione** (season) **system**, their two-centuries-old practice of repeating one work night after night, or a couple of works in alternation, for a good part of the season, until the next new work was ready. They gradually introduced a **repertory system**, in which a larger number of works were presented in rotation.[2] Now a subscriber was less apt to hear the same work repeatedly in the same season and get to know it from beginning to end by dint of repeated exposure. Composers working under the new system would naturally have considered how to make the opera memorable without

relying on the listener hearing the work repeatedly. Repeating a musical motive within the work, associating it each time with the same character or idea, was one answer. Meanwhile, the increasing practice of dimming the house lights during performances (made feasible by gas and then electric lighting) encouraged listeners to stay attentive to the work from beginning to end. Nowadays, of course, opera broadcasts and recordings supplement the live experience, changing beyond recognition the process of getting to know an opera and therefore changing once again the listener's need for internal musical reminders.

Political Melodrama Around the Time of the French Revolution

Prerevolutionary Melodrama: Grétry, *Richard Coeur-de-Lion*

Late in the eighteenth century, even before the French Revolution (1789), which would help shape profound change in the subject matter and stylistic resources of opera, some remarkable steps in that operatic revolution were already being made. In André-Ernest-Modeste Grétry's *Richard Coeur-de-Lion* (*Richard the Lion-Hearted*, 1784), for example, the vehement musical tone characteristic of nineteenth-century opera is present, along with a musical theme that recurs throughout the work. Neither of these features is associated with a tragic sense of destiny; in fact, the ending is exultantly happy. But they are both associated with a kind of political turbulence that had not been represented on the operatic stage before.

The opera was created in Paris, not at the Opéra but at the Comédie-Italienne, home of *opéra comique*, the form of French opera that used spoken dialogue between the musical numbers. Despite the relatively restricted resources of the Comédie-Italienne, it was the scene of tremendous creative ferment in the 1780s, especially in the works of Grétry and Michel-Jean Sedaine, the librettist of *Richard Coeur-de-Lion*. Until the Revolution all theatrical performance in Paris was under the control of the monarchy, and revolutionary or antimonarchical subject matter was consequently unthinkable onstage. But subjects that expressed the anxieties of a nation living in an autocratic political system were potentially permissible. In fact, Sedaine and Grétry turned out several works about individuals unjustly imprisoned and then rescued through the devotion of a spouse or friend—a type sometimes known as the "rescue opera."[3] The whole history of opera had been filled

with prison scenes, but traditionally it was rivalry in love that led tyrannical rulers to imprison heroes. In *Richard Coeur-de-Lion* the motive was political, and the rescue of the prisoner therefore an act of resistance to political injustice. The subject was tolerated by the French monarchy because the imprisoned hero is a king.

Finding power in a song The story concerns the twelfth-century English king Richard I and takes place in Austria, where the historical Richard was captured on his way home from a Crusade and held for ransom in the castle overlooking the town of Dürrenstein. In the opening act the stage shows the daily life of the medieval town, as young and old, powerful and powerless, natives and visitors go about their business, almost all unaware of the royal prisoner being held in the castle. Part of the medieval coloration comes from the pseudo-medieval songs sung or played on the violin by a visiting troubadour, Blondel, who is actually Richard's faithful friend and fellow poet-songwriter, come in search of him. One of these songs turns out to play a central role in the opera. "Une fièvre brûlante" ("A burning fever") is supposedly the song Richard wrote for his beloved Marguerite before their betrothal was interrupted by the Crusade. Now Marguerite is passing through Dürrenstein, and Blondel plays it for her on his violin.

In the second act Blondel stands at the foot of the prison tower and sings the song, thinking that if Richard is being held there, he can respond to it without his captors understanding that he is identifying himself. It not only works; it produces an effect unlike anything ever known before in opera. The effect depends on the traditional comic practice of doubling. Blondel is not just Richard's countryman and fellow troubadour, but his fellow tenor. When he begins singing Richard's love song, he is standing in for Richard:

Blondel (1841), by the English painter George Frederic Watts, depicts the twelfth-century French troubadour (probably the historical Jean de Nesle), who was connected in legend to the English king Richard I. In Watts's version Blondel holds a harp, a less anachronistic instrument than the violin he plays in Grétry's opera, composed a half century earlier.

©Trustees of the Watts Gallery, Compton, Surrey/Bridgeman Art Library

Une fièvre brûlante	*A burning fever*
Un jour me terrassait . . .	*struck me down once . . .*

In his speaking voice and therefore as an aside, not giving himself away, Richard exclaims that he recognizes the voice. And because Blondel played the song earlier on the violin, the audience too recognizes it and hears it as a reminder of Richard's happy earlier life as king, lover, and troubadour. Blondel continues:

Et de mon corps chassait	*driving my languishing soul*
Mon âme languissante.	*away from my body.*
Ma Dame approche de mon lit,	*My lady comes toward my bed,*
Et loin de moi la mort s'enfuit.	*and death runs far away from me.*

Now Richard stands in for Blondel, his tenor voice smoothly replacing Blondel's as he completes the song with its refrain:

Un regard de ma belle	*One look from my beloved*
Fait dans mon tendre coeur	*makes happiness*
A la peine cruelle	*replace cruel suffering*
Succéder le bonheur.	*in my tender heart.*

It is an uncanny moment. For Richard it is as if the song has given him back his voice—and with it his old life and attachments. For Blondel it is as if he has brought his missing king back to life by singing. And because the audience already knows the song and can almost feel itself singing along with Richard, he seems to come to life within listeners as well.

Blondel starts a second verse, evidently his own since it describes the present situation. In that sense it has changed from a song from Richard's past to one about his present. But in the sense that Blondel is now composing the song, he has become Richard.

Dans une tour obscure	*In a dark tower*
Un roi puissant languit.	*a powerful king is languishing.*
Son serviteur gémit	*His servant groans*
De sa triste aventure.	*at his sad fate.*

Just when Blondel has become Richard, Richard announces (again in his speaking voice) that he recognizes him as Blondel, and then he completes Blondel's verse with a thought that could come only from Richard:

Si Marguerite etait ici,	*If Marguerite were here,*
Je m'écrierais: plus de souci.	*I would cry, "No matter!"*

Finally, the two singers, each other's doubles, join their voices to sing the final couplet as a duet in parallel thirds. This is a duet of solidarity and even, on the two little notes they have in unison, one of complete identity. Literally a scene of discovery, it seems more like a conjuring scene, in which each character makes the other appear, out of his own identity, in the medium of a song. In its way, this is the one politically revolutionary moment in the opera. While it romanticizes the monarch, it also makes the monarch and his subject (and even the audience, humming along) not just equal, but identical. The comic device of doubling has here become a musical device of magical political transformation.

Transformation is not the same thing as rescue, however. For that, Blondel enlists the townspeople of Dürrenstein. Although in the first act they did not appear politically discontented, they now participate willingly in Blondel's plot against their own rulers. They hold a dance, to which the governor of the prison is lured, then captured and held, while soldiers enlisted by

André-Ernest-Modeste Grétry

Grétry's *Memoirs, or Essay on Music* (1789; enlarged edition, 1797) is invaluable not only as a source of information about that composer's works and thoughts, but as a window into the process of creating operas more than two centuries ago. The following passage gives us the kind of insight into the creation of the romance "Une fièvre brûlante" in *Richard Coeur-de-Lion* that would be welcome from many other composers.

Sedaine, in sending me his manuscript, told me: "I have already entrusted this poem to one composer; he didn't accept it because he didn't believe he could do justice to the romance it contains. Read it, decide for yourself, and don't feel any compulsion about it."

Even though I accepted this fine dramatic work without hesitation, I admit that the romance troubled me as much as my colleague: I composed it in several ways without finding what I sought, namely the old style that was capable of pleasing the moderns. My struggle to choose the eventual song from among my ideas lasted from 11:00 at night until 4:00 the next morning. We entrusted the role of Richard to [the singer] Philippe, who had not yet created any role and who, since his success in this one, has earned more and more plaudits from the public. After several rehearsals, the beauty of the situation and the actor's sensitivity, combined with his desire to perform the role well, exalted his imagination, to the point where he choked on his tears when he was to reply to Blondel: "Un regard de ma belle . . ."

The day of the first performance the actor, filled with ardor and zeal, suddenly lost his voice. There wasn't time to put on a different show: the hall was full. He summoned me to his dressing room. "Let's see," I said, "sing me your romance." He produced several sounds painfully. "There it is," I told him, "the voice of a prisoner. You'll produce the effect that I'm looking for. Sing and don't worry about it."

Mémoires, ou Essais sur la musique (Paris, 1797; reprinted New York: Da Capo Press, 1971), vol. 1, pp. 368–70.

Blondel storm the prison and liberate Richard. This was an ending that the librettist and composer did not originally envision, but devised once the opera was up and running, when audiences found an ending without a popular uprising unconvincing.[4] It reveals something about the political climate in Paris in the years before the Revolution that public opinion could force the creators of this work and the administrators of the opera house to change the ending so as to show an aroused populace resisting unjust authority.

In the sense that the uprising liberates a foreign king at the instigation of his faithful servant, the new ending was just as monarchist as Blondel's passionate first-act air of allegiance and devotion to his king, "O Richard, ô mon Roi" ("O Richard, O my king"). But in the new ending the vehemence of the music, matching the noise and bluster of the stage action, helps turn the populace into a character in its own right, rising up against authority. In that sense—not just for its sheer noise—the scene foreshadows many scenes of revolutionary uprisings in later operas. When it is over, amid the general celebration at Richard's liberation, Marguerite, Richard, and Blondel sing a quiet but grand final version of "Une fièvre brûlante" to new words. This song has not only recurred in each act, but has developed as it recurred, ending the work in a triumphant transformation—what is sometimes called a musical **apotheosis**. In

effect, the song has led a life of its own in the drama. We might even call it the hero of the story. Since then, songs have played that role in many kinds of show ("Can't Help Lovin' Dat Man of Mine," for instance, in the Jerome Kern / Oscar Hammerstein musical *Show Boat* of 1927); in 1784 it was a revolutionary idea.

Postrevolutionary Melodrama: Beethoven, *Fidelio*

In 1805, two decades after *Richard Coeur-de-Lion* was produced in Paris, Ludwig van Beethoven's *Fidelio*, another opera with spoken dialogue telling a story of unjust imprisonment and rescue, premiered in Vienna. But it was created in the aftermath of the French Revolution and expresses a postrevolutionary outlook. The Revolution overthrew the monarchy in France and utterly altered every other institution of French society in the last decade of the eighteenth century. It brought France into conflict with the monarchies that ruled elsewhere in Europe. By the time Beethoven was composing his opera, French armies had defended France against the armies of those monarchies and had invaded other countries in turn, threatening the traditional political order everywhere they went, including the Austrian monarchy seated in Vienna.

The French government was no longer pursuing revolutionary ideals, nor was it executing its real and imagined enemies, as it had in the Reign of Terror of 1793–94. French public opinion recoiled from those excesses, and an opportunistic military leader, Napoleon Bonaparte, had taken control of the country. But even when monarchies were restored, as they were in France and throughout Europe by 1815, Europeans would never again think of a political order as unchangeable. Instead, everyone looked out at a world in a state of perpetual division and potential conflict over the most basic principles of political power. Opera, like all the arts, came to express this outlook and to explore the consequences of living in this new, polarized world.

Postrevolutionary consciousness At the height of revolutionary fervor in France, the opera houses of Paris had produced works, some based on current events, celebrating the heroism of ordinary citizens in the face of tyranny. After the Reign of Terror passed, these same houses produced operas sympathetic to aristocrats who were victims of tyranny. But the public was weary of ideological shouting matches that had erupted even between factions in the audience, and the creators of postrevolutionary operas were careful to set them in remote times or places, with oppressor figures who did not resemble any French authorities. One of these works was *Léonore*, produced in Paris in 1798, with music by Pierre Gaveaux to a libretto by Jean-Nicolas Bouilly. This was the libretto that Beethoven would soon

recompose as *Fidelio*. *Léonore* is set in Spain at an unspecified date, and it concerns an aristocrat, Florestan, vindictively imprisoned by a tyrannical governor of the local prison. The prisoner's wife, Leonore, disguises herself as a young man named Fidelio—thus making us see her double through most of the opera—to get work in the prison and discover if her husband is still alive. She prevents him from being executed, and the king's minister completes the rescue and punishes the guilty governor.

The action hinges on a commoner who is caught between fear of disobeying an unjust authority figure and sympathy for that figure's victims. The commoner, Roc the jailer, agrees to take Leonore/Fidelio to see the secret "state prisoner" in the dungeon, agrees to her request to let the prisoners out of their cells for a few minutes of air and sun, and refuses the governor's demand that he kill the secret prisoner (though he does agree to dig a grave for the body to fill once the governor himself has killed him). Roc may not have the courage to defy injustice, but he is a commoner who sees aristocrats like Florestan as fellow human beings. He is the bearer of what was then a new, postrevolutionary consciousness: a will to ignore class differences for fear of the violence that could be unleashed by either the monarchist insistence on upholding them or the revolutionary insistence on eliminating them.[5]

If French audiences of the late 1790s, in the aftermath of the Terror, were ready to see a new political consciousness embodied in operas, it is hardly surprising that these operas were soon being exported to other countries, where people were riveted by news of the revolutionary events in France and where the upper classes trembled at the approach of French armies. It is telling that in Vienna, with the Austrian emperor Franz a nephew of the executed French queen Marie Antoinette, there was a great vogue for postrevolutionary operas. Starting in 1802 a stream of *opéras comiques* of this type was performed there. When *Léonore* joined this stream in 1805, the libretto was translated into German, and Beethoven provided it with new music. It was billed as *Fidelio* to distinguish it from several earlier versions titled *Léonore*, and it has been known as *Fidelio* ever since.

Beethoven has sometimes been described as the embodiment of the French Revolution in music. But his politics look more complicated than that when we consider the support he received from the antirevolutionary Austrian power structure in getting *Fidelio* composed, produced, and successfully received in Vienna. The secretary of the imperial court theaters translated the French libretto for him at a time when Austria was at war with France. The government censor initially held up the performance of *Fidelio*, but then allowed it when assured that it could not be construed as antimonarchical and that the Austrian empress herself supported the work.[6] By the time *Fidelio* was produced in 1805, the French army under

Napoleon was occupying Vienna, and the opera failed, in part because the nobility that patronized opera and supported Beethoven had mostly fled the city. In 1814, however, when Beethoven and a new librettist altered the work, it was revived with great success. By then the French were gone, and Napoleon was in exile.

The Austrian political establishment would never have supported *Fidelio* if its members had thought the work advocated revolutionary ideas that threatened them. Yet it does deal with tyranny and liberty in terms shaped by the French Revolution. Evidently Beethoven, along with those Austrian nobles who were implacable foes of Napoleon, accepted the need to come to terms with the Revolution through artistic works like this opera. Evidently they accepted that they were now living in a world of endless struggle over political principles. Beyond that, to discover what political attitudes *Fidelio* embodies, we need to examine the dramatic shape and musical character Beethoven and his librettists gave this French story.

Images of injustice and freedom *Fidelio* is set entirely in a prison. When the prisoners sing of their yearning for freedom, spectators do not have to ask themselves what form of freedom these prisoners have in mind. In Act 1, scene 9 (examined in Chapter 3), all the prisoners except Florestan are allowed out into the garden, and the music to which they enter conveys their squinting at the sunlight and their coming to life in the fresh air, as their "timid voices," in Hector Berlioz's description half a century later, "slowly come together to reach an expansive harmony, which is like a sigh of happiness issuing from all these oppressed breasts."[7] Because the sights and sounds of the scene convey to us the sensations of imprisonment, we can feel how this tiny taste of freedom makes them contemplate the real thing, their voices rising to the bursting point:

O Himmel! Rettung! Welch' ein Glück!	O Heaven! Rescue! What happiness!
O Freiheit, Freiheit, kehrst du zurück?	O freedom, are you coming back?

Likewise, in Florestan's monologue (Act 2, scene 1) the stage shows us a dark underground cell, which our eyes get to penetrate during several long minutes of gloomy, pulsing, pained music before Florestan utters his first words: "Gott! Welch' Dunkel hier!" ("God, how gloomy this is!"). Before his voice rises out of the gloom, then, we know what freedom means to him because we have imagined what it is like for him to be deprived of it. And by the end of his monologue, when his suffering leads him to believe he sees his wife before him as an angel leading him to "freedom in the heavenly realm," his rapturous singing helps us imagine how a desperate prisoner could contemplate death as an ecstatic liberation.

These scenes give us such power to imagine the experience of imprisonment that we can hardly separate ourselves from the prisoners embodied onstage. Why are they in prison? We are not told. Florestan reveals in his monologue that he was imprisoned because he dared to utter the truth, and the wicked prison governor has already told us (Act 1, scene 5) that vengeance drove him to imprison Florestan and now to plot his death. In other words, all we know of Florestan's case is that he is a victim of arbitrary power.

A prison is a place that symbolically raises questions about justice and injustice, freedom and the deprivation of freedom. The French Revolution itself was symbolically initiated by a mob action that seemed to come straight out of an opera: the storming of the Bastille and the freeing of its prisoners. But both sides in the conflict could wield that symbol. Antirevolutionary forces throughout Europe countered the image of the Bastille with that of the deposed queen of France languishing in prison before being executed. Beethoven seems to have grown up in a climate of Enlightenment thinking, espousing the principle of liberty from arbitrary and despotic power without advocating the abolition of monarchy or social ranks generally. In *Fidelio* he expressed the urge for liberty so concretely in human terms yet so indefinitely

The prisoners' chorus in a production of *Fidelio* staged at the prison block on Robben Island (where leaders of the African National Congress were imprisoned for decades), off Capetown, South Africa, 2004. This performance marked the tenth anniversary of South African freedom from apartheid. Because it is both so moving as a celebration of resistance to injustice and so ambiguous in its application to the political situation of its own time and place, *Fidelio* lends itself to adaptations of this sort in radically different situations two centuries later.
Kim Ludbrook/EPA/Newscom

in political terms that listeners from all sides of the raging political conflicts could find their own deepest political anxieties confirmed in the cries of Florestan and his fellow prisoners.[8]

There is no mass action as in many revolutionary operas of the 1790s, no battle scene as in *Richard Coeur-de-Lion*. It is individual action that frees Florestan, the action of his disguised wife Leonore in pulling a pistol on the governor when he arrives to dispatch Florestan. Beethoven composed part of this scene (Act 2, scene 2) in **melodrama**—that is, in spoken dialogue punctuated or underscored by orchestral music. This may be considered an extreme form of the acting style of music. But the whole scene is melodramatic in the ordinary sense of the word: heavy with suspense and a sensational outcome. With this melodramatic action at its dénouement, *Fidelio* is a political thriller.

By brandishing her pistol, Leonore stops the governor from killing Florestan, but she does not have the power to get him released. That is accomplished by a second melodramatic event in the same scene. Just as she is threatening to shoot the governor, an offstage trumpet call signals the arrival of the king's minister to inspect the prison. The characters have been alerted to expect this signal, and so when the trumpet call is heard, it is clear that Florestan's life has been saved and that justice will prevail. Sure enough, in the finale that follows, the minister has the governor arrested, releases Florestan, and offers to help the rest of the prisoners. The source of injustice here, in other words, is a renegade local official; the king is actually the source of justice, which is restored by his representative. In this sense *Fidelio*, following Bouilly's text of *Léonore*, can be considered a counterrevolutionary work, advocating faith in a wise king rather than in those who take power into their own hands.

The political and the personal in *Fidelio* One critic, Stephen Meyer, finds that Beethoven cancels "the political rhetoric of liberation" in the opera and makes its action hinge instead on individuals' moments of "spiritual breakthrough."[9] Florestan's breakthrough in the monologue from his gloomy cell in Act 2, scene 1 ("Gott! Welch' Dunkel hier!"), is preceded by a monologue of Leonore's in Act 1, scene 6, that follows a similar course from despair to triumphant resolution: "Abscheulicher! Wo eilst du hin?" ("You abomination! Where are you rushing off to?"). This emphasis on the personal is reinforced in the finale, where the protagonists are joined by the chorus of prisoners and townspeople in praising not the liberating role of the king's minister, but the wifely devotion of Leonore. In fact, the subtitle of the opera is "The Triumph of Marital Love." Is the celebration of Leonore's devotion a testament to the power of personal relationships to triumph over

the politics of the public arena? Or is it a symbol of the power of devotion within the political arena? And if so, does Leonore's loyalty represent a revolutionary image of equality between the sexes? (She is, after all, disguised as a man through much of the opera and achieves her goal by wielding a gun.) Or does her rescue of her husband restore the traditional hierarchy of the family, just as the intervention of the king's minister at the prison restores the traditional hierarchy of the kingdom?

Such ambiguities allowed Beethoven's opera (like its French predecessor) to speak to his controversy-weary age. They have also enabled directors and performers in highly charged political climates over the subsequent two centuries to place the action in new settings and give it new interpretations. Through all these changes audiences have felt that the work sings of freedom and devotion in a way meaningful to them.

Partisan Conflict and Grand Opera: Meyerbeer, *Les Huguenots*

By the 1830s, approaching half a century since the beginning of the Revolution, France seemed like a nation permanently at war with itself. One part was as immovably committed to the authority of the monarchy and the Catholic Church as the other part was to freeing France from the power of those institutions. Even after the defeat of Napoleon and the restoration of monarchy in 1815, the tensions between the sides would break out into armed struggle every few years, a new government would be formed, and the tensions would continue. In the twenty-first century it may seem normal that the populace of a nation is divided into groups of people holding opposed sets of political beliefs and that these groups are represented by formal political parties. But in the early nineteenth century this condition was quite new.

For centuries, under the *ancien régime* (the "previous order," meaning the centuries-long era of royal rule), France was officially constituted of three "estates," or social identities, each of which theoretically performed a different function for king and country and therefore had a claim to its share of the benefits of power: the clergy, the nobility, and the commoners. Except for the clergy, one did not choose one's estate, but was born into it. The Revolution abolished these distinctions and substituted a government of political parties that competed with each other for control of the state. This change, which persisted even under the restored monarchy, required citizens to rethink profoundly their relationships to the state and to members

of other groups. What did it mean to choose a political identity on the basis of one's beliefs, rather than to be born into it? What did it mean to be "in power" or "in opposition," as opposed to "in favor" or "out of favor" with the king? How were you to treat members of a competing party, as opposed to people of a different rank?

Operas on Reformation history The arts were essential in modeling the challenges of living in this changed political world. Several grand operas created at the Paris Opera in the 1830s and 1840s were landmarks in this process, especially Fromental Halévy's *La Juive* (*The Jewish Woman*) in 1835, Giacomo Meyerbeer's *Les Huguenots* in 1836, and Meyerbeer's *Le Prophète* (*The Prophet*) in 1849. All three had texts by the leading librettist of the nineteenth century, Eugène Scribe. These operas were among the greatest blockbusters of the operatic world, not simply because they were stirring as

The *St. Bartholomew's Day Massacre* by François Dubois (1529–1584). Dubois was a Huguenot who escaped the massacre and fled to Lausanne in Switzerland, where he was commissioned to create this record of the event. His painting shows, besides the general slaughter across the public spaces of Paris, the body of the Huguenot leader Admiral Coligny being thrown out of a window and the Catholic Queen Mother, Catherine de' Medici, in widow's black toward the back, standing between the river Seine and the Louvre palace, looking at the bodies of Huguenot victims. Musée Cantonal d'Art et d'Histoire, Lausanne.
Scala/White Images/Art Resource, NY

music, drama, and spectacle, but also because they helped people think their way into the roles and modes of behavior demanded by the partisan structure of political life that was taking hold throughout the Western world.

The stories come from the era of European history before there was a partisan political order, yet from a particular time within that era when people had divided into opposing camps on the basis of their religious beliefs: the sixteenth century, the time of the Protestant Reformation. But while the beliefs at stake were religious, the struggle was political. Individuals in the sixteenth century might want to adhere to the denomination that expressed their beliefs, but they were expected to accept the denomination chosen by their ruler. Untold numbers of Europeans in this era died struggling to impose their religious choices on each other. It was easy for nineteenth-century Europeans to see their own partisan political struggles prefigured in the partisan religious wars of the Reformation.

The operas depicting Reformation history are tragic tales of unequal struggles between fanatical religious parties and the human toll caused by the intolerance of the party in power. To the French, one Reformation event in particular seemed to foreshadow the bloody history of their recent Revolution: the Massacre of St. Bartholomew's Eve in 1572, when militant Catholics slaughtered thousands of French Calvinist Protestants, called Huguenots, in the name of the Catholic king. Author Germaine de Staël, for instance, wrote in 1818 that in the Reign of Terror "eighty people a day were sacrificed, as if the massacre of Saint Bartholomew were to be repeated drop by drop."[10] Meyerbeer's opera on this subject, Les Huguenots, which created a stir and exerted an influence unmatched by any other opera in the nineteenth century, will provide a focus for the discussion here of the theme of conflicting allegiances.

The list of other works on the theme is long. Among French operas Meyerbeer's Le Prophète deals with the uprising of Anabaptist Protestants in Reformation Flanders; Halévy's La Juive involves Catholic intolerance of Jews at a time when the church was suppressing a pre-Reformation group of dissenters, the Hussites; and Verdi's Don Carlos (created at the Paris Opera in 1867) depicts the resistance of Dutch Protestants to Spanish Catholic rule during the Reformation. In Russia, where there had been no Protestant Reformation, the struggles of dissenters called the Old Believers against the established authority of the Russian Orthodox Church was considered a comparable prefiguring episode, and Modest Musorgsky's Khovanshchina (The Khovansky Matter, composed in the 1870s) dramatizes that struggle.

In each of these operas two lovers dramatize the conflict in their society by loving each other across the divide that polarizes it. Religious affiliation is presented as a family matter, and in most cases a daughter who dares to

love a man of a different religion has to contend with her father, who insists on her allegiance to the family's affiliation. Fathers not only held the greatest power in nineteenth-century families, but also represented the lineage, the name, and hence the social and political identity of their family. Conversely, it was a daughter, not a son, who had the potential—by marrying outside her family's identity group—to give her father an heir of an unwelcome identity. This was no longer an era when marriage was seen as a means for powerful families to forge alliances that would reconcile differences of identity; now it was seen as a means of reinforcing shared identities of nationality, religion, or social standing.

Conflicting religious identities are represented as irreconcilable in these operas, and characters who place love over identity are doomed. The works tantalized audiences with the possibility that the unbounded spirit of love could break down the barriers of identity. Spectators may then have felt shocked when, as in *Les Huguenots*, the lovers were cut down brutally. That shock was the means by which the authors protested the cruelty of the identity divisions in their own society. Nothing in these operas suggests that those divisions could be overcome.

History Onstage: Act 1

Since grand operas dramatized specific historical events, unprecedented efforts were made to render those events visually and musically specific as well (see "Staging the Nation's Past," pp. 276–77). The first act of *Les Huguenots*, for instance, presents a remarkable musical portrait of sixteenth-century France. The scene is a drinking party of French noblemen at the chateau of the Count of Nevers. In the course of this scene the audience hears number after number imitating the aristocratic styles of earlier centuries: choral and ensemble numbers in courtly dance rhythms; a romance for the tenor accompanied by an antique string instrument, the viola d'amore; and a lighthearted canon, almost a round, sung by the carousing gentlemen. In the midst of all this secular singing, the one Huguenot nobleman, Raoul de Nangis, is joined by his old servant Marcel, who—sharing none of his master's desire to get along with the Catholics—launches into a Protestant hymn, hoping to remind Raoul to shun the sinful pleasures of the Catholics. The Catholics are so amused that they then prevail on Marcel to sing a Protestant battle song.

Exact historical references in music would have been lost on audiences in 1836, when there was little opportunity to

Les Huguenots

PRINCIPAL CHARACTERS

Catholics:
- **Queen Marguerite de Valois** (sister of the king, Henri III)
- **Count of Saint-Bris**
- **Count of Nevers**
- **Valentine**, daughter of Saint-Bris, betrothed to Nevers

Huguenots:
- **Raoul de Nangis**, in love with Valentine
- **Marcel**, his servant

hear sixteenth-century music. Accordingly, Meyerbeer chose the rhythm of the gavotte, a courtly dance of the seventeenth and eighteenth centuries, for the first two numbers, and an eighteenth-century instrument (that viola d'amore) to accompany Raoul's romance.[11] Marcel's hymn is a different case. It is an authentic Protestant hymn from the sixteenth century, written in fact by the German initiator of the Reformation, Martin Luther: "Ein feste Burg ist unser Gott" (traditionally translated as "A mighty fortress is our God"). In the opera it is sung in French:

Seigneur! rempart et seul soutien   Lord! Rampart and sole support
Du faible qui t'adore.   of the weak who adore you.
Jamais dans ses maux un Chrétien   Never does a Christian in trouble
Vainement ne t'implore.   call on you in vain.

The catch is that the French Protestants—the Huguenots—were followers not of Luther, but of the French theologian Jean Calvin. Why would Meyerbeer have decided to represent them with a hymn belonging to a different sect?

He was in a sense simply exploiting the history of "Ein feste Burg" as a political song: it was the hymn that Lutherans sang at their yearly commemoration of the Reformation. For that reason Heinrich Heine, a German poet working in Paris, compared it with the battle song of the French Revolution, dubbing it "the Marseillaise of the Reformation." "Ein feste Burg" appears throughout the opera as the badge of the Huguenot party and the touchstone of their fortunes. It is first heard proudly as the theme of the overture. Marcel is apt to sing it defiantly whenever he appears onstage. While he is singing it at the drinking party in Act 1, Raoul helpfully explains to the Catholic company that it is "Luther's protective song, which we always sing at a moment of danger." And in the final act all the Huguenots of Paris sing it as they are being slaughtered by Catholics. This pervasive, evolving use of the hymn led one reviewer to observe caustically that "it would be more natural to suppress the title *Les Huguenots* and to say quite frankly: *The Hymn of Luther in Five Acts, Set to Music by Meyerbeer*."[12]

In Protestant practice, church congregations sing hymns not only to praise God, but also to create communal solidarity. Meyerbeer is therefore recasting the function of a hymn when he has "Ein feste Burg" sung for the first time by a single character, Marcel, as an act of defiance in Catholic company. As the opera proceeds, the hymn gradually assumes a more communal expression. In fact, it is characteristic of operas about religious strife that the oppressed minority sect (the Jews in *La Juive*, the Anabaptists in *Le Prophète*, the Old Believers in *Khovanshchina*) defines itself and maintains its spirit of opposition by singing a communal song, or hymn. The members of the majority sect tend not to band together this way in hymns. They don't need to. They are represented by different kinds of music, and that musical

Staging the Nation's Past

The production of grand operas like *Les Huguenots* at the Paris Opera revolutionized the staging of history. Instead of the fantastic sets and costumes of most earlier opera, with their generic references to classical or medieval or Oriental styles, the stage designers lovingly recreated historic buildings and the costume designers lovingly recreated attire from the time of the opera's setting. In Act 2 of *Les Huguenots* they presented the picturesque royal chateau of Chenonceaux straddling the river Cher; in Act 3, the Pré-aux-Clercs, an open space on the banks of the Seine in Renaissance Paris, with its surrounding buildings. Italian composer Gaetano Donizetti, after seeing Parisian stage spectacle in *La Juive* in 1835, wrote home: "This is no longer illusion; it's reality."[13] Soon the creative teams at other opera houses and theaters were producing the same kind of **costume drama**. The vogue continues today, in movies as well as onstage.

© Grand Tour/Corbis

The royal chateau at Chenonceaux in the Loire Valley of France, as it appears today (above) and as it was depicted in the scenery by Edouard Despléchin for Act 2 of Meyerbeer's *Les Huguenots* at the Paris Opera in 1836. Lithograph by C. Deshayes.

Bibliothèque Nationale de France

To depict historical sites onstage was to treat them as tourist sites (and to help turn them into tourist sites, which is what the chateau of Chenonceaux soon became). The scenery transported spectators to a place and time where they could imagine themselves taking part in the events that transpire in the opera. A costume drama like *Les Huguenots*, by making its audience feel like tourists in their nation's past, could make them feel that the work was speaking to them about their present.

Cathedral Square in the Kremlin, Moscow, as it appears today (above) and as it was depicted in the scenery by Mikhail Il'yich Bocharov for Scene 2 of the Prologue to Musorgsky's *Boris Godunov* at the Mariinsky Theater, St. Petersburg, in 1874.

difference dramatizes the unequal nature of the struggle. In *Les Huguenots* the party of power (the Catholics) performs music of public religious ceremony, political authority, and military force—music designed to create solidarity between the ruling class and the majority of the people and to cow the minority of dissenters.

Refuge and Confrontation: Acts 2 and 3

The second act of *Les Huguenots*, set in the garden of the fairy-tale chateau at Chenonceaux, is the bucolic moment in the opera. Operas about political strife often include, early on, a country scene in which the most sympathetic characters find temporary refuge from the strife of the city. Just as it is generally men who are represented as generating the political strife, the refuge usually belongs to women. In this case the chateau is the home of the king's sister, Queen Marguerite de Valois, the figure most actively engaged in making peace between Catholics and Huguenots. She herself, a Catholic, is engaged to marry the Huguenot Henri de Navarre, who would later become King Henri IV. The second act begins with Marguerite rejoicing at being in the beautiful countryside of Tourraine province ("O beau pays de la Tourraine"), far from the bloody disputes of the theologians and their followers. Then the idea of refuge is presented in sexual terms. The ladies of Marguerite's court go down to the river for a swim, relying on their location to protect them from men's leering eyes. The issue is made explicit when the young page Urbain is discovered hiding and watching (the comic effect is enhanced by the fact that his role is played by a woman), and the bathers flee.

If this action demonstrates the fragility of refuge in the world of *Les Huguenots*, the rest of the act underlines the point. Marguerite gathers a group of Huguenot and Catholic nobles and proposes to help end their strife by marrying the Huguenot Raoul to his beloved Valentine, the daughter of the Catholic Count of Saint-Bris. But Raoul, who mistakenly believes Valentine has betrayed his love for her, refuses her hand, setting off a sectarian row right in the queen's supposed Garden of Eden, and even she can barely contain it. Violence is deferred rather than quelled. Later in the opera the idea of refuge will become a vanishing dream for the protagonists. In Act 4 Raoul and Valentine, confessing their love to each other even though she has now been married against her will to a fellow Catholic, will long for a refuge in the duet "Ô ciel! où courez-vous?" ("O heaven! Where are you running to?"). Whereas operas like *Richard Coeur-de-Lion* and *Fidelio*, from the era of the French Revolution, celebrated the engagement of individuals in political struggles, by the 1830s operas were expressing the instinct to escape politics, while dramatizing the impossibility of escape.

In Act 3 of *Les Huguenots* Protestant soldiers and civilians (on the left, including one with a cross-shaped sword) face off against Catholic civilians (on the right, including the vengeance-seeking Count of Saint-Bris, standing commandingly on the steps). Production directed by Olivier Py, Opéra de la Monnaie/De Munt, Brussels, 2011.

Matthias Baus/De Munt/ La Monnaie

Dramatic confrontation / "musical amalgam" That message is not simply made through the deaths of the hero and heroine at the end of an opera, but accumulates in the course of a work. In *Les Huguenots*, after two acts of sectarian disagreement intruding on innocent recreation in the country, the action moves to Paris, the center of the troubles—and of what Anselm Gerhard tells us is always the underlying subject of grand opera: the nineteenth-century urban experience.[14] The setting of the third act is also the first in the opera that is laid in a public space. This is the Pré-aux-Clercs, one of the few open spaces in sixteenth-century Paris, where people of every class and calling gather to amuse themselves. In particular it is a place where Catholics and Huguenots congregate separately but at close quarters. The stage maps their confrontation: Catholic students and young women sit in front of a tavern on one side, Huguenot soldiers in front of a tavern on the other. Sunday strollers sing of the pleasures of the day of rest; the Huguenot soldiers sing a battle song in which they mouth a drum roll ("Rataplan"); and the wedding procession of Valentine and her Catholic bridegroom, the Count of Nevers, crosses the stage, accompanied by a chorus of Catholic girls and women singing a litany in the spare two-voiced modal polyphony of the medieval church:

Vierge Marie,	*Virgin Mary,*
Soyez bénie,	*be blessed.*
Votre voix prie	*Let your voice pray*
Pour le pêcheur.	*for the sinner.*

The three groups cannot seem to leave each other alone. Marcel outrages the strollers (apparently Catholics) by refusing to remove his hat and bow before the wedding procession. As the women's choir continues its litany, the Huguenot

soldiers enter the sonic fray, tenors resuming their rat-a-tat while basses sing, "Long live war—let's drink, friends, to our father Coligny" ("Rataplan! Vive la guerre, buvons amis à notre père, à Coligny"). The strollers curse them as "blasphemous! sacrilegious! hard-hearted!" ("profanes! impies! dont les âmes sont endurcies"; see Example 10.1). This overlapping of previously heard themes, which represent opposed forces in the plot, is known by a French term, **réunion des thèmes** (literally a joining together, or a reconciliation, of themes).

Because the *réunion des thèmes* is a characteristic resource of nineteenth-century opera, it should be differentiated from the eighteenth-century thematic combination examined earlier: the overlapping of different dance tunes in the ball scene of *Don Giovanni* (Chapter 9). There, the sound of three onstage bands playing in three different meters dramatizes the separate worlds in which people of different social classes live, even when they are at the same ball. That music makes the head spin because the bands play alongside each other without any rhythmic reconciliation; like the dancers, they seem oblivious of each other. In the ensemble from *Les Huguenots*, by contrast, the musical elements are rhythmically compatible (all in 9/8 meter), though opposed in character. In this case no one is oblivious of anyone else, and the character of one group's music infects that of the other groups. The serene lilt of the litany, for instance, is disturbed by the agitated rhythms of the "Rataplan" and the abrupt interjections of the strollers. The themes are not so much reconciled as irreparably transformed by their contact with each other. Berlioz wrote that "from this joining together there results the most magnificent musical amalgam."[15]

In a way the wedding is also irreparably marred by this confrontation outside the chapel. The marriage is supposed to be a pure match—between two aristocrats of the same religious sect. But the conflict tearing at France does not allow Valentine a happy marriage. If religious politics did not intrude and she could follow her heart, she would choose her Huguenot suitor Raoul over her Catholic suitor Nevers. But she cannot choose the impure match, and since she does not want the pure one, she is doomed. The quarrel of Huguenots and Catholics that mars the music of her wedding procession does not stop the wedding from taking place, but the array of forces disturbing it reminds the audience that society depends on marriage for the perpetuation of all its institutions, not just of families. Many grand operas (including *Aida* and *Boris Godunov*) include scenes like this one, in which a ceremony that is meant to mark the continuity of the social order is interrupted, revealing the threats to that continuity.

Conspiracy and Massacre: Acts 4 and 5

The conspiratorial oath Act 3 of *Les Huguenots* continues with a planned act of sectarian violence. Raoul is ambushed by Valentine's father and his accomplices, who want to kill him for refusing her hand (though the father

10.1 Meyerbeer, Les Huguenots: Act 3, *Réunion des thèmes*

would not in any case have allowed the match). Battle is joined between Huguenot and Catholic groups until Queen Marguerite arrives and stops it. In Act 4 Catholics plan another act of violence against Huguenots, this time on a citywide scale. Catholic nobles, soldiers, and monks gather at the home of Valentine's husband, the Count of Nevers, and swear an oath to exterminate all the Huguenots of Paris later that night (the eve of St. Bartholomew). The conspiratorial oath, like the interrupted wedding ceremony, is a commonplace in nineteenth-century opera. The example in *Les Huguenots*, however, is unusual in several respects. In the first place, operatic conspirators usually represent an oppressed party fighting for freedom; here they represent the monarchy and the established church. Conspiracies by freedom fighters can appeal to an audience's sympathies; conspiracies by intolerant ruling classes can only repel them. In the second place, conspiracy scenes by nature tend to exclude any opponents. But the conspiracy here is remarkable for the presence of Catholics who do not go along, as well as one Protestant who secretly observes the proceedings.

At the beginning of Act 4 Raoul appears without warning before Valentine, who is alone in her new home. He realizes that she tried to save him from the ambush in the previous act, and now he will not leave her alone, even though she is married to the Count of Nevers. At the approach of her husband, her father (the Count of Saint-Bris), and several other Catholic noblemen, she hides Raoul in the room where those men are gathering (but in view of the audience). At her husband's insistence and over her father's objection, she remains present as her father reveals to the others the plan by the king's strong-willed mother, Catherine de Médicis, to exterminate the Huguenots. When he asks the noblemen to swear obedience to the king's commands, Nevers questions the enterprise. Glaring at his son-in-law, Saint-Bris then leads the oath of obedience:

Pour cette cause sainte	For this holy cause
J'obéirai sans crainte	I will fearlessly obey
À mon Dieu, à mon roi!	my God and my king!

In a famously vituperative review of *Les Huguenots*, the composer Robert Schumann called this melody "nothing but a revamped Marseillaise,"[16] and indeed the first phrase of the melody is closely modeled on the first phrase of the "Marseillaise" (see Example 10.2). If the hymn "Ein feste Burg" serves in this opera as the "Marseillaise" of the Huguenot Reformation, "Pour cette cause sainte" represents an opposing "Marseillaise" for the Catholic conspirators. But it operates very differently here from "Ein feste Burg": it appears in just this one scene, as part of an oath-swearing. Within the scene, however, it is heard three times. Three is a ritual number, and ritual scenes in nineteenth-century opera are almost invariably formed, like this one, around a three-fold musical repetition. In this case each repetition marks a change in the dramatic situation.

10.2 Beginning of "La Marseillaise" compared with *Les Huguenots*, Act 4, "Pour cette cause sainte"

The first stanza begins with Saint-Bris's words "Pour cette cause sainte," setting out the oath he wants his fellow noblemen, including Nevers, to swear to God and king. In the remaining lines of that stanza, sung to a continuation of the melody that is warmed by violin doubling and a wavelike accompaniment, Saint-Bris entrusts himself to those who would follow his lead:

Comptez sur mon courage!	*Count on my courage.*
Entre vos mains j'engage	*Into your hands I commit*
Mes serments et ma foi.	*my pledges and my faith.*

As he repeats these lines to the same music, others join in. His shocked son-in-law Nevers doubles his notes, but to words that contradict Saint-Bris's:

Quel est donc ce langage?	*What kind of language is this?*
À l'honneur seul j'engage	*To honor alone do I commit*
Mes serments et ma foi!	*my pledges and my faith.*

The other noblemen punctuate Saint-Bris's lines with phrases that repeat or second his: "Grand Dieu . . . sauvez . . . la foi!" ("Great God . . . save . . . the faith!"). And Valentine pours out her terror:

Comment tromper leur rage?	*What would divert their rage?*
Dieu! Soutiens mon courage	*God, sustain my courage*
Et prends pitié de moi!	*and take pity on me!*

What seemed at the start like an aria has turned into a complex ensemble, in which the principal singer's lines are dogged to the end by others' lines, some joining and others resisting the ritual he has begun. In opera of earlier centuries most ensembles likewise begin as solos. What is new in this scene is that the solo initiates the solemn, repetitive form of a ritual that is meant to encompass everyone onstage, and yet Nevers and Valentine find ways within the ritual to express their opposition to it. This uneasy amalgam

As the Count of Saint-Bris (Philippe Rouillon, center) leads his followers in the conspiracy to slaughter the Huguenots, his daughter Valentine (Mireille Delunsch, right) looks on and comments in horror. Act 4 of *Les Huguenots*, directed by Olivier Py, Brussels, 2011.

Matthias Baus/De Munt/La Monnaie

of the mass event and the individual assertion tells us how far opera, which began as a courtly wedding drama about individual identities and relationships, had been transformed into a national drama about the plight of individuals within a struggle over the fate of their nation.

After all the Catholic noblemen except Nevers have pledged their support, Saint-Bris challenges Nevers's silence. Nevers, announcing that his proud ancestral line includes many soldiers but no assassins, breaks his sword in two. This elicits a quiet declaration from his bride, Valentine, that now she really belongs to him (even though she still loves Raoul). At that moment the doors open to admit a crowd of civic officials, all ready to take the oath. This evidence of an inexorably expanding conspiracy makes the principled stand Nevers is about to take seem all the more futile, and admirable. He takes that stand by singing a new verse of Saint-Bris's oath music, twisting the words into an oath of resistance:

Ma cause est juste et sainte!	*My cause is just and holy!*
Je puis, je dois sans crainte	*I could, I must without fear*
Résister à mon Roi.	*oppose my king.*

His verse is joined by disparate voices from the start: Valentine sides with him, while the half dozen noblemen quietly confront each of his phrases with Saint-Bris's original words.

Blessing the conspirators The real response to Nevers comes as soon as he is done with his verse: he is removed from the room under guard, to keep him from betraying the conspiracy. As the scene proceeds, it grows ever more chilling, dramatically and musically. One martial-sounding passage follows

another as Saint-Bris gives orders for the massacre; Valentine (who has taken refuge in the next room) calls out to God to protect her beloved Raoul; and a trio of monks, accompanied by a crowd of novices, enters to sing "Glory to the vengeful God" and to bless the daggers and swords that the conspirators raise before them. In an opera that Berlioz praised as a "musical encyclopedia,"[17] the monks' music is perhaps the single most strangely colored entry, by turns churchly, military, and exotically ritualistic. The anointed conspirators advance to the front of the stage, crying in a frenzy, "Let's strike them, let's strike them!" They pause and kneel for a final blessing, and then rise to swear the oath that Saint-Bris set out at the beginning of the scene.

This crowd, now singing "in exaltation" and in unison (actually in octaves because the novices are played by the women's chorus), accompanied by one rising and crashing wave after another from the orchestra, sings this final verse of "Pour cette cause sainte" with irresistible power. But the music they are now singing in such triumphant unity reminds us of the voices of dissent that have been stifled since the previous two times we heard it. Furthermore, the presence of both Raoul and Valentine onstage even now, silenced and hidden but visible to us, makes the song utterly terrifying because the potential victims are right before our eyes, within reach of the murderous singers.[18] In other words, what makes this music overwhelmingly thrilling the third time we hear it is exactly what makes it blood-curdling.

The voices of those who protested have been silenced by the time the oath music reaches its climax. When the conspirators have finished singing, they disperse in a hush, leaving the orchestra to continue playing the oath music, but now in a sequence of distortions and fragmentations that render the theme grotesque, validating the audience's instinct to resist what that music represents (see Example 10.3). This too is a characteristic technique of

10.3 Meyerbeer, *Les Huguenots*: Act 4, orchestral oath music

nineteenth-century opera (and all later dramatic music), called **thematic transformation**: the transformation of a well-established musical motive or theme, through which the composer comments on the progress of the story.

The toll of fanaticism The rest of the opera traces the progress of the love between Valentine and Raoul as they are swept up into the St. Bartholomew Massacre. Act 4 ends, as it began, with the two of them conferring secretly (they are still in her husband's house). Now, in a desperate attempt to induce him to stay with her rather than lose his life warning his fellow Huguenots, she astonishes Raoul by confessing her love to him, and they sing a duet famous for capturing the intensity and wonder of love in the face of pressing danger: "Tu l'as dit: oui, tu m'aimes" ("You said so: yes, you love me").[19] He heads off into that danger, and in Act 5 she comes upon him and Marcel in a churchyard where Huguenots are seeking refuge from the slaughter and offers him means to find safety if he will convert to Catholicism. He is tempted, especially once he learns that her husband, Nevers, has died preventing assassins of his own religion from killing Marcel and that Valentine is therefore free to marry him. But Marcel persuades Raoul to hold to his Huguenot faith unto death, whereupon Valentine declares that she will convert to his faith so that they can be "together on earth and in eternity." Marcel agrees to marry them.

In Act 5 of *Les Huguenots* Marcel stands between Valentine and Raoul, whom he has just joined in marriage, when they are set upon by armed Catholics intent on massacring Huguenots. Color print by Achille Devéria of the original production of the opera.

Private collection/Archives Charmet/ Bridgeman Art Library

Valentine's second wedding makes a striking contrast with her first. In place of the pomp and choral splendor of the Catholic wedding procession in Act 3, Marcel conducts a stern Huguenot examination of the bridal pair in the cemetery, accompanied by nothing more than a mournful bass clarinet, and pronounces them married. But Catholic assassins immediately set upon them, and in a volley of gunfire—one more example of the violence and noise introduced into opera in the nineteenth century—Raoul is wounded. Shortly thereafter another band of Catholics, led by Saint-Bris, comes upon them, and though Valentine tries to stop him, Raoul proclaims himself a Huguenot, whereupon Valentine and Marcel declare that they are too, and Saint-Bris orders them all shot, only to discover that he has killed his own daughter.

In this final act Raoul, who from the start has tried to cross the divide between Catholics and Huguenots, finally succumbs to intransigence, refusing to save his life and Valentine's by converting to her faith or even by keeping quiet about his when Catholic guns are pointed at him. Wavering between the unflinching fanaticism of both Saint-Bris and Marcel and the unflinching commitment to tolerance that costs Nevers his life, Raoul therefore embodies the lesson of this opera: fanaticism breeds more fanaticism. Valentine, on the other hand, represents a principle of accommodation that is explicitly identified as feminine (she converts to Raoul's faith, telling him he will learn the fullness of a woman's love) and a principle of forgiveness in the face of the fanatics' brutality (she dies telling her father that she is going to pray for him).

The opera offered its original audiences a horrifying image of the power of religious fanaticism in the past. Some commentators, like the writer George Sand and the musical activist Joseph Mainzer, understood the religious fanaticism portrayed in the work as a metaphor for fanaticism of any kind in political life.[20] But others felt that the opera slandered their own religion, whether Catholic or Protestant. At a time in European history when the alliance of church with state persisted everywhere and was persistently controversial, an opera blaming religious power for inflaming political hostility was bound to stir impassioned responses, and it did. And in a number of countries, whether the established church was Catholic or Protestant, the authorities were so frightened of sectarian feelings that they allowed the work onstage only after it was rewritten as a drama about some other conflict, making nonsense of Meyerbeer's musical references, to say nothing of Scribe's libretto.[21]

Many other nineteenth-century grand operas similarly challenged the political power of religion by showing how religious belief could breed official intolerance and communities of fanaticism, making an inclusive national spirit of community impossible. These operas often had troubles with

censors and critics. Apparently they made the political power of religion seem a real problem of their own time, not merely a metaphor drawn from history. And to judge by the terrifying power that works like *Les Huguenots*, *Don Carlos*, and *Khovanshchina* can still exert, these operatic episodes from a history that grows ever more remote nevertheless cry out about a danger that continues to haunt the world.

National Conflict and Grand Opera

Nationalism and *Bel Canto*: Bellini, *Norma*

In the course of the nineteenth century people throughout the Western world were moving gradually toward a modern sense of national identity: a sense that a person's primary political identity was as a citizen of a nation, connected to the rest of the nation by bonds that might include language, culture, and religion. Opera, along with other arts, helped to move people's thinking in that direction. The ideology of nationalism—and the demand for nationalist arts—was especially urgent among people who lacked a national state, including those who lived under the control of foreign powers (Italians, Hungarians, Czechs, and Poles) and those whose land was divided among many small states (especially Germans and Italians).

The sacred grove of the Druids, in the opening scene of *Norma*, produced at the Théâtre Italien in Paris with sets by Domenico Ferri in 1835 (four years after the premiere in Milan). Bibliothèque-Musée de l'Opéra National de Paris.
Bridgeman Art Library

In France and Russia, nations that had recently survived threats to their independence, operas idealizing national liberation were tolerated or even encouraged by the governing authorities. In Russia, for example, the tsars used opera to promote a form of nationalism that was defined as loyalty to the tsar. In Mikhail Ivanovich Glinka's opera *A Life for the Tsar* (*Zhizn' za tsarya*, 1836) Russian national identity is defined in terms of peasant culture, while nationalist fervor

is expressed in the willingness of a peasant to sacrifice his life to save the tsar. In France the royal censors nervously allowed the production of several works that depicted historical insurrections in other countries. Two examples are Daniel-François-Esprit Auber's *La Muette de Portici* (*The Mute Woman of Portici*, 1828) and Gioachino Rossini's *Guillaume Tell* (*William Tell*, 1829). These works did in fact inflame nationalist and anti-authoritarian feelings in France and elsewhere: a performance of *La Muette* in Brussels touched off the revolution in which the Belgians freed themselves from Dutch rule.

In Italy, much of which was under the control of the Austrian Empire, opera librettists had to contend with the imperial censors whenever they created stories of national struggle for independence. One of their strategies was to set their works in distant times and places—even though the librettists and censors both knew that politically restive audiences would easily see through the strategy. Vincenzo Bellini's *Norma* (1831), for example, is a story of the ancient Gauls (the inhabitants of what became France) seething under Roman occupation in the first century BCE. The title character is the high priestess of the Druids, the chief religious authority of the Gauls and their de facto political leader, since the Romans have deprived them of their political autonomy. But though her oath as priestess requires her to be a virgin, she has secretly had an affair with Pollione, the Roman proconsul who governs Gaul, and given birth to two children. As in *Les Huguenots* (written five years later) the political conflict is embodied in the forbidden love between lovers from opposite sides of a fatal divide. But in *Les Huguenots* the lovers at least know what to hope for: tolerance of each religion by the other. *Norma* has no hope because she has betrayed her religious oath and her people before the opera begins.

The conflict between the political and the personal in *Norma* is embodied in music that pits tremendously powerful effects of chorus and orchestra against solos of long phrases full of expressive embellishment. Like *Les Huguenots*, *Norma* was created in a transitional moment in musical style when the eighteenth-century art of florid solo singing was maintained in the face of an increasing force of orchestral and choral sound. In Italian opera this stylistic moment is referred to as **bel canto** (beautiful singing). The term may suggest continuity with the singing of the previous century, but the solo lines in operas like *Norma* were deployed in ways that pushed traditional vocal technique to its limits and beyond.

In the first and last scenes of *Norma* the title character stands before her people, in the first case challenging their political judgment, in the second pleading her personal needs in the face of their disapproval. Her solos here, such as the aria "Casta diva" ("Chaste goddess") in the first scene, are as florid as soprano solos by Handel or Mozart, yet unlike Cleopatra or Donna Anna she is joined at times by the massed sound of the full chorus and

orchestra and has to make her voice heard as a distinctive dramatic presence above that sound. In other words, the florid style that could be produced with a light delivery in earlier opera needs to be produced at a high volume in a high register for long stretches of *Norma* and other *bel canto* operas. It is hardly surprising that the role of Norma, requiring a dramatic intensity to match that vocal intensity, is considered one of the most demanding in the entire operatic repertory. Nor is it surprising that as those large-scale musical forces continued to be used to treat themes of political conflict, the florid style of solo singing would be squeezed off the operatic stage in just a few decades.

The Plight of the Exiled: Verdi, *Aida*

By 1871, as that transformation in vocal technique was occurring, Italians had achieved independence and unity. During the long struggle toward that goal, Giuseppe Verdi had contributed a number of operas on the theme of national struggle against oppression, and this year he explored the theme one more time in *Aida*. In this story the oppressor nation is ancient Egypt, and its victim is ancient Ethiopia. The choice of subject is remarkable because the work was commissioned for the opera house of Cairo, built by the khedive (ruler) of modern Egypt, who was at war with modern Ethiopia. As Ralph Locke writes, "the metaphors of empire and conquest can resonate many ways at once" in this opera.[22]

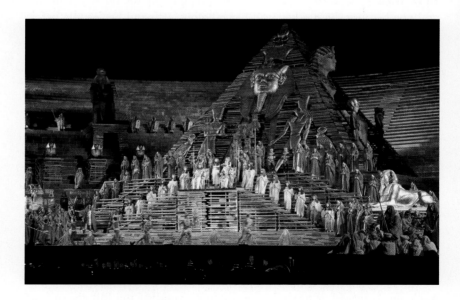

The ancient Roman arena in Verona, Italy, on a summer night provides an evocative setting for imagining the splendor of pharaonic Egypt. The Triumphal Scene (Act 2, scene 2) of *Aida* in a production by Franco Zeffirelli, photographed in 2010.

Ronald Naar/ANP/Newscom

Since *Aida* is set entirely in Egypt and the Ethiopian characters are shown only as slaves or prisoners of the Egyptians, there is an imbalance of music and spectacle between the two nations, as there is between the Catholic and Huguenot groups in *Les Huguenots*. The rituals of the Egyptian priests and priestesses, the might of the Egyptian military, and the grandeur of the Pharaoh are all displayed with music that is magnificent enough to please the khedive. There is even a stirring national anthem, "Gloria all'Egitto" ("Glory to Egypt"), sung as if by the entire Egyptian nation in a parade celebrating their victory over the Ethiopian enemy (the Triumphal Scene, Act 2, scene 2). By contrast, there is only one number representing the Ethiopians as a nation, and that is the moving prayer for mercy that the captured Ethiopian soldiers, led onstage in chains at the end of that parade, sing to the Pharaoh: "Ma tu, Re, tu signore possente" ("But you, King, you powerful lord"). The prayer is powerful enough to bring disruption to the celebration, as the sympathizing Egyptian people take up the Ethiopians' plea while the Egyptian priests plead with the Pharaoh to deny them mercy.

The vast spectacles of Egyptian public life in this opera make us feel Aida's isolation as an enslaved foreigner all the more whenever she steals a moment for reflection. Leontyne Price as Aida at the Metropolitan Opera in 1961.
Louis Mélançon/Metropolitan Opera Archives

Otherwise the task of representing the Ethiopian nation falls largely to a single character and her music, which includes a yearning theme that follows her throughout the opera. Hers is the yearning of the exile. This character is Aida, the daughter of the Ethiopian king, who has been captured and enslaved by the Egyptians some time before the battle marked in the Triumphal Scene, but who has kept her royal identity secret. She has also fallen in love with the commander of the Egyptian army, Radamès, and he with her. But union between Aida and Radamès is impossible. It would symbolize union between their two nations, and that union is incompatible with the basic premise of nineteenth-century nationalism that every nation should lead a separate existence from every other.

In the Triumphal Scene the Pharaoh promises his daughter, Amneris, to Radamès in marriage, an offer he can't refuse. In the following scene Aida, cut off now from both her Egyptian lover and her Ethiopian roots, steps out alone onto the banks of the Nile at night and sings of her grief and homesickness in the aria "O patria mia" ("O my fatherland"). The still and resonant sounds of strings and flute that open the scene evoke the night, their open harmonies inviting a dreamer to fill in the darkness with memories, hopes, and fears. The first sounds that fill that dreamy void are the voices of the Egyptian priests and priestesses, praying for a happy marriage for

Amneris and Radamès. As their voices die away, Aida enters to the sound of her recurring motive, the prospect of that marriage weighing on her. She is here to meet Radamès secretly and expects it will be their last meeting. She imagines drowning herself in the Nile, and the swirling of the lower strings helps us fill the darkness with that image. Then she hears an exotic wailing of the oboe around two adjacent pitches (F and E; see Example 10.4), and she responds: "O patria mia, mai più ti rivedrò" ("O my fatherland, I will never see you again"), sung as if to a remembered voice from her past.

10.4 Verdi, *Aida*: Act 3, oboe introduction to "O patria mia"

The oboe voice repeats its call, and Aida repeats her regret. Then she and her music move on to specific memories of her homeland—its azure skies, its cool valleys—and of her departed dreams of a happy love. Each set of memories ends with a cry that she will never see her homeland again, and then the oboe melody returns, three times in all and exactly the same each time. This returning (or rondo) form of the aria gives her thoughts the structure of nostalgia: a pain that keeps returning unchanged because the dreamer has no way of recovering the past or moving beyond it. Like Norma, she doesn't know what to wish for. She can't win politically, and she can't escape from politics.[23]

Her father, the Ethiopian king, emerging from the shadows, interrupts her reverie. He does know what to wish for. He is ready to raise a new Ethiopian army and attack the Egyptians again. He just needs to know what route the Egyptian army is to set out on, and since he knows Aida is about to meet Radamès, he demands that she extract that information from him. But she is horrified at the idea of asking Radamès to betray his country. There ensues a battle of wills between father and daughter as compelling as that between Violetta and Germont in *La traviata*. Here too we know from the start that the man will win because he is willing to use an argument that the young woman cannot counter: she alone can make it possible for her "vanquished and tormented" country—the country for which she has just expressed such desperate longing—to rise up again. A love that is doomed anyway can hardly stand up to the call of her national identity.

Aida gets the information from Radamès, but his treason is discovered, and he is condemned to be buried alive. Aida, rather than live without him, sneaks into the tomb to suffocate with him. Meanwhile, the apparently disastrous fate of her country in its struggle with the Egyptians gets no further attention. That turning away from the political conflict is not apt to seem strange in the opera house, however, because the lovers' death scene carries the audience's attention to another realm. The very last moments are devoted to a duet in which Aida and Radamès, in their air-starved delirium, bid farewell to the earth and picture heaven opening up before them:

O terra addio, addio valle di pianti,	*O earth, farewell; farewell, vale of tears,*
Sogno di gaudio che in dolor svanì.	*dream of happiness that has vanished in sorrow.*
A noi si schiude il ciel e l'alme erranti	*Heaven opens to us, and the wandering souls*
Volano al raggio del'eterno dì.	*fly to the rays of the eternal day.*

The music of this duet, with its gently swaying rhythms and endless repetitions of the opening phrase, creates the effect of a lullaby.[24] Ending the opera with a lullaby is a formula not for resolving the warfare that has brought Radamès and Aida to this tomb, but for making it "vanish" along with the whole earthly "vale of tears." Harp chords and string harmonics convey their vision of heaven opening up. And as they repeat their stanza, the chorus of Egyptian priests and priestesses, along with the princess Amneris, poised on a second stage over the tomb and unaware that Aida is with Radamès, add their chanted prayers for his soul. The Egyptian political establishment, in other words, joins the lovers in diverting the plot at its conclusion from the fate of two nations to that of two individuals in love.

The final scene of *Aida* showing—like the score cover reproduced at the beginning of this chapter—Aida and Radamès buried alive, but also Amneris and the priests and priestesses of Vulcan above, praying for peace. Staging by Franco Zeffirelli at La Scala, Milan, in 2006, with Violeta Urmana as Aida, Roberto Alagna as Radamès, and Ildikó Komlósi as Amneris.
Marco Brescia © Teatro alla Scala

Nation, People, and Ruler: Musorgsky, *Boris Godunov*

In Modest Musorgsky's *Boris Godunov* (1874), by contrast, the connection between the fate of the nation and that of individual rulers is the point of the work, even though the rulers

Fyodor Shalyapin as Tsar Boris Godunov sitting uneasily on the throne of Russia The photo was taken in 1910, when Shalyapin, one of the most imposing singing actors in opera history, was making Musorgsky's opera an international sensation.

General Photographic Agency/ Getty Images

and the ruled are shown to be incapable of speaking to each other. This opera, drawn largely from a historical play of 1831 by the Russian poet Alexander Sergeyevich Pushkin, is set in Russia at the beginning of the seventeenth century. This period, when the Russian lands were relatively small and at risk of conquest by more powerful neighbors, was regarded by nineteenth-century Russians as a crucial and troubling moment in the formation of their nation. The opera enacts the disintegration and death of Tsar Boris, haunted by guilt for murdering the child tsar Dmitri in order to gain the throne for himself, and the path to power taken by a novice monk who pretends to be Tsar Dmitri, risen from the dead. The work is famous for its engagement with questions about who and what shape a nation's history; for its gripping musical representation of Boris's descent into madness; and for the compelling "acting style" in which the characters and even the chorus sometimes sing. (There is no trace of *bel canto* here.) Yet no less remarkable is the series of ironic twists Musorgsky gives to the theme of conflicting national allegiances.

The first twist is that the people of Russia, represented in choral scenes that open and close the opera, are not symbolically identified with any of the high-ranking solo characters. Though their suffering is exacerbated by the struggles for the throne, they are shown as unreliable in their support for any leader, let alone for the cause of Russia. The people always appear out in the cold, excluded from the indoor scenes in which the competitors for power work out their schemes. In the opening scene, for instance, they stand in the courtyard of a monastery near Moscow, where they are bullied by a police officer to get on their knees and beseech Boris Godunov, who is inside the monastery, to accept the vacant throne as tsar. They comply, but no one could believe that their performance has any effect on Boris. Musorgsky presents the people throughout in an extraordinarily bold way for nineteenth-century opera: they are as apt to break into quarrelsome packs or solos as to join their voices in solidarity; to bully as to be bullied; to display every conceivable musical style; and thus to embody an unmoored state of political identity.

The few times when the rulers or would-be rulers appear outdoors among the people, the opportunity for solidarity between them and the people is conspicuously missed. The second scene is set in the Kremlin in Moscow, in front of the church in which Boris is being crowned tsar. This scene, famous for its orchestral rendering of the Kremlin bells' joyful pealing, is one of

René Pape, Tsar Boris at the Metropolitan Opera in 2010, exposes the terrors and humanity of the role for our age.
Ken Howard

those public ceremonial scenes, like the Triumphal Scene in *Aida*, in which the celebration of solidarity between ruler and ruled is unexpectedly disrupted. Here the disruption comes not from the people but from Tsar Boris. Instead of using his crowning moment to draw the people into his field of power, he gloomily proclaims his self-doubt. What other coronation address by a ruler begins: "My soul is grieving"?

It is the Pretender (the false Dmitri) who introduces the conflict of national allegiances into the opera. We hear this young monk learn that Boris was responsible for the death of the young tsar-apparent and figure out that he and Dmitri were the same age. We follow him as he sneaks across the border, betraying a fellow monk along the way, now convinced that he can pass himself off as Dmitri returned to life. And in the version of the work that Musorgsky saw onto the stage (agreeing to the demands of the theater authorities that he include some love interest),[25] we watch the Pretender court the daughter of a Polish governor in order to use her father's troops to invade Russia and claim its throne. She meanwhile lets a Jesuit priest persuade her that marrying the Pretender will put her in a position to convert the Russians from Orthodox to Catholic.

The Pretender and his Polish princess Marina cannot represent a conflict between love and country, as Aida and Radamès do, because they lack the nobility of character to represent the ideals of their nations. Musorgsky does use conventional musical contrasts to label Poland as aggressor and Russia as victim: the Polish characters, all aristocrats, step and sing to the rhythms of Polish ballroom music, while folk-song styles fill the speech of all the Russian characters, from the mob in the street to the tsar's family. Marina sings so relentlessly in the rhythm of one Polish dance, the mazurka, that it comes to mark her single-minded ambition, not just her

nationality. Nevertheless, there is enough feeling between the Pretender and Marina to sustain a beautiful love duet. But because they are bringing a foreign army onto Russian soil, Musorgsky does not have to worry about the audience's sympathy for these lovers, and he ends the opera without showing what becomes of them and their self-serving alliance.

Tsar Boris is the individual whose fate holds the interest of the audience. In two scenes set in rooms of the Kremlin (Act 2 and Act 4, scene 1), we see him as a fond father, counseling his son on how to be a wise and successful tsar; as the tsar in action, letting his closest counselor and an old monk terrify him with stories of the dead Dmitri and of the new Dmitri approaching Moscow to overthrow him; and as a guilt-ridden soul, hallucinating visions of the dead child and—in the second of these scenes—dying in the throes of that hallucination.

The scenes are extraordinary for showing such warring sides of a single personality in musical speech, and especially for the harrowing portrayal of his hallucinations, in which the real chiming of a clock sets off tortured musical phrases in the orchestra that suggest his reeling imagination. In his hyperpersonal struggle between reality and madness, it might seem as if the conventional dramatic struggle of a ruler weighing his personal needs against those of his nation gets lost. But part of what makes these scenes so affecting is that it does not. Even after episodes in which he hallucinates and faints in front of his noblemen, Boris manages to bid a calm and extended farewell to his young son just before he dies ("Proshchay, moy sïn, umi-rayu"/ "Farewell, my son, I am dying"), giving him elaborate advice, commending his daughter warmly to his son's care, and in an orchestral halo of celestial sound praying to the angels to watch over his children. Though he then dies in a paroxysm of guilt, he has provided as best he could for his legacy as tsar, and so for the fate of his nation.

The final twists on the theme of conflicting national allegiance appear after Boris's death, in the last scene, which shows a crowd of miserable Russians hailing the Pretender as their tsar when he and his Polish retinue pass them en route to Moscow. They are a people, it seems, as willing to invite foreign occupation as those in other operas are to seek liberation from it. Furthermore, the very last utterance in the opera is a prophecy, sung by a Holy Fool (an idiot popularly believed to have visionary powers). In his madness he is the double of Tsar Boris. One dies with a mind in musical chaos; the other sings in the simplicity of a nursery rhyme. The tsar can't tell whether what he sees before him is real or not; the fool looks at what is happening and sees the future without illusion: "Soon the enemy will come and the darkness will begin."

Nineteenth-Century Operas Testing Twenty-first-Century Beliefs

Nineteenth-century operas depict nationalism as an ideology of exclusion. Over and over again they seem to teach the lesson that Anita sings to Maria in *West Side Story*: "Stick to your own kind!" But the operas put that lesson in terms of political duty. They insist that your nation has the right to tell you to stick to your own kind, that the loyalty you owe your nation overrides any personal loyalties. Aida, forced by her father to trick her lover into betraying his country, sings, "O fatherland, what you cost me!" and then does what it demands of her. But like *West Side Story* these operas create their dramatic tension and draw our tears through precisely the opposite ideology. They ask us to believe in the possibility that love can override the obstacle of different nationality, even though we know that political imperatives are almost bound to crush that possibility in the end. The tragic plots allowed nineteenth-century audiences to have it both ways: to indulge a sentimental attachment to the idea that love should conquer all while acknowledging the right of nationality to destroy "misplaced" love.

Audiences today are separated from that era by a century and more filled with horrible wars fueled by nationalism. Nevertheless, they continue to find meaning in these operas. In fact, in our day *Aida* has lent its story to a successful musical of the same name (music by Elton John, 2000), through which even more people have come to care about the fate of Aida and Radamès. No doubt audiences continue to believe, maybe more strongly than ever, in love that crosses the boundaries of nationality. Do they also continue to grant that for the good of their nation people should stick together, should even marry within their own kind?

In 1978, when *Aida* was about a century old, Julian Budden wrote that the work did not altogether suit the present age because this age "is suspicious of authority" and "in *Aida* state authority is never called into question" except by the Egyptian princess.[26] In fact, recent stagings of the opera have sometimes depicted the authority of the Egyptian state in darker terms than would have been conceivable in Verdi's lifetime (particularly at the premiere, which was sponsored by the Egyptian state). *Boris Godunov* offers a far bleaker view of state authority than *Aida*, no matter how it is performed. But even there audiences are expected to accept the nation as the natural unit of human community—to an extent that they may not do in our globally conscious day. It is a question, then, whether these operas retain their power today because operagoers view the claims of nations metaphorically (standing for any obstacle to love) or because they concede the enormous power that nations continue to exert over their citizens' private lives.[27]

FURTHER READING

On the life and works of Grétry, David Charlton, *Grétry and the Growth of Opéra-Comique* (Cambridge and New York: Cambridge University Press, 1986). On Beethoven's *Fidelio*, Paul Robinson, *Ludwig van Beethoven: "Fidelio"* (Cambridge and New York: Cambridge University Press, 1996). On nineteenth-century grand opera, David Charlton, ed., *The Cambridge Companion to Grand Opera* (Cambridge and New York: Cambridge University Press, 2003); Anselm Gerhard, *The Urbanization of Opera: Music Theater in Paris in the Nineteenth Century*, trans. Mary Whittall (Chicago: University of Chicago Press, 1998). On Bellini's *Norma*, David Kimbell, *Vincenzo Bellini: "Norma"* (Cambridge and New York: Cambridge University Press, 1998).

On Verdi's *Aida*, Hans Busch, *Verdi's "Aida": The History of an Opera in Letters and Documents* (Minneapolis: University of Minnesota Press, 1978); Katherine Bergeron, "Verdi's Egyptian Spectacle: On the Colonial Subject of *Aida*," *Cambridge Opera Journal* 14/1 & 2 (March 2002):149–159; Steven Huebner, "'O patria mia': Patriotism, Dream, Death," *Cambridge Opera Journal* 14/1 & 2 (March 2002):161–75; Ralph P. Locke, "Beyond the Exotic: How 'Eastern' is *Aida*?" *Cambridge Opera Journal* 17/2 (July 2005):105–39.

On Musorgsky's *Boris Godunov*, Caryl Emerson and Robert W. Oldani, *Modest Musorgsky and "Boris Godunov": Myths, Realities, Reconsiderations* (Cambridge and New York: Cambridge University Press, 1994); Richard Taruskin, *Musorgsky: Eight Essays and an Epilogue* (Princeton: Princeton University Press, 1993).

FOR RESEARCH AND REFLECTION

1. *Fidelio* dealt with explosive political issues of its day, somewhat neutralizing them with a setting that was distant in time and place from its audience. In recent times stage directors have worked to keep the work vital by giving it new settings, whether historical or contemporary, that are not so distant from their audiences. Imagine a setting for this opera (or any other nineteenth-century opera of political conflict) that would make it particularly meaningful today. How would you adapt the work to that setting?

2. A grand opera like *Les Huguenots* presents a world of enormous sonic and visual color and variety. If you take that variety as a metaphor for social diversity, what happens to it by the end of the opera?

3. In operas of political conflict or national liberation, considerable trouble and expense is often devoted to evoking the land that a people either inhabit (even if they do not control it) or are deprived of (if they are in exile). How is that sense of a land, or country, created in these operas?

4. How is the traditional operatic medium of the love duet adapted to the new dramatic needs of operas of political and national conflict?

5. Violence—from duels between individuals to battles between nations—and death are common on the nineteenth-century operatic stage; in earlier centuries they were rare. Once they are introduced into opera, do the serious and heroic works of the earlier centuries, from which onstage violence and death are generally excluded, seem like cop-outs?

6. Nationalities, religious denominations, and partisan political causes are often given identifying anthems in nineteenth-century operas. Give some examples of these anthems, and consider how the device is used to play on the sympathies of audiences.

 Additional resources available at wwnorton.com/studyspace.

Opera on Themes
of Domestic Conflict

Interracial Relationships:
Bizet, *Carmen*

Grand operas of the nineteenth century incessantly explore the connections between public and private life. Another set of operas from the same century—sometimes comic, more often tragic—shines a steady light on the private sphere alone. Within that intimate, domestic sphere, often in familiarly local and contemporary settings, these works—the soap operas of opera—explore the mundane but disturbing ways in which parent and child, girlfriend and boyfriend, husband and wife, torment each other. The characters are usually ordinary people, not leaders, and their individual struggles are not depicted as part of larger political or social conflicts. Nevertheless, serious social and political divisions are at stake in these stories.

Racial division is one. In operas of conflicting national allegiances there is no suggestion that individuals from neighboring countries—an Ethiopian and an Egyptian in *Aida*, a Russian and a Pole in *Boris Godunov*—could not make a success of life together if the politics of their nations allowed it. There is no suggestion, that is, that their difference in nationality makes them incompatible. But in other operas the conflict lies between individuals whose homelands are more remote from each other, and who are more

Édouard Manet, *Portrait of Émilie Ambre as Carmen*, 1880. Ambre performed the title role in Bizet's *Carmen* in the United States just a few years after the work was premiered in Paris, and Manet's portrait makes her a bewitching Carmen. Philadelphia Museum of Art.
Art Resource, NY

strongly differentiated in race (or "color"). In these works the conflict is internalized within the lovers themselves: they are shown to be so different from each other in their racial nature that their relationship is bound to fail.

The most famous opera of this type—and one of the most universally popular—is Georges Bizet's *Carmen* (1875), written to a libretto by Ludovic Halévy and Henri Meilhac that was based on a novella by Prosper Mérimée. This is not a grand opera. It was created at the Opéra Comique in Paris, with spoken dialogue between the musical numbers, as was required at that house. But its violent and tragic ending went against the tradition of the Opéra Comique, and the work achieved real success only when it was produced later the same year at a grander opera house, the Vienna Court Opera, where tragic subjects were the rule. For that production the dialogue, shortened for the purpose, was set as recitative by Ernest Guiraud (Bizet having died in the interim), and for a long time, except in France, that was the standard version of the opera. In fact, the competition between the spoken-dialogue and fully sung versions, over the performance history of the work, can be seen as reflecting the ambiguous nature of the opera, part comedy and part tragedy.[1]

Carmen is set in Spain, and all its characters are natives of Spain, but they are nevertheless divided by race. The leading male character, Don José, is a soldier from the northernmost part of the country and therefore, from the perspective of the French authors and the operagoers for whom they were writing, practically a stand-in for a Frenchman. He is stationed in Seville, the capital of Andalusia, the southernmost province, close to Africa. From the French perspective, this was the most exotic corner of Europe. Don José is enchanted by Carmen, a Gypsy woman of Seville—a woman, that is, whose people (the Romani) were originally from India and who, though they had lived in Spain for centuries, remained culturally distinct from the rest of the population. "Culturally distinct" is a twenty-first-century formulation. In this nineteenth-century opera the distinctness was presented as an inborn and insurmountable racial difference.

The possibility never arises that Don José might give up his Spanish identity to become Carmen's Gypsy husband or that Carmen might give up her Gypsy identity to become his Spanish wife. It is not a story of lovers devoted to each other in the face of external obstacles, whether political, religious, or familial. Rather, it is a story of seduction: of a European man who is ready to be seduced, ready to give over his soldier's life and his engagement to his hometown sweetheart in pursuit of a more exotic fantasy, and an exotic woman who is ready to exploit his susceptibility as an exercise of her own freedom.

Seduction in Song and Dance

The assignment of roles in this scheme is not at all arbitrary. In *Les Huguenots* it does not matter which lover is Huguenot and which is Catholic. In *Aida* it does not matter which lover is Egyptian and which is Ethiopian. But in an opera of racial difference like *Carmen*, the male lover is almost invariably the seduced European because he is the one with everything to lose—worldly power (Don José is a soldier) and the pride that goes with it—and the female is the exotic because her only power is the power to seduce. In *Les Huguenots* or *Aida*, where there is no seduction, the dramatic issue is the cost, not the cause, of the lovers' attraction to each other; in fact, they are already in love before the curtain goes up. But Carmen's seduction of Don José takes up half of their opera, and when she has accomplished it, she is finished with him.

In the first two acts Carmen displays her seductiveness not just to Don José, but to every male character she encounters. She displays it in her voice, to which she draws attention by singing wordlessly, as in Act 1 when a fight between her and a woman who works with her in a cigarette factory leads to Carmen's being arrested and hauled before the commander of the local garrison. She answers his questions and threats with wordless defiance, sinking provocatively lower and lower in her mezzo-soprano range. And in Act 2 she sings wordlessly, both in the Gypsy Song with which she and two friends entertain at a tavern and later, when Don José arrives and she dances for him alone, accompanying herself with castanets.

Carmen's dancing too displays her seductiveness. The standard practice in opera is to assign the dancing to specialists, who are not given individual identities or words to deliver. They dance and then get out of the way. In that context Carmen is a famously (though not uniquely) demanding role for a singer, one who does her own dancing. Carmen is defined by her dancing as Orfeo is by his singing. In the seductive first half of the opera, she dances practically every time she sings: in the sultry Habanera that introduces her in Act 1; in the Seguidilla, which shows her under arrest, her hands bound, but nevertheless suggesting to Don José how she wants to dance for him (see Chapter 3); and in the Gypsy Song and the castanet dance in Act 2. All of these numbers are hypnotic, not only in their dance rhythms, but also in their harmonies—whether hypnotically static (the Habanera) or hypnotically fluid (the opening of the Gypsy Song, which dispenses with the logic of classical modulation and instead anticipates the free harmonic shifts of later popular music).

In the first two acts, in fact, every number seems to be song and dance music, even when no one is actually dancing—the Toreador Song, for

example, which simply marks that character's grand entry. The endless, colorful parade of numbers — derived, as Susan McClary points out, mostly from the "Spanish" or "Gypsy" styles of cabaret music in Bizet's Paris — makes the first half of *Carmen* seem like a musical comedy.[2] In the third and fourth acts, however, the action and music turn increasingly tragic. In the third act a playful game of fortune-telling turns grim when Carmen reads her own impending death in the cards, and Don José almost shoots his sweetheart by mistake and then fights a nearly deadly duel with the toreador, his rival for Carmen's attentions. In the fourth act an obsessed Don José, unable to comprehend that Carmen wanted to be free of him the moment she seduced him, stalks her and stabs her to death in revenge.

Racial Difference and Gender Difference

The comic and tragic halves of the story can seem extraordinarily different in tone. It is not surprising, then, that it is *Carmen* the French feminist writer Catherine Clément is speaking of when she tells the story of a poor old woman who, unable to afford opera tickets, used to sneak into the opera house to see just the last act, saying, "I come for the death."[3]

Nevertheless, the two halves are inextricably connected. Already in the overture, a musical warning of the tragic outcome is sounded by means of a portentous five-note motive in a "Gypsy" mode, heard in sequential repetition (see Example 11.1). Through the rest of the opera that motive reappears in different guises, in the orchestral soundtrack only, always connected to Carmen's power to turn Don José's head. The motive comes to embody his obsession with her, which dooms them both. In classical tragedy the characters doom themselves by committing acts that offend a god or goddess, who punishes them. In *Carmen* there are no gods or goddesses to offend. Instead, the brief attachment of Carmen and Don José violates the presumed difference in nature between the Spanish and Gypsy races, and nature punishes them for it.

11.1   Bizet, *Carmen*: Overture

Andante moderato

Carmen was created in what is known in the English-speaking world as the Victorian age—an age when nature was thought to create strict differences of character not just between races, but also between the sexes. In fact, this opera rests on the assumption that differences of race and gender reinforce each other. It is already so difficult for any man and woman to understand each other, the opera seems to tell us, that it would be almost impossible for a man and a woman of different races to sustain a relationship. Today, well over a century later, debates about human nature are framed in drastically different terms. In particular, such differences are explained much more by reference to cultural formation than to nature. Nevertheless, Bizet's opera remains unsurpassed in popularity, while its story and music continue to inspire a steady flow of new versions in other media, including theater, film (even a film "hip hopera"), and dance.[4] Why, then, might people still be fascinated by the impossible relationship between Carmen and Don José?

One answer might be that this work allows us to understand both sides in a doomed relationship, both characters' incomprehension of the other. Take the moment when Don José, called to his barracks just as Carmen is offering herself to him in song and dance at the tavern, nevertheless tries to prove the sincerity of his love in the passionate aria

Enrico Caruso as Don José in *Carmen*, knife in hand, ready to kill for a love that he can never possess. Through his pioneering recordings Caruso (1873–1921) forms the beginning of the line of opera singers whose performances remain canonic today.

Art Resource, NY

"La fleur que tu m'avais jetée" ("The flower that you had thrown me"). The audience can both sympathize with his dilemma and realize why she refuses to sympathize, as she responds—quietly carrying the music to the most alien new key possible: "No, you don't love me!" ("Non, tu ne m'aimes pas!").

In one sense Carmen is the exotic answer to the yearnings of a man with dull prospects: she is almost a figment of his imagination. But in the opera (unlike in Mérimée's novella, where she has no existence except as one male narrator, Don José, describes her to another) she is also a real woman singing and dancing on the stage. Through this actress the opera expresses an archetypal experience of women in a world controlled by men. More than most operas *Carmen* is one work for women spectators and another for men. Men tend to respond to Carmen's exotically colored songs and dances as if they themselves were the objects of her seduction; women tend not just to identify with Carmen, but to see her performances as acts of liberation more than of seduction. Likewise, they are more apt to feel the courage in what Clément has called this "image, foreseen and doomed, of a woman who refuses masculine yokes and who must pay for it with her life."[5] This is not to say that women experience the opera exclusively from Carmen's vantage point and men exclusively from Don José's. But it is hard to imagine the aged French operagoer who "came for the death" as a man.

Despite its exotic musical colors, *Carmen* is a story about people of no great social status—a common soldier infatuated with a Gypsy woman—in a nearly contemporary setting (the opera, created in 1875, is set around 1830). In earlier centuries only comic operas dealt with contemporary, everyday life. Well into the nineteenth century tragic operas were still usually set in the fairly distant past and peopled by the high and mighty—even tragic operas dealing with racial difference, like Meyerbeer's *L'Africaine* (*The African Woman*), produced in Paris in 1865. *Carmen*, ten years later, showed the power of opera to present racial difference as a contemporary issue in a period when Western nations were extending their power over much of the rest of the world. The most famous opera to follow its lead is Giacomo Puccini's *Madama Butterfly* (1904), about the American imposition of power on contemporary Japan.

Other operas of this period, almost all by New World authors, raise the possibility of a multiracial society, though their tragic endings invariably show that possibility being crushed. These include several early twentieth-century

works composed in the United States that deal with doomed love affairs between white and native Americans.[6] An earlier example (premiered in Italy five years before *Carmen*) is *Il Guarany* (1870), by the Brazilian composer Carlos Gomes, about the encounter of Portuguese settlers with the Guaraní people in sixteenth-century Brazil. This work faced the difficulty of defining nationality in a multiracial country at a time when the prevailing ideology equated nationality with race. The conceptual audacity of the opera shows in the unusual gender construction of the couple at the heart of the plot: the man belongs to the exotic people, the Guaraní, while the woman is European.

Trials of Young Love

Age and Class: Rossini, *The Barber of Seville*

Gioachino Rossini's *The Barber of Seville* (*Il barbiere di Siviglia*, 1816) dramatizes a kind of struggle over love that has a much older dramatic history: the resistance of an older generation to letting young people choose their own partners. In fact, though this is a nineteenth-century opera, it is based on an eighteenth-century play, the first play (1775) in Pierre-Augustin Beaumarchais' Figaro trilogy (the second of which is *The Marriage of Figaro*). Its theme was one of the oldest in comedy even then: the foolish old man who is the guardian of a beautiful young woman and tries to thwart her handsome young suitor so that he can marry her himself.

Rossini's opera is great fun, and the fun depends on the audience being delighted to see the young lovers, the high-born orphan Rosina and her suitor (apparently a poor student), outwit the old guardian, Dr. Bartolo. Even parents who might try to control their own children's matches have presumably always laughed at Bartolo's lecherous desire to take advantage of his legal power over Rosina. And he is made even more ridiculous because the match that he tries in vain to prevent is more advantageous than he could have imagined: Rosina's suitor turns out to be a nobleman, the Count Almaviva, trying to win her heart without impressing her with his status. The four decades between the first staging of Beaumarchais' play and of Rossini's opera were the decades of the French Revolution, the Industrial Revolution, and the Napoleonic Wars, which brought social, economic, and cultural upheaval to Europe. Nevertheless, the social premises of Beaumarchais' prerevolutionary *Barber of Seville* did not need to be altered for Rossini's postrevolutionary audiences (or for audiences

today): the difference in age between Rosina and her guardian make it impossible not to feel that the noble Rosina and the noble Almaviva are meant for each other.

Nevertheless, Rossini's music creates a characteristically nineteenth-century comedy, based on a characteristic nineteenth-century attitude toward social class. This is not at all the kind of comic music that Mozart wrote in *The Marriage of Figaro* (1786). Whereas Mozart balances funny numbers (especially ensembles) with serious (especially arias), in *The Barber of Seville* every single number is humorous. What's more, Rossini's fun derives from a relentless energy that seems to sustain every vocal and orchestral line, creating irrepressible tension when things get stuck dramatically and madcap explosiveness when they come unstuck. How does that energy embody an attitude toward social class?

Throughout this opera the traditional art of **patter**—a flood of words to the simplest, most repetitive of melodic formulas—appears in a new transformation. In eighteenth-century comedies like Mozart's, patter conveys the cleverness but also the lack of verbal or musical "class" of servants like Figaro, Leporello, and Despina. It is the poor man's or poor woman's virtuosity. In *The Barber of Seville* patter has this function in the aria "Largo al factotum" ("Make way for the jack-of-all-trades"), in which Figaro, the Barber of Seville, advertises his services—especially as a go-between in aristocratic love affairs and courtships—to the young and amorous Count Almaviva. Here, the flood of Figaro's words allows him to depict himself as coping with a flood of demands from all around him:

Figaro qua, Figaro là,	*Figaro here, Figaro there,*
Figaro qua, Figaro là,	*Figaro here, Figaro there,*
Figaro su, Figaro giù,	*Figaro up there, Figaro down there,*
Figaro su, Figaro giù!	*Figaro up there, Figaro down there!*

But then the patter slips into a very different (and much less traditional) function, making precisely the opposite effect. His notes run ahead of his ability to supply them with words, and he has to fill in the notes with nonsense syllables. Now instead of indicating his ability to cope with anything, his patter seems to reveal his limits.

Patter in Rossini almost always reaches a point of excess, carrying singers past the effect they hoped to make and therefore making them look foolish. And it is not only servant or lower-class characters. The most extraordinary patter in *The Barber* comes from Bartolo, precisely when he is bragging that he is a doctor, far too distinguished and intelligent to be the victim of deceit. In his Act 2 aria "A un dottor della mia sorte" ("To a doctor of my status") he has caught his ward Rosina lying to cover her secret contacts with her

young suitor. He warns her that he is no fool and will take measures to keep her and the young man apart:

E Rosina innocentina	And innocent little Rosina,
Sconsolata, disperata,	disconsolate and desperate,
In sua camera serrata	will stay locked in her room
Fin ch'io voglio star dovrà.	as long as I wish.

In Rossini's setting the singer delivers this neat stanza as a frenzied diatribe, at the top of his range and at a furious, steady clip, repeating each line of verse in turn while taking no breaths. His repetitious musical phrases circle around and around, drawn ever more relentlessly to one pitch, that of the unmoving bass note underlying the whole passage. In this music we hear that Bartolo has reached the limit of his power over Rosina. Old and unattractive to his ward, he is more trapped than she is, despite the confines he is threatening to impose on her. And as he patters on, his frustration emerges in the only sonic outlet available to him: his voice (and the orchestra with him) grows louder and louder. This effect of a *crescendo* that embodies the rising energy of an endlessly repeating musical loop—that is, an energy that has nowhere to go—is so characteristic of the composer that it is known as the "Rossini *crescendo*."

The aristocratic characters, Count Almaviva and Rosina (whom the middle-class Dr. Bartolo controls because she is an orphan), do not sing patter. Instead, like the aristocratic characters in Mozart's operas, they sing their own "aristocratic" style of quick notes: florid passages of many notes on a single vowel. If anything, Rossini marks class differences more strictly with this musical distinction than Mozart does. Yet Rossini, unlike Mozart, was writing in the wake of that experiment in class leveling, the French Revolution. *The Barber of Seville* comes from the period known in political history as the Restoration (1815–30), when the old royal and aristocratic order was being restored all across Europe and the forces of revolution were being suppressed. But the term should not be understood to mean that anything was actually as it had been before the Revolution, either in social and political life or in the arts. Depicting the highhandedness and cruelty of aristocrats on the operatic stage, as Mozart had done in *The Marriage of Figaro* and *Don Giovanni*, was now no longer as permissible as it had been before the aristocratic

Nathan Gunn as Figaro (right) gives directions to Juan Diego Florez as Count Almaviva in the duet "All'idea di quel metallo" in Act 1 of *The Barber of Seville*, performed at the Los Angeles Opera, 2009.
© Robert Millard

order had actually come under attack. Instead of being mocked, the aristocrat is now romanticized. Whereas Mozart's Count Almaviva insists on his right to take advantage of those beneath him, Rossini's Count Almaviva, a singer of elegant serenades, simply knows he will win his love. By the same token, the exchange of roles and musical styles between masters and servants—which provided so much provocative fun in eighteenth-century comic opera—virtually disappears in the comic operas of Rossini.

The Barber of Seville instead provides a socially leveling humor, a mocking of all the characters, no matter what their class, simply for being human. In Act 1, for instance, when Count Almaviva asks Figaro to find a way for him to enter the suspicious Dr. Bartolo's house to declare his love to Rosina, their plotting takes the form of a duet ("All'idea di quel metallo" / "At the idea of that metal") in which Figaro cooks up a suitable scheme and the Count accepts it. But then, predictably, the characters get carried away. They express themselves so excessively and repetitively that they seem to have turned into robotic spokesmen for themselves. The Count sets this second section of the duet in motion by asking directions to Figaro's barbershop, and Figaro, who could simply point to it down the road, instead gives him endless directions and descriptions, all sung on a single note ("Numero quindici" / "Number fifteen"). Later in this section Figaro relishes the money the Count is paying him, while the Count relishes the love he is about to find with Rosina, yet both of them sing to music that turns like clockwork between two chords (see Example 11.2):

11.2 Rossini, *The Barber of Seville*: Act 1, "All'idea di quel metallo"

Figaro:

Delle monete	The sound of money
Il suon già sento!	I hear already!
Già viene l'oro,	Here comes the gold,
Viene l'argento,	here comes the silver,
Eccolo qua.	it's right here.

Count:

Ah, che d'amore	Ah, how I feel
La fiamma sento ...	the flame of love ...

The social distinction between the two characters is not lost in the music. True to long-standing operatic convention, the barber Figaro sings in patter, one syllable to each note, while the aristocratic Count Almaviva sings in long, artful passages on single syllables. In this passage, for instance, Figaro sings four times as many syllables as the Count to exactly the same number of notes. The effect of the duet, however, is not to distinguish the two characters but to demonstrate that human beings of every class behave in utterly predictable ways, like cogs in a machine, even when they are in the throes of love. Rossini's comic art is both cynical and tolerant because it is not really about differences between people, but about what is ridiculous in human nature. In an age when revolutionary ideas of political and social equality were not permitted in the theater, Rossini showed his audiences

how readily anyone could be reduced to behaving like an automaton and so got them, through their laughter, to embrace one sense in which everyone is created equal.[7]

Controlling Families: Donizetti, *Lucia di Lammermoor*

The resistance of young people to marriages arranged by their families is a theme with a long history in the theater: Shakespeare's *Romeo and Juliet*, for example, was produced in the 1590s; it was then turned into opera several times, notably by Charles Gounod in 1867. Nineteenth-century treatments of the theme have a particular edge because a Romantic ideology of individual autonomy had taken hold in Western society by then, supporting the idea of marriage by choice, even while the practice of arranged marriages was far from over. As Michelle Perrot writes of the nineteenth-century French family: "The more rigorous a family's marital strategy, the more it sought to channel or stifle desire. As individualism became a more powerful force, people began to rebel against arranged marriages — the source of many a romantic drama and of countless crimes of passion."[8] Among those dramas were Walter Scott's novel *The Bride of Lammermoor* (1819), a work read across Europe, and the equally famous Italian opera based on it, Gaetano Donizetti's *Lucia di Lammermoor* (1835).

In the opera (on a libretto by Salvadore Cammarano), set in seventeenth-century Scotland, the conflict lies between Enrico Ashton, the Laird of Lammermoor, and his sister Lucia. In order to save his family's fortunes, Enrico arranges for his sister to marry a wealthy suitor, but she loves Edgardo Ravenswood, a man of no such means whose family has long feuded with her own. Lucia and Edgardo meet in secret by a fountain to exchange vows. In the process we learn about Lucia's overactive imagination: at that same spot she has been terrified by the ghost of a young woman (one of her ancestors) murdered long ago by a Ravenswood. She expresses herself in *bel canto* melodies that represent the utmost hypersensitivity: long-breathed, embellished melodies, sometimes chromatic and plaintive, sometimes giddily excited. Using a forged letter appearing to show that Edgardo is unfaithful to her, her wicked brother tricks her into agreeing to the arranged marriage. Edgardo appears at the wedding, too late to stop the ceremony but shocking her with the realization that he still loves her. She goes mad, murders her husband, and dies. Edgardo, hearing of her death, kills himself.

Death is in fact the classic escape path of young lovers from familial and social control in nineteenth-century opera. Suicide provides that escape for male characters: Gherman in Tchaikovsky's *The Queen of Spades* (*Pikovaya dama*, 1890) and the title character in Jules Massenet's *Werther* (1892), along with Edgardo. Female characters also commit suicide: Gilda in Verdi's *Rigoletto* (1851), Liza in *The Queen of Spades*, and the title character in Amilcare Ponchielli's *La Gioconda* (1876). But female characters are at least as likely to find escape into death involuntarily, through disease (Violetta in *La traviata*) or frailty (the title character Manon Lescaut in operas by Massenet [1884] and Giacomo Puccini [1893]), or madness, as Lucia does.

In this pattern of involuntary deaths there may seem to be a consistent characterization of women as passive by nature — so passive that death simply, or perhaps conveniently, overtakes them. But these women are more rebellious than passive, resisting the fates that their families and societies decree for them. Consequently, the ailments to which they succumb seem more like sentences imposed on them by fate for failing to exhibit the passivity expected of a marriageable woman. These are some of the most heartbreakingly sympathetic characters in all of opera, because they appear so strong in spirit as they stand up for their right to love and so weak in constitution as their resistance fails. Audiences, that is, love them for singing their resistance to the power of the family and love them even more for singing their victimhood as they succumb to death, leaving the power of the family intact.

Lucia's mad scene Lucia's madness presents itself on her wedding night, when she has stabbed her husband and enters the large hall where the rest of the wedding party is gathered, knife in hand and blood on her white dress. She performs a **mad scene**, a kind of scene especially characteristic of the heroines of Italian *bel canto* opera. This is a long, complex solo number with commentary provided by the wedding guests (including her brother, who appears halfway through the scene and registers in horror what his actions have achieved). A mad scene is the portrayal of a character hallucinating, and the presence of the guests here is crucial because it shows the audience the discrepancy between what is actually happening to Lucia (where she is and who is around her) and what she believes is happening. She fails to acknowledge the guests, or for that matter the bloodstains on her dress, and instead addresses her lover, who is absent.

Through much of the scene the flute plays a part that is not only musically prominent (like the *obbligato* parts in arias of Handel and Mozart), but integral to the representation of her madness. The free-floating sound of the flute

Lucia's mad scene in *Lucia di Lammermoor*. In this staging by Mary Zimmerman at the Metropolitan Opera in 2011, Natalie Dessay plays Lucia, the huge background moon symbolizing her lunacy, her dress stained with the blood of the husband she has just murdered, and the sounds in her head taking her away from the here and now.

© Ken Howard, Metropolitan Opera

reminds us of two melodies from her love scene with Edgardo by the fountain. Lucia does not sing them this time, but seems to be hearing them in her head. While they come back to her, she sings delighted greetings to Edgardo, as if he were there. She is clearly not hearing the flute sounds as memories of her past, but hallucinating them as mistaken markers of her present.

As the scene progresses, she undergoes a different hallucination: she sees a specter, which separates her from Edgardo. But she recovers and imagines herself and Edgardo getting married ("Ardon gl'incensi" / "The incense is burning"). In formal terms this is the *cantabile* (slow part) of a slow-fast aria (like Violetta's "Ah! fors'è lui" in Act 1 of *La traviata*; see Chapter 4). But Lucia does not sing the opening of the melody; she lets the flutes take it, as she describes the course of the wedding in increasingly rhapsodic asides to her imagined Edgardo. When she does eventually take up the melody herself, it becomes a crazily embellished duet with the flute, utterly absorbing music representing a character utterly absorbed in her imagined reality. The chorus of stunned onlookers punctuates the passage with prayers for her.

Gustave Flaubert

The French writer Flaubert (1821–1880) published *Madame Bovary* in 1857. The novel tells the story of Emma Bovary, a woman raised on Romantic novels about passionate love who can't help being disappointed in her marriage to a small-town physician. On a trip to the opera in the provincial capital of Rouen to see a performance of *Lucia di Lammermoor*, she crosses paths with an old flame and, under the influence of the tragic love story unfolding in the opera, begins an affair with him.

Lucie [Lucia] came on, half borne up by her women; there was a wreath of orange blossoms in her hair, and she was paler than the white satin of her gown. Emma thought of her own wedding day: she saw herself walking toward the church along the little path amid the wheatfields. Why in heaven's name hadn't she resisted and entreated, like Lucie? But no—she had been light-hearted, unaware of the abyss she was rushing toward. Ah! If only in the freshness of her beauty, before defiling herself in marriage, before the disillusionments of adultery, she could have found some great and noble heart to be her life's foundation! Then virtue and affection, sensual joys and duty would all have been one; and she would never have fallen from her high felicity. But that kind of happiness was doubtless a lie, invented to make one despair of any love. Now she well knew the true paltriness of the passions that art painted so large. So she did her best to think of the opera in a different light: she resolved to regard this image of her own griefs as a vivid fantasy, an enjoyable spectacle and nothing more; and she was actually smiling to herself in scornful pity when from behind the velvet curtains at the back of the stage there appeared a man in a black cloak.

Madame Bovary, trans. Francis Steegmuller (New York: Random House, 1957), pp. 253–54.

The arrival of Enrico coincides with a new stage in her hallucination, as she recalls her awful confrontation with Edgardo (who knew nothing about the forged letter) at her wedding. Here, her hallucination almost makes contact with the reality around her: her brother is standing right there as she pleads to the imagined Edgardo that she was "the victim of a cruel brother." Then the progression of her thoughts—a rational progression in its own terms—takes her past her death, and in the upbeat *cabaletta* (fast part) of her aria, a waltz tune ("Spargi d'amaro pianto" / "Cover with bitter tears"), she tells Edgardo that she is in heaven, praying for him to join her. Her family having made an unbearable reality of her life, Lucia escapes through madness into a false reality where her desires triumph over her adversities. And in its "happy ending" at least, the narrative of her mad scene does prove real: she does lead Edgardo with her into death.

Respectability and Disease: Verdi, *La traviata*

Verdi's *La traviata* (The Woman Gone Astray, 1853) dramatizes another obstacle that families throughout history—including literary and dramatic history—have put in the way of young lovers: their difference in social class.

In the nineteenth century, when inherited rank meant less and less, bourgeois (middle-class) families focused their anxieties on wealth and respectability as markers of their social position. For that era *La traviata* serves, in Catherine Clément's words, as "the exemplary history of a woman crushed by the bourgeois family."[9] It is "exemplary" even though it is the man's bourgeois family, not her own, that crushes her.

Our study of the first half of the opera in Chapter 4 showed how Violetta Valéry, a poor girl from the country, became a courtesan to escape from poverty into the glamorous life maintained by some of the richest men in Paris. But in the first act, finding her new life a spiritual desert, she allows herself to be tempted by a middle-class student, Alfredo Germont, into making a second escape. They do so in the second act, leaving the high life of Paris and setting up what seems like a middle-class life in the suburbs. But they cannot actually attain a middle-class life or indeed any life together because of her disreputable past, and we pick up the story now as it follows her through another cycle of would-be escapes.

Escaping the controlling family Violetta doesn't tell Alfredo that the reason she is leaving him is to spare his family's middle-class respectability. In any case, when he set up house with her, he disregarded the social impact of his actions on his family. Now, humiliated by Violetta's apparent betrayal and in particular by her return to her aristocratic lover, the Baron Douphol, Alfredo finds a new means to spurn his class. Crashing a party at the Paris house of her friend Flora, where he knows he will find Violetta and the Baron, he heads straight for the gambling table. In a scene that manifests the obsession of the gambler in an endlessly repeating orchestral figure (Act 2, scene 2, starting at Flora's line "Qui desiata giungi" / "You're most welcome here"), Alfredo plays recklessly and with amazing success. In one sense he is gambling to humiliate Violetta in front of her Paris friends, since he then hurls his winnings at her feet to repay her, as he says, for what she spent on him. In another sense he is gambling to free himself of his middle-class identity. By playing against the Baron, who can afford to gamble, Alfredo is acting as if he could escape from middle-class existence, which is perpetually concerned about money and responsibility, into the apparently carefree life of the upper class.

Gambling is also a sign of social striving in other operas of domestic conflict, notably Massenet's *Manon* and Tchaikovsky's *The Queen of Spades*. In all three cases the young lover competes at the gambling table with a man who is not only richer and nobler, but also his rival for the love of the heroine. Taking the rival's money therefore means both equaling him in

Gherman (Maksim Aksënov) in Tchaikovsky's *The Queen of Spades* becomes so possessed by winning at the gambling table that he loses all thought of his beloved, all awareness of his rival and his surroundings. Production directed by Denis Krief in 2009 at the Teatro Regio, Turin, Italy.

Ramella & Giannese / © Fondazione Teatro Regio di Torino

class and displacing him in love. The young lover has extraordinary luck at cards (though in *The Queen of Spades* his luck runs out in the last round), but gambling provides no escape from his confining social status. Even Alfredo, who wins a fortune, simply brings disgrace on himself when he casts the money at Violetta's feet. Furthermore, he lands himself in a duel with Baron Douphol.

In its dramatic function dueling is just another form of gambling—another action that offers male characters the hope of release from an imprisoning social status, in this case into death. And like gambling, dueling does not pay off. The young protagonist, whether it is Alfredo or the title character in Tchaikovsky's *Yevgeny Onegin* (1879), survives the duel and therefore wins no release from anything. His death wish is unfulfilled, he goes into exile to avoid the disgrace of having participated in a duel, and later returns to find his situation worse than ever. The duel itself is not staged in *La traviata*, but Violetta hears that Alfredo has injured the Baron and left the country.

In the final act Alfredo learns that it was his father who drove Violetta away, and he returns to Paris, hoping for a second chance with her. But her tuberculosis has advanced, her aristocratic patrons have abandoned her, and he finds her living impoverished, isolated, and on the point of death. Though they are now reconciled, they focus for the rest of the opera on two possible paths of escape from the social constraints on their love. The

first is a return to their earlier idea of escaping Paris and finding a love nest in the country. To music of a caressing, almost lulling lilt, they sing the duet "Parigi, o cara":

Parigi, o cara,	*Paris, my beloved,*
Noi lasceremo,	*we'll put behind us;*
La vita uniti	*we will spend*
Trascoreremo.	*our life together;*
De' corsi affanni	*you will be quit*
Compenso avrai,	*of past anguishes;*
La tua/mia salute	*your/my health will*
Rifiorirà.	*bloom again.*

This duet can be heard as an expression of the Suburban Dream, the dream that you can evade your troubles by moving away from the urban center of things to a more natural, less socially entangling setting. Expressions of this sentiment, sung to dreamy music, issue frequently from the lips of operatic young lovers who find that their love cannot overcome the social obstacles of family and class. Even in operas where political or racial conflicts, not just family and class issues, stand against them, the lovers often voice their dreams of escape to a country retreat. Aida, for instance, offers to lead Radamès to the "virgin forests" of her homeland (in Act 3: "Là, tra foreste vergini" / "There, amid virgin forests"). But "Parigi, o cara" ends in Violetta collapsing, and they are forced to recognize that she will die before they can manage any other escape.

Violetta's tuberculosis, like Lucia di Lammermoor's madness, provides an opportunity for the portrayal of hallucination. Her disease plays a crucial role in her relationship with Alfredo from the beginning: in the first scene, when everyone else is only too happy to leave her to her coughing fit, his concern makes her take his expression of love seriously. The symptoms of her disease are less in evidence later, in her scene with Alfredo's father (though he uses her condition to argue that his son's love will not last) and the gambling scene. But the final act, from its first note to its last, is dedicated to taking us through the dying stages of her disease.

It was plausible for this act to be organized around a pair of false recoveries because tuberculosis, a familiar killer in nineteenth-century Europe, had a reputation for allowing its victims deceptive bursts of renewed vitality just before it carried them off. Early in the last act Violetta undergoes one false recovery when Alfredo returns to her, giving her renewed hope and strength. After "Parigi, o cara" her second false recovery comes when Alfredo's father and Violetta's doctor and maid have entered the room and it is clear to them that she is on the point of death. She reaches into a

drawer, finds a small portrait of herself from healthier days, and hands it to Alfredo:

> Prendi, quest'è l'immagine
> De' miei passati giorni,
> A rammentar ti torni
> Colei che sì t'amò.

> Take this, it is the image
> of my past days;
> turn your thoughts back to her
> who loved you so.

She delivers these words initially on a monotone, her wasted-sounding voice hanging pathetically in the air because the orchestra does not accompany her so much as punctuate her words with funereal drum-roll chords. It could be a funeral march, except that it is in three. When the Germonts, son and father, have protested her mention of dying, she continues, now accompanied by a sustained and sweetly rocking pattern in the strings, still punctuated by the drum roll: a slow funeral lullaby-waltz.

To this macabre dance of death she sings her macabre vision of the future. It is not, however, a delusion (like Lucia's), but a brutally clear-sighted vision of what her death makes possible for Alfredo in the real world she is leaving. She imagines Alfredo marrying a "chaste virgin" (an image that is not just a contrast with herself, but a reminder of Alfredo's sister, for the sake of whose respectable marriage Violetta gave him up earlier), and she gives this imagined marriage her blessing:

> Se una pudica vergine
> Degli anni suoi sul fiore,
> A te donasse il core,
> Sposa ti sia, lo vo'.

> If a chaste virgin
> in the best years of her life
> should give you her heart,
> let her be your wife: I wish it.

This is in every sense a devastating moment, in which she not only prepares to escape from the unrespectable life she has led, but also erases the past that she and Alfredo have shared. The erasure even includes her recalling two phrases from his declaration of love in Act 1 (the minor-mode phrases to "Misterioso, altero" / "Mysterious and proud"), singing them now to new words about the future she imagines for him: "Le porgi quest'effigie, dille che dono ell'è" ("Present this portrait to her, tell her it is the gift"). She thereby allows him to escape to that respectable course from the social dead end in which his love waylaid him. Shrinking her presence in his life to a tiny portrait, she waltzes slowly into oblivion.

This clear vision then gives way to a delusional one. Like the flute in Lucia's mad scene, a small and intensely quiet group of violins and violas plays—apparently in Violetta's head—a reminder of happier days when she imagined that their impossible love was possible: the melody of "Di quell'amore ch'è palpito" ("In that love which is the pulse") from Alfredo's

Alfredo (José Bros, left) weeps and his father, Giorgio Germont (Renato Bruson), comforts as Violetta (Irina Lungu) slips into death at the very end of *La traviata*, in a production directed by Lilian Cavani at La Scala, Milan, 2008.

Marco Brescia © Teatro alla Scala

declaration when he first met her. As the violins spiral up sequentially with that melody and then the woodwinds and the rest of the strings add urgency, she ecstatically declares herself revived. In this burst of energy she is enacting her second false recovery, even as she unknowingly reveals the only way a *traviata*—a woman who has strayed from a moral life—could actually escape the punishment of her moralistic social world: leaping on the word "Joy!" ("gioia!") to a *fortissimo* high B-flat that seems to overshoot its accompanying chord, she falls dead.

Beyond the Reach of Family: Puccini, *La bohème*

Nineteenth-century audiences—and especially the parents in those audiences—could weep sentimentally over Lucia, Violetta, and similar heroines even though they agreed that it was the duty of a head of family to make a child's romantic love yield to the family's social needs. But the social realities of courtship were changing. As the century progressed, larger and larger masses of young people found themselves living away from the controlling force of their families. Middle-class young men left the provinces to study at universities in the cities, and young women as well as men from peasant families left farming villages to seek work there. By mid-century Paris in particular (at once a national capital, a university

town, and a center of commerce and culture) harbored a large population of young people starting out in life detached from their families and more or less committed to the idea that they could make their marital choices for themselves. Novels and plays by writers like Honoré de Balzac, George Sand, and Henry Murger were giving the French public its image of this independent youth culture, this "Bohemian life," in Paris.[10] Later in the century even greater numbers of young Europeans became separated from their families at the marrying time of life when they migrated for work across national boundaries and across the ocean, especially to the Americas.

But except for a few works like *La traviata*, this growing reality of Western culture was not represented in opera until practically the end of the nineteenth century, when it found its muse in the Italian composer Giacomo Puccini. In 1896 (a year before a rival composer, Ruggero Leoncavallo, produced an opera with the same title and subject) Puccini presented *La bohème* (*Bohemian Life*), set in Paris in the 1830s and based on stories that Henry Murger published in 1847–49 and then turned into the play *La Vie de bohème* (*Bohemian Life*) in 1849.[11] This was a drama of the lives and loves of Bohemian artists and intellectuals (representing the young men with the freest ideas of social behavior) and a seamstress (representing the impoverished young women who flooded into cities from the countryside). Not only has it been one of the most beloved of all operas almost from its premiere, but its theme of young love unfettered by family constraints made it just about the only nineteenth-century opera that could be effortlessly transplanted to a contemporary setting and musical style a century later, as it was in Jonathan Larson's rock Broadway show *Rent* (1996).

La bohème is in fact like a retelling of *La traviata* in which the young man's father never arrives to break things up, and in Puccini's operas generally, romance has no parental opposition to contend with. The lovers live in a youth culture, in constant contact with their peers. In the whole opera there is only one moment when a character is alone onstage, and the dramatic point of it is that he is ready not to be alone. The poet Rodolfo stays behind when the three friends with whom he shares an apartment head for a cafè; he tries to write, but declares that he is not in the mood; and a knock at the door brings the seamstress Mimì into his life.

Rodolfo's friends may provide a substitute for family, but they do not create any allegiance that conflicts with his love for Mimì. As a result, we might wonder where the drama in an opera like *La bohème* comes from. The answer on the whole is that the conflict is internal: these are operas

The Puccini Sound

More than any other composer, Puccini draws from singers the sound that listeners today, whether fans or not, associate with opera, a sound that expresses the frailty of love. It is the sound of a voice full-bodied up to its highest notes, always on the breaking point and frequently succumbing to vocal "sobs" or emotional shrieks, a sound that in the late nineteenth century allowed the high voices of tenors and sopranos to dominate opera as never before. They no longer thrilled listeners by the lightness and agility that tenors and sopranos of earlier centuries had exhibited in their top ranges, but by a new vocal technique that projected relentless emotionalism with incredible power on the highest notes.

This technique is not required exclusively for Puccini's operas, nor did it develop overnight. Already by the middle of the century star tenors were giving up head tones, or falsetto, in their upper registers for full-voiced high notes (the "high C from the chest"). Composers like Verdi, Wagner, and Tchaikovsky pushed female as well as male singers for greater power in their upper registers well before Puccini came along. And contemporaries of his like Jules Massenet and Pietro Mascagni called for much the same from singers. This sound was developed in part to project commandingly over larger orchestras and choruses in the larger opera houses built in both hemispheres in the second half of the nineteenth century. Through the recording industry, which developed during Puccini's career, the tenor Enrico Caruso and other great singers of the day popularized this vocal sound with an unprecedented mass of listeners around the world.

about lovers who, having chosen each other freely, fall to quarreling and desertion. In the first act Rodolfo and Mimì no sooner meet by accident than they fall in love, but by the third act they fall out, she complaining of his jealousy and he admitting to a friend that he pretends to be jealous in order to cover his true feelings: he loves her so much that he cannot bear to see her dying of tuberculosis while he lacks the money to provide for her. Whereas in La traviata Violetta's tuberculosis draws Alfredo in sympathy toward her, in La bohème the same disease makes Rodolfo shrink in fear from his commitment to Mimì. Despite their mutual love, they agree to stay together only until winter loses its grip, but the disease carries her off before winter ends. Puccini's operas are perennially appealing in no small part because they show the human frailty of love, its capacity to turn to doubt, selfishness, and cruelty of its own accord, rather than the side of love that opera had traditionally shown: its capacity to grow strong when challenged from outside.

Sound textures of love The frailty of love is suggested in the full-throated, emotionally vulnerable sound that opera singers developed for music like Puccini's. It is not the sound of any one voice that gives Puccini's music its dramatic effect, however, but the relationship he creates between one voice and another and especially between voice and orchestra. In the third act of *La bohème*, for instance, where Mimì, shivering on a snowy street, overhears Rodolfo admit his fear of watching her die, she sings what amounts to an aria, pathetically announcing that in that case she will leave him. Someone who looked simply at her vocal line in the opening of this number would see a traditional switch from the repeated notes of an acting-style delivery on her first lines—

Donde lieta uscì	*From where she gladly emerged*
Al tuo grido d'amore,	*at your cry of love,*
Torna sola Mimì	*Mimì will return alone*
Al solitario nido.	*to her solitary nest —*

to a more songful style of delivery on the succeeding lines (see Example 11.3):

Ritorna un'altra volta	*She returns once again*
A intesser finti fior!	*to braiding artificial flowers!*

When her lines are heard with the orchestra, though, the effect is more complex. Far from merely accompanying her, the orchestra provides a constant stream of melody, to which Mimì's melodies constantly adjust. Her unsongful opening lines allow listeners to notice the violin melody against which she delivers them, a melody that creates nostalgia for the past moment she is describing, since it is what she sang as she introduced herself to Rodolfo in the first act ("Mi chiamano Mimì" / "I'm called Mimì"). But while she is proposing to return to the life she led before meeting him, the clarinet introduces a more agitated melody, which she then takes up, doubled by the violins. The switch here is from a wistful moment in which her words and memories are articulated in separate planes to a more decisive moment when her thoughts come together and cadence on a resolution about her future.

Mimì is not as decisive as she seems. A minute later she and Rodolfo have decided to stay together while the winter lasts and go their separate ways in the spring. It is a lovely mutual deception: without admitting that they are still in love or that Mimì is about to die, they agree on a course of action that assumes both things are true. And they agree in a love duet that explains why spring is the right time for lovers

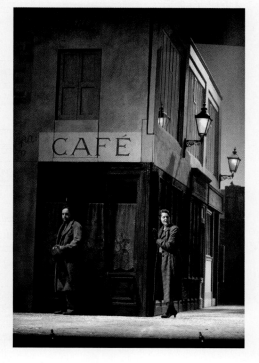

Melody Moore as Mimì and Alfie Boe as Rodolfo, concealing their love and fears for each other, work out how long they should stay together, in Act 3 of *La bohème*. In Jonathan Miller's production at the English National Opera in London, 2009, Isabella Bywater's designs present a starkly chilly cityscape.
Tristram Kenton/Lebrecht Music & Arts

to part. Puccini's music of constantly fluctuating textures suits drama that is marked by such constant wavering and ambiguity.

Even what seems like the simplest of all textural techniques—the doubling of voices by instruments (as in the second line of Example 11.3)—is in Puccini's hands a liquid device. It appears incessantly in his scores, yet he seldom uses it in a consistent way for more than a single phrase. Instrumental doubling of a singer's part had been a standard procedure in opera since at least the time of Gluck as a means of enveloping the audience in the character's consciousness. Puccini creates that effect on nearly every climactic phrase of every number of his operas, but he also goes well beyond it. In moments delicate as well as stentorian, he often makes the

11.3 Puccini, *La bohème*: Act 3, "Donde lieta uscì"

bass line double the melody, sometimes harmonizing that line with inner parts. And in his love duets, especially at their most memorable phrases, the singers are far more likely to unite their voices in riveting octave doubling than to harmonize in the traditional sweet texture of parallel thirds or sixths.

The cover of the original English vocal score of *La bohème* emphasizes the playful side of the scene just after Mimì and Rodolfo's duet in Act 3, when they are joined onstage by the quarreling lovers Musetta and Marcello. London: G. Ricordi, 1897.

This third-act duet of Mimì and Rodolfo is a remarkable case. It is a prolonged moment of half-acknowledged yearnings, incredibly placid harmonically (at least five minutes of music that hardly leave the tonic and dominant chords of G-flat major), yet built on irony: the two lovers bring their voices together in octaves in the middle of a line about being apart from each other:

Soli d'inverno	*To be separate in the winter*
È cosa da morire!	*is a thing to die of,*
Mentre a primavera	*whereas in the spring*
C'è compagno il sol!	*there is the sun for companion!*

Puccini underlines the irony by breaking off this texture rich in doublings (voices, strings, and woodwinds in three octaves) for a single measure of just Mimì's voice, doubled by just a quartet of woodwinds, on the word "soli" (separate, or alone).

The ironies multiply as the opera's other couple, quarreling jealously nearby, turn Mimì and Rodolfo's duet of tranquil yearning into a duet of contrasting duets, all within the ongoing spell of Mimì and Rodolfo's still music. Just before the end of this duet-turned-quartet (and of Act 3), all four singers unaccountably unite their voices, in three octaves, to three different sets of words, if for only one measure. The meaning of this phrase is complex: Mimì and Rodolfo, singing of leaving each other, are walking offstage in each other's arms, while the other two, enjoying their own quarrel, are just playing at leaving each other. Doubling may be the most ordinary device in Puccini's practice, but at this moment of dramatic complexity the sound of so many voices and instruments united, all at the peak of their range, while the bass and harmony drop out, is unique and unforgettable.

Trials of Married Life: Verdi, *Otello*

Marriage did not stop being interesting for operatic purposes once the knot was tied. Operas about the trials of married life include some masterpieces of the repertory, especially the Italian: works by Donizetti (*Anna Bolena*, 1830; *Lucrezia Borgia*, 1833) and Verdi (*Stiffelio*, 1850; *Un ballo in maschera* [*A Masked Ball*], 1859; *Otello*, 1887), and the single most famous works by Amilcare Ponchielli (*La Gioconda*, 1876), Pietro Mascagni (*Cavalleria rusticana* [*Rustic Chivalry*], 1890), and Ruggero Leoncavallo (*Pagliacci* [*Clowns*], 1892).

In all of these operas a marriage is tested—and in most of them it is destroyed, with the loss of at least one life—by a husband's suspicions, justified or not, of his wife's fidelity. It is almost always the husband who is suspicious of his wife. This disparity hardly seems remarkable: the jealous

husband is an age-old fixture in many dramatic traditions, including the whole history of opera. Nevertheless, we might ask what sense it made for nineteenth-century opera to continue the tradition. No doubt librettists and composers of the day, who as in previous centuries were almost all men, were in some sense expressing their own anxieties. In a broader sense they were exploring and reinforcing the prevailing, and legally ordained, ideas of their era about marriage as a relationship built on an inequality of roles. Because the husband was recognized as the more powerful partner and the wife bore the next generation of the family, a wife's infidelity was considered to undermine the stability of a marriage more than a husband's did.

Operas about couples were dramas of conflicting allegiances in that they showed husbands and wives committed to marital roles so disparate that they could not fail to conflict. The role of the wife was characteristically to embody true love. This was understood as a dangerous trait because a wife's affection might become fixated, to her shame, on someone other than her husband. In that case she might become that man's lover (Lina in *Stiffelio*, Lola in *Cavalleria rusticana*) or decide to run away with him (Laura in *La Gioconda*, Nedda in *Pagliacci*) or be discovered in a compromising situation with him, even while she is resisting his pleas (the title character in *Anna Bolena*, Amelia in *Un ballo in maschera*). In *Lucrezia Borgia* the wife's fixation is actually maternal rather than sexual, but since her husband does not know the identity of her grown son by a previous marriage, he takes that son to be her lover. In all these cases except *Stiffelio*, no matter what the wife has actually done, the husband assumes she has been unfaithful and takes his revenge.

In Verdi's *Otello* (to a libretto adapted from Shakespeare's *Othello* by the poet Arrigo Boito) the title character, the Moorish commander of a Venetian army in the fifteenth century, is entirely unjustified in his jealousy. His wife Desdemona loves him alone, as their joint recounting of their courtship makes clear in the Act 1 love duet, "Già nella notte densa" ("Already in the thick night"). Later, through the treacherous scheming of his ensign Iago, he will come to believe that Desdemona is unfaithful. But in this initial duet Otello shows himself to be no less true in his love than Desdemona is in hers. In fact, we later find his capacity for jealousy credible precisely because through this duet we have come to believe in the depth of his love. He is based after all on Shakespeare's Othello, who at the moment of his death tells us he is "one that lov'd not wisely, but too well" (5, ii, 344).

Husbandly violence The operatic husband's status as a married man confers on him a treasured social identity, and any doubt about his wife's fidelity puts his public figure, not just his private happiness, at risk. This feeling of being betrayed in both the private and the public spheres is

more than a suspicious husband can stand. It turns him violent. Otello's violence against his wife, like Saint-Bris's against his daughter in *Les Huguenots* or Don José's against Carmen, is a soldier's violence. Otello's is all the more frightening because he is a soldier of fortune (a mercenary) formidable enough on the battlefield to have been entrusted with the command of Venice's armies.

When Otello begins to be disturbed by the suspicions Iago has planted in his mind, his first thought (Act 2, scene 5), expressed in Boito's clamorous

Otello (Vladimir Galuzin) knocks Desdemona (Kallen Esperian) to the ground before the crowd of Venetian visitors, soldiers under Otello's command, and civilians, in the finale of Act 3 of *Otello*, directed by David Kneuss at the Metropolitan Opera, 2003.
© Ken Howard, Metropolitan Opera

verse and Verdi's surging march music, is that by betraying him, his wife has stripped him of his soldierly manhood:

Clamori e canti di battaglia, addio! . . .	*Noises and songs of battle, farewell!*
Della gloria d'Otello è questo il fin.	*This is the end of Otello's glory.*

Then he exhibits violence for the first time. He seizes Iago by the throat and throws him to the ground. Eventually, though, he enlists Iago's help in punishing Desdemona for her supposed adultery. The two join in a conspiratorial oath ("Sì, pel ciel marmoreo giuro!" / "Yes, I swear by the marbled heaven!") as terrifying in its martial solemnity and stridency as the oath of the Catholic conspirators in *Les Huguenots*. But here the conspiring soldiers are not swearing to wipe out their political enemies; one is swearing to help the other kill his wife and her presumed lover.

In the third act Otello turns his violence for the first time on Desdemona. In a private conversation, her innocent answers to his questions succeed only in reinforcing his belief in her adultery, and he shoves her from the room. Left alone, he falls into an abyss of self-pity in which, once again comparing the martial and marital signs of his manhood, he declares that he would have sacrificed his reputation as a soldier sooner than his bliss as a husband (Act 3, scene 3: "Dio! mi potevi scagliar tutti i mali" / "God! You could have hurled at me all the ills"). Later in the same act (scene 8) he demonstrates the public side of the humiliation he feels she has brought on him when he humiliates her at a public ceremony, pushing her down and cursing her. Then in the last act he comes into their bedroom, wakes her, and smothers her.

Wifely fortitude *Otello* is compelling musical theater because of the way in which it incessantly opposes—in word, action, and above all music—Otello's uncontrolled violence to Desdemona's meek fortitude. She is, as Verdi expressed it in a letter, "not a woman, she is a type! She is the type of goodness, of resignation, of sacrifice!" She embodies, in other words, a certain nineteenth-century ideal of a wife. Desdemona is powerless to protect herself from her husband's fury, but she matches him with a sort of staying power, maintaining her identity, self-control, and calm in the face of his incomprehensible attacks. This calm is embodied in her songfulness, which she sustains even as she suffers more and more verbal and physical abuse from Otello. In Verdi's words, "Desdemona is a part in which the thread, the melodic line, never ceases from the first note to the last."[12] In the public ceremony when she falls to the ground, two

companions lift her up physically, but musically she picks herself up. At first she blurts out scattered impressions of her humiliation to a stumbling accompaniment —

A terra! . . . sì . . . nel livido	*On the ground . . . yes . . . in the black-and-blue*
Fango . . . percossa . . . io giacio	*mud . . . beaten . . . I lie —*

but after just a few more such lines she pulls herself together to begin a long, noble solo marking the sudden extinction of her husband's love:

E un dì sul mio sorriso	*Whereas once on my smile*
Fioria la speme e il bacio . . .	*flowered hope and kissing . . .*

As she repeats this tragic declaration of defeated love, her voice soars over those of Otello and Iago and the multitude of shocked and sympathetic bystanders who fill the stage, giving the act a thrilling climax of a sort derived from grand opera. But the musical dominance of her voice over this huge ensemble serves only to dramatize how utterly isolated she is by husband's public cruelty.

Even more extraordinary in their dramatic power are the two songs Desdemona sings, one right after the other, at the beginning of Act 4 as she gets ready for bed on her final night. One is the Willow Song ("Piangea cantando" / "She wept as she sang"), a funereal song of betrayed love that she remembers hearing as a child from her mother's servant; the other is an Ave Maria that she sings as her nightly prayer, adapting the ecclesiastical words as she goes so that they cover her own victimized condition. These are both songs of conventional and straightforward expression, except for a few moments when she allows her foreboding to intrude. Those moments include the outburst with which she ends the Willow Song, a shatteringly final-sounding farewell to her companion Emilia ("Ah! Emilia, addio!"), and the lines in the Ave Maria that point in wrenching music to her own situation:

Prega per chi sotto l'oltraggio piega	*Pray for any who bend their brows*
La fronte e sotto la malvagia sorte	*under the force of outrage and evil fortune.*

These startling outbursts bring to the forefront of our consciousness the violence that we know Otello is bound to visit on Desdemona and that her singing is powerless to stop. They show us by contrast the enormous strength of character it takes in all the other phrases to suppress her fears and sing with the simple expression that these songs demand.

In pitting Desdemona's serene self-control against Otello's uncontrolled violence, the opera is not simply telling the story of two individuals locked in a doomed marriage. If Desdemona is a type of the feminine, Otello is likewise a type of the masculine. And just as his identity is constructed out

of his allegiance to the exclusively male military world in which he has lived, so Desdemona's identity is constructed out of her allegiance to an exclusively female world. This world is most fully revealed when she sings the Willow Song and Ave Maria, the first a tale of suffering in love, handed down in domestic settings from woman to woman, and the second an appeal to the Virgin Mary, the figure of female power within a Catholic Church that in Verdi's day was identified as a spiritual haven for women far more than for men. In this way *Otello* dramatizes what were regarded in Verdi's culture as universal differences in identity, sphere, and nature between men and women. Accordingly, it is hardly surprising that he and Boito played down the importance of racial difference between the Moor Otello and the Venetian Desdemona.[13] Instead of portraying a marriage beset by the particular incompatibility of race, their opera can be understood as showing how the supposedly innate differences between all men and all women can imperil even the most loving of marriages.

At the same time, *Otello* allows us to understand domestic conflict as a metaphor for larger-scale conflicts. Perhaps more than any other opera about the trials of married life, *Otello* derives its musical terms of distinction — the march and conspiracy oath that help constitute Otello's male identity, the folk song and hymn that help constitute Desdemona's female identity — from nineteenth-century operas about political conflict. But the lovers in *Otello* do not represent two sides in a political conflict, as

the lovers do in *Les Huguenots* and *Aida*, or even two hostile parts of a racially divided world, as the lovers do in *Carmen*. They represent simply the two sides in a conflicted relationship between women and men. And if the musical terms of distinction allow us to see the domestic conflict of *Otello* as political (men and women as irreconcilable political factions within the human nation), they also allow us to see the political conflict depicted in other operas as domestic conflict writ large. They allow us, that is, to see operas from *Fidelio* and *Les Huguenots* to *Aida*, *Boris Godunov*, and *Carmen* as depictions of people who, living close together despite different political ideology, religious affiliation, national allegiance, or racial identity, suspect and resent and attack each other like ill-matched spouses.

FURTHER READING

On domestic life in nineteenth-century Europe, Michelle Perrot, ed., *From the Fires of Revolution to the Great War*, vol. 4 of Philippe Ariès and Georges Duby, eds., *A History of Private Life*, trans. Arthur Goldhammer (Cambridge and London: Belknap Press of Harvard University Press, 1990). On race and exoticism in opera, Ralph Locke, *Musical Exoticism: Images and Reflections* (Cambridge and New York: Cambridge University Press, 2009), esp. ch. 7 on Bizet's *Carmen*. Also on *Carmen*, Susan McClary, *Georges Bizet: "Carmen"* (Cambridge and New York: Cambridge University Press, 1992).

On Rossini's *The Barber of Seville*, Emanuele Senici, *The Cambridge Companion to Rossini* (Cambridge and New York: Cambridge University Press, 2004). On Donizetti's *Lucia di Lammermoor*, Richard Taruskin, *Oxford History of Western Music* (Oxford: Oxford University Press, 2005), 3:46-59. On Puccini's *La bohème*, Arthur Groos and Roger Parker, *Giacomo Puccini: "La bohème"* (Cambridge and New York: Cambridge University Press, 1986). On Verdi's *Otello*, James Hepokoski, *Giuseppe Verdi: "Otello"* (Cambridge and New York: Cambridge University Press, 1987).

FOR RESEARCH AND REFLECTION

1. Compare the finale of Act 1 of *The Barber of Seville* with a Mozart mid-point finale (the finale to Act 2 of *The Marriage of Figaro*, to Act 1 of *Don Giovanni*, or to Act 1 of *Così fan tutte*). What similarities and differences do you find in their respective dramaturgical and musical elements? How much alike are the two finales in their dramatic and musical effects?

2. In the nineteenth century European and American opera audiences expected to see all-white casts in the opera house, even in works like

Bizet's *Carmen* and Meyerbeer's *L'Africaine*, both of which deal with racial difference. In recent decades, as more and more nonwhite singers have entered the opera house, how have white and nonwhite roles been cast?

3. Nineteenth-century operas of domestic conflict like *La traviata*, *La bohème*, and *Otello* often employ the full resources of grand opera — grand sets, a huge chorus, and a symphonic orchestra — even though the work is concerned with an intimate subject: the trials of a love affair or marriage. Are these grand resources misplaced in such works? Are they used simply because they are available? Or are they put to a valid dramatic purpose?

4. Fathers don't get any respect — or do they? The fathers and substitute fathers in operas of domestic conflict play the heavies with their daughters (sisters, wards), and yet, representing the needs of respectable families, they can claim some respect from audiences. Consider what makes any of these fathers (and substitute fathers) sympathetic or unsympathetic characters: Giorgio Germont in *La traviata*; the title character in Verdi's *Rigoletto*; Enrico Ashton in Donizetti's *Lucia di Lammermoor*; Pogner in Wagner's *Die Meistersinger von Nürnberg*; the Countess in Tchaikovsky's *The Queen of Spades*.

5. How is the obsession of gambling conveyed musically in the gambling scenes of *La traviata*, Massenet's *Manon*, Tchaikovsky's *The Queen of Spades*, or Prokofiev's *The Gambler*?

 Additional resources available at wwnorton.com/studyspace.

Opera on Legendary Themes

Struggles for a Soul

The cult of medieval legends, a craze in the mid-eighteenth century, grew into a dominant current of cultural life in the nineteenth. From medieval or imitation-medieval legends, nineteenth-century readers and audiences learned to thrill to the terror of the supernatural. They considered their own times an age of reason and the Middle Ages an age of faith, but also of superstition. That distant and alien era when the supernatural seemed a part of daily life provided an artistic setting in which people could explore the inexplicable anxieties and suppressed "demons" that unsettled their own lives, but that could scarcely be acknowledged, let alone described, in the setting of their own supposedly rational society.

In the largely rural, largely illiterate culture of medieval Europe, legends commonly took the form of narrative song or poetry, handed down orally from one storyteller to another. It was a simple matter for those storytellers to portray the supernatural as a part of daily life because their medium left everything to the imagination. Listeners could close their eyes and imagine ghosts and demons as easily as fishermen and stepmothers, magical transformations as easily as horses galloping and lovers embracing. But when medieval tales of the supernatural were transferred to the operatic stage, the fantastic had to be realized in the flesh: actors with the help of stage effects had to embody supernatural characters enacting magical deeds. And music had to be devised to evoke both the human and the supernatural sides of those characters.

Arthur Rackham, "Brünnhilde the Valkyrie," from *The Rhinegold and the Valkyrie*, by Richard Wagner (London: William Heinemann, 1910). Rackham, an important English book illustrator, brings an Edwardian fairy-tale tone to the sixty-six drawings he made for this and a companion volume telling the story of Wagner's cycle *The Ring of the Nibelung*.

Stapleton Collection/Art Resource, NY

Pacts with the Devil: Gounod, *Faust*

One of the most prominent themes in legendary opera is the struggle over a character's soul. A number of famous operas tell of a man who offers his soul to the devil in payment for magical power and then struggles to deny the devil what he owes him—or finds himself caught between the devil's claims and the pleas of a woman who loves him. These operas include Carl Maria von Weber's *Der Freischütz* (*The Freeshooter*, 1821) and Meyerbeer's *Robert le Diable* (*Robert the Devil*, 1831), as well as musical settings of Johann Wolfgang von Goethe's poetic drama *Faust* (Part 1, published in 1808) by Hector Berlioz (*La Damnation de Faust* / *The Damnation of Faust* [1846], a "dramatic legend" intended for concert performance but sometimes staged as an opera); Charles Gounod (*Faust*, 1859); and Arrigo Boito (*Mefistofele/Mephistopheles*, 1875). Gounod's *Faust*, to a French libretto by Jules Barbier and Michel Carré, the version examined here, was long one of the most popular works in the operatic repertory.

Though the story of *Faust* originated in a folk narrative tradition stretching back to the Middle Ages, Goethe's drama and Gounod's opera express a nineteenth-century sensibility. The nameless, depressive discontent suffered by its protagonist is a condition characteristic of the time. That was an age of boundless belief in self-reliance, when young men were being freed from the traditional expectation that they would follow in their fathers' professional footsteps and would marry the women their parents chose for them. But this freedom produced a corresponding anxiety about the challenge of self-reliance: having to compete for one's position in society, for one's identity, for love, for everything. What drives Faust is his sense of inadequacy to fulfill any of his needs on his own. He is a philosopher who is tired of his studies and longs for the knowledge that study cannot bring, for his lost youth, for wealth, power, and love.

His unhappiness is answered by the appearance of the devil, Méphistophélès, who tempts him with the promise of an effortless cure. Before proving his supernatural powers, Méphistophélès wins Faust's confidence by displaying the human self-confidence that the scholar so painfully lacks. He matches Faust's own scholarly nature, deflecting with philosophical skill Faust's questions about who he is and then putting their unholy bargain into the legalistic form of a contract through which Faust signs away his soul.

The musical characterization of Méphistophélès as a figure both human and superhuman is crucial to the imaginative appeal of the work. Portrayals of devils, as of Christian religious figures, were usually not allowed in European theaters before the French Revolution, but in its aftermath that prohibition began to yield, and in the course of the nineteenth century conventions were established for representing the devil in music. Gounod's Méphistophélès, like

Staging the Supernatural

Just as operas of conflicting allegiances posed the challenge of how to bring history to life onstage, legendary operas posed the challenge of how to make magic events seem real: the dwarf Alberich turning himself into a dragon and then a toad in Wagner's *Das Rheingold*, the hero Ruslan doing battle with a giant's head in Glinka's *Ruslan and Lyudmila*, the sinking of a ghost ship in Wagner's *The Flying Dutchman*. A subtler challenge was the characterization of legendary and even supernatural characters. Like aliens in movies, these characters had to sound and look somehow different from ordinary humans, but the mere fact that they were played by singers meant that they were bound to seem *somewhat* human, not as purely fantastic as a creature we might imagine. Onstage, even the devil can become a sympathetic character. Before there were movies, opera was the most natural dramatic medium for legendary subjects: the music gave the drama the power both to evoke the unearthly and to endow a character with humanity. In fact, by bringing both these sides of the power of music to bear on supernatural characters, legendary opera often humanizes evil to such an extent that it shows how the choice between good and evil can be a genuine dilemma.

A backstage view of the machinery used to represent the dragon Fafner in his battle with Siegfried in Wagner's *Siegfried*, as staged at the Paris Opera in 1902. The conductor in the top hat is cueing the singer who is singing Fafner's lines into the megaphone. This drawing by Georges Redon appeared in *Scientific American* 86/13 (March 29, 1902), supplement 1369.

Bildarchiv Preussischer Kulturbesitz, Berlin/Art Resource, NY

A century later, low-tech, labor-intensive machinery is often still used for stage monsters. Here, in a 2005 production of *Siegfried* at the Lyric Opera of Chicago, sixteen puppeteers in black manipulate the dragon (designed by Lisa Aimee Sturz of Red Herring Puppets) in battle with Siegfried (John Treleaven). Placing the monster toward the back of the stage and the hero facing it, with his back to the audience, is an effective way to make the spectators feel that the monster is attacking them.

Dan Rest/Lyric Opera of Chicago

practically all operatic devils then and since, has a bass voice, and when he first appears, summoned by Faust (a tenor), he announces himself in deep tones, accompanied by a blast from deep brass instruments and by creepy string chords. He is a conjurer who tempts his victims with wonders, and as he conjures each new wonder, his music takes on a new character. Leading Faust into a garden to meet the woman of his dreams (Act 3), for instance, Méphistophélès sings in ravishing, light tones against nocturnal nature music as he casts a love spell on the garden. Finally, since his role is to trick humans into forfeiting their souls, part of his character is playful: he is traditionally dressed in a version of a court jester's costume, and he mocks his victims in song. When Faust's love brings disgrace to his beloved, Marguerite, Méphistophélès taunts him in a mock serenade (Act 4) full of diabolical sung laughter.

The musical magic of the garden scene transforms Méphistophélès' sound, but it transforms Faust's even more. There, the weary, suicidal old scholar becomes what a tenor is expected to be in nineteenth-century opera: an ardent, young-sounding lover. By contrast, Marguerite stays true to herself and her sound throughout the opera. Like Desdemona in *Otello*, Marguerite sings always with a pure melodiousness, all the more remarkable given how severely her character is tested. She is an innocent young woman who allows herself to be seduced by the pleasure-seeking Faust and is then abandoned by him. She

The Polish bass Édouard de Reszke (1853–1917) dressed for the role of Méphistophélès in *Faust*. His costume invokes the traditional association of devil with court jester.

Private collection/Lebrecht Music & Arts

murders the baby she has by Faust, goes to church and prays to God, haunted by guilt and taunted—even in church—by Méphistophélès and a choir of demons for her illicit love affair.

Because she loves Faust, she struggles to pull him away from the devil and perdition. The struggle for his soul, then, is not simply a contest between Faust and the devil. Just as Méphistophélès represents Faust's desire for relief from his own inadequacy, Marguerite represents his ability to withstand the easy solution with which the devil tempts him. Her prayers supply Faust with the connection to godliness that he has needed to discover for himself all along. At the same time, her capacity to pray—again, like Desdemona's—is a touchstone of female moral character in nineteenth-century opera, just as Faust's incapacity to pray is a touchstone of a distinctively male moral dilemma.

Marguerite is imprisoned and condemned to death, and in the end she cannot save Faust by her steadfast love. Instead, Faust tries to rescue her from execution, but she dies, and he is simply left behind. That failure to resolve his fate indicates that Marguerite has become the real focus of the opera. In the final scene, leading Faust and Méphistophélès in the trio

"Anges pures, anges radieux" ("Pure, radiant angels"), the woman whose prayers could not save her lover's compromised soul succeeds through her prayers in saving her own. She dies to the sounds of salvation (another convention developed in nineteenth-century opera): harp, organ, and a chorus of angelic voices that proclaim her forgiven. In an opera full of the supernatural sounds of the devil, the final stroke of the supernatural is a sound from heaven.

Fulfilling a Legend: Wagner, *The Flying Dutchman*

An opera on a legendary theme often contains, early in its course, the narration of a legend, giving the back story to the action being played out onstage. The content of this story is legendary in that it reveals one of the characters in the opera to be a demon or a human who fell under a magic spell. The story is also legendary in its **ballad** form, with stanzas all sung to the same tune. This is a song sung to an onstage community that has likely heard it before.

The German opera *The Flying Dutchman* (*Der fliegende Holländer*, 1843), by Richard Wagner, revolves around a legend told and then fulfilled. By the beginning of the second act, when we hear the Ballad of the Flying Dutchman, we have already heard the stormy sea (the setting of the legend) in the overture. We have met the Dutchman (the only name he bears in the opera) and know that he lives a cursed life at sea. We have seen him encounter another sea captain, Daland, who promises him the hand of his daughter Senta. But not until we hear Senta sing this Ballad do we learn what his curse is or how he can be freed of it.

She and other women, awaiting the return of their men from a long sea voyage, sing as they work at their spinning wheels. Senta, mocked by the others for staring at a portrait on the wall, orders them to stop their "stupid song" and asks her former nursemaid, Mary, to sing instead the Ballad of the Flying Dutchman (who is the subject of the portrait). When Mary says that she has had enough of that song, Senta announces that she will sing it herself. From the conversation leading up to the Ballad, then, we learn that the Dutchman is a legendary figure to these women, since they endlessly hear the story of his life; that at least one of them (Mary) has contempt for the legend; that others enjoy listening to it; but that only one (Senta) believes in it wholeheartedly.

Senta begins singing unaccompanied, and that sound along with the stanzaic form helps us understand that she is telling her tale in song. Her first phrases suggest a sea chanty in both their leaping vocalization and their nonsense syllables ("Johohoe! Johohohoe!"). That melody is already associated with the Flying Dutchman: the orchestra played it in the first

Undated photographic portrait of Richard Wagner by the lithographer and photographer Franz Hanfstaengl. Portrait Collection of the Munich City Museum.

Ullstein Bild/Granger Collection

measures of the overture and in Act 1, punctuating the Dutchman's appearances and his most portentous pronouncements. Wagner makes sure we hear the connection now by giving the bass instruments that familiar melody just before Senta sings it to "Johohoe!" What's more, the opening phrase of her Ballad proper — when she begins to relate the Dutchman's story — has virtually the same rhythm (see Example 12.1).

12.1 Wagner, *The Flying Dutchman:* Act 2, Senta's Ballad

Each stanza of Senta's Ballad consists of two quatrains capped by a **refrain** — a concluding passage that comments on the story. In the first stanza's opening quatrain we meet the Dutchman as he is now.

Traft ihr das Schiff im Meere an,
blutroth die Segel, schwarz der Mast?
Auf hohem Bord der bleiche Mann,
des Schiffes Herr, wacht ohne Rast.

Have you met on the sea the ship
with blood-red sail and black mast?
On the bridge the pale man,
the ship's commander, watches
without rest.

There follows the second quatrain, which is more musically descriptive (with its sea-chanty calls and orchestral storm music), but also suggests the Dutchman's state of mind:

Hui! —Wie saust der Wind! Jo ho he!
Hui! —Wie pfeift's im Tau! Jo ho he!
Hui! —Wie ein Pfeil fliegt er hin,
ohne Ziel, ohne Rast, ohne Ruh'!

Whoosh! — How the wind rushes! Yo ho he!
Whoosh! —What whistling in the rigging! Yo ho he!
Whoosh! — Like an arrow he flies away,
without destination, without stop, without rest!

Then comes the refrain, telling us what would lift the curse under which the Dutchman suffers. That is a remarkable thing to learn at this point in the Ballad, before we are even told what the curse is and how he fell under it.

And these lines make a plea that is remarkably personal for a ballad; it is the singer's own wish for the lifting of the curse:

> Doch kann dem bleichen Manne Erlösung einstens noch werden,
> fänd' er ein Weib, das bis in den Tod getreu ihm auf Erden! —
> Ach! Wann wirst du, bleicher Seemann, sie finden?
> Betet zum Himmel, dass bald
> ein Weib Treue ihm halt'!

> Yet redemption can still come someday to the pale man,
> if he should find on earth a woman who is true to him till death!
> Ah! When will you find her, pale seaman?
> Pray to heaven that soon
> a woman stays true to him!

The music too marks the refrain apart from the opening two quatrains as more personal. The tempo slows, the mode changes from minor to major, the accompaniment is left to a small group of wind instruments, and the melody, warmer and less dramatic than what came before, seems especially significant because we have heard it already in the overture. Senta's wording and musical delivery turn the lifting of the curse from an impersonal prophecy into her own crusade.

The second and third stanzas tell the story of the curse. Long ago the Dutchman, struggling to navigate his ship around a stormy cape, swore that he would stay that course if it took forever. Satan, taking him at his word, cursed him to sail the seas forever. Every seventh year he can come ashore to search for a woman who can free him of the curse by being faithful to him till death, but so far he has found no such woman. This is the situation that prompts Senta's prayer in the refrain. The music is exactly the same for all three stanzas of her Ballad, but the refrain, which in many ballads repeats the same words and music every time, here features different words and a different mode of performance in each stanza.

In the second refrain the principal change is that the chorus of Senta's fellow spinners joins in on the last two phrases, harmonizing her melody. The refrain is perhaps a normal place for listeners to join in; in fact, another term for refrain is "chorus." But here the added voices make a particular dramatic effect: Senta's performance has moved her companions to think of the Dutchman not as a figure of legend, but as a real man in distress. The third refrain, which ends the song, is even more dramatically changed. Senta, exhausted by her involvement in the story, collapses and stops singing, leaving it to her companions to take up the refrain unaccompanied, asking where the woman is who will fulfill the prophecy. A resurgent Senta, altering the end of the refrain musically, begs to be that woman: "Through me you will achieve redemption!"

Senta, holding the portrait of the Flying Dutchman, sings the ballad about his fate, drawing her own fate into the story. Deborah Voigt plays Senta in Act 2 of *The Flying Dutchman*, directed by Stephen Pickover at the Metropolitan Opera, 2010.

©Cory Weaver, Metropolitan Opera

Senta's Ballad is a story within a story, both predicting and impelling the outcome of the opera. Because the character who sings the Ballad is also the one inspired by it, she is in a position to adapt it as she goes along: she announces within its structure her intention to fulfill the legend by being true to the Dutchman till death. In Thomas Grey's words Senta "breaks free of the balladic narrative," and in this way Wagner is "transforming the narrative ballad into a dramatic action that will bring closure to the open-ended story."[1]

That closure comes after a series of events: the Dutchman asks for her love and she pledges it to him; he then discovers her in heated conversation with another suitor and, mistakenly believing that Senta is being unfaithful, abandons her and sets sail once more. To keep her pledge, Senta now throws herself off a cliff to her death, thereby lifting the curse on the Dutchman, whose ship sinks into the sea. At these actions the orchestra plays once more the third refrain of Senta's Ballad, the music to which she sang, "Through me you will achieve redemption." The return of this music—which was first heard at the end of the overture—does not simply bring closure to the opera. It binds the promise in Senta's Ballad to its fulfillment in the drama and thus in a general sense binds together Ballad and action, legend and life. In fact, to show us the Dutchman redeemed by Senta's sacrifice, Wagner returns to what could be considered the supernatural realm of the opera. Just before the curtain falls, Senta and the Dutchman appear to rise up out of the sea together, embracing and looking toward heaven.

The Dutchman is a demonic figure, tempting Senta into surrendering her life and soul to satisfy his needs. That might make her seem like a female Faust. But she does not bargain with her demon like Faust. Senta wants exactly what her demon wants. He wants her to sacrifice herself to free him, and she wants to do just that. As Carl Dahlhaus writes, *The Flying Dutchman* belongs to the category of "martyr plays, which lay down the paths along which the protagonists, bent on self-sacrifice, can go to meet their ends."[2]

Being a martyr for love (rather than for religion) requires a psychology in which a yearning for death doubles as sexual attraction. Wagner, like other male nineteenth-century composers and artists generally, treats this as a syndrome characteristic of women. In his works it is always the women figures who, like Senta, are dying to die for love: Elisabeth in *Tannhäuser* (1845), Isolde in *Tristan und Isolde* (1865), Brünnhilde in *Der Ring des Nibelungen* (1876). The male characters present a complementary condition: Tannhäuser, Tristan, and Siegfried (in *Der Ring des Nibelungen*), like the Dutchman, die in need of the redemption that those female characters sacrifice themselves to grant.

Quest Legends

Legends of struggle over a soul have enjoyed great prestige in the past two centuries, in part because important operas like *Faust* and *The Flying Dutchman* have been made of them. But more widely known, in part because people learn them in childhood, are legends of a young person on a quest: a young man who fights with dragons and through hostile terrain to rescue his beloved, or a female spirit who falls in love with a male human and seeks to be transformed into a human in order to be his lover. Such legends have been told for much more than two centuries, though it was only in the nineteenth that they too became operatic subjects. They are stories of struggle against evil represented by a sorcerer or sorceress, not a devil. A legend of struggle over a soul requires a devil because it is a tale of moral temptation. A quest legend, on the other hand, involves a sorcerer or sorceress to prompt the self-doubts and test the readiness of a young person during the transition to a new stage or status in life.

Interrupted Weddings: Glinka, *Ruslan and Lyudmila*

Quest legends, found in the folklore and literature of many peoples, take certain nearly universal forms. The quest to rescue a bride, for instance, is often built around the framing device of the Interrupted Wedding. The hero and

heroine are just married or on the point of being married when the wedding is interrupted by an uninvited visitor of supernatural powers, who suspends the proceedings, often by casting a spell on the bride and abducting her. The bridegroom then sets out to rescue her, facing down enemies and dangers of many kinds, but also developing friends who provide invaluable assistance, until the bride is brought back home, the wedding is completed, and the couple can live happily ever after. Mikhail Glinka's *Ruslan and Lyudmila* (*Ruslan i Lyudmila*, 1842), based on the poem of the same title that established the young Alexander Pushkin's fame as a Russian poet in 1820, is the classic translation of the Interrupted Wedding theme into opera.

The opera opens on the wedding of Lyudmila, a princess of Kiev (the capital of the medieval Russian kingdom), to a Russian knight, Ruslan, a ceremony marked by bardic songs and wedding choruses inspired by age-old Russian folk practice. This colorful image of Russia signifies the country as part of the real, natural world, at least until magic intrudes into the scene. The lights go out, thunderclaps are heard, and the sound of the folk-style wedding chorus is replaced by the most alien music Glinka could write: a slowly descending whole-tone scale (a mysterious progression because every step of it is indistinguishable in size from every other), played by the full orchestra.

When the lights come back on, Lyudmila has been dragged away, the rest of the wedding party is frozen in place (their voices bound in a slow canon over an unchanging bass note), and the sorcerer responsible for the abduction has escaped unidentified. But the action has now moved into a magical realm. Lyudmila's father promises that the hero who rescues her can marry her, and Ruslan and two previously unsuccessful suitors now set out on a quest through mysterious and dangerous places, until Ruslan finds her spellbound and returns her to the natural world of her father's palace. There, he awakens her with a magic ring—an act of sorcery balancing the one by which she was abducted—and they are ready to start their life together.

This quest of Ruslan and his rivals is the heart of the work, occupying the middle three acts. Each rival travels to strange places and meets strange people, who all have tales to tell. Instead of a central legend that is told and then fulfilled, a quest requires a series of encounters between the protagonist (or one of his associates) and characters who appear along the way, providing either obstruction or assistance. In order for spectators to understand the functions of these encounters, they have to hear the characters tell their own stories.

The strangest of these characters is one Ruslan meets on a battlefield strewn with corpses in Act 2. Ruslan, having lost his sword and shield, expresses his discouragement in an aria, "O pole, pole!" ("O field, field!"), but then thoughts of Lyudmila give him the strength to carry on. In this crucial number, looking death in the face, Ruslan struggles with doubts that he has

the maturity to meet the challenges of adulthood, and specifically of marriage, while the manliness of his music paradoxically assures the audience that he has now achieved precisely that maturity. It is immediately after this very human scene of introspection that Ruslan encounters a monstrously large Head, who tries to blow him down with his breath. Ruslan strikes the Head with his spear and takes away the sword that the Head is hiding. The Head now tells his story: he is the giant brother of the dwarf Chernomor, the evil sorcerer who abducted Lyudmila. His brother tricked him out of his sword, cut his head off with it, and then left the sword in his safekeeping. From the Head's story and his own questioning along the way, Ruslan learns that the sword he has just won from the Head is the magic weapon that will enable him to cut off Chernomor's extremely long beard—the beard that gives him his strength—and rescue Lyudmila. It is the key to his quest.

This severed but singing Head is represented onstage by a prop big enough to be filled with men, like the Trojan horse: a chorus of tenors and basses who sing his story in unison. Their music is fittingly awesome for a giant living head, built in ponderous stanzas that are largely identical in melody but different in accompaniment. The first stanza, for instance, is accompanied by mysteriously whispering violas over cellos and basses that first hold a pedal point and then shadow the voices—"Nas bïlo dvoye, brat moy i ya" ("We were two, my brother and I")—while in the last stanza the voices are eerily surrounded by a twisting flute solo high above and a shadowing cello and bass line well below: "I poletel on s bednoy glavoy" ("And he flew with my poor head").

The orchestration, in other words, adds its own spare weirdness to the weird use of a unison chorus to represent one giant voice. The Head's relating his story in the form of a song with repeating melodic verses is, like Senta's Ballad, a standard sign of storytelling in opera. For the orchestra to provide a constantly transformed background to that repeating melody was such a specialty of Glinka's that the technique has become known in Russia as

"Glinka variations." It is found several times just in *Ruslan and Lyudmila*, especially in narrative songs that relate amazing marvels. As Richard Taruskin writes, "the appropriateness of such a technique to an opera about sorcery is obvious."[3]

In Act 4 the action reaches the magic garden where Chernomor is holding Lyudmila captive, but the sorcerer has no need to tell his own story since his brother has already told it. His bizarre nature is represented in the alternately weird and enchanting music of his entrance march, in music of the dances performed for him, and even in music of his courtiers, who comment as he does battle with Ruslan. Chernomor loses his beard, the battle, and his captive in this climactic action. Through all this, in fact in the entire opera, he sings not a word. A silent sorcerer in opera makes a comic effect, even though his evil is the driving force in the plot. When he loses his beard and his power and leaves the stage, Ruslan still has to deal with that evil. Just before the battle Chernomor cast a sleeping spell over Lyudmila, and Ruslan now must take her back to the scene of their wedding, ward off one last rival, and employ a magic ring to wake her before his quest can be completed and their wedding can be celebrated.

Rimsky-Korsakov, *The Legend of Kitezh*

Some composers indebted to Glinka set stories that are not such straightforward examples of the quest legend. Among the masterpieces of legendary opera by Nikolay Rimsky-Korsakov, for instance, is one that combines Russian legendary history with political allegory, and the life of a medieval saint with pre-Christian nature worship, all within the framework of an Interrupted Wedding quest: *The Legend of the Invisible City of Kitezh and the Maiden Fevroniya (Skazanie o nevidimom grade Kitezhom i deve Fevronii*, 1907). Like *Ruslan and Lyudmila*, the opera dramatizes the difference between a purely human world and a world with supernatural forces, but here the human world is itself divided into the natural world of the forest and the urban world of two medieval towns, Lesser Kitezh and Greater Kitezh. There is no separate supernatural realm, but instead these human realms are both magically transformed, and their inhabitants with them. For each of these worlds in each of its conditions, Rimsky-Korsakov devised its own distinctively colored world of sound.

The whole first act, for instance, set in the forest, seems to pulse with quavering figures that suggest the warbling of birds and the rustling of leaves. This act introduces the forest as the natural site of the Russian national identity and Fevroniya, a maiden who lives in the forest with her brother, as a figure at home with the birds and flowers and trees and hence at home in that identity. Part of her natural Russianness is her religious practice. She feels no need for churches, but instead worships the world around her: God and Heaven and Mother-Earth together. In the forest she meets Prince Vsevolod of Kitezh—a figure from urban, civilized Russia—when he is separated from

his hunting companions. The two fall in love at first sight, though she does not learn he is a prince (this being a legend) until she has agreed to marry him. She is abducted on the way to her wedding, and he takes up arms to rescue her, but in this unusual quest opera it is the bride, Fevroniya, whose quest is at the center of the work.

In terms of political allegory the two medieval Russian towns in the opera represent the urban Russia of Rimsky-Korsakov's own day. He creates their sound world from evoca-

Konstantin Korovin's 1908 stage design for Act 1 of *The Legend of Kitezh* shows the Russian forest, alive with light and color, the object of the maiden Fevroniya's nature worship. State Central A. A. Bakhrushin Theater Museum, Moscow.

Culture-images/Lebrecht Music & Arts

tions of two bodies of Russian music with medieval roots: folk song (especially in Act 2, set in Lesser Kitezh, where Fevroniya arrives on the way to her wedding) and the choral music of the Russian Orthodox Church, the national denomination of Russia (especially in Act 3, set in Greater Kitezh). Rimsky's political commentary emerges from the invidious comparison that the opera presents between two visions of Russia. In Act 1 we find Fevroniya living in harmony with all species of plants and animals (the picture of an "original" Russia?), while in Act 2 Lesser Kitezh appears as a place rent by destructive social divisions—the snobbery of the rich, the misery of the poor, and the taunting and mocking of one group by another (Russia in Rimsky's day?).

There is political commentary too in the way the Russian towns meet a threat to their survival. In Act 2 a bridal song the people of Lesser Kitezh are singing to Fevroniya, their princess-to-be, is brought to a stop by an invading force of Tatar soldiers (depicted as uncouth and murderous enemies of Russia), who capture the town, kill many of its inhabitants, and drag Fevroniya and the town drunk away with them on their way to attack Greater Kitezh. As she is being abducted, Fevroniya prays to God to make Greater Kitezh and its righteous people invisible.

In Act 3 the people of Greater Kitezh gather an army under the command of Prince Vsevolod to march against the Tatars, but they also pray for the same miracle Fevroniya has sought. Unlike her, they resort to the poetic and musical language of the Russian Orthodox Church. Three times they pray to the Virgin Mary, the Miraculous Queen of Heaven ("Chudnaya nebesnaya tsaritsa"), to cast her protective veil over the city. Each verse relates in a different way to the

tradition of *a cappella* (unaccompanied) choral singing in the Russian Orthodox Church: the first in traditional unison chant (but with a halo of string sound); the second in the three-part harmony of nineteenth-century Russian church composers (but doubled by instruments); and the third in four-part imitation, a Western rather than Russian ecclesiastical texture, but strictly *a cappella*—all in all, a stunning means of making Russian operagoers feel as if they are in church. This prayer creates such an aura of quiet, fervent expectancy that even the gathering of the army—the action that immediately follows the prayer—is done under its spell.

Once the army has left the city, the miracle begins. Church bells begin to ring by themselves. A boy who had been sent up a tower to report on the advancing foe now declares that a miracle is at hand. A golden mist descends over Greater Kitezh to render it invisible to the Tatars. And in the golden glow of sound that the master orchestrator Rimsky-Korsakov creates for this moment, part of the musical miracle lies in the way he orchestrates with the human voice: the boy in the tower sings a melody that sounds like a bell chiming (see Example 12.2):

Vozlikuyte, lyudi,	*Rejoice, citizens,*
poyte Bogu slavï!	*all praise to God!*
On trezvonom chudnïm	*Through this miraculous ringing*
k nam s nebes vzïvaet.	*He is calling to us from heaven.*

The battle of Prince Vsevolod's army with the Tatars is dramatized in the middle of Act 3 by an orchestral entr'acte (interlude) while a "cloud curtain" covers the stage. By this time the Tatars can be recognized by their own sound world of bad-guy music, consisting of raucous themes built on unsettling or exotic scales. In the galloping music of the battle, a sinister Tatar theme with its exotic interval (the augmented second from D-flat to E-natural in Example 12.3, m.2) is heard in the bass, below the melody of the battle hymn to which we heard the Russians march off to fight. But soon the Russian theme drops out and only the Tatar theme is heard, signaling that the Tatars have defeated the Russians. Prince Vsevolod, we learn later, fought heroically and died with

12.2 Rimsky-Korsakov, *The Legend of Kitezh*: Act 3, "Vozlikuyte, lyudi"

12.3 Rimsky-Korsakov, *The Legend of Kitezh*: Act 3, orchestral entr'acte (Battle of Kerzhenets)

forty wounds. But in a quest legend the hero is not expected to die fighting, and in a Russian opera the Russian army should not be destroyed in battle. The opera—composed just before and premiered just after the country's disastrous defeat in the Russo-Japanese War of 1905—seems to challenge reliance on armed exploits in both the construction of legends and the conduct of political policy. Relying on miracles is made to sound like a much better idea.

The opera has now entered its miraculous phase, an unparalleled creation in the repertory. Whereas most legendary operas feature brief scenes showing magic spells (usually evil ones) being cast or broken, in *The Legend of Kitezh* we spend the whole second half of the opera observing the transfiguring effects of holy magic on all the worlds and characters we encountered in the first half. The miraculous in this work is as encyclopedic as it is radiant. In Act 3, scene 2, the Tatars, coming to a spot across a lake from Kitezh, see the reflection of the city in the lake but not the city itself. They flee in terror. In Act 4 Fevroniya, wandering in the woods at night with the town drunk still by her side, takes up the role of the hero on a quest. She begins with a religious quest, attempting to redeem the drunkard, who by now has gone mad. The way he tests her patience and yet she keeps working to save him reminds us that she is destined to become a saint. But when he runs away, she turns her attention to the legendary quest posed earlier, the

Viktor Vasnetsov's stage design for Act 3, scene 2, of *The Legend of Kitezh* shows the reflection of the city of Greater Kitezh in the waters of Lake Svetlïy Yar, but the city itself, miraculously, no longer visible on the hillside behind. From the original production, Mariinsky Theater, St. Petersburg, 1907.

Culture-images/Lebrecht Music & Arts

completion of her Interrupted Wedding. Unfortunately her bridegroom, Prince Vsevolod, is now dead. Another miracle is called for.

She falls asleep in the forest, and while she sleeps, the forest is transformed from a natural to a supernatural place, where she can meet the ghost of her lover. In part the transformation appears as an extension of the nature religion she extolled in Act 1: the quavering forest music returns, unearthly flowers bloom, and bird spirits of pre-Christian Russia appear before her. In part, though, the process is designed to remind audiences of church: from tree to tree on the darkened stage, the light of candles spreads, gradually filling the darkened opera house the way it fills an Orthodox church during the midnight Easter vigil. In the realm of the miraculous the primordial Russia of the forest and the modern Russia of the church become one. This synthesis is preserved in the final scene, when Fevroniya sings one moment with the quavering accompaniment of rustling leaves and the next in the unaccompanied chant of an Orthodox priest: "Otchego u vas zdes svet velik?" ("Why do we have this great light here?")

Truths are conveyed in this opera by the juxtaposition of opposites. But by now she and Vsevolod are no longer in the forest; they are in Greater Kitezh to resume their wedding, and Greater Kitezh, no longer invisible, is in Paradise. This is not the way Interrupted Weddings are supposed to resume in legends. The bride and groom have had to die, not just grow into adults, and the disparate Russian worlds they came from have been gloriously transfigured and united. In this legend there is no going home.

Wagner, *Lohengrin*

In Wagner's Lohengrin (1850) no spells are cast at all, though a spell is broken at the very end. But besides the fact that one character is under that spell (turned into a swan) until the final scene, the plot includes other ingredients of a good quest legend: a wicked sorceress whose spell impels the plot, an interrupted marriage, a bride who is sworn not to ask the name of the man she is marrying but cannot resist asking, a knight who relates the story of his quest, and a trial by combat. Still, this is no ordinary quest-legend opera, because the order and relationships of those ingredients are scrambled. The sorceress Ortrud—a noblewoman in Christian Flanders in the eleventh century who worships Nordic gods as well as practicing sorcery—has secretly transformed the young heir to the throne of the Duchy of Brabant into a swan before the opera begins. Ortrud's husband, Telramund, has accused the young man's sister Elsa of murdering him, but the knight Lohengrin appears and rescues Elsa from the charge by defeating Telramund in a trial by combat. Elsa and Lohengrin wed, but on their wedding night she asks him his name—exactly what he made her swear not to do when he came to her rescue. He not only reveals his name, as legends decree that he must, but also tells the story of how

he came to be in Brabant. In the process he explains his quest, but he also ensures that their marriage will remain interrupted for good.

Above all *Lohengrin* differs from traditional quest legends in the extent to which it focuses our attention on the motivation of the characters. This is Wagner's trademark. Here, for instance, it seems inevitable that Elsa will ask the question forbidden to her: in legends a character forbidden to ask a question invariably ends up asking it, with dire consequences. Modern scholars may explain the significance of this pattern in archetypal, mythical, anthropological, or psychological terms, but within a traditional telling of a legend, very little explanation of a character's motivation is apt to be given. A good part of Wagner's opera, however, is spent exploring what moves Elsa from accepting it as her duty not to ask Lohengrin his name to insisting that he tell her.

In this illustration of Act 1 of *Lohengrin* in its original production at the Court Theater in Weimar, 1850, Elsa has been accused of murdering her brother by Telramund (right front) as King Henry sits in judgment under the Oak of Justice. Elsa's response, a prayer for a knight to defend her, is answered by the arrival of Lohengrin (center rear) in his swan boat. The illustrator gives the scene the storybook-historical look of nineteenth-century costume drama, but also places Lohengrin in an oddly uncertain space relative to the other characters, as if he were a mirage conjured up by Elsa's wish. *Illustrirte Zeitung*, Leipzig, April 12, 1851.

Much of the music that has always made this opera popular comes in scenes of public ceremony: stirring martial music such as the Prelude to Act 3, along with the Bridal Chorus to which newly wed Lohengrin and Elsa are escorted to their bridal chamber, "Treulich geführt" ("Faithfully led"—better known in English-speaking countries as "Here comes the bride"). Nevertheless, the crux of the opera lies in the scenes of private conversation that determine whether Elsa will ask Lohengrin the Forbidden Question and explain why she does.

There are three of these conversational scenes. Elsa is not even present in the first (Act 2, scene 1), in which the sorceress Ortrud proposes to Telramund two paths by which they can defeat Lohengrin's power and prevent him and Elsa from ruling Brabant: either Telramund should wound Lohengrin (any loss of blood would deprive him of his power), or Elsa should be persuaded to ask him his name (thereby ending their marriage). Besides casting magic spells, Ortrud practices psychological sorcery, based on her knowledge of everyone's weaknesses. In this scene she exploits her husband's gullibility and ambition. In the next scene, the second conversation, she goes after Elsa's "proper suspicion," as she puts it, of a man who expects her to marry him without knowing who he is.

Elsa, after being accused of murder by Ortrud's husband, has every reason to be suspicious of them both. Nevertheless, in this chilling encounter (Act 2, scene 2) Ortrud ingratiates herself with Elsa until she is able to play Iago to Elsa's Otello. In the guise of wishing her well, Ortrud plants doubt in Elsa's mind about the man she is about to marry: "May he never leave you in that magical way that he came here to you!" Elsa's naïve response allows further evidence of Ortrud's duplicity: while Elsa assures her that "trust" and "belief" bring "happiness without regret," Ortrud joins her in a sweetly, contentedly harmonious duet. Ortrud's words, however, which are not for Elsa to hear, mock every word of these innocent sentiments, promising an attack on her "trust" that will turn her arrogance into "regret."

What follows (Act 2, scenes 3–5) is no private conversation, but the gathering of participants on the steps of the church where Elsa and Lohengrin are to be wed. Their entry into the church is twice interrupted, first by Ortrud, who publicly dares Elsa to ask her bridegroom whether he employs magic, and then by Telramund, who demands that Lohengrin reveal his name and origin. In reply Lohengrin declares that only Elsa has the right to ask him that. She responds that her love will stand up to any doubt. But in between his declaration and her response comes a prolonged moment of suspense in which Lohengrin—and the audience—can see that the challenges from Ortrud and Telramund have unnerved Elsa.

This moment is filled by a "contemplative ensemble" (like the trio of maskers in the Act 1 finale of *Don Giovanni*) in which the principals and chorus of wedding guests express their shock at Elsa's hesitation, a static passage of slow-moving and overlapping voices that is dramatic precisely in that it holds up Elsa's

response and the wedding. Like Interrupted Ceremony scenes in grand operas (*Les Huguenots*, Verdi's *Don Carlos*, *Aida*) and unlike the Interrupted Wedding scenes of most legends (*Ruslan and Lyudmila*), this interruption reveals a weakness in the social bonds that the ceremony is supposed to celebrate, but it does not actually put a stop to the ceremony. In *Lohengrin* the wedding is held offstage, between acts, and the real interruption, which we witness, is to the wedding night.

Escorted into their bridal chamber with the famous Bridal Chorus, Elsa and Lohengrin immediately launch into an operatic form of pillow talk. This is the third and last of the private conversations, the one that ends in Elsa asking the Forbidden Question. Just as the elements of a legend are scrambled in the opera as a whole, so are the elements of a love scene here (Act 3, scene 2). At the beginning of the scene comes what would normally be last, the overlapping and joining of the two lovers' voices in sweet intervals. Then they slip into an involved and increasingly heated debate that reveals why living with the Forbidden Question is intolerable to Elsa. Her initial argument is that she needs to know him to be able to help him the way he has helped her. This comparison prods him into counterarguments that provoke her in turn into confessing the doubt that Ortrud put into her mind: if she allows him to retain the mystery of who he is and what magic brought him to her, she will live in dread that the same magic will one day take him away. Having plumbed her doubts, Elsa then asks what she must not.

That action delivers us from a dialogue of lovers, in which we have been studying the motivation of a deeply conflicted human being, into the fairy-tale world where fair maidens ask mysterious princes who they really are. Wagner marks this arrival of the crucial legendary action by switching from an unobtrusive dialogue style of music to a portentous style in which

Elsa (Petra Maria Schnitzer) can't resist asking Lohengrin (Stuart Skelton) the Forbidden Question of his identity on their wedding night, in the staging by Götz Friedrich at the Deutsche Oper Berlin in 2008.
© Bettina Stoess

we hear that Elsa's words are no longer just words; they constitute a deed from which there is no going back. The change of style is marked above all by a tremolo note sustained in three octaves by the high strings, separating the Forbidden Question off from the rest of the scene. As she is about to begin asking, the orchestra plays and then Lohengrin sings the melodic phrase on which he earlier made her swear not to. This phrase (see Example 12.4), because it appears repeatedly in the opera, always associated with the same idea (the Forbidden Question), counts as a **leitmotif** (leading motif, or motive). Wagner would develop this musical-dramatic device into a pervasive system in his later works. Here, Lohengrin sings this motive in a last effort to silence Elsa: "Elsa, was willst du wagen?" ("Elsa, what risk are you taking?")

12.4   Wagner, *Lohengrin*: Act 3, "Elsa, was willst du wagen?"

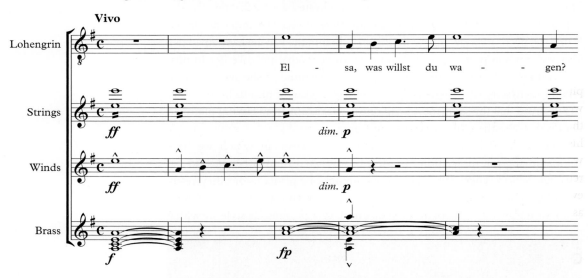

She ignores this and his subsequent interjections, posing her question in one form after another, all the while climbing slowly and inexorably in pitch (as do her accompanying chords) until she finishes on a trumpeted high B:

Elsa:
Unselig holder Mann,   You fatally benign man,
hör' was ich dich muss fragen!   listen to what I must ask you!
Den Namen sag' mir an!   Tell me your name!

Lohengrin:
Halt' ein!   Stop!

Elsa:
Woher die Fahrt?   From where did you journey?

Lohengrin:
Weh' dir!   *Woe to you!*

Elsa:
Wie deine Art?   *Of what race are you?*

The deed is done, and Lohengrin has no choice but to answer her.

He chooses, however, not to answer immediately. (In any case, Telramund rushes in at this moment, intent on wounding Lohengrin, who dispatches him.) Instead, he brings Elsa before the king and the whole court (Act 3, scene 3) and tells them all not just his name but his story. This too is a standard legendary action. But as Berthold Hoeckner explains, Lohengrin's narrative (beginning with the words "In fernem Land" / "In a distant land" and usually called the Grail narrative) comes too late.[4] It is too late to play any of the roles that a narrative ordinarily plays in a legend: it neither explains (like the narratives in *Ruslan and Lyudmila*) nor does it prophesy (like Senta's Ballad). We already knew how his quest could be fulfilled (but it is too late for that, thanks to Elsa), and we do not learn why he withheld his identity from Elsa.

In a musical sense this narrative is itself a fulfillment, since much of it recapitulates the Prelude to the opera, only this time with the signifying power of words. But dramatically it fulfills nothing except Lohengrin's duty to answer the Forbidden Question, and in doing that he abandons his quest. In telling his listeners onstage and off that he is Lohengrin, a Knight of the Holy Grail who came to Brabant to rescue Elsa, he has to abandon her and Brabant and return to the Temple of the Grail in Spain. Their marriage is interrupted forever, Elsa dies of grief, and the legendary device of the Forbidden Question, as Carl Dahlhaus writes, gives *Lohengrin* the unlegendary ending of a tragedy.[5]

Quests of Becoming: Dvořák, *Rusalka*

Quest legends typically tell of young people conquering their unreadiness for adulthood. In one subset, quests of becoming, the protagonist is not just coming of age, but acquiring a new identity in the process: an oppressed person achieves a higher station in life or a spirit becomes human. These quests often link changes in identity to the cyclical changes that time brings in nature and human history, from one season to another or one generation to another.

A coming-of-age legend about a boy, for instance, will often entail the passing of political power from one generation to the next. In both Wagner's *Parsifal* (1882) and Rimsky-Korsakov's *The Tale of Tsar Saltan* (*Skazka o Tsare Saltane*, 1900), a boy's mastery of supernatural powers symbolizes his acquisition of the maturity and wisdom needed to become a ruler. A coming-of-age legend about a girl is more apt to tell about a character who passes, or tries to pass, into an identity for which she seems not to be destined. The legend

of Cinderella, for example, who rises above her status as an oppressed step-daughter, is told in two nineteenth-century operas: Rossini's *La Cenerentola* (1817) and Massenet's *Cendrillon* (1899). These works bear comparison especially because Rossini's nonlegendary treatment, which excludes all the magical elements, asks us to consider that social status is in the eye of the beholder, whereas Massenet's legendary treatment makes social inequality seem natural because magical interventions are needed to overcome it.

Other operas tell of female spirits who long to experience human love. An example from the Czech repertory is Antonín Dvořák's *Rusalka* (1901), its libretto drawn by the poet Jaroslav Kvapil from nineteenth-century legends of water spirits. The title character is a spirit who lives in a lake, falls in love with a prince who swims in the lake, and wants to become human so that she can acquire a human soul and be loved by the prince. The witch Ježibaba gives Rusalka a magic potion that makes her human, but the transformation leaves her unable to speak to other humans. The prince acknowledges her magical power over him, and despite recognizing that such magic is fleeting, he takes her back to his palace with him. There, a foreign princess is competing for his affection, and in his frustration he drives Rusalka away. This rejection changes her condition. When he returns to the lake looking for her, she can speak to him, but only to tell him that her kiss would kill him. He begs for that kiss, she gives it to him, and as he dies she gives up her quest to become human and plunges back into the lake as a spirit.

Both of these characters feel a compulsion to leave their own world behind and enter the other's, attracted to what they know they cannot have. What are these worlds? Rusalka's is the world of nature, which comes alive with spirits and magic at night. In Act 1 this world is fully displayed in the cavorting of forest spirits, the stern warnings of Rusalka's wood spirit father, and the weird sounds of Ježibaba mixing her magic brews. Above all, the sound of nocturnal nature is heard in the muted strings and ethereal soprano tones of Rusalka's aria "Měsíčku na nebi hlubokém" ("O moon deep in the sky"), as she sits on a tree branch by the lake and calls on the moon to tell the prince about her. The human world infiltrates this scene as dawn breaks and the horn calls of the prince's hunting party announce his arrival. His is the world of daylight and of human activities and relationships. Act 1, like the other two acts, seems to carry us between worlds with no change in scene, simply by a gradual change between night and day (something that electrical lighting was newly capable of depicting when the opera was created) and comparable gradual changes in the coloring of the orchestral music.

Night and day turn into each other, but cannot coexist because each is the absence of the other. Likewise, the two characters enter each other's worlds briefly, but they cannot live there. In the final scene of Act 1 the prince reaches the shore of the lake, sends his hunting party away, and meets Rusalka for

the first time. He senses that he is in the presence of magic, and the sound of her sister water spirits calling out to her give voice to that presence. But Rusalka's own voice is silent. That is a sign to the prince that she is a magical being who is bound to vanish soon: he calls her "my fairy tale."

In that way he signals the metaphorical nature of his love and of the whole opera, inviting us to interpret it as allegory. Its two opposed worlds can be seen as the worlds of women and of men; as nature and human society; as traditional society (with its magical ways) and modernity (which has left them behind); as the confined world of a native people (the Czechs, for instance) and the larger world that impinges on them. In any interpretation the work honors the impulse of both Rusalka and the prince to cross the boundary that divides them, at the same time that its tragic tone springs from the belief that each depicted world is defined by its difference from the other.

The middle act is set on the palace grounds, where Rusalka's muteness prevents her from standing up for herself in competition for the prince's favor. At most, she provokes the foreign princess into behaving so arrogantly as to turn the prince against her. The change of light in this act is from day to night, and when night falls, we watch as lamps are lit in the palace, imposing manmade daylight on the darkness of nature. Then we spot Rusalka's water-spirit father standing on the darkened grounds, looking in as the human guests sing and dance. His presence and his stern comments let us feel, as we listen to Dvořák's splendid party music, both the attraction this world exerts on Rusalka and the regret it inspires in her father that she is attracted to a world where she does not belong.

In the final act the scene returns to the lake, and as the sun sets, that scene returns to the moonlit state in which we first encountered it. The music

too brings back the themes and colors (such as the muted strings) with which it began, and the prince arrives to meet Rusalka one last time. As it displays the natural cycles of time, the opera dramatizes the changes that those cycles bring. Now for the first time Rusalka can speak to the prince, but their dialogue is heartbreaking both because it has been so long delayed and because of its desperate tone as it leads inexorably to the kiss that kills him. Once that has happened, the moonlight music turns into a funeral march, and Rusalka undergoes her final transformation, playing a priestly role as she intones a plea for God to have mercy on the prince's human soul.

Legendary Epic: Wagner, *Die Walküre*

The most ambitious operatic treatment of a legendary subject is Wagner's *Der Ring des Nibelungen* (*The Ring of the Nibelung*, 1876). Rather than a story about the decisive episode in the life of one or two characters, it is an epic tale involving intersecting casts of gods, spirits, and mortals, incorporating a variety of quests and struggles for souls, set in obscure and widely scattered locales, and taking place across generations. It is not a single work, but a sequence of four operas, designed to be presented on four successive days—the way folk epics were once recited over the course of days—in a theater in Bayreuth, Germany, built expressly for the purpose. The cycle was ambitious not only in scale but also in the originality of its musical and theatrical concepts. In fact, Wagner insisted that the work (and others he wrote after *Lohengrin*) be called **music drama**, not opera. The *Ring*, as it is familiarly known, has been endlessly influential in opera, in the movies (a medium Wagner could not have imagined), in music not linked to drama or story, and in legendary stories told in media that use no music.

Part of the originality of the *Ring* lay in Wagner's practice of setting virtually the whole libretto (which he wrote himself) in his version of acting style. This is a kind of musical prose, an expressive recitative with hardly any text repetition or vocal embellishment or rounded musical forms (hence, hardly any arias in a traditional sense), though there are short stretches in songlike phrasing and longer stretches (especially of narration) that constitute musically coherent numbers. Likewise, there are hardly any ensembles of a traditional kind, since Wagner condemned the overlapping of voices as unnaturalistic. This relentless use of the acting style might have deprived his listeners of the pleasure of instant familiarity, of being able to sing silently along with a phrase as it is repeated within an aria or ensemble. But Wagner compensates for this loss by embedding the vocal parts in a web of orchestral phrases that do reappear many times, not in close succession, but over the course of the entire cycle.

Richard Wagner

Wagner (1813–1883) was the rare opera composer not content to leave the theory of opera to others. His many volumes of writing about opera include much that is grandly self-justifying, but also challenging to centuries of received opinion. The following passage from his *Opera and Drama* (1852) is characteristic in that it celebrates his practice, unusual at the time, of writing his own librettos; this he considers to be a matter of reconciling different life experiences rather than different artistic skills.

Poet and Musician herein are like two travelers who have started from *one* departure-point, from thence to journey straight ahead in opposite directions. Arrived at the opposite point of the Earth, they meet again; each has wandered round one half the planet. They fall a-questioning one another, and each tells each what he has seen and found. The Poet describes the plains, the mountains, valleys, fields, the men and beasts, which he has met upon his distant journey through the mainland. The Musician has voyaged across the seas, and recounts the wonders of the ocean: on its breast he has often been nigh to sinking, and its deeps and strange-shaped monsters have filled him half with terror, half with joy. Roused by each other's stories, and irresistibly impelled to learn for themselves the Other which each has not yet seen,—so as to make into an actual experience impressions merely taken up in fancy,—they part again, each to complete his journey round the Earth. At their first starting-point they meet at last once more; the Poet now has battled through the seas, the Musician has stridden through the continents. Now they part no more, but both now *know* the Earth: what they earlier had imagined in their boding dreams, as fashioned thus and thus, has now been witnessed by them in its actuality. They are One; for each knows and feels what the other feels and knows. The Poet has become musician, the Musician poet: now they are *both* an entire Artistic Man.

Opera and Drama, trans. W. Ashton Ellis (London, 1900); reprinted by University of Nebraska Press (Lincoln, 1995), p. 300.

These phrases, the leitmotifs that we encountered in *Lohengrin*, are a much more continuous part of the musical fabric in the *Ring*, where they provide a pervasive dramatic function as musical signifiers. Each is associated with a particular element of the story and appears whenever that element is at issue. Trying to identify precisely what every leitmotif signifies is notoriously problematic, though such attempts have been published on the dubious assumption that listeners should be able to name and keep track of dozens of different motives scattered across four evenings of music. Some of them—like the phrase to which the hero Siegmund pulls his sword out of a tree—are easy to identify and remember. Others are much more elusive and disputable. But it is indisputable that a system of orchestral motives that connect what the characters are saying and doing with deeds performed in the past or predicted for the future makes an especially apt medium for the musical dramatization of legends—tales of fates predicted and fulfilled.

The sources of the *Ring* are in epic Nordic poetry, originally oral narrations that were compiled in medieval Scandinavian and Germanic written languages around the thirteenth century. There is an overarching story to the cycle: Wotan, king of the Norse gods, has a fortress called Valhalla built as home of the gods, and to pay for it, he has to surrender a magic gold ring that bestows world-ruling power. That ring is cursed by the Nibelung dwarf Alberich, from whom Wotan wrested it by trickery. In his quest to reclaim

the ring, but obliged not to resort to trickery or force of his own, Wotan places his hopes in a succession of human heroes. In the end all these heroes die, and Valhalla goes up in flames with the gods in it.

The allegorical significance of the story has always been controversial. Created at a time when German nationalists were hailing Norse mythology as a cultural treasure,[6] the *Ring* has sometimes been made a vehicle for the promotion of German national pride, despite its bleak ending. Utopian critics starting with the socialist British playwright George Bernard Shaw have interpreted that ending as a cleansing destruction of the old order (anything from monarchy or capitalism to the institution of marriage).[7] A pessimistic interpretive tradition, by contrast, has focused on Wagner's turn to the bleak philosophy of Arthur Schopenhauer as he was working on the *Ring* or his turn away from revolutionary politics as he became financially dependent on the largesse of the king of Bavaria to realize his operatic projects.[8] One philosopher, Wagner's younger contemporary and sometime friend Friedrich Nietzsche, even moved over the course of a few decades from hailing Wagner as the hope of modern culture to denouncing him for his nihilism.[9]

Although Wagner wrote more about his own works than any other opera composer in history, his pronouncements only complicate the debates about the meaning of his works. The fact that his writings are filled with anti-Semitism, for instance, has prompted readings of the *Ring* as a racist vision of a primordial Germany inhabited by heroes exhibiting a German character unspoiled by alien influences, or as a racist vision of a world under the control of capitalists, who are caricatured as Jews; it has also been argued that Wagner's anti-Semitism does not show itself in the *Ring*.[10] In Nazi Germany Wagner's music dramas were ready instruments of Hitler's racist nationalism and genocidal campaign against Jews, and that association of Wagner with Nazism has given more urgency than ever to the question of how his beliefs may be embedded in his works. What's more, stage directors and designers are understood as participants in the debates, their visual concepts projecting certain allegorical interpretations and implicitly demoting others. In the aftermath of World War II, for instance, Wagner's grandsons Wieland and Wolfgang Wagner designed productions of the *Ring* at Bayreuth that emphasized psychological archetypes in the legend while erasing any nationalist imagery.

The *Ring* as a whole tells a complete story. In fact, it creates a closed narrative circle, or ring: in the opening scene of the first work (*Das Rheingold* / *The Rhine Gold*) the Nibelung dwarf Alberich steals from three water spirits living in the Rhine River the gold from which he fashions the magic ring, and at the end of the final work (*Götterdämmerung* / *Twilight of the Gods*) those Rhine maidens reclaim the ring. The individual works in the cycle have no such dramatic wholeness, and yet opera houses all over the world frequently produce them as stand-alone works.

The second work in the cycle, *Die Walküre* (*The Valkyrie*, first performed by itself in 1870), will be examined here on its own. It is, as Carl Dahlhaus writes, dramatically "disjointed," deriving its "overwhelming spell . . . less from the whole, for it is no whole, than from individual acts."[11] In terms of its cast, for instance, the three acts are barely connected: the first involves three human characters in a triangular relationship; the second is almost entirely occupied with a dispute among gods, in which the three human characters intrude only at the end; and by the third act, two of the humans are dead, the remaining one is quickly sent packing, and the gods get down to worrying about themselves. *Die Walküre* works, in other words, less like a play or movie than like an episode of a television series in which we know the characters and track their changing lives from week to week; each episode follows several threads and ends on a chord of suspense. *Die Walküre* is nevertheless the most successful of the *Ring* music dramas on its own, as well as the source of some of Wagner's greatest stand-alone music and a remarkable showcase of the practices found in other legendary operas, now turned to the purposes of a music-drama epic.

> ### Die Walküre
> #### PRINCIPAL CHARACTERS
>
> - **Wotan**, king of the gods
> - **Fricka**, goddess of marriage, Wotan's wife
> - **Brünnhilde**, Wotan's daughter by Erda, goddess of the Earth
> - **Siegmund** and **Sieglinde**, Wotan's twin son and daughter by a mortal woman
> - **Hunding**, Sieglinde's husband

Act 1 It opens, like many other operatic legends, with the sounds of nature, in this case a musical storm whose course is charted by a rising and falling bass line (see Example 12.5) that intensifies to a peak and then subsides to its original form. At this point the curtain rises to show a room of a house in the forest —as we can deduce from the fact that an ash tree is growing in the middle of the room. The storm music disappears as the first character we meet steps wearily into the house and falls asleep. Our experience of the storm has prepared us to think of this character as storm-tossed, and we will find that he remains so, in some sense, even indoors.

12.5 Wagner, *Die Walküre*: Prelude

Stürmisch

A woman comes from the next room and discovers him asleep on her hearth. She brings him water; he asks her who she is; she tells him that she is the wife of Hunding, whose house this is; and she asks him about himself. Hunding enters and seconds her request that the stranger tell them who he is. The stranger doesn't give his name, identifying himself only through the stories he relates of his life as a solitary. From one of these stories Hunding recognizes

that the stranger is an enemy of his clan, and he tells him that while he may spend the night there, the two of them must face off in combat the next day. Once Hunding goes off to bed, the stranger longs for a sword to fight with, and Hunding's wife returns to tell him about a sword lodged in the ash tree, waiting to be pulled out by a great hero. In helping the stranger defeat her husband, she is asking him to rescue her from her miserable marriage. They are falling in love.

As they do, they discover their identities: they are twins, separated from each other at an early age. This is no coming-of-age story, no Interrupted Wedding legend (for her, it is more of an Accelerated Divorce). The goal of their shared quest is incest, and that too is a traditional subject of legend. In nineteenth-century culture it was hardly an acceptable artistic subject except when given the distancing, symbolic treatment it found in legend, whether of folk origin or classical (as in Sophocles' tragedy *Oedipus*). There is plenty of symbolism in Wagner's treatment of this incestuous relationship. Both lovers speak, for example, of their love as a recognition of themselves in each other. The stranger says: "You are the image that I harbored in myself." What was far from traditional, and shocking, was that Wagner also made them express their physical passion for each other.

As they declare their love, a transformation of their surroundings occurs that seems as magical as it is symbolic. The door springs open, the moonlight of a spring evening floods in, and the stranger sings a love song, or aria. When Wagner wanted his characters to express passion, he could relax his resistance to arias, it seems. There is symbolism as well as passion in the ways he depicts the lovers' shared sense of bad times giving way to good. He does this by means of the thematic transformation of the minor-mode bass line of the earlier storm music into the major-mode bass line that introduces this love song (compare Example 12.5 with Example 12.6) and the corresponding metaphor of transformation in its opening words:

Winterstürme wichen dem Wonnemond,
in mildem Lichte leuchtet der Lenz.

Winter storms have given way to the month of delight;
in gentle light shines springtime.

The wife responds with her own love song: "You are the springtime I longed for" ("Du bist der Lenz nach dem ich verlangte"). Arias were one thing, but even in this rapturous exchange Wagner did not relax his resistance to joining the voices in a duet.

In one sense the lovers have discovered their identities, but in another sense they are creating a new mutual identity, and for that purpose they need new names. The wife now names her brother-lover Siegmund and herself Sieglinde. Siegmund—like Ruslan, or the future King Arthur or

12.6 Wagner, *Die Walküre*: Act 1, "Winterstürme"

Luke Skywalker—needs a sword for the battle that lies ahead. To a richly accompanied fanfare played by three trumpets (the Sword motive), he pulls from the trunk of the ash tree the sword that Sieglinde watched their disguised father plant there long ago and that many strong men have subsequently tried and failed to dislodge. And to ecstatic music they fall into each other's arms as the curtain hurries down.

Act 2 The gods, it turns out, have been watching this love quest unfold. The twins do not know that their mysterious father is Wotan, king of the gods, or that he now desperately needs help from his son Siegmund. Wotan orders his daughter and right-hand gal Brünnhilde to make sure Siegmund wins the combat with Hunding. But before the combat begins, Wotan faces the objections of his wife Fricka, the goddess who protects marriage. Fricka has no patience for the twins (Wotan's children by a mortal woman) or for Brünnhilde, the Valkyrie (his daughter by the earth goddess Erda). Her

The set design by Josef Hoffmann for Act 1 of *Die Walküre* at the opening season of the Bayreuth Festival in 1876. The drawing shows the action in Hunding's hut at the moment when Siegmund, rapturously encouraged by Sieglinde, pulls out the sword planted in the tree by their father, Wotan.

© Lebrecht Music & Arts

confrontation scene with Wotan over the outcome of the impending combat (Act 2, scene 1) is like the Bridal Chamber scene between Lohengrin and Elsa: a duel of arguments in which the characters' deepest motives eventually emerge, so that these figures seem more like characters in a novel than like those of a traditional legend.

At the beginning of this exchange Fricka demands that Wotan support Hunding, the offended husband, in the combat and punish the twins for their incestuous adultery, while Wotan protests that the twins' love is holier than the loveless marriage of Sieglinde and Hunding. So long as the two gods conduct their argument on this level of principle, Wagner uses his web of leitmotifs to favor Wotan's side. Fricka asks, for instance:

Wann ward es erlebt,	*When was such a thing ever seen*
dass leiblich Geschwister sich liebten?	*as a sister and brother as lovers?*

The orchestra then brackets Wotan's reply—"Heut' hast du's erlebt!" ("Today you have seen it!")—with the rapturous opening motive of Siegmund's love song, "Winterstürme wichen dem Wonnemond" (compare Example 12.6 with Example 12.7). There is no such familiar and appealing musical material supporting Fricka's lines; her music consists largely of stark accompanied recitative. This contrast is calculated to make the audience more sympathetic to Wotan's defense of free love than to Fricka's defense of marriage. It does not, however, win him any points with her. Wotan's defense of an adulterous

love simply allows Fricka, now sustained by the orchestra in a passionate outburst that is almost an aria, to remind him of his own endless adulteries, including the one that resulted in the birth of the twins. Helpless against this charge, he changes his tack, revealing a stronger, more selfish reason for favoring Siegmund in the combat.

12.7 Wagner, *Die Walküre*: Act 2, "Wann ward es erlebt"

This reason derives from the overarching action of *The Ring of the Nibelung*: Wotan's struggle with Alberich to control the power-giving ring. As Wotan now explains to Fricka, he himself is not able to fight Alberich for the ring; he must leave his side of the struggle, and hence the fate of the gods, to a mortal without even lending him divine protection. Because he has decided that Siegmund is the mortal for the job, he wants him first to survive the fight with Hunding. Fricka sees this argument as a trick, though Wotan is perfectly serious about it, and she now defeats him not by any further argument, but by invoking her divine status. She simply insists that she, a goddess and Wotan's wife, not be put in a position of inferiority to Siegmund, a mortal and Wotan's slave. Her voice rising higher and louder in commanding phrases, she makes Wotan, much against his will, his voice now reduced to feeble, low, unaccompanied muttering, promise to let Siegmund fall.

With this promise, Wotan sets events on the course that will lead eventually to the destruction of Valhalla and the gods. He orders Brünnhilde to let

Hunding win the duel. But she challenges this change of plan, and he now has to face down his daughter when she is making the case for what he actually wants. In the course of this argument he recovers the strength of his voice, as if he is learning to accept Fricka's position as his own. In these successive scenes, then, Wotan is caught in a tug-of-war between his wife and daughter, one representing the claims of propriety and the other his own will. It is a struggle for his soul, set out much like the struggle between the devil and Marguerite for Faust's soul, except that in this case neither of the contending parties can be characterized as a devil. The upshot of this struggle is that the king of the gods comes to acknowledge the limits of his powers. In fact, Brünnhilde disobeys her father and supports Siegmund in the fight. Wotan then smashes Siegmund's sword, causing him to die. Brünnhilde protects Sieglinde by leading her away. In the third and last act of *Die Walküre* Wotan will punish Brünnhilde for disobeying him.

Act 3 The act opens with a gathering of Brünnhilde's eight Valkyrie sisters, who, following Wotan's standing directive, have ridden on horseback to a rocky mountaintop carrying the corpses of dead warriors. These warriors are to be revived to fight against Alberich's army in defense of the gods at Valhalla. The galloping orchestral music, to which the Valkyries soon add their whooping battle cry "Hojotoho!," is the Ride of the Valkyries, the most famous example of cavalry-charge music in Western culture. Within *Die Walküre* the Ride is one of several episodes (along with the opening storm music and the concluding Magic Fire music), more orchestral than vocal, that provide the thrill of obsessive rhythms, steady harmonies, and full-throttled orchestration to balance the generally spare, concentrated style of the dialogue.

That is not to say that these episodes are musical breaks from the drama. The Ride of the Valkyries, for instance, provides a picture of Brünnhilde's nature by portraying her sisterhood. She and her sisters are typical foot soldiers in a great enterprise. Having no responsibility for the outcome of the cosmic battle for which they are preparing, they have turned their grisly body-collecting assignment into a joy ride—as their music tells us. They have a tomboy spirit, riding around armed and armored on horseback, making ready for war. This spirit expresses itself in their battle whoop, which though playful is like the Sword motive in its martial rhythm and triadic fall and rise. The whole episode, moreover, is dramatic in an ironic sense. The whooping Valkyries do not yet know, as we do, that they are wasting their effort: now that Wotan has seen the futility of resisting Alberich by force, he has already decided to cancel their collecting of dead warriors.

Brünnhilde arrives before Wotan and gets Sieglinde, who is now pregnant by Siegmund, out of the way of Wotan's wrath. When he arrives, he directs that wrath at Brünnhilde, condemning her to a "defenseless sleep" in which she will

belong to the first man who comes along and wakes her. Once again Brünnhilde challenges her father. Their dialogue crystallizes the duality of meaning between the legendary (or symbolic) mode and the realistic (or novelistic) mode that lies at the heart of the Wagnerian music drama. In the legendary mode Brünnhilde represents the side of Wotan that he is trying to suppress. In the realistic mode she represents the daughter he punishes all the more severely because she is his favorite. The musical language supports the duality throughout this scene, combining a rich orchestral texture of symbolically referential leitmotifs with a humanly expressive eloquence in the vocal lines.

At first Brünnhilde insists on her symbolic relationship to Wotan. In disobeying him, she says, she was only following his better instincts, only acting on his love for Siegmund. She cannot win that argument. But when she shifts her appeal and begs her father not to subject her to the disgrace of being won by the first man who happens upon her, she makes him see her less as a symbolic part of himself and more as his daughter in distress. She proposes that he ring her around with flames so that no cowardly man will dare to approach her, and he, suddenly moved by her plight and by the thought that in turning his beloved daughter out of his life he is punishing himself, agrees.

Adolphe Appia, design for Act 3 of *Die Walküre*, showing Wotan, spear in hand, about to leave Brünnhilde, asleep under his spell on the right, looking as if she has become part of the terrain. Appia's theories (see "In Their Own Words," Chapter 1) and designs had a wide influence on twentieth-century theatrical staging, but especially on Wieland Wagner's productions of his grandfather Richard's works at the Bayreuth Festival.

Schweizerische Theatersammlung Bern

His speech of farewell and concession ("Leb wohl, du kühnes, herrliches Kind!"/"Farewell, you bold and splendid child!"), crowned by a heartbreakingly expressive orchestral passage, serves as a hinge on which the scene turns from the symbolic to the personal realm.

The ring of magic fire that Wotan now summons up will protect Brünnhilde, as she herself prophesies, until Sieglinde's baby is born and grows into the fearless hero Siegfried, who will walk through the flames and become her lover. She, meanwhile, a Sleeping Beauty figure, will not age but will mature. She will be transformed from a boyish girl, a tomboy of the gods, into a woman in love, hoping to use that self-sacrificing love to redeem the gods. The music to which the Magic Fire springs up at the end of *Die Walküre* therefore casts a spell not just to protect Brünnhilde's virginity until the right man comes along, but also to alter her identity in time for that event. As woodwinds, harps, and strings provide a lullaby of dancing flames for her to sleep by, Wotan puts the spell into words:

Wer meines Speeres Spitze fürchtet,	*Whoever fears the tip of my spear*
durchschreite das Feuer nie!	*shall never step through the fire!*

The melody to which he sings, doubled by French horns, allows us to understand his words as a prophecy as well as a spell. We heard that melody half a dozen times in the preceding dialogue, connected each time to Brünnhilde's plea to be awakened only by a fearless hero, and even earlier in the act, when she prophesied that Sieglinde's baby would grow up to be "the noblest hero in the world." The melody has by now become a leitmotif referring to that hero. And sure enough, in the two succeeding works in the cycle, *Siegfried* and *Götterdämmerung*, the same leitmotif is identified with Siegfried, who is fearless enough to penetrate the magic fire as well as to recapture the ring (though that will do the gods no good). Even as Wotan casts his forbidding spell, then, the leitmotif to which he is singing it predicts who will be able to break that spell, naming him in notes. Used systematically, as in *The Ring*, leitmotifs not only communicate messages above and beyond what the characters say, but more importantly allow audiences to feel how the past and the future are present in every action the characters take. The leitmotif system perfectly suits the stories that legends tell: it exhibits the power of knowing that exceeds the power of doing in a world where fate controls everything.

That is not to say that the characters in operatic legends move robotically through their own stories. Wotan and Faust, Senta and Rusalka, all choose their fates. But at the same time, they undergo transformation into a more fully human state. The god Wotan, as he walks sadly away from Brünnhilde and the ring of magic fire at the end of *Die Walküre*, has turned into a very human figure, learning like Faust that even superhuman power cannot prolong the happiness of a relationship with someone he loves. The demigoddess

Brünnhilde, meanwhile, is undergoing a different but equally human transformation, the same one in fact as Lyudmila, Fevroniya, Senta, and Rusalka, and for that matter Ruslan. She is crossing into adulthood, which is defined as readiness for a mature love relationship. Such transformations as these are the real subjects of legends and consequently of legendary opera. For legends to represent them as the realization of prophecies and the product of magic spells is not fanciful, or simply an excuse for special musical and stage effects. It is a way of acknowledging that in real life these transformations result from processes beyond human control. They result from the passage of time and the experience that comes with the passage of time.

FURTHER READING

Legendary operas use many of the narrative motives catalogued in Stith Thompson's standard *Motif-Index of Folk-Literature: A Classification of Narrative Elements in Folktales, Ballads, Myths, Fables, Mediaeval Romances, Exempla, Fabliaux, Jest-Books, and Local Legends*, rev. ed., 6 vols. (Bloomington: Indiana University Press, 1955–58). On Gounod's operas, Steven Huebner, *The Operas of Charles Gounod* (New York: Oxford University Press, 1990). On Glinka's *Ruslan and Lyudmila*, Marina Frolova-Walker, "On Ruslan and Russianness," *Cambridge Opera Journal* 9/1 (March 1997): 21–45. On Rimsky's *The Legend of the Invisible City of Kitezh and the Maiden Fevroniya*, Richard Taruskin's entry on the opera in *New Grove Dictionary of Opera*. On Dvořák's *Rusalka*, John Tyrrell, *Czech Opera* (Cambridge and New York: Cambridge University Press, 1988).

On Wagner's music dramas, Carl Dahlhaus, *Richard Wagner's Music Dramas*, trans. Mary Whittall (Cambridge and New York: Cambridge University Press, 1979). On *The Flying Dutchman*, Thomas Grey, *Richard Wagner: "Der fliegende Holländer"* (Cambridge and New York: Cambridge University Press, 2000). On *Lohengrin*, Berthold Hoeckner, "Elsa Screams, or The Birth of Music Drama," *Cambridge Opera Journal* 9/2 (July 1997): 97–132. On *Die Walküre*, see the listings in Barry Millington, *The New Grove Wagner*.

FOR RESEARCH AND REFLECTION

1. Describe how the presence of magic is portrayed musically in one or more operas on legendary themes.

2. If you were going to stage *Faust* or *The Flying Dutchman* or *Ruslan and Lyudmila*, would you make the demonic or cursed characters look and sound as human as possible or as demonic? Why?

3. Operas on legendary themes are typically set largely in the wild. Nature can be a benign or a threatening force, but it is almost always powerfully present. Examine some of the natural settings and their music in these operas, and explain what roles nature plays.

4. What makes the leading female characters so often the touchstone of humanity in operas on legendary themes, even when they are saints (the princess Fevroniya) or spirits struggling to be human (Rusalka)?

5. Story-telling or story-singing possesses a supernatural power in *The Flying Dutchman*, *Lohengrin*, and *Die Walküre*. Explain how that power operates in the drama and manifests itself in the music.

6. Wagner was not the first composer to attach musical motives to characters or dramatic ideas. But he developed and intensified the practice to an extent unknown in earlier opera. In a given work by Wagner do the leitmotifs seem more like signs of a narrator's voice intruding into the story, or the power of fate, or the legendary nature of the story?

 Additional resources available at wwnorton.com/studyspace.

TWENTIETH-CENTURY MILESTONES

1902
Debussy's *Pelléas et Mélisande*, begun in 1893, premieres in Paris.

1903
Staging of Rameau's *Hippolyte et Aricie* (1733) in Geneva, a milestone in the revival of early opera.

1904
Janáček's *Jenůfa*, begun in 1894, premieres in Brno.

1905
Premiere of Strauss's *Salome* in Dresden, quickly followed by productions in many other cities, despite moral objections by church and cultural authorities.

Rimsky-Korsakov is dismissed as professor at the Saint Petersburg Conservatory for supporting students' right to demonstrate against the tsar's government. *The Legend of Kitezh*, composed 1903–4, premieres in 1907.

1906
Meyerbeer's *Les Huguenots* (1836) becomes the first work performed 1,000 times at the Paris Opera.

1914–18
World War I

1917
October Revolution establishes Communist rule in Russia (later reconstituted as the Soviet Union).

1925
Berg's *Wozzeck*, begun in 1914, premieres in Berlin. It was widely produced, but the start of the Nazi regime in 1933 brought German productions to an end.

1936
An editorial attack in the Communist newspaper *Pravda* drives Shostakovich's successful opera *The Lady Macbeth of the Mtsensk District* from the stage in the Soviet Union.

1939–45
World War II

1948
Aldeburgh Festival founded in Suffolk, England, for the performance especially of operas and other works of Benjamin Britten.

1957
First staged performance of Schoenberg's *Moses and Aaron*, as he left it at his death. He set the first two acts of his own libretto in 1930–32 and never set the third.

1964
Revolutionary ballet *The Red Detachment of Women* premieres in China. A 1972 performance attended by the Nixons in Beijing is represented in Adams's *Nixon in China*, premiered in Houston in 1987.

1966
The Metropolitan Opera opens its new house at Lincoln Center, New York, with premiere of Barber's *Antony and Cleopatra*.

1972
Joplin's *Treemonisha*, completed and published in 1911, premieres in Atlanta.

1976
Glass's *Einstein on the Beach* premieres at the Avignon Festival, France, and other sites, including a visiting performance at the Metropolitan Opera.

1983
Messiaen's *Saint Francis of Assisi*, begun in 1975, premieres in Paris.

1985
Gershwin's *Porgy and Bess* is produced at the Metropolitan Opera, after being performed around the world in the fifty years since its original production on Broadway.

1989
The fall of the Berlin Wall symbolically marks the end of Communist governments in Central and East Europe.

2000
Premiere of Saariaho's *L'Amour de loin* in Salzburg.

PART V

Opera of the Twentieth Century and Beyond

By the beginning of the twentieth century, opera houses had become revival houses. In the course of the nineteenth, their repertories had shifted from almost exclusively new to mostly classic works. The history of opera may be written (as in this book) largely as the history of new works, but operagoers in the twentieth century did not regularly encounter new works. Likewise, hardly any librettists or composers received enough commissions to derive a steady income from opera. Often they set out on their own, spending years or even decades to produce something that could take its place in the repertory beside the masterpieces of past centuries. That was a challenge that Mozart and even Verdi and Wagner had not faced, having launched their works in the context of other new, untested operas. The result is that librettists and composers in the twentieth and twenty-first centuries, aiming for a place in the canon, have become more fertile and daring than ever before in exploring what an opera can be, what kind

The burning of Moscow in Prokofiev's *War and Peace*, a twentieth-century grand opera based on Tolstoy's grand-operatic novel of 1869, composed during World War II and revised up to 1952. The scene, based on the historic fire during Napoleon's occupation of the city in 1812, is seen here in the Mariinsky Theatre / Metropolitan Opera coproduction, directed by Andrei Konchalovsky, with set designs by George Tsypin, at the Metropolitan Opera in 2007.
© Ken Howard, Metropolitan Opera

of story it can tell, and how—in both dramaturgical and musical terms—it can tell it. The treasury of singular, sometimes solitary works that they have devised, each representing a composer's deepest thought and highest hopes, gives this repertory its enduring importance.

CHAPTER 13

Human-Interest Opera

Struggles of the Poor

One thematic innovation is exceptionally widespread in twentieth-century opera: a focus on the lives of ordinary people. In the eighteenth century ordinary people were often the subjects of comic opera, and in nineteenth-century grand opera individuals and choruses representing the masses were an obligatory element of the panorama of a nation's history. But in twentieth-century operas the lives of ordinary individuals are treated seriously in themselves. Life—usually contemporary life—in the lower classes often forms the whole subject of a work, and the work is often melodramatic rather than comic in tone. This new focus first appeared in operas composed in the 1890s, such as Pietro Mascagni's *Cavalleria rusticana* (*Rustic Chivalry*, 1890), Alfred Bruneau's *L'Attaque du moulin* (*The Attack on the Mill*, 1893) and *Messidor* (1897), and Gustave Charpentier's *Louise* (1900).

This period around 1900 is known in America as the Gilded Age and in Europe as *la Belle Époque* (beautiful era), terms that emphasize the unprecedented prosperity of the fortunate few without acknowledging the unprecedented disparity between the lives of the rich and the poor or the discontent and unrest that disparity created. In opera houses the patrons' wealth underwrote productions of unprecedented lavishness. Why would those patrons have spent a fortune on entertainments designed to make them feel bad about the plight of the poor?

Susan Graham as Sister Helen Prejean and John Packard as Joseph de Rocher in Heggie's *Dead Man Walking*, in the original production, staged by Joe Mantello at the San Francisco Opera, 2000. The story of murder and punishment, drawn from the news and dramatizing current public concerns (in this case the death penalty), typifies the whole history of human-interest opera.

© Ken Friedman, San Francisco Opera

In part the answer lies in a new attitude that the rich had developed toward the poor. Until the nineteenth century it was easy for the privileged throughout the world to believe that poverty was the natural and inevitable fate of the majority of mankind. In Christendom this belief was characteristically reinforced by quoting out of context a line spoken by Jesus in the Gospel of St. John, 12:8: "For the poor always ye have with you." In the course of the nineteenth century, thanks to interrelated revolutions in agriculture and manufacture, communication and transportation (not just the Industrial Revolution), the material needs of greater numbers of people were being abundantly supplied. For the first time in human history, it became possible to imagine that poverty could be eradicated from the earth and therefore to believe that the persistence of poverty was a social injustice.

The arts were crucial in promoting this belief. In the mid-nineteenth century social researchers like the English journalist Henry Mayhew made the poor visible to the rich and educated. But it took artists like the English novelist Charles Dickens and the French caricaturist Honoré Daumier to let the rich and educated contemplate the faces and lives of the poor with fellow feeling. Toward the end of that century the detached reporting technique of journalism and the sympathetic voice of the novel came together in a new style of fiction and spoken drama, which made the most heartrending stories out of the difficulties that poor people faced in their daily lives. The novel *Maggie: A Girl of the Streets* (1892) by the American writer Stephen Crane and the play *The Lower Depths* (*Na dne*, 1902) by the Russian writer Maxim Gorky are typical of these **human-interest stories**. It was from stories like these that composers derived the first operatic melodramas about the struggles of the poor, the first human-interest operas. Mascagni based *Cavalleria rusticana*, for example, on a human-interest play by Giovanni Verga, while Bruneau's operas derive from human-interest novels by Émile Zola.

In twentieth-century opera lower-class protagonists are often found in contemporary settings—uncomfortably close to home for their original audiences—and seldom exhibit traits that those audiences identified with. They are typically individuals who, whether by their own actions or for reasons beyond their control, are cut off from everyone around them. They no longer even fit into the lower-class society into which they were born. They include an unwed mother abandoned by the father of her child in Leoš Janáček's *Jenůfa* (1904); a deranged soldier who murders his unfaithful wife in Alban Berg's *Wozzeck* (1925); a cripple who fails to hold a woman's love in George Gershwin's *Porgy and Bess* (1935); and a fisherman who alienates his community, especially by his abusive treatment of his apprentices, in Benjamin Britten's *Peter Grimes* (1945). There is even a prison opera, Janáček's *From the House of the Dead* (*Z mrtvého domu*, 1930), about a whole community of people cut off from society by their criminal status.

Twentieth-century operagoers, drawn from the most comfortable and respectable classes of society, might feel pity for some of these characters, but how would they be able to imagine themselves living the lives and experiencing the feelings of such characters, as operagoers of previous centuries had entered the lives and feelings of classical heroes, bourgeois lovers, and national heroes? Isn't that the imaginative process on which opera depends for its appeal?

In a way, a human-interest opera appeals to audiences the way any other opera does: by transporting them to a different world. To the fortunate class of people who go to operas, the world of the unfortunate depicted in a human-interest story may be a very alien world, even if the setting is in their own city and their own day. It is not an exotic or fantastic or beautiful or exalted place, but it may be strangely compelling precisely because it is so close at hand and yet so unfamiliar. For people who have never been inside a cold-water flat, at a murder scene, or in a prison cell, it may be as fascinating to be transported imaginatively to a place like that—through the music as well as the scenery and costumes—as to ancient Egypt or Mt. Olympus.

Even the most privileged people are capable of sensing that their privilege is circumstantial, that their social identity depends on their connections to others, and that if they somehow got cut out of their social network, all their advantages and their very identity would disappear. An operatic character who is cut off from any social status embodies with a vengeance the spectators' imagined capacity to lose their own status and so makes the unimaginable seem all too real. In the human-interest opera the audience's anxieties are engaged in the protagonist's effort to maintain his or her humanity in the face of dehumanizing isolation.

In order to take audiences inside the experience of such characters, composers had to evoke by musical means the humble, sometimes degraded, social worlds in which they lived; their feeling of disconnection from that world; and their struggle to preserve their humanity despite being lost souls. This complex of effects could not be achieved with any single musical style, only with a system of extreme contrasts in musical expression, leading the audience into the heart of human suffering and out again.

In the Gilded Age: Janáček, *Jenůfa*

Leoš Janáček's *Jenůfa* (1904), based on the play *Její pastorkyna* (*Her Stepdaughter*) by Gabriela Preissová, more than just an early example of this genre, is a trail-blazing work in which a great composer found his artistic voice in the process of bending the expressive resources of opera to the purposes of a human-interest story. One of the resources he bent was nationalism. *Jenůfa* is

an opera on a Czech subject and in the Czech language, written within the musical tradition that helped sustain the national aspirations of the Czech people in the decades before 1918, when they became free from Austrian rule for the first time in centuries. According to the nationalist theories of the age, peasants embodied the spirit of a nation more purely than city folks. Accordingly, *Jenůfa* honors the Czech national spirit by representing the musical life of a village in the region of Moravia: in the first act, as we are meeting characters from all walks of village life, we hear a song of religious devotion, a folk song complaining about military conscription, and a folk song and dance about mating, while the third act opens with a wedding scene full of dance music and a bridal song for women's chorus. In all these numbers Janáček was drawing pervasively, if indirectly, on the Moravian folk music he had studied.[1]

But the opera is hardly a celebration of Czech folk culture. On the contrary, it depicts a village constantly tearing at itself over distinctions of social status. Everyone there feels that his or her claim to respectability is threatened by the behavior of others, and consequently everyone is constantly passing moral judgment on relatives and neighbors. It is a suffocating social environment. The sound with which the opera opens, a haunting xylophone roll in the overture, apparently symbolizing the turning of the village mill wheel, recurs throughout the first act until it seems to represent a threat of violence. The threat is realized in a series of brutal actions taken against the title character.

Jenůfa is a young woman from a highly respectable family in the village: her family owns the mill, and her stepmother (and guardian) is an official of the parish church, referred to by her church status as the Sexton (*Kostelnička*). Jenůfa has spent time away from the village getting educated, and she expects to marry her cousin Števa, who has become the chief proprietor of the mill. But her respectability is at risk because she has become pregnant by him, and her prospect of saving face by marrying him is at risk because he may be conscripted into the army. In the course of Act 1 the village learns that Števa has avoided conscription, but he celebrates that good fortune so drunkenly, taunting Jenůfa with his interest in other women, that her stepmother intervenes and forbids her to marry Števa until he has remained sober for a year. Not knowing that Jenůfa is pregnant, the stepmother cannot know she is condemning Jenůfa to the shame of bearing her child out of wedlock. Nevertheless, Jenůfa's lover and her stepmother together have made it impossible for her to maintain a respectable position in the village. At the end of the act another cousin of Jenůfa's, Laca, who loves her far more deeply than Števa does, becomes

Jenůfa

PRINCIPAL CHARACTERS (all members of the Buryja family)

- **Kostelnička** (the **Sexton**), a widow and sexton of the church in a Moravian village
- **Števa**, owner of the family mill
- **Laca**, his older half-brother
- **Jenůfa**, orphan, stepdaughter of the Kostelnička, cousin of Števa and Laca

enraged at her unrequited devotion to Števa and slashes her cheek with a knife. This whole string of punitive actions against Jenůfa is especially horrifying because the people who commit them are the people closest to her. One by one her most important personal ties are severed, and by the end of the act the scene of communal life, symbolized by folk music, has given way to a scene of Jenůfa cast into total social isolation.

Patricia Racette in the title role of *Jenůfa*, as staged by Francesca Zambello at the San Francisco Opera in 2001. This shot of Jenůfa desperately clutching her newborn captures the isolation of the young mother within her own community.

© Larry Merkle, San Francisco Opera

Acting style of music in *Jenůfa* In the middle of the act, though, even as it is becoming clear that Jenůfa cannot stop this process, she asserts her resistance in a powerfully expressive musical number. Left alone with Števa, she complains to him that, knowing she is pregnant with his baby, he has nevertheless made things impossible for her by behaving brutishly in front of her stepmother. Janáček sets this complaint in an acting style of music that is significantly different from the traditional acting style in opera, recitative. The traditional formula for recitative is metered language, sung and punctuated by instrumental chords in such flexible rhythm that it sounds unmetered—like people actually talking to each other. Jenůfa's complaint by contrast, like the whole libretto, is written in prose, but set against an exceptionally inflexible orchestral motive:

Bez toho bude	Anyway I'll have
od mamičky těch výčitek	from mother reproaches
dost, dost!	enough, enough!
Víš, jak si na mně zakládá,	You know what store she sets by me;
včil, včils ju měl slyšet,	you should have heard her now,
včils měl slyšet!	you should have heard her now!
Nevím, nevím,	I have no idea, I have no idea,
nevím, nevím,	I have no idea, I have no idea,
co bych udělala, kdybys ty	what I would do if you didn't
mne včas nesebral,	marry me in time,
nevím, nevím,	I have no idea, I have no idea,
nevím, nevím,	I have no idea, I have no idea,
co bych udělala	what I would do
také já	either
také já	either
nevím, co bych udělala také já!	I have no idea what I would do either![2]

The astonishing orchestral accompaniment to these lines comes in twenty-six one-measure phrases, each made up of a rhythmically identical four-note melodic motive that creates a catch in the throat: each phrase starts just after the downbeat and stops just short of the next downbeat, leaving a held-over note sounding on the downbeat itself (see Example 13.1). This is no mere accompaniment, let alone punctuation, to the singer's lines, but an orchestral embodiment of the spirit of her plea, endlessly launched and never arriving.

The singer sometimes doubles these orchestral phrases, but also departs from them. Her prose words, after all, do not fit into four-note melodic phrases, and Janáček, who modeled vocal melodies closely on the musical features of spoken Czech, makes her irregular phrases even more irregular with unexpected breaths and word repetitions. The utter regularity of the orchestral phrases throws into relief the unmetricality, the spontaneity, the desperate outpouring of emotion in her vocal phrases. Though her first

13.1 Janáček, *Jenůfa*: Act 1, "Bez toho bude"

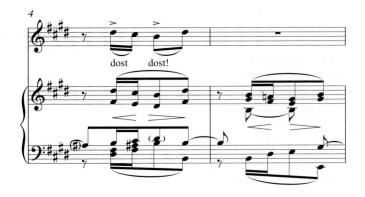

phrase ("Bez toho bude"/"Anyway I'll have") fits with just a tiny adjustment into the four-note melody of the orchestral phrase, her longer second phrase ("od mamičky těch výčitek"/"from mother reproaches") takes up two orchestral phrases, riding over the "catch" between them. Later—when she gets going on the subjects of her stepmother's expectations and her own need for Števa to marry her soon—her phrases take up three or even four orchestral phrases. Meanwhile the orchestral phrases evolve harmonically, in a sequence that suggests the coherence of Jenůfa's thought, while her own irregular and inconclusive phrases suggest that she is not able to deliver that thought coherently.

After she has announced to Števa that she has no idea what she will do if he doesn't hurry up and marry her, Jenůfa shows her frustration by repeating the sentence, and especially the "no idea" part of it, over and over. Without departing from the orchestral phrase structure, Janáček gives her new ways to sound distraught. On a sudden surge of sound and with a distorted version of the four-note motive, the orchestra pulls us to a minor key (G-sharp minor), while—to the words for "I have no idea" ("Nevím, nevím")—Jenůfa sings the orchestra's phrases, but out of sync with it, sounding as if she has literally lost her place. The rest of the passage is full of other unsettling shifts: after a calming moment ("také já"/"either") in a major key, she soars impulsively (on one last assertion that she has no idea what to do), then ends her complaint in a hush of resignation.

In basing his acting style on a figure that endlessly evolves as it repeats, Janáček was anticipating composers of a later generation, like the American minimalists Philip Glass and John Adams, more than following any earlier acting style. But his acting style has proven inimitable in one respect, which is in the nature of the rhythms that he so relentlessly repeats. Often, as in this case, there is an abrupt, even heartrending catch in the rhythm, which triggers our sympathetic response to the character. Whatever her plight is, however her social standing has been undermined, that catch draws our hearts to her as a fellow human.

Isolation, forgiveness, reintegration In the second act we find Jenůfa isolated from everyone but her stepmother, who has hidden her in her own house to keep the village from discovering her pregnancy. This act's gloomy overture, subject to stormy eruptions, portrays the bleakness of the wintry nighttime scene and of Jenůfa's situation, eight days after the birth of her baby. Her stepmother, having earlier driven Števa away, is now trying to persuade either him or Laca to salvage Jenůfa's honor by marrying her. But Števa is put off by her scarred cheek, and Laca, learning about the baby from the stepmother, is so reluctant to raise his rival's child that the stepmother tells

him the baby has died. Once Laca has left the house, she turns her thoughts to making good on that lie. In her blood-curdling soliloquy of rationalization ("Co chvíla"/"In a moment"), her voice rises quickly from whispered self-pity to a blasting assertion that it would be a godly act for her to kill the inconvenient baby. Then, while Jenůfa naps, she steals out of the house with the infant and drowns it in the nearby millstream.

Meanwhile Jenůfa awakens in the empty house, searches deliriously for her baby, and kneels to sing a Hail Mary ("Zdrávas královno"), unknowingly answering her stepmother's calculating view of God the Father with luminous trust in the Mother of God. The stepmother now returns to tell her the child has died, and while she is coming to terms with that news, Laca enters and proposes marriage. At this moment, when Jenůfa sees hope of becoming less cut off from those around her, her stepmother is overcome by remorse—she becomes cut off in her own mind, that is, from the respectability that had defined her social standing. An icy wind blows a window open, and the stepmother screams in terror, proclaiming that "it is as if Death were looking in!" ("Jako by sem smrt načuhovala!"). The orchestra picks up the motive of five repeated notes on which she sings the last word of that line and turns the motive into a postlude of breath-stopping timpani outbursts (each ending with a characteristic Janáček catch) and chord shifts, expressing the terror of a guilty conscience.

In the third and final act the music of village life returns, the music of isolation returns more brutally than ever, and the music of Jenůfa's humanity triumphs. As the village is gathering with folk dance and song to celebrate Jenůfa's marriage to Laca, the wedding is interrupted, just as the grander weddings in operas from *Les Huguenots* to *Ruslan and Lyudmila* and *Lucia di Lammermoor* are. The news is brought in that a dead baby has been found in the stream; Jenůfa reveals that it is hers, and the villagers threaten to stone her for murdering her own child. This is the point of ultimate isolation for Jenůfa, surrounded by everyone in her village, to the accompaniment of pounding orchestral rhythms, all with stabbing catches in them.

Then silence breaks out, and when the music resumes, it loses those rhythmic catches that have dominated the opera for two and a half acts. Instead, for what feels like the first time, we hear a steady flow of sound with long, long chords and even longer pedal points. It is at this moment that a set of amazing

Anja Silja (right) as the Kostelnička, pleading with her stepdaughter Jenůfa (Karita Mattila) after confessing to having killed Jenůfa's baby, in Act 3 of *Jenůfa*, staged by Olivier Tambosi at the Metropolitan Opera, 2007.

© Beatriz Schiller/Metropolitan Opera

acts of reconciliation bring Jenůfa to a new, trusting and loving relationship with her world. The first such act is her stepmother's public confession that she is the murderer. As she fills in the details, sinking to her knees, the orchestra fills in a background of persistent repeated notes and repeating motives. Jenůfa, at first unable to cope with the terrible story, quickly comes to see how her stepmother could have thought she was acting in her interest. To a series of softly radiant, sustained major chords with harp, she goes to the older woman, makes her stand up, and consoles her.

Her stepmother, now apparently suicidal with guilt, starts to run to the bedroom but stops, realizing that if she did not face justice for her crime, Jenůfa would:

Já nesmím!	I mustn't do that!
Oni by tebe soudili, Jenůfo!	They would only take you to court, Jenůfa!

She sings this line with no accompaniment, while Jenůfa's answer is bathed in the warmth of a long-sustained major chord:

A ta moje pestounka,	But my foster mother,
Uz to chápu, uz to chápu.	now I understand, now I understand.

What's more, as she sings these words, she reestablishes their severed bond by the most direct and indelible of musical means: she simply enters on her stepmother's note just as her stepmother is finishing on it. The effect, which almost has to be seen onstage to be heard, is to let us feel Jenůfa's empathy with her stepmother even before she tells her that now she understands her motivation. As the warm, sustained chords continue, Jenůfa announces that the Redeemer will shine even on her stepmother, who accepts Jenůfa's magnanimity by echoing that line.

The opera could have ended with this act of forgiveness, which John Tyrrell justly calls "one of the great moments of opera."[3] Instead, Janáček binds up another cut-off relationship. Laca and Jenůfa are left onstage; another radiant texture emerges from the orchestra; Laca pledges his love in these trying new circumstances; and Jenůfa, discovering a new trust in him and in her own capacity to be loved, welcomes his appeal as never before. The opera ends, then, through a chain of interdependent acts in which individuals reach out to those who have hurt them the most, changing the moral climate of Jenůfa's world. From the beginning, it is not just Jenůfa whose relationships have gotten cut off; the entire society of her village has been in a fragmented state, just as the entire opera has been dominated by motives with a catch in them, cut off from each other on every downbeat. And the world of the village, not just Jenůfa, is made whole again at the moment when her stepmother takes the blame for the baby's death, the moment when those cut-off motives are replaced by chords of uninterrupted harmony.

Between the World Wars: Berg, *Wozzeck*

Alban Berg's *Wozzeck*, composed from 1914 to 1922 and premiered in Berlin in 1925, was created two decades later than *Jenůfa* and seems to come from a different world. Its title character is cut off from those around him not by socially defiant behavior, at least to begin with, but by his psychological condition: he is falling into madness. The music, in turn, makes the spectators feel as if they are observing everything through a distorting lens, but that lens cannot be associated entirely with the character's psychological state.

Janáček's musical language is full of rhythmic and harmonic jolts that disrupt forcefully established rhythms and keys. Berg's musical language, by contrast, is full of forceful rhythms and pitches, but for long stretches he denies them a point of reference. The most dissonant chords cannot disrupt the harmony when no key is established in the first place (such harmony is called **atonal**), and the opera ends with an oscillating passage for wind instruments that is cut off just before a downbeat that they never reach. Filled with elaborate and self-conscious, if sometimes obscure, musical games,[4] Berg's score is like a model in notes of a mind working overtime because it cannot orient itself.

Wozzeck is based on a play written in 1837 by Georg Büchner, who drew on the trial record of a man executed for murdering his girlfriend. *Woyzeck* (the title of the play, after the convict's actual name) was not pieced together and performed until 1914, when Berg saw it and determined to make an opera of it. Since he used a selection of scenes from the play as his libretto rather than a freshly written text, the opera has the same dramatic focus as the play: it is more concerned with the politics of madness than with its psychology. The protagonist's madness, which is fatal to him and those closest to him, is contrasted with that of the powerful, fatal only to those beneath them. Like *Jenůfa*, then, and all human-interest stories about the struggles of the poor, *Wozzeck* is a work about the tyranny of class.

The social politics of madness The opera conveys its message about the relationship of madness to class through a systematic structure of dramatic and musical contrasts. All but three of the fifteen scenes show us encounters between the protagonist, Franz Wozzeck, and one or more other characters, and we gauge his descent into insanity from his responses to these other characters, who range from his commanding officer and his doctor to his girlfriend and his best pal. Furthermore, we comprehend the other characters and Wozzeck not just from their words, but also from their music, which uses a striking range of styles and references to popular music (even if they are filtered through the lens of distorting harmonies) to map the power structure of their world.

In the opening scene, for instance, Wozzeck, a common soldier, is shaving his Captain. The Captain, at first telling him to work more slowly, soon moves to crazed assertions about time and eternity. He finds it terrifying, he says, that the whole world rotates in a day. As the Captain's thoughts grow increasingly hysterical, his tenor voice rises to heights uncomfortable even for a tenor. Wozzeck, meanwhile, responds repeatedly with noncommittal agreement—"You're right, Captain"—on a single note right in the middle of his baritone range. We can read any number of attitudes into this deadpan delivery: Wozzeck is deferring to his officer or frightened of him or hiding his feelings or resisting being infected with his hysteria or too depressed to put any expression into his voice. In any case, our first impression of Wozzeck is not of someone out of control, but of someone coping with a superior who is out of control. It is only when the Captain taunts him with having a child out of wedlock that Wozzeck's voice comes to life. Suddenly singing in forceful intervals, he makes a surprisingly cogent argument, supported by biblical quotation, that "we poor folk" simply cannot afford to live and raise children by the same moral code as the rich. His eloquent reasoning throws the Captain into comic confusion.

Leo Schützendorf as Wozzeck in the original production of *Wozzeck* at the Staatsoper, Berlin, in 1925. The actor and photographer create an image of the suffering and dispirited proletarian to match those of contemporary German visual artists like Käthe Kollwitz.
© Private Collection/Lebrecht Music & Arts

Later in the opera Wozzeck's engagements with his superiors continue to demonstrate the insanity of a world in which the powerful get to determine who is mad and who is sane. In Act 1, scene 4, the Doctor treating Wozzeck for his supposed madness reveals an insane delight in diagnosing his condition without curing it. Still later, in Act 2, scene 2, the Captain and the Doctor, coming upon Wozzeck on the street, taunt him unmercifully with the suggestion that Marie, his girlfriend and the mother of his child, is cheating on him with an officer, the Drum Major. This scene, one of the longest in the opera, makes us feel how easily the powerful can use their power to push a troubled person over the brink.

In other scenes we see Wozzeck in the company of his own class of people, especially his friend Andres and Marie and their child. Characters like these are always singing folk songs and even dancing—things that the higher-class and better-educated characters like the Captain and the Doctor do not do. It is as if music, or popular culture in general, serves as a psychological refuge for the downtrodden, their means of staying sane. It is striking that Wozzeck, though often a bystander, hardly ever participates in these performances of folk music.

The first time we meet Marie, for instance (Act 1, scene 3), she sings a little march tune in admiration of the Drum Major as he steps past her window on parade. When the parade has gone by, she rocks her child back to sleep with what appears to be a commonplace lullaby. Its words, though, describe her own situation as an unwed mother:

Mädel, was fangst Du jetzt an?	*Maiden, what are you going to do?*
Hast ein klein' Kind und kein' Mann!	*You have a little child, but no husband!*
Ei, was frag' ich darnach,	*Oh, why should I ask about that;*
Sing' ich die ganze Nacht.	*I'll just sing all night.*

Likewise the music, though built on the simple, repetitive rhythmic motives of a lullaby, slides constantly and disturbingly—unlike real folk song—away from any single key. Folk song may be a refuge within the world of this opera, but it is not a refuge that can be relied on.

Nature is no refuge, either. While the powerful control the town, the out of doors belongs to the poor. But it is a terrifying place. In Act 1, scene 2, Wozzeck and his friend Andres go out into the countryside at the end of the day to gather firewood. But while Andres staves off his fear in the darkening natural world by singing a silly song about hunting, Wozzeck instead attends closely to the sights and sounds of the fields, which are depicted in the eeriest musical figures, harmonies, and instrumental colors. He imagines the place to be haunted by the dead, the setting sun to be a fire rising from the earth, and the very quiet to be a sign that the world could be dead.

Michael Volle (left) as Wozzeck and Kevin Connors as Andres, gathering kindling in a field in Act 1, scene 2, of *Wozzeck,* staged by Andreas Kriegenburg at the Bavarian State Opera, Munich, 2008. Stefan Bollinger's lighting makes even this natural setting seem conducive to Wozzeck's hallucinations.

© Wilfried Hoeal, courtesy Bayerische Staatsoper

Jealousy and madness Within this social landscape the opera presents a conventional story of an individual driven to madness and murder by jealousy. Marie takes up with the Drum Major, Wozzeck is made suspicious, he confronts Marie, the Drum Major boasts of his conquest to Wozzeck, and Wozzeck stabs Marie to death. But we do not follow the psychological process of Wozzeck's descent into the "madness" of jealousy the way we follow that of Verdi's Otello. Here, the protagonist's jealousy is continuous with the madness he already suffers from at the beginning of the opera, before his suspicions are aroused: the "madness" of being so conscious of his downtrodden social condition that he hallucinates. It is also continuous with the blindly megalomaniacal lunacy of his social superiors; the unsettled self-consciousness of his social equals, especially Marie, who suffers guilt as she cheats on him; and even the hauntedness of the natural world, a sign of a "world of hysteria," as Joseph Kerman calls it.[5]

Even in his one tiny soliloquy before he murders Marie, Wozzeck expresses his troubles in universal, not personal, terms. This comes in Act 2, scene 3, one of several scenes in which characters utter their lines in a melodramatic half-sung delivery known in German as **Sprechstimme** (speech voice). He and Marie quarrel, she leaves, and he describes his situation as if from outside it: "Der Mensch ist ein Abgrund, es schwindelt Einem, wenn man hinunterschaut" ("Man is an abyss; it makes one dizzy to peer down into it"). He then personalizes his reflection: "mich schwindelt" ("it makes me dizzy"). But even that apparently personal language connects him to the insanity of those around him: the Captain opened the opera by saying to Wozzeck, "Er macht mir ganz schwindlich!" ("You make me quite dizzy!").

The scene in which Wozzeck kills Marie (Act 3, scene 2) exemplifies this drama of interconnected disconnections. He leads her out on a walk by a pond in the darkening woods, where thoughts and memories and observations of nature, all relevant to their broken relationship, float so incoherently in and out of their dialogue and of the orchestral music surrounding it that we realize the conversation can reach no rational conclusion, but will end in violence. Wozzeck notices the dark. Wind instruments remind us of the rhythm of Marie's lullaby. Wozzeck takes stock of their years together, challenges her fidelity again, and then kisses her. He notices her shivering from the cold. A passage of slowly rising trombone notes marks the rising of the moon. Marie notices how red it is. Wozzeck compares it to a "bloody iron," drawing his knife. She notices him shivering, not from the cold. He stabs her. She collapses and dies. The orchestra, from which we have been hearing the colors of individual instruments or families of instruments, now comes together in a frightening *crescendo* on a single note that has been sounding deep

Expressionist scene design by V. Hofman for Act 3, scene 2, of *Wozzeck*, as produced at the National Theater in Prague, 1926. This is the setting where Wozzeck kills Marie under a blood-red moon (the color doesn't show here) and where he later drowns himself (scene 4).

Courtesy Hekman Digital Archive at Calvin College, Grand Rapids, MI

in the bass all along. In a scene full of references to the characters' lives and world but empty of any hope of bringing reason and order to them, there is suddenly a new order, a new reality, achieved in the monotone of death.

From the solitude into which he casts himself by murdering Marie, Wozzeck seeks refuge in society: the monotone of death gives way to a fast polka on an out-of-tune piano in a tavern, where he is resorting to wine, woman, and song to drown his sorrows. But when blood is discovered on his arm, he runs back to the pond; seeing Marie's body there, he slips from guilt-obsessed to lunatic. When the moon rises again blood-red, making the pond water look red as well, he wades in to wash the blood off himself with blood, and drowns. This could be the end of the opera, but it's not even the end of the scene. As the action continues, we may wonder what will become of the disorienting lens that the music has provided now that Wozzeck is gone.

A world still mad Wozzeck drowns to a chilling sound of chromatically rising pitches in one group of instruments after another, at a gradually slowing pace. We seem to be hearing the bubbles of his last breaths welling up to the surface of the pond, slower and slower as they become feebler. Against this sound the Captain and the Doctor wander into the scene, speaking rather than singing, stopping to listen to what seems like a groaning sound. They decide that it is the last gasp of someone drowning (though it is the resumption of the frog-croaking heard earlier in the scene), and they hurry fearfully offstage. It is fitting that the music during their moment onstage remains as distorted as it was before Wozzeck died, since however

correct they are about a man drowning in the pond, it is their paranoid misreading of the frogs' croaking that leads them to that idea.

The orchestra then plays an emotionally powerful interlude in a more conventional style than we have heard earlier. In 1923, before *Wozzeck* had even been staged, Fritz Heinrich Klein praised this interlude as "Wozzeck's tragic story . . . retold as a grandiose lament."[6] But more than thirty years later Joseph Kerman, praising the *frisson* of terror that Berg's atonal landscape gave audiences up to this point but insisting that "*frisson* is not tragedy," criticized this interlude for its sentimentalizing change of perspective: "it is not of the action, but *about* the action."[7] And more recently Richard Taruskin has argued that in this interlude Berg, by resorting to tonal (if still highly dissonant) music to make "his most direct appeal to empathy in his audience," reduces the atonal language that had come to seem like normality earlier in the opera to abnormality. In his metaphor "all the rest of the opera is now placed 'in quotes.'"[8] All of these writers could at least agree with Berg that the interlude "is to be understood as an 'Epilogue' following Wozzeck's suicide, as a confession of the author who now steps outside the dramatic action on the stage. Indeed, it is, as it were, an appeal to humanity through its representative, the audience."[9]

The controversial interlude is followed by one more dramatic episode, the shortest in the opera, powerful and controversial in its own way. Some children are singing a nursery rhyme like "Ring around the rosie," simple in its outline, though rendered through the lens of atonality, like the folk and popular music earlier in the work. These children come upon a much younger child, Marie and Wozzeck's son, who is riding a hobbyhorse. With the heartlessness of childhood they tell him his mother is dead, then they run off to look at her corpse, and he, uncomprehending, singing a two-note riding song ("Hopp, hopp!"), hops off after them, to an accompaniment of fluctuating chords that do not reach any conclusion, but continue into inaudibility after the curtain falls. The final perspective, dramatically and musically, is one of innocence about to be lost.

For Kerman this scene, though overwhelming in its appeal to the audience's sympathy, is "disjoined from the essential business."[10] But it can be considered joined to the essential business if we regard that business as larger than the psychological case of Wozzeck. If, that is, we take the opera to be a drama about a world driven mad by social injustice, then Wozzeck and Marie are not its only victims. Their child is too, and in a political sense his case is the most damning of all, since the opera leaves us with an image of how the abuse of power that we have seen all along in the Captain and the Doctor eventually infects even the youngest and most innocent. By this interpretation, the death of Wozzeck does not end the story or even close off his clear-sighted as well as mad perspective. And this interpretation fits with Berg's own claim that in watching this opera, no one in the audience "gives heed to anything but the vast social implications of the work which by far transcend the personal destiny of Wozzeck."[11]

Gershwin, *Porgy and Bess*

Porgy and Bess is an opera about a man who is cut off within his own impover-ished and oppressed community because he is a cripple. As he says at his first appearance (Act 1, scene 1): women pass him by . . . they look in at his door and they keep on moving . . . when God makes a cripple, He means him to be lonely . . . by night or by day he has to take the lonesome road. In other words, Porgy's condition deprives him not just of love and companionship, but of his identity as a man. In the course of the opera, though, he does find love and companionship from Bess, a woman who needs him to rescue her from an abusive lover and from her life of drinking, drug addiction, and easy sex. It is an unlikely match, and she does not sustain it for long. The abusive former lover returns and forces himself on her again; Porgy kills him, but is then taken into police custody; and while he is away, his protective influence over Bess evaporates. When she abandons him and heads far away, he sets out in pursuit, giving up even his lonely place within his community in the hope of restoring the identity Bess has given him as her lover. *Porgy and Bess* is comparable to both *Jenůfa* and *Wozzeck* as a story of difficulties in love that precipitate a crisis in a character's place within a community.

But the story is complicated by a factor that does not enter into either of those earlier works: race. It is an opera about the struggles of an African American community in the South in the early twentieth century, a time when, despite emancipation from slavery, African Americans there suffered from a system of racial segregation that excluded them by law from the means to better themselves. Set in the fishing village of Catfish Row on the waterfront of Charleston, South Carolina, the opera is derived from the novel *Porgy* (1925) by DuBose Heyward, a white Charlestonian who took an exceptional interest in the lives, language, and music of his black neighbors.

From this novel Heyward created the libretto for a white New Yorker, composer George Gershwin, the two of them working with Gershwin's constant lyricist, his brother Ira. The opera (premiered in 1935) is therefore a white representation of black culture and life. But the controlling force of whites over the lives of blacks is apparent in the opera only in a few brief intrusions by white characters, who are, suitably, officers of the law. As the historian Darlene Clark Hine puts it, "*Porgy and Bess* should remind us of an earlier time when black men and women, against a backdrop largely absent of overwhelming white power, still struggled to love each other, to build a community, to sustain heroic, even transcendent identities."[12]

This is an opera about a character cut off from his community by his disabled condition, but also about that community, cut off from the rest of American society by its disabling racial status. The "dramatic centrality of the community," writes Howard Pollack, "manifests itself most obviously

in the prominence of the chorus,"[13] which is almost always onstage, endlessly singing with the soloists. The village is represented as tight-knit and distinctively colorful in its funeral rituals and prayers, lullabies, work songs, street cries, and everyday speech. In other words, Catfish Row is a place chosen for its isolation and celebrated for its exoticism. Thus, it functions more like the Gypsy Spain of *Carmen* than like the Czech village of *Jenůfa* or the proletarian Germany of *Wozzeck*.

Representing African Americans in opera

But while Bizet wrote the Gypsy parts in *Carmen* for Parisian performers, not Spanish Gypsies, to play, Gershwin wrote the parts in *Porgy and Bess* (all but the few, extremely brief roles of white characters) to be played by black performers. This was a serious opera about the lives of African Americans, and audiences in the 1930s would not have taken it seriously without African Americans playing the roles. That meant these performers would participate in portraying themselves as exotics within their own country. It is no surprise, then, that blacks have often felt repelled or at least ambivalent about *Porgy and Bess*. As the literary and cultural scholar Gerald Early writes about growing up African American in the 1960s, "No black person I knew liked *Porgy and Bess* but everyone knew the songs."[14]

By 1935 Gershwin, the son of Russian Jewish immigrants, was an enormously successful composer of songs and musicals for Broadway and Hollywood, and had been working his way into the classical concert hall with innovative works (like *Rhapsody in Blue*, 1924) touched by jazz and blues. For at least ten years he had also been dreaming of writing an opera, imagining that he would conquer that most daunting musical medium with a work in jazz style on an African American subject. In 1926 he read Heyward's *Porgy* and proposed an opera on that subject to its author. But when Gershwin was commissioned in 1929 to write an opera for the Metropolitan Opera, he turned to a very different subject: Szymon Ansky's play *The Dybbuk*, based on East European Jewish legend. He was unable to secure the rights to the play, though, and he set to work instead on the *Porgy* project. He seems to have designed this opera for a Broadway theater from the start, and even when Otto Kahn, president of the Metropolitan Opera, offered to produce

A game of craps occupies the whole community of Catfish Row in Act 1, scene 1, of *Porgy and Bess*, photographed in the tryouts at the Colonial Theatre, Boston, before the Broadway opening in 1935.
Culver Pictures

it there, he turned the offer down on the grounds that it was not practical for the Met to hire an all-black cast to give a limited number of performances of one work.[15]

Gershwin had written his opera at a moment in American history when there were African American singers trained and ready to sing opera, but kept off the stages by systematic racial discrimination. Anne Brown, who originated the role of Bess in the opera's first run at the Alvin Theatre in New York, had studied classical singing at the Peabody Conservatory and the Juilliard School of Music. Todd Duncan, the first Porgy, taught singing at Howard University and auditioned for Gershwin with a classic Italian aria.[16] Gershwin was on the one hand tapping into a pool of talented and frustrated singers who were more than eager to show the world what they could do, and on the other hand condemning his work to be shut out of opera houses for the foreseeable future. In the event, although *Porgy and Bess* brought great African American singers success in Europe in the 1950s, it was not until the work's fiftieth anniversary, in 1985, that it was finally produced at the Met.

An opera about African Americans created by a white novelist and a white composer, written for a Broadway theater, to be performed by singers who were excluded from opera houses—these ambiguities growing out of the political circumstances of American life in the 1930s made for ambiguities in the nature of the work. *Porgy and Bess* has long faced doubt about its authenticity

Anne Brown as Bess and Todd Duncan as Porgy in the original Broadway production of *Porgy and Bess* at the Alvin Theatre, New York, 1935.
© ML/Lebrecht Music & Arts

in representing African American experience (just as *Carmen* has faced doubt about its representation of Spanish and Gypsy experience) and at the same time doubt about whether its music marks it as an opera rather than a musical. The two doubts go together, and both are best handled by being willing to find depth rather than compromise in the hybrid nature of the work.

Crossing stylistic boundaries The singers who first auditioned for the roles may have sung classical vocal music, but at Gershwin's insistence they also, reluctantly, sang spirituals. In the history of *Porgy and Bess* on stage and recording, the great performers of the lead roles have been opera singers who could color their sound with inflections from traditional African American vocal styles, whether spirituals, blues, jazz, or gospel. In the recordings of Leontyne Price as Bess, for instance, you can hear the voice of one of the greatest Verdi sopranos of the twentieth century in one phrase and the sound of the blues from her native Mississippi in the next. Gershwin created one role for a Broadway song-and-dance man: Sportin' Life, the high-living character who supplies dope to Bess and eventually entices her to seek out the bright lights of New York City. The famous performers of the role — including John Bubbles (John W. Sublett), Cab Calloway, and Sammy Davis Jr. — have all skipped nimbly from one vocal style to another. Mocking the sermon of a black preacher in "It Ain't Necessarily So," they have alternated in a flash between blue-note intonation, jazz scat-singing, and a whooping gospel *glissando*, ending by belting out a big, chorus-supported Broadway *crescendo*.

Gershwin was right, it seems, to insist on a cast of black singers, not just because the characters had to look right onstage, but even more because only those singers had the right combination of training and experience to cross the borders of vocal style that his music required. The music allows us to perceive the drama of Porgy and Bess and their neighbors in Catfish Row one moment as a story unmistakably bearing the stamp of early twentieth-century African American experience and the next moment as a story of human relationships that in its essence could happen in other settings.

Gershwin's demands for incessant shifts in vocal style are evident in the score. In "It Ain't Necessarily So," for instance, a few measures are enough to show the scat syllables ("Hoodle ah da wa da / Scatty wah"), the preacherly whoop ("Yeah!"), and the blue-note effect of D against D-flat and C against C-flat at the return of the line "It ain't necessarily so" (see Example 13.2). In other places the stylistic alternations work on a much larger scale. They shape the whole second scene, for instance, which shows the wake for Robbins, a character killed in the previous scene fighting with Crown, Bess's abusive lover. The scene is framed by long choral numbers modeled on spirituals, built on call and response between soloists and the chorus of mourners. The middle of the scene, by contrast, contains the most decisively European, operatic number in the opera: "My Man's Gone Now," the lament of Robbins's widow Serena.

13.2 Gershwin, *Porgy and Bess:* "It Ain't Necessarily So"

In this lament Gershwin turns his back on African American musical traits. Even the triple rhythm that makes Serena's listeners sway to her wailing is unusual in black music. Gershwin further rejects the African American scales (blues, pentatonic, and diatonic) that he uses elsewhere in favor of a chromaticism that pervades the chord progressions and Serena's texted phrases and wordless wailing. The chorus joins her not in call and response, but in modulatory passages and in chords undergirding her phrases. And at the end, after an orchestral trumpeting of the lament tune—an effect worthy of Puccini—and a chromatic moan for the chorus, Serena sings a final, embellished wail that recalls laments from the synagogue more than any African American tradition. It is characteristic of opera that the traits anchoring a work in its particular setting fall away at such a moment of intense dramatic gravity, and it is characteristic of the focus on community spirit in *Porgy and Bess* that the most intense expression of grief in the opera is given to a subsidiary character.

At the other stylistic extreme are numbers that Gershwin modeled on African American song practices he had observed in a couple of visits to Charleston and nearby coastal communities. These include the street cries of

the strawberry woman, the honey man, and the crab man, representing the ongoing commercial life of Catfish Row as we wait (Act 2, scene 3) for Bess to recover from delirium in the wake of being raped by Crown. They also include the healing prayer ("Oh Doctor Jesus") that Serena sings just before, to draw Bess out of that delirium, and the choral prayer (also beginning "Oh Doctor Jesus") that members of the community sing at the beginning and end of the scene in which they are waiting out a hurricane (Act 2, scene 4). This is not so much a chorus in the operatic sense as a long moment of simultaneous chanting by six members of the chorus, each singing in a different rhythm and to different words, while the rest of the chorus hums an unchanging chord.

These numbers are among the most distinctive musical creations in *Porgy and Bess*. Together they help an audience imagine this particular time and place and community by showing them what resources of ritual and song that community has for getting through crises and going about its business. But these are not the songs that Gerald Early says everyone knew. Numbers like "Oh Doctor Jesus" are too dependent for their effect on their dramatic function in the opera to have a life of their own. The songs the whole world knows are the solo songs that cross elements of African American with Broadway or even operatic styles, including Porgy's "I Got Plenty o' Nuttin'," Sportin' Life's "It Ain't Necessarily So," and—most popular of all—Clara's "Summertime."

Lullaby and spiritual "Summertime" has lent itself to arrangement in any number of styles, Howard Pollack explains, in part because it mixes such contrasts of style in itself, from the simplicity of its melody to the "sophisticated harmonic palette" of its accompaniment.[17] Even the way it is reprised in the course of the work inserts a Broadway practice into this opera. "Summertime" is the lullaby that Clara, a nervous young mother, sings to her baby in the scene-setting sequence at the opening of the opera. At first hearing, it is possible to think that the singer believes in the vision of tranquility she offers: a life in which "the living is easy," the baby's family is prosperous, and his prospects are secure. But the song returns several times in the opera, and each time—as in a Broadway reprise—the dramatic situation is changed. Soon after the opening Clara sings it again, but by now her husband Jake is worrying her by risking all his earnings in a game of dice. Later, when Jake is out at sea fishing in the midst of the hurricane, she sings "Summertime" again (Act 2, scene 4), this time to calm herself and her neighbors as much as her infant. Then after Jake is drowned and she dies trying to find him, it is Bess who sings the song's now deeply ironic words of comfort to the orphaned baby (Act 3, scene 1).

In other ways, though, the reprising of "Summertime" does not represent simply a Broadway touch that Gershwin imported into his opera. For one thing, the first reprise has a particularly operatic character. When Clara sings it in the middle of Jake's dice game, her soothing strains are heard against the very unsoothing phrases of the dice players calling out for the numbers they need. This is a *réunion des thèmes* straight out of nineteenth-century opera. Furthermore, we first hear "Summertime" before the dramatic situation of its singer is at all clear. It is in effect a song prior to its dramatic meaning, ready to be detached from the opera and performed in a thousand different arrangements. In another sense, this first hearing could be considered just another reprise. "Summertime" is a lullaby, and there is never a first time for a lullaby. It is simply sung again whenever it is needed.

The final number in the opera is simpler in its stylistic origins, but no less complicated in its dramatic meaning than "Summertime." When Porgy learns from his neighbors that Bess has left to seek her fortune with Sportin' Life in New York, he resolves to follow her. The neighbors have no more idea of how far away New York is than he does, but they know that a cripple can't get there in his goat cart, and so they try to dissuade him. But he sets out, as the orchestra plays the jazzy passage with which the overture began, now identified as the beckoning sound of New York. That breaks off, and Porgy begins the final number, "Oh Lawd, I'm on my way." There can be no doubt about the style Gershwin had in mind here: he marks it "quasi Spiritual" and directs that Porgy sing it "with religious fervor." He even recognizes the communal nature of the traditional African American spiritual by having all of Catfish Row join Porgy from the second phrase to the end of the song.

Yet while the participation of the chorus gives the opera a rousing finale, it also makes for dramatic complication. The words have no simple meaning. "I'm on my way to a Heav'nly Lan'," in the tradition of the spiritual, could mean escaping slavery either by going north—as Porgy is doing—or by dying and going to heaven. Porgy surely means the first, but his neighbors might be imagining the other possibility. In any case, the very fact that they are singing with him needs to be reconciled with the symbolic meaning of his departure. The character cut off by his handicap from full participation in the life of his community and full opportunity for happiness suddenly finds himself in the unusual position of being joined in song by all his neighbors—just at the moment when he is leaving them.

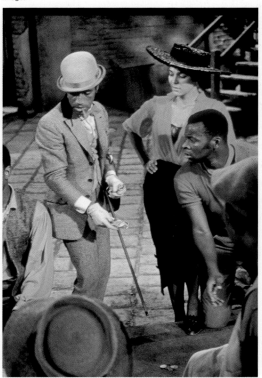

A Hollywood solution to the long-running issues of casting in *Porgy and Bess*: in the 1959 movie version, directed by Otto Preminger, actors Sidney Poitier and Dorothy Dandridge played Porgy and Bess, and their singing was dubbed by the singers Robert McFerrin Sr. and Adele Addison. Sammy Davis Jr. (left), a vaudeville song-and-dance man by training, did his own singing as Sportin' Life, as did Brock Peters (far right) as Crown. The dialogue in this version is spoken.

Gjon Mili/Time & Life Pictures/Getty Images

Should we interpret the choral singing, then, as a sound that could echo in Porgy's head as he heads north by himself? If so, would it make him feel all the more lonely, remembering what he gave up to pursue his desperate quest for Bess, or would he feel that he carried his community inside him, in the form of a song? The song does not signify that he can feel justified in his hopefulness, as the final phrases do in *Jenůfa*. But neither does it signify hopeless aloneness, as the child's "Hopp, hopp!" does at the end of *Wozzeck*. Instead, it gives Porgy the strength to set off on his journey by providing a promise to cling to—an idea of a Promised Land—in the face of his heartbreak, sacrifice, and loneliness. For expressing such hope in the face of despair, no kind of song could be more appropriate than the spiritual.

Postwar Themes of Mob Justice: Britten, *Peter Grimes*; Operas of Floyd and Heggie

While stories about the violation of communal taboos have been around at least since Sophocles' *Oedipus*, many operas and other dramas written since the end of World War II (1945) give the theme a new twist. These are stories of ordinary individuals who not only offend by their presumed criminal or nonconforming behavior, but who seem willing to cut themselves off from their community rather than repent. This attitude offends the community more than the behavior itself does, since it amounts to a reproach to those who claim to uphold the norms. And that reproach of the powerful crowd by a powerless individual provokes a response of uncontrolled rage.

The English composer Benjamin Britten launched this theme in postwar opera with *Peter Grimes* (1945). It tells the story of a nineteenth-century fisherman in an isolated English town whose negligent and abusive behavior leads his fellow villagers to believe him responsible for the death of first one young apprentice and then another; the villagers hound Grimes to his death. Among postwar American operas on the theme, the most popular has been Carlisle Floyd's *Susannah* (1955), in which the church elders of an Appalachian town (like their counterparts in the Apocryphal story of Susannah) have come upon a beautiful young woman bathing in a mountain stream and decide that she must be lewd; when she is falsely accused of seducing a simple-minded neighbor boy, what really convicts her in the eyes of the community is that she refuses to absolve herself of any guilt at a revival meeting. More recently, in Jake Heggie's *Dead Man Walking* (2000), based on the memoir by Sister Helen Prejean, a man convicted of a brutal double murder in rural Louisiana expects no sympathy from anyone and gets none until a nun assigned to be his spiritual adviser persuades him to face his conscience. In these operas and others like them, the confrontation between individual and community

may be understood on its own terms or as a stand-in for other confrontations that the creators did not feel free to raise explicitly — from the anti-Communist witch hunts during the McCarthy era (which Floyd said "terrified and enraged" him at the time he composed *Susannah*) to the repression of homosexuals (which has been identified as a powerful force driving Britten in creating *Peter Grimes*).[18]

The operatic medium gives a composer (as opposed to the writer of a play or film) a unique means of representing the fearful power of a single-minded community: the voice of the chorus. The chorus, accordingly, deserves special attention in all these works. In *Susannah* it is particularly associated with the church, around which the life of the town revolves. Susannah's chief accusers are the church elders and their wives, and she cannot go into town without encountering the supper and square dance taking place on the church grounds and the revival meetings held there night after night. Her only refuges, accordingly, are the mountain home she and her brother share (they are orphans) and the secular folk music of their region. When she is singled out at the revival meeting and asked to repent of sins she hasn't committed, her response is to run home and comfort herself by singing a song with a folk-revival first-person text and a melody that hauntingly borrows the form and style of an Appalachian ballad: "The trees on the mountains are cold and bare" (Act 2, scene 3).

There could be no resolution of the moral standoff between the righteous-minded community and the nonconforming individual in these operas if it were not for the go-betweens — characters who fit in comfortably enough, but who understand the plight of the characters who do not. In *Susannah* the revival preacher Blitch becomes a go-between only because he compromises himself morally. After his relentless and terrifying preaching in the revival meeting fails to draw a confession out of Susannah (Act 2, scene 2), he follows her to her house, where he seduces her. Knowing now that she was a virgin until that moment, he fails to persuade the townspeople of her previous innocence because he won't reveal his own role in ending it. He is the great operatic portrait of the hypocrite preacher.

The go-between in *Dead Man Walking* is another religious figure, Sister Helen Prejean, but she is by contrast the heroine of her opera, its true subject. In her efforts to reach out to the murderer Joseph De Rocher, she becomes a social pariah herself, hearing the voices of the community in her head, including the relatives of both murderer and victims. And in forgiving De Rocher, she enables him, just before his execution, to ask forgiveness of his victims' parents. Though she does not understand him, she

Peter Grimes (Peter Pears) strikes Ellen Orford (Joan Cross) for interfering with his treatment of his apprentice (Leonard Thompson), in Act 2, scene 1, of the original production of *Peter Grimes*, staged by Eric Crozier at Sadler's Wells, London, 1945.
Courtesy of *Opera News*

creates—through her actions, her sympathy, and her song "He will gather us around"—a symbolic equality and emotional closeness with the condemned man. In an opera of moral confrontation, that bond seems more extraordinary than understanding.

Peter Grimes In *Peter Grimes* there are two go-betweens, and though they are not connected to the church like Blitch and Sister Helen, they offer the audience a moral footing, a vantage point for contemplating all sides with unprejudiced clarity. One is Ellen Orford, the woman whom Grimes has hopes of marrying and who has taken responsibility for the treatment of his second apprentice; she is drawn to help Grimes, perhaps to become part of his life, until she sees all her hopes for him dashed. The other is Balstrode, a retired skipper, who protects and advises Grimes, but discovers the death of the second apprentice before anyone else and, to spare Grimes being lynched, urges him to drown himself. Neither of these characters has the power that Blitch has to affect the course of events in *Susannah* or that Sister Helen has to bring moral closure to *Dead Man Walking*. Theirs is a different power: by standing

Desmond Shawe-Taylor

Shawe-Taylor (1907–1995) was the music critic for the British political and cultural magazine *New Statesman* in the late 1940s and 1950s and later of the *Sunday Times*. The following paragraphs come from his review of the original 1945 production of *Peter Grimes* at Sadler's Wells (later the English National Opera) in London. The first paragraph shows a concern that many human-interest works have provoked, from *Wozzeck* and *Lady Macbeth* to *Dead Man Walking* and *The Death of Klinghoffer*: how to reconcile sympathy for a character's social situation with revulsion at his or her behavior. The second exemplifies another side of the reviewer's task: evaluating the many different contributions that any opera production requires.

I know that operas are not ethical treatises, and that I shall be accused of taking too literal a view of a poetic creation. Maybe. But is there not something shocking in the attempt to win our sympathies for a character *simply because* he is an outlaw and an enemy of society—and no more questions asked? What I am quite prepared (especially after the Wigmore Hall concert) to believe is that the richness and dramatic power of Britten's music will enable us to ignore (for the time being) an adolescent conception of man and society which is in sober truth indefensible. In the theatre we may well be lulled into acquiescence; but at home, shall we not begin to wonder? . . .

All the singers clearly felt the unusual happiness of singing a text that did not sound (as so many English operas do) like a translation. The chorus, though on the first night the public-house 'round' went badly, rose to their great moments, and, like the soloists, were wonderfully free of that depressing one-eye-on-the-conductor tradition. Eric Crozier's production was imaginative and effective, though it was a mistake not to make the fog visible, and there were times when I could have done with a little more light, and a more specifically early morning *kind* of light at the beginning and end of the main action.

New Statesman, June 9 and 16, 1945; reprinted in Philip Brett, ed., *Benjamin Britten: "Peter Grimes"* (Cambridge: Cambridge University Press, 1983), pp. 155, 158.

outside the standoff between Grimes and the rest of the townspeople, they provide us with the eyes to see Grimes go to his death neither convicted nor acquitted of what the others believe he has done.

The chorus possesses a particularly disturbing power in *Peter Grimes* precisely because it represents the intolerant townspeople in such a believable way, with all the personality and contradictions of a real human society. We hear them carousing in the tavern and singing in church. We meet a remarkable number as distinct individuals, we see them going about their many different tasks on a working day, and we hear them turned into a lynch mob when they learn that the second apprentice has died in Grimes's service, egging each other on in overlapping phrases and finally uniting their voices in bloodthirsty calls of "Peter Grimes" as they set out to hunt him down (Act 3, scene 1). Even more chilling is the final scene, when they go about their tasks once again, while a couple of them notice a boat sinking offshore—it is Grimes, hounded but at least out of their reach, drowning himself—and no one bothers about it.

This chorus is an inescapable presence in the opera, heard in every scene, even when it is not onstage. In fact, its presence is especially frightening when it is offstage. The second act finds the new apprentice on the shore, just in front of the church, on a Sunday morning with Ellen Orford. In the course of their conversation she discovers a tear in the boy's coat and a bruise on his neck and realizes that Grimes is never going to meet standards that she, let alone the town, considers humane. Her grim discovery is made even more unsettling by the sounds of community righteousness coming from the offstage church: the voices of the pastor and the congregation singing the praises of God.

At the end of this scene the suspicious mob sets off for Grimes's seaside hut, where their threatening approach actually precipitates the disaster they believe they are preventing: Grimes hurries his apprentice out the door of the hut, and the boy slips down a cliff to his death. Later (Act 3, scene 2) the crowd sets out again, this time believing in the boy's still unconfirmed death and crying out for retribution. Its offstage shouting reaches Grimes, standing "weary and demented" on a deserted street, and invades his soliloquy. The voices of the mob, calling his name, intrude into his thoughts, and by responding to them rather than fleeing them, he gives us a better picture than anything else could of how broken his mind and spirit are.

Grimes defines himself as unfit for society by talking to his fellow townspeople when they are absent, yet withdrawing into himself when they are present. Earlier he has walked into a crowded tavern and delivered himself of a dreamy poetic vision—"Now the Great Bear and Pleiades where earth moves" (Act 1, scene 2)—that makes the tavern crowd declare him "mad or drunk." But above all, just as Susannah seeks refuge in her mountain retreat, Grimes seeks refuge in the sea. The entire opera is played on the border between land and water, and if the land is dominated for him by the incessant, uncomprehending voices of the townspeople, the sea—the place of his livelihood—is comfortingly wordless, if far from silent. Its presence is marked by the orchestra, which bridges the scenes with interludes, each of which portrays the sea in different weather, at a different time of day, in a different mood. The sea in *Peter Grimes* is as richly realized a character as the chorus, but it passes no judgment.

Grimes's unwanted arrival and his unsociable behavior cast a large shadow over the celebrations of the townspeople at the tavern in Act 1, scene 2, of *Peter Grimes*, staged by Willy Decker at the Royal Opera House, Covent Garden, 2004. Ben Heppner appears as Grimes.
© 2011 Royal Opera House/Clive Barda

The Unfulfilled Housewife: Shostakovich, *The Lady Macbeth of Mtsensk District*

A young woman, married but childless, lives in the provinces. Her husband is prosperous enough—this is no story about the struggles of the poor—but preoccupied with running his family's business, and he still answers to the demands of his surviving parent. Our heroine feels imprisoned in her marriage, surrounded by dull provincials, trapped in her reality. She is cut off from love, from any real company, from anything she ever dreamed of. Another man becomes available to her, and she has an affair with him. Guilt assails her, and she kills herself.

Give or take a detail, this is the story of some of the most sensational and important works of nineteenth-century fiction: Gustave Flaubert's novel *Madame Bovary* (1857), Alexander Ostrovsky's play *The Storm* (*Groza* in Russian, 1860), and Leo Tolstoy's novel *Anna Karenina* (1877) among them. Not until the twentieth century, though, did it become an important theme in opera. Variants of the theme are found in two operas set in working-class locales within great cities: Puccini's *Il tabarro* (*The Cloak*, 1918) and Kurt Weill's *Street Scene* (1946). Janáček turned Ostrovsky's *The Storm* into the opera *Kát'a Kabanová* (premiered in 1921). And the Soviet composer Dmitri Shostakovich made an opera called *The Lady Macbeth of Mtsensk District* (*Ledi Makbet Mtsenskogo uyezda*, 1934) from an 1865 story by the Russian writer Nikolai Leskov.

The title sets the tone for all these works. Lady Macbeth may be a figure from Shakespearian tragedy, but a Lady Macbeth from the District of Mtsensk (a farming area south of Moscow) could be the subject of tragedy only in the most careless sense of the term, a back-page human-interest story from a small-town newspaper. Leskov himself described his story as a "sketch," giving it the form of an account by a local reporter, suitable for use in a criminal court case.[19] The fascination that stories like this held for him and ambitious writers like Flaubert and Tolstoy apparently comes from the very banality of these housewives' lives. Because their ordinary circumstances make them seem so much like the rest of us, when we look into the question of how boredom could drive them to commit adultery, suicide, and other acts of violence, we are also asking whether in similar circumstances we might do the same. What drives them is the same in every case: a sense that life has cheated them out of the happiness they dreamed of as girls, that the simplest creatures around them seem to enjoy.

Soliloquies of a banal existence In Shostakovich's *Lady Macbeth* the title character, Katerina Izmailova, envies the happiness, and in particular the sexually satisfied lives, of animals (Act 1, scene 3):

Zherebyonok k kobylke toropitsya,	*The colt goes after the filly,*
Kotik prositsya k koshechke,	*the tomcat begs for the female cat,*
A golub' k golubke stremitsya,	*the dove seeks his mate,*
I tol'ko ko mne nikto ne speshit.	*and only I have no one hurrying to me.*

A minute after she sings this, someone does hurry to her and forces himself on her. Katerina heads down the path of adultery and death out of self-pity, the easiest sentiment in the world for any of us to succumb to, and she uses the tritest comparisons in the world to justify it.

The narrator of Leskov's story, as Caryl Emerson puts it, "rarely reproduces an inner thought as direct discourse, assumes no responsibility for the tale, and demonstrates little sympathy for (or even interest in) the heroine."[20] But when Shostakovich and his co-librettist, Aleksandr Preis, turned the story into a dramatic text, they saw to it that Katerina got plenty of soliloquies and other opportunities to reveal her inner thought. Furthermore, at the time he was composing the opera, Shostakovich insisted that the text "must be a singing one, it must give the composer maximum possibility for freely flowing song." And in *Lady Macbeth*, as he wrote elsewhere, "all the vocal parts . . . are melodious, lyrical."[21] In Katerina's confessional soliloquies, as a result, we get to understand her state of mind not just through her words, but also through the nature of the "freely flowing song" to which she sings them.

The opera opens on one such soliloquy. Katerina is in bed, yawning and complaining that she has so little to do she can't sleep. Here already she expresses her complaint as envy of lowlier creatures: ants and cows, along with farm hands, have more to do than she does. As she sings, her music switches from aimless arioso into a simple and repetitive folk-song idiom. Her musical style, in other words, is as trite as her similes. In her later soliloquy, in which she muses that the animals all find sexual partners, her music takes the form and style of a traditional Russian parlor song, a Romance. This style makes for a far more expressive number than the earlier one, building its effect patiently from one harmonically restless, long-arched phrase to the next. Her singing of this "Romance," much more than of the earlier "folk song," can make listeners feel more at home with Katerina's misery, and in that way they can sympathize with her plight, even though her own self-pity will eventually lead her to commit three murders as well as adultery and suicide. In fact, Shostakovich wrote: "Despite the fact that [she] is the murderer of her husband and father-in-law, I sympathize with her nonetheless."[22]

Agrippina Sokolova as Katerina Izmailova in the original production of *The Lady Macbeth of Mtsensk District* at the Maly Opera House, Leningrad (now St. Petersburg), 1934.

© Lebrecht Music & Arts

Still, this Romance is not a song about the pangs of love, as Romances conventionally are; it expresses her resentment that she alone is denied any part of love, either its pangs or its fulfillment.

Katerina's soliloquies represent the stories she tells herself about her state of mind. We don't have to regard them as privileged insights into her motivation. In fact, we should probably expect them to be full of banal half-truths. Nor do we have nothing else to go on; after all, we see her interact with the other characters in the opera. They are there, it seems, simply to provoke Katerina into revealing something about herself to us. And when we put together what we learn about her in private and in company, it seems that there is no simple truth about her. Her contradictions are what make her—and the music of her opera—fascinating.

An elusive case It tells us something, for instance, that in the first act Katerina interacts more with her father-in-law than with her husband. It is the father-in-law who openly suspects her of adulterous intentions and makes her kneel to her husband, in front of all the workers on the family estate, and swear to stay faithful to him when he is about to leave to tend to family business elsewhere (Act 1, scene 1). She never speaks of this humiliation in her soliloquies, but it is hard to imagine that it has no effect. Her eventual lover, the clerk Sergei, arrives to work on the estate just when her husband is leaving, and her first interaction with him comes when she intervenes to stop him and other male workers from molesting a female worker (Act 1, scene 2). In this scene Katerina displays her boldness, first in a speech chiding the men for their arrogance toward women (a "freely flowing song" as self-possessed as her opening soliloquy is self-pitying), and then in her acceptance of Sergei's challenge to a wrestling match.

It is presumably this side of her that emboldens Sergei to knock on her bedroom door that night. She lets him in and barely resists when he forces himself on her. But when her father-in-law catches Sergei later sneaking out of her window and whips him mercilessly, what leads her to respond by feeding her father-in-law rat poison and watching coldly as he dies in front of her? Is it the self-pitying loneliness expressed in her opening soliloquy, or the humiliation she accepted silently from her father-in-law, or the boldness she exhibited to Sergei, or outrage at her father-in-law's viciousness to her new lover, or all those different impulses accumulating force together?

And once she and Sergei have buried her father-in-law, what drives them to murder her husband several days later, when he returns home and discovers that she is having an affair? Is she, with Sergei's help, still working out her self-pity or outrage at her loveless married state? Or have they by now developed such a firm commitment to each other that they feel they need to take drastic action to free her from her marriage? Or shall we think of them as the Bonnie and Clyde of nineteenth-century Russia, freed by their first crime to exercise selfish and violent options outside the constraints of lawful behavior? Their actions and language and music give us some means of thinking about these possibilities, but no clear way of deciding among them.

An example of these ambiguous possibilities can be found in what the orchestral music of two scenes suggests about the sexual relationship between Katerina and Sergei. In their first sexual encounter (Act 1, scene 3) Sergei disregards her objections and takes her behind a curtain, leaving it to the orchestra to suggest the headlong sexual frenzy that actors in a Soviet opera house in the 1930s were not at liberty even to fake onstage. In fact, that music so graphically and energetically evokes the sexual act, complete with post-climactic downward trombone slides, that this music was cut in some early productions.[23] If there is anything besides physical excitement between Katerina and Sergei in this scene, the music doesn't show it. But in the later scene in which her husband discovers them together (Act 2, scene 5), the curtain rises on the two lovers in bed after making love, and the scene-setting music, which continues as they begin their pillow talk, expresses the utmost tenderness. Of course, the first scene represents them in the heat of passion and the second in its afterglow, but it is also possible to imagine the total contrast in musical character as an indication that in the intervening days, sexual attraction has matured into love. Can we even accept the possibility that partners in a murder spree can develop a loving relationship? And is the journalistic crime story a genre that makes room for its criminal characters (or even one of them, Katerina) to be in love?

In this case, at least, the genre certainly makes plenty of room for them to feel guilt. If the fascination of the genre lies to a great extent in trying to understand what could drive a housewife to murder and murder again, the morality of the genre can be maintained only by making her accept responsibility in the end. Katerina certainly takes on a load of guilt. Already in the scene when she and Sergei are in bed, about to be disturbed by the return of her husband, she is frightened by a visit from the ghost of her father-in-law. The fact that Sergei cannot see the ghost tells us that it is a figment of her guilty conscience. Later she stands so often staring at the door to the cellar in which she and Sergei have dumped her husband's body that a curious peasant decides to see what her staring is about and discovers the body. In

The wedding of Katerina (in white, standing in front of the table) to Sergei is interrupted by the arrival of the police, come to arrest them both for the murders of Katerina's father-in-law and husband. Stanislavsky-Nemirovich-Danchenko Music Theater, Moscow, 1934.

RIA Novoeti/Lebrecht Music & Arts

that inadvertent way her guilt leads to Katerina and Sergei being arrested and sent to Siberia.

At a stop on the convict trail to Siberia (Act 4, scene 9), Sergei takes advantage of her continuing devotion to obtain a pair of stockings from her that he then uses to obtain sex with Sonyetka, another convict. Katerina, discovering the betrayal and mocked for it by the rest of the women convicts, delivers herself of the grimmest musical number in the opera ("V lesu" / "In the woods"), a vision of a lake with waters "as black as my conscience." This is the crux of the drama, the moment when the audience hears Katerina acknowledge the horror of what she has done and face the fact that she will die for her sins. But as ever, there is an ambiguity in her motivation here. What sets off this confessional moment, after all, is not a new pang of conscience or insight into her guilt; it is jealousy. And her response is not simply to throw herself into an icy river, but to grab her rival, Sonyetka, and pull her into those black waters with her. By drowning her rival, she continues to exact revenge on all those who continue to cheat her out of happiness; by drowning herself, she expiates her guilt for those acts of revenge. Even in her death her case is fascinating to contemplate because it is too contradictory to adjudicate.

During the period when the opera was created and first performed, the Communist Party was formulating requirements that artistic works produced in the Soviet Union were to be simple, uplifting, and politically correct entertainments for the masses; eventually these requirements were summed up in the term "socialist realism." But the requirements were not clearly established when *Lady Macbeth* was premiered in 1934, and in fact it was a huge success, running for over two years in productions in Leningrad and Moscow, as well as in the provinces, on the radio, and abroad. Then in 1936 the Soviet leader

Stalin went to see the opera and left before it was over. Shortly thereafter an anonymous denunciation appeared in the official Soviet newspaper *Pravda*, under the title "A Muddle Instead of Music." It is likely that *Lady Macbeth* was attacked less for the specific traits listed in the *Pravda* article than for the generally experimental attitude it exhibited, with its morally ambiguous stance toward its criminal heroine, its obsessive focus on her quest for private happiness, its eroticism, and its riotous play of musical styles.[24] *Lady Macbeth* became the lead case in a crackdown on free artistic expression that lasted for just about the remaining half century of the Soviet regime. The opera was not seen or heard again in the Soviet Union for another three decades, and then only in a bowdlerized version.

Even now that that regime is gone, the question of the opera's moral stance toward its heroine continues to provoke controversy. Richard Taruskin, for instance, has found irony in the punishment of Shostakovich by Stalin's government, since he sees something akin to Stalinism in an opera that he feels justifies Katerina's crimes.[25] In all this controversy it is important to notice that a mere human-interest story has shown itself capable of revealing the political dimensions of private behavior, not just through the condemnations of the opera by a totalitarian state, but also through the debates within freer societies about how this representation of an unfulfilled housewife's private behavior is to be judged in the public arena.

Ordinary People Caught Up in Great Events

Poulenc: *Dialogues of the Carmelites*

Nineteenth-century works like *Aida* and *Les Huguenots* cannot be called human-interest operas because the central characters' private woes are created by their public positions of power. Although this model continued to be followed in twentieth-century works like Samuel Barber's *Antony and Cleopatra* (1966) and Thea Musgrave's *Mary, Queen of Scots* (1977), a more characteristic theme takes the human-interest story into the realm of political affairs without losing its human-interest character: the theme of ordinary people caught up in political forces they want no part of. The twentieth century was an era of totalitarian politics, of political regimes that attempted to bring people's every thought, word, and move under their arbitrary control. The experience of totalitarianism could lead to an intense desire to be free of politics altogether. Especially in countries that had recently known that experience, artists often gave voice to that desire. Such a portrayal occurs in Francis Poulenc's *Dialogues*

of the Carmelites (*Dialogues des Carmélites*, 1957), a French opera about a group of nuns who were executed during the French Revolution.

The French Revolution, and especially the phase of mass executions known as the Reign of Terror, was such a formative event in the political imagination of the Western world that artists throughout that world have resorted to it ever since as a mythical stage on which to play out the scenarios of terror that their own times inspire. Nowhere but in France itself, however, has the Revolution served as the touchstone of all political and cultural stances for over two centuries. It would be a tremendous project, consequently, to trace all the historical, political, religious, and cultural resonances of *Dialogues of the Carmelites*. The work is based on the true story of the sixteen Carmelite nuns of Compiègne who were guillotined in the final days of the Reign of Terror, evidently for their aristocratic origins as well as their refusal to give up their religious vocation. Later the question of whether or not to restore the privileged pre-Revolutionary position of the Catholic Church in France was an ongoing subject of dispute. As a result, the beatification of the Compiègne nuns by the Pope in 1906 was viewed in France not just as a tribute by the church to the steadfast faith of its adherents, but also as part of its ongoing reproach to all those who continued to identify themselves as heirs of the Revolution.

In the following decades the story of the Carmelites of Compiègne kept acquiring new political implications. It provided the basis for the 1931 novella *Die Letzte am Schafott* (*The Last One at the Scaffold*) by the German Catholic writer Gertrud von le Fort. No doubt the fate of the nuns resonated for her with the threats posed by the competing Communist and Fascist movements in her own day. By 1948, when the French writer Georges Bernanos turned Von le Fort's novella into a play, France had endured five years of totalitarianism in the form of Nazi occupation during World War II. Although Bernanos was Catholic and had once even been an old-fashioned royalist, his play is no mere polemic for a given political side. Instead, it consists largely of philosophical dialogues among the nuns and others on how to cope with the fear of death in oppressive circumstances.

Those dialogues spoke strongly to Francis Poulenc, who was Catholic but no royalist. In fact, his lifelong habit of shunning politics, which had served him well during the terrors of the Nazi occupation, fitted him to appreciate better than Bernanos the dread of politics that animates the nuns in the story. Poulenc claimed to have read Bernanos's script "telling myself at the end of each scene, 'But obviously, it's made for me!'" He pared down that lengthy text, but otherwise kept its language intact as the libretto to his opera.[26]

Dialogues focuses on the fate of a single character, a young aristocratic woman named Blanche de la Force. Overprotected by her father and brother and dreading life in the world, Blanche decides to join the Carmelite Order

just as the Revolution is beginning. Her story personalizes the fate of the whole convent for the audience, her outlook giving us a stake in the theological disputes that dominate the early scenes especially. Hers is certainly not a human-interest story like Jenůfa's or Porgy's or Peter Grimes's or Katerina Izmailova's, unfolding from a sensational misdeed or doomed love affair. In the end, though, it becomes as sensational as any of theirs: having fled from the Carmelites when her fear of their impending fate overwhelmed her, she returns to their side just as they are being guillotined and joins in their death.

Private dialogues, communal songs Apart from the prolonged and gripping scene in which the Prioress of the convent dies, the first two of the opera's three acts run the risk of not being sensational or dramatic enough. From one scene to the next the nuns engage each other in intense dialogues over what it means to be a religious, how they should live, and how they should die. Compared with most other protagonists in human-interest operas, these nuns are fearsomely articulate. But they are speaking of abstract matters, and their words are in prose, set in a conversational melodic style against a steady flow of chords. Poulenc described the style of the opera as "Monteverdi (please excuse me) of the twentieth century," suggesting that he was lopsidedly favoring an acting style of music over a song style.[27] The only real concessions to song style come when the nuns take a break from their talk to sing their prescribed Latin

In Nicolas Joel's production of *Dialogues of the Carmelites*, presented at the Théâtre du Capitole in Toulouse, France, in 2009, the wooden frames of Hubert Monloup's scenery eerily suggest both the protective arches of the nun's cloister and the guillotine that eventually awaits them.
© Patrice Nin

prayers in choral harmony. And even that change of pace leaves another kind of uniformity intact: for five scenes and two interludes (shorter scenes), except for a single line sung by the Prioress's doctor, we hear women's voices all the time. All in all, for much of the opera Poulenc runs the risk that his music, however beautiful, will lack dramatic variety.

Being patient with all this musical conversation brings two rewards. The first is that we are taken deep into the moral struggles of Blanche and her religious community. Among all the characters described in this chapter as cut off from everyone around them, only these Carmelite nuns live apart from society by their own conscious choice. And a couple of them—the Prioress who heads the convent and Blanche—articulate the implications of that choice with a fierce clarity. Here they are at their first meeting (Act 1, scene 2), as the Prioress tests whether Blanche is fit for holy orders:

> Blanche:
> *Il doit être doux, ma Mère, de se sentir si avancée dans la voie du détachement qu'on ne saurait plus retourner en arrière.*

> La Prieure:
> *Ma pauvre enfant, l'habitude finit par détacher de tout. Mais à quoi bon, pour une religieuse, être détachée de tout, si elle n'est pas détachée de soi-même, c'est-à-dire de son propre détachement?*

> Blanche:
> *It must be sweet, Mother, to realize that you have advanced so far on the path of detachment that you wouldn't know how to come back from it.*

> The Prioress:
> *My poor child, habit ends up cutting us off from everything. But what good is it for a nun to be detached from everything if she is not detached from herself, that is, from her own detachment?*

This acute consciousness of their need to practice detachment does not prevent the Carmelites from forming the strongest of attachments to each other. This reveals itself equally in their relentless engagement in dialogue and in their harmonious choral singing. In the end it is clearly this attachment to each other that gives each of them the strength to face her senseless execution with serenity.

The world intrudes The second reward for hearing out the nuns' dialogues is a dramatic one: the shattering musical effect of the second half of the opera, when the outside world forces itself inside the convent walls and destroys that detached communal life. The first intrusion (Act 2, scene 3) is by Blanche's brother, the Chevalier de la Force. As the Revolution has proceeded, it has increasingly threatened the safety of the Catholic clergy and religious orders, and in this political atmosphere the Chevalier visits the Carmelite

convent to urge Blanche to abandon her life there in the interest of her safety. He already appeared in the first scene, when she was deciding to become a nun, and his overprotectiveness in that scene is reestablished here. But his exchange with Blanche now makes a more striking effect because it has an obsessive charge that none of the intervening exchanges between Blanche and her fellow nuns have had.

Musically the obsessiveness is embodied particularly in the rising two-note motive heard in the orchestra almost without break throughout their conversation—whereas in the nuns' conversations hardly any motive is ever repeated persistently. In this repeating motive alone, to say nothing of the strident vocal lines, we hear the emotional strain characteristic of a difficult sibling relationship, a bond not chosen and not severable, full of misunderstandings that are endlessly reiterated and inequalities that can never be rectified. Feeling "harassed" by her brother's (and by implication her father's) pity, "disgusted by their kindness" (as she says once he is gone), Blanche rejects her brother's help, but in the process we have learned how unsure she is of herself.

The next intrusion (Act 2, scene 4) brings the Revolution itself into the convent. The nuns' chaplain announces that he is being forced to stop saying mass for them, and the nuns begin to speculate on whether they will need to become martyrs for their faith. A knocking at the gate announces the arrival of a government commissioner, at the head of an intemperate mob, to inform the nuns that they must vacate the convent. At this point the intimate drama of dialogues, focused on Blanche's struggle to understand her personal destiny, turns into grand opera: a political confrontation between the two sides in a struggle over the destiny of a nation. The conjoined voices of the nuns, accomplished as a choir but small in number, are now set against those of the mob, practically inarticulate but frightening in their numbers, as they burst into the convent, growling wordlessly on dissonant chords or chanting the "Ça ira," the rallying cry of the Revolution. The personal fears that have dominated the dialogues until this moment (Blanche's fear of life, the Prioress's fear of pain and death) are now exchanged for political fears as the nuns debate whether to martyr themselves by inviting the Revolution to crush them. In the history of opera there are few cases of a work so transformed at its midpoint from one type of opera, one level of focus, to another.

The private scenes continue, however. The nuns take counsel with themselves and, against the advice of their new prioress, join together in a vow to stay together as a convent, an act the revolutionary government is bound to punish as seditious, but one they see as patriotic as well as holy. Blanche, afraid to support this plan, flees the sisterhood and returns to her home, only to find that her father has been guillotined and there is no safety there. In the meantime most of the other nuns are arrested and condemned to death.

In the final scene of *Dialogues of the Carmelites* the nuns sing together as they march one by one toward the guillotine, taunted by the crowd. The original production of the opera, staged by Margherita Wallmann, at La Scala, Milan, 1957.

Erio Piccagliani © Teatro alla Scala

The final scene, which brings the action back into the public arena, puts an ending of grand-opera spectacle and horror on what began as a drama of cloistered dialogue. The spectacle is unforgettably dramatic and moving: the nuns are brought to the Place de la Révolution, mount the steps to the guillotine one by one, and are beheaded — Blanche joining them at the last moment and submitting herself to the same fate. Nevertheless, Poulenc was justified in claiming that the death of Blanche — he could have said the whole last scene — was "overwhelming in its simplicity, in its resignation, and . . . in its peace."[28] It is so because there is no dialogue at all: musically the whole scene consists of the nuns singing the last of their prayers, the Salve Regina, together as they are guillotined. At first they sing quietly, but gradually their voices grow louder, conveying a gathering courage, as their numbers are slowly diminished by the strokes of the blade. Those disturbingly lovely strokes sound at unpredictable moments, unnervingly, against the steady flow of the song without interrupting it. At times the crowd that has been attracted to the spectacle sings

wordlessly, inarticulately, during the nuns' prayer. Beneath the voices the orchestral bass marches in repeated notes that step up a minor third and down again—a figure that throughout the opera has been associated with fear. But the nuns' words speak of hope:

Salve Regina, Mater misericordiae,	Hail, Queen and Mother of mercy!
Vita, dulcedo, et spes nostra, salve.	Life, sweetness, and our hope—hail!

What conveys their hopeful spirit and makes their song "overwhelming in its simplicity" is above all that they sing this, unlike any of their previous prayers, in unison (or at certain points, in octaves), harmonized by the orchestra. The wordless mob sings in parts, and those parts convey a feeling of disunity against the audible unity of the nuns. Because the nuns sing in unison, the silencing of one voice after another does not alter the texture of their song, though toward the end it softens it. And when Blanche arrives on the scene, just as the remaining other nun completes the Salve Regina and is beheaded, the unity allows Blanche to maintain the sensation of continuous singing. She takes up a different prayer—the last verse of the Veni Creator Spiritus—yet the nuns' song seems to be continued without interruption a little longer. The unison singing makes a dramatic point that words could not convey. Each of these women individually decided even before the Revolution to detach herself from politics, from the world, by entering the Carmelite order. Now with the help of their communal song, which feeds their sense of attachment to each other and thus of belonging to a community, they are able to conquer their fears and face a horribly public death, singing their defiance to the end. Their song's unified texture signifies that the nuns have not shunned politics after all, but have chosen their own path of political solidarity.

Adams, *The Death of Klinghoffer*

A more recent American opera, John Adams's *The Death of Klinghoffer* (1991), is also based on a true story, but in this case one taken fresh from the news. This is an opera about how ordinary people are thrust into the political arena against their will by an act of modern political terrorism. It is based on the hijacking of an Italian cruise ship, the *Achille Lauro*, by four members of the Palestinian Liberation Front as it left the harbor of Alexandria, Egypt, on October 7, 1985. The hijackers shot and killed a wheelchair-bound Jewish American passenger, Leon Klinghoffer, before they negotiated the release of the hundreds of other passengers and crew.

Operas have rarely been made out of such recent and unsettling pieces of news. It seems more like the stuff of television movies, and in fact a

TV movie called *Voyage of Terror: The Achille Lauro Affair* (1990) appeared shortly before the opera was produced. It is hardly surprising, then, that some people have greeted this opera with an outrage, over both the choice and handling of its subject, that is usually reserved for works of popular culture. In 2003, more than ten years after its premiere, the Brooklyn Academy of Music set up metal detectors in its lobby to guard against violent protest when it staged a revival of the work.[29]

As Brian Jenkins has written: "Terrorism is aimed at the people watching, not at the actual victims. Terrorism is a theater."[30] In a hostage-taking, the audience for that theatrical action is in a narrow sense those involved in securing the release of the hostages—here, the Israeli government, which was asked to release fifty Palestinian political prisoners in exchange for the passengers. In a wider sense, at least in a modern political hostage-taking, the audience is public opinion. The public, brought into the "theater" through the power of the news media, applies pressure on governments to respond or not. In this case public opinion in a number of countries was involved: the United States and various European countries, whose citizens made up most of the passengers; Italy, the home country of the ship; Israel, on whose government the hijackers made their demands; and Egypt and Syria, whose ports were chosen as possible destinations by the hijackers.

A hostage-taking occurs in a severely confined space—much like a stage—in which two small groups, hijackers and hostages, interact with each other. The hijackers are attempting to influence a large-scale political conflict by reducing it to the scale of a standoff between themselves and their hostages, whose lives matter to the other side. The news media and the governments concerned perform a complementary function: they magnify the standoff into a crisis so that public opinion will support a response that maintains the governments' positions, optimally without loss of lives.

In a way there are two dramas in a hostage crisis, the human-interest drama of hijackers and hostages locked together in the confined space, and the political drama that connects them with the powerful forces that are kept at bay by the threat of violence. The challenge in creating an opera out of this real-life theater is to encompass both dramas within one work, on one stage, without the larger political conflict and the perspective of the outside world diminishing the intense, claustrophobic experience of those inside, who both long for and dread a resolution.

In *The Death of Klinghoffer* the claustrophobic atmosphere is sustained by setting the work entirely within the cruise ship—there could hardly be a space more dramatically cut off from the world than a ship at sea—and by restricting the cast entirely to those on board: the four hijackers, the captain and first officer, and a sampling of the passengers. Like other human-interest operas,

this one centers on characters who are cut off from the rest of society, but it is exceptional for the whole cast to be in this position. What's more, the Palestinian hijackers, by cutting themselves off in the company of people they consider their enemies (especially the Israeli, British, and American passengers), create a bizarre reversal of their normal situation, locking themselves in confrontation with the very people from whom they are ordinarily most isolated.

Experiencing and reporting The creators of this opera use an alternation of present-time dialogue with past-time narration and unspecified-time choral commentary to bring the larger drama of the outside world to bear without shattering the atmosphere of isolation on board the ship. The composer John Adams and the stage director Peter Sellars (who instigated the work's creation and staged its first productions) both cited as their models the Bach passions and religious works from other cultures—all models that combine narration and enactment, dialogue and commentary. The librettist, Alice Goodman, asserted that she constructed the text on a more novelistic narrative model, and the narrative structure is in fact complex.[31] The narrators are certain characters: those who survived to tell their stories when the ordeal was over. When those characters are relating what happened, as opposed to acting their roles within the event, it is as if they are reporting on the experience to the press, or testifying later at the trials of the hijackers. In fact, when the opera was adapted into a movie (directed by Penny Woodcock) in 2003, this alternation in types of speech was highlighted by an alternation of shots from the dock in Egypt, showing the disembarked passengers telling reporters their experience, with shots back on the ship, showing them living through the experience. This cinematic fluidity of location necessarily deprives the movie of the claustrophic concentration that marks the staged version.

The "reporting" side of the opera emphasizes the human-interest nature of the story, reminding us that the human-interest story has always been a journalistic genre. At the same time, connecting the characters who survived with the news audience emphasizes the wider political context of the event. In the staged version neither the hijackers nor the hostages receive any evidence of how the media is representing their situation or what public opinion makes of it. But between the scenes choruses tell their own stories, which may be regarded as background to and reflection on the hijacking of the *Achille Lauro*: historical background (the Chorus of the Exiled Palestinians and the Chorus of the Exiled Jews), biblical analogy (the Chorus of Hagar and the Angel), and reflections on the universality of human experience (the Ocean Chorus, Desert Chorus, Night Chorus, and Day Chorus). The wider context that the opera proposes for its audience to consider, then, is not so much a political way to identify the

The cruise ship *Achille Lauro*, the stage for the actual hijacking drama on which Adams's *The Death of Klinghoffer* is based, in a news photo taken on October 1, 1985, when hijackers, crew, and surviving passengers disembarked in Port Said, Egypt.

Peter Turnley/Corbis

issues at stake as a poetic way to identify a ground of common experience between people who are inclined to fear and hate and punish each other for being different.

Poetic insight also emerges from the disconcerting thoughts and feelings the characters display, either in moving through events on the ship or in recollecting them. The first scene of action begins, for instance, with the Captain describing how he learned that his ship had been taken over (Act 1, scene 1: "It was just after one fifteen"). But before he really gets started on that story, he falls into reflections about how life at sea differs from life on land, singing to an atmospheric marine accompaniment of rolling string arpeggios and gull-like oboe intervals. What does this introduction tell us? Is it important for us to understand that at sea "good and evil are not abstract"? Or are we supposed to gather that our Captain is too much of a dreamer to cope with the coming crisis? Or is it crucial to the story that the hijacking crept up on everyone when their minds were on other things?

What people's minds were on, all the way through the hijacking, turns out to be the heart of the story this opera tells. There are, of course, tense exchanges. In one of these (Act 2, scene 1) the most vicious of the hijackers, referred to as Rambo, provokes Leon Klinghoffer, confined to his wheelchair, with anti-Semitic taunts and physical threats. In another (Act 2, scene 2), just after Klinghoffer is shot, the hijacker Mamoud tells the Captain they intend to go on killing a passenger every fifteen minutes. Such exchanges remind the audience of the fear that rules the hostages every second of their two-day captivity. But two days of enforced idleness make some very long, empty hours for strained minds to fill, and Goodman and Adams take the opportunity to show us how differently people respond to the challenge.

They let the hijackers reveal something about what kind of men they are and what might have drawn them into the life of the terrorist. Of these, Mamoud seems the reflective one because we catch him musing in quiet moments, while guarding the equally reflective Captain. In a long aria, "Now it is night" (beginning of Act 1, scene 2), sung as he tunes a radio to bring in stations from Lebanon that play his favorite songs, his analysis of what he likes about the songs ("It's good that these songs are sad") lead him in to the brutal saga of loss that constitutes his family history. At the end of the same scene ("Those birds flying above us") he compares the morality of birds ("Ritual song defends their nesting grounds") favorably with that of humans. These metaphorical turns of thought, along with the

long, elaborate phrases to which he sings them and the equally elaborate melodic lines or dignified chords accompanying his phrases, all paint him as the poet among the hijackers. The leader Molqi, by contrast, reveals his commitment to the Palestinian cause only in the blunt rhetoric he shouts to the hostages ("We are men of ideals!"). Rambo reveals his pathology in his abuse of Klinghoffer. The female voice of the fourth hijacker, Omar, indicates that he is really just a boy trying mightily to prove himself a man. We do not learn what has brought any of them to the point of killing for their cause (any more than we learn what makes a killer of Wozzeck or Peter Grimes or Katerina Izmailova), but we get a sense, especially from Mamoud's arias, that the four Palestinians, despite their utterly different characters, share a life experience that could well bring them to a shared course of action.

None of the passengers shows as reflective a nature as the Captain or Mamoud. What makes them so affecting is precisely that they confront the hijacking—and with it the possibility of their untimely deaths—so prosaically. They remind us that in the same situation our minds would likely be occupied with mundane rather than heroic concerns. A Swiss grandmother (Act 1, scene 1) recounts how she kept her grandson calm by what we might consider small-minded devices, and she admits with shame that she thought, "At least we are not Jews." An elderly Austrian woman, who happened to be in her stateroom when the hijacking was launched, reports (Act 1, scene 2) that she decided to hide there and wait out the crisis. Her thoughts, she tells us, were fixed on the details of surviving, like rationing her fruit and chocolate to last as long as possible. She is at the same time the character in the opera who speaks most straightforwardly about death: "I have no fear of death. I'd rather die alone, if I must, though I'd hate to drown."

One of the most remarkable features of this opera is the way in which Adams sometimes overlays the testimony of these passengers with other kinds of speech: Molqi's real-time commands or the Captain's indeterminate-time musings. In purely musical terms these moments may sound like those traditional operatic ensembles in which characters voice (ostensibly to themselves) conflicting responses to the same turn of events. The overlaid speeches of Molqi and the Swiss grandmother, for instance, are about the chaos at the beginning of the hijacking. But Molqi's speech is in real time (his initial orders and explanations to the Captain), and the grandmother's is recollection in the aftermath of the hijacking (see Example 13.3). Their duet, sung over a neutral accompaniment that is no more associated with one of them than with the other, is like a split-screen effect in a movie, indicating here a difference in both place and time. It brings experiencing and reporting momentarily together. But hearing these two sets of words from two different time frames can also make us realize that the minds of the hostages and hostage takers were largely in two different worlds.

13.3 Adams, *The Death of Klinghoffer*: Act 1, "Horrible, horrible"

Expressing the here and now Leon Klinghoffer and his wife Marilyn are as mundane in their thoughts as any of the other passengers; they don't know he is going to be killed and she is going to be widowed. Sitting on deck in his wheelchair under the blazing sun, he speaks his mind to Rambo without giving a thought to the best way to deal with a hostage taker, let alone a sadistic one. When Rambo finishes his anti-Semitic diatribe, Klinghoffer can say only, "You're crazy." He then turns to his wife and tries to cheer her up: "We'll bring home a tan anyway." As he is wheeled away, he says to her, "I should have worn a hat." We are reminded of the power that the here and now has over people when danger presses on them.

Though Klinghoffer is never poetic, he becomes poeticized when he is dead. We don't see him get shot, but a long stately aria (Aria of the Falling Body: Gymnopédie) makes a slow-motion ritual of his body being dropped over the side of the ship (or, in the movie adaptation, of his body and wheelchair sinking into the sea). The body of Klinghoffer is now represented by both a dancer and the original singer, the dancer dragging the singer, who

sings impersonal words about going away and leaving possessions behind. Those words resemble the texts of the choruses more than the words of any living character. And the orchestra plays a dance of slow but inexorable sinking, the dance of the corpse doing what none of the living characters can do: freeing itself from the prison—the stage—of the ship.

With *The Death of Klinghoffer*, much more than with any other opera considered in this chapter, it is unclear whose story we are mainly hearing. Is it the story of the hijackers, who commit the act we are scrutinizing? The story of the passengers, whose responses to that act draw our sympathy? Or is this the human-interest story of both groups, thrown together by chance and by force? The ending gives one answer, but does so by excluding so many of the recurring elements of the work that we might well distrust it. All the characters besides Leon Klinghoffer do get off the ship alive, though the opera does not mark that event. The hijackers disappear from the story without being accounted for. But the Captain stays on board and has Marilyn Klinghoffer brought to him so that he can give her the news that has been kept from her until now. The opera ends with her grief-stricken response, which makes her story seem like the real point of the opera.

In a still from Penny Woodcock's 2003 movie version of *The Death of Klinghoffer*, Tom Randle as Molqi, leader of the hijackers, takes aim at wheelchair-bound hostage Leon Klinghoffer (Sanford Sylvan) aboard the cruise ship *Achille Lauro*.

© Joshua Paul, courtesy Channel 4, UK

Like her husband and the other passengers, she has been occupied with mundane concerns before this. She in particular has been occupied with pain, her husband's and her own: she evidently suspects that she has cancer. On learning of Leon's death, she cannot easily leave thoughts of the here and now behind. In fact, the news reminds her that she has not been keeping her mind on the big issues:

> We heard them fire.
> It didn't register.
> And Leon Klinghoffer,
> My husband,
> My best friend,
> Is killed by a punk
> While I think
> Of this and that.

A chorus of women joins her aria, and at times takes it over, wailing what might be her lamentations. But in the end we hear her solitary voice, drained of feeling, singing in recitative style, that operatic equivalent of plain speech: "They should have killed me. I wanted to die." The political context of events—something she never admitted into her thoughts—is

banished from this ending. The choral voices we heard lamenting a moment before, which raised poetic questions of universal meaning all through the opera, are now banished as well. The reflections of the reflective characters are gone. All that remains is an impassive report from a broken heart.

FURTHER READING

On *Jenůfa*, John Tyrrell, ed., *Janáček's Operas: A Documentary Account* (Princeton: Princeton University Press, 1992). On Berg's works, Anthony Pople, ed., *The Cambridge Companion to Berg* (Cambridge and New York: Cambridge University Press, 1997). On *Wozzeck*, Douglas Jarman, *Alban Berg: "Wozzeck"* (Cambridge and New York: Cambridge University Press, 1989). On Gershwin's life and career, Howard Pollack, *George Gershwin: His Life and Work* (Berkeley and Los Angeles: University of California Press, 2006); Larry Starr, *George Gershwin* (New Haven and London: Yale University Press, 2011).

On Britten's life and career, Humphrey Carpenter, *Benjamin Britten: A Biography* (New York: C. Scribner's Sons, 1992). On *Peter Grimes*, Philip Brett, *Benjamin Britten: "Peter Grimes"* (Cambridge and New York: Cambridge University Press, 1983). On Shostakovich's life and career, Laurel E. Fay, *Shostakovich: A Life* (Oxford and New York: Oxford University Press, 2000). On Poulenc's life and career, Carl B. Schmidt, *Entrancing Muse: A Documented Biography of Francis Poulenc* (Hillsdale, N.Y.: Pendragon Press, 2001). On John Adams's works, Thomas May, ed., *The John Adams Reader: Essential Writings on an American Composer* (Pompton Plains, N.J.: Amadeus, 2006).

FOR RESEARCH AND REFLECTION

1. Take a recent story about an ordinary person from the news, and design an opera about it. What makes your story suitable for operatic treatment, and what would make it difficult to turn into a successful opera?

2. Jenůfa is not a saint, but her twin acts of forgiveness in the last scene produce what seem like miraculous effects on her relationships with others and on the character of the music. What other characters in human-interest operas have saintly qualities, and how does their music give them a saintly aura?

3. The protagonists of human-interest operas are victims of social and political circumstances, but not necessarily sympathetic characters in themselves. What kind of bond does the music create between the audience and a given protagonist, and how does it do that?

4. How has dance, sometimes merely a pleasant diversion in opera, been put to the service of the drama in these works?

5. In most human-interest operas the music is more in acting style than in singing style. Why might that be appropriate? In what kinds of situations does singing style nevertheless emerge?

6. How do the protagonist and the chorus relate to each other musically in a given human-interest opera?

 Additional resources are available at wwnorton.com/studyspace.

CHAPTER 14

Operas of Dreaming

Preview: Saariaho, *L'Amour de loin*

L'Amour de loin (Love from Afar, 2000), an opera in French by the Finnish composer Kaija Saariaho, takes us far from the world of the human-interest opera. This work represents the main alternative strand in the twentieth-century repertory: operas about extraordinary people who inhabit dream realms. These may be symbolic characters—Everyman or Everywoman—who live in undefined or fabled times and places. They may be adults lost in a poetically or satirically nightmarish world. They may be children lost in an imaginary world until it is time for them to grow up. Or they may have actually lived, in which case they are apt to be gifted with extraordinary powers to imagine, to create, to transform the world around them: artists, saints, charismatic leaders.

Saariaho's opera brings to life an artist from history: a twelfth-century troubadour (aristocratic songwriter in southern France) named Jaufré Rudel, the lord of Blaye, whose half-dozen surviving love lyrics include a famous song about "love from afar": "Lanquan li jorn son lanc en may" ("When the days are long, in May"), which Saariaho weaves into the opera. A later medieval biography, short and impossibly romantic, provided Saariaho's librettist, Amin Maalouf, with the basis for a story about the power of a songwriter

Dawn Upshaw as the Countess Clémence in her tower, in Saariaho's *L'Amour de loin*, staged by Peter Sellars at the Santa Fe Opera, New Mexico, 2002.
© Ken Howard, Santa Fe Opera

to imagine an object of love, to bring her to life in words and melody, to become possessed by the idea of her, and to inspire a corresponding love in her, purely by means of his song. *L'Amour de loin* is like every opera of dreaming in dramatizing the power of the imagination to transform unreality into reality. Some follow the course of a dream from wishing to fulfillment, some from entering the dream to escaping from it, some from the casting of a spell to the breaking of it.

This work begins with the troubadour Jaufré falling in love with the idea of a woman who lives so far away that he can assure himself she does not really exist: "Never shall this lady be mine," he sings, "but I am hers forever" (Act 1, scene 2). The transformation of his dream requires not only an actual lady, but a means of communication between them. For this purpose Maalouf and Saariaho create a go-between, the Pilgrim (a male role performed by a female singer), who hears his song and sails from France to Tripoli in the Holy Land (the first of several trips back and forth), where he sings it to the Countess Clémence, assuring her that she is the object of the songwriter's love.

Clémence, a Frenchwoman who lives exiled in Tripoli and feels incapable of being loved, finds the same kind of safety in her troubadour lover's distance that he does in hers:

Troubadour, je ne suis belle que dans le miroir de tes mots.

Troubadour, I am beautiful only in the mirror of your words.
(Act 2, scene 2)

But Jaufré is scandalized when the Pilgrim returns to report that he has sung her the song, and doubly so when he says he "merely hummed it": "Merely!" exclaims the composer, proud of his melody. His outrage is soon transformed into a belief that if his beloved is going to hear his love songs, "she must hear them from my own mouth" (Act 3, scene 1). And so, while Clémence is content with a love fed by distance and music ("Between our two lives sails music," Act 3, scene 2), Jaufré sets out across the sea with the Pilgrim to declare his love in person. Like many other operas of dreaming, this one turns into a quest.

As he sails, Jaufré is subject to illness and dreams (Act 4, scene 2), from which we learn that his love will not survive the transformation it is about to undergo ("I'm afraid of not finding her and afraid of finding her"). He arrives in Tripoli at the point of death, and he and Clémence declare their love for each other as he dies in her arms. One final transformation remains. Clémence, who curses God upon Jaufré's death, quickly comes to accept God as love and pardon and passion and ends by declaring: "You are the love from afar" (Act 5, scene 3). Having first fulfilled Jaufré's quest to exchange

Operatic Technology and Media

Before 1900 the opera house was the proving ground of many innovations in theatrical spectacle. Since then, it has been a conservative place for stage technology and especially for sound technology, shunning new instruments and systems of amplification. Electronic supertitles, however, have been widely adopted since they were introduced at the Canadian Opera Company in 1983. These have made opera comprehensible to audiences, whatever language it is sung in, diminishing the pressure on companies to perform foreign-language operas in translation, while significantly boosting the popularity of opera all over the world.

Domestic performance of operatic excerpts has always been part of the life of opera, but commercial audio recordings of excerpts, available since around 1900, created a new and wholly aural version of the public spectacle in private spaces. Regular radio broadcasts (starting at the Metropolitan Opera in 1931) did the same. Television broadcasts began on a limited scale in the late 1930s, and video recordings became available in the 1980s. Both TV and video reunited sight with sound, creating a new paradox: the whole spectacle became available in intimate spaces. Sound and video recordings both contributed vitally to the teaching of opera as an academic subject. By the early twenty-first century operagoing could mean going to your local cinema, and operagoing of any sort could be just one facet of a life rich in opera.

his distant love for a physical one, she now apparently denies that quest by transferring the source of her "love from afar" to God.

Dreams were long interpreted as valuable symbolic bearers of secret meaning. In ancient stories (like Jacob's Ladder in the biblical Book of Genesis) dreams are visited on humans from the divine or spirit world, often as portents. By the twentieth century dreams were being considered as products of the dreamer's own uncontrolled imagination, as symbolic bearers of the secrets of past experiences and present desires and anxieties. Psychologists—most famously Sigmund Freud in *The Interpretation of Dreams* (1900)—developed systems for decoding the symbols and elucidating the patterns in their patients' dreams. Artists, both anticipating and drawing on these new concepts, began to construct works more and more self-consciously on the illogical logic and defamiliarized familiarities that they assumed to be the markers of everyone's dreams. Dreams in operas unlock secrets of how people channel their desires and anxieties into creativity.

Because dream operas are concerned with the representation of the imagined, the unreal, and the symbolic, they tend to be more experimental or at least less straightforward in their dramaturgy than human-interest operas.

A single singer is more apt to play several roles. Time and space may be jumbled. *L'Amour de loin*, for instance, lays out time and space vaguely. The individual roles, just three in number, are stably cast, but the cross-gender casting of the Pilgrim creates an ambiguity in his dealings with both Jaufré and Clémence. There is a different ambiguity in the choruses, a male chorus that challenges Jaufré's seriousness about a lover he has imagined and a female chorus that challenges Clémence in the same way; at the end the two choruses unite in expressing a conventional morality. But since the choruses never appear onstage to confront the principals, their voices could easily represent the principals' own doubts.

Because dream operas may have historic settings, they are more apt to employ historic musical styles than human-interest operas are. In *L'Amour de loin*, the melodic style of the medieval troubadour, sung by all three principals, creates a language of love that they share long before the two lovers meet. We also feel how possessed both Jaufré and Clémence are by their dreamed love, in the obstinacy of the musical language: the repetitions of simple motives, the sustaining of chords, the thick clustering of instrumental sounds, the unyielding sonority of the electronic instruments in the orchestral mix, and the singers' long, long lines. For four acts, that sound accumulates within it the sexual tension of the distance they keep between each other, until that tension is released, and they surrender their dream of love from afar, when they finally meet on the beach in Tripoli and he dies at her kiss.

Fantasies of Desire and Attachment

Fatal Attractions: Debussy, *Pelléas et Mélisande*

The fatal attraction of Jaufré toward a woman he has never met connects *L'Amour de loin* thematically to other operas of dreaming, from as much as a century earlier. Many of these derive their dream nature from one character's quest to unlock another's secret, to know the unknowable. That is the fatal attraction. In Giacomo Puccini's *Turandot* (unfinished at the composer's death in 1924, completed by Franco Alfano, and performed in 1926) it is the quest of the Tartar prince Calaf to answer the three riddles with which the Chinese princess Turandot tests any man who wants to marry her. In Béla Bartók's *Duke Bluebeard's Castle* (*A Kékszakállú herceg vára*, 1918) the Duke's new wife is drawn

to her husband by rumors that he kills every woman he marries; he is drawn to her by his instinct that despite his warnings she will pursue the rumors until she makes herself another victim. In Leoš Janáček's *The Makropulos Case* (*Věc Makropulos*, 1926) and Alban Berg's *Lulu* (unfinished at the composer's death in 1935, completed by Friedrich Cerha, and performed in 1979) the fatal spell that the leading female character casts on men depends on something secret about her identity and nature. And in Claude Debussy's *Pelléas et Mélisande* (1902) two brothers share a fatal attraction to the same woman of mystery.

An "atmosphere of dreams" The first scene of *Pelléas* establishes both a dreamlike setting and the secrecy of Mélisande's identity. The scene is set deep in a forest, where the widowed prince of Allemonde, Golaud, has gotten lost hunting a wild boar and comes upon Mélisande, weeping by a spring. She is fearful ("Don't touch me," she keeps saying) and evasive about what has made her afraid and whom she is fleeing. When Golaud spots a crown fallen in the water and offers to retrieve it for her, she says it is the crown that "he" gave her, but won't say who "he" is and protests that she would rather die than have it back. Golaud asks how old she is, and she answers that she is starting to get cold. The most he can get out of her is her name. Yet he not only refuses to let her stay in the darkening forest; he marries her. Six months after this first encounter, as we learn in the next scene, he has still learned nothing about her, and we never learn more than he does.

The mysteriousness of Mélisande is inseparable from what Debussy called his opera's "dream atmosphere." In a note published at the time of the premiere, he claimed to have derived that atmosphere, along with a very human mode of expression, from the play by his contemporary Maurice Maeterlinck that he set verbatim (allowing for some cuts):

> The drama of *Pelléas* [Maeterlinck's play]—which despite its atmosphere of dreams contains much more humanity than those so-called documents of real life [and here he could mean human-interest stories in any medium]—seemed to suit my purpose admirably. It has an evocative language whose sensibility is able to find an extension in the music and in the orchestral setting [*décor orchestral*] . . . the characters of this opera try to sing like real people. . . . A character cannot always express himself melodically: the *dramatic* melody has to be quite different from what is generally called melody.[1]

How could Debussy make it seem as if his characters were singing like real people at the same time that they inhabited an "atmosphere of dreams"?

Pelléas et Mélisande
PRINCIPAL CHARACTERS

- **Arkel**, King of Allemonde
- **Golaud and Pelléas**, half-brothers, grandsons of Arkel
- **Geneviève**, their mother
- **Mélisande**, Golaud's wife
- **Yniold**, Golaud's young son by his previous wife

Paul Gay as Golaud, lost on a hunt in the forest, encounters Mélisande (Patricia Petitbon) in Act 1, scene 1, of Debussy's *Pelléas et Mélisande*, staged by Peter Stein at the Opéra de Lyon, France, 2003–4.

© Gérard Ameellem/Lyon-France

His account of "dramatic melody" makes it sound like the acting style of the earliest operas: not songful in an ordinary sense, but closely tied to the sound of spoken language. In fact, the vocal writing in *Pelléas et Mélisande* observes many of the rules of that acting style, and with almost no lapses—something Monteverdi never even set out to do. Debussy's word setting is strictly syllabic, with considerable intoning on a single pitch, shifting at times to a new pitch that is rarely more than a fourth higher or lower, just as a speaking voice would rise and fall in the course of a sentence, and all in a fairly even rhythm, faster or slower according to the character's state of mind. Yet his *Pelléas* never sounds like early opera, above all because his orchestra provides a far fuller "setting"—fuller in figuration (patterns of moving parts), orchestration, rich harmonies, and recurring motives—than any early opera, even while it is designed never to obscure the singers' words.

The texture of this opera is in a sense a Wagnerian web of orchestral motives more or less associated with characters or ideas, against which the characters sing; they are free of such repeating motives because their dramatic melody is tied at every moment to their words. Debussy's orchestral motives, however, all seem to come not from the same family, as Wagner's do, but from different musical worlds, each with its own atmosphere. In the first six measures of the Prelude, for instance, we hear two such different motives. The first (mm. 1–4 in Example 14.1) is a somber, modally harmonized chant motive in the low strings and bassoons that transports us to a time long ago and a place deep in the forest. The second (mm. 5–6) is a restless motive in higher woodwinds, each instrument vacillating between two adjacent pitches; collectively they hover around an unsettling chord built from the whole-tone scale (a scale in which each note is a whole step from the next). This motive will be associated with the character Golaud from the moment he begins to sing.

What makes this second motive in particular different from Wagner's orchestral motives is its melodic nature. The vacillation between its two pitches is controlled by a changing rhythm that throws first one note and then the other into relief. It embodies energy without direction. But while its distinctive rhythms and harmonization make it count as a melody here, the two-note structure allows it to slip out of a melodic role and into the background of our consciousness when it is stripped of those distinguishing features. A few measures later, when the curtain has risen and Golaud enters, we hear the two notes turned into a bass line that vacillates in a

14.1 Debussy, *Pelléas et Mélisande:* Prelude

steady triplet rhythm, so that the two notes are still thrown alternately into relief (see Example 14.2). Now instead of forming a motive that can stand for Golaud, they create a backdrop, a décor, to his steps and words as well as a bass to the chant motive that returns from the opening of the Prelude. But this décor is like a wallpaper pattern or natural backdrop in a painting by Henri Matisse or Édouard Vuillard, French painters contemporary with Debussy: a background that demands attention as forcefully as the human figures it surrounds. The orchestral motives constantly devolve in this way into the restless rhythmic figuration of a single instrumental line or a throbbing progression of offbeat chords, allowing the voices to make their words clearly heard. In one form or the other the orchestral "background" is always looming in the foreground, always creating the atmosphere of dreams in which the characters breathe, think, and move.

14.2 Debussy, *Pelléas et Melisande:* Beginning of Act 1

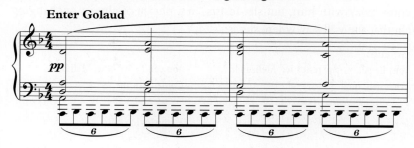

A "palpitating voice" When the English poet Arthur Symons saw a performance of Maeterlinck's play in English, he gave this extraordinary account of the speaking voice of Mrs. Patrick Campbell, the actress playing Mélisande: "Her palpitating voice, in which there is something like the throbbing of a wounded bird, seemed to speak the simple and beautiful words as if they had never been said before."[2]

In Debussy's opera this effect comes equally from the singers' voices and the sounds of the orchestra. The orchestral music does not address the audience on a separate plane from the characters' words, as soundtrack music in a movie does. Instead, vocal phrases ride on the throbbing of the orchestra, contributing their share to the creation of the atmosphere of dreams. Each vocal phrase has a distinctive profile, often a simple rise and fall, like a breath, allowing the actors to "sing like real people." And the cumulative effect of their phrases, drawing breath from the same palpitating orchestral atmosphere without breaking into song (except once, at the beginning of Act 3), is hypnotic. The characters, while casting this hypnotic spell on the audience, do not seem hypnotized; they seem like real people trapped in a dream, inhabiting the "hermetic world of Allemonde," as Roger Nichols calls it.[3]

The effect of Debussy's vocal writing in *Pelléas* is easy to mock. In fact, Igor Stravinsky described people in the foyers at early performances of the opera "making fun of the *récit* style and intoning little sentences à la *Pelléas* to each other."[4] But that mockery is an unacknowledged admission that the style is achieving its paradoxical effect: for all its commitment to clear declamation over melody, it can get under your skin. In a way it resembles a style that it does not sound at all like: the equally speech-bound acting style of French opera in the period from Lully to Rameau. There, vocal embellishments on downbeats, resolving on after-beats, incessantly produce an alternation of tension and release as sensually addicting in its way as Debussy's rhythm of rising and falling breaths.

An example of Debussy's method can be found at the end of the first scene, that first encounter between Golaud and Mélisande. Having failed to learn anything about Mélisande except her name, Golaud has invited her to come away with him, but she insists, in a phrase of almost unchanging pitch, that she will stay where she is:

Golaud:
Vous ne pouvez pas rester ici, Mélisande. You can't stay here, Mélisande.
Venez avec moi. Come with me.

Mélisande:
Je reste ici. I am staying here.

He counters that she cannot stay in the forest by herself at night:

Vous aurez peur, toute seule,	*You will be afraid, all alone.*
On ne sait pas ce qu'il y a ici . . .	*Who knows what's out here . . .*
toute la nuit . . . toute seule.	*all night long . . . all alone.*

Agitated whole-tone lines and chords support his voice. But his vocal phrases move at a measured pace, in a steady rise and fall, within a comfortable range, making his voice a source of reassurance against the terrors of the forest at night. Even the whole-tone harmonies melt into more tonal chords as he renews his invitation to her: "Ce n'est pas possible. Mélisande, venez, donnez-moi la main" ("That's not possible. Melisande, come, give me your hand"). But she is not ready for that. Instead, in one last act of resistance she exclaims for the last time, "Don't touch me!" ("Ne me touchez pas!"), her voice leaping to a high F-sharp. Golaud's reassurance grows more insistent:

Ne criez pas . . .	*Don't cry out . . .*
Je ne vous toucherai plus.	*I won't touch you again.*
Mais venez avec moi.	*But come with me.*

And then something extraordinary happens. His words continue in the same vein:

La nuit sera très noire et très froide.	*The night will be very black and very cold.*
Venez avec moi.	*Come with me.*

But Golaud's voice now intones slowly, staying on a single pitch for almost two measures. And his orchestral music is changed quite magically: the first violins in high octaves return to the somber scene-setting motive that opened the whole opera (Example 14.1), while the flutes play the vacillating triplet figuration that accompanied his entrance (Example 14.2), and the second violins play the same notes but in a slower and simpler rhythm, warbling eighth notes. In the midst of the characters' tense exchange, this is a moment of ravishing stillness and delicacy. It evidently belongs with his words describing the night.

Yet while his words suggest that the blackness and coldness of the night are something to flee, this music—including his own hushed intonation, swimming in the orchestral radiance—portrays it as enticing. In its poetry of the night Golaud's music, as opposed to his words, offers Mélisande his love. She cuts his poetry short, but with a question that allows him to humble himself before her:

Mélisande:	
Où allez-vous?	*Where are you going?*

Golaud:

Je ne sais pas . . .	*I don't know . . .*
Je suis perdu aussi . . .	*I'm lost too . . .*

And at that she allows herself to be enticed away.

In a drama that is going to deal with a husband suspecting his wife of adultery, it is important for the audience to feel what the relationship was like before things started going bad. Verdi accomplishes that at the end of the first act of *Otello* with the long, reminiscence-filled love duet of Otello and Desdemona. Here, at the end of the first scene of *Pelléas*, Debussy does the same with just three measures of sensuous night music in which Golaud's attraction to Mélisande silences all his questions, followed by a couple of measures in which Mélisande without saying a word goes along with his love. Her feelings, which he does not think to ask her about, remain her secret.

Interchangeable brothers: Pelléas Golaud and Mélisande go away and marry; after six months they return, and Golaud's half-brother Pelléas meets Mélisande and is also attracted to her. The fact that they are half-brothers signals that they serve interchangeable functions in the dream. In a sense the opera examines two opposed ways in which a man might pursue the mysterious attraction of Mélisande. But their competition is what makes the attraction fatal: eventually Golaud catches Pelléas and Mélisande declaring their love, kills Pelléas, and wounds Mélisande in a way that may or may not cause her death at the end of the opera. That too is a mystery.

The structure of scenes emphasizes the dreamlike interchangeability of the two men. In most scenes we see Mélisande with either Golaud or Pelléas but not with both, except for two scenes that end with Golaud intruding into an intimate exchange she is having with Pelléas (Act 3, scene 1; and Act 4, scene 4). Other than those two moments, there is only a pair of short scenes (Act 3, scenes 2 and 3) in which Golaud and Pelléas appear together onstage. Since the opera consists largely of the two parallel tracks of attraction to Mélisande—Pelléas's increasingly open admission of love and Golaud's increasingly desperate suspicion—it may be helpful to follow them separately through most of the opera.

Six of the fifteen scenes bring Mélisande together with Pelléas. In the first of these (Act 1, scene 3) she has just come for the

The set for the scene at the "Blindmen's Well," Act 2, scene 1, designed by Lucien Jusseaume, in the original production of *Pelléas et Mélisande* at the Opéra Comique, Paris, 1902.

© Lebrecht Music & Arts

first time to the family castle. Like the first scene with Golaud, this one establishes a starting point for a relationship, but the possibilities are hedged in by Mélisande's married status and the presence of his mother. There is only pleasant family idleness in this scene, three people standing in front of their castle, looking out to sea, until the mother suddenly leaves Mélisande and Pelléas by themselves. At that moment the violins play a motive (Example 14.3) first heard in the Prelude, described by Debussy as Mélisande's "initial theme" and sounded here, as there, over a whole-tone chord.[5] Its warning tone, heard at this awkward moment between the new bride and a brother-in-law who seems more her age and type than the man she has married, marks the moment as significant. The motive will sound throughout the opera, often with a warning tone. Mélisande freely lets Pelléas take her by the arm as they walk back to the castle (something she emphatically did not do when she first met Golaud), and she expresses alarm when he announces that he may be going away the next day.

14.3   Debussy, *Pelléas et Mélisande*: Act 1, Mélisande's initial theme

The next scene (Act 2, scene 1) brings them together again, and that in itself suggests that they find comfort in each other's company. They visit what he calls the "Blindmen's Well," and she tosses her wedding ring in the air until it falls into the well. Pelléas is practically a bystander to what she displays about her feelings toward Golaud here. Mélisande and Pelléas appear together again in Act 2, scene 3. She has lied to Golaud about where and how she lost the ring, and he has told her to go find it. He can't go with her because he has fallen from his horse and injured himself, and so she and Pelléas turn up at a cave by the sea in the dark, looking for what they know is not there. At the sight of three paupers asleep in the cave, she leads Pelléas away. Nothing happens, but the scene has brought them to a place where the dark and threatening side of nature—evoked by Debussy's lapping musical waves and cavernous sonorities—draws them ominously close together. Here Pelléas displays for the first time the protective interest in Mélisande that his brother showed

Édouard Vuillard painted the "Blindmen's Well" scene from *Pelléas et Mélisande* as a wall decoration in the foyer of the Comédie des Champs-Élysées, a theater that opened in Paris in 1913. The painting was one of a series commemorating famous theatrical productions, and Vuillard seems to have worked from a photograph of the original production, to judge by Jusseaume's set. At the same time, he gave the scene an "atmosphere of dreams" appropriate to Debussy's music.

Scala/White Images/Art Resource, NY

in the forest, and she for the first time resists him the way she resisted Golaud. The interchangeability in this opera is not all on the brothers' side, it seems.

The next scene (Act 3, scene 1) features more song and dance than any other. It opens with the hypnotic sounds of a summer night, then with Mélisande leaning out her tower window and singing an unaccompanied song in medieval style. Pelléas appears at the foot of the tower, full of himself, bursting with love for Mélisande and heedless of what danger that could create. Mélisande now seems conscious of the danger. But the night and its music, much of it in a meter that sways effortlessly between duple and triple rhythms, belong to him. After his entrance she drops her singing and gives herself over to fearful protests as his lines grow lyrical with excitement. When he can't persuade her to lean far enough out the window that he can touch her hand, her hair tumbles down instead and covers him. She is out of his reach, but that gives him the freedom to fondle her hair.

Much the same happens in the music. Pelléas sings a bizarre solo love "duet," an unrestrained rhapsody to Mélisande about her hair ("It loves me more than you"), while she cries to him to let her go

Denise Duval as Mélisande and Henri Gui as Pelléas in the Tower scene (Act 3, scene 1) of *Pelléas et Melisande,* **as staged at the Opéra Comique, Paris, in 1962. The design gives the scene a fairy-tale atmosphere.**

Roger Viollet/Getty Images

("Laisse-moi, laisse-moi") as insistently as she once cried to Golaud not to touch her. Her warning that "someone might come"—heralded by a remarkably threatening close interval from two bassoons—draws a response from him that is careless to the point of cruelty: he ties her hair to the branch of a tree and keeps singing. Meanwhile a solo viola joins his voice, completing the texture of the duet that is not a duet. Her complaint that he is hurting her does not get him to leave her alone; her doves suddenly taking flight do that. But then Golaud arrives, denounces them as "children," and leads Pelléas away.

Interchangeable brothers: Golaud From this midpoint let us go back and trace Golaud's path, especially his meetings with Mélisande since their first encounter in the forest. Immediately after she lets her ring fall into the well, she goes into the castle and tends Golaud, who has fallen off his horse (Act 2, scene 2). She suddenly bursts into tears, and in the process of asking why she is unhappy, he takes her hand and discovers that her wedding ring is no longer on her finger. From being a solicitous husband, he now turns in a flash into a furious one (like Otello pursuing the handkerchief that Desdemona lost), though he does not yet suspect that any attraction is developing between Mélisande and Pelléas. Like Pelléas's passion, Golaud's suspicion builds slowly from scene to scene. In Act 3 he has no scene alone with Mélisande, but he does (as we've seen) discover Pelléas wrapping himself in Mélisande's hair at the tower, and though he scolds them for behaving like children, from then on he worries about worse than that.

The next two scenes form the sole encounter of the two brothers without Mélisande. In the first (Act 3, scene 2) Golaud leads Pelléas into the crypt beneath the castle, where Debussy's music of deep, hushed, unclear sonorities (the music of virtually the whole scene is constructed from whole-tone scales) creates a threatening atmosphere worthy of Edgar Allan Poe, a writer Debussy greatly admired. In fact, the unprecedented concentration on a single, unsettling harmony in this scene makes the crypt seem like the source of everything fearful and secretive in the opera. But here, where there is a real danger of Pelléas hurting himself or falling into a bottomless pit in the dark, Golaud actually protects him by taking his arm—treating him, that is, as interchangeable with Mélisande, whom both he and Pelleas have taken by the arm in previous scenes. It is only when they emerge from the crypt (scene 3), into the sunlight and sea-scented

Anne Sofie von Otter as Mélisande and William Burden as Pelléas in the Tower scene, staged by Jonathan Miller at the Metropolitan Opera in 2005. Here the staging emphasizes how the characters are locked away in separate mental worlds, even as Pelléas expresses his love.

© Marty Sohl, Metropolitan Opera

air (which through Debussy's exultant music we can feel revive Pelléas), that Golaud threatens Pelléas. He reveals his suspicions, tells him Mélisande is pregnant, and warns him to stay clear of her. In the two scenes together, mood and action are dissociated just as they might be in a dream.

Golaud is now looking for evidence of betrayal, and in Act 3, scene 4, Pelléas, ignoring his brother's warning, feeds his suspicions by visiting Mélisande in her room at night. The scene takes place on the ground just below the window of her room, where they are just out of sight of Golaud and his son Yniold, the principals in the scene, and out of our view as well. Yniold spends a lot of time with his uncle and stepmother, and Golaud pumps him for information about what he has seen going on between them. But Yniold is too young to understand what his father's questions are getting at, and in one of the longest exchanges in the opera he gives inconsistent and ambiguous answers, driving Golaud to greater and greater frustration.

True to the dream structure of the whole opera, this exchange shows Golaud displacing his fury against Pelléas and especially Mélisande onto his son. Debussy wrote the role of Yniold for a boy soprano (a voice in the same range as Mélisande's), and the sound of his sweet voice distills everything that makes her as well as him a vulnerable figure and everything about them both that frustrates Golaud. Golaud takes Yniold by the arm and hurts him, just as Pelléas hurt Mélisande when he pulled her hair and Golaud is soon to hurt her. Yniold self-consciously takes on the role of Mélisande when he tells his father that he saw her and Pelléas kiss once, and in reply to Golaud's demand to know how they kissed, he laughingly plants a kiss on his father's mouth. At the end of the scene Golaud lifts Yniold on his shoulders so that he can see into Mélisande's room. What Yniold reports is less than Golaud feared: she and Pelléas are standing in silence, looking at the light. Yet from this point Golaud is convinced, more from what he has imagined than from anything he, or we, can learn for sure, that Pelléas and Mélisande are lovers.

He displays that certainty when he enters a room where his grandfather, King Arkel, is conversing with Mélisande (Act 4, scene 2). He makes Mélisande fetch his sword and then insists that he is not going to kill her with it (just as he took Pelléas into the crypt and made a show of not threatening him there). Stung by Arkel's praise of her innocent eyes, Golaud launches into a tirade against her appearance of innocence, makes her kneel, grabs her long hair, and pulls her this way and that. This is the moment when the threatening music of the opera finally breaks into violence, and it is followed by the most painfully expressive of the orchestral interludes that Debussy wrote to allow set changes between the scenes. Mélisande has now

felt the brutality of Golaud's jealousy and knows that it will only get worse, while Pelléas knows nothing of it. We are ready to join the two of them (Act 4, scene 4) outside the castle, in the darkening garden where they have arranged to meet one last time before Pelléas is to set out on a long trip. In an hour the castle doors are due to be shut for the night.

Death and aftermath Mélisande is late, and as Pelléas waits for her, he admits that until now he has been playing childishly and has never even really looked into her eyes. He wants to capture her look and store it in his memory, tell her everything he has never told her, and leave. This soliloquy is one of the least dreamlike moments of the opera. Dream progressions are not narratives of growing up, becoming self-conscious, learning from experience, and moving on. Nevertheless, it is necessary for the dream structure of the scene that Pelléas's sense of being able to leave the past behind collides with Mélisande's fatalism as the victim of Golaud's violence. That collision is evident immediately. Pelléas is worried about the time left to them, worried they will be caught, anxious for her to move into the shadows, where they can't be seen from the castle. She says she wants to be seen.

Pelléas declares that this is the last time he will see her. He has to leave because — and here the orchestra drops out, as he kisses her abruptly — he loves her. She loves him too, she sings in a barely audible voice. But now, hearing the words he feared he might never hear and forgetting his resolution to move on, he launches into love music not so different from what he sang at the tower, poetic lines with a delicate lilt in their flow: "On dirait que ta voix a passé sur la mer au printemps!" ("It is as if your voice came over the sea in springtime!") Here too his phrases are formed into a "duet" by an instrumental line, because here too he is singing to her, not with her. This instrumental line is tossed from one wind instrument to another and later given to the violins and cellos as he grows passionately confident in her love. But he cuts himself short to ask her to step into the light, where they can see how happy they are. That thought shows how completely transformed he is since the beginning of the scene; he is now throwing away his careful, grown-up plans, all for a moment's unguarded embrace.

His declaration of love, meanwhile, has turned her cautious, and after earlier refusing to move out of the light, she now refuses to move out of the darkness. It may be that at first she was willing to risk being seen because her future looked so bleak anyway, but that now, feeling the depth of his love, she wants to survive with him. At any rate, over the warning motive from their first meeting (Example 14.3), she sings: "Je suis heureuse, mais je suis triste"

("I am happy, but I am sad"). Nothing in the whole opera is more dreamlike than this trading of roles, so sudden and so symmetrical.

At that moment they hear the castle doors creak shut, and they know they are trapped. Pelléas recognizes that his dream is shattered, and Mélisande reverts to her fatalism: now she repeats "Tant mieux!" ("So much the better") as frequently as she once repeated "Don't touch me!" or "Let me go!" As the violins rework the instrumental duet line from Pelléas's love music just before, he begins what will be a real love duet with Mélisande—"Ah! qu'il fait beau dans les ténèbres" ("Oh, how beautiful it is in the darkness"). But Mélisande hears Golaud creeping up on them, and though they try to conquer their fears by singing in alternating poetic lines, they break down in frantic whispers. Finally Mélisande frees them both from their fear with two more utterances of "So much the better!" They give themselves over to a fatal embrace and resume their duet. Now they sing with total abandon, though still without violating Debussy's notion of dramatic melody. Just as in the first scene he distilled the enchantment of the love duet from Verdi's *Otello* into a few measures, here he distills the ecstasy of an even longer love scene, the famous one in Wagner's *Tristan und Isolde* (1865), into a few phrases. These lovers even sing in octaves together for two measures before Golaud rushes in, kills Pelléas with his sword, and sends Mélisande fleeing in terror.

It is not just the track of Pelléas's pursuit of Mélisande that ends with his death; the spell of the whole dream seems to be broken. In the final scene (the single scene of Act 5) Golaud's track runs its course, but he has learned nothing. He continues to press Mélisande for her secrets, but she is even less capable of revealing them now. Having given birth to a baby girl, Mélisande is lying in bed, dying of unknown causes and delirious. "I can no longer say what I mean," she says. And so when Golaud insists that she tell him whether she loved Pelléas, her answer simply shows him the ambiguity of his question: "Mais oui; je l'ai aimé" ("But of course; I loved him"). And then she adds, confirming her delirium, "Where is he?" Golaud is silenced, and his quest to understand her ends when her life slips away. Two versions of a dream, two visions of how to unlock the secrets of Mélisande's heart, have ended, the first one successfully but fatally, and now the other emptily and fatally.

But from the start of Act 5 the music tells us that the whole act represents the aftermath of the dream. The singers carry on in the same acting style as before, but the strange, especially whole-tone harmonies that have given the whole opera up to this point its atmosphere of dreams, both frightening and magical, are now dissipated. Almost the only exceptions are a few phrases in

which Golaud raises his voice, as if to frighten Mélisande into telling him what he wants to know. Otherwise, the music is stiller and sweeter than any in the previous acts. It is music for an awakening from dream to calm reality. But it has a magic of its own, the magic of natural process. Before Mélisande dies, she holds her daughter, and once she is dead, King Arkel proclaims, "It is the turn of the poor little one." At this the harmony of the opera reaches its final cadence, but the orchestra plays on for a while, and in its lulling strains can be felt the onset of one last displacement: the displacement of one generation by the next.

Tests of Love: Strauss, *Die Frau ohne Schatten*

In other dream operas the lovers are involved not in a fatal attraction, but in a tested attachment. Two masterpieces on this theme are *Die Frau ohne Schatten* (*The Woman Without a Shadow*, 1919) by the German composer Richard Strauss and *The Rake's Progress* (1951) by the Russian composer Igor Stravinsky.

Tests of love are the stuff of fairy tales, and the librettist of *Die Frau ohne Schatten*, Hugo von Hofmannsthal, cooked up from elements of the world's fairy tales a story of two couples whose marriages are tested by childlessness. The Emperor and Empress of a mythical island empire are the lead couple. She—the daughter of Keikobad, ruler of the spirit world—once had the ability to transform herself at will into any creature. When the Emperor hunted her down as a gazelle, she turned back into a woman but lost the talisman that gave her the power to transform herself. Now she has been married for a year, but is neither quite a spirit nor quite human. Her lack of humanity is shown by the fact that she casts no shadow, and the voice of a falcon informs her that unless she can acquire a shadow in three days, she will not be able to bear children and her husband will turn to stone. Following the lead of her worldly old Nurse, she sets out on a quest into human society to find someone willing to sell his or her shadow.

Like legendary operas in the nineteenth century *Die Frau ohne Schatten* is filled with supernatural elements that are easily represented in storytelling, but can be daunting to represent when the story is dramatized. It is difficult, for instance, to show one character casting no shadow while all the others on the same stage cast unmistakable shadows. In the first scene the secret of the Empress's lack of shadow and the imminent danger to the Emperor's life is known only in the spirit world, and a falcon is sent as an emissary from that world to convey the knowledge to the Empress. The difficulty is to convey to the audience that the Empress, who herself comes

Inga Nielsen as the Empress listens to the Falcon's song (worded version sung by Elena Cassian), as the Nurse (Reinhild Runkel) looks on, in Act 1, scene 1, of *Die Frau ohne Schatten*, staged by Jean-Pierre Ponnelle at La Scala, Milan, in 1999.

Andrea Tamoni © Teatro alla Scala

from the spirit world, apprehends the falcon's message from its wordless twitterings, yet at the same time to make that message clear to the audience, who can understand it only through words. Strauss's solution is to announce the voice of the falcon wordlessly in the twittering monotone of the piccolo and other woodwind instruments, then have a singer imitate those sounds with words:

Die Frau wirft keinen Schatten,	*The woman casts no shadow,*
Der Kaiser muss versteinen!	*the Emperor must turn to stone!*

The sign that the Empress and even her Nurse understand this message is that they repeat the words at their own pitches, replicating the monotone but stripping it of its twitter, as if translating the words into their own terms.

This news launches the Empress on her quest for a shadow. The Nurse takes her in disguise to the hut of a poor Dyer named Barak. He and his wife have been childless even longer than the Emperor and Empress: they have been married for two and a half years. The strain in their marriage makes the Dyer's Wife vulnerable to her visitors' suggestion that she sell her shadow to them; in doing so, she would give up any prospect of fertility for the promise of tempting pleasures. The plight of the Dyer and his Wife is in some ways like a human-interest story set in the middle of a fairy tale. In scene after scene they act out their frustration with each other, culminating in one (Act 2, scene 5) in which she tells her husband she

Hugo von Hofmannsthal

The Austrian writer Hofmannsthal (1874–1929) is today remembered above all as the librettist of seven operas for Richard Strauss, of which *Die Frau ohne Schatten* (1919) was the fourth. Their letters, exchanged throughout these collaborations, preserve a remarkable ongoing conversation about the making of operas. In this excerpt from a letter Hofmannsthal wrote while at work on *Die Frau ohne Schatten* (January 20, 1913), he sets a challenging dramatic task for the music to perform—a task that Strauss evidently took to heart.

There are eleven significant, almost pantomimically incisive situations, but it is their combination—in which two worlds, two pairs of beings, two interwoven conflicts take their turn, reflect each other, enhance each other and eventually find their equilibrium—which gives unity to the whole work. Even seen merely as a spectacle, it would be most remarkable and attractive; through the music it will receive its final consummation, through the music which will merge both worlds, will reflect the one in the other, will indeed transform one into the other, as an alchemist transmutes the elements.

The Correspondence Between Richard Strauss and Hugo von Hofmannsthal, trans. Hanns Hammelmann and Ewald Osers, introduction by Edward Sackville-West (Cambridge: Cambridge University Press, 1980), p. 154.

---

has been sleeping with a stranger in his absence, he threatens her, and she admits she was lying and yet invites him to kill her in punishment. Barak and his Wife are subjected to their share of magic in this opera, yet their all-too-human relationship is what holds the sympathies of an audience above all, even more than the troubles of the imperial couple. In the subsequent scene (Act 3, scene 1) they are trapped in separate quarters on a divided stage, both realizing how deeply they love each other after all, and sing a bizarre love duet (neither character aware of the other's presence), justifiably described by Bryan Gilliam as "unquestionably the most moving passage in the entire opera."[6]

Nevertheless, Barak and his Wife are merely fixtures in the Empress's quest, instruments for instructing her about the human condition. As the librettist Hofmannsthal wrote to Strauss, in the Empress "the humanity is missing; to acquire this humanity—that is the meaning of the whole work, even in the music." Those are not the terms in which she understands her quest; she is simply trying to get a shadow, to save her husband from being turned to stone. But as the Nurse tries to persuade the Dyer's Wife to sell her shadow, the Empress has the freedom to observe, and in observing she comes to realize that buying the Wife's shadow would be tricking them out of the chance for happiness that she and her husband want for themselves. In other words, the Empress discovers in herself the capacity for human sympathy. As Hofmannsthal pointed out, she is present in every scene of the opera, and even when she does not speak, "everything turns exclusively on her."[7]

The Empress's dream The dilemma of how to save one couple without sacrificing another forces itself on the Empress in the form of a dream (Act 2, scene 4), dramatized by showing her calling out in her sleep: "Barak, I am to blame for you." Then as she continues to sleep, the vision of her dream is enacted: the Emperor appears at a bronze door leading into a mountain; an unseen chorus calls him forward; the voice of the falcon is heard again, proclaiming that "the Emperor must turn to stone"; and he goes through the door, which closes behind him. Through all this, and in long interludes when there is no stage action, Strauss throws the full resources of a mighty orchestra into a restless depiction of the Empress's mind in turmoil. In the process he calls up one musical motive after another from earlier scenes, motives associated with her father's divine power, the Emperor's love for her, the Emperor being turned to stone, Barak's humble aspirations, and her own quest for the shadow.[8] Each thought makes its claim on her conscience, and each gets pushed aside by another thought. At the end of the scene she wakes up and at first blames herself for the stony death her husband is about to suffer, just as she earlier blamed herself for Barak's troubles. But then she sees her dilemma whole:

Da und dort	*On this side and that,*
Alles ist meine Schuld —	*everything is my fault —*
Ihm keine Hilfe,	*No help to one,*
Dem andern Verderben —	*the ruin of the other —*
Barak, wehe!	*Woe to Barak!*
Was ich berühre,	*Whatever I touch,*
Töte ich!	*I kill!*
Weh mir!	*Woe to me!*
Würde ich lieber	*I would rather*
Selber zu Stein!	*turn to stone myself!*

From this dream she comes to understand her dilemma, but not its resolution. She reaches that only when her love is tested in the third and last act. She along with Barak and his Wife and the Nurse are all transported to the spirit realm, where she can see her husband already becoming embedded in stone. Her trial consists of repeated offers to drink the Water of Life and thereby gain a shadow, which will allow her to bring the Emperor back to life and to have children by him. The cost would be to deny the same happiness to Barak and his Wife, and throughout the Empress's agonized decision-making, their voices are repeatedly heard, letting her (and us) know that although they are still kept apart from one another, they have both realized how committed they are to each other. The Empress, meanwhile, has realized that she does not need to drink the Water of Life, because "love is in me, and that is greater."

That is, in enduring her test, she has learned that she cannot love her husband without loving all of humanity.

The temptations are offered in the most fearfully supernatural-sounding musical voices and colors, but the Empress now stops singing and instead uses a deliberate speaking voice over the orchestra. The sound of her voice here marks this decision as her release from the clouded mindset in which she has understood the human

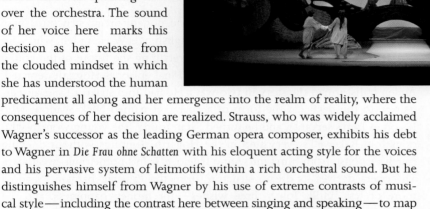

predicament all along and her emergence into the realm of reality, where the consequences of her decision are realized. Strauss, who was widely acclaimed Wagner's successor as the leading German opera composer, exhibits his debt to Wagner in *Die Frau ohne Schatten* with his eloquent acting style for the voices and his pervasive system of leitmotifs within a rich orchestral sound. But he distinguishes himself from Wagner by his use of extreme contrasts of musical style—including the contrast here between singing and speaking—to map radically different worlds: not only the spirit, intermediate, and human worlds, but also the different mental states through which the Empress migrates.

Furthermore, he uses these musical contrasts to transform, in Hofmannsthal's words, one world into the other, "as an alchemist transmutes the elements" (see "In Their Own Words," p. 441). At this moment the Empress turns to her stone-encased husband and says that since she refuses to save him, she wishes to die with him. Then, in a pained, groaning shriek—a sound that is not mere speech, but not singing, either—she refuses the Water of Life one last time: "I will not." And here she is accompanied by an instrumental sound distinct from any of the opera's orchestral worlds, simply a long rising and falling scale on the harp. To her amazement, the Emperor is freed from stone and informs her that she has a shadow and that they will have children. The two couples are united in a love quartet, within which the Empress and Emperor share their first love duet of the opera. The quartet is joined in turn by an offstage children's choir representing both couples' not yet born children. There is no suggestion of magic at work here. The opera's message is that there was never a dilemma after all: the Empress's courage has shown that the reality of being human is that to have love in you for one person is to have it in you for all others as well.

The two couples are reunited in the final scene of *Die Frau ohne Schatten*. Wolfgang Brendel as Barak the Dyer, Linda Watson as the Dyer's Wife, Inga Nielsen as the Empress, and Robert Dean Smith as the Emperor in the Los Angeles Opera production, with set design by David Hockney, 2004.
© Robert Millard

Stravinsky, *The Rake's Progress*

The inspiration for *The Rake's Progress* (1951), the only full-length opera by Igor Stravinsky and the only one in English, came from a series of eight paintings with the same title by the eighteenth-century English satirical artist William Hogarth. These paintings depict the moral decline of a young man who comes into a fortune, wastes it on the temptations of the city, marries foolishly, goes to prison for debt, and loses his mind, ending his young days in a madhouse. Stravinsky was drawn to Hogarth's art, he wrote, by its "theatricality," its "clear moral, a moral that I wanted to retain," and its "essence" of eighteenth-century London.[9]

Hogarth's *Progress* had no Test of Love theme, nor any dream structure. These were introduced into the scenario by the English poet W. H. Auden, who with Chester Kallman wrote the libretto. While retaining the figure of the young man, Tom Rakewell, and most of the individual episodes Hogarth depicted, Auden transformed the story in two ways. He had Tom strike a Faustian bargain with the devil (in the form of a character named Nick Shadow, who becomes Tom's servant), and he turned Sarah Young (the young woman who dogs Tom Rakewell's every step in the Hogarth paintings without drawing much response from him) into Anne Truelove, Tom's hometown sweetheart. The opera derives its dream structure from the Faustian bargain (Shadow more or less fulfills Tom's three wishes—for money, happiness, and the means to perform a good deed) and its Test of Love from Anne, who stays faithful to him when he abandons her to seek his fortune in London.

Neoclassical pastiche Stravinsky said he "wanted to set to music" what Hogarth captured about eighteenth-century London in his images. In both language and music *The Rake's Progress* is a twentieth-century imitation, or **pastiche**, of an eighteenth-century opera. It is constructed as a succession of discrete musical numbers: recitatives (of which some are accompanied by harpsichord), arias, ensembles, and choruses. The texts for the recitatives are written in prose, those for the arias and larger numbers in verse, usually rhymed stanzas. The musical numbers adopt conventions of eighteenth-century form and style, from the florid melodic writing to the patterned movement of the accompaniments, and the orchestra (including the harpsichord) matches older models in its size and make-up. In earlier operas like Tchaikovsky's *The Queen of Spades* (1890) and Richard Strauss's *Der Rosenkavalier* (1911), eighteenth-century settings had also inspired the imitation of eighteenth-century musical style. But no opera takes that imitation (known as **Neoclassicism**) to such an extreme as does *The Rake's Progress*.

Neoclassical style is present throughout the text and music. At the same time, the words and music give away at every turn that they are not

really Classical. In stopping short of true imitation, they make the listener constantly conscious of the imitation. Stravinsky never repeats the lines of text in his numbers the way Mozart unfailingly does, and his numbers are both wordier and shorter than Mozart's. His harmonies are more dissonant, his melodies spikier in both pitch and rhythm, his orchestration more changeable. The result is a work that evokes the world of eighteenth-century England through language based on the poetry of Alexander Pope, music based on the operas of Mozart, and sets and costumes based on the images of Hogarth, but then renders these familiar and comfortable styles unfamiliar and uncomfortable through distortion and distancing.

In "The Rake in Bedlam," the eighth and last painting of William Hogarth's series *A Rake's Progress* (1733), Tom Rakewell, naked and manacled, is ending his days in Bedlam, the faithful Sarah Young weeping over him while fashionable Londoners, in the background, visit the asylum for their amusement. Sir John Soane's Museum, London.

The London we see in Hogarth's paintings is no site of dreams, compared with the castle of Allemonde in *Pelléas et Mélisande* or the island empire of *Die Frau ohne Schatten*. What makes it so in Stravinsky's opera is the self-conscious irony, the false note, of its eighteenth-century style. The process of defamiliarization is not uniform throughout the opera. In the opening scene in the country, where Tom and Anne sing relatively unclouded love duets, Stravinsky evokes, almost without irony, an eighteenth-century dream of paradise in the innocent, lilting pastoral style. Likewise in the last scene, set in the insane asylum at Bedlam, Anne sings a lullaby to soothe the lunatic Tom, and her simple stanzaic song, accompanied just by two flutes and punctuated by choruses of Tom's fellow inmates, takes us to a paradise of imagined childhood. But through all the intervening scenes, which are set in London and encompass both the test of Tom's love and the struggle for his soul, the world of the opera is more a nightmare than a dream of paradise. Stravinsky, Auden, and Kallman create that nightmare by locking their characters, with no possibility of escape, into a world of eighteenth-century words and sounds that are never simple, innocent, or comfortable, but always alienating in style.

Following the Test of Love in *The Rake's Progress* means following a pair of intertwined trails, because Anne's love is tested as well as Tom's. At the end of Act 1, when Tom has already abandoned her and gone to spend his fortune in London, Anne decides—in the soliloquy beginning "No word from

Tom"—to track him down and offer him the help he clearly needs. This is answered, at the beginning of the next scene (Act 2, scene 1), by Tom's soliloquy "Vary the song," in which he complains about how false he finds all the pleasures of the great city. But in the midst of this complaining he sings two phrases so bracketed off from the rest of the number and so unrelated to it musically that they sound like a confession of love for Anne that he hardly dares make even to himself: "Who's honest, chaste, or kind? One, only one, and of her I dare not think." After that, his aria takes its course, rounded off by a heartbreaking string phrase reprising the French horn theme that opened the number—a phrase that ends with a paradoxically sad turn from minor to major on the final chord. Then Tom speaks the second of his wishes (just as he speaks his other two): "I wish I were happy." Nick Shadow appears and persuades him that he can prove he is truly free only by taking an action that runs counter to both desire and reason; he should therefore marry a fairground freak, Baba the Turk.

"The heart for love dares everything" The following scene (Act 2, scene 2) is worth examining in detail because it brings the paths of the two separated lovers together. Anne has come to London and has found Tom's house. She stands in front of his door and wonders that she has come all this way and yet is afraid to knock: "How strange!/Although the heart for love dare everything,/ The hand draws back and finds no spring of courage." "How strange" could also describe the orchestral music that has introduced these lines. Short bursts of fanfare from the whole orchestra alternate with quiet, murmuring passages for the violins in parallel thirds—an effect borrowed almost slavishly from a trio in Mozart's *Così fan tutte* ("Soave sia il vento"/ "Let the wind be mild"), in which the heroines wish a safe voyage to their departing sweethearts, who are sailing off to war. Here there is no breeze and no sailing for the murmuring figure to refer to, and the singer is not singing farewell to her lover, but expecting to meet up with him again. Furthermore, the murmuring effect is disturbed here, as it is not in the Mozart trio, by stops and starts. Stops and starts are not natural for murmuring sounds, whether they depict breezes or waves. But then, an unnatural sound is just what the dramatic situation here calls for. It fits Anne's sense of "How strange" it is for her to be hesitating—starting and stopping—just when she has reached the goal of her search.

In the end she doesn't need to knock on the door. A sedan chair is carried to the front of the house, and Tom steps from it. He is just as astonished to find Anne waiting there as she is to see him arrive in such splendor. In their first exchange since their innocent love duets of Act 1, they sing an anti–love duet: an exchange with the musical progression of a love duet, but words that don't match the form. He urges her to give up on him and

return home. She says she can't go without him. At this point, as in the conventional form, they move from singing alternately to joining together in harmony. But their words, instead of joining together, go underground, into asides. Though they both acknowledge love for the other, Tom does so by wishing for the strength to resist that love, while she wishes for the strength to get through to him:

Tom:
O willful powers, pummel to dust
And drive into the void, one thought — return!

Anne:
Assist me, Heaven, since love I must,
To calm his raging heart, his eyes that burn.

Words like these belong in an ensemble of conflicting emotions, not a love duet. And from here things get both funnier and sadder.

They return to conversation, and just as he seems on the point of wavering ("O Anne!"), the curtain of the sedan chair parts to reveal Baba the Turk inside, her face below the eyes covered in a veil, calling on Tom to escort her into the house. Tom is now forced to admit to Anne that this is his bride, and she is mortified: "I see, then it is I who was unworthy." They launch into a long, slow passage of duet in which their voices overlap, neither answering each other nor joining together. They are both swimming in their own sad reflections. In the midst of this, Baba renews her demands on Tom. The one character who is really present in the situation, she turns the anti–love duet into a three's-a-crowd trio. Near the end Tom's and Anne's different texts coincide on the word "never," and Stravinsky turns this word into a cadenza for the two singers, traditionally a sign of a harmonious relationship at the culmination of a love duet. Here, where the characters are not even aware of their vocal synchrony, it is instead a sign of the beautiful relationship that Tom is not allowing to exist. Anne hurries off, and Baba, urged by the crowd that has gathered, removes her veil to reveal her freakish claim to fame, a full beard, all to the rhythm of a sarabande, the most majestic of eighteenth-century dances.

Tom, like the Empress in *Die Frau ohne Schatten*, has a dream in the course of the opera. Yet his has a satirical side: it is a comic revelation of his capacity to deceive himself. Tom dreams of a machine that creates bread from stone, telling himself that he wants to save mankind with it, when all he really wants is to save himself from the debt and disgrace into which he is falling. Shadow pretends to produce that machine. This scene (Act 2, scene 3) and the following one (Act 3, scene 1), in which his goods and even his wife Baba are auctioned off to pay his debts, mark the high point of comedy in *The Rake's Progress*. But even the auction scene ends in a surprisingly touching

duet of reconciliation between Baba and Anne, in which Baba concedes that Anne is the sole object of Tom's affection. At this point the test of Anne's love is essentially finished.

Gambling in the graveyard, forgiveness in the madhouse A year and a day have passed, and it is time for Shadow to claim Tom's soul. The scene (Act 3, scene 2) moves to a graveyard, a setting not taken from Hogarth but perhaps inspired by the graveyard scene in Mozart's *Don Giovanni*. This graveyard scene, like that one, embodies real fears (Tom's) in genuinely fearful music (starting with the lugubrious Prelude), but they have to compete with Shadow's bravado, embodied in the silly nursery-rhyme tune in which he informs Tom of his fate ("A year and a day"). He also offers Tom a chance to retain his soul by guessing three cards drawn from a deck, and in a further display of bravado he gives Tom hints for the first two. The tone for this part of the scene is set by the harpsichord, which no longer plays chords as in eighteenth-century recitative, but provides a continuous undercurrent of overlapping arpeggiated chords in clashing keys (F-sharp minor against F major, etc.), making a creepy effect worthy of an old-time horror movie. The effect is over the top, yet everything that matters in the story of our rake's progress comes to a head here. Not only does the game decide what price he is to pay for his career in wish fulfillment; the test of his love for Anne Truelove is also decided here. On the

Leanne Kenneally as Anne Trulove sings her lullaby to Tom Rakewell (John Heuzenroeder) in the Bedlam scene (Act 3, scene 3) of *The Rake's Progress*, in the Opera Australia production at the Sydney Opera House, 2006. The patterns on the black and white sets and costumes by David Hockney recall the crosshatching used in the engravings that Hogarth made from his paintings of *A Rake's Progress*.
Patrick Riviere/Getty Images

first card Shadow hints that he should think of Anne, and Tom correctly guesses the Queen of Hearts. For the third guess Shadow refuses to give him a hint, thinking he'll outfox Tom by drawing the Queen of Hearts again. But Anne's voice is heard offstage, singing of the power of love, and Tom names the card correctly.

He has won his Test of Love, but Shadow in his rage turns Tom's dream back into a nightmare by making him insane. The final scene (Act 3, scene 3) then takes us where the final painting in Hogarth's series takes us: to Bedlam, the asylum in which Tom is confined, where we hear an uninterrupted sequence of the most serenely Classical music of the whole opera. Anne's visit brings on the dénouement. Within the duet "In a foolish dream," he declares his repentance — "Forgive thy servant, who repents his madness" — and she offers her forgiveness: "What should I forgive? Thy ravishing penitence/Blesses me, dear heart, and brightens all the past." This simple exchange takes on a religious gravity by being set not as in a Mozart opera, but in the style of a Bach cantata duet, concluding with a passage of gorgeous love-harmony ("Rejoice, beloved"). Because he had to lose his mind to come to his senses about her, it is too late for them to enjoy their love, but they have finally learned to express it unstintingly. Singing her lullaby "Gently, little boat," with Tom's head in her lap, Anne lulls him to sleep, and knowing that there is nothing more she can do for him, she slips away. Tom wakes up, misses her, and, after an insane rant in rapturously florid style, collapses and dies. The chorus mourns him in an extraordinarily stark lament.

This culminating scene, like the scene of infernal punishment in *Don Giovanni*, is powerful beyond anything the opera has prepared its audience for. And like Mozart's work, the opera is rounded off by an epilogue: the characters stand outside the action (in this case in front of the curtain, with the house lights turned up) and sing what they announce as the moral of the tale: "For idle hands and hearts and minds the Devil finds a work to do." As in *Don Giovanni*, the drama has not been simply a comedy, and the disconcerting effect of following a moving finale with a tritely moralizing epilogue is to prompt listeners to consider just what kind of drama it has been, after all. This is not simply a question of how a comedy can have a sad ending. It is more a question of how an opera can work so hard to keep its audience from taking its premises seriously — from the eighteenth-century opera style, which never for a moment sounds real, to the bargain-with-the-devil routine, which could just be in Tom's head, for all the other characters know about it — and yet can play for such serious effect in its closing scene of reconciliation and death. The epilogue only intensifies this ambiguity.

Exemplary Lives

Both *Die Frau ohne Schatten* and *The Rake's Progress* can be seen as twentieth-century versions of the morality plays that were popular in Europe in the fifteenth and sixteenth centuries: dramas of moral choice involving characters who embody abstract qualities. Some musical dramas of this type appeared in the early years of opera (Cavalieri's *Rappresentatione di Anima et di Corpo*, 1600), but the type soon became identified with oratorio rather than opera. In the twentieth century not only did the morality play return to opera, but so did a related kind of drama: the saint's life. In fact, if that term is understood broadly to mean the exemplary life story of a revered, not necessarily religious, figure, then quite a number of important twentieth-century operas can be considered saints' lives. And these can be considered operas of dreaming because they involve people with the power to dream a new way of life into existence for themselves and others.

Saints' Lives: Messiaen, *Saint Francis of Assisi*

One of the most remarkable of these operas is a real saint's life: *Saint François d'Assise* (*Saint Francis of Assisi*, 1983) by the French composer Olivier Messiaen. The composer's culminating work and his only opera, it brings onto the stage the same elements he had combined in concert music all his life: experiments with musical time and color, transcriptions of bird-songs that he collected himself, and his personal Catholic mysticism. Paul Griffiths gets at an important quality of *Saint Francis of Assisi* when he describes it as "an iconic opera."[10] An icon is not just an image of a revered person or action, but an image that is itself revered because it is believed to embody the spirit of its subject; the icon acts as a medium of communication between the believing viewer and the divinity or saint depicted. An iconic opera, then, could be an opera designed to serve not simply as a representation of a saintly life, but as a ritual that summons up the spiritual force of that life. It is not a dramatized biography in the sense of a story covering the major events in a person's life or an attempt to explain how the person became a saint. It is rather the enactment of a spiritual progression, and like a dream, it takes a preordained course, typically from wish to fulfillment — that is, from a wish for faith, through doubt and trial to the realization of that faith, even in death. It is therefore a progression in the character's mind as much as a sequence of actions, but it requires following both private ruminations and public manifestations of faith.

Messiaen wrote his own libretto for *Saint Francis of Assisi*, excluding some episodes from the medieval Lives of St. Francis that might have provided highly effective drama: the story, for instance, of Francis's struggles with his wealthy father, who resisted his calling to a life of poverty and prayer. Messiaen included whatever he thought would allow him, in Claude Samuel's formulation, "to trace, in the spirit of the saint, the development of grace." That included Francis's own song text, the Canticle of the Creatures (or Canticle of the Sun), which is sung almost in its entirety in the course of the opera.

Francis's "development of grace" can be followed in the opera's eight scenes. The first two show him already a monk, but still searching for the "perfect joy" that he knows will come when he learns to bear the sufferings of Christ. In the crucial third scene he faces the challenge of overcoming his fear and repulsion at leprosy and performs a miracle: he embraces a leper, who is instantly cured of his disease. As Messiaen described his subject's spiritual journey, Francis is now a saint. He further manifests his saintliness in the fifth and sixth scenes by responding to the divine concert that an Angel plays on a viol and by preaching to the birds in a voice they understand. In the seventh scene Saint Francis becomes, in Messiaen's words, "super-Saint Francis" when he receives the stigmata, the wounds of Christ on the cross. And in the final scene he dies and enters a new life in Paradise, represented by overwhelming bursts of sound and light.

The task Messiaen set himself in this opera was to represent the connection between the human reality of Francis's life and its path to the spiritual. As a result, his stage requirements range from detailed replications of sites where Francis lived to lasers and other special lighting effects to represent the miracles. One of the longest operas ever staged, *Saint Francis* taxes the musical and staging resources of any opera house. To people who objected that the work was "too rich to describe a saint who was poor and didn't want to own anything," Messiaen replied: "A stylized staging would have been a contradiction to the spirit of Saint Francis, who never ceased to glorify all things on earth, who called the sun and the moon his brother and sister. These are tangible realities, even if they are at the same time symbols of invisible realities."[11]

Music in the spirit Messiaen uses his musical language likewise to connect the material and spiritual worlds. The dialogue is conducted in a ritualistic recitative, the syllables ringing out in solemn order, impervious to the pace

Willard White as St. Francis in Nicolas Brieger's production of *St. Francis of Assisi* at the San Francisco Opera, 2002. In this costume by Andrea Schmidt-Futterer, White looks like a Gothic stone sculpture of the saint.
Marty Sohl, San Francisco Opera

and rhythm of conversation, while the incessant repetition of melodic formulas, especially the interval of the rising tritone (three whole steps), casts a powerful spell. Orchestral motives associated with characters and ideas do not so much accompany the dialogue, the way they do in Debussy and Wagner, as punctuate it, producing "an effect of text and commentary," according to Griffiths, "or perhaps, if one were to think in terms of a medieval manuscript, of text and illumination."[12] This dialogue music, mixed with lyrical passages in which Francis and the other monks sing their daily praises to God, make up the "tangible reality" of the opera. More extraordinary musical effects, coupled to extraordinary effects of staging and lighting, embody the miracles: still, organ-like chords for Francis's embrace of the leper, crazed music for the cured leper's dance of joy, fearful rumblings and a piercing *crescendo* for the moment when Francis receives the stigmata.

The legendary episode of St. Francis preaching to the birds is depicted enchantingly in this predella panel at the bottom of an altarpiece whose main panel shows St. Francis receiving the stigmata. The altarpiece, thought to have been painted for the Church of St. Francis in Pisa around 1300, is signed by Giotto di Bondone (c. 1266–1337), whose various paintings of St. Francis contributed to the cult of the saint in the century after his death and canonization. **Louvre, Paris.**

Louvre, Paris/Bridgeman Art Library

Nothing makes a more extraordinary effect (or taxes the orchestral resources more) than the other-than-human music in the fifth and sixth scenes. In the fifth scene the Angel appears, bringing God's musical response to Francis's prayer. We see the Angel play this on the viol, but the sound we hear comes from three Ondes Martenot, electronic instruments (in use since 1928) that move from one pitch to another in a glissando of an otherworldly timbre. Here, the sound of the three Ondes, coming from three different places and supported by the simplest harmonies, at first played by the strings and then sung by offstage chorus, should transport the listener, Messiaen says, to another world.[13] The Angel's playing arouses other sounds from the orchestra—"the forest resounds," says the libretto—but the effect of its "intolerable sweetness" on Francis is to render him unconscious, almost to make "his soul quit his body." His role in the scene, then, is to receive God's blessing by listening to heavenly music. As the Angel says: "Hear this music that suspends life from the ladders of heaven; hear the music of the invisible."

The other-than-human music in the sixth scene is birdsong. Throughout the opera Messiaen's renderings of birdsong cling to Francis and other characters, serving a mediating role between the human and the spiritual, opening the world of humans to the larger world of God's creation. In the sixth scene, based on one of the most famous episodes in the medieval Lives of St. Francis, the birds become characters in the drama. After singing their individual songs, the birds sit in silence when Francis preaches to them and then blesses them with the sign of the cross, only to erupt afterward into a "tumultuous concert" in which the sounds of many different species resound together. Then they fly off together in cross formation. In terms of the development of grace in this saint's iconic life, the concert of birdsong is a miracle because it confirms that he has communicated his love of God beyond the human world and therefore that his faith has reached a new stage of connection to God.

Schoenberg, *Moses and Aaron*

Moses was a Jewish prophet, not a saint. The story of Moses and the Exodus of the Jewish people from Egypt is dramatic enough to make a grand opera, and that is what Rossini made of it (*Mosè in Egitto*/*Moses in Egypt*) in 1818. More than a century later the Austrian composer Arnold Schoenberg wrote a very different kind of opera, *Moses and Aaron* (*Moses und Aron*). He finished the libretto by 1930 and the music for two of the three acts by 1932 in Berlin, where he was teaching composition, as German politics grew increasingly infected with the violent anti-Semitism of Hitler and the Nazi Party. When Hitler came to

power in 1933, Schoenberg, by then an internationally influential composer, was dismissed from his teaching position for being a Jew. He fled Germany and settled shortly thereafter in the United States. He put off composing the music to the third act for the remaining two decades of his life, with the result that the first two acts (which are now treated as a complete opera) were not staged until 1957, six years after his death.

It seems natural that a Jewish composer witnessing a rising tide of anti-Semitism in Germany and interested in the Zionist project of creating a homeland for Jews would be attracted to the biblical story of Exodus as an operatic subject.[14] It is surprising, then, that his opera (unlike Rossini's) omits the crucial action of Moses wringing freedom for his people from the oppressive Egyptian Pharaoh and leading them across the parted Red Sea to safety. In Schoenberg's opera the escape from Egypt is an unmentioned event that would have occurred between the first and second acts. Neither the text nor the scenic directions even anchor the story specifically in Egypt and Sinai: this is an Exodus without a Promised Land.[15]

Schoenberg's recasting of the story in fact pushes it in the direction of a saint's life. It begins, for instance, with the episode of the young Moses, in exile from Egypt, coming upon the Burning Bush, in which he hears the voice of God, who gives him the mission of leading his people out of captivity in Egypt. This is the scene that follows the biblical narrative most closely.[16] But as an episode in which an individual hears a religious calling, doubts his worthiness, but nevertheless undertakes to answer the call, this scene closely parallels the openings of many saints' lives, including Messiaen's *Saint Francis*. Schoenberg even designates this first scene "Moses' Calling."

Thereafter, the analogy with a saint's life grows more complicated. In the biblical episode of the Burning Bush (Exodus 4:1–9) God shows Moses how to convince the Jewish people that he is God's messenger, by turning his rod into a snake and back and turning his hand leprous and then healthy again. In *Moses and Aaron* Schoenberg saves this demonstration for the scene in which Moses meets the people, so that it becomes more like a saint's miracle: a public manifestation of God's superhuman power residing in the saintly individual. But by then Moses has met up with his brother Aaron (Act 1, scene 2), whom God has designated to provide the eloquence that Moses lacks, and it is Aaron who performs, or at least presents, the miracles (Act 1, scene 4).

In that action Aaron serves as Moses's able assistant, just as he does in the Bible. Yet on the whole, Schoenberg's Aaron is more his opponent than his assistant.[17] All through the opera the brothers are locked in argument, Moses insisting that the people must learn to worship a God who is impossible to see or visualize and Aaron insisting that they will do so only if they are given

a little help in imagining that God. This unresolvable debate is the dramatic core of the opera, as Schoenberg recognized in calling it not *Moses*, but *Moses and Aaron*. In that sense the work is not so much a saint's life as the embodiment of a theological dispute.

A musical opposition Schoenberg builds this opposition between the brothers into the musical language of the opera. He avoids giving the music a key or tonal center, just as his pupil Alban Berg did in *Wozzeck*, but Schoenberg does so by means of a systematic technique of pitch construction: the **twelve-tone technique** that he invented (and that many other composers later adopted). His melodies or chordal progressions use a "row" of all twelve different chromatic pitches in a predetermined order before starting in on an alternate version of that row. Aaron, like most of the other characters as well as the choral groups and the instruments of the orchestra, sings lines constructed of twelve-tone rows. But the role of Moses is not sung; it is delivered in speech-song (*Sprechstimme*). Since the other singers almost always sing, Aaron's singing makes him seem more in touch with his fellow Jews than Moses is. It may also make him, as Robert Weaver writes, "the sympathetic character," while Moses is "arbitrary, inhibited and powerless."[18]

John Daszak (left) as Aaron and John Tomlinson as Moses in Schoenberg's *Moses and Aaron*, staged by David Pountney at the Bavarian State Opera, Munich, 2006. Moses' insistence that God be understood as a concept—that is, through words—rather than visualized is rendered visually here by covering his body with Hebrew script.
Picture-alliance/Newscom

The difference in their modes of delivery constantly reminds us of how much at odds Moses and Aaron are. When they begin their mission, for instance, they approach a crowd of Jews from the back of the stage, moving without appearing to move, and then they both speak at once. Moses proclaims his austere idea of an incomprehensible but demanding God:

> Der Einzige, Ewige, Allmächtige, Allgegenwärtige, Unsichtbare, Unvorstellbare verlangt kein Opfer von euch; er will nicht den Teil, er fordert das Ganze.

> The Only, Eternal, Almighty, Omnipresent, Invisible, Unportrayable One requires no sacrifice from you; he does not want a part, he demands the whole.

Aaron offers an attractive vision of a God who has bestowed his special favor on Jews:

> Er hat euch vor allen Völkern auserwählt und will euch allein seine ganze Gnade schenken. Werft euch nieder, ihn anzubeten!

> He has chosen you before all other peoples and will give you alone his full mercy. Prostrate yourselves and pray to him!

Moses propounds his idea in a forceful but monotonously speechy delivery (see Example 14.4, where the crosses for note heads indicate *Sprechstimme*), while Aaron propounds his softly, in a tone-row line that is not melodious, but reasonable sounding.

In this scene the brothers collaborate in performing their miracles, and the witnesses affirm the special status of those through whom God has shown His power. In a saint's life that status is sainthood. In this Judaic drama, where there is no sainthood, Moses and Aaron achieve the status

14.4 Schoenberg, *Moses and Aaron*: Act 1, "Der Einzige" / "Er hat euch"

of leaders of their national struggle, and the Jews, in a powerful fugal chorus, recognize their own special status as God's chosen people ("Er hat uns auserwählt"/"He has chosen us"). That recognition counts as the crucial act of self-liberation, and the acts of God that make the liberation happen—the plagues, the Passover, the parting of the Red Sea—can be skipped over.

In the second act the Jewish people have been left waiting for forty days in the Sinai Desert while Moses goes to seek God. In their impatience they threaten Aaron and the elders, and Aaron, who in any case has always wanted to offer them a way of visualizing God, casts the Golden Calf for them. Given this chance to release the energies that Moses's strictly abstract model of belief and worship has frustrated, they lose themselves in an orgy of drunkenness, dancing, sacrificial suicide, and sexual slaughter (Act 2, scene 3). Returning from Mount Sinai as this orgy is ending, a furious Moses destroys the Golden Calf and resumes his dispute with Aaron. When Aaron suggests that the Ten Commandments that Moses has brought back from the mountain inscribed on tablets are also "just an image," Moses smashes the tablets. And when the pillar of fire appears before them, the people decide to follow it into the Promised Land. Aaron calls it a sign from God, and Moses decries it as yet another idol. It is another miracle, but performed with no human agent, identifying no one as saint or intermediary with God or leader. It may provide divine protection and guidance to the Jews, but it leaves both their quarreling leaders out in the cold.

To Pierre Boulez, a famed conductor of *Moses and Aaron:* "The chorus . . . is the most important character in the opera. It's like a chameleon, speaking for or against, sometimes even internally divided or emphatic in its support of one particular party; it is angry, it is docile, it comments on the action."[19] To describe the chorus in this way is to connect it to the choruses of Greek tragedies. The opera does not end like a tragedy. None of the characters learn from experience the way tragic protagonists do. They all believe at the end what they have believed all along (and this is equally true whether we consider just the two acts to which Schoenberg wrote music or all three acts of the libretto). The opera does not end like a traditional saint's life either. Moses's faith is tested by the cult of the Golden Calf and survives the test, but the experience produces no transcendence. It gives him no sense of union with God, such as Saint Francis achieves. And yet by withstanding the test, he deprives Aaron of any sense of triumph when the people follow the pillar of fire. What makes it hard for different listeners to agree on whether Moses or Aaron or the chorus is the principal character is exactly what makes it hard to decide whether this opera is more of a tragedy or a saint's life or some other genre: Schoenberg has created an opera around a dispute that resists any resolution.

Political Saints: Operas of Thomson, Glass, and Davis

The idea of the saint's life can be extended to stories about figures whose calling may not have been religious, but who stood by their principles when those principles were tested in the public arena. A number of twentieth-century operas, for instance, depict artists of the sixteenth century who, caught in the religious and political strife of the Protestant Reformation, struggled to find the strength of purpose to carry on their creative work: Hans Pfitzner's *Palestrina* (1917), Paul Hindemith's *Mathis der Maler* (*Mathis the Painter*, 1938), and a kind of anti–saint's life, Peter Maxwell Davies's *Taverner* (1972). In the Soviet Union, which was ruled by an atheist ideology, political saints were celebrated in place of religious ones, and usually these were ordinary people who suffered and triumphed in defense of the Communist cause, like the title character of Sergei Prokofiev's *Semyon Kotko* (1940). An American opera that celebrates the heroism of an equally ordinary character is *Treemonisha* (completed by 1915, first performed in 1972) by the ragtime composer Scott Joplin. The title character of this work is a young woman who assumes the leadership of her community of African Americans in the rural South and whose saintliness ironically consists in using her education to free her people from the religious forces in the community, both the superstitious practices of the traditional conjurors and the ineffective leadership of the Christian clergy. In the end she dances the community into a hopeful future to the secular, syncopated rhythms of a "Real Slow Drag," "Marching Onward."

Other American operas make saints' lives out of the careers of political leaders. Two of them tell of American leaders of liberation movements: Virgil Thomson's *The Mother of Us All* (1947), about Susan B. Anthony (1820–1906), the leader of the women's suffrage movement; and Anthony Davis's *X: The Life and Times of Malcolm X* (1986), about the African American civil rights leader assassinated in 1965. Two of Philip Glass's trilogy of "portrait" operas deal with figures who were spiritual as well as political leaders of other countries, in other times: *Satyagraha* (1980), about the early career of Mahatma Gandhi, when he organized the Indian community in South Africa to resist political oppression nonviolently; and *Akhnaten* (1984), about the Egyptian pharaoh of the second millennium BCE, who introduced monotheism to Egypt. In all these works the mark of the central figure's saintliness, or moral power, is truth-telling.

Thomson, *The Mother of Us All* Susan B. Anthony's life, as the librettist Gertrude Stein and the composer Virgil Thomson created it in *The Mother of Us All*, may have the structure of a saint's life, but she displays no saintly meekness.

She harps endlessly, if wryly, on the idea that in a man's world being right is a way for a woman to get men to listen to her:

> And in a way,
> Yes, in a way,
> Yes, really in a way,
> In a way, really in a way,
> It is useful to be right.
> (Act 1, scene 1)

Anthony undercuts her political opponents (who include Daniel Webster and Ulysses S. Grant) with unholy zeal, yet without undercutting the seriousness of her own political mission. At the beginning of Act 1, scene 5, in which one of her protégées gets married, she sings a soliloquy ("Will they remember that it is true") in which she examines her doubts about marriage in a culture of gender inequality, and her hymn-like melody affirms that she is bringing a prayerful humility to the examination. When the wedding party arrives, she reiterates her doubts, but also intervenes to keep the ceremony moving forward, and when it is completed, she declares — to a thunderous version of her hymn melody — that the couple's children of both sexes will have the vote. Her doubts and her faith come together powerfully here.

In the second act male politicians test her faith by working to write into the Constitution that only men shall vote, and she endures that test with both irony and earnestness, mocking the hypocrisy of the men who allow her to address political assemblies and delivering what amounts to a sermon to her companion Anne about the fears that rule men and those that rule women. The immense range of tones and attitudes that all the characters, but especially Anthony, display in their words can come across in their singing because Thomson set most of the text in a style as plain and flexible as the plainest recitative in seventeenth- or eighteenth-century opera. The opera does not dramatize the miracle of Anthony's success, since she did not live to see women's suffrage guaranteed in the Constitution. Instead, the final scene shows her statue being dedicated in the U.S. Capitol after the passage of the suffrage amendment. When everyone has departed, the ghost of Susan B. Anthony is left quietly singing one more reprise of her hymn, now to words about how "life is strife." The actual statue in the Capitol depicts Anthony and two other suffragettes, but while Gertrude Stein had called for that statue to be replicated in the opera, the scenarist, Maurice Grosser, suggests in the score that instead there should be "a statue of Miss Anthony alone." That emphasizes the solitary side of her struggle and makes the finale seem more like a weary but saintly transfiguration.

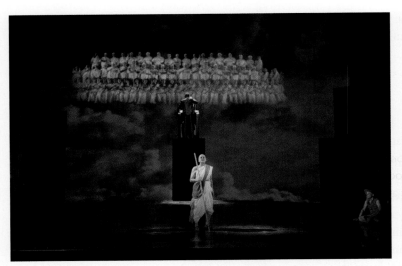

Richard Croft as Gandhi, with an actor representing Martin Luther King Jr. at the podium and a projection of men and women arranged like divinities in a Hindu painting, in Act 3 of Phelim McDermott's staging of Glass's *Satyagraha* at the Metropolitan Opera, 2011.
© Ken Howard, Metropolitan Opera

Glass, *Satyagraha* and *Akhnaten* In Philip Glass's two operas on political lives, the idea of saintliness is embedded in the words being sung. The very title *Satyagraha* is a Sanscrit word translated as "truth-force"; it is the name that Gandhi gave to his movement for political rights in South Africa. Though the work stages events from the decades Gandhi lived and worked in South Africa before World War I, its text, sung in Sanskrit, is taken entirely from the *Bhagavad-Gita*, the portion of the ancient epic poem *Mahabharata* in which the god Lord Krishna discusses the Hindu philosophy of life with the mortal Prince Arjuna. In the first scene Gandhi joins in this conversation, while the Russian pacifist writer Leo Tolstoy looks down on them from his desk. In the rest of the opera Gandhi and his associates organize their political movement and lead a protest march of Indian workers and their families against the white South African government, while singing more philosophical verses from the *Bhagavad-Gita*. The preexisting text gives a ritualistic character to the drama, and Glass's minimalist music adds to the ritualistic effect: against a background of rapid and unceasingly repeated figuration, the singers move as if in a trance through words the audience is not expected to understand.

In *Akhnaten* the characters likewise sing preexisting texts, in this case from a variety of sources, not only ancient Egyptian. The role of truth-telling is more ambiguous. The historic Pharaoh Akhnaten evidently saw himself as a religious visionary uniquely possessed of truth about God. The text of the Hymn to the Sun attributed to him and sung by the character Akhnaten in the opera (Act 2, scene 4) says about the Sun-God: "There is no other that knows thee save thy son, Akhnaten." But the opera also shows Akhnaten being overthrown (Act 3, scene 2) because "the two eyes of the king . . . do not see" the truth of what is happening in his land. In this repertory of political operas the formula of doubt, testing, and miracle that makes up a traditional saint's life is adjusted to relate stories of politicians learning to see and tell the truth.

In different ways both *Satyagraha* and *Akhnaten* are concerned with the creation of sacred communities, united in belief and action, similar to *Dialogues of the Carmelites* as well as *Treemonisha* and *Moses and Aaron*. But while the community in *Satyagraha* achieves a considerable political victory with

its organizing and protests, that is not shown in the opera. And in *Akhnaten* the action indicates that the Pharaoh is overthrown, his new religion wiped out, and the city he founded reduced to ruins inhabited in the final scene by his ghost and those of his family. The ending is not occupied with the fate of the community, but with the leader's individual attainment of a status equivalent to sainthood. *Satyagraha* likewise ends with a long solo by Gandhi, contemplating at night while his comrades sleep. In an extraordinarily simple melody of aspiration—each phrase a new statement of the same rising scale—he sings verses of Lord Krishna's wisdom from the *Bhagavad-Gita*. By making these verses his own, Gandhi comes to seem godlike: "For whenever the law of righteousness withers away and lawlessness arises, then do I generate myself on earth."

Davis, X: X: *The Life and Times of Malcolm X* is the most fully biographical of these operas, starting with the night when Malcolm as a young boy learns that his father has been murdered by white supremacists and ending with his own murder as he is addressing a meeting in Harlem. It is also the one that most clearly invokes the music of its subject's time and place. Anthony Davis's score mixes elements of jazz and other African American music with operatic style to create an operatic portrait of black society in the middle of the twentieth century. The music contains more of both jazz and opera and less of Broadway than *Porgy and Bess*. (At the same time, Davis tips his hat to *Porgy* by modeling the minor character Street after Gershwin's Sportin' Life.) The singers' lines are for the most part very even in rhythm, almost like the vocal lines in *Saint Francis of Assisi* or the Glass operas, but their effect is seldom ritualistic. In the aria "Momma, help me" in the first scene, for instance, the steady, uninflected lines of the young Malcolm, being taken from his mother by a social worker after the death of his father, give his voice an affectless quality that suggests how traumatized he is.

For all its biographical verisimilitude, *X* is also shaped as a saint's life. Malcolm's character and beliefs are tested from the first scene to the last. His doubts become acute when he is jailed for petty crime as a young man, and he sets out to resolve those doubts when his brother visits him there and introduces him to the message of the Black Muslim leader, Elijah. But though he is consecrated to a political and religious mission from this time and though he develops a powerful effectiveness as a preacher, Malcolm never stops trying to discover his true mission, even his true name. If there is a miraculous event in this story, it occurs on his pilgrimage to Mecca, where, feeling "tied in a silence unknown," he prays during a trumpet interlude and emerges "new born today." There is no Hollywood moment when the protagonist's struggles pay off and a once-doubtful community cheers his success. Instead, he is shown being

harassed to the end by white reporters and murdered by black opponents. Of all these political operas, X has the bleakest ending. Yet it shares with most of the rest its mixed message about truth-telling: the dire need of society to be told unpleasant truths, yet the terrible human cost to the saintly individual who dares to do so. As the young Malcolm sings (Act 1, scene 3), alone onstage but apparently addressing a white police interrogator: "You want the truth, / But you don't want to know."

Fantasy Worlds: Ligeti, *Le Grand Macabre*

A detail from *The Triumph of Death*, painted around 1562 by Pieter Breughel the Elder, an apparent inspiration for Ligeti's *Le Grand Macabre*, which is set in "Breughelland." The singer and lute player carrying on in the lower right corner, virtually the only figures in the vast scene not succumbing to death, could be the inspiration for Ligeti's Amanda and Amando. Museo del Prado, Madrid.

Scala/Art Resource, NY

All operas of dreaming construct fantasy worlds, if only the better worlds or lives that religious or secular saints imagine and then work to bring about. Certain twentieth-century operas can be considered fantasy-world operas in the special sense that the characters treat what looks and sounds crazy from the outside as normal. An example is György Ligeti's *Le Grand Macabre* (*The Great Macabre*, or *The Grim Reaper*, 1978; revised 1996), based on a play by Michel de Ghelderode and set "in the Principality of Breughelland, an imaginary country, no particular century." The imagining of that country seems nevertheless to be associated with the sixteenth-century Flemish painter Pieter Breughel, who created the horrifying panorama of war and destruction known as *The Triumph of Death*. But before we encounter the stage decked out as Breughelland, we hear the overture. The orchestra is gathered in the pit, the conductor comes out as usual and gives the downbeat, and we hear music—played on twelve car horns. The sound of car horns may seem to come from a particular century very far from Breughel's, but no one onstage acts as if things are out of joint. In fact, the first character we hear, from offstage, sings:

> O golden Breughelland
> That never knows a care,
> Fill all your children
> With delight!
> O long-lost paradise,
> Where are you now?

Fantasy operas are apt to be as crazy in genre as in setting. They frequently end like comedies, with the cast coming forward in chorus to sing the moral of the tale, but they do this as if it is all in a day's work for them,

whether or not it is clear to the audience that the work is a comedy. *Le Grand Macabre*, for instance, is hard to call a comedy because its subject is the Triumph of Death, and even though it has been filled with silliness from the first honk of those car horns, it is still disconcerting at the end, when the Grand Macabre has shriveled to nothingness, to find the rest of the cast singing a comic moral about death:

> *Fear not to die, good people all!*
> *No one knows when his hour will fall!*
> *And when it comes, then let it be . . .*
> *Farewell, till then in cheerfulness!*

Musical style is one more realm of craziness in fantasy operas. The characters seem not to know what the norms of operatic style are. In fantasy operas by Shostakovich (*The Nose/Nos*, 1930) and Prokofiev (*The Love for Three Oranges/ Lyubov' k tryom apel'sinam*, 1921) as well as *Le Grand Macabre*, characters make musical numbers out of laughing, belching, sexual sighing, and other inarticulate sounds. But they perform them with a straight face. As Shostakovich wrote of *The Nose*: "Gogol [who wrote the story behind the opera] tells of the comic events in a very serious tone, and it is precisely here that the force and merits of his humor lie. He is not trying to be witty. The music, too, does not try to be witty."[20]

A clear-eyed perspective and two visions of sexuality There is often, however, one character who does notice the craziness of the fantasy world, and that character gives the audience a way to put the craziness in perspective. Paul Griffiths finds such a character in *Le Grand Macabre*: Piet the Pot, who opens the opera looking for golden Breughelland, "the opera's common man and the single person on stage with whom the audience might be tempted to identify."[21] Piet the Pot is a drinker, and his drunkenness might explain how he can notice what a crazy world he lives in without letting it drive him crazy. In Scene 1, for instance, he watches the Grand Macabre climb out of an open grave, bears physical abuse from him, hears him threaten to kill not only Piet but all of humanity, hears him give his name as Nekrotzar (Emperor of Death), is forced to gather his scythe and trumpet for him out of the tomb, and only then recognizes "That bony face / Those hollow eyeball sockets / Those grinning jaws" as the features of Death: "O God, now I'm in deep shit!" Nekrotzar commandeers him for his horse and rides him offstage. No one can miss the point that we are all the slaves of death.

The other characters in this first scene are a pair of lovers, who spend the whole scene locked in an embrace and singing an ecstatic love duet as they repeatedly go on- and offstage, looking for a place where they can be undisturbed. They find the tomb that Nekrotzar has vacated, and they remain in it until the end of the last scene, when they emerge rejoicing that while the world

was collapsing around everyone else, "for us too the world ceased to be,/and yet how ecstatic were we!" These two lovers are described in Ligeti's synopsis of the opera as "the beautiful loving couple, Amanda and Amando, who look as if they could have come straight out of a Botticelli painting." He characterized the roles as female and male, but composed them for a soprano and mezzo-soprano. Their voices intertwine in close range with an ecstatic abandon like that of Poppea (a female soprano) and Nerone (a soprano castrato) in Monteverdi's *The Coronation of Poppea*, one of the operas Ligeti cited as a model for his.[22]

In the craziness of his casting Ligeti is, like Gogol and Shostakovich, "not trying to be witty." He is not making fun either of heterosexual love or of the long operatic tradition—stretching from Monteverdi's *Poppea* in the seventeenth century to Richard Strauss's *Der Rosenkavalier* in the twentieth—of cross-voiced portrayals of heterosexual love. He is extending the expressive possibilities of that tradition. He left it to other composers of his day (Mauricio Kagel in *Staatstheater*, 1970; John Cage in *Europeras 1 & 2*, 1987) to scramble the traditional resources of opera so as to suggest wittily that their original force and purpose were now spent. Ligeti criticized a production of *Le Grand Macabre* that promoted the idea of "the death of opera, which is absolutely not what I intended. I wanted the destruction of the world, which is quite different."[23]

We might ask what the ecstatic love music of Amanda and Amando, however crazily they are cast, is doing in an opera about "the destruction of the world." In part the answer could be that they escape destruction by hiding out in a tomb and making love. In part they balance the couple who appear in the second scene: the astrologer Astradamors, sung by a bass wearing women's clothes, and his wife Mescalina, a soprano in leather who whips him, strikes him, and threatens him with a poisonous spider, but can't get any sexual satisfaction from him. Astradamors ranges from highest falsetto to profoundest bass in a single line—"Oh, my dreary nights, dark with bitterness!"—that leads him into dreaming of all the ways he might kill her. Nekrotzar intrudes and offers Mescalina the violent love-making she craves, but since he is, after all, Death, he ends by biting her on the throat like a vampire, killing her and leaving Astradamors triumphant. In comparison with Astradamors and Mescalina, whose sex roles are as crazy as their vocal casting is "normal," the vocal ranges of Amanda and Amando seem to symbolize equal and reciprocal affection as a formula for love that can resist even the destruction of the world.

A satire of totalitarianism The third scene moves the fantasy from sex to politics, to the royal palace of Breughelland, where the ruling Prince, Go-Go (a countertenor), is being bullied by his two quarrelsome ministers, the Black Minister and the White Minister (a baritone and a tenor). The childishness of the Prince is attested by his high-pitched voice, as well as by the rocking horse

he rides. Gepopo, the Chief of the secret police, enters and through an endless and evolving stream of nonsense syllables (he calls it code, or rather "cococoding"), manages to warn the Prince that his people are headed angrily to the palace. Gepopo (whose name is no doubt a reminder of Hitler's secret police, the Gestapo) is played by a woman with an extremely high soprano range.

In a way this is traditional political satire, making fun of rulers and their associates as idiotic, bad-tempered, childish, effeminate, and impotent behind their façade of wisdom, manliness, and power. The specific political object of satire in *Le Grand Macabre* is the kind of tyranny that depends on secret police: modern totalitarianism. Ligeti himself had experienced totalitarianism as a Hungarian Jew who barely survived the Nazi occupation of his homeland during World War II and afterward suffered from the oppression of Soviet-style Communism in Hungary. Anyone who can imagine that kind of experience can enjoy the revenge he takes on totalitarian regimes in this scene. Anyone can take pleasure in finding that the "intelligence" offered by Gepopo is gobbledygook that only rarely, and it seems accidentally, produces any meaningful information. It is harder to know what he is up to in the musical style of this scene.

Ligeti makes Gepopo sing his/her coded words in an esoteric style of vocal extremes—stratospherically high notes, superhumanly long notes, impassively disconnected phrases, tonally tortured melodies, rhythms that would render the words incomprehensible if they weren't so already. This is the vocal style, challenging for performers and listeners alike, that avant-garde composers in Western Europe favored after World War II—composers like Karlheinz Stockhausen, Pierre Boulez, Luciano Berio, and to an extent Ligeti himself. In this scene, then, he portrays Gepopo and the whole function of the secret police as crazy by the astonishingly self-deprecating gesture of making Gepopo sing in the style of Ligeti and Company.

This third scene is completed by the arrival of the greatest of all tyrants, Death—that is, Nekrotzar—intent on exterminating all of humanity, but at the same time making a ludicrous appearance as he rides in on the back of Piet the Pot. Griffiths tells us that Ligeti sees in him "a low but hugely insidious clown on the model of Hitler: one intoxicated with annihilation on the grandest scale."[24] Nekrotzar makes this entrance to music that may refer to an earlier tyrant: it is built on a bass line using the distinctive rhythm of the bass line theme of the finale of Beethoven's Third (*Eroica*) Symphony, which the composer intended originally as a tribute to Napoleon.

Frances Bourne as Amando and Rebecca Bottone as Amanda in the production of *Le Grand Macabre* staged by Valentina Carrasco and La Fura dels Baus at the English National Opera, London, 2009.

© Laurie Lewis/Lebrecht Music & Arts

The chorus of the people of Breughelland, cowering before Nekrotzar, sings: "Punish all the rest, / But not me, me, me; / Do not kill me!" At the same time, Piet the Pot and Astradamors resourcefully get Nekrotzar so drunk that he loses himself in singing an increasingly incoherent catalogue aria of all the destroying he has done. Lightning and earthquakes shake the stage, the sun and moon are extinguished, a comet grows bright, and darkness descends. The Triumph of Death proceeds even while Nekrotzar, the Emperor of Death, tumbles from Prince Go-Go's rocking horse to the ground in a drunken stupor. Is the apocalypse that he claims to have set in motion going on without him? Or has the destruction of the world that Ligeti said he wanted to stage even occurred?

Destruction, beauty, survival Likewise it is hard to make sense of the fourth and final scene, which follows an Interlude in which we seem to hear the comet streak by. Is it more like the aftermath of an apocalypse or like an awakening from a bad dream? All the characters we have previously met are now present, asking themselves if they are alive or dead. Three new characters appear, announcing that they have "risen from the grave." Some of the survivors carry on as badly as before, and it is at least clear that we are not in heaven but still in Breughelland. Nothing has happened, it seems, except that humanity has had a lucky reprieve from death. But that is really something. We can hear it in a change that comes over the music, which sheds its former craziness and begins to flow in steady rhythm, clear chords, and coherent melody. A calm string passage in the form of a mirror canon (one part answered by an inversion of itself) quietly accompanies the rising of the sun, as Nekrotzar shrivels to nothingness and disappears.

These are quiet events, yet they ought to be momentous: the dawn of a new era? the death of Death? Amanda and Amando emerge from the tomb and resume their love duet, no longer in uncontrolled gasps of ecstasy, but in sweet, lyrical phrases regulated by the stately repeating phrases of a passacaglia (the grandest dance in a Lully opera). Their words express joy that their strategy of lying low and loving each other has allowed them to survive. Their music offers beauty as an antidote to craziness. As the passacaglia progression continues, the rest of the cast joins the lovers in singing the moral quoted earlier, urging the audience not to fear death, but to be cheerful till then.

Le Grand Macabre is a survivor's opera about survival, an artist's testimony to the power of beauty as a counterweight to destruction. Survival may not seem a particularly decisive ending, compared with death or marriage, the typical endings of tragedy and comedy. But in fantasy-world operas the survival of the protagonists signifies their release from the world of bad dreams.

Here, the shriveling of Nekrotzar lets its inhabitants enjoy a reprieve of uncertain duration. The audience too has been trapped for the duration of the opera, and when it leaves at the end, it needs to be sure which side of the line between the crazy and the real it is on. The concluding moral sung by the cast is one way that assurance is given. The moral itself may not be reassuring: "No one knows when his hour will fall!" What matters is that the cast, addressing the audience directly, is removed from the world of the drama, and the audience knows it can be confident that when the lights come up, the dream is over.

Dreams of Childhood: Ravel, *L'Enfant et les Sortilèges*

The twentieth century saw the development of the first substantial repertory of operas for and about children. That development sprang from a growing belief that one kind of subject suited adults and another kind suited children. Of course, operas designed for young people might interest adults too, just as children's books and movies do. Given that parents and other adults read books to kids and sit through movies with them, it is no accident that artworks created for children often contain references or messages that go over their heads. But when artists reach the point of pitching their "children's" works to those looking back longingly on childhood, they may not have an easy time holding the interest of those presently enduring it.

One opera about childhood that takes on that challenge is Maurice Ravel's "lyric fantasy" *L'Enfant et les Sortilèges* (*The Child and the Magic Spells*, 1925). Children certainly enjoy its story (by the French novelist Colette) and its music. In fact, some features of the work, such as its succession of short episodes in dazzlingly contrasting musical styles, seem specially calculated to hold the interest of children. Other features may go harmlessly over their heads and engage adults, like the musical references to, in Ravel's words, everything "from Bach up to . . . Ravel" and "from opera to American operetta, with a bit of jazz band."[25]

Yet though the opera focuses our attention utterly on the child protagonist, the action places the Child's emotions in contexts that only an adult would understand, while the music colors his experience with a regret that only an adult could feel. The Czech choreographer Jiří Kylián, introducing his danced staging of the opera on video, speaks of the "beautiful experience of being able to go back into your own childhood,"

adding that he wishes anyone who sees his production would "feel like someone who is looking into a child's book that was lost for a long time."[26] He is suggesting that *L'Enfant et les Sortilèges* can speak to adults by presenting a fantasy in which they think they recognize their childhood.

Childishness and guilt The Child of the title is a boy of six or seven. The part is written for a mezzo-soprano and has generally been taken by a woman. As the curtain rises on the Child in his room in a country house, two oboes move in parallel intervals with an "apparent aimlessness" that, as Roger Nichols explains, captures the spirit of the Child doing his homework in what the score calls "a full-blown crisis of boredom."[27] The sets and furniture are to be outsized, so that the audience sees them as they appear to the Child. His mother, or rather the looming figure of a giant mother, enters the room, finds that he has done nothing, and punishes him by locking him in the room with unsweetened tea and dry bread. The Child smashes the teapot and cup, hurts the caged squirrel and the cat, disturbs the fire, tears the wallpaper, pulls the pendulum out of the grandfather clock, and finally shreds his homework along with some books.

The rest of the opera consists largely of the revenge that these defenseless victims, brought magically to life and given to reproachful speech, take on him, along with his responses. From an adult perspective, the story is unmistakably like a dream shaped by a child's developing psyche. It may represent his growing capacity for guilt. It may represent his attempt to cope with parental power. In fact, within two years of the premiere the psychoanalyst Melanie Klein published a Freudian interpretation of the libretto, exploring the Child's sadistic displacement of anger at his mother onto the material and animal objects around him.[28]

Elisa Cenni, as the Child, behaves with childish impudence to Aude Extrémo, as the Mother, in a production of *L'Enfant et les Sortilèges* staged by Jean Liermier at the Paris Opera, 2009.
Pascal Victor/ArtComArt

Each of the objects and animals the Child attacked gets back at him in turn, but their revenge has the orderly progression of art, not dream. First the armchair he tries to slump into moves out of the way, joining with another armchair in a stiff minuet (to music in Ravel's faux-eighteenth-century style), singing

that they will never let the wicked boy sit in them again. The grandfather clock, the teapot and cup, and the fire come to life in turn, each to crazy music. The Wedgwood teapot sings nonsense British phrases ("I boxe you, marm'lad' you") to a nonsense rag, while the Chinese teacup sings nonsense Chinese phrases ("Kengçafou, Mahjong") to a nonsense foxtrot. However silly their words and music, these mute objects breed fear in the Child simply by coming to life. They appear to have the power to exact the revenge that his guilt suggests he deserves. At the end of this sequence he sings simply, "I'm afraid."

The next set of victims raises a different emotion in him. These are the shepherds and shepherdesses from the wallpaper he has stripped off and the Princess from his favorite storybook, which he has torn up. Their reproach is that they could have loved forever, in the eternity of their paper worlds, if the Child had not torn up those worlds. The Princess makes him feel that in tearing up her picture, he has destroyed his budding potential for romantic love. In both episodes the pastoral sweetness of the music intensifies the singers' reproach. And when the Princess is sucked down into a trap door, calling out for help, the Child is left alone onstage to sing a song of regret over his lost Princess: "Toi, le coeur de la rose" ("You, the heart of the rose"). In the simplest and most devastating music of the opera so far, he sings that what is left of her is just a single golden hair and "les débris d'un rêve": the remains of a dream. This is not simply the regret of guilt—something a child could feel—but an adult regret over a moment in life that can never be recaptured. Without that adult sentiment, the music is meaningless.

After a drilling by a mad arithmetic teacher, reminding him that he has also torn up his homework, the Child is visited by the black cat, whose tail he pulled. The moon has risen. A white cat appears, and the two cats, male and female, sing a love duet in meows to the most seductive music, reminiscent of Ravel's music for the ballet *La Valse*. For once the Child has no response. The episode, which scandalized some early audiences, calls out for some interpretation, and one stage director, Frank Corsaro, perhaps inspired by Melanie Klein's Freudian analysis of the work, responded by revealing the white and black cats to be the Child's mother and father, whom he sees in a sexual embrace.[29] Even in a production that does not enact that scenario, the music for this number can be understood to suggest that the Child is becoming conscious of sexual issues he is not ready to face.

Costume design by the poster artist Paul Colin for the black cat in Scene 1 of Ravel's *L'Enfant et les Sortilèges*, as produced at the Paris Opera in 1939. At the end of a scene in which inanimate objects come to life to protest against the Child, it is fitting that the last protester is a cat made to look like an Art Deco vase. Bibliothèque-Musée de l'Opéra National de Paris.
© 2012 ARS, NY/ADAGP, Paris/Archives Charmet/Bridgeman Art Library

Maturity and benediction It is a great relief to him when, at the beginning of the second part of the opera, he finds himself in the moonlit garden. The garden is portrayed as a place of tranquil mystery, where the nightmarish magic of his room gives way to the natural magic of the outdoors at night. Ravel's orchestral evocation of this magic is extraordinary: hollow, widely spaced chords in the strings shift in an eerie progression, while two high flutes fill the night air with the fluttering sounds of insects and birds. Eventually an unseen chorus adds the croaks of frogs. When the Child spreads his arms and sings "What a joy to find you again, Garden!" it is clear that his relief comes from being in a world without articulate voices, a world of natural but blessedly inarticulate sounds.

But in expressing his joy, he breaks the spell of the natural, and a new round of complaints begins. A tree he has slashed with his knife claims it is still bleeding sap. A dragonfly sings what Ravel labels an "American waltz," a relaxed, sentimental song embodying the love that the Child has destroyed by killing her mate. She continues singing as the frogs and nightingale resume their night sounds. Another version of the waltz is heard as the bats play and dance. A squirrel sings still another version about what it meant to him when the Child caged him. Meanwhile, in Colette's words, "the garden, palpitating with wings, glowing with squirrels, is a paradise of animal tenderness and joy." The Child, beginning to recognize the signs of love and learn that the world doesn't revolve around him, exclaims: "They love each other! They are happy! They have forgotten me!" And "in spite of himself," needing his share of all this love, he calls out: "Maman!" ("Mamma!").

But that sound brings the animals' attention back to him, and they all attack him. In the mêlée a little squirrel is wounded, and the Child—now able, in Klein's words, to "conquer his sadism by means of pity and sympathy"—binds up the squirrel's wounds, then sinks down lifeless from the struggle.[30] The rest of the animals are taken aback. They recognize that he has learned an important lesson. They see that he is hurt and that they cannot do for him what he has done for the squirrel. So they carry him back to his house, acting with the responsibility of adults and so embodying within the drama an adult perspective that until now only adults among the spectators have brought to bear.

Approaching his house and needing to get the attention of his family, they try calling out the sound they have just heard him make: "Maman." Eventually, putting more and more voices into the effort, they see a

light go on. As the Child stands on his own feet, they sing a hymn in his honor:

Il est bon, l'Enfant,	*He is good, the Child,*
Il est sage, bien sage, si sage,	*he is wise, quite wise, so wise,*
Il est si doux.	*he is so kind.*

Ravel sets these words in a style borrowed from Renaissance sacred music: long, calm vocal lines in imitation, the chorus sometimes entirely unaccompanied, sometimes subtly harmonized or doubled by instruments, and at the end absorbing into its serenely assured harmony the "aimless" duet of oboes that characterized the Child's boredom at the opening of the opera. In place of a moral sung by the cast, this ending is a benediction sung by the chorus of animals, from a perspective that seems angelic.

They are honoring the process of growing up that they have witnessed in the Child, and in a sense that is what operas (or other stories) about childhood generally do. The Child returns to his house in a grown-up spirit of acceptance. As the chorus of animals reaches the end of its benediction, he puts a cadence to that chorus, and the opera, by repeating his "Maman." But this time, thanks to the intervening action — the fight, his care of the little squirrel, the animals' care of him, and the blessing that their hymn bestows on him — the word takes on a new significance. He seems to call to his mother not just out of his own need, but also to show her that he has learned to accept the needs of others and his own role in his family.

In Conclusion

The magnificent final chorus of *L'Enfant et les Sortilèges*, in a style derived from church music of the sixteenth century, may seem like a curious note on which to end an opera about a twentieth-century child who throws a tantrum. But it strikes an apt note on which to conclude this historical survey of the operatic canon, and not just because the sound of the chorus takes us back to the period when opera was born. That sound, after all, was simply a current choral style when Peri and Monteverdi imported it into their operas, while it was centuries old when Ravel reworked it for his. Its antiquity gave the style a nostalgic charge that Ravel harnessed to evoke the sentimentality of the Child's yearning for his mother. And the nostalgia in turn was part of what was new about the opera: its sophisticated

use of musical style to produce a sentimental adult view of childhood. Learning the history of opera allows us to appreciate this paradox.

Studying the canon, whether in an academic course or in a lifetime of operagoing, gives us a mental map of operatic experiences. Any new experience, whether of a brand-new opera or one new to us, produces a double effect. It adds something distinctive to our map (in this case, a sophisticated musical rendering of childhood), and it also casts a new light on everything already on the map (the choral movements in Monteverdi's operas as fashionable music in their day, the overwhelming focus on young adults in most operas). Likewise, every new production of a canonic opera can open us to new thoughts about the work, as well as prompting adjustments to the way we judge earlier productions. In that way the story of opera is not simply the history of a centuries-old tradition in which the emotional power of music is linked to the human issues that can be enacted as stories. It is also a frame within which your operatic experiences can engage, enrich, and deepen each other.

FURTHER READING

On Saariaho's life and career, Pirkko Moisala, *Kaija Saariaho* (Urbana: University of Illinois Press, 2009). On Debussy's life and career, Roger Nichols, *The Life of Debussy* (Cambridge and New York: Cambridge University Press, 1998). On *Pelléas*, Roger Nichols and Richard Langham Smith, *Claude Debussy: "Pelléas et Mélisande"* (Cambridge and New York: Cambridge University Press, 1989).

On Strauss's life and career, Bryan Gilliam, *The Life of Richard Strauss* (Cambridge and New York: Cambridge University Press, 1999). On *The Rake's Progress*, Paul Griffiths, *Igor Stravinsky: "The Rake's Progress"* (Cambridge and New York: Cambridge University Press, 1982). On *Saint Francis of Assisi*, Peter Hill, ed., *The Messiaen Companion* (Portland, Ore.: Amadeus Press, 1994); Robert Scholl, ed., *Messiaen Studies* (Cambridge and New York: Cambridge University Press, 2007). On Schoenberg's life and career, Joseph Auner, *A Schoenberg Reader: Documents of a Life* (New Haven: Yale University Press, 2003). On Thomson's life and career, Anthony Tommasini, *Virgil Thomson: Composer on the Aisle* (New York: Norton, 1997).

The librettos of the three "portrait" operas by Glass — *Einstein on the Beach*, *Satyagraha*, and *Akhnaten* — along with essays about them by Glass and

others are in Philip Glass, *Music by Philip Glass*, ed. and with supplementary material by Robert T. Jones (New York: Harper & Row, 1987). On *Le Grand Macabre*, Richard Steinitz, *György Ligeti: Music of the Imagination* (Boston: Northeastern University Press, 2003). On *L'Enfant et les Sortilèges*, Richard Langham Smith, "Ravel's Operatic Spectacles: *L'Heure* and *L'Enfant*," in Deborah Mawer, ed., *The Cambridge Companion to Ravel* (Cambridge and New York: Cambridge University Press, 2000).

FOR RESEARCH AND REFLECTION

1. *L'Amour de loin* starts out as a poet's dream of love, then becomes a dream he shares with his beloved, and ends as her dream alone. In what other operas of dreaming does the ownership of the dream shift? Whose story — whose dream — is *Pelléas et Mélisande*? How can you tell?

2. What do the changes of setting signify in *Pelléas*? in *Die Frau ohne Schatten*? in *Le Grand Macabre*?

3. How is the portrayal of a saint's life — even a political or artistic, as opposed to a religious, saint's life — different from the portrayal of a hero's life?

4. Dreams may not be amusing to the dreamer, but operas of dreaming can be funny, at least intermittently, to the audience. What kind of humor do you find in *The Rake's Progress*, *The Mother of Us All*, *Le Grand Macabre*, or *L'Enfant et les Sortilèges*? What does it say about your relationship to the action and characters that you can laugh at them?

5. In what operas of dreaming does the musical language create a separate dream world? When a protagonist enters or leaves the dream world, how is the music adapted to reflect that change?

6. What indications do you find within *L'Enfant et les Sortilèges* that the world it takes us to is an adult reconstruction of a child's dream world, rather than a representation of a child's imagining?

 Additional resources available at wwnorton.com/studyspace.

GLOSSARY

Capitalized words have their own definition elsewhere in the Glossary. Further definitions of musical terms can be accessed on Wikipedia (which offers illustrative sound files) and the Virginia Tech Multimedia Music Dictionary (www.music.vt.edu/musicdictionary/).

Accompanied recitative (in Italian: *recitativo accompagnato* or *recitativo obbligato*) RECITATIVE accompanied by a good part of the orchestra, punctuating the singers' lines with more than simple chords. This kind of accompaniment normally signifies a speech or dialogue of particular significance, sometimes a decisive reflection.

Acting style (in Italian: *stile rappresentativo*) or **declamatory style** (*stile recitativo*) Style of sung declamation that projects the intonations and pacing of an actor's delivery more than the elaborations and repetitions of song. The creation of an acting style was the defining musical requirement for the invention of opera, and the subsequent history of the genre has relied on the continuing evolution of that style. Compare SINGING STYLE.

Afterbeat A weak beat succeeding a DOWNBEAT or other strong beat.

Apotheosis The triumphant final transformation of a melody that has been repeated numerous times throughout an opera.

Appoggiatura A note that creates dissonance on a strong beat and then slides to a consonant adjoining note after the beat.

Aria A solo operatic speech accompanied and framed by the orchestra. The character's text is usually in stanza form. Textual and musical repetitions and returns shape the speech into a musical number embodying some form of STROPHIC PROGRESSION.

Arioso (Italian, "aria-like") Style of operatic speech in which the text is declaimed as in recitative, while the accompaniment has the constant rhythms and independent melodies of an ARIA.

Arpeggio A chord performed with its notes spread out in sequence, as if strummed on a harp.

Aside Thoughts that a character addresses to no one else present onstage. In a LIBRETTO or score, an aside is indicated by parentheses around the words; in performance, usually by the singer turning away from other characters.

Atonal music Music in which no key is established.

Augmented second An interval equal to a WHOLE STEP plus a HALF STEP, producing a striking effect when it occurs between successive notes of a SCALE, as it does between the sixth and seventh notes in a version of the MINOR scale.

Backdrop Screen at the back of a stage, painted in perspective to provide the background setting of a scene.

Ballad Medieval form of narrative song, imitated in opera to suggest the sung narration of a legend. A ballad relates its story through a series of stanzas, each set to more or less the same music; sometimes each stanza ends in a refrain.

Ballad opera English-language genre of COMIC OPERA, both satirical and sentimental, with spoken dialogue and simple songs, including familiar BALLADS and other popular songs of the day, outfitted with new words to suit the dramatic situation. *The Beggar's Opera* (London, 1728) established the genre.

Ballet corps Ensemble of dancers, generally with no individual identities or names within the drama, though their dances may be connected more or less closely to the action.

Baritone Male vocal range lower than the TENOR and higher than the BASS. In opera since about 1800, the role of the male protagonist's rival or enemy or best friend has typically been assigned to a baritone.

Bass The lowest male vocal range. A father or someone of considerable age and authority is often cast as a bass.

Bass part The lowest part playing in the ORCHESTRA at any given time.

Basso continuo (Italian, "continuous bass"; also known as *figured bass*) Instrumental BASS PART in most numbers (vocal and instrumental) of a seventeenth- or eighteenth-century opera. The written bass line may be played by one or more chord instruments, filling in the harmonies according to the figures written under the notes (hence *figured bass*). A melodic bass instrument may double the bass line.

Bel canto (Italian, "beautiful singing") Classic vocal technique; more specifically, the florid vocal technique of the eighteenth century as it was continued and transformed in Italian opera in the first half of the nineteenth century.

Blue note A somewhat lowered note within an otherwise MAJOR SCALE, typically occurring on the third and seventh and even the fifth note of the scale in the blues and related traditions.

Breeches role Male role played by a woman.

Cabaletta The brilliant concluding part of a nineteenth-century Italian ARIA, contrasting with the slower, more soulful first part, known as the CANTABILE.

Cadence The move that brings a phrase or longer musical unit to an end.

Cadenza (Italian, "cadence") Wordless, unaccompanied, and theoretically improvised flourish that holds off the final cadence of an ARIA.

Canon An imitative texture, in which one voice or part performs the same melody as another, following it at a fixed time interval, whether proceeding from the same pitch or a different one.

Cantabile (Italian, "singable") The slow, soulful first part of a nineteenth-century Italian ARIA, contrasting with the brilliant concluding part, the CABALETTA.

Castrato (Italian, "castrated") Male singer who was castrated before puberty so that he would retain a high singing range when his voice matured. In the first two centuries of Italian opera, castrati were the greatest stars.

Chord A cluster of three or more pitches sounded together.

Chorus Group of singers representing characters with a group identity, but no individual identities.

Chromatic scale or harmony A rich SCALE or harmony that uses more HALF STEPS than are found in a DIATONIC SCALE or harmony.

Comic opera Opera on a nonclassical subject, though not necessarily comic.

Conductor Musical director of an opera, responsible for coordinating players, singers, and dancers, as well as for overall musical interpretation of the score.

Consonance The harmonious effect produced by certain notes sounded simultaneously or successively.

Contralto (or alto) The lowest female vocal range. The role of an older woman or a woman of evil character is often played by a contralto.

Costume drama Drama that evokes a particular place at a particular moment in the past by means of costumes and sets derived from that world.

Countermelody A secondary melody sounded against a principal one.

Counterpoint The play of simultaneous musical lines against each other.

Crescendo Growing louder.

Da capo aria (Italian, "from the head") An ARIA in which the music to the first of two stanzas is reprised after the music to the second. The da capo form became ubiquitous in arias in the early-eighteenth century.

Declamatory style See ACTING STYLE.

Dénouement (French, "unravelling") The turn of events that allows the plot to resolve and the work to end.

Descant A harmonizing part sounding above the main melody.

Diatonic scale A seven-note scale, such as the major- and minor-mode scales of tonal music.

Diegetic Belonging to the scene that the characters inhabit. Diegetic music in opera is music that the characters are understood to be hearing within the action.

Dissonance The disharmonious effect produced by certain notes sounded simultaneously or successively.

Divertissement (French, "diversion") A dance episode within an opera, belonging barely, if at all, to the action of the opera.

Dominant The note of a SCALE, or CHORD, of a KEY, that exerts the strongest countervailing force to the TONIC and leads back most directly to it.

Dominant pedal A PEDAL POINT on the dominant pitch of the scale, often employed for the tension it creates as the listener waits for that pitch to resolve to the tonic.

Downbeat The strong and organizing beat in the repeating pattern of beats that constitutes a measure. It is signaled in a conducting pattern by a downward motion of the conductor's arm.

Drag role Female role played by a man.

Dramaturgy The layout of the action to be staged.

Dramma giocosa (Italian, "humorous drama") A term sometimes used for COMIC OPERA in the late eighteenth century.

Duet ENSEMBLE of two characters.

Eighth note A note length often used to represent half a beat.

Ensemble Musical number in which two or more individual characters sing together.

Entr'acte (French, "between the acts") Entertainment between the acts of an opera. Instrumental pieces, dance suites, and dramatic episodes have all served this function.

Figuration A patterned movement of notes within a given musical line.

Finale ENSEMBLE or uninterrupted sequence of numbers that ends an act of an opera.

Flat An indication to lower a pitch by a HALF STEP.

Fourth The INTERVAL between two notes of a SCALE that are separated by two others.

Glissando A smooth slide of the voice (or on an instrument) between two pitches.

Grand opera Opera designed to employ the resources of a great opera house to spectacular effect. Opera of this type was initiated at the Opéra in Paris in the early nineteenth century and was soon taken up elsewhere.

Ground bass A short, usually stepwise bass line that repeats many times in the course of a slow, dance-like number.

Half cadence A cadence on a dominant chord, which leaves the phrase feeling half-resolved.

Half step One of the smaller STEPS in a MAJOR or MINOR SCALE, half as large as a WHOLE STEP.

Human-interest story In either journalism or fiction beginning at the end of the nineteenth century, a heart-rending story about the difficulties that ordinary people face in their daily lives.

Intermezzo Brief COMIC OPERA in two scenes, performed between the acts of a serious opera (to which it was unconnected) in early eighteenth-century Italian opera houses.

Interval The relationship, or distance, between two pitches.

Introduzione (Italian, "introduction") ENSEMBLE or uninterrupted sequence of numbers that opens an act of an opera.

Key The tone around which the harmony of a musical work or passage is organized.

Lament Solo number (usually soliloquy) expressing loss.

Legato Connected, of a melodic line.

Leitmotif (German, "leading motif") A musical (usually orchestral) phrase that recurs many times, each recurrence reinforcing its association with an idea or object or person in the drama. The term is especially applied to Wagner's music dramas.

Librettist Author of a text to be set to music as an opera.

Libretto (Italian, "little book") The dramatic text of an opera, traditionally published and sold to operagoers in the form of a "little book." Where an opera is performed in a language foreign to the audience, a translation may appear opposite the original text.

Local color (in French: *couleur locale*) Telling detail (visual, musical, or other) that locates a work in place or time.

Love duet A duet expressing the characters' love for each other.

Mad scene A complex solo number that shows a character hallucinating.

Major mode One of the two types of SCALE and KEY in tonal music, conventionally used for happier or more tranquil music. Compare MINOR MODE.

Maxim Pithy saying or general statement of a human truth.

Measure A unit of musical time comprising the prevailing pattern of strong and weak beats; bar.

Melismatic Flowing (referring to vocal passages sung on a single vowel).

Melodrama 1. Dialogue spoken over orchestral accompaniment. 2. Suspenseful drama with a sensational ending.

Mezzo-soprano The female vocal range lower than SOPRANO and higher than CONTRALTO. Roles of rival to or confidante of the heroine are often written for mezzo-sopranos.

Minor mode One of the two types of SCALE and KEY in tonal music, conventionally used for sadder or stormier music. Compare MAJOR MODE.

Modal polyphony Composition in several voices or parts using the modes of the medieval Catholic Church rather than tonal scales, and therefore tending, in opera, to evoke the sound world of medieval or Renaissance Western Europe.

Mode In tonal music, one of the two principal kinds of SCALE, MAJOR or MINOR.

Modulation Migration from one key to another in the course of a musical number.

Motive A short, distinctive melodic and/or rhythmic figure that insinuates itself into the listener's consciousness through frequent repetition and reworking.

Neoclassicism Imitation of eighteenth-century style in twentieth-century music.

Obbligato aria Aria with an "obligatory" part, that is, a part for a particular instrument that creates an elaborate duet with the singer.

Octave The interval between two equivalent pitches (with the same letter name) in adjoining REGISTERS.

Opera buffa (Italian, "comic opera") Eighteenth-century Italian opera performed by comic actors.

Opéra comique (French, "comic opera") French opera with spoken dialogue.

Opera seria (Italian, "serious opera") Eighteenth-century Italian opera on a classical subject.

Oratorio Sacred musical drama, partly narrated and partly dramatized, using operatic forms and styles.

Orchestra Instrumental ensemble for an opera.

Overture Orchestral number that introduces an opera.

Pantomime Action carried out through wordless movement and gesture.

Parallel sixths A movement of two voices or parts at a constant interval of a SIXTH, often producing an effect of sweetness.

Parallel thirds A movement of two voices or parts at a constant interval of a THIRD, often producing an effect of sweetness.

Part-writing Composing in several voices or parts so as to control both the melody of the individual parts and the harmony of the whole.

Patter A flood of words sung to the simplest, most repetitive of melodies.

Pedal point A note sustained in the bass while the harmony changes several times above it; a drone.

Pentatonic scale A five-note scale, such as those from which much traditional music in many parts of the world is made.

Period Musical sentence made of complementary phrases, often opening identically and ending differently.

Phrase A melodic or musical thought that might be performed in a breath.

Prelude A short overture.

Quarter note A note length often used to represent the prevailing beat.

Quartet Four-voice ensemble.

Quatrain Four-line poetic stanza (or part of a stanza).

Recitative (from the Italian *stile recitativo*) Reciting style. Operatic dialogue in blank verse (nonstrophic poetry), set to talky melodies that allow the singers to control the pacing of their delivery, with spare instrumental punctuation.

Refrain A recurring phrase or section at the end of each strophe of a song. The refrain may have the same or nearly the same words each time and may contain a moral or other comment on the story unfolding in the song. In opera the refrain to a solo song may be sung by the chorus.

Register A segment of a singer's or instrument's pitch range.

Repertory system The scheduling system in which an opera house presents a number of works in steady rotation. Compare with STAGIONE SYSTEM.

Réunion des thèmes (French, "reconciliation of themes") Culminating passage in which two or more contrasting musical themes, previously heard in succession, are heard simultaneously.

Rhetoric The art of persuasion. In ancient Greece and Rome, an art of courtroom and political speaking that also shaped the language of tragedy. Opera was developed with the ambition of creating a sung rhetoric for drama.

Ritornello (Italian, "refrain") An orchestral passage that introduces an aria or other vocal number and returns to mark off stages of that number, including the ending.

Rondò A form of aria used for sentimental statements by noble characters in late eighteenth-century opera: a slow movement of simple character followed by a virtuosic fast movement.

Scale The collection of pitch STEPS that define a KEY.

Scenario The layout of scenes and action in a drama.

Seventh chord A four-pitch chord made from alternate notes of a scale.

Sharp An indication to raise a pitch by a HALF STEP.

Simile aria (in Italian: *aria di paragone*) ARIA on a text that proposes and develops a poetic comparison between some natural or human condition and the present dramatic situation.

Simple recitative (in Italian: *recitativo semplice*; also known as *recitativo secco*) In eighteenth-century opera, recitative sung to BASSO CONTINUO accompaniment.

Sinfonia (Italian, "symphony") An instrumental number within an opera.

Singing style Songlike style that characters in opera use when they are expressing themselves most poetically or supposed to be actually singing. This style is characterized by regularity of phrases, melismatic melody, and considerable repetition of both text and musical phrases. Compare ACTING STYLE.

Sixth The harmonious interval between two notes of a SCALE separated by four others.

Socialist realism In the Soviet Union and other Communist countries in the twentieth century, the official artistic doctrine, prescribing simple and uplifting expression in praise of working-class heroes in their struggles against oppression.

Soprano The highest female vocal range (and in the age of the CASTRATO, the highest male range as well). The leading female role is ordinarily written for a soprano; typically it is a young woman in love, often with a TENOR character.

Sprechstimme (German, "speaking voice") In twentieth-century opera in German, a melodramatic and rhythmic declamation that is less fully pitched than singing.

Staccato Disconnected, of a melodic line.

Stagione system The scheduling system in which an opera house presents the same work night after night, or a couple of works in alternation, for weeks at a time. Compare REPERTORY SYSTEM.

Step The difference in pitch between successive notes in a SCALE.

Stile rappresentativo See ACTING STYLE.

Stile recitativo See ACTING STYLE.

Strophic progression Stanzas of text set to musical units that are not identical, but equivalent in length and related to each other in such a way that the whole sequence of units suggests a reasoned progression of thought.

Strophic repetition Each stanza of a song sung to the same music.

Strophic song A song in which each stanza of text is sung to the same music.

Strophic text A poetic text constructed in stanzas identical in form.

Suspension A harmonized note that is sustained into a new chord with which it does not harmonize and is then resolved into a note that does belong in that new chord.

Syncopation A rhythmic displacement, such as a strong beat played on an upbeat that is sustained through the downbeat.

Tenor A high male vocal range. Starting in the nineteenth century, the leading male role is typically written for a tenor; usually it is a young man in love with a SOPRANO character.

Texture The number and relationship of the lines or parts sounding together.

Thematic transformation Transformed version of a previously heard musical motive or theme, its new character marking a new stage in the dramatic action.

Third The harmonious interval between two notes of a SCALE separated by one other.

Tonic The home note of a SCALE, or home CHORD of a KEY, or home key of a musical number or work.

Tragédie en musique Seventeenth- or eighteenth-century French opera on a classical subject.

Tremolo (Italian, "trembling") A rapid repetition of a single pitch or alternation between two pitches.

Triad A three-pitch chord made from alternate notes of a scale. Triads are the defining chords of a key.

Trill Embellishment of a sustained note by fluttering between that note and an adjoining one.

Tritone An interval (found, for example, between the fourth and seventh notes of a major scale) that is traditionally treated as particularly dissonant and unstable.

Vanishing point In a perspective stage set, the ostensibly distant spot to which all the ostensibly horizontal lines in the set point.

Whole step One of the larger STEPS used in a MAJOR SCALE, twice as large as a HALF STEP.

Whole-tone scale A six-note SCALE consisting entirely of WHOLE STEPS, producing an effect of tonal ambiguity because it is the characteristic distribution of whole steps and half steps that gives a tonal (DIATONIC) scale its tonal orientation, or TONIC.

Wing flats In a seventeenth- or eighteenth-century stage set, narrow vertical boards arranged on both sides of the BACKDROP and receding toward it; the scene painted on the backdrop continues onto the wing flats, extending the illusion of depth.

Word painting The use of a vivid musical image to illustrate a word or idea in the sung text.

NOTES

Chapter 1

1. Tommasini 2006.
2. Shaw 1961, 255–56.
3. Renoir 1962, 189.
4. Ossi 1998.
5. Viale Ferrero 1998, 2.
6. Kimbell 1991, 120.
7. Solie 1997, 197.
8. Marcello [1720] 1948, 390.
9. Langhans 1992, 3:123.
10. Johnson 1995, 245.

Chapter 2

1. Yung 1984, 150.
2. Harris-Warrick 2000.
3. Spitzer and Zaslaw 1992, 1:915.

Chapter 3

1. Kerman 1988, 17.
2. Bentley, 1968, 6:226.
3. Heller 2003, 34, 4.
4. Rosselli 1992, 58.
5. Poizat 1992, 32.
6. Brown 1997, 69–70.
7. Betzwieser 2000, 4, n. 13.
8. Hansell 2002, 191; Smith 2003, 103–4.

Chapter 4

1. Dumas [1848] 1986, 67–68.
2. Kimbell 1981, 657.
3. Ibid., 420.
4. Budden 1978, 2:38.
5. Galilei [1581] 1984, 167–68.
6. Ober and Strauss 1990, 270.

Chapter 5

1. Greenblatt 1980, 2.
2. Pico della Mirandola [1496] 1956, 7.
3. Bianconi 1982, 173–74.
4. Pirrotta 1982, 262–63;
   Bianconi 1982, 175.
5. Ovid, *Metamorphoses* 15:875–76; see Simpson, Michael, trans. 2001.
6. Cusick 1994, 36.
7. Peri [1601] 1981, xlii.
8. Fenlon 1986, 12–16.
9. Whenham 1986, 68.
10. Pirrotta 1982, 277.
11. Kerman 1988, 27.

Chapter 6

1. Alm 2003, n. 96.
2. Piperno 1998, 6, 9.
3. Bjurström 1975, 109–10.
4. Bianconi 1982, 184.
5. Ivanovich 1984, 304.
6. Zoppelli 1992, 4:915; Bianconi and Walker 1984, 268–70.
7. Rosand 1991, 335–38.
8. Rosand 1985, 45–47.
9. Taruskin 2005, 2:27.

Chapter 7

1. Zaslaw 1989, 7–23.
2. La Gorce 1985, 150, 158.
3. Rosow 1992, 3:84.
4. Bianconi 1982, 251.
5. Dryden [1685] 1976, 15:15.
6. Lecerf de la Viéville [1705] 1950, 498–99.
7. Cowart 1981, 37.
8. Wood and Sadler 2000, 32–33.
9. La Gorce 1985, 40–41.
10. Titon du Tillet [1743] 1998, 572–73.
11. Lecerf de la Viéville [1705] 1950, 499.
12. Anthony 1997, 94–95.
13. Rosow 1992, 1:201.
14. Harris-Warrick 2007.
15. Anthony 1997, 104.
16. Masson 1930, 210–12.
17. Howard 1989, 143–45.
18. Anthony 1997, 95, 99.
19. Titon du Tillet [1743] 1998, 573.

Chapter 8

1. Dean and Knapp, 1995, 498.
2. Heartz 2003, 69–78; Rosselli 1992, 91–100.
3. Brosses [1739] 2002, 86.
4. Grout 1988, 208.
5. Martello [1715] 2002, 80.
6. Ibid., 79.
7. Weiss 1982, 391.
8. Dean and Knapp 1995, 487, 496.
9. Emslie 2003, 188.
10. Dean and Knapp 1995, 7.
11. Anonymous in *Almanach des Spectacles*, 1765; quoted in Malherbe, ed., 1900, 6:lix.
12. Anthony 1997, 162.
13. Girdlestone 1969, 550.
14. Brown 1992, 1:694.
15. Gluck [1769] 2002, 119–20.
16. Johnson 1995, 59.
17. Vincent-Buffault 1991, 58.
18. Ibid., 10; Johnson 1995, 61.
19. Johnson 1995, 51.

Chapter 9

1. Fiske 1986, 99.
2. Lindgren 1992.
3. Fiske 1986, 102.
4. Cook 1992.
5. Fiske 1986, 101–02, 109.
6. Carter 1987, 35–36.
7. Hunter 1999, 81.
8. Allanbrook 1983, 327.
9. Carter 1987, 97.
10. Allanbrook 1983, 286–87.
11. Ibid., 43–44, 172.
12. Ibid., 33.
13. Platoff 1989, 218.
14. Rushton 1981, 15–16.
15. Platoff 1989, 219.
16. Hunter 1999, 147.
17. Ibid., 88.
18. Brown 1995, ch. 4.
19. Hunter 1999, 97–98.

Chapter 10

1. Berlioz [1853] 1994, 66.
2. Smith 2003, 94.
3. Charlton 1992, 1992a.
4. Charlton 1986, 248–50.

5. Charlton 1996.
6. Thayer 1964, 1:385–86.
7. Berlioz [1860] 1994, 48.
8. Solomon 1977, ch. 4; Robinson 1996, 75–80.
9. Meyer 2002, 515.
10. Staël [1818] 1983, 306.
11. Gerhard 1998, 162–70.
12. *La France Musicale*, 13 May 1838.
13. Donizetti 1948, 369.
14. Gerhard 1998.
15. Berlioz [1836] 1998, 2:433.
16. Schumann 1964, 196.
17. Berlioz [1836] 1998, 2:419.
18. Gerhard 1998, 228–31.
19. Dahlhaus 1989, 12–13; Taruskin 2005, 3:225–27.
20. Sand [1836] 1971, 2:918; Mainzer [1836] 1998, 211.
21. Kelly 2004, ch. 3; Brzoska 2003, 206–07.
22. Locke 2005, 135.
23. Huebner 2002.
24. Budden 1978, 3:254–55.
25. Taruskin 1992, 1:554–56; Taruskin 1993.
26. Budden 1978, 3:258.
27. Locke 1993, 58–62; Said 1994, 111–32.

Chapter 11

1. Wright 2000, ix–xxi.
2. McClary 1992, 51–61.
3. Clément 1988, 49.
4. McClary 1992, ch. 7.
5. Clément 1988, 48.
6. Parakilas 1993/94.
7. Johnson 2004, 167.
8. Perrot 1990, 181.
9. Clément 1988, 60.
10. Perrot 1990, 186–87, 249–51.
11. Seigel 1986, 1–11.
12. Verdi [1887] 1988, 1:301, 310.
13. Parakilas 1997; Hepokoski 1987, 163–78.

Chapter 12

1. Grey 2000, 80–81.
2. Dahlhaus 1979, 17–20.
3. Taruskin 1992, 4:96.
4. Hoeckner 1997, 131.
5. Dahlhaus 1979, 35–38.
6. Millington 1992; Millington 1992a, 286.
7. Shaw 1967; Borchmeyer 2003; Williams, 2004.

8. Reinhardt 1992, 287–96; Millington 1984, 222–27.
9. Nietzsche 1967.
10. Rose 1992, 66–72; Borchmeyer 1992, 183–85; Millington 1992a, 161–64.
11. Dahlhaus 1979, 119.

Chapter 13

1. Tyrrell 1988, 246–48.
2. English text adapted from uncredited translation in London recording 414 483-2.
3. Tyrrell 1992, 2:891.
4. Jarman 1989, 42, 149–70.
5. Kerman 1988, 185.
6. Jarman 1989, 138.
7. Kerman 1988, 186, 188.
8. Taruskin 2005, 4:520.
9. Jarman 1989, 153.
10. Kerman 1988, 190.
11. Jarman 1989, 153.
12. Hine 1999.
13. Pollack 2006, 583.
14. Allen and Cunninghman 2005; Early 2006, 32.
15. Pollack 2006, 574.
16. Wyatt and Johnson 2004, 221–36.
17. Pollack 2006, 661.
18. Abarbanel 1994, 9; Brett 1983, 180–96.
19. Emerson 1989, 60–61.
20. Ibid., 67.
21. Shostakovich 1989, 69; Shostakovich 2000, 69.
22. Shostakovich 2000, 69.
23. Fay 1995, 165, 174–76; Fanning 1993, 18.
24. Emerson 2004, 196, n. 30.
25. Taruskin 1997, 498–510.
26. Poulenc 1954, 211; Schmidt 2001, ch. 12.
27. Poulenc 1999, 297.
28. Poulenc 1991, 220.

29. May 2006, 297–342; Tommasini 2003.
30. Jenkins 1975, 4; see also Weimann and Winn 1994.
31. May 2006, 11, 253.

Chapter 14

1. Debussy [1902] 1977, 75.
2. John 1982, 28.
3. Nichols 1989, 172.
4. Stravinsky [1962] 1981, 131, n. 1
5. Nichols and Smith 1989, 144.
6. Gilliam 1999, 106.
7. Hofmannstahl 1980, 184, 209.
8. Del Mar 1986, 2:194–5.
9. Stravinsky 1996.
10. Griffiths 1994, 504.
11. Messiaen 1994, 214; 214, 224; 211, 247.
12. Griffiths 1994, 492.
13. Messiaen 1994, 234.
14. Stuckenschmidt 1977, 367–70, 541–2.
15. Goldstein 2000, 161–3.
16. Weaver 1981, 294–8.
17. Goldstein 2000, 167–84.
18. Weaver 1981, 300.
19. Boulez 1996, 13.
20. Shostakovich 1981.
21. Griffiths 1983, 98.
22. Ligeti 2003, 222.
23. Steinitz 2003, 237.
24. Griffiths 1983, 104.
25. Ravel 1990, 436.
26. Kylián 1986.
27. Nichols 1992, 3:48.
28. Klein 1948.
29. Corsaro 1987.
30. Cited in Smith 2000, 201.

WORKS CITED

For further reading: The most comprehensive English-language reference work on opera is *The New Grove Dictionary of Opera*, ed. Stanley Sadie (London: Macmillan and New York: Grove's Dictionaries of Music, 1992), available online through Oxford Music Online. Important documents from the history of opera, translated into English, are collected in Piero Weiss, *Opera: A History in Documents* (New York and Oxford: Oxford University Press, 2002). A multi-author history of opera is *The Oxford Illustrated History of Opera*, ed. Roger Parker (Oxford and New York: Oxford University Press, 1994).

The Cambridge University Press series of *Cambridge Opera Handbooks* provides detailed analysis and commentary on many individual operas in the standard repertory. Scholarly articles on opera are published in the *Cambridge Opera Journal* (Cambridge University Press) and *The Opera Quarterly* (Oxford University Press), as well as in general musicological journals.

Abarbanel, Jonathan. 1994. Program note in the booklet of Kent Nagano recording of Carlisle Floyd, *Susannah*, Virgin Classics VCD 5 45039 2.

Allanbrook, Wye Jamison. 1983. *Rhythmic Gesture in Mozart: "Le nozze di Figaro" & "Don Giovanni."* Chicago and London: University of Chicago Press.

Allen, Ray, and George P. Cunningham. 2005. "Cultural Uplift and Double-Consciousness: African-American Responses to the 1935 Opera *Porgy and Bess*." In *Musical Quarterly* 88/3 (Fall 2005): 342–69.

Alm, Irene. 2003. "Winged Feet and Mute Eloquence: Dance in Seventeenth-Century Venetian Opera." In *Cambridge Opera Journal* 15/3 (Nov 2003): 216–80.

Anthony, James R. 1997. *French Baroque Music, from Beaujoyeulx to Rameau*. Rev.ed. Portland, Ore.: Amadeus Press.

Bentley, Gerald Eades. 1968. *The Jacobean and Caroline Stage*. Oxford: Clarendon Press. Quoting Thomas Brandes.

Berlioz, Hector. 1994. Reviews in *Journal des Débats* 6 February 1853 (Rossini) and 19 and 22 May 1860 (Fidelio). Repr. in *A Travers Chants*. Paris, 1862. New ed. by Léon Guichard. Paris: Gründ, 1971. Eng. trans. by Elizabeth Csicsery-Rónay in *The Art of Music and Other Essays (A Travers Chants)*. Bloomington: Indiana University Press.

———. [1836] 1998. Reviews of 6 and 13 March 1836 in *Revue et gazette musicale de Paris*. Repr. in Hector Berlioz, *Critique musicale, 1823–1863*, ed. Yves Gérard. Vol. 2: 1835-36. Paris: Buchet/Chastel.

Betzwieser, Thomas. 2000. "Musical Setting and Scenic Movement: Chorus and *Choeur dansé* in Eighteenth-Century Parisian Opéra." In *Cambridge Opera Journal* 12/1 (March 2000). Quoting published letters by Abbé François Arnaud and Nicolas le Bouguinon de La Salle.

Bianconi, Lorenzo. 1987. *Music in the Seventeenth Century*, trans. David Bryant. Cambridge and New York: Cambridge University Press. Original Italian ed, 1982.

———, and Thomas Walker. 1984. "Production, Consumption and Political Function of Seventeenth-Century Opera." In *Early Music History 4: Studies in Medieval and Early Modern Music*, ed. Iain Fenlon. Cambridge and New York: Cambridge University Press.

Bjurström, Per. 1975. *Giacomo Torelli and Baroque Stage Design*. Ann Arbor, Mich.: Xerox University Microfilms, 1975. Original ed., Stockholm: Nationalmuseum, 1962.

Borchmeyer, Dieter. 1992. "The Question of Anti-Semitism." In *Wagner Handbook*, ed. Ulrich Müller and Peter Wapnewski, trans. John Deathridge. Cambridge and London: Harvard University Press.

Boulez, Pierre. 1996. "Boulez on Schoenberg's *Moses und Aron*: An Interview with Wolfgang Schaufler." In the libretto of the recording of *Moses and Aaron* conducted by Boulez. Deutsche Grammophon 449 174–2.

Brett, Philip. 1983. *Benjamin Britten: "Peter Grimes."* Cambridge and New York: Cambridge University Press.

Brosses, Charles de. [1739] 2002. *Lettres d'Italie du Président de Bosses*, ed. Frédéric d'Agay. Paris: Mercure de France, 1986. Eng. trans. in Piero Weiss, *Opera: A History in Documents*. New York and Oxford: Oxford University Press.

Brown, Bruce Alan. 1992. "Calzabigi, Ranieri de'." In *New Grove Dictionary of Opera*.

———. 1995. *W. A. Mozart: "Così fan tutte."* Cambridge and New York: Cambridge University Press.

———. 1997. "Lo specchio francese: Viennese Opera Buffa and the Legacy of French Theatre." In *Opera Buffa in Mozart's Vienna*, ed. Mary Hunter and James Webster. Cambridge and New York: Cambridge University Press.

Brzoska, Matthias. 2003. "Meyerbeer: *Robert le Diable* and *Les Huguenots*." In *The Cambridge Companion to Grand Opera*, ed. David Charlton. Cambridge and New York: Cambridge University Press.

Budden, Julian. 1978. *The Operas of Verdi*. Vol. 2: From *"Il Trovatore"* to *"La Forza del Destino."* Vol. 3: From *"Aida"* to *"Falstaff."* New York: Oxford University Press.

Carter, Tim. 1987. *W. A. Mozart: "Le nozze di Figaro."* Cambridge and New York: Cambridge University Press.

Charlton, David. 1986. *Grétry and the Growth of Opéra-Comique*. Cambridge and New York: Cambridge University Press.

———. 1992. "On Redefinitions of 'Rescue Opera.'" In *Music and the French Revolution*, ed. Malcolm Boyd. Cambridge and New York: Cambridge University Press.

———. 1992a. "Rescue Opera." In *New Grove Dictionary of Opera*.

———. 1996. "The French Theatrical Origins of Fidelio." In *Ludwig van Beethoven: "Fidelio,"* ed. Paul Robinson. Cambridge and New York: Cambridge University Press, pp. 62–67.

Clément, Catherine. 1988. *Opera, or the Undoing of Women*, trans. Betsy Wing. Minneapolis: University of Minnesota Press. Original French ed., 1979.

Cook, Elisabeth. 1992. "Querelle des Bouffons." In *New Grove Dictionary of Opera*.

Corsaro, Frank. 1987. Staging in videorecording of Ravel, *L'Enfant et les Sortilèges*, at Glyndebourne Festival Opera, conducted by Simon Rattle. Framingham, Mass.: Home Vision.

Cowart, Georgia. 1981. *The Origins of Modern Musical Criticism: French and Italian Music, 1600–1750*. Ann Arbor: UMI Research Press.

Cusick, Suzanne. 1994. " 'There Was Not One Lady Who Failed to Shed a Tear': Arianna's Lament and the Construction of Modern Womanhood." In *Early Music* 22/1 (February 1994): 21–41.

Dahlhaus, Carl. 1979. *Richard Wagner's Music Dramas*, trans. Mary Whittall. Cambridge and New York: Cambridge University Press.

———. 1989. *Nineteenth-Century Music*, trans. J. Bradford Robinson. Berkeley and Los Angeles: University of California Press. Original German ed., 1980.

Dean, Winton, and John Merrill Knapp. 1995. *Handel's Operas, 1704–1726*. Rev. ed. Oxford: Clarendon Press.

Debussy, Claude. [1902] 1977. "Why I Wrote Pelléas." Repr. in *Debussy on Music*, ed. François Lesure, trans. Richard Langham Smith. New York: Knopf. Original French ed., 1971.

Del Mar, Norman. 1986. *Richard Strauss: A Critical Commentary on His Life and Works*. Ithaca, N.Y.: Cornell University Press. First publ. 1969.

Donizetti, Gaetano. [1835] 1948. Letter of 16 March 1835 to Antonio Dolci. In Guido Zavadini, *Donizetti: Vita, Musiche, Epistolario*. Bergamo: Istituto Italiano d'Arti Grafiche.

Dryden, John. [1685] 1976. Prologue to *Albion and Albanius*. In *The Works of John Dryden*. Berkeley and Los Angeles: University of California Press.

Dumas, Alexandre fils. [1848] 1986. *La Dame aux Camélias*, trans. David Coward. Oxford and New York: Oxford University Press.

Early, Gerald. 2006. Review of *At Canaan's Edge: America in the King Years, 1965–1968*, by Taylor Branch. *The Nation*, March 27, 2006.

Emerson, Caryl. 1989. "Back to the Future: Shostakovich's Revision of Leskov's *Lady Macbeth of Mtsensk District*." In *Cambridge Opera Journal* 1/1 (March 1989): 59–78.

———. 2004. "Shostakovich and the Russian Literary Tradition." In *Shostakovich and His World*, ed. Laurel E. Fay. Princeton: Princeton University Press.

Emslie, Barry. 2003. "Handel the Postmodernist." In *Cambridge Opera Journal* 15/2 (July 2003):185–98.

Fanning, David. 1993. Introduction to the libretto of Shostakovich, *Lady Macbeth of Mtsensk District*,

recording conducted by Myung-Whun Chung. Deutsche Grammophon 437 511-2.

Fay, Laurel E. 1995. "From *Lady Macbeth* to *Katerina*: Shostakovich's Versions and Revisions." In *Shostakovich Studies*, ed. David Fanning. Cambridge and New York: Cambridge University Press.

Fenlon, Iain. 1986. "The Mantuan 'Orfeo.'" In *Claudio Monteverdi: "Orfeo,"* ed. John Whenham. Cambridge and New York: Cambridge University Press.

Ferrero. See Viale Ferrero, Mercedes.

Fiske, Roger. 1986. *English Theatre Music in the Eighteenth Century*, 2nd ed. Oxford: Oxford University Press.

Galilei, Vincenzo. [1581] 1984. *Dialogo della musica antica e della moderna*, trans. Richard Taruskin. In *Music in the Western World: A History in Documents*, ed. Piero Weiss and Richard Taruskin. New York: Schirmer.

Gerhard, Anselm. 1998. *The Urbanization of Opera: Music Theater in Paris in the Nineteenth Century*, trans. Mary Whittall. Chicago and London: University of Chicago Press. Original German ed., 1992.

Gilliam, Bryan. 1999. *The Life of Richard Strauss*. Cambridge and New York: Cambridge University Press.

Girdlestone, Cuthbert. 1969. *Jean-Philippe Rameau*. Rev. ed. New York: Dover.

Gluck, Christoph Willibald. [1769] 2002. Dedication to *Alceste*. Vienna, 1769. Eng. trans. by Piero Weiss. In Weiss, *Opera: A History in Documents*. Oxford and New York: Oxford University Press.

Goldstein, Bluma. 2000. "Schoenberg's *Moses und Aron*: A Vanishing Biblical Nation." In *Political and Religious Ideas in the Works of Arnold Schoenberg*, ed. Charlotte M. Cross and Russell A. Berman. New York and London: Garland.

Greenblatt, Stephen. 1980. *Renaissance Self-Fashioning: From More to Shakespeare*. Chicago and London: University of Chicago Press.

Grey, Thomas. 2000. *Richard Wagner: "Der fliegende Holländer."* Cambridge and New York: Cambridge University Press.

Griffiths, Paul. 1983. *György Ligeti*. London: Robson.

———. 1994. "*Saint François d'Assise.*" In *The Messiaen Companion*, ed. Peter Hill. Portland, Ore.: Amadeus Press.

Grout, Donald J. 1988. *A Short History of Opera*, 3rd ed., with Hermine Weigel Williams. New York: Columbia University Press.

Hansell, Kathleen Kuzmick. 2002. "Theatrical Ballet and Italian Opera." In *Opera on Stage*. Vol. 5 of *The History of Italian Opera*, ed. Lorenzo Bianconi and Giorgio Pestelli. Chicago and London: University of Chicago Press. Original Italian ed., 1988.

Harris-Warrick, Rebecca. 2000. "The Phrase Structures of Lully's Dance Music." In *Lully Studies*, ed. John Hajdu Heyer. Cambridge and New York: Cambridge University Press.

———. 2007. "Lully's On-Stage Societies." In *Opera and Society in Italy and France from Monteverdi to Bourdieu*, ed. Victoria Johnson, Jane F. Fulcher, and Thomas Ertman. Cambridge and New York: Cambridge University Press.

Heartz, Daniel. 2003. *Music in European Capitals: The Galant Style, 1720–1780*. New York: Norton.

Heller, Wendy. 2003a. *Emblems of Eloquence: Opera and Women's Voices in Seventeenth-Century Venice*. Berkeley and Los Angeles: University of California Press.

Hepokoski, James. 1987. *Giuseppe Verdi: "Otello."* Cambridge and New York: Cambridge University Press.

Hine, Darlene Clark. 1999. Commentary in *"Porgy and Bess": An American Voice*, directed by Nigel Noble. Princeton: Films for the Humanities and Sciences.

Hoeckner, Berthold. 1997. "Elsa Screams, or The Birth of Music Drama." In *Cambridge Opera Journal* 9/2 (July 1997): 97–132.

Hofmannstahl, Hugo von. [1913] 1980. Letter of 28 December 1913 to Richard Strauss. In *The Correspondence Between Richard Strauss and Hugo von Hofmannsthal*, trans. Hanns Hammelmann and Ewald Osers. Cambridge and New York: Cambridge University Press. Original German ed., 1952.

Howard, Patricia. 1989. "Lully and the Ironic Convention." In *Cambridge Opera Journal* 1/2 (July 1989): 139–53.

Huebner, Steven. 2002. "'O patria mia': Patriotism, Dream, Death." In *Cambridge Opera Journal* 14/1 & 2 (March 2002): 161–75.

Hunter, Mary. 1999. *The Culture of Opera Buffa in Mozart's Vienna: A Poetics of Entertainment*. Princeton: Princeton University Press.

Ivanovich, Cristoforo. [1681] 1987. "Le memorie teatrale di Venezia." Appendix to *Minerva al tavolino* (Venice). Excerpt in Bianconi, *Music in the Seventeenth Century*, trans. David Bryant. Cambridge and New York: Cambridge University Press.

Jarman, Douglas. 1989. *Alban Berg: "Wozzeck."* Cambridge and New York: Cambridge University Press.

Jenkins, Brian. 1975. *International Terrorism.* Los Angeles: Crescent.

John, Nicholas, ed. 1983. *English National Opera Guide to Claude Debussy: "Pelléas et Mélisande."* New York: Riverrun Press.

Johnson, James H. 1995. *Listening in Paris: A Cultural History.* Berkeley and Los Angeles: University of California Press.

Johnson, Janet. 2004. "*Il barbiere di Siviglia.*" In *The Cambridge Companion to Rossini,* ed. Emanuele Senici. Cambridge and New York: Cambridge University Press.

Kelly, Thomas Forrest. 2004. *First Nights at the Opera.* New Haven: Yale University Press.

Kerman, Joseph. 1988. *Opera as Drama.* Rev. ed. Berkeley and Los Angeles: University of California Press. Original ed., New York: Knopf, 1956.

Kimbell, David. 1981. *Verdi in the Age of Italian Romanticism.* Cambridge and New York: Cambridge University Press.

———. 1991. *Italian Opera.* Cambridge and New York: Cambridge University Press.

Klein, Melanie. 1948. "Infantile Anxiety-Situations as Reflected in a Work of Art and in the Creative Impulse." Originally presented March 23, 1927. Repr. in Klein, *Contributions to Psycho-Analysis, 1921–1945.* London: Hogarth Press.

Kylián, Jiří. 1986. Introduction to videorecording of his ballet production of Ravel, *L'Enfant et les Sortilèges.* Framingham, Mass.: Home Vision.

La Gorce, Jérôme de. 1985. "L'Opéra et son public au temps de Louis XIV." Repr. in *The Garland Library of the History of Western Music,* vol. 6/1, ed. Ellen Rosand. New York: Garland.

Langhans, Edward A. 1992. "Machinery." In *New Grove Dictionary of Opera.*

Lecerf de la Viéville, Jean-Laurent. [1705] 1950. *Comparaison de la musique italienne et de la musique française.* Excerpt in *Source Readings in Music History: From Classical Antiquity Through the Romantic Era,* ed. and trans. Oliver Strunk. New York: Norton.

Lindgren, Lowell. 1992. "*Astianatte.*" In *New Grove Dictionary of Opera.*

Locke, Ralph P. 1991. "Constructing the Oriental 'Other': Saint-Saëns's *Samson et Dalila.*" In *Cambridge Opera Journal* 3/3 (November 1991): 261–302.

———. 1993. "Reflections on Orientalism in Opera and Musical Theater." In *Opera Quarterly* 10/1 (Autumn 1993):48–64.

———. 2005. "Beyond the Exotic: How 'Eastern' is *Aida?*" In *Cambridge Opera Journal* 17/2 (July 2005): 105–39.

Mainzer, Joseph. [1836] 1998. Review of *Les Huguenots* in *Neue Zeitschrift für Musik,* September 1836. Quoted in Anselm Gerhard, *The Urbanization of Opera: Music Theater in Paris in the Nineteenth Century,* trans. Mary Whittall. Chicago: University of Chicago Press. Original German ed., 1992.

Malherbe, Charles, ed. 1900. "Commentaire bibliographique to Jean-Philippe Rameau, *Hippolyte et Aricie.*" Vol. 6 of *Oeuvres complètes.* Paris: Durand.

Marcello, Benedetto. [1720] 1948. "*Il teatro alla moda,* Part I," trans. Reinhard G. Pauly. In *Musical Quarterly* 34:371–403.

Martello, Piero Jacopo. [1715] 2002. *Della tragedia antica e moderna,* Eng. trans. in Piero Weiss, *Opera: A History in Documents.* New York and Oxford: Oxford University Press.

Masson, Paul-Marie. 1930. *L'Opéra de Rameau.* Paris: Henri Laurens.

May, Thomas, ed. 2006. *The John Adams Reader: Essential Writings on an American Composer.* Pompton Plains, N.J.: Amadeus Press.

McClary, Susan. 1992. *Georges Bizet: "Carmen."* Cambridge and New York: Cambridge University Press.

Messiaen, Olivier. 1994. *Music and Color: Conversations with Claude Samuel,* trans. E. Thomas Glasow. Portland, Ore.: Amadeus Press. Original French ed., 1986.

Meyer, Stephen. 2002. "Terror and Transcendence in the Operatic Prison, 1790–1815." In *Journal of the American Musicological Society,* 55/3 (Fall 2002): 477–523.

Millington, Barry. 1984. *Wagner.* London: J. M. Dent.

———. 1992. "*Ring des Nibelungen, Der.*" In *New Grove Dictionary of Opera.*

———, ed. 1992a. *The Wagner Compendium: A Guide to Wagner's Life and Music.* New York: Schirmer.

Nichols, Roger, and Richard Langham Smith. 1989. *Claude Debussy: "Pelléas et Mélisande."* Cambridge and New York: Cambridge University Press.

Nichols, Roger. 1992. "*L'Enfant et les Sortilèges.*" In *New Grove Dictionary of Opera.*

Nietzsche, Friedrich. 1967. *The Birth of Tragedy* and *The Case of Wagner*, trans. Walter Kauffman. New York: Vintage. Original German ed., 1888.

Ober, Josiah, and Barry Strauss. 1990. "Drama, Political Rhetoric, and the Discourse of Athenian Democracy." In *Nothing to Do with Dionysos? Athenian Drama in Its Social Context*, ed. John J. Winkler and Froma I. Zeitlin. Princeton: Princeton University Press.

Ossi, Massimo. 1998. "*Dalle machine . . . la maraviglia*: Bernardo Buontalenti's *Il rapimento di Cefalo* at the Medici Theater in 1600." In *Opera in Context: Essays on Historical Staging from the Late Renaissance to the Time of Puccini*, ed. Mark A. Radice. Portland, Ore.: Amadeus Press.

Parakilas, James. 1993/94. "The Solder and the Exotic: Operatic Variations on a Theme of Racial Encounter." In *Opera Quarterly* 10/2 (Winter 1993/94): 33–56, and 10/3 (1994): 43–69.

———. 1997. "Religion and Difference in Verdi's *Otello*." In *Musical Quarterly* 81/3 (Fall 1997): 371–92.

Peri, Jacopo. [1601] 1981. *Euridice: An Opera in One Act, Five Scenes*, ed. Howard Mayer Brown. Madison, Wis.: A-R Editions.

Perrot, Michelle, ed. 1990. *From the Fires of Revolution to the Great War*. Vol. 4 of *A History of Private Life*, ed. Philippe Ariès and Georges Duby, Eng. trans. Arthur Goldhammer. Cambridge and London: Belknap Press of Harvard University Press.

Pico della Mirandola, Giovanni. [1496] 1956. *Oration on the Dignity of Man*, trans. A. Robert Caponigri. Chicago: Henry Regnery.

Piperno, Franco. 1998. "Opera Production to 1780." In *Opera Production and its Resources*, trans. Lydia Cochrane. Vol. 4 of History of Italian Opera, ed. Lorenzo Bianconi and Giorgio Pestelli. Chicago and London: University of Chicago Press; original Italian ed., 1987.

Pirrotta, Nino. 1982. "Early Opera and Aria." Repr. in Nino Pirrotta and Elena Polovedo, *Music and Theatre from Poliziano to Monteverdi*, trans. Karen Eales. Cambridge and New York: Cambridge University Press.

Platoff, John. 1989. "Musical and Dramatic Structure in the Opera Buffa Finale." In *Journal of Musicology* 7/2 (Spring 1989).

Poizat, Michel. 1992. *The Angel's Cry: Beyond the Pleasure Principle in Opera*, trans. Arthur Denner. Ithaca: Cornell University Press; original French ed., 1986.

Pollack, Howard. 2006. *George Gershwin: His Life and Work*. Berkeley and Los Angeles: University of California Press.

Poulenc, Francis. 1954. *Entretiens avec Claude Rostand*. Paris: R. Julliard.

———. 1991. *Selected Correspondence 1915–1963*, trans. and ed. Sidney Buckland. London: Victor Gollancz.

———. 1999. Letter of 12 October 1953 to Henri Hell. English trans. of cited passage in Claude Gendre, "*Dialogues des Carmélites*: The Historical Background, Literary Destiny and Genesis of the Opera," trans. William Bush. In *Francis Poulenc: Music, Art and Literature*, ed. Sidney Buckland and Myriam Chimènes. Aldershot, U.K.: Ashgate.

Ravel, Maurice. [1925] 1990. Interview publ. in *Le Gaulois*, 20 March 1925. English trans. in *A Ravel Reader*, ed. Arbie Ornstein. New York: Columbia University Press.

Reinhardt, Hartmut. 1992. "Wagner and Schopenhauer." In *Wagner Handbook*, ed. Ulrich Müller and Peter Wapnewski, trans. John Deathridge. Cambridge and London: Harvard University Press.

Renoir, Jean. 1962. *Renoir, My Father*. Trans. Randolph and Dorothy Weaver. Boston: Little, Brown.

Robinson, Paul. 1996. *Ludwig van Beethoven: "Fidelio."* Cambridge and New York: Cambridge University Press.

Rosand, Ellen. 1985. "Seneca and the Interpretation of *L'Incoronazione di Poppea*." In *Journal of the American Musicological Society* 38/1 (Spring 1985).

———. 1991. *Opera in Seventeenth-Century Venice: The Creation of a Genre*. Berkeley and Los Angeles: University of California Press.

Rosow, Lois. 1992. "*Armide* (1)." In *New Grove Dictionary of Opera*.

Rosselli, John, 1992. *Singers of Italian Opera: The History of a Profession*. Cambridge and New York: Cambridge University Press.

Said, Edward. 1994. *Culture and Imperialism*. New York: Vintage.

Sand, George. 1971. Letter of September 1836 to Giacomo Meyerbeer, *Lettres d'un voyageur*, XI. Repr. in *Oeuvres autobiographiques*, ed. Georges Lubin. Paris: Gallimard.

Schmidt, Carl B. 2001. *Entrancing Muse: A Documented Biography of Francis Poulenc*. Hillsdale, N.Y.: Pendragon Press.

Schumann, Robert. 1964. *Robert Schumanns Gesammelte Schriften über Musik und Musiker*, 5th ed., Martin Kreisig, ed. Leipzig: Breitkopf & Härtel, 1914. Selected Eng. trans. by Paul Rosenfeld in *On Music and Musicians: Robert Schumann*, ed. Konrad Wolff. New York: McGraw-Hill.

Seigel, Jerrold. 1986. "The Rise of Bohemia." In *Giacomo Puccini: "La bohème,"* ed. Arthur Groos and Roger Parker. Cambridge and New York: Cambridge University Press.

Shaw, George Bernard. [1905] 1961. "Sumptuary Regulations at the Opera." Letter to the *London Times*, 3 July 1905. Repr. in *How to Become a Musical Critic*, ed. Dan H. Laurence. New York: Hill and Wang.

———. [1898] 1967. *The Perfect Wagnerite*. Repr. New York: Dover.

Shostakovich, Dmitri. [1930] 1981. "Why *The Nose*?" Original publ. in *Rabochi i Teatr* 3 (1930) 11. Cited in Editor's Note to Shostakovich, *Sobraniye Sochineniy* (Collected Works), vol. 18. Moscow: Muzyka.

———. 1989. "Plakat' i smeiat'sia." Original Russian publ. 1933. Cited and trans. Caryl Emerson in "Back to the Future: Shostakovich's Revision of Leskov's *Lady Macbeth of Mtsensk District*." In *Cambridge Opera Journal* 1/1 (March 1989): 59–78.

———. 2000. "Tragediya—satira." Cited and trans. Laurel E. Fay in *Shostakovich: A Life*. Oxford: Oxford University Press. Original Russian publ. 1932.

Simpson, Michael, trans. 2001. *The Metamorphoses of Ovid*. Amherst: University of Massachusetts Press.

Smith, Marian. 2003. "Dance and Dancers." In *The Cambridge Guide to Grand Opera*, ed. David Charlton. Cambridge and New York: Cambridge University Press.

Smith, Richard Langham. 2000. "Ravel's Operatic Spectacles: *L'Heure* and *L'Enfant*." In *The Cambridge Companion to Ravel*, ed. Deborah Mawer. Cambridge and New York: Cambridge University Press.

Solie, Ruth A. 1997. "Fictions of the Opera Box." In *The Work of Opera: Genre, Nationhood, and Sexual Difference*, ed. Richard Dellamora and Daniel Fischlin. New York: Columbia University Press.

Solomon, Maynard. 1977. *Beethoven*. New York: Schirmer.

Spitzer, John, and Neal Zaslaw. 1992. "Conductor." In *New Grove Dictionary of Opera*.

Staël, Germaine de. [1818] 1983. *Considérations sur la Révolution française*, ed. Jacques Godechot. Paris: Tallandier.

Stravinsky, Igor. 1996. "Comments on Hogarth and *The Rake's Progress*." Repr. in libretto of recording of *The Rake's Progress* conducted by Kent Nagano. Erato 0630-12715-2.

———, and Robert Craft. [1962] 1981. *Expositions and Developments*. Berkeley and Los Angeles: University of California Press.

Stuckenschmidt, H. H. 1977. *Schoenberg: His Life, World and Work*, trans. Humphrey Searle. New York: Schirmer. Original German ed., 1974.

Taruskin, Richard. 1992. "Boris Godunov." "Ruslan and Lyudmila." In *New Grove Dictionary of Opera*.

———. 1993. *Musorgsky: Eight Essays and an Epilogue*. Princeton: Princeton University Press.

———. 1997. *Defining Russia Musically: Historical and Hermeneutical Essays*. Princeton: Princeton University Press.

———. 2005. *The Oxford History of Western Music*. 6 vols. Oxford: Oxford University Press.

Thayer, Alexander. 1964. *Life of Beethoven*, rev. ed. by Elliott Forbes. Princeton: Princeton University Press.

Titon du Tillet, Evrard. [1743] 1998. First Supplement to *Le Parnasse françois*. Trans. Margaret Murata in Strunk, *Source Readings in Music History*, ed. Oliver Strunk. Rev. ed. by Leo Treitler. New York: Norton.

Tommasini, Anthony. 2003. Review of Adams, *The Death of Klinghoffer* at Brooklyn Academy of Music. *New York Times*, December 5, 2003.

———. 2006. "Bayreuth Journal: Anthony Tommasini at the Bayreuth Festival: Day 4: What to Wear?" *New York Times*. July-August 2006.

Tyrrell, John. 1988. *Czech Opera*. Cambridge and New York: Cambridge University Press.

———. 1992. "Jenůfa." In *New Grove Dictionary of Opera*.

Verdi, Giuseppe. [1887] 1988. Letter of 22 April 1887 to Giulio Ricordi, trans. Hans Busch. In *Verdi's "Otello" and "Simon Boccanegra" (Revised Version) in Letters and Documents*, ed. Hans Busch. Oxford: Clarendon Press.

Viale Ferrero, Mercedes. 1998. "Stage and Set." In *Opera on Stage*, vol. 5 of *The History of Italian Opera*, ed. Lorenzo Bianconi and Giorgio Pestelli, trans. Kate Singleton. Chicago: University of Chicago Press; original Italian ed., 1988.

Vincent-Buffault, Anne. 1991. *The History of Tears: Sensibility and Sentimentality in France*, trans. Teresa

Bridgeman. New York: St. Martin's Press. Original French ed., 1986.

Weaver, Robert. 1981. "The Conflict of Religion and Aesthetics in Schoenberg's Moses and Aaron." In Essays on the Music of J. S. Bach and Other Divers Subjects: A Tribute to Gerhard Herz, ed. Robert Weaver. Louisville: University of Louisville Press.

Weimann, Gabriel, and Conrad Winn. 1994. The Theater of Terror: Mass Media and International Terrorism. New York and London: Longman.

Weiss, Piero. 1982. "Metastasio, Aristotle, and the Opera Seria." In Journal of Musicology 1/4 (October 1982):385–94.

Whenham, John. 1986. "Five Acts: One Action." In Claudio Monteverdi: "Orfeo." Cambridge and New York: Cambridge University Press.

Williams, Simon. 2004. Wagner and the Romantic Hero. Cambridge and New York: Cambridge University Press.

Wood, Caroline, and Graham Sadler, eds. 2000. French Baroque Opera: A Reader. Aldershot, U.K.: Ashgate.

Wright, Lesley A. 2000. "Looking at the Sources and Editions of Bizet's Carmen." In Mary Dibbern, Carmen: A Performance Guide. Hillsdale, NY: Pendragon Press.

Wyatt, Robert, and John Andrew Johnson, eds. 2004. The George Gershwin Reader. Oxford and New York: Oxford University Press.

Yung, Bell. 1984. "Model Opera as Model: From Shajiabang to Sagabong." In Popular Chinese Literature and Performing Arts in the People's Republic of China 1949–1979, ed. Bonnie S. McDougall. Berkeley and Los Angeles: University of California Press.

Zaslaw, Neal. 1989. "The First Opera in Paris: A Study in the Politics of Art." In Jean-Baptiste Lully and the Music of the French Baroque: Essays in Honor of James R. Anthony, ed. John Hajdu Heyer. Cambridge and New York: Cambridge University Press.

Zoppelli, Luca. 1992. "Venice." In New Grove Dictionary of Opera.

CREDITS

INDEX

Note: Page numbers in *italics* indicate illlustrations or music examples.

Rimsky-Korsakov, Nikolay
  The Legend of the Invisible City of Kitezh, 346–50, *347, 349, 370*
  The Tale of Tsar Saltan, 355
Rinaldo and Armida (Poussin), *163*
Ring des Niebelungen, Der (Wagner), 358–70
  Brünnhilde's character in, 257, 261, 343, 367–70
Rinuccini, Ottavio
  Arianna, 99, 101, 102, 111
  Dafne, 99, 101
  Euridice, 99, 100–101
ritornello(s), 104–5, 110, 113–17, 177–78, 195, 196–97, 202
Ritorno d'Ulisse in patria, Il (Monteverdi), 120–21
Robert le Diable (Meyerbeer), 32, 336
Robinson, Anastasia, 186
Roi s'amuse, Le (Hugo), 52
Roland (Lully), 154, 155
Romans, ancient, 13, 47
  myths of, 98–118
  as opera subject, 185
  rhetoric of, 83
rondò, 243–46
Roqueplan, Camille-Joseph-Etienne, *Marie Du Plessis at the Theater*, *64–65*
Rosenkavalier, Der (Strauss), 444, 464
Rosow, Lois, 147
Rospigliosi, Giulio, *Sant'Alessio*, 97
Rossini, Gioachino
  The Barber of Seville, 38, 307–12, *309*
  La Cenerentola, 356
  Guillaume Tell, 38, 289
  Mosè in Egitto, 453, 454
  Le Siège de Corinthe, 260
Rouillon, Philippe, 284
Rousseau, Jean-Jacques, 194–95
  Le Devin du village, 233
  La nouvelle Héloïse, 211
Royal Opera House (Covent Garden, London)
  Cendrillon production, 42–43
  Peter Grimes production, 401
  Rigoletto production, 53

La traviata production, 76
Rubens, Peter Paul, *Jupiter and Callisto*, *124*
Rusalka (Dvořák), 355–58, *357, 369*, 370
  "Měsíčku na nebi hlubokém," 356
Ruslan and Lyudmila (Glinka), 337, 343–46, *345*, 355, 370
  interrupted wedding in, 344, 353, 382
  "Nas bïlo dvoye," 345
  "O pole, pole!," 344–45
Russia. *See also specific composers and operas*
  nationalism in, 288–89, 293–96
  opera in nineteenth century, 293–96, 343–50
  opera in twentieth century, 402–7
  socialist realism in, 406–7
Russian Orthodox Church, 273–74
Russo-Japanese War of 1905, 349

Saariaho, Kaija, *L'Amour de loin*, 422–23
Saccà, Roberto, *74*
Sacrati, Francesco
  Bellerofonte, 121–22, *123, 125*, 126–27, *129*
  Venere gelosa, 20
Sadler's Wells (London), *Peter Grimes* production, 399
Saint-Aubin, Gabriel de, *Lully's Opera "Armide" Performed at the Palais-Royal, 1761*, *3*
Saint Francis of Assisi (Messiaen), 450–53, *451*
  Ondes Martenot and birdsong in, 453
  recitative style in, 451–53
Saint-Quentin, Jacques Philippe Joseph de, 230
Salome (Strauss), *66*
Salzburg, Italian opera in, 145
Salzburg Festival
  Così fan tutte production, 250
  Idomeneo production, *8*

Samuel, Claude, 451
San Cassiano Theater (Venice), 121
Sand, George, 287, 321
San Diego Opera, *Pearl Fishers* production, 45
San Francisco Opera
  Dead Man Walking production, 374–75
  Don Giovanni production, 239
  Jenůfa production, 379
  Saint Francis of Assisi production, 451
San Marco (Venice), 111
San Salvatore Theater (Venice), *Germanico sul Reno* production, 128
Santa Fe Opera (New Mexico)
  L'Amour de loin production, 422–23
  outdoor venue, 15
Sant'Alessio (Landi), 97
Sartorio, Antonio, *Giulio Cesare*, 183, 184, 192
Satyagraha (Glass), 458, 460, *460–61*
Schaefer, Christine, *53*
Schenk, Otto (director), *55*
Schmidt-Futterer, Andrea, 451
Schnitzer, Petra Maria, 353, *365*
Schoenberg, Arnold, *Moses and Aaron*, 54, 453–57, *455*, 460
Schopenhauer, Arthur, 360
Schrott, Erwin, *234*
Schumann, Robert, Meyerbeer's *Les Huguenots* reviewed by, 282
Schützendorf, Leo, *385*
score, 66
Scott, Walter, *The Bride of Lammermoor*, 312
Scribe, Eugène, 83, 272–73, 287
Séchan, Charles (stage designer), 257
Sedaine, Michel-Jean, 262–63, 265
seguidilla, 34, 35, 57, 303
Seiffert, Peter, *365*
self-denial as opera subject, 154–55
self-sacrifice as opera subject, 184–93, 211–14, 407–13
Sellars, Peter (director), 61, *415*, 422–23
semi-operas, 166–72